SERVICES MARKETING AND MANAGEMENT

[For M.B.A., P.G. Diploma in Business Administration and other Management Courses]

B. BALAJI

B.E. (ECE), MBA, M. Phil, Diploma in Training & Development, Ph.D., UGC-NET
Professor in Management and Incharge, Research Centre
Acharya Institute of Management and Science, Bangalore

(Formerly, Senior Manager - Administration
Pan Clothing & Consolidated Company Ltd.)

S. CHAND
PUBLISHING

S Chand And Company Limited
(ISO 9001 Certified Company)

S Chand And Company Limited
(ISO 9001 Certified Company)
Head Office: D-92, Sector–2, Noida – 201301, U.P. (India), Ph. 91-120-4682700
Registered Office: A-27, 2nd Floor, Mohan Co-operative Industrial Estate,
New Delhi – 110 044, Phone: 011-49731800
www.**schandpublishing.com**; e-mail: **info@schandpublishing.com**

Marketing Offices:

Chennai : Ph: 23632120; chennai@schandpublishing.com
Guwahati : Ph: 2738811, 2735640; guwahati@schandpublishing.com
Hyderabad : Ph: 40186018; hyderabad@schandpublishing.com
Jalandhar : Ph: 4645630; jalandhar@schandpublishing.com
Kolkata : Ph: 23357458, 23353914; kolkata@schandpublishing.com
Lucknow : Ph: 4003633; lucknow@schandpublishing.com
Mumbai : Ph: 25000297; mumbai@schandpublishing.com
Patna : Ph: 2260011; patna@schandpublishing.com

First Edition 2002
Second Revised Editions 2006
Reprints 2008, 2009, 2010, 2012 (Twice), 2013, 2014, 2021, 2022, 2023

Reprint 2025

ISBN : 978-81-219-2161-9 **Product Code :** H8SMM60BMGT10ENAB06R

PRINTED IN INDIA

By Vikas Publishing House Private Limited, Plot 20/4, Site-IV, Industrial Area Sahibabad, Ghaziabad – 201 010 and Published by S Chand And Company Limited, A-27, 2nd Floor, Mohan Co-operative Industrial Estate, New Delhi – 110 044.

FOREWORD

The service sector has increased dramatically in importance over the last decade, both internationally and in India, where it now accounts for nearly two-thirds of the economy by income and jobs.

Deregulation of services, growing competition, fluctuations in demand, and the application of new technologies are presenting a considerable challenge to service companies. Banks, insurance companies, airlines, retailers and telecommunication companies, as well as professional service firms such as accountants and lawyers, need new approaches to address the challenge.

The foundation of the text is the recognition that services present special challenges that must be identified and addressed. Problems commonly encountered in service businesses - the inability to inventory, difficulty in synchronising demand and supply, and challenges in controlling the performance quality of human interactions - need to be articulated and tackled by managers. Many of the strategies required include information that is new to marketing.

This text provides an in-depth coverage of services marketing and management and is aimed primarily at students of management courses besides practising managers, across the country. The textual material includes twenty-four chapters followed by a resourceful appendix and index. The text adopts a logical flow starting with the basics and progressing smoothly to more complex issues.

This text comprises many distinguishing features:

* Chapters progress in a logical manner
* Lucid language
* Exhaustive tables that provide a quick summary of details
* Exhaustive figures that, besides providing a visual treat, enable the reader to understand the relationships better
* Self-contained sections that highlight the nuances of each topic
* Resourceful definitions throughout the chapters
* Numerous examples from day-to-day life
* Integration of theory and practice
* Invaluable information from journals, magazines, managers, general public and marketers
* Question Bank comprising short and essay-type questions that test basic theory and inter-relationships
* Exercise Corners that stimulate creative thinking, a zest for field research and application skills
* Appendix that relates to the corporate world from various angles
* Case studies the test comprehension of concepts
* Recent concepts like Service Leadership, Relationship Marketing, Service Profitability and Productivity, Service performance and measurement and Globalisation of services
* Separate chapter on service mix scenario covering innumerable services

The author, Mr. Balaji. B, has had a good grounding in the basics of engineering and management. A recipient of several national and international awards for outstanding contribution and leadership, he has presented papers in a variety of fields at various conferences and symposia. He possesses a zest for continuing research and leaves no stone unturned with regard to collection of details. His industrial experience has added that extra edge to his academic endeavours. This text has stemmed from his special interest in the challenging world of services. He has been awarded the Doctoral Degree in Business Administration for his thesis titled "A Study on Quality Gaps in Service Industry". He received Gold Medals for his MBA and Diploma in T&D programmes.

I am extremely pleased to recommend this book for all those who recognise the vital role that services play in the economy and its future. This book is a culmination of extensive research, innovative ideas, tactful mentoring, creative approach and practical thinking. I wish the author many more laurels that would provide the student and business community with such enriching experiences.

DR. N. BALASUBRAMANIAM
PROFESSOR, DEPARTMENT OF MANAGEMENT STUDIES,
UNIVERSITY OF MADRAS, CHENNAI.

This book is dedicated to
my beloved parents

Shri. K. Balasubramaniam

and

Smt. Saroja Balasubramaniam

PREFACE TO THE SECOND REVISED EDITION

The recognition that service is vital to the product sector as well as to the service sector formed the backdrop for this book. The title ***Services Marketing and Management*** accentuates the fact that emphasis has been given to aspects like service delivery and improving service over time, and not merely about marketing services. Another important aspect of this book is its multifunctional perspective. Business executives continually complain that students too often learn subjects in isolation, while in the business world everything connects to everything else. It is impossible to talk seriously about service without considering the relationship to strategy, human resources and organisational behaviour, accounting, finance, and operations. The last 10 years have brought tremendous attention to the issues of customer satisfaction and service quality. These topics have been dealt like never before, consistent with the importance they now command in the business world.

The book can be broadly divided into 8 parts, which comprises 24 chapters, an appendix and an index, as follows:

Section 1: Introduction (Chapters 1 to 3)

These chapters deal with the basic concepts, characteristics and expectations about services. Starting with the definition of services, services marketing and service management, the evolution of services and emergence of the service sector have been described. The merits, limitations and competitive trends have been highlighted along with the distinction between services and goods. The extended marketing mix for services and components of the internal and external environments have been detailed. This is followed by the discussions on expectations and their implications.

Section 2 : Service Mix elements (Chapters 4 to 10)

The mix elements, namely, Product, Place, Price, Promotion, Process, Physical Evidence and People have been dealt with in depth. For each element, its determinants, requirements, characteristics, strategies and models have been detailed.

Section 3 : Organisation for services (Chapter 11)

Activities like research, concept testing, communicating, analyses, segmentation, planning, rethinking, focussing, positioning, etc. have been presented in order to understand the background for delivery of services.

Section 4 : Planning, design, delivery and its determinants (Chapters 12 to 14)

The different stages of designing the service have been explained with models and examples. The concept of Blueprinting and Service Mapping have been explained exhaustively. The reasons for possible service failures and ways of overcoming them have been discussed. The strategies to manage demand and supply, the related issues, constraints and determinants have been detailed. The process of service delivery, the intermediaries, flowcharting, reception, and failures have been presented followed by problem resolution and quality function deployment.

Section 5 : Performance and quality (Chapters 15 to 16 & 22)

The impact of service quality, various approaches, dimensions, gaps, information system, measurement and costs have been detailed. The measures for monitoring and stabilising to enable optimisation follows. Performance is linked to productivity where sample indicators have been provided. The service-profit chain has been explained.

Section 6 : Examples from daily life (Chapter 17)

About two dozen services have been explained in terms of the extended marketing mix for services.

Section 7 : Internal and external interactions (Chapters 18 to 21)

The different types of Service encounters including Triadic Sorting (Kelly's repertory grid), Customer service scripts, Laddering, Critical Incident Techniques, Blueprinting, Leading edge user studies, Role playing have been explained. The concept of guarantees and management of customer complaints and queries have been detailed. The importance of customer retention and an in-depth discussion of Relationship Marketing follows. The types of leadership styles, dimensions and vision are also covered.

Section 8 : Global aspects (Chapter 23)

The concept of transnational strategies, processes, barriers, modes and model have been presented.

Section 9 : Case Studies (Chapter 24) & Appendices

The concept of transnational strategies, processes, barriers, modes and model have been presented.

The appendix comprises a collection of checklists and questionnaires that provide insights into the concepts of Leadership, Teamwork, Management, Vision, Consumer expectations, Climate, Moments of Truth, Quality standards, Measurement and Culture, besides strategies for breakthrough services.

This book provides a logical approach that integrates theory and practice and is presented in a lucid manner. The exhaustive compilation tables and figures provide rich and concise information. The chapters are amply supported by definitions, self-contained sections, numerous examples from daily life, thought-provoking question banks and exercises. This book covers the syllabi of all universities across India. Not just students of management courses would be benefited; any employee serving in the service sector can gain valuable insights into the concepts of services marketing and management. This book can also be used for training and development.

I owe an enormous debt to S. Chand and Company Limited for encouraging my maiden venture. The publishers are constantly striving to provide quality books for all. I profusely thank Shri. Ravindra Kumar Gupta, Managing Director and Shri. R. S. Saxena, Adviser, for their encouragement and guidance.

My special thanks to Shri. A. M. Arunachalam, Regional Manager, S. Chand & Company Limited, who laid the foundation for this book. His services and vision have greatly benefited the learning community.

Behind the strenuous efforts have been pillars of support, without whom, this book would not have been completed. I would like to extend my special thanks to Ms. B. Rajeshwari and other family members for extending their resources and for sharing their experiences and knowledge. I would also like to specially thank M/s. Xcellent Xerox and Prints Pvt. Ltd., Chennai for their DTP assistance.

I would also like to acknowledge the contributions of my ex-student, Mrs Bhuvana Devi, for her proof-reading and editing efforts. I would like to specially thank Dr. N. Balasubramaniam, Professor, Department of Management Studies, University of Madras, for his foreword.

A book of this nature calls for drawing upon the subject matter from different sources - publications, practising professionals, retired persons, the World Wide Web, statistics and professional bodies. It is not possible to include all those references and names here. I express my thanks to all such contributors.

Do share your personal and company experiences including feedback about this book at:

prof_bbalaji@yahoo.co.in

BALAJI. B

Flat 12, Subarag Apartments,

Old 12, New 25, Shenoy Road, Nungambakkam,

Chennai - 600 034.

CONTENTS

1

Concept of Service

1.1 WHAT IS SERVICE ?

A service is an act or performance offered by one party to another. Although the process may be tied to a physical product, the performance is essentially intangible and does not normally result in ownership of any of the factors of production.

Services are economic activities that create value and provide benefits for customers specific times and places, as a result of bringing about a desired change in - or on behalf of - the recipient of the service. Service are those separately identifiable, essentially intangible activities which provide want-satisfaction, and that are not necessarily tied to the sale of a product or another service. To produce a service may or may not require the use of tangible goods. However when such use is required, there is no transfer of title (permanent ownership) to these tangible goods.

One common method of defining a service is to distinguish between the 'core' and 'peripheral' elements of that service. The 'core' service offering is the 'necessary outputs of an organisation which are intended to provide the intangible benefits customers are looking for'. Peripheral services are those which are either 'indispensable for the execution of the core service or available only to improve the overall quality of the service bundle. Services include all economic activities whose output is not a physical product or construction, is generally consumed at the time it is produced, and provides added value in forms (such as convenience, amusement, timeliness, comfort or health) that are essentially intangible concerns of its first purchaser. Examples of services are : Transportation & public utilities, Hotels and other lodging places, Rail-road transportation, Personal services, Local and inter-urban passenger transit, Business services, Trucking and warehousing, Auto repair, services and garages, Water transportation, Miscellaneous repair services, Air transportation, Motion pictures, Pipelines except natural gas, Amusement and recreation services, Health service, Communication, Legal services, Telephone and telegraph, Educational services, Radio and television broadcasting, Social services and membership organizations, Electricity, Gas, Sanitary services, Miscellaneous professional services, Wholesale trade, Private household services, Retail trade, Finance, insurance, and real estate, Banking, Military, Credit agencies other than banks, Government enterprises Security & commodity brokers, Local government, Real estate, Education, Holding and other investment companies and Other services.

The classification of services based on various criteria is shown in Figure 1.1

1.2 THE SERVICES MARKETING TRIANGLE

Figure 1.2 suggests that there are three types of marketing that must be successfully carried out for a service organization to succeed, and that all of them revolve around making and keeping promises to customers. On the right side of the triangle are the external marketing efforts that the firm engages in to set up its customers' expectations and make promises to customers regarding what is to be delivered. Anything that communicates to the customer before service delivery can be viewed as part of this external marketing function. In service firms there are many factors that communicate to

FIGURE 1.1 : CLASSIFICATION OF SERVICES

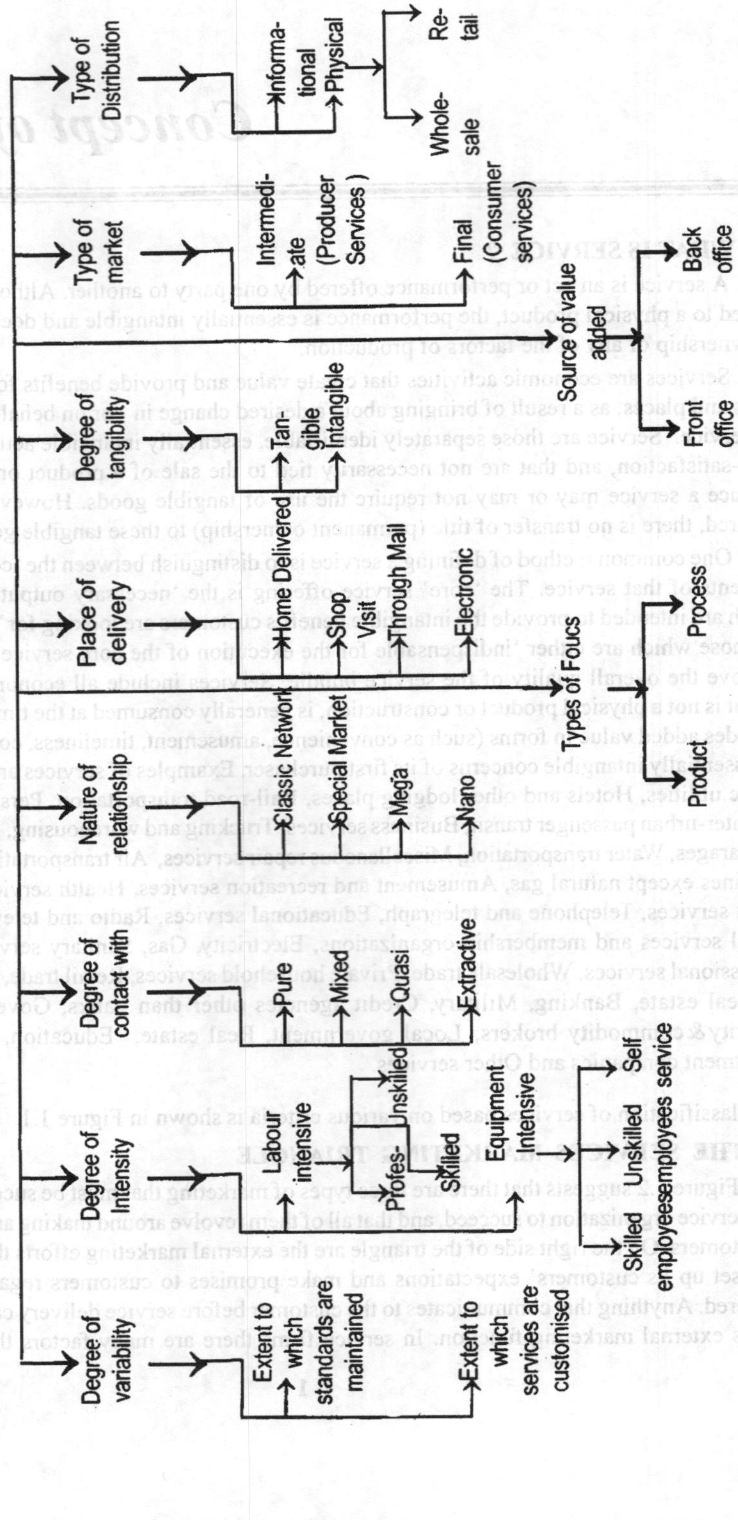

customers beyond the traditional elements of advertising, special promotions, sales, and public relations, for example, the firm's personnel and the physical facilities themselves. On the bottom of the triangle is what has been termed interactive marketing, or what some refer to as real-time marketing. Here the actual service delivery takes place-the firm's employees interact directly with customers. It is at this point that the promise is delivered (or not delivered). Having a positive link between what is promised through external marketing and what is delivered through interactive marketing is critical. All the external marketing in the world is useless if promises cannot be kept. The left side of the triangle suggests the critical role played by internal marketing, which enables employees to keep the promises that have been made to customers.

Figure 1.2: SERVICES MARKETING TRIANGLE

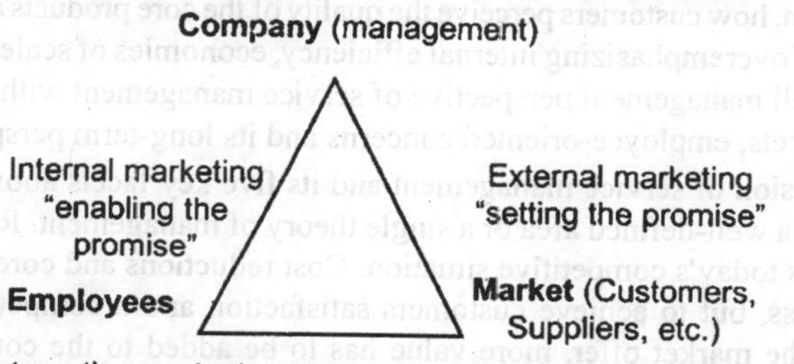

Internal marketing refers to the activities the firm must carry out to train, motivate, and reward its employees. Unless service employees are able and willing to deliver on the promises made, the firm will not be successful in keeping its promises and the services marketing triangle will collapse. Internal marketing hinges on the assumption that employee satisfaction and customer satisfaction are inextricably linked.

1.3 SERVICE MANAGEMENT

Service management draws insights from business practice and from marketing, operations, human resources, service quality management, organizational theory and economics. Its five key facets are (a) an overall perspective that guides decisions in all areas of management, (b) customer focus, (c) a holistic approach to cross-functional collaboration, (d) an emphasis on quality and (e) internal development personnel.

Service management is:

1. **To understand the utility customers receive by consuming or using the offerings of the organization and how services alone or together with physical goods or other kinds of tangibles contribute to this utility, that is, to understand how total quality is perceived in customer relationships, and how it changes over time;**
2. **To understand how the organization (personnel, technology and physical resources, systems and customers) will be able to produce and deliver this utility or quality;**
3. **To understand how the organization should be developed and managed so that the intended utility or quality is achieved; and**
4. **To make the organization function so that this utility or quality is achieved and the objectives of the parties involved (the organization, the customers, other parties, the society, etc.) are met.**

Service management is a total organizational approach that makes quality of service, as perceived by the customer, the number one driving force for the operations of the business.

1. It is an overall management perspective which should guide decisions in all areas of management (not only provide management principles for a separate function such as customer service);
2. It is customer-driven or market-driven (not driven by internal efficiency criteria);
3. It is a holistic perspective which emphasizes the importance of intra-organizational, cross-functional collaboration (not specialization and the division of labour);
4. Managing quality is an integral part of service management (not a separate issue); and
5. Internal development of the personnel and reinforcement of its commitment to company goals and strategies are strategic prerequisites for success (not only administrative tasks).

The overall management perspective

Service management as an overall management perspective gives high priority to the external efficiency of the firm, how customers perceive the quality of the core products and the total performance of a firm, instead of overemphasizing internal efficiency, economies of scale and cost reduction. This combines the overall management perspective of service management with its customer-driven and quality-oriented facets, employee-oriented concerns and its long-term perspective.

As the discussion of service management and its five key facets above demonstrates, service management is not a well-defined area or a single theory of management. Rather it is a management perspective that fits today's competitive situation. Cost reductions and core product quality are still important to success, but to achieve customers satisfaction and a competitive advantage through differentiation of the market offer, more value has to be added to the core product. This is done through a variety of services and by turning activities such as deliveries, technical service, claims handling, telephone exchange, invoicing, etc. into customer-oriented, value-adding services.

The eight components of integrated service management are:

- Product elements.
- Place and time.
- Process.
- Productivity and quality.
- People.
- Promotion and education.
- Physical evidence.
- Price and other costs of service.

1.4 THE EVOLVING ENVIRONMENT OF SERVICES

Around the world, innovative newcomers offering new standards of service have succeeded in markets where established competitors have failed to please today's demanding customers. Many barriers to competition are being swept away, allowing the entry of eager newcomers, ranging from tiny start-up operations like garden maintenance or baby-sitting services to well-finished multinational firms importing service concepts previously developed and tested in other countries. Established businesses often find it hard to maintain customer loyalty in the face of competition from innovative firms offering new product features, improved performance, price-cutting, clever promotions and the introduction of more convenient, technology-driven delivery systems.

Depending on the industry and the country in which the service firm does business, the underlying causes of such changes may include any of the twelve forces listed below:

- Changing patterns of government regulation.
- Relaxation of professional association restrictions on marketing.
- Privatisation of some public and nonprofit services.
- Technological innovations.
- Growth of service chain and franchise networks.

- Internationalization and globalization.
- Pressures to improve productivity.
- The service quality movement.
- Expansion of leasing and rental businesses.
- Manufacturers as service providers.
- Need for public and nonprofit organizations to find new income.
- Hiring and promotion of innovative managers.

Changing patterns of government ownership and regulation

Traditionally, many service industries were highly regulated. Government agencies set price levels, placed geographic constraints on distribution strategies and, in some instances, even defined the product attributes. Reduced government regulation has already eliminated or minimized many constraints on competitive activity in such industries as airfreight, airlines, railways, road transport, banking, securities, insurance and telecommunications. Barriers to entry by new firms have been dropped in many instances, geographic restrictions on service delivery have been reduced, there is more freedom to compete on price and existing firms have been able to expand into new markets or new lines of business.

Privatization and relaxation of restrictions

The transformation of such service operations as national airlines, telecommunication services and utilities such as gas, electricity and water into private enterprise services had led to restructuring, cost-cutting and a more market-focused posture. When privatization is combined with a relaxing of regulatory barriers to allow entry of new competitor, the marketing implications can be dramatic. The privatization of utilities has led to a trend towards international ownership, which many authorities see as irreversible. Privatisation can also apply to regional or local government departments. At the local level, for instance, services such as refuse collection and cleaning have been shifted from the public sector to private firms. Not everyone is convinced, however that such changes are beneficial to all sectors of the population. When services are provided by public agencies, there are often cross-subsidies, designed to achieve broader social goals. With privatization, there are fears that the search for efficiency and profits will lead to cuts in service and price increases. The result may be to deny less affluent segments the services they need at prices they can afford.

Technological innovations

New technologies are radically altering the ways in which many service organizations do business with their customers - as well as what goes behind the scenes. Perhaps the most powerful force for change today comes from the integration of computers and telecommunications. Companies operating information-based services, such as financial service firms, are seeing the nature and scope of their businesses totally transformed by the advent of national (or even global) electronic delivery systems, including the internet and its best-known component, the World Wide Web. Technology does more than enable the creation of new or improved services. It may also facilitate re-engineering of such activities as delivery of information, order-taking and payment, enhance a firm's ability to maintain more consistent service standards, permit the creation of centralized customer service departments, allow replacement of personnel by machines for repetitive tasks and lead to greater involvement of customers in operations through self-service technology.

Growth of service chains and franchise networks

Franchising involves the licensing of independent entrepreneurs to produce and sell a branded service according to tightly specified procedures. It is an increasingly popular way to finance the expansion of multi-site service chains that deliver a consistent service concept. Large franchise chains are replacing (or absorbing) a wide array of small, independent service businesses in fields as diverse as bookkeeping, car hire, dry-cleaning, hairdressing, photocopying, plumbing, fast-food restaurants and estate agency services.

Internationalization and globalization

The internationalization of service companies is readily apparent to any tourist or business executive travelling abroad. Airlines and airfreight companies that were formerly just domestic in scope today have extensive foreign route networks. Numerous financial service firms, advertising agencies, hotel chains, fast-food restaurants, car hire agencies and accounting firms now operate on several continents. This strategy may reflect a desire to serve existing customers better, to penetrate new markets, or both. The net effect is to increase competition and encourage the transfer of innovation in both products and processes from country to country.

Pressures to improve productivity

Historically, the service sector has lagged behind the manufacturing sector in productivity improvement, although there are encouraging signs that some services are beginning to catch up, especially when allowance is made for simultaneous improvements in quality. Using technology to replace labour (or to permit customer self-service) is one cost-cutting route that has been followed in many industries. Re-engineering of processes often results in speeding up operations by cutting out unnecessary steps. However, managers need to be aware of the risk that cost-cutting measures driven by finance and operations personnel without regard for customer needs may lead to a perceived deterioration in quality and convenience.

The service quality movement

With the growing realization that improving quality was good for business and necessary for effective competition, a radical change in thinking took place. Traditional notions of quality (based on conformance to standards defined by operations managers) were replaced by the new imperative of letting quality be customer-driven, which had enormous implications for the importance of service marketing and the role of customer research in both the service and manufacturing sectors. Numerous firms have invested in research to determine what their customers want on every dimension of service, in quality improvement programmes designed to deliver what customers want, and in regular measurement of how satisfied their customers are with the quality of service received.

Expansion of leasing and rental businesses

Leasing and rental businesses represent a marriage between service and manufacturing businesses. Increasingly, both corporate and individual customers find that they can enjoy the use of a physical product without actually owning it. Long-term leases may involve use of the product alone - such as a lorry - or provision of a host of related services at the same time. In road transport, for instance, full-service leasing provides almost everything, including painting, washing, maintenance, tyres, fuel, licence fees, road service, substitute vehicles and even drivers. Personnel, too, can be hired for short periods rather than employed full-time, as evidenced by the growth of firms supplying temporary workers, from secretaries to security guards.

Manufacturers as service providers

Service profit centres within manufacturing firms are transforming many well-known companies in fields such as computers, motor vehicles and electrical and mechanical equipment. Supplementary services once designed to help sell equipment - including consultation, credit, transportation and delivery, installation, training and maintenance - are now offered as profit - seeking services in their own right, even to customers who have chosen to purchase competing equipment.

Pressure on public and nonprofit organizations to find new income sources

The financial pressures confronting public and nonprofit organizations are forcing them not only to cut costs and develop more efficient operations, but also to pay more attention to customer needs and competitive activities. In their search for new sources of income, many 'non-business' organizations are developing a stronger marketing orientation, which often involves rethinking their product lines, adding profit-seeking services such as shops, retail catalogues, restaurants and consultancy, becoming more selective about the market segments they target and adopting more realistic pricing policies.

Hiring and promotion of innovative managers

Managers tended to spend their entire careers working within a single industry, even within a single organization. Each industry was seen as unique and outsiders were suspect. Relatively few managers possessed degrees in business, such as an MBA, although they might have held an industry-specific diploma in a field such as hotel management or healthcare administration. In recent years, however, competition and enlightened self-interest have led companies to recruit better qualified managers who are willing to question traditional ways of doing business and able to bring new ideas from previous work experience in another industry.

1.5 MYTHS ABOUT SERVICES

A myth is a popular belief, usually oversimplified, that tends to explain only part of the phenomena. The following are commonly held myths about services. While there is some truth in each of the myths, the ideas are generally overly simplistic and logically flawed.

Myth 1 : A Services Economy Produces Services at the Expense of Other Sectors

There are those who fear that because services continue to grow at an accelerated pace, eventually advanced economies will produce only services, and there will be no manufactured goods output at all. A related belief is that because service production is growing, other sectors cannot grow simultaneously. These fears are largely unfounded. First, in an absolute sense, both manufacturing and services have grown. There are more workers in the manufacturing sector now than there were twenty years ago, and total industrial production has grown as well. Second, much of the employment in the service sector is linked directly to manufacturing; there has been an increasing need for services in support functions (that is, to hire someone outside the firm to provide services that used to be provided by company employees) will result in continued growth of services in support of manufacturing, but not at the expense of manufacturing.

Myth 2 : Service Jobs Are Low Paying and Menial

Many people believe that service employees are primarily small retailers, fast-food employees, hairdressers, store clerks, and low-skilled workers. There is some truth to this perception in that many small businesses are services and when people are laid off in low-skilled manufacturing jobs they typically see their employment alternatives as limited to low-paying, low-skilled service jobs. However, easily half of all service workers are in highly skilled, white-collar occupations such as law, accounting, education, banking, and medicine. And much of the growth in service jobs has come in the more highly skilled sectors. People in these professional service jobs are not at the low-pay end of the wage scale.

Myth 3 : Service Production is Labor Intensive and Low in Productivity

Common images of the service economy suggest businesses where investments in labour far outweigh capital investments and where productivity is sluggish, creating a drag on the entire economy. Such images are certainly not very positive. While some service industries are labour intensive (e.g. many personal services, restaurants, professional services), as many or more are high in capital intensity. One simply has to think of examples of highly capital intensive service industries - airlines, telecommunications, utilities - to known that the labour intensity myth is not generally true. Gains in productivity generally show up as either lower costs (for the same value/quality) or higher value/quality to the customer (for the same costs). The problem for many services is in determining how to measure value or quality.

1.6 THE SERVICE AS A SYSTEM

When receiving a haircut, for example, customers come into contact with receptionist and stylists, the physical dimensions of the salon itself, heating, seating etc., and other customers within the salon. The model draws the distinction between visible elements and invisible components of the system. The latter would include all the other organizational activities taking place 'backstage', for instance, staff training and administration. According to the model, in order to receive the benefits from the service experience the customer must be part of the system thus explicitly acknowledging the inseparability characteristic of services.

The components of the service system are (1) the service operations system, (2) the service delivery system, and (3) the service marketing system.

The model illustrates how the three functional areas - marketing, operations and human resources of the service business - are integrated together.

Figure 1.3 identifies the various components of the services marketing system as related to a hairdressing service.

FIGURE 1.3 : THE SERVICE SYSTEM

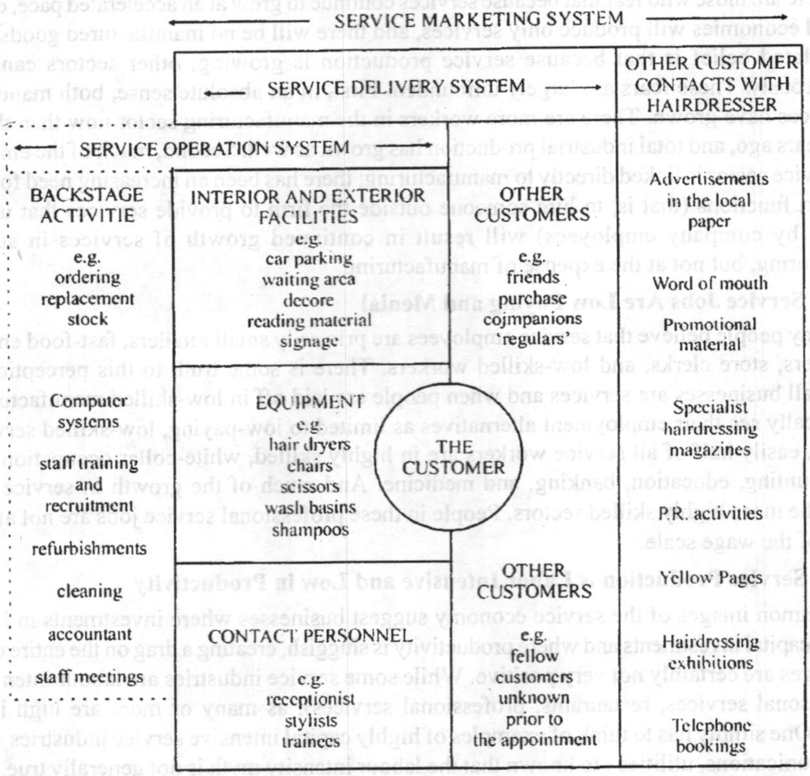

The distinction between frontstage and backstage elements of the system is maintained, with backstage activities taking place out of sight of the consumer.

The Service Operations System

The service operations system comprises backstage activities, such as staff training, stock replenishment, etc., as well as the frontstage aspects of the operation experienced directly by the customer, such as how they are treated by employees as soon as they enter the parlour, or how quickly they are moved around from the washbasins to the cutting chair (if they are receiving a cut and blow for example). Although there is generally no need for the customer to see most aspects of service operations (therefore they are kept backstage), some service providers deliberately expose customers to backstage activities in an attempt to influence positively their perceptions of the quality of the service provided. Restaurants frequently invite customers to visit kitchens where the food is being prepared either before or after they have eaten. This is designed to reinforce an image of fresh food prepared in a hygienic cooking environment which may influence their perception of the overall quality of their experience.

The Service Delivery System

The service delivery system encompasses not only the visible elements of the service operating system, employees and the physical facilities, but also includes exposure to other customers. In many service businesses, positive on-site interaction can have a significant impact on customers' overall perception of their experience. In the hairdressing parlour,, customers may find themselves waiting for a period of time for their particular stylist in a communal reception area. Conversations frequently take place at this point between customers who have never met prior to entering the delivery system. Although the discussions may consist largely of banter and pleasantries not directly connected with the hairdressing service (e.g. conversations about the weather, traffic in town, etc.), the exchanges can for many customers improve their overall experience by making the time pass more quickly. Occasionally, when conversations turn to the service itself, the provider can benefit positively from the exchange. For instance, one customer who has visited the parlour several times may comment on the skill and expertise of a certain stylist, and the generally professional attitude of all employees. To new customers attending for the first time the comments might have a positive influence on their opinion of the parlour.

The Service Marketing System

The service marketing system incorporates elements of the service experience which may contribute to the customer's overall view of the organisation but are not specifically part of the delivery system. Clearly, many of these are the elements which the organisation may not be able to control, such as conversations customers may have about the parlour with friends or relatives at home, or exposure to the service they may get from reading a hairdressing editorial in the local paper.

Lovelock feels that by conceptualising the service experience as three overlapping systems, services managers are forced to consider their business from a customers rather than a purely operations perspective. It highlights the importance of managing all elements of the business that are visible to customers.

1.7 ATTITUDES TOWARDS SERVICES AND THE SERVICE SECTOR

There is a need for a change in attitude towards services and the service sector of the economy, services are still not regarded as valid forms of wealth; that services are treated still as 'unproductive.' This narrow view of the unimportance of service is reflected in a number of ways. Some examples are:

(a) The manufacturing sector is accorded higher status than the service sector: 'It is probably a consequence of services' lower status than the quantity and quality of data on the sector is poor-which itself has discouraged research.

(b) The basic measurement problems of defining the quantity and quality of services remain unresolved. More attention needs to be devoted to the measurement of productivity in the service sector. As recent work has identified, this remains a fundamental and difficult problem and hampers any attempted objective discussion of the service economy.

(c) Emphasis upon manufacturing only, at the expense of services - and particularly through cut backs in public service - perpetuates the myth of services as invalid forms of wealth. In a modern advanced economy there are close links between manufacturing and services.

Modern economic theory has come to the conclusion that there is no point in the distinction between productive and unproductive activities. If the product of an activity is wanted by the individuals who are consuming it, then that activity must be productive. This criterion applies both to products that are bought and sold (either physical goods or services) and to products that are allocated through the State (again, either physical goods or services).

Many service organizations are complacent about the level and the quality of service that they give.

Figure 1.4 : CONSUMER PERSPECTIVES OF SERVICE

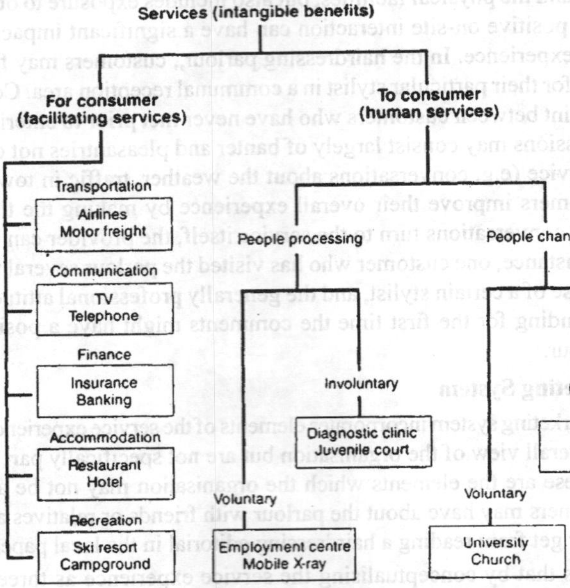

Challenges and Questions for Service Marketers

Because of basic differences between goods and services, marketers of services face some very real and distinctive challenges. The challenges revolve around understanding customer needs and expectations for service, tangibilizing the service offering, dealing with a myriad of people and delivery issues (Figure 1.4), and keeping promises made to customers. Answers to questions such as the ones listed here still elude managers of services.

How can service quality be defined and improved when the product is intangible and non-standardized?

How can new services be designed and tested effectively when the service is essentially an intangible process?

How can the firm be certain it is communicating a consistent and relevant image when so many elements of the marketing mix communicate to customers, and some of these elements are the service providers themselves?

How does the firm accommodate fluctuating demand when capacity is fixed and the service itself is perishable?

How can the firm best motivate and select service employees who, because the service is delivered in real-time, become a critical part of the product itself?

How should prices be set when it is difficult to determine actual costs of production and price may be inextricably intertwined with perceptions of quality?

How should the firm be organized so that good strategic and tactical decisions are made when a decision in any of the functional areas of marketing, operations, and human resources may have significant impact on the other two areas?

How can the balance between standardization and personalization be determined to maximize both the efficiency of the organization and the satisfaction of its customers?

How can the organization protect new service concepts from competitors when service processes cannot be legally patented?

How does the firm communicate quality and value to consumers when the offering is intangible and cannot be legally patented?

How can the organization ensure the delivery of consistent quality service when both the organization's employees and the customers themselves can affect the service outcome?

1.8 THE EVOLUTION OF SERVICES MARKETING

Fisk, Brown and Bitner identify three distinct stages in the evolution of services marketing that are reflected in the literature:

1. the 'Crawling Out' stage which took place prior to 1980;
2. the 'Scurrying About' stage between 1980 and 1986;
3. the 'Walking Erect' between 1986 and 2000.
4. the 'Galloping' stage from 2000 till date.

'Crawling Out' Stage

In the 'crawling out' stage, discussion centered around the need for a separate body of literature to deal with the specific problems of the service sector.

Specific areas of marketing theory were examined and found to be insufficient or inappropriate when it came to handling service sector problems and concerns. Donnelly, for example, highlighted the differences between the marketing 'channels' used for services and those used for physical goods and implications for marketing strategy.

Marketing traditionalists argued that service organisations did not need a separate body of theory, and that existing marketing theories could, and should, be applied to service organisations. They argued that services could not be defined tightly enough to deserve special treatment and, in many instances, were so closely linked to the physical product that they needed to be considered as part of the 'offer' when developing marketing strategy. For example, the after sales service guarantee supplied with a motor car could be valued as highly as the interior design features of the car itself.

Distinctive Characteristics of Service

Services Marketing academics and practitioners argued that services required special treatment as a result of their distinctive characteristics; intangibility, inseparability, heterogeneity and perishability. These characteristics were outlined during the 'crawling out' stage.

Intangibility refers to the fact that a large component of many service offers is immaterial or intangible and cannot be presented in a concrete manner to consumers prior to purchase. A customer cannot touch an aerobics class, for example, prior to taking part, and can only make a full assessment of the quality of the service offered after having attended the class.

Inseparability refers to the notion that, in many service operations, production and consumption cannot be separated, that is, a service is to a great extent consumed at the same time as it is produced. For example, although the hairdresser may prepare in advance to carry out the service (i.e. gather the necessary equipment, undergo specialised training, etc.), most of the hairdressing service is produced simultaneously as the customer consumes the service (i.e. sits in the chair).

Heterogeneity is closely linked to inseparability as it is very difficult to apply quality standards to services to ensure an identical service output, when so much depends on the cooperation and participation of individual customers.

Perishability refers to the fact that unlike physical goods, services cannot be stored. An appointment with a dentist, in contrast, at a given time on a given day, cannot be stored and offered again to customers.

'Scurrying About' Stage

In the 'scurrying about' stage between 1980 and 1985 efforts were made to classify services more clearly and attention focused heavily on the crucial issue of managing quality in service operations. Zeithaml, Berry and Parasuraman developed their pioneering 'gaps model' of service quality which highlighted the importance of Efforts made to assess quality in services. Other topics emerged as being particularly important to the management of service organisations, including a better understanding of the components of the 'service encounter' (i.e. the interpersonal aspects of the service), 'relationship marketing' and 'internal marketing'. Booms and Bitner developed their expanded 'marketing mix' for services which took into account the distinctive characteristics of service identified in the 'crawling out' stage: intangibility, inseparability, heterogeneity and perishability. Booms and Bitner added three more Ps to this original marketing mix to make it more appropriate to services; People, Process and Physical evidence. For the first time textbooks on Services Marketing began to be produced, establishing it more firmly as a legitimate field of academic study.

'Walking Erect' Stage

In the 'walking erect' stage since 1986, there has been 'almost no discussion of whether services are different from goods, but rather the literature has focused on specific marketing problems of service organisations'. They include consideration of Service Encounters, Service Design, Perceived Service Quality and Customer Satisfaction, Internal Marketing and Relationship Marketing.

'Galloping' Stage

In the 'Galloping' stage since 2000, there has been an increase in the growth of the service sector and services are the main contributors to the GDP of the country.

1.9 REASONS FOR THE GROWTH OF THE SERVICE ECONOMY

A number of reasons have been put forward to explain the growth of the service economy. Three of the main explanations are examined here. They are:

(a) the lag in growth in labour productivity in services compared with the rest of the economy;

(b) the growth in intermediate demand from firms;

(c) the growth in final demand from consumers.

The Lag in Growth in Labour Productivity in Services

Part of the explanation for the growth of services is attributed to the slower growth of labour productivity, as measured by volume of output per employee, that is, the amount of labour required to produce a given volume of output in other sectors of the economy like manufacturing, fell more rapidly than in services. Lower output per man in services was the major explanation for the shift in employment into the service sector. A number of reason why this was so, included:

(a) A greater decline in hours worked per man in service than in industry.

(b) A more rapid increase in the quality of labour in industry than in service.

(c) A difference in the physical capital per worker available in industry compared with service.

(d) More rapid technological change in industry than in service; and that industry benefited more from scale economies.

The weakness with these suggestions is the problem of measuring output changes in services.

The Growth in Intermediate Demand from Firms

Another part of the explanation for the growth of services is attributed to the growth of intermediate demand from firms (i.e. providing inputs to manufacturing and other sectors of the economy). Specialist firms have been set up to provide services previously carried out by existing firms (e.g. engineering services, personal services). Alternatively specialist firms have been set up to provide new services (e.g. data processing).

Business buyers have always used an array of services like accounting, construction, banking, insurance, legal, research, advertising, public relations, training, transport, shipping and consultancy services. As advanced economies have developed so too have markets for service provision. Companies and other organizations increasingly rely on the services of specialists because of the complexity of economic organization and to obtain the economies involved in the division of labour: technological and competitive pressures require the use of services to keep up-to-date in a constantly changing environment; organizations are able to retain their flexibility by hiring in services which provide 'use' without 'ownership'; time pressures and lack of available internal resources encourage organizations to use outside services rather than having services provided internally.

The Growth in Final Demand from Consumers

Another part of the explanation for the growth of service is attributed to the growth of final demand from consumers. As society gets wealthier and as the marginal utility derived from additional increments of goods declines, then people turn to services expenditures. This argument therefore rests on the assumption of a relationship between income and spending patterns on goods and services. Consumers spend increases in income on travel, recreation, education, health care and similar services rather than on cars and clothing.

Other elements of the growth of final demand from consumers include changed life-styles, more leisure time, longer life expectancy and the increasing complexity of life. Technological developments mean more goods-which require specialist service in fields like motor cars, stereophonic equipment, video equipment and home computers. Affluence and more discretionary income allow consumers to delegate tasks to others; this delegation of responsibility generates new types of services and service organizations. For example, part of the increase in employment in services is due to the transfer of certain kinds of households jobs (not shown in conventional employment or output measures) into the officially paid and recorded workforce (e.g. welfare services). Services formerly provided unpaid by household members are now provided by institutions recognized in official statistics.

A summary of some of the reasons for the growth of consumer service industries is given in Table 1.1 .

Table 1.1 : REASONS FOR THE GROWTH IN SERVICE INDUSTRIES

1. Increasing affluence	Greater demand for lawn care, carpet cleaning, and other services that consumers used to provide for themselves.
2. More leisure time	Greater demand for travel agencies, travel resorts, adult education courses.
3. Higher percentage of women in the labour force	Greater demand for day care nurseries, maid service, away-from-home meals.
4. Greater life expectancy	Greater demand for nursing homes and health care services.
5. Greater complexity of products	Greater demand for skilled specialist to provide maintenance for such complex products as cars and home computers.

6. Increasing complexity of life	Greater demand for income tax preparers, marriage counsellors, legal advisers, employment services.
7. Greater concern about ecology and resource scarcity	Greater demand for purchased or leased services, such as door-to-door bus service and car rental instead of car ownership.
8. Increasing number of new products	The computer-sparked development of such service industries as programming, repair, and time sharing.

1.10 HOW TECHNOLOGY IS LEVERAGING CUSTOMER SERVICE

As service firms grow larger and extend their operations across broader geographic areas, corporate managers may become far removed from the day-to-day operations of the business-and thus from their customers. This development requires new efforts to achieve service consistency across time and geography. Information technology can often help provide the solution.

Service firms with multi-site operations are trying to develop programmes for building closer ties with customers by centralizing certain functions that don't require face-to-face contact. Computer technology and telecommunications make it possible to provide national (or even global) on-line service from a central location to serve customers who require information, wish to place orders or seek to resolve problems. At the same time, technology is creating opportunities for real-time feedback from the marketplace.

Technology is used in services businesses to lower costs, increase productivity, improve the way service is delivered, put more information in the hands of service representatives, personalize the service, collect data on customer needs, add value for the customer, differentiate the service, and build relationships with customers. Technological advances such as relational data bases, expert systems, image processing, and local area networks are but a few of the technologies that offer service opportunitics. Consumers can make their own airline reservations, choose restaurants in cities far from their home computer, talk to other users through electronic billboards, and check the weather in all parts of the world. Other electronic services offer the customer access to extensive library services and on-demand cable programming and movies.

Technology also revolutionizes the types of new services created by companies. Perhaps the most exciting emerging technology is virtual reality, the use of simulated environments This technology uses multiple sensory information and data to render, recreate, and simulate a 'world' that is described in data.

Marketing Opportunities Arising from New Technology

New technology (or more sophisticated use of existing technology) offers service businesses a variety of ways to improve their competitive stance (Figure 1.5). These include:

Creation of new or improved services: Spurred by advances in both computers and telecommunications, the whole field of remotely accessed, information based services is expanding rapidly. Banking and certain types of retailing services are being transformed by telecommunications and the so-called Information Superhighway. Soon it may be hard for many people to imagine how they coped without E-Mail or the rapidly growing array of services offered through the World Wide Web.

Figure 1.5 : IMPACT OF TECHNOLOGY

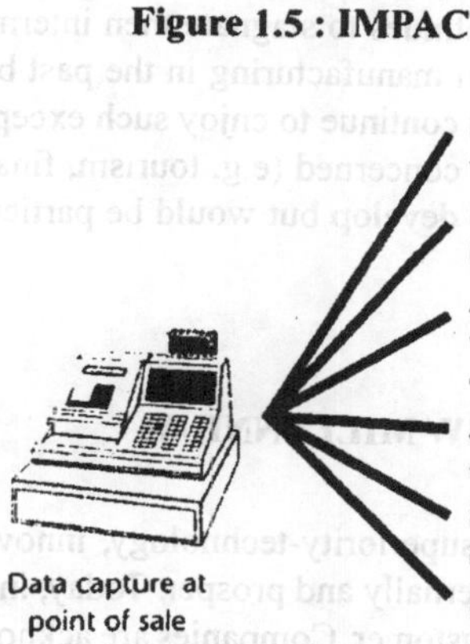

More involvement of customers in self-service operations: Well-established examples include automated teller machines in banks and self-service petrol or diesel pumps. These options are often available 24 hours a day in locations where personal service would be infeasible.

Creation of centralized customer service departments backed up by computerized file systems and accessed by toll-free telephone calls: Examples include airlines, credit firms, and car rental businesses. These departments may enable multi-site service operations to maintain higher standards for providing information, taking reservations, and handling problems and complaints than when such responsibilities are assigned to individual local service outlets.

Recording customer information in easily accessible data banks: This strategy offers several major advantages. Knowledge of customer usage patterns may suggest new ways of grouping customers into market segments, help improve pricing decisions, and lead to better targeted selling and advertising efforts. Database marketing is becoming a key tool for both service and goods marketers, allowing marketers to customize their communications with consumers. There may also be opportunities to personalize machine interactions with customers.

1.11 THE FUTURE OF THE SERVICES SECTOR

There are the likely trends in the service sector for the different kinds of services.

Old Services

Demand will continue to fall (e.g. public transport, laundries). However because these services have a fairly small share in service consumption and output they will have little influence upon services as a whole.

New Services

Demand will be fairly close to the trend of output and income in the overall economy (e.g. health, education, tourism). Private consumer demand for leisure and recreation-related services may tend to increase faster than personal income if the economy is growing. The resources devoted to new services that are publicly provided (e.g. health and education) will be influenced by political decisions. The complexion of the government in office will clearly influence what share of resources will be devoted to public services, although this decision in turn will be influenced by factors like the general health of the economy and general demographic trends (e.g. the increasing numbers of old people).

Complementary Services

Demand for these will be influenced by the health of the sectors which use them. If the fortunes of the manufacturing sector improve then intermediate services will grow (e.g. computing, finance, research). If on the other hand manufacturing continues to stagnate then intermediate services will suffer too. Generally they have growth faster than manufacturing in the past but it is unlikely that under stagnant conditions in the 1980s they could continue to enjoy such exceptional growth.

As far as internationally traded services are concerned (e.g. tourism, financial services) their growth is less constrained and could continue to develop but would be particularly influenced by two factors:

(a) Competition
(b) Exchange Rates

1.12 COMPETITIVE TRENDS FOR THE NEW MILLENNIUM

Customer Satisfaction and Customer Focus

Many of the historic sources of company superiority-technology, innovation, economies of scale-allowed companies to focus their efforts internally and prosper. Today, internal focus in many companies is shifting to an external focus on the customer. Companies are acknowledging that unless customer needs are taken into account in designing and delivering both services and goods, all the technical superiority in the world will not bring success.

When customers become scarce in an industry and competition heats up, however, the customer gains power. In the 1990s, when competition for master of business administration students intensified and Business today conducted " customer surveys" of students to rank the best business schools in India, the business school "customer" assumed a more central position in these organizations. What students wanted in courses and experiences began to drive curricula, content, and peripherals associated with business degrees. Business Schools overhauled their MBA programs to make them more relevant to the students and the business environment. Many B-schools revamped the course content of their programmes, recognized their key constituents (students, faculty, administrators, alumni, and corporate recruiters), and acknowledged that they needed research to understand their customer's expectations.

Value

Another key competitive factor defining the way services are bought and sold is value. In the words of the business observer, the marketing of value has "gone from a ground swell to a tidal wave." Value reflects the growing customer concern of getting more for money, time, and effort invested. Experts can point to many reasons why value is critical to today's consumers: economic problems, loss of jobs due to company restructuring, and a return to the real and practical. While the 1980s could easily have been termed the decade of extravagance, the customer priority of the 1990s is turning out to be value. To thrive, companies must understand the demographic and psychographic changes that reflects this new perspective.

Total Quality Management and Service Quality

Many experts considered the 1980s the decade of manufacturing quality because efforts to improve quality-to make products that conformed to requirements-were initiated in some form in many companies during that time. Total quality management (TQM) is the term widely used to capture the movement, although this concept is used in a myriad of ways. In a general sense, TQM has most often been defined as a management philosophy or way of doing business based on continuous quality improvement. TQM has subsumed a diverse group of quality techniques and strategies, among them statistical process control, process management, employee participation, management commitment and leadership, empowerment, and team building.

Emphasis on Service as a Key Differentiator in Manufacturing Firms

Competitive parity has been reached in many manufactured goods (such as personal computers, video cassette recorders, and other electronic products, to name just a few) meaning that product quality alone no longer differentiates one producer from another. Low price as a differentiating strategy is also disappearing, especially as companies face the reality that they and their competitors accomplish little more in price wars than to eliminate their own margins. One of the few remaining strategies that can set one goods company apart from others is customer service, broadly defined as developing strong relationships with customers. Goods firm in industries such as automobiles, computers and most industrial firms are heavily focusing on service.

New Measurement Systems That Link Customer Satisfaction with Financial Goals and Operational Measurements

Before the early 1990s, few companies had measurement systems that viewed the customers as a focus. While most companies were drowning in measurement, emphasis was typically on short-term financial performance, productivity, and efficiency-not on long-term customer satisfaction and value. Focusing on customers' priorities led the company to many changes, one of the most important being a company-wide measurement effort emphasizing customer satisfaction. When committing resources to improve service quality, company executives want to be sure that these investments will pay off. To document the payoff, many organizations have put in place measures that capture both the costs and gains of service quality.

Internationalization of Services

At one time-and indeed, not so long ago-the potential for services to be provided on a global basis was limited by the belief that services cannot be transported. That time is now past, for the internationalization of services has become a reality.

Probably the most dramatic examples of global service markets are in the airline and financial services industries.

1.13 LIMITATIONS ON GROWTH IN SERVICE INDUSTRIES

The overall conclusion from the previous section that services will continue to be important in the economy and that growth is likely in some sub-sectors is reasonable. Even in times of economic decline and stagnation there is evidence to suggest that demand for services is less sensitive to economic fluctuations. But any optimistic forecasts should take account of possible limitations on growth in the service sector. Two forces which could limit their growth are external forces and internal forces.

A. External Forces

Some constraints on growth include:

- customers can perform services themselves. The degree of essentiality of service purchases varies (e.g. people can eat at home instead of eating in restaurants);
- manufactured goods will be produced which replace service roles (e.g. TV replaces cinemas, tools replace the service of skilled labour, like carpenters, easy-care fabrics replace cleaning and laundry services);
- manufactured goods will be produced which require less service attention (e.g. cars with longer service intervals, equipment with throwaway replaceable parts).

B. Internal Forces

Some internal constraints on growth include:

- the small size of the average service firm;
- the shortage of people with certain special skills (e.g. doctors);
- the limited competition in some service sub-sectors (e.g. rail transport, local authority services);
- little emphasis on research and development in many service fields; the general failure to recognize the importance of marketing in some service businesses.

1.14 SERVICES IN THE MODERN ECONOMY

As consumers, we use services every day. Turning on a light, watching TV, talking on the telephone, catching a bus, visiting the dentist, posting a letter, getting a haircut, refuelling a car, writing a cheque or sending clothes to the cleaners are all examples of service consumption at the individual level. In addition to educational services, the facilities at today's colleges and universities usually comprise libraries and cafeterias, counselling services, a bookshop and careers offices, copy services, telephones and Internet connections, and may be even a bank. If you are registered at a residential university, additional services are likely to include halls of residence, health care, indoor and outdoor sports and athletic facilities, a theatre and, perhaps, a post office.

Unfortunately, customers are not always happy with the quality and value of the services they receive. People complain about late deliveries, rude or incompetent personnel, inconvenient service hours, poor performance, needlessly complicated procedures and a host of other problems. They grumble about the difficulty of finding sales assistants to help them in shops, express frustration about mistakes on their credit card bills or bank statements, shake their heads over the complexity of new self-service equipment, mutter about poor value and sigh as they are forced to wait for service or stand in queues almost everywhere they go.

Suppliers of services often seem to have a very different set of concerns. Many complain about how difficult it is to make a profit, how hard it is to find skilled and motivated employees, or how difficult to please customers have become. Some firms seem to believe that the surest route to financial success lies in cutting costs and eliminating 'unnecessary frills'.

Happily, in almost every field of endeavour there are service suppliers who know how to please their customers while also running a productive, profitable operation, staffed by pleasant and competent employees. The growth of the services economy is shown in Table 1.2.

Table 1.2 : THE GROWTH OF THE SERVICES SECTOR IN INDIA

	Period	Agriculture (% share of GDP)	Industry	Services
1	1998 - 1999	26.83	22.01	51.16
2	1997 - 1998	26.44	22.32	51.24
3	1996 - 1997	28.05	22.05	49.91
4	1995 - 1996	27.64	22.27	50.08
5	1994 - 1995	29.68	21.18	49.15
6	1993 - 1994	29.50	24.88	45.62
7	1992 - 1993	30.19	24.47	45.34

1.15 GOODS VERSUS SERVICES

Goods differ from services in numerous ways as summarised in Table 1.3.

Table 1.3 : A COMPARISION OF SERVICES AND GOODS

	Dimensions	*Services*	*Goods*
A.	***Characteristics***		
1.	Entity	Intangible	Tangible
2.	Storage	Not possible	Possible
3.	Quality	Varies with time and person	Standardised
4.	Producer status	Inseparable from service	Separate from goods
5.	Labour intensity	Tends to be high	Lower
6.	Life	Stillborn	Longer
B.	***Marketing Planning***		
7.	Demand	Fluctuating	Stabilised
8.	Supply	Constrained	Flexible
9.	Title	No ownership	Ownership possible
10.	Seasonality	Present	Goods specific
11.	Consumer reaction	Spontaneous	Delayed
12.	Pricing	Labour based	Material based
13.	Need satisfied	More emotional	More physical
14.	Basis of competition	Personalisation	Technology
15.	Channels	Shorter	Longer in most cases
16.	Repairs	Impossible	Possible
17.	Replacement	Rare	Common
18.	Forecasting	Short-run	Long-run
19.	Forecast	Consumer behaviour and arrival time	Products to place to inventory
20.	Image	Corporate	Brand
21.	Physical movement	Of the provider	Of the goods
22.	Cost allocation	Difficult	Easier
C.	***Marketing Strategy***		
23.	Orientation	External & Internal	External
24.	Focus	Customer expectations	Customer needs
25.	Approach	Focussed	Can be diffused
D.	***Operations***		
26.	Production	Spontaneous	Time-spread
27.	Customer involvement	High	Low / absent
28.	Physical presence of the customer	Essential	Hardly necessary
29.	Physical surrounding	Very important	Not so important
30.	Standardisation	Only for routine services	All over
31.	Facility location	Close to customer	Near supply
32.	Facility design	To accommodate	To enhance production

33.	Product design	Physical / psychological needs Environmment plays a vital role	Only physical product
34.	Process design	Immediate effect on consumers	Customer not involved
35.	Scheduling	As per customer interest	Completion dates
36.	Production planning	Smoothing results in losses	Possible
37.	Inventory	Personnel	Raw material
38.	Quality control	Variable standards	Fixed
39.	Quality objective	Zero defection	Zero defect
40.	Worker skill	Interaction	Technical
41.	Time standard	Loose	Tight
42.	Capacity planning	Fluctuation	Average
43.	Wage payment	Time based	Unit based
44.	Type of technology	Generally soft	Generally hard
45.	Delivery	Along with production	Separate from production
E.	***Organisation***		
46.	Structure	Flatter	Taller
47.	Role of higher levels	Supportive	Demanding
48.	Communication	Criss-cross	Mainly vertical
49.	Desired design	Organic	Rational

1.16 LPG SYNDROME

The buzzwords of today's economy are Liberalisation, Privatisation and Globalisation.

Liberalisation of the economy refers to the changing nature of policies and procedures to facilitate more growth and ensuring better standards of living. The economy is thrown open and the best goods and services compete in the market. The consumer then has a choice and monopolies disappear.

Privatisation connotes a wide range of ideas. In a narrow sense privatisation implies the induction of private ownership in publicly owned enterprises, but in a broader sense, it connotes besides private ownership (or even without a change in ownership), the induction of private management and control in public sector enterprises. The various modalities of privatisation can thus be grouped under three sets of measures: (a) Ownership transfer, (b) Management transfer and (c) Marketisation.

(a) Ownership Transfer: The set of measures, which transfer ownership of public enterprises, fully or partially, lead to privatisation through ownership measures. The higher the proportion of transfer of ownership to the individual or co-operatives or corporate sector, the greater is the degree of privatisation (subject to one qualification, namely, that the government infact as a shareholder might, in practice, tend to be out of proportion to its ownership interest). Privatisation through ownership measures can take three forms: (i) Total denationalisation, (ii) Joint ventures and (iii) Liquidation.

(b) Management Transfer: Management transfer may or may not involve ownership transfer. Several options are available to transfer management rights to the private sector important amongst them being: (i) Leasing, (ii) Franchising and (iii) Sub-contracting.

(c) Marketisation: These are the least spectacular, but very meaningful, measures of privatisation. Such measures are intended to inject the spirit of commercialisation and market discipline in public enterprises. The measures include:

- introduction of incentive payments not only to the blue collar workers but to the white collar employees also;
- allowing a public enterprise to acquire an input across the market, instead of producing it from within itself, i.e., by contracting out;
- by insisting that the public enterprise should go to the capital markets for capital funds exception being made for non-commercial projects; and
- by allowing private sector to enter into areas hitherto reserved for public sector.

The principal characteristics of globalisation consist of the following:

- the globalisation of financial markets
- the internationalisation of corporate strategies, in particular their commitment to competition as a source of wealth creation;
- the diffusion of technology and related R & D and knowledge worldwide;
- the transformation of consumption patterns into cultural products with worldwide consumer markets;
- the internationalisation of the regulatory capabilities of national societies into a global political economic system;
- the diminished role of national governments in designing the rules for global governance.

Suggested Indian Approach

The Indian approach in the present wave of globalisation, liberalisation and privatisation could be:

1. India should adopt the approach of selectivity in regard to globalisation, liberalisation and privatisation. The onus of making the right kind of choices should not be left to the bureaucracy or the political system alone, but it should be the joint responsibility of four wings of the society namely, intellectuals, businessmen, bureaucracy, and the politicians.

2. There should not be any doubt about the strong role that the State has to play even in the context of market driven paradigm of development. The legal system, the regulatory system, and the monitoring functions of the State need to be strengthened and made effective.

3. Foreign direct investment should be permitted and encouraged only in those sectors which would significantly contribute to income generation, employment creation, and net export earnings. The stipulations that the right to invest by the multinationals should become a legal right without any interventions of the State, which is envisaged in the proposed Multilateral Agreement on Investment (MAI) should not be acceded to, under any circumstances. On the contrary, India along with other like minded countries, should mount pressures in the WTO and other fora to include code of conduct and the obligations of the multinationals for transferring technology, sharing information and promoting employment, in any multilateral agreement.

4. The approach of globalising the financial markets without commensurate globalisation of the real sector, could have dangerous consequences of excessive short term debt resulting in instabilities and crisis situations of the Mexican type. There are already many signals of instabilities driven by volatile capital markets, and these need to be checked by enforcement of proper disciplines on the capital markets.

5. It is not yet the right time for bringing about total convertibility of the Indian currency since many of the necessary conditions for total convertibility to be successful are not yet met.

6. India should endeavour to strengthen the infrastructure, and human resources covering areas such as universal literacy and health for all, for improving what one may call as the social capability of the economy for taking advantages of the globally competitive environment.

7. As indicated by the recent theories of the industrial organisations, it is necessary that the industrial organisation structure should be based upon the principles of blending competition and

cooperation on the lines of industrial clusters and cooperative societies, for facilitating optimum utilisation of the scarce resources of knowledge and information. The sweeping statement that competition alone promotes efficiency in resource use and resource allocation has been belied by the recent experiences of flexible forms of industrial organisations which combine competition with cooperation.

8. India should take leadership role on various international economic issues for mobilising support from like minded countries of the world for strengthening the bargaining positions of the developing countries on the current issues of negotiations. For example, the Singapore meeting on WTO has decided to set up a working group for setting the implications of the proposed multilateral agreement on investment. The developing countries will have to get ready to present their stand on this issue. Similarly, the issues of social clause and labour standards would be soon becoming major issues of negotiations in the WTO. India should take initiatives to organised intellectual debates and consultations at the political level for evolving a consensus.

9. Liberalisation should necessarily mean democratisation of the decision making process in the economy. This kind of liberalisation would require significant effort to reform and remotivate the bureaucracy both at the level of the central government and at the state governments. India's image in the global scene would be very poor unless the bureaucratic procedures are streamlined and the delay of bureaucratic sanctions and permits are considerably reduced. Unfortunately, there have not been adequate initiatives to bring about this revolution in the functioning of the bureaucracy. Concerted efforts are required in this regard to enable India to take full advantage of the emerging competitive environment.

10. India is best suited to continue to be in the framework of mixed economy, in which the public sector, private sector and the cooperative sector coexist. The present exercise of privatising even the profit making public sector is not warranted because privatisation is only a modality for improving the efficiency in resource use and resource allocation. In any case, selling a few scrips of the public sector to the people at large does not at all mean privatisation. For a truly effective privatisation, the approach of preserving power for appointments of the executive and also interventions in the commercial decision making process of the public sector need to be fully eliminated. Privatisation should not be pursued as an end in itself. In fact, many of the private sector units are also suffering from endemic sickness and as such privatisation per se cannot be considered as a virtue in itself for an efficient production system. The weaknesses of corporate management both in the public and the private sectors need to be addressed in an objective way instead of viewing the problem as an ideological issue.

11. The final point which needs to be made with all emphasis at our command is that India should not give up its aspirations for maintaining and strengthening the paradigm of intellectual self-reliance for taking its own decisions to serve its national interest in the best possible manner without denying to itself the advantages of the emerging new opportunities and challenges of development.

SHORT ANSWER QUESTIONS

1. Define the following
   (a) Service
   (b) Services Marketing
   (c) Services Management
   (d) TQM
   (e) Internal marketing
2. What are the myths about services?
3. Briefly mention the reasons for the growth of the service economy.
4. Has technology leveraged customer service? If so, what has been its impact?

5. Does the growth of service industries suffer from limitations?
6. Differentiate goods from services.
7. What is the significance of services marketing?
8. Identify the vertices of the services marketing triangle. What is the relationship between these vertices?
9. What is meant by the term 'the Service Economy'?
10. Have all sub-sectors of the service economy experienced growth?
11. Identify three features associated with employment in services in recent years.

ESSAY QUESTIONS

1. Trace the evolution of economic activity highlighting the importance of the service sector.
2. Can service activities be considered as belonging to a system? Substantiate.
3. How are services classified? Elaborate.
4. "The services sector has been growing in direct proportion to the environmental changes occurring in India". Comment.
5. What are the challenges facing service managers?
6. How have the economic, demographic and social environmental changes been influential in ushering the services boom?
7. Describe the impact of Liberalisation, Privatisation and Globalisation on the services sector in India.
8. "The need and variety of services would depend on economic and social factors". Illustrate this viewpoint with examples.
9. What type of environment prevails for services?
10. What is the need for service management? Explain.
11. What trends do you visualize for services in the new millennium? Give examples.
12. What are the various industries that are categorized as service industries? What are their distinctive features?

EXERCISE / ASSIGNMENTS

1. Make a list of all service industries operating in your city. How many of them are controlled by the government?
2. Trace the growth of any two service industries in your neighbourhood and analyse the factors that have influenced their growth.
3. Have any service industries failed in your locality? What were the reasons? Could the failures have been prevented?
4. Consider any five services being offered and mention the myths surrounding them? How would you endeavour to dispel such myths?
5. Assess the impact of technology on any service industry, of your choice, over the last two decades.
6. Choose an organizational context you are familiar with. Discuss each of the three sides of the services marketing triangle in the context of that organization.

●●●

2

Service Characteristics

2.1 REVISED MARKETING MIX FOR SERVICES

The seven elements in marketing mix for services are :

(a) Product

(b) Price

(c) Place

(d) Promotion

(e) People

(f) Physical evidence

(g) Process

The marketing concept dictates that marketing decisions should be based upon customer needs and wants. Buyers purchase goods and services to satisfy their needs and wants. Thus when a buyer engages in a market transaction he perceives a bundle of benefits and satisfactions to be derived from that transaction. However he does not usually divide the market offering into its component parts. From the sellers' view point however the market offering can be divided into its component parts. The marketing mix is the convenient means of organizing all the variables controlled by the marketer that influence transactions in the marketplace. It is a 'checklist approach' where marketer's attempt to list and organize the variables under their control which may be important in influencing transactions in the market place.

The formulation process of marketing mixes in services markets is much the same as in other types of markets Typically this involves:

(a) separating the offering into its components or sub mixes;

(b) co-ordinating the sub mixes into the marketing mix.

The specific marketing mix adopted by a particular organization will of course vary according to circumstances (e.g. level of demand, range of service being offered). The marketing mix process then is a constant one of fashioning and reshaping the component elements in response to changing market circumstances and needs. Inevitably there is much overlap and interaction between the various components of a marketing mix. Decisions cannot be made on one component of the mix without considering their impact upon the other components. Also the precise elements and their importance within any marketing mix at any point in time will vary. The outline that follows therefore indicates some of the key areas to which marketing managers need to devote their attention in formulating their marketing mixes for services markets. It is illustrative not comprehensive. Service organizations will almost certainly need to adapt it in their strategy planning. Each element is considered in more detail in subsequent chapters.

Table 2.1 : EXPANDED MARKETING MIX FOR SERVICES

Product	Place	Promotion	Price	People	Physical evidence	Process
• Physical good features	• Channel type • Exposure	• Promotion blend • Salespeople	• Flexibiliity • Price level	• Employees Recruiting	• Facility design Aestheiics	• Flow of activities Standardardized
• Quality level	• Intermediaries	Number	• Terms	Training	Functionality	Customized
• Accessories	• Outlet locations	Selection	• Differentiation	Motivation	Ambient conditions	• Number of steps
• Packaging	• Transportation	Training	• Discounts	Rewards	• Equipment	Simple
• Warranties	• Storage	Incentives	• Allowances	Teamwork	• Signage	Complex
• Product lines • Branding	• Managing channels • Accessibility	• Advertising Targets	• Commissions • Perceived value	• Customers Education	• Employee dress • Reports	• Level of customer involvement
• Service lines	• Coverage	Media types		Training	• Business Cards	• Policies
• After sales service		Type of ads		• Communicating	• Statements	• Procedures
		Copy thrust		culture	• Guarantees	• Employee discretion
		• Sales promotion		and Values	• Furnishing	• Customer
		• Public Relations		• Employees research	• Colour	Involvement
		• Publicity		• Attitudes	• Layout	
					• Noise level	

TRADITIONAL MIX

Product

The service product requires consideration of the range of services provided, the quality of services provided and the level of services provided. Attention will also need to be given to matters like the use of branding, warranties and after-sale service. The service product mix of such elements can vary considerably and may be seen in comparisons of service range between a small local building society and one of the largest in the country; or between a small hotel offering a limited menu range and a four star hotel offering a wide range of meals.

Price

Price considerations include levels of prices, discounts allowances and commissions, terms of payment and credit. Price may also pay a part in differentiating one service from another and therefore the customers perceptions of value obtained from a service and the interaction of price and quality are important considerations in many service price sub mixes.

Place

The location of the service providers and their accessibility are important factors in services marketing. Accessibility relates not just to physical accessibility but to other means of communication and contact. Thus the types of distribution channels used (e.g. travel agents) and their coverage are linked to the crucial issue of service accessibility.

Promotion

Promotion includes the various methods of communicating with markets whether through advertising, personal selling activities, sales promotion activities and other direct forms of publicity, and indirect forms of communication like public relations.

EXPANDED MIX FOR SERVICES

Because services are usually produced and consumed simultaneously, customers are often present in the firm's factory, interact directly with the firm's personnel, and are actually part of the service production process. Also, because services are intangible customers will often be looking for any tangible cue to help them understand the nature of the service experience. These facts have led services marketers to conclude that they can use additional variables to communicate with and satisfy their customers. For example, in the hotel industry the design and decor of the hotel as well as the appearance and attitudes of its employees will influence customer perceptions and experience.

Acknowledgment of the importance of these additional communication variable has led services marketers to adopt the concept of an expanded marketing mix for services shown in the three remaining columns in Table 2.1. In addition to the traditional four Ps, the services marketing mix includes people, physical evidence, and process.

People

All human actors who play a part in service delivery and thus influence the buyer's perceptions; namely, the firm's personnel, the customer, and other customers in the service environment.

All of the human actors participating in the delivery of a service provide cues to the customer regarding the nature of the service itself. How these people are dressed, their personal appearance their attitudes and behaviors all influence the costumers perceptions of the service. The service provider or contact person can be very important. In fact, for some services, such as consulting, counselling, teaching, and other professional relationship - based services, the provider is the services. In other cases the contact person may play what appears to be a relatively small part in service delivery, for instance, a telephone installer, an airline baggage handler, or an equipment delivery dispatcher. Yet research suggests that even these providers may be the focal point of service encounters that can prove critical for the organization.

Physical Evidence

The environment in which the service is delivered and where the firm and customer interact, and any tangible components that facilitate performance or communication of the service.

The physical evidence of service includes all of the tangible representations of the services such as brochures, letterhead, business cards, report formats, signage, and equipment. In some cases it includes the physical facility where the service is offered, for example, the retail bank branch facility. In other cases, such as telecommunication services, the physical facility maybe irrelevant. In this case other tangibles such as billing statements and appearance of the repair truck may be important indicators of quality. Especially when consumers have little on which to judge the actual quality of service they will rely on these cues, just as they rely on the cues provided by the people and the service process. Physical evidence cues provide excellent opportunities for the firm to send consistent and strong messages regarding the organization's purpose, the intended market segments, and the nature of the service.

Process

The actual procedures, mechanism and flow of activities by which the service is delivered - the service delivery and operating systems.

The actual delivery steps the customer experiences, or the operational flow of the service, will also provide customers with evidence on which to judge the service. Some services are very complex, requiring the customer to follow a complicated and extensive series of actions to complete the process. Highly bureaucratized services frequently follow this pattern, and the logic of the steps involved often escapes the customer. Another distinguishing characteristic of the process that can provide evidence to the customer is whether the service follows a production-line/standardized approach or whether the process is an empowered/customized one. None of these characteristics of the service is inherently better or worse than another. Rather, the point is that these process characteristics are another form of evidence used by the consumer to judge service. For example, two successful airline companies, Southwest in the United States and Singapore Airlines, follow extremely different process models. Southwest is no-frills (no food, no assigned seats), no exceptions, low-priced airline that offers frequent, relatively short length domestic flights. All of the evidence it provides is consistent with its vision and market position. Singapore Airlines, on the other hand, focuses on the business traveler and is concerned with meeting individual traveler needs. Thus, its process is highly customized to the individual, and employees are empowered to provide nonstandard service when needed. Both airlines have been very successful.

The three new marketing-mix elements (people, physical evidence, and process) are included in the marketing mix as separate elements because they are within the control of the firm and any or all of them may influence the customer's initial decision to purchase a service, as well as the customer's level of satisfaction and repurchase decisions. The traditional elements as well as the new marketing-mix elements will be explored in depth in future chapters. Certainly Marketing managers in services markets need to undertake research about the markets and market segments for which their respective marketing mixes are shaped. Wherever possible the services marketing manager will need to research and analyses the characteristics of the markets served. It is these problems of conducting such analysis and research that we now examine (Figure 2.1).

1 Developing a marketing strategy involves two tasks. These are selecting target markets and formulating marketing mixes.

2 In services marketing adaptations and adjustments may be required, although the processes of devising marketing strategies and formulating marketing mixes are similar irrespective of market type.

Figure 2.1 : BUILDING THE MARKETING MIX

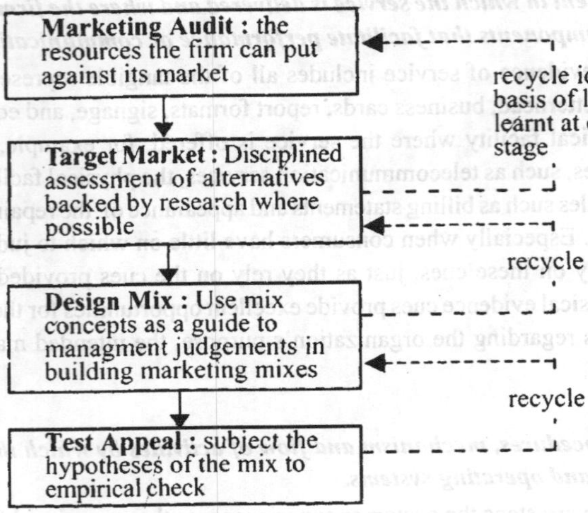

3 In the analytical stage preceding strategy formulation, common questions posed about all products may give rise to different answers for services.

4 The marketing mix may have to be revised for use in services contexts. In particular people, processes and physical evidence may have to be incorporated into the marketing mix framework.

2.2 CHARACTERISTICS OF SERVICES

Services possess some key distinguishing characteristics. They are:

a. Intangibility
b. Inseparability
c. Variability
d. Perishability
e. Simultaneity
f. Heterogeneity
g. Lack of Ownership

2.3 INTANGIBILITY

Services cannot generally be seen, tasted, felt, heard or smelt before being bought. The potential customer is unable to perceive the service before (and sometimes during and after) the service delivery. For many customers of car repair, for example the service is totally intangible - they often cannot see what is being done and many indeed are unable to evaluate what has been done.

Implications

Intangibility presents problems in that consumer may experience difficulty in knowing and understanding what is on offer before, and even after, receipt of the service. The challenge for the service provider is to determine the extent of intangibility and the management action required to make the service more tangible (Figure 2.2). The first task implies resort to some form of measurement, and the second task involves the provision of tangible evidence, e.g. a brochure to help consumer understanding of the service.

Figure 2.2 : SOME IMPLICATIONS OF SERVICE INTANGIBILITY

INTANGIBILITY OF SERVICE

↓

leads to customers:

1. Having difficulty in evaluating competing service
2. Perceiving high levels of risk
3. Placing great emphasis on personal information
4. Using price as a basis for assessing quality

↓

results in management response through :

1. Reducing service complexity
2. Stressing tangible cues
3. Facilitating word-of-mouth recommendation
4. Focusing on service quality

Pure services have no tangible properties which can be used by consumers to verify advertising claims before the purchase is made. The intangible process characteristics which define services, such as reliability, personal care, attentiveness of staff, their friendliness, etc., can only be verified once a service has been purchased and consumed.

Intangibility has a number of important marketing implications. The lack of physical evidence that intangibility implies increases the level of uncertainty which a consumer faces when choosing between competing services. An important part of a services marketing programme will therefore involve reducing consumer uncertainty by such means as adding physical evidence and the development of strong brands. It is interesting to note that pure goods and pure services tend to move in opposite directions in terms of their general approach to the issue of tangibility. While service marketers seek to add tangible evidence to their product, pure goods marketers often seek to augment their products by adding intangible elements such as after-sales service and improved distribution.

Evidence Creation

The ability to picture a service may be assisted by the service organization providing something tangible. This may be in the form of tangible evidence, e.g. computerized representation of hairstyles or a tangible possession, e.g. a university prospectus. The aim would be to help the potential customer form expectations before using the service. Equally, tangible evidence and possessions could assist customer judgement of the service during and after usage.

2.4 INSEPARABILITY

There is a marked distinction between physical goods and services (Figure 2.3) in terms of the sequence of production and consumption.

Figure 2.3 : SEQUENCE OF PRODUCTION AND CONSUMPTION

Physical goods	***Services***
Production	Sale
↓	↓
Storage	Produced and consumed at the same time
↓	
Sale	
↓	
Consumption	

Whereas goods are first produced, then stored, and finally sold and consumed, services are first sold, then produced and consumed simultaneously. For the production of many services (e.g. counselling, museums, hairdressing, rail travel, hotels), the customer must be physically present. Some services may be produced and delivered in circumstances where the customer's presence is optional, e.g. carpet cleaning, plumbing. Other services may rely more on written communication, e.g. distance learning course, or on technology, e.g. home banking. Whatever the nature and extent of contact, the potential for inseparability of production and consumption remains.

Implications

The involvement of the customer in the production and delivery of the service means that the service provider must exercise care in what is being produced and how it is produced. The latter task will be of particular significance. How teachers, doctors, bank tellers, lawyers, car mechanics, hairdressers conduct themselves in the presence of the customer may determine the likelihood of repeat business. Therefore, proper selection and training of customer contact personnel are necessary to ensure the delivery of quality. The production and consumption of a tangible good are two discrete activities. Companies usually produce goods in one central location and then transport them to the place where customers most want to buy them. In this way, manufacturing companies can achieve economies of scale through centralized production and have centralised quality-control checks. The manufacturer is also able to make goods at a time which is convenient to itself, then make them available to customers at times which are convenient for them. Production and consumption are said to be separable. On the other hand, the consumption of a service is said to be inseparable from its means of production. Producer and consumer must normally interact in order for the benefits of the service to be realized - both must meet at a time and a place which is mutually convenient in order that the producer can directly pass on service benefits. In the extreme case of personal care services, the customer must be present during the entire production process - a doctor cannot provide a service without the involvement of a patient. For services, marketing becomes a means of facilitating complex producer - consumer interaction, rather than being merely an exchange medium. Inseparability occurs whether the producer is human, as in healthcare services, or a machine, as in the case of a bank ATM machine. The service of the ATM machine can only be realized if the producer and consumer interact. In some cases, it has been possible to separate service production and consumption, especially where there is little need for personal contact.

Inseparability has a number of important marketing implications for services (Figure 2.4). First, whereas goods are generally first produced, then offered for sale and finally sold and consumed, inseparability causes this process to be modified for services. These are generally sold first, then produced and consumed simultaneously. Second, while the method of goods production is to a large extent (though by no means always) of little importance to the consumer, production processes are critical to the enjoyment of services.

Figure 2 . 4 : SOME IMPLICATIONS OF SERVICE INSEPARABILITY

INSEPARABILITY OF SERVICES

↓

leads to customers :

1. Being co-producers of the service
2. Often being co-consumers of a service with other consumers
3. Often having to travel to the point of service production

↓

results in management response through :

1. Attempts to separate production and consumption
2. Management of consumer-producer interaction
3. Improvement in service delivery systems

2.5 VARIABILITY

An unavoidable consequence of simultaneous production and consumption is variability in performance of a service. The quality of the service may vary depending on who provides it, as well as when and how it is provided. One hotel provides a fast efficient service and another a short distance away delivers a slow, inefficient service. Within a particular hotel, one employee is courteous and helpful while another is arrogant and obstructive. Even within one employee there can be variations in performance over the course of a day.

Implications

Reducing variability involves determining the causes. It may be due to unsuitable personality traits in an employee which are very difficult to detect at the selection stage. There is nothing much that can be done about this except hope that the employee decides to terminate his employment! However, there may be good sound reasons for variations in performance. For example, it could be due to poor training and supervision, lack of communication and information and generally a lack of regular support.

Some have argued for a replacement of labour with automation and a production line approach to service operations. This would mean a reduction in employee discretion and an increase in standardization of procedures. The operation of pizza restaurants is put forward as an ideal model of vice industrialization.

For services, variability impacts upon customers in terms not just of outcomes but also of process of production. It is the latter point that causes variability to pose a much greater problem for services, compared to goods. Because customer are usually involved in the production process for a service at the same time as they consume it, it can be difficult to carry out monitoring and control to ensure consistent standards. The opportunity for pre-delivery inspection and rejection which is open to the goods manufacturer is not normally possible with services-the service must normally be produced in the presence of the customer without the possibility of intervening quality control. Particular problems can occur where personnel are involved in providing services on a one-to-one basis-such as hairdressing - where no easy method of monitoring and control is possible.

The variability of service output can pose problems for brand building in services compared to tangible goods - for the latter it is usually relatively easy to incorporate monitoring and a quality control procedures into production processes in order to ensure that a brand stands for a consistency of output. It is often difficult to achieve standardization of output in services.

2.6 PERISHABILITY

Services cannot be stored for later sale or use. Hotel rooms not occupied, air line seats not purchased, and college places not filled cannot be reclaimed. As services are performances they cannot be stored. If demand far exceeds supply it cannot be met, as in manufacturing, by taking goods from a warehouse. Equally, if capacity far exceeds demand, the revenue and/or value of that service is lost.

Implications

Fluctuations in demand characterize service organizations and may pose problems where these fluctuations are unpredictable. Strategies need to be developed for producing a better match between supply and demand. Services differ from goods in that they cannot be stored. A producer of cars which is unable to sell all its output in the current period can carry forward stocks to sell in a subsequent one. The only significant costs are storage, financing and the possibility of loss through obsolescence. In contrast, the producer of a service which cannot sell all is output produced in the current period has no chance to carry it forward for sale in a subsequent one. An airline which offers seats on 9.00 a.m. flight from Mumbai to Delhi cannot sell any empty seats once the aircraft has left. The service offer disappears and spare seats cannot be stored to meet a surge in demand which may occur at, say, 10.00 a.m. The perishability of services results in greater attention having to be paid to the management of demand by evening out peaks and troughs and in scheduling service production to follow this pattern as far as possible. Pricing and promotion are two of the tools commonly adopted to tackle this problem.

2.7 HETEROGENEITY

Even though standard systems may be used, for example to handle a flight reservation, to book in a customer's car for service or to quote for insurance on his life. Each 'unit' of a service may differ from other 'units'. Franchise operations, attempt to ensure a standard of conformity, but ultimately it is difficult to ensure the same level of output in terms of quality. From the customers' viewpoint too it is difficult to judge quality in advance of purchase; although this element also applies to some product marketing.

Capacity level should be available on cope with surges in demand before service levels suffer. Equally, attention has to be given in times of low levels of usage on whether spare capacity will lie idle or whether short-term policies (e.g. differential pricing, special promotions), will be adopted to even out fluctuations in demand. Some illustrations of programmes that may be adopted to compensate for fluctuating demand are shown in Table 2.2.

Table 2.2 : PROGRAMMES TO COMPENSATE FOR UNEVEN DEMAND

Industry	*Programme*
Airlines	Night rates, group and tour fares, family discounts, advance purchase super savers, 24-hour round-trip discounts, and low season fares.
Hotels	Off-season and group rates, theme weekends (Valentine getaway), sports packages, family and senior citizen discounts.
Telephone	Evening, night, and weekend rates.
Barber shops	Evening appointments and family rates
Automobile	Specials (tyre balancing, tuneups, and lubrication)
Dentists	Call-back reminders and family discounts.
Education	Weekend classes, adult education and military programmes.
Movies	Weekend specials, Film festivals
Theme Parks	Off-season specials, group and senior citizen rates, family rates, advance purchase discounts.

2.8 LACK OF OWNERSHIP

Lack of ownership is a basic difference between a service industry and a product industry because a customer may only have access to or use of a facility (e.g. a hotel room, a credit card). Payment is for the use of , access to or hire of items. With the sale of a tangible good, barring restrictions imposed say by a hire purchase scheme, the buyer has full use of the product.

A summary of these characteristics of services with some implications is shown in Table 2.3.

Table 2.3 : SOME CONSTRAINTS ON THE MANAGEMENT OF SERVICES AND WAYS OF OVERCOMING THEM

Characteristics of service	*Some implications*	*Some means of overcoming characteristics*
Intangibility	Sampling difficult. Places strain on promotional element of marketing mix. No patents possible. Difficult to judge price and quality in advance.	Focus on benefits. Increase tangibility of service (e.g. physical representations of it). Use brand names. Use personalities to personalize service. Develop reputation.
Inseparability	Requires presence of producer. Direct sale. Limited scale of operations.	Learn to work in larger groups. Work faster. Train more competent service providers.
Heterogeneity	Standard depends upon who and when provided. Difficult to assure quality.	Careful personnel selection and training. Ensure standards are monitored. Pre-package service. Mechanize and industrialize for quality control. Emphasize bespoke features.
Perishability	Cannot be stored. Problems with demand fluctuation.	Better match between supply and demand (e.g. price reductions off peak).
Ownership	Customer has access to but not ownership of activity or facility.	Stress advantages of non-ownership (e.g. easier payment systems).

2.9 ELEMENTS OF CUSTOMER SERVICE

Pre-transaction elements

- Written customer service policy
  (Is it communicated internally or externally, is it understood, is it specific and quantified where possible?)
- Accessibility
  (Are we easy to contact/do business with? Is there a single point of contact?)
- Organization structure
  (Is there a customer service management structure in place? What level of control do they have over their service process?)
- System flexibility
  (Can we adapt our service delivery systems to meet particular customers needs?)

Transaction elements

- Order cycle time
  (What is the elapsed time from order to delivery? What is the reliability / variation?)
- Inventory availability

(What percentage of demand for each item can be met from stock?)

- Order fill rate

  (What proportion of orders are completely filled within the stated lead-time?)
- Order status information

  (How long does it take us to respond to a query with the required information? Do we inform the customer of problems or do they contact us?

Post-transaction elements

- Availability of spares

  (What are the in-stock levels of service parts?)
- Call out time

  (How long does it take for the engineer to arrive and what is the 'first call fix rate'?)
- Product tracing / warranty

  (Can we identify the location of individual products once purchased? Can we maintain/extend the warranty to customers' expected levels?)
- Customer complaints, claims etc.

  (How promptly do we deal with complaints and returns? Do we measure customer satisfaction with our response?)

2.10 PROBLEMS ARISING FROM THE CHARACTERISTICS

Heterogeneity

Where services are people processing (e.g. an interview at a job centre) or people changing (e.g. a haircut), the degree of heterogeneity will be greater than where a facilitating service is being provided for a consumer (e.g. a telephone service).

The problems associated with this characteristic largely revolve around the inability to standardize either the product or the procedures needed to deliver the service. One of the aspects of delivering a quality product, is the requirement of identifying customer requirements and writing a specification for the product. The actual product produced can then be compared with the specification to judge quality and consistency of delivery. When the product specification changes every time, there is no way of ensuring that the mode of delivery is the best possible. There is no time to study, test, adapt or refine the product. Training is difficult, as each encounter with the customer will be different and will not follow a prescribed pattern. As the method of delivery will differ on subsequent occasions, the customer will not know what to expect. Mood will often play a large part in the quality of a delivery of a service. When a person is preoccupied, or not feeling well, the delivery of the service may well be affected. Even during the course of a day, a receptionist who was friendly and helpful at the beginning of the day may become tired, irritable and most unhelpful by the end of a trying few hours.

Simultaneity

Quite apart from the fact that every time a service is reproduced it will be different, making standardization difficult and quality hard to define and ensure, the very fact that the customer is present throughout the production process, or during part of the process, means that factors which would not normally be an issue in a factory have to be considered.

Safety

The safety of employees is always a factor, but customers are not trained, may not be familiar with safety regulations, or may be children. As a consequence, the layout and design of facilities is very important. Nursery schools are a good example : barred gates need to be in place where there are stairs, while colouring crayons need to be non-toxic, just in case the child decides to eat the crayon!

Signposting

Customers arriving for the first time at any facility will need to know where to got. Most organizations will have a reception, which will be the first point of contact for either new members of staff or customers. New employees will usually be told, or shown, where to report on their first day. After that, they will either be given a tour of the parts of the factory they need to know, or be told by fellow workers. A visitor to a hospital, however, will not necessarily have been given any instructions on how to find Ward 'X'. Unless there is clear signposting, visitors could inadvertently wander into isolation wards or operating theatres! Out-patients frequently have to find their way round hospitals, maybe to have an X-ray or other specialized tests. One solution has been to paint different coloured lines on the floor, so that a nurse need only tell the patient to follow the red line to reach the X-ray department, or maybe the green line for the exit.

Layout

The actual layout will need thought, not just from a safety point of view, but also from an ease of access perspective. Is there adequate car parking? Will the customer's trolley fit between the displays?

Decor

Decor influences the atmosphere of a facility. There may be a trade-off between functionality and atmosphere. In a hospital, thick carpets would be so much nicer to step out of bed on to in the morning (or at any time of day). In some private hospitals, carpets, are in place. However, from a cleaner's perspective, or a hygiene perspective, easily washable floors would be much more functional.

Manner of delivery

Because the customer is present during the production process, he or she can observe how the product is produced. May be a new employee is serving a customer in an insurance office. A form is not filled in correctly, and a colleague, unobtrusively observing the operation, corrects the new employee. The customer will be aware that it has taken two attempts to fill the form in correctly. He or she may lose confidence in the competence of the employee and may then take their business elsewhere.

No pre-test

In many cases, because production and consumption take place simultaneously, it is impossible to pre-test the service. Once a hairdresser has cut a customer's hair, there is no sticking it back on again ! How many times have you heard someone say, 'the barber/hairdresser took much off or 'the colour hasn't come out how I wanted it to, it's too reddish'? A car may be taken out for a test run. A suit may be tried on in the fitting room. The kettle which did not work when you got it home may be taken back. One of the problems with the hairdresser may have been poor communication skills on the part of the customer. On the other hand, the hairdresser may have lacked the necessary interpersonal skills, and was unable, or not prepared, to find out just what was required.

Unpredictability

Quite apart from the fact that no two customers will ever want exactly the same service, the fact that the customer is present during the conversion process leads to inevitable surprises which may lead to disruptions of the service. Customers turn up late for appointments. They get lost going from the emergency department of a hospital to the X-ray department. Students ask too many or too few questions in the lecture. A passenger on a long-haul flight is vegetarian and has not previously informed the carrier at the time of booking.

The effect of unpredictability can have a major impact on scheduling/capacity management. Customers take longer than expected and create bottlenecks and queues which negatively affect the experience of other customers. Customers who do not turn up on time, or who do not take as long to process as expected, lead to under-utilization of resources. In the case of the students, the planned amount of ground that was to be covered in a lecture may be impossible because of too many questions. On the other hand, more ground than planned could have been covered because the students did not ask any questions.

Customer as unpaid employee

One aspect of the customer's presence within the system may be seen as very positive. Customers can actually be considered as unpaid employees, fulfilling tasks that would otherwise have to be done by paid employees. Any kind of self-service situation falls into this category. Self-service petrol stations mean that perhaps ten cars can be served simultaneously without the need for ten petrol pump attendants. The implications for an operations manager of using the customer as an unpaid employee are mainly related to the reduced need for paid employees. However, to do this successfully, as with any employee, there is a need for training. The customers will need to know what their role is.

Labour intensive

Car washes may not involve the customer in any contact whatsoever with service personnel. The purchase of a token from a machine, which is then placed in the slot at the entrance of the car wash, may be all that is required to obtain the service. At the other extreme, counselling will usually preclude the use of equipment, and is purely people based. A tape recorder may be used to keep a record of sessions with patients, but mechanization of the actual process is impossible. The option to mechanize services is often, therefore, precluded by other considerations. A particular problem arising from this is the need for training employees. As services cannot be stored, fluctuations in demand are often met by adjusting the number of employees and the length of hours worked. This often results in part-time working or temporary staff being taken on to meet peaks in demand. High rates of labour turnover are also common.

High levels of personal judgement

It is difficult in a service setting, when there is a high level of contact with the customer, to produce procedures and guidelines to fit every situation. The frontline employee who is dealing with a customer will be making judgements about how to provide the service. A successful taxi driver will try and judge whether or not a particular customer wants to be talked to. Is a running commentary of the areas of interest en route appropriate? Are the passengers tourists who would welcome the information, or would the passenger prefer the time to collect his or here wits for the forthcoming job interview?.

Numerous outlets

Another characteristic of services is the need for outlets near to the customer. If the customer needs to be present during the transformation process, e.g. the customer has to be present to have a haircut, then usually the location of the service needs to be convenient. Problems associated with this dispersal of units thus include the inability to take advantage of economies of scale, difficulty in controlling widespread units, and hence difficulty in ensuring consistency and required service quality levels. For example, if a customer stays in a hotel which is part of a chain in one part of the country, and has a bad experience, then he or she will be very unlikely to stay in any other hotels which are part of that particular chain. The image of the whole chain may be damaged by one or two inferior outlets.

Distribution

Many services are provided on the customer's premises: for example, home helps, gardening services, and servicing of gas and electrical equipment within the home. There is an increasing trend for restaurant and fast (or semi-fast) food establishments to provide a delivery service. Distribution and routing problems and solutions are common to both the service sector and the manufacturing sector. What is different, however, is the need actually to carry out a service in the customer's home. Equipment has to be transported to the site of provision of service.

Intangibility

If customers are buying something intangible, how can they know just what it is they are buying, if it cannot be described precisely? Subjectivity is inevitable. What makes an exciting and pleasurable experience for one person may constitute a frightening and nightmarish experience for another. Take flying - for some, the takeoff, when the aeroplane accelerates down the runway, is exhilarating; for others, the takeoff represents the start of what seems like a lifetime of fear. When a service involves providing an experience of any kind, whether exciting, relaxing, entertaining, romantic or exhilarating, defining the dimensions of that service is fraught with difficulties. Even if surrogate measures can be made, they tend to be of the form describing the surroundings or conditions for providing the service, rather than definition of the service itself. In terms of what the customer perceives the service to be, that service, provided in the same manner on two different occasions, may also seem different, because of the mood of the customer. A happy customer is more likely to see an experience in a favourable light than a customer in a bad temper.

Perishability

Perishability is one of the characteristics of service most frequently presented. If is a direct consequence of the intangibility of the product. Whenever there are elements of the product which are not tangible, and which cannot therefore be stored in a warehouse for later use, the option to produce for later consumption does not exist. Services are even more perishable that fruit, which does have some storage life.

Easy to imitate

Service firms often differentiate themselves by the way the service is delivered. The actual core service provided may not differ substantially, but the way it is 'packaged' may give one firm a competitive edge over another. It is very difficult to gain a sustained competitive edge in services. It is not possible to obtain patents for intangibles services, and as such, no long-lasting benefit can be obtained by being the first to design and introduce a new product, as can be the case with a physical product.

Accounting/pricing/charging

Air travel is notorious for the range of prices which may be charged on just one flight. Quite apart from the difference in fares charged between first-business and economy-class seats, when the flight was booked, the ability to alter a booking, whether or not the return flight was within a week, but covered a Saturday night, etc. may mean that, although each price clearly related to a slightly different product, two passengers sitting next to each other on a flight receiving the same service in terms of checking-in and in-flight service, could be paying fares different from each other by a factor of five or more.

Customers do not always know how much a service will cost. Lawyers charge for their time, for the number of phone calls made, and for the number of letters written. Sceptics would say that many of the letters written are unnecessary and that lawyers have little incentive to hurry a case along- after all, the longer it takes, the more they can charge. Because, in most cases, there will be a large gap in knowledge between the lawyer and client, the client is not in a position to challenge the manner in which the lawyer operates.

2.11 THE COMPONENTS OF A SERVICE

The products that firms market do differ in the extent to which they involve the transfer of ownership of physical goods. However, intangible components inevitably play a pivotal role in winning and maintaining a satisfied customer. To stress this point, we will refer to all the market offerings of firms as their services, and point out that these services can be broken down into four main components: physical product, service product, service environment, and service delivery (Figure 2.5). All of them must be managed to meet customer needs.

FIGURE 2.5
THE FOUR COMPONENTS OF A SERVICE

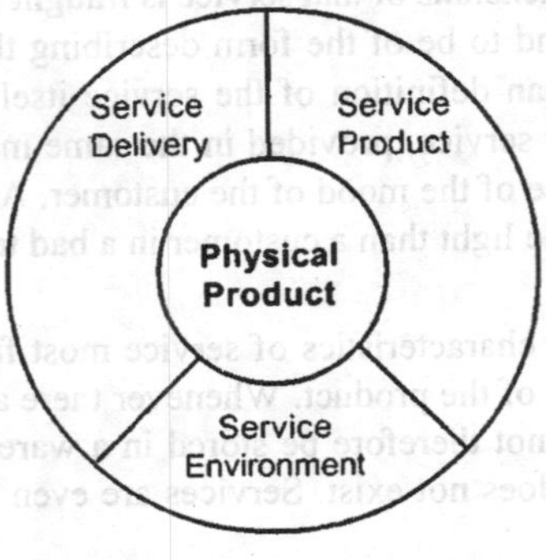

The physical product is whatever the organization transfers to the customer that can be touched. It is tangible and physically real. Examples include houses, automobiles, computers, books, hotel soap and shampoo, and food. As with the rest of the service offering, product design must be customer-oriented. There is a well-developed method for ensuring that product design matches customer needs, called Quality Function Deployment (QFD), or more popularly, the House of Quality. The procedure was developed in Japan in the 1970s as a way to help marketing managers and engineers to talk to each other and to work toward a common goal of meeting customer needs. By linking engineering design features to specific customer needs QFD assures that design improvements improve the product's value to customers. At the same time, it helps the firm to avoid costly engineering improvements that "better engineering" but do not meet customer needs. Spending time and effort on unnecessary engineering is known as "over-engineering," and it is seen most often in technology-driven companies.

The service product is the core performance purchased by the customer, the flow of events designed to provide a desired outcome. It refers to that part of the experience apart from the transfer of physical goods and typically includes interactions with the firm's personnel'. For example, at some car dealer showrooms customers are allowed to look at the cars in the showroom without being approached by sales representatives. Only when shoppers ask to speak to someone will a sales rep speak to them. To further reduce anxiety, actual sales prices, set to be competitively low, are posted on the cars, so that customers don't have to worry about negotiating the price, as at most other auto dealerships. The cars come with strong service guarantees, and dealer personnel are trained and empowered to make exceptional efforts to keep customers happy and solve their problems. All of these aspects of the firm's interaction with customers must be planned, and they help determine the nature of the overall service experience. The service environment is the physical backdrop that surrounds the service, sometimes referred to as a "servicescape." For example, going to see a movie is more enjoyable if the theater is clean, has comfortable seats, and has a spacious, well-lit parking lot. Even though the customer doesn't take any of that home, it has an important impact on the service experience.

The service environment (Table 2.4) can also signal the intended market segment and position the organisation. For example, a restaurant near a university campus might signal that it is catering to college students by putting college memorabilia and pictures of students on the walls. A car dealer might use its service environment to position itself as upscale by decorating its showroom in the service environment: the ambient conditions, the spatial layout, and the signs and symbols. The ambient conditions include things such as the lighting and background music. What may be appropriate for some businesses may be inappropriate for others, depending upon the market positioning. For example, bright lighting is appropriate for fast food restaurants, but would be inappropriate for an expensive, romantic restaurant. The spatial layout can also influence customer satisfaction. For example, Disney World found that long waiting lines seem shorter if the lines go around frequent turns, and there is some entertainment along the way. Signs and symbols are also important. The service delivery refers to what actually happens when customers buy the service. The service product defines how the service works in theory, but the service delivery is how the service works in actual practice. We often hear the adage, "Plan your work, and work your plan. " The service product is the result of "planning your work, " and the service delivery is the result of "working your plan." For example, the service design may be that a fast-food customer is greeted cheerfully within ten seconds, but the actual service delivery may be hindered by the counter employee joking in the back of the store for five minutes with other employees. What is designed does not always occur.

Table 2.4 : COMPONENTS OF SERVICE : INDUSTRY EXAMPLES

Industry	*Physical product*	*Service Product*	*Service Environment*	*Service Delivery*
Auto	The Car	Title transfer Warranty Loans	Showroom Grounds Car lot	Test drive and sales pitch Repair time Negotiation
Hotels	Shampoo, etc. Food	Messages Shuttle Wake-up calls	The room Pool Lobby	Front desk performance Room cleaning Promptness of room service
University	Diploma	Majors Residence Placement	Classrooms Dormitories Sports fields	Teaching performance Janitorial Job interview schedules
Retail store	Goods	Assistance Credit Inventory	Sales floor	Knowledgeability Friendliness Speed

2.12 CATEGORIES IN THE DECISION-MAKING PROCESS

The basic consumer decision-making process (Figure 2.6) comprises 1. information search 2. evaluation of alternatives, 3. purchase and consumption, and 4. post-purchase evaluation. In purchase of services, these categories do not occur in a linear sequence in the way they mot often do in the purchase of goods. One of the major differences between goods and services is that a greater portion of the evaluation of services succeeds purchase and consumption than is the case with goods.

A. Information Search

Use of Personal Sources: Consumers obtain information about products and services from personal sources (e.g., friends or experts) and from non-personal sources (e.g., mass or selective media). When purchasing goods, consumers make generous use of both personal and non-personal sources because both effectively convey information about search qualities. When purchasing services on the other hand, consumers seek and rely to a greater extent on personal sources, for several reasons. First, Mass and selective media can convey information about search qualities but can communicate little about experience qualities. By asking friends or experts about services, however, the consumer can obtain information vicariously about experience qualities. Second, non-personal sources of information may not be available because (1) many service providers are local, independent merchants with neither the experience nor the funds for advertising; (2) "cooperative" advertising, or

Figure 2.6 : CATEGORIES IN CONSUMER DECISION-MAKING AND EVALUATION OF SERVICES

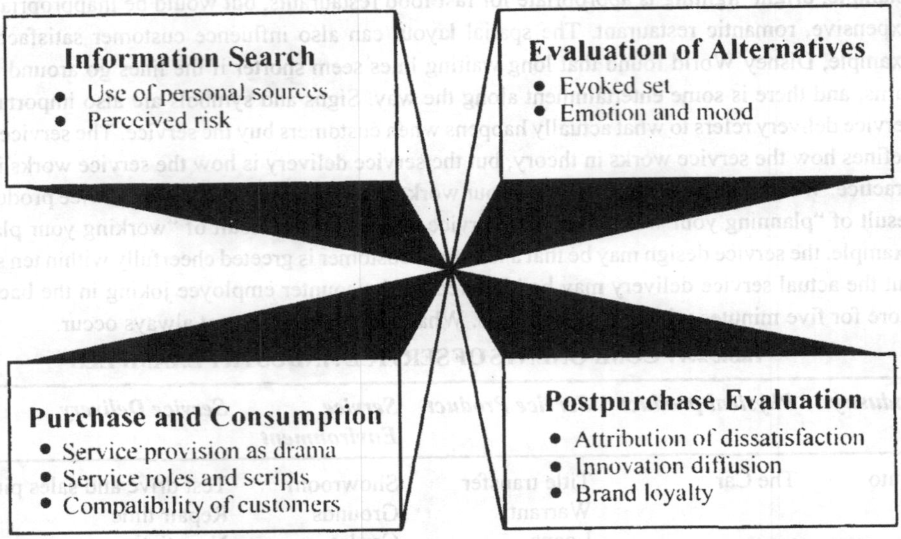

advertising funded jointly by the retailer and the manufacturer, is used infrequently with services because most local providers are both producer and retailer of the service; and (3) professional associations banned advertising for so many years that both professionals and consumers tend to resist its use even though it is now permitted. Third, since consumers can discover few attributes before purchase of a service, they may feel greater risk in selecting a little-known alternative.

Personal influence becomes pivotal as product complexity increases and when objective standards by which to evaluate a product decrease (i.e., when experience qualities are high). Most managers in service industries recognize the influence of word of mouth in services.

Perceived Risk: While some degree of perceived risk probably accompanies all purchase transactions, more risk would appear to be involved in the purchase of services than in the purchase of goods because services are intangible, non-standardized, and usually sold without guarantees or warranties.

First, the intangible nature of services and their high level of experience qualities imply that services generally must be selected on the basis of less pre-purchase information than is the case for products.

Second, because services are non-standardized, there will always be uncertainty about the outcome and consequences each time a service is purchased.

Third, service purchases may involve more perceived risk than product purchases because, with few exceptions, services are not accompanied by warranties or guarantees. The dissatisfied service purchaser can rarely "return" a service, since he has already consumed it by the time he realizes his dissatisfaction.

Finally, many services (e.g., medical diagnosis, pest control) are so technical or specialized that consumers possess neither the knowledge nor the experience to evaluate whether they are satisfied, even after they have consumed the service.

B. Evaluation of Service Alternatives

Evoked Set : The evoked set of alternatives - that group of products a consumer considers acceptable options in a given product category-is likely to be smaller with services than with goods.

One reason involves differences in retailing between goods and services. To purchase goods, consumers generally shop in retail stores that display competing products in close proximity, clearly demonstrating the possible alternatives. To purchase service, on the other hand, the consumer visits an establishment (e.g., a bank, a dry cleaner, or a hair cutting parlour) that almost always offers only a single "brand" for sale. A second reason for the smaller evoked set is that consumers are unlikely to find more than one or two business providing the same services in a given geographic area, whereas they may find numerous retail stores carrying the identical manufacturer's product. A third reason for a smaller evoked set is the difficulty of obtaining adequate pre-purchase information about services.

Emotion and Mood : Emotion and mood are feeling states that influence people's (and therefore customers) perceptions and evaluations of their experiences. Moods are distinguished from emotions in that moods refer to transient feeling states that occur at specific times and in specific situations, whereas emotions are more intense, stable, and pervasive.

Because services experiences, moods and emotions are critical factors that shape the perceived effectiveness of service encounters. If a service customer is in a "bad mood" when he enters a service establishment, service provision will likely be interpreted more negatively than if he were in a buoyant, positive mood. Similarly, if a service provider is irritable or sullen, her interaction with customers will likely be coloured by that mood. Furthermore, when another customer in a service establishment is cranky of frustrated, whether from problems with the service or from existing emotions unrelated to the service, his or her mood affects the provision of service for all customers who sense the negative mood. In sum, any services characterized by human interaction is strongly dependent on the moods and emotions of the service provider, the service customer, and other customers receiving the service the service at the same time.

C. Service Purchase and Consumption

Service Provision as Drama : Researchers and managers of service business have compared service provision with drama, observing that both aim to create and maintain a desirable impression before an audience, and both recognize that the way to accomplish this is by carefully managing the actors and the physical setting of their behavior. In fact, the service marketer must play many drama-related roles (including director, choreographer, and writer) to be sure the performances of the actors are pleasing to the audience. The skill of the service "actors" in performing their routines, the way they appear, and their commitment to the "show" are all pivotal to service delivery. While service actors are present in most service performances, their importance increases when the degree of direct personal contact increases (such as in a hospital, resort, or restaurant), when the services involve repeat contact, and when the contact personnel as actors have discretion in determining the nature of the service and how it is delivered (as in education, medical services, and legal services).

Service Roles and Scripts : If we think of services performances as drama, we can view each player as having a role to perform. Roles have been defined as combinations of social cues that guide and direct behavior in a given setting. The success of any service performance depends in part on how well the "role set" or players-both service employees and customers-act out their roles. Service employees need to perform their roles according to expectations of the customer; if they do not, the customer may be frustrated and disappointed. The customer's role must also be performed well. If customers are informed and educated about the expectations and requirements of the service (i.e. if the customer plays the proper role), and if the customer cooperates with the service provider to deliver the best possible service (i.e., if he or she is reading from the same script), the service performance is likely to be successful.

The Compatibility of Service Customers : We have just discussed the roles of employees and customers receiving service. We now focus on the role of other customers receiving service at the same time. Consider how central the mere presence of other customers is in churches, restaurants, dances, bars, lounges, and spectator sports. If no one else shows up, customers will not get to socialise with others, one of the primary expectations in these types of services. However, if the number of customers becomes so dense that crowding occurs, customers may also be dissatisfied. The way other customers behave with many services such as airlines, education, clubs, and social organizations also exerts a major influence on a customer's experience. In general, the presence, behavior, and similarity of other customers receiving services has a strong impact on the satisfaction and dissatisfaction of any given customer.

Customer compatibility has been identified as important in service experience, especially in situations where:

- Customers are in close physical proximity to each other, such as in crowded airlines,
- Verbal interaction among customers is likely, such as in full-service restaurants, and bars,
- Customers are engaged in numerous and varied activities, such as in a library or swimming pool,
- The service environment attracts a heterogeneous customer mix, such as public parks or bowling alleys,
- The core service is compatibility, such as matrimonial services,
- Customers must occasionally wait for the service, such as in physicians' offices or waiting for a table in a restaurant,
- Customers are expected to share time, space, or service utensils with one another the way patrons in health clubs share shower facilities and residents of a retirement community share laundry facilities.

Customers can be incompatible for many reasons-differences in beliefs, values, experiences, abilities to pay, appearance, age, and health, to name just a few. The service marketer must anticipate, acknowledge, and deal with heterogeneous consumers who have the potential to be incompatible. The service marketer can also bring homogeneous customers together and solidify relationships between them, which increases the cost to the customer of switching service providers.

D. Post-Purchase Evaluation

Attribution of Dissatisfaction : When consumers are disappointed with purchases-because the products did not fulfill the intended needs, did not perform satisfactorily, or were not worth their price-they may attribute their dissatisfaction to a number of different sources, among them the producers, the retailers, or themselves. Because consumers participate to a greater extent in the definition and production of services, they may feel more responsible for their dissatisfaction when they purchase services than when they purchase goods.

The quality of many services depends on the information the customer brings to the service encounter: a doctor's accurate diagnosis requires a conscientious case history and a clear particular of symptoms; a dry cleaner's success in removing a spot depends on the consumer's knowledge of its cause; and a tax preparer's satisfactory performance relies on the receipts saved by the consumer. Failure to obtain satisfaction with any of these services may not be blamed completely on the retailer or producer, since the consumer must adequately perform his or her part in the production process also.

Innovation Diffusion : The rate of diffusion of an innovation depends on consumers' perceptions of the innovation with regard to five characteristics: relative advantage, compatibility, communicability, divisibility, and complexity. An offering that has a relative advantage over existing or competing products; that is compatible with existing norms, values, and behaviors; that is communicable; and that is divisible (i.e., that can be tried or tested on a limited basis) diffuses more quickly than others. An offering that is complex, that is, difficult to understand or use, diffuses more slowly than others.

Considered as a group, services are less communicable, less divisible, more complex, and probably less compatible than goods. They are less communicable because they are intangible (e.g., their feature cannot be displayed, illustrated, or compared) and because they are often unique to each buyer (as in a medical diagnosis or dental care). Services are less divisible because they are usually impossible to sample or test on a limited basis (e.g., how does one "sample" a medical diagnosis? A lawyer's services in setting a divorce? Even a haircut?). Services are frequently more complex than goods because they are composed of a bundle of different attributes, not all of which will be offered to every buyer on each purchase.

Finally, services may be incompatible with existing values and behaviours, especially if consumers are accustomed to providing the service for themselves.

Brand Loyalty : The degree to which consumers are committed to particular brands of goods or services depends on a number of factors; the cost of changing brands (switching cost), the availability of substitutes, the perceived risk associated with the purchase, and the degree to which they have obtained satisfaction in the past. Because it may be more costly to change brands of services, because they may have more difficulty being aware of the availability of substitutes, and because higher risks may accompany services, consumers are more likely to remain customers of particular companies with services than with goods. Because of the difficulty in being aware of the availability of substitutes, and because higher risks may accompany services, consumers are more likely to remain customers of particular companies with services than with goods.

Greater search costs and monetary costs may be involved in changing brands of services than in changing brands of goods. Because of the difficulty of obtaining information about services, consumers may be unaware of alternatives or substitutes for their brands, or may be uncertain about the ability of alternatives to increase satisfaction over present brands. Monetary fees may accompany brand switching in many services: Physicians often require complete physicals on the initial visit; dentists sometimes demand new X-rays; and health clubs frequently charge "membership fees" at the outset to obtain long-term commitments from customers.

2.13 ECONOMIC DISTINCTIONS

The characteristics of various entities like commodities, goods, services and experience differ in terms of economic offering. Table 2.5 shows the distinctions in terms of economic offerings including Economic Function, Nature of offering, Key Attribute, Method of Supply, Seller, Buyer and Factors of Demand.

Table 2.5 : ECONOMIC DISTINCTIONS

Economic offering	*Commodities*	*Goods*	*Services*	*Experiences*
Economy	Agrarian	Industrial	Service	Experience
Economic Function	Extract	Make	Deliver	Stage
Nature of Offering	Fungible	Tangible	Intangible	Memorable
Key Attribute	Natural	Standardized	Customized	Personal
Method of Supply	Stored in bulk	Inventoried after production	Delivered on demand	Revealed over a duration
Seller	Trader	Manufacturer	Provider	Stager
Buyer	Market	User	Client	Guest
Factors of Demand	Characteristics	Features	Benefits	Sensations

SHORT ANSWER QUESTIONS

1. What are the elements in the marketing mix for services?
2. "Services possess some key distinguishing characteristics". Comment.
3. How do direct customers differ from indirect customers?

4. What constitutes the expanded mix for services?
5. How does simultaneity differ from variability?
6. Why are services intangible?
7. What are the implications of 'inseparability'?
8. What are the components of a service?
9. Give examples for service processes.
10. Write short notes on:
    (a) Physical Evidence.
    (b) People.
11. What are the economic distinctions between commodities, goods, services and experiences?

ESSAY QUESTIONS

1. What do you understand by 'services'? Describe the characteristics of services and service operations.
2. What are the various 'customer groups'? What are their distinctive characteristics?
3. What are the steps involved in decision-making? What characteristics are associated with them?
4. Does research need to be undertaken for shaping the mix elements? If so, how?
5. How are customer relationships maintained?
6. Who are 'decision-makers and opinion leaders'? What is their role?
7. What are the elements of customer service? What are the related issues?
8. List some constraints on the management of services and ways of overcoming them.
9. Give examples of the components for the following services:
   (a) Airlines (b) Financial services (c) Tourism.
10. Give examples of decision makers and opinion leaders for the following services:
    (a) Telecommunications (b) Internet (c) Insurance.

EXERCISE / ASSIGNMENTS

1. Prepare the elements of the marketing mix for the following services:
   (a) Civil Services
   (b) Waterways
   (c) Water & Sanitation
   (d) Town Planning
   (e) Agricultural
   (f) Counselling
   (g) Maintenance & Repairs
   (h) Advertising.
   [Note: Refer Chapter on "Service Mix Scenario" for assistance].
2. Select any five service industries of your choice. For each such service industry, identify the various customer groups associated with the industry. Make a list of prominent companies institutions for such customer groups and their activities.
3. In your business courses, how much attention is paid to the distinct issues facing service businesses? Why have services received relatively little attention in business schools and management strategies compared with packages and other manufactured goods?

3

Service Expectations

3.1 EXPECTATIONS

Satisfaction and delight are both strongly influenced by customer expectations. By "expectations," behavioral researchers mean an array of possible outcomes that reflect what might, could, should, or had better not happen. There are several different kinds of expectations. Figure 3.1 show a hierarchy of expectations that might exist for a typical customer.

The will expectations comes closest to the mathematics definition. It is the average level of quality that is predicted based on all known information. This is the expectation level most often meant by customers (and used by researchers). When someone says that "service exceeded my expectations," they generally mean that the service was better than they had predicted would be.

The should expectation is what customers feel they deserve from the transaction. Very often what should happen is better than what the customer actually thinks will happen. For example, a student may think that each lecture should be exciting, but doubts that a particular day's lecture actually will be exciting. Or, professors may think that students should be lively and intelligent, but think that actually they will sit in class passively.

The ideal expectation is what would happen under the best of circumstances.

Figure 3.1 : THE EXPECTATION HIERARCHY

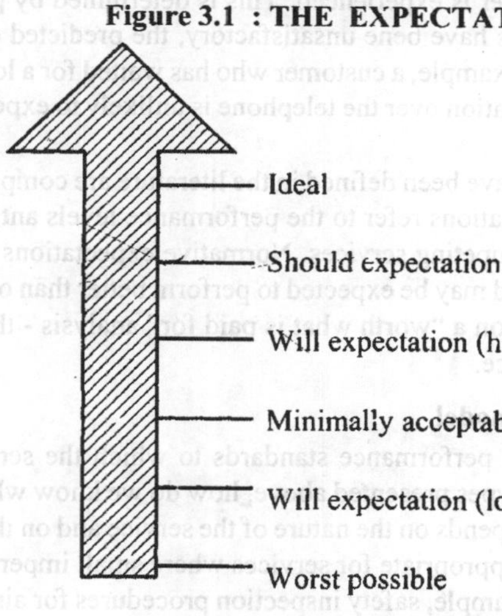

It is useful as a barometer of excellence. On the other end of the scale are the minimally acceptable level (the threshold at which mere satisfaction is achieved), and the worst possible levels (the worst outcome that can be imagined).

Expectations are affected strongly by experience. For example, if the customer has a bad experience, then the will expectation will decline. A good experience will tend to raise the will expectation. Generally speaking, the should expectation will go up, but never decline. Very good experiences tend to bring the should expectations up to that level. Thus expectations change over time, often for the better.

An example of this is the U.S auto industry. General Motors, Ford, and Chrysler had instilled a level of quality expectations in the U.S population that was low by today's standards. Then the Japanese started exporting cars of significantly higher quality. Expectations jumped, as customers saw that a higher level of quality was possible. The complacent U.S. automakers, making cars of the same quality as always, suddenly found themselves faced with millions of customers who have significantly higher expectations. The result was disastrous for the auto manufacturers.

Experience is not the only thing that shapes expectations. Expectations may also be affected by advertising, word of mouth, and personal limitations.

Types of expectations

What do we mean when we talk about a customer's expectations of performance? Do we mean the performance level that a customer would ideally expect from a service? Or, do we mean the performance level that the customer would desire that service to have, or the level that is acceptable? Is it the performance level that the customer would predict for a particular service encounter? Or can we think about comparative expectations based on the customer's experience with similar services?

Ideal expectations refer to the performance wished for in a perfect service. Desired expectations are the performance levels that customers want the service to meet in practice. If the service provider cannot deliver service at the desired level, customers may be willing to tolerate deviations in performance up to their acceptable expectations with relatively small degradation in satisfaction. Dissatisfaction results if the performance falls below this level.

The predicted expectation is the performance level that the customer anticipates will be achieved by a service encounter before this encounter is experienced. This is determined by past experience with the service. If past service encounters have bene unsatisfactory, the predieted expectation for the next encounter is likely to be low. For example, a customer who has waited for a long time during previous attempts to make an airline reservation over the telephone is unlikely to expect that the next call will result in a short wait.

Some other types of expectation that have been defined in the literature are comparative, normative, and value-based. Comparative expectations refer to the performance levels anticipated for the service derived from experiences with competing services. Normative expectations of services are based on brand names - a well-known brand may be expected to perform better than one that is lesser known. Value-based expectations depend on a "worth what is paid for" analysis - the performance expectations of a service depend on its price.

Selecting the appropriate expectations model

Expectations are used to develop the performance standards to which the service should be designed. Given the range of expectation types presented above, how do we know which type to use for a particular application? The answer depends on the nature of the service and on the objectives of the firm. The ideal expectations model is appropriate for services where small imperfections in performance have large consequences. For example, safety inspection procedures for aircraft should be designed to meet ideal, or close to ideal, expectations. Companies that wish to use the quality of their service as a marketing vehicle should attempt to achieve their process to meet the ideal level. Any firm that wants to compete profitably in the market should adopt the comparative expectations model and design a service that performs at least as well as the competitors, or, in accordance with value-based expectations, should design a service that maximizes the customers' sense of what they get for what they pay. The normative expectations model is appropriate for the designing a new service for a firm with an already established name or service line. The new service should be designed to match the performance expectations commensurate with the reputation of the firm or of the service line.

In summary, researchers have identified many different kinds of expectations, each of which applies under different circumstances. In practice, there is a need to develop to optimal combination of performance standards that will allow the designed service to satisfy customers, to compare favourably with competitors' services, and to be delivered at a cost that will allow the company to sell the service profitably. Depending on the application, the design or service management team may have to combine different types of expectations in order to define this set of standards. Some examples are presented in Table 3.1

Table 3.1 : SERVICE CUSTOMERS WANT THE BASICS

Type of service	*Type of customer*	*Principal expectations*
Automobile repair	Consumers	Be competent ("Fix it right the first time"). Explain things ("Explain why I need the suggested repairs - provided an itemized list") Be respectful ("Don't treat me like a dumb female").
Automobile Insurance	Consumers	Keep me informed ("I shouldn't have to learn about insurance law changes from the newspaper"). Be on my side ("I don't want them to treat me like I am a criminal just because I have a claim
Hotel	Consumers	Provide a clean room ("Don't have a deep-pile carpet that can't be completely cleaned... you can literally see germs down there"). Provide a secure room ("Good bolts and peephole on door"). "Treat me like a guest ("It is almost like they're looking you over to decide whether they're going to let you have a room"). Keep your promise ("They said the room would be ready, but it wasn't at the promised time").
Property and Casualty insurances	Business customers	Fulfill obligations ("Pay up"). Learn my business and work with me ("I expect them to know me and my company"). Protect me from catastrophe ("They should cover your risk exposure so there is no single big loss"). Provide prompt service ("Fast claim service").
Equipment repair	Business customers	Share my sense of urgency ("Speed of response. One time I had to buy a second piece of equipment because of the huge down time with the first piece"). Be competent ("Sometimes you are quoting stuff from their instruction manuals to their own people and they don't even know what it means"). Be prepared ("Have all the parts ready").
Truck and tractor rental/leasing	Business Customers	Keep the equipment running ("Need to have equipment working all of the time - that is the key"). Be flexible ("The leasing company should have the flexibility to rent us equipment when we need it"). Provided full service ("Get rid of all the paperwork and headaches").

3.2 EXPECTED SERVICE : TWO LEVELS OF EXPERIENCE

Customers hold several different types of expectations about service. The first can be termed desired service and defined as the level of service the customer hopes to receive - the "wished for" level of performance. Desired service is a blend of what the customer believes "can be" and "should be" - For example, consumers who sign up for matrimonial service expect to find compatible, attractive, interesting people to marry. The expectation reflects the hopes and wishes to these consumers - without these hopes and wishes and the belief that they may be fulfilled, they would probably not purchase the service. In a similar way, you will engage the services of your college's placement office when you are ready to graduate. What are your expectations of the service? In all likelihood, you want the office to find you a job - the right job in the right geography for the rights salary - because that is what you hope and wish for.

However, you probably also see that the economy may constrain the availability of ideal job openings in companies. In this situation and in general, customers hope to achieve their service desires but recognize that this is not always possible. For this reason they hold another, lower level expectation for the threshold of acceptable service. This lower expectation has been termed adequate service - the level of service the customer will accept. Many college graduates in the early 1990s, trained for high-level, highly skilled jobs, accepted entry-level positions at fast-food restaurants and mail-order retailers or internships for no pay. Their hopes and desires (that is, their desired service expectations) were still high but they recognized that they could not attain those desires in the market that existed at the time. This standard of adequate service was much lower than that of their desired service. Some graduates accepted any job for which they could earn a salary, and others agreed to non-paying, short-term positions as interns to gain experience. Adequate service represents the "minimum tolerable expectation", the bottom level of performance acceptable to the customer, and reflects the level of service customers believe they will get, on the basis of their experience with services.

3.3 THE ZONE OF TOLERANCE

Services are heterogeneous in that performance may vary across providers, across employees from the same provider, and even within the same service employee. The extent to which customers recognize and are willing to accept this variation is called the zone of tolerance. If service drops below adequate service - the minimum level considered acceptable - customers will be frustrated and their satisfaction with the company undermined. If service performance is outside the zone of tolerance at the top end - where performance exceeds desired service - customers will be very pleased and probably quite surprised as well. You might consider the zone of tolerance as the range or window in which customers do not particularly notice service performance. When it falls outside the range (either very low or very high), the service gets the customer's attention in either a positive or negative way. As an example, consider the service an airline passenger receives from the ticket counter when checking luggage. Most customers hold a range of acceptable times for this service encounter - probably somewhere between five and ten minutes. If service consumes that period of time, customers probably do not pay much attention to the wait. If a customer enters the line and finds sufficient airline personnel at their stations to serve her in the fist two or three minutes, she may notice the service and judge it as excellent. On the other hand, if a customer has to wait in line for fifteen minutes, he (and most likely all the other passengers in the line) begins to grumble, looks at his watch, and glares at the personnel behind the stations marked "position not open" who are not waiting on customers. The longer the wait is outside the zone of tolerance, the more frustrated he becomes.

Customer's service expectations are characterized by a range of levels, bounded by desired and adequate service, rather than a single level. This tolerance zone, representing the different between desired service and the level of service considered adequate, can expand and contract within a customer. An airline customer's zone of tolerance will narrow when he is running late and is concerned about making his plane. A minute seems much longer and his adequate service level increases. On the other hand, a customer who arrives a the airport early may have an expanding tolerance zone, making the wait in line far less noticeable than when he or she is pressed for time. This example shows that the marketer must understand not just the size and boundary levels for the zone of tolerance but also when and how the tolerance zone fluctuates within a given customer.

Another aspect of variability in the range of reasonable services is that different customer possess different tolerance zones. Some customers have narrow zones of tolerance, requiring a tighter range of service from providers, while other customers allow a greater range of service. For example, very busy customers would likely always be pressed for time and therefore desire short wait times in general and also hold a constrained range for the length of acceptable wait times. When it comes to meeting plumbers or repair personnel at their homes for appliance problems, customers who work outside the home have a more restricted window of acceptable time duration for that appointment than would customers who work in their homes or do not work at all.

3.4 SOURCES OF DESIRED SERVICE EXPECTATIONS

Two of the targets influences on desired service level are personal needs and philosophies about service. Personnel needs, those states or conditions essential to the physical or psychological well being of the customer, are pivotal factors that shape the level of desired service. Personal needs can fall into many categories, including physical, social, psychological, and functional. A fan who regularly goes to cricket games right from work, and is therefore thirsty and hungry, hopes and desires that the food and drink vendors will pass by his section frequently, whereas a fan who regularly has dinner elsewhere has a low or zero level of desired service from the vendors. A customer with high social and dependency needs may have relatively high expectations for a hotel's ancillary services, hoping, for example, that the hotel has a bar with live music and dancing.

Some customers are more demanding than others, having greater sensitivity to, and higher expectations of, service. Enduring service intensifiers are individual, stable factors that lead the customer to a heightened sensitivity to service. One of the most important of these factors can be called derived service expectations, which occur when customer expectations are driven by another person or group of people. A niece from a big family who is planning a ninetieth birthday part for a favourite aunt is representing the entire family in selecting a restaurant for a successful celebration. Her needs are driven in part by the derived expectations from the other family members. A parent choosing a vacation for the family, a spouse selecting a home-cleaning service, an employee choosing a rental office for the firm - all these customer's individual expectations are intensified because they experience derived expectations from other parties who will receive the service. In the context of business-to-business service, customer expectations are driven by the expectations of their own customers. The head of an information services department in an insurance company, who is the business customer of a large computer vendor, has expectations based on those of the insurance customers he serves: when the computer equipment is down, his customers complain. His need to keep the system up and running is not just his own expectation but is derived from the pressure of his customers.

Business-to-business customers may also derive their expectation from their managers and supervisors. Employees of a marketing research department may speed up project cycles (i.e., increase their expectations for speed of delivery) when pressured by their management to deliver the study results. Purchasing agents may increase demands for faster delivery at lower costs when company management is emphasizing cost reduction in the company.

Another enduring service intensifier is personal service philosophy -the customer's underlying generic attitude about the meaning of service and the proper conduct of service providers. If you have ever been a waitress or a waiter in a restaurant, you are likely to have standards for restaurant service that were shaped by your training and experience in that role. You might, for example, believe that waitresses should not keep customers waiting longer than fifteen minutes to take their orders. Knowing the way a kitchen operates, you may be less tolerant of lukewarm food or errors in the order than others who have not held the role of waiter. In general, customers who are themselves in service businesses or have worked for them in the past seem to have especially strong service philosophies.

3.5 SOURCES OF ADEQUATE SERVICE EXPECTATIONS

A different set of determinants affect adequate service, the level of the service the customer finds acceptable. In general, these influences are short term in nature and tend to fluctuate more than the somewhat stable factors that influence desired service: **1.** transitory service intensifiers, **2.** perceived service alternatives **3.** customer self-perceived service role **4.** situational factors and **5.** predicted service.

The first set of elements, ***transitory service intensifiers***, are temporary, usually short term, individual factors that make a customer more aware of the need for service. Personal emergency situations in which service is urgently needed (such as an accident and the need for automobile insurance, or a breakdown in office equipment during a busy period) raise the level of adequate service expectation, particularly the level of responsiveness required and considered acceptable. A mail-order company that depends on toll-free lines for receiving all customer orders will tend to be more demanding of the telephone service during peak periods of the week, month, and year. Any system breakdown or lack of clarity on the lines will be tolerated less during these intense periods than at other times.

Problems with the initial service can also lead to heightened expectations. Performing a service right the first time is very important, because customers value service reliability above all other dimensions. If the service fails in the recovery phase, fixing it right the second time (that is, being reliable in service recovery) is even more critical than it was the first time. Automobile repair service provides a case in point. If a problem with your automobile's brakes sends you to a car repair provider, you expect the company to fix the brakes. If you experience further problems with the brakes after the repair (a situation that is not all that uncommon with car repair), you adequate service level will increase. In general, service recovery expectations are higher than initial service expectations. As one auto repair customer put it: "I am willing to be understanding the first time but would expect much more and be more impatient the second time around." In these and other situations where transitory service intensifiers are present, the level of adequate service will increase and the zone of tolerance will narrow.

Perceived service alternatives are other providers from whom the customer can obtain service. If customers have multiple service providers to choose from, or if they can provide the service for themselves (such garden care of personal grooming), their levels of adequate service are higher than those of customers who believe it is not possible to get better service elsewhere. An airline customer who lives in a very small town with a tiny airport, for example, has a reduced set of options in airline travel. This customer will be more tolerant of the service performance of the carriers in the town because few alternatives exist. She will accept the scheduling and lower levels of service more than the customer in a big city who has myriad flights and airlines to choose from.

A third factor affecting the level of adequate service is the ***customer's self-perceived service role***. Customer perceptions of the degree to which customers exert an influence on the level of service they receive. In other words, customers' expectations are partly shaped by how well they believe they are performing their own roles in service delivery. One role of the customer is specifying the level of service expected. A customer who is very explicit with a waiter about how less he wants his beef cooked in a restaurant will probably be more dissatisfied if the meat comes to the table overcooked than a customer who does not articulate the degree of work expected. The customer's active participation in the service also affects this factor. A customer who doesn't show up for many of her allergy shots will probably be more lenient on the allergist when she experiences symptoms than one who conscientiously shows up for every shot.

A final way the customer defines his or her role is in assuming the responsibility for complaining when service is poor. A dissatisfied customer who complains will be less tolerant than one who does not voice his or her concerns.

Levels of adequate service are also influenced by ***situational factors***, defined as service performance conditions that customers view as beyond the control of the service provider. For example, where personal emergencies such as serious automobile accidents would likely intensify customer service expectations of insurance companies (because they are transitory service intensifiers), catastrophes that affect a large number of people at one time (earthquakes) may lower service expectations because customers recognize that insurers are inundated with demands for their services. Customers who recognize that these contingencies are not the fault of the service company may accept lower levels of adequate service given the context. In general, situational factors temporarily lower the level of adequate service, widening the zone of tolerance.

The final factor that influences adequate service is ***predicted service***, the level of service customers believe they are likely to get. This type of service expectation can be viewed as predictions made by customers about what is likely to happen during an impending transaction or exchange. Predicted service performance implies some objective calculation of the probability of performance or estimate of anticipated service performance level. If customers predict good service, their levels of adequate service are likely to be higher than if they predict poor service. For example, full-time residents in a college town usually predict faster restaurant service during the summer months when students are not on campus. This will probably lead them to have higher standards for adequate service in restaurants during the summer than during college months. On the other hand, customers of telephone companies and utilities know that installation service from these firms will be difficult to obtain during the first few weeks of college when people are setting up their apartments for the year. In this case, levels of adequate service decrease and zones of tolerance widen.

3.6 SOURCES OF BOTH DESIRED AND PREDICTED SERVICE EXPECTATIONS

When consumers are interested in purchasing services, they are likely to seek or take in information from several different sources. For example, they may call a store, ask a friend, or deliberately track newspaper advertisements to find the needed service at the lowest price. They may also receive service information by watching television or hearing an unsolicited comment from a colleague about a service that was performed well. In addition to these active and passive types of external search for information, consumers may conduct an internal search by reviewing the information held in memory about the service. This section discuses one internal and three external factors that influence both desired service and predicted service expectations: **1.** explicit service promises **2.** implicit service promises **3.** word-of-mouth communications, and **4.** past experience.

Explicit service promises are personal and non-personal statements about the service made by the organization to customers. The statements are personal when they are communicated by salespeople or service or repair personnel; they are non-personal when they come from advertising, brochures, and other written publications. Explicit service promises are one of the few influences on expectations that are completely in the control of service provider.

Promising exactly what will ultimately be delivered would seem a logical and appropriate way to manage customer expectations and ensure that reality fits the promises. However, companies and the personnel who represent them often deliberately overpromise to obtain business or inadvertently overpromise by stating their best estimates about delivery of a service in the future.

Explicit service promises influence both the levels of desired service and predicted service: They shape what customers desire in general as well as what they predict will happen in the next service encounter from a particular service provider or in a certain service encounter.

Implicit service promises are service-related cues other than explicit promises that lead to inferences about what the service should and will be like. These quality cues are dominated by price and the tangibles associated with the service. In general, the higher the price and the more impressive the tangibles, the more a customer will expect from the service. Consider a customer who shops for insurance, finding two firms charging radically different prices. She may make the inference that the firm with the higher price should and will provide higher quality service and better coverage. Similarly, a customer who stays at a posh hotel is likely to desire and predict a higher standard of service than from a hotel with less impressive facilities.

The importance of ***word-of-mouth communication*** is shaping expectations of service is well documented. These personal and sometimes non-personal statements made by parties other than the organization convey to customers what the service will be like and influence both predicted and desired service. Word of mouth tends to be very important in services that are difficult to evaluate before purchase and direct experience of them. Experts (including consumer Reports, friends and family) are also word-of-mouth sources that can affect the levels of desired and predicted service.

Past experience, the customer's previous exposure to service that is relevant to the focal service, is another force in shaping predictions and desires. The service relevant for prediction can be previous exposure to the focal firm's service. For example, you probably compare each stay in a particular hotel with all previous stays in that hotel. But past experience with the focal hotel is likely to be a very limited view of your past experience. You may also compare each stay with your experiences in the other hotels and hotel chains. Customers also compare across industries: hospital patients, for example, compare hospital stays against the standards set by telephone service, one reason why cable service is often judged to be poor. In a general sense, past experience may incorporate previous experience with the focal brand, typical performance of a favorite brand, experience with the brand last purchased or the top-selling brand, as well as the average performance a customer believes represents a group of similar brands.

3.7 A MODEL OF CUSTOMER SERVICE EXPECTATIONS

The full model of customer expectations and the forces that influence them is shown in Figure 3.2. At the center of the model is the detailed view of expectations showing the two levels, desired and adequate, and the zone of tolerance that separates them. The sources of antecedents of each type of expectation are shown along the sides of the model.

How might a manager of a service organization use this model to create, improve, or market services? First, managers need to know the pertinent expectation sources and their relative importance for a customer population, a customer segment, and perhaps even a particular customer. They need to know, for instance, the relative weight of word of mouth, explicit service promises, and implicit service promises in shaping desired service and predicted service. Some of these sources are more stable and permanent in their influence (e.g., enduring service intensifiers and personal needs) than the others, which fluctuate considerably over time (e.g., perceived service alternatives and situational factors).

Figure 3.2 : NATURE AND DETERMINANTS OF CUSTOMER EXPECTATION OF SERVICE

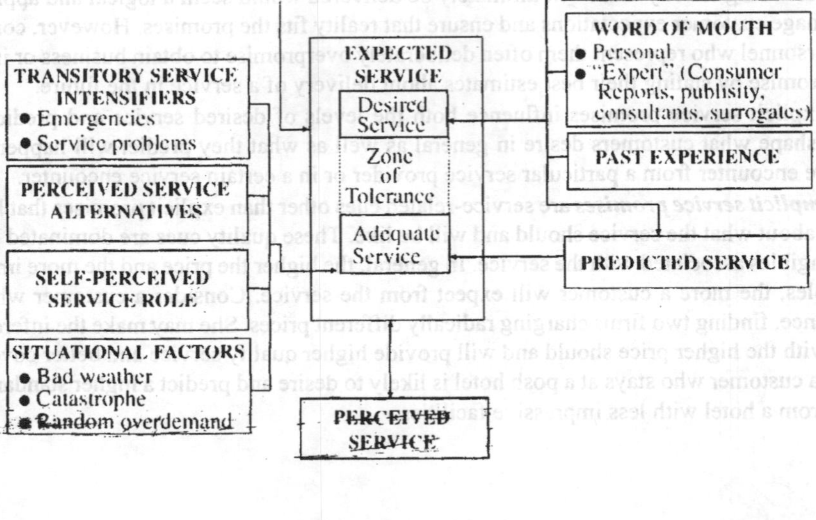

3.8. INFLUENCE STRATEGIES

Factors which can be controlled by service marketers include explicit and implicit service promises. On the other hand, less service controllable factors include enduring service intensifiers; personal needs; transitory, perceived and self-perceived factors; word-of-mouth; past experience; predicted service and situational factors. The possible influence strategies for these factors is summarised in Table 3.2.

Table 3.2 : WAYS SERVICES MARKETERS CAN INFLUENCE FACTORS

Controllable factors	*Possible influence strategies*
Explicit service promises	Make realistic and accurate promises that reflect the service actually delivered rather than an idealized version of the service.
	Ask contact people for feedback on the accuracy of promise made in advertising and personal selling.
	Avoid engaging in price or advertising wars with competitors because they take the focus off customers and escalate promises beyond the level at which they can be met.
	Formalize service promises through a service guarantee that focuses company employees on the promise and that provides feedback on the number of times promises are not fulfilled.
Implicit service promises	Assure that service tangibles accurately reflect the type and level of service provided.
Less controllable factors	***Possible influence strategies***
Enduring service intensifiers	Use market research to determine sources of derived service expectations and their requirements. Focus advertising and marketing strategy on ways the service allows the focal customer to satisfy the requirements of the influencing customer.
	Use market research to profile personal service philosophies of customers and use this information in designing and delivering service.
Personal needs	Educate customer on ways the service addresses their needs.
Transitory service intensifiers	Increase service delivery during peak periods or in emergencies.
Perceived service alternatives	Be fully aware of competitive offerings and, where possible and appropriate, match them.
Self-perceived service role	Educate customers to understand their roles and perform them better.
Word-of-mouth communications	Simulate word-of-mouth in advertising by using testimonials and opinion leaders.
	Identify influencers and opinion leaders for the service and concentrate marketing efforts on them.
	Use incentives with existing customers to encourage them to say positive things about the service.

Past experience	Use marketing research to profile customers' previous experience with similar services.
Situational factors	Use service guarantees to assure customers about service recovery regardless of the situational factors that occur.
Predicted Service	Tell customers when service provision is higher than what can normally be expected so that predictions of future service encounters will not be inflated.

3.9 RETHINKING THE TRADITIONAL ORGANIZATION

The three businesses - customer relationship management, product innovation, and infrastructure management- rarely map neatly to the organizational structure of a corporation. Product innovation, for example, typically extends beyond the boundaries of a product development unit to include such activities as conducting market research, qualifying component suppliers, training sales and support people, and designing marketing materials. Rather than representing discrete organizational units, the three businesses correspond to what are popularly called "core processes" - the cross-functional work flows that stretch from suppliers to customers and, in combination, define a company's identity.

Managers talk about their key activities as "processes" rather than as "businesses" because, with rare exceptions, they assume that the activities ought to coexist. Nearly a century of economic theory underpins the conventional wisdom that the management of customers, innovation, and infrastructure must be combined within a single company. If those activities were disbursed to separate companies, the thinking goes; the interaction costs required to coordinate them would be too great. It's cheaper to do them yourself.

As interaction costs fall, companies will come under pressure to unbundle their core processes, each of which has very different economic, cultural, and competitive imperatives as shown in Table 3.3 and Figure 3.3.

Figure 3.3 : RETHINKING THE TRADITIONAL ORGANIZATION

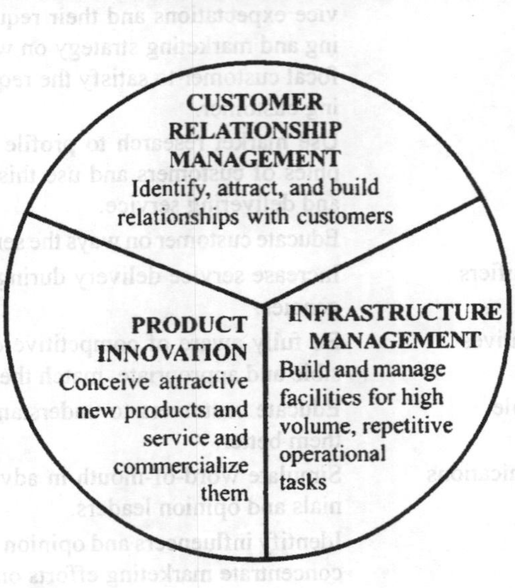

Table 3.3 : DETERMINANTS OF "PROCESSES"

Product Innovation	Customer Relationship Management	Infrastructure Management
Economics		
Early market entry allows for a premium price and large market share; speed is key	High cost of customer acquisition makes it imperative to gain large shares of wallet; economies of scope are key	High fixed costs make large volumes essential to achieving low unit costs; economies of scale are key
Culture		
Employee centered coddling the creative "stars"	Highly service oriented; "customer comes first"	Cost focused; stress on standardization, pre dictability, efficiency
Competition		
Battle for talent; low barriers to entry; many small players thrive	Battle for scope; rapid consolidation; a few big players dominate	Battle for scale; rapid consolidation; a few big players dominate

SHORT ANSWER QUESTIONS

1. What is the difference between desired service and adequate service?
2. Why would a service marketer need to understand both types of service expectations?
3. What do you mean by "expectation"?
4. Explain the expectation hierarchy.
5. What are the determinants of customer expectations?
6. What is 'zone of tolerance'?
7. What are the sources of adequate service expectations?

ESSAY QUESTIONS

1. Consider a recent service purchase that you made. Which of the factors influencing expectations were the most important in your decision? Why?
2. Why are desired expectations more stable than adequate service expectations?
3. What are the ways in which service marketers influence service factors?
4. What is the relationship between customer relationship management, infrastructure management and product innovation?
5. What are the sources of desired and adequate service expectations?

EXERCISE / ASSIGNMENTS

1. What factors do you think influenced your professor to adopt this textbook? In the case of textbook adoption, what do you think are the most important factors? After you have formulated your ideas, ask your professor in class to talk about the sources of his or her expectations.

2. List five incidents when a service company has exceeded your expectations. How did you react to the service? Did these incidents change the way you viewed subsequent interactions with the companies? In what way?
3. Intuitively, it would seem that managers would want their customers to have wide tolerance zones for service. But if customers do have these wide zones of tolerance for service, is it more difficult for firms with superior service to earn customer loyalty? Would superior service firms be better off to attempt to narrow customers' tolerance zones to reduce the competitive appeal of mediocre providers?
4. Describe several instances where a service company's explicit service promises were inflated and led you to be disappointed with the service outcome.

4

The Service Product

4.1 UNDERLYING CONCEPTS

Central to any definition of a service product, from a marketing viewpoint, is the linkage that must be established between the service product from the consumers' or users' viewpoint. Service marketing organizations may find it helpful in tracing this linkage to analyse their service product (s) at four levels. These levels are:

(a) the consumer benefit concept

(b) the service concept

(c) the service offer

(d) the service delivery system.

The Consumer Benefit Concept

This terminology is used by Bateson. He argues that it is only from the idea of a consumer benefit that the service concept can be defined. The consumer's view, so the marketing concept suggests, should be central to the shaping of any good or service for offer. As Bateson says:

"The true nature of a product can be perceived only by the consumer. That is, the manufacturer can specify the function of the product. He can even specify the kinds of psychological benefits that will be offered in advertising. The consumer, however, takes away from the product only that part of the bundle he/she needs at that point of time".

The clarification, elaboration and translation of the consumer benefit concept poses a number of problems for service marketers. First the services offered should be based upon the needs and benefits sought by consumers and users. But consumers and users may be clear or unclear about what they require, articulate or inarticulate in the expression of their requirements. Difficulties may stem from their ignorance of what to expect, inexperience of what is required or basic inability to elucidate latent need. Secondly, benefits sought may change over time through good or bad experiences in service use, through new expectations' sets, through sophistication in service usage and consumption. Thirdly there are practical measurement problems for service marketers in deriving consumer-based measures of the importance of services' benefits sought, preferences between them and changes in their importance. Also it may be necessary to measure the trade-offs between elements of services offered that consumers are prepared to make.

The definition and monitoring of the consumer benefit however, is of central importance to all service product design and delivery decisions. The constant task of the service marketer is to try to come to grips with what benefits customers seek; benefits which are so central to the success of the service marketing operation, but so elusive to define.

The Service Concept

The service concept is the core of the service offering. Two levels of service concept are possible. The 'general' service concept refers to the essential product being offered (e.g. a car hire company offers solutions to temporary transportation problems). In addition there will be 'specific' service concepts at the core of specific service (e.g. candle-lit dinners or oriental foods for restaurants). The service concept has to be translated into the 'service formula'. This translation process, implies not only a clear definition of the service concept (i.e. what consumer benefits is the service firm aiming to serve; which service attributes best express the consumer benefit). It also demands attention to the service process; that is the ways and means the service is produced distributed and consumed; the market segment has to be identified; the organization - client interface has to be organized in a network; the service image has to facilitate clear communication between the service organization and its potential clients. The service concept is the definition of the offer in terms of the bundle of goods and services sold to the consumer plus the relative importance of this bundle to the consumer. It enables the manager to understand some of the intangibles, elusive and implicit that affect the consumer decision and to design and operate his organization to deliver a total service package that emphasizes the important elements of that package.

The Service offer

The service offer is concerned with giving more specific and detailed shape to the basic service concept notion. The shape of the service offer stems from managerial decisions concerned with what service will be provided, when they will be provided, how they will be provided, where they will be provided, who will provide them.

Management of the service offer is concerned with making decisions and thinking through the implications of actions affecting at least three components.

These are:

(a) service elements;
(b) service forms;
(c) service levels.

Service Elements

The service elements are the ingredients of a total service offer; they are the particular bundle of tangibles and intangibles which compose the service product. Service managers face two particular problems in defining the composition of a service offer. First there is the difficulty of articulating all of the elements that could make up a service offer. It is usually easier to articulate the tangible elements than the intangible. Secondly there is the difficulty of deciding upon the particular set of elements the service organization will actually use in its service offer.

The management and the marketing of a service operation is largely about the management of the tangible and intangible elements of the service offer. Management must try to control the tangible and intangible elements that make up the service offer to ensure that they conform with standards laid down. So the cleanliness of a hotel or the size of food portions served in a restaurant are controllable elements of a service. So too is the attention given by an air hostess to passengers or the speed with which telephones are answered in a car rental branch.

But some elements of a service offer are less controllable. Management can ensure that all guests signing in at a hotel reception desk are formally greeted by the receptionist. There is less control over the warmth of the greeting. Nevertheless management must try to anticipate some of these uncontrollable elements and ensure that the climate of the organization contributes to rather than detracts from the service offer.

Service Forms

Service elements are offered to the marketplace in different forms. Service form is concerned with examining in detail the various options relating to each service element. The particular decision taken on the precise form of each service element will depend upon a number of factors including market requirements, competitors' policies and the need to obtain balance within, and between, the various elements that make up the service product offer- what is called 'cohesiveness and coherence of the set of services offered'. An additional consideration is to try to achieve the lowest level of complexity from the customer and service marketing organization points of view. Service products with a high degree of complexity are difficult to manage from the service marketers' perspective (e.g. in terms of quality control, staff knowledge of options) and difficult to understand from the users' point of view.

Service Levels

An offer can be viewed at several levels (Table 4.1 and Figure 4.1) as follows:-

Core or generic. For consumer or industrial products this consists of the basic physical product, i.e. 2 kg of sugar, a packet of self-tapping screws, or a camera. The core elements for a camera, for example, consists of the camera body, the viewer, the winding mechanism, the lens and the other core basic physical components which make up the transactional utility in the form of deposits and withdrawals.

Expected : This consists of the generic product together with the minimal purchase conditions which need to be met. When a customer buys a video cassette recorder they expect an instruction book which explains how to programme it, a warranty for a reasonable period should it break down, and a service network so that it can be repaired.

Augmented: This is the area which enables one offer to be differentiated form another. For example, IBM have a reputation for excellent customer service although they may not have the most technologically advanced core product. They differentiate by 'adding value' to the core, in terms of service reliability and responsiveness.

Potential: This consists of all potential added features and benefits that are or may be of utility to some buyers. The potential for redefinition of the product gives advantages in attracting new users or 'locking in' existing customers. This could make it difficult or expensive for customers to switch to another supplier.

Table & Figure 4.1 : THE TOTAL PRODUCT CONCEPT

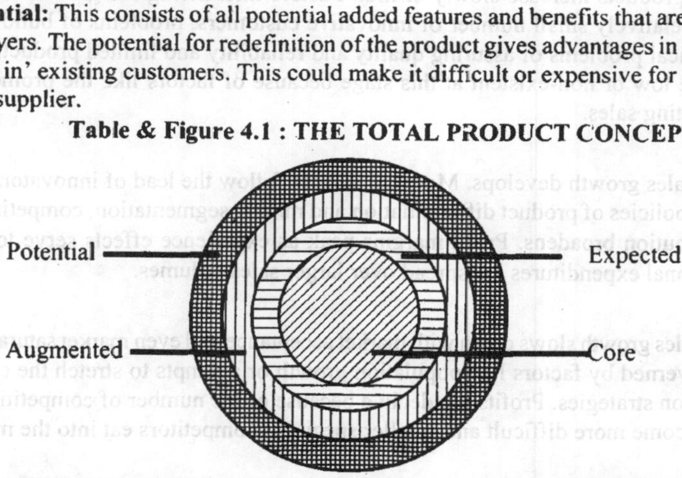

Product level	*Customer's view*	*Marketer's view*	*Personal computer example*
Core Product	Customer's generic need which must be met	Basic Benefits which make product of interest	Data storage, processing. speed of processing, retrieval
Expected Product	Customer's minimal set of	Marketer's product decisions intangible component	Brand name, warranty service support, the
Augmented	Seller's offering over and above what customer expects or is accustomed to	Marketer's other mix decisions on price, distribution and promotion	Diagnostic software, trade-in allowance, base price plus options, dealer network. user clubs, personal selling
Potential product	Everything that potentially can product that is of utility to the customer	Marketer's actions to attract regarding changed conditions or new applications	Use as a system controller, facsimile machine, music composer, application

Thus a firm's offer is a complex set of value-based promises. People buy to solve problems and they attach value to any offer in proportion to this perception of its ability to achieve particular ends. In other words, values is assigned by buyers in relationship to the perceived benefits they receive matched against their expectations.

Camera Example: The expected offer may include a series of lens choices, attractive packaging, easy-to-read operating instructions, a network of service agents, and so on. The augmented offer could include a wide range of differentiating factors such as longer warranties, etc. The potential offer involves creative options or innovations which will add value for the customer. This might involve new applications being worked on, new materials being used in the camera constitution, or new ideas for varying the camera's features for different user requirements.

4.2 THE PRODUCT LIFE-CYCLE

One of the most common ideas in marketing in the concept of the Product Life-Cycle (Figure 4.2). Almost without exception basic marketing texts refer to and illustrate the meaning of this concept. Briefly, it is suggested that products pass through a number of stages over time. These are usually described as

Introduction

Sales of new products increase slowly at first. Factors influencing the growth of sales at this stage include the relatively small number of innovative customers, problems of building effective distribution, technical problems of assuring quality and reliability and limited production capacity. Profits too may be low or non-existent at this stage because of factors like the promotional costs involved in promoting sales.

Growth

In this stage sales growth develops. More consumers follow the lead of innovators, the market broadens through policies of product differentiation and market segmentation, competitors enter the market, and distribution broadens. Profit margins peak as experience effects serve to reduce unit costs and promotional expenditures are spread over larger sales volumes.

Maturity

In this stage sales growth slows down with market acceptance and even market saturation. Growth is increasingly governed by factors like population growth or attempts to stretch the cycle through market segmentation strategies. Profits too decline because of the number of competitive offerings, cost reductions become more difficult and smaller specialist competitors eat into the market.

Decline

In this stage sales decline through factors like changing tastes and fashions and technical advances causing product substitution. Declining sales are accompanied by reducing profit margins as too many competitors fight for the remaining market. Price cutting may be active and marginal competitors fall out of the industry.

Example: The transatlantic airline industry is believed to have progressed to the maturity phase of the lifecycle. The introductory stage, involving competition with sea travel from the end of the Second World War until 1958 was on the basis of speed and convenience rather then price. The introduction of jet passenger transport and air economy fares in 1958 led to the growth phase of the lifecycle and much harsher competition for sea transport. The maturity phase from the early 1970s to the present time has been marked by increasing price sensitivity and the growing success of charter flights and cheap fare offers.

An interesting illustration of the lifecycle is that applied by Sasser and others to the multisite service firm. They generalize that based on experience of multisite companies like McDonalds, Holiday Inns and Hertz the multisite firm passes through five stages. These stages are :

- entrepreneurial;

- multisite rationalization;
- growth;
- maturity;
- decline / regeneration;

Each stage of the lifecycle is described and examined in the context of the five major functional areas of the firm

- finance/ control;
- operations;
- marketing;
- development;
- administration;

From their examination of each stage of the lifecycle and these main functional areas they believe that by identifying a company's position in the lifecycle, the major objectives, decisions, problems and organizational transitions needed for the future can be anticipated. They develop their analysis further to consider how a firm's costs might behave as it passes through the lifecycle (e.g. economies may flow from learning and volume increases).

The lessons service managers can extract from their analysis are that the successful growth of a multisite firm depends upon the ability of its executive to manage the present and the future. As the firm progresses through the lifecycle the following management actions must be undertaken:

(a) Management must understand there are four basic functions to manage (new unit development, operations, marketing, concept development);

(b) the founder (s) must delegate;

(c) the management team must develop or acquire the competencies required to manage a larger firm;

(d) management motivation must be maintained;

(e) sloppy (i.e. haphazard) growth must be avoided;

(f) the firm must change a mature concept;

(g) the firm must not diversify too quickly. Communication channels must be kept open.

Stage 1- *Entrepreneurial* In this stage, an individual identifies a market need and offers a service to a small number of people, usually operating from one location. While most entrepreneurs stay at this stage, some begin to think about growth, often entailing a move to larger and /or additional sites.

Stage 2 - *Multi-site rationalization* In this stage, the successful entrepreneur starts to add to the limited number of facilities. It is during this stage that the skills required for being a multi-site operator begin to be developed. By the end of this stage, the organization gains a certain degree of stability at a level of critical mass. At this point franchising starts to be considered.

Stage 3- *Growth* Here the concept has become accepted as a profitable business idea. The company is now actively expanding through the purchase of competitors, franchising/licensing the concept, developing new company-operated facilities or a combination of the three. Growth is influenced not only by the founder's desire to succeed but also from the pressures placed upon the company by the financial community.

Stage 4- *Maturity* The number of new outlets declines and revenues of individual facilities stabilize and, in some cases, also decline. This tends to be caused by a combination of four factors: changing demographics within the firm's market, changing needs and tastes of consumers, increased competition and 'cannibalization' of older services by service firms' newer products.

Stage 5- ***Decline /regeneration*** Firms can become complacent, and unless a new concept is developed or new markets found, decline and deterioration soon follows.

Figure 4.2 : A HYPOTHETICAL PRODUCT LIFECYCLE FOR TYPESETTING

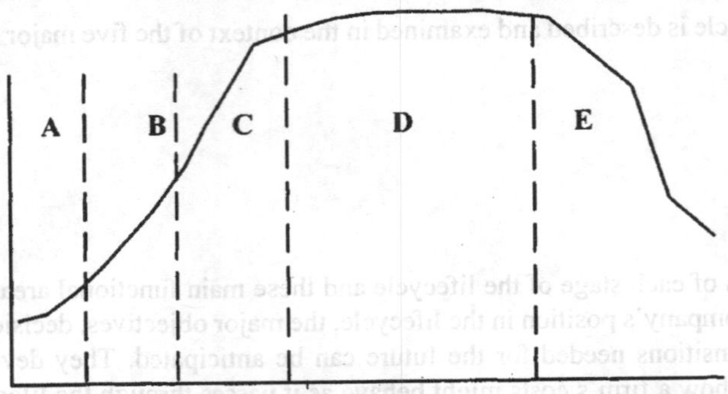

A : INTRODUCTION - New Technology appears. Early adopters.
B : GROWTH - Greater awareness of benefits. Rapid growth in demand.
C : MATURITY - Increasing level of competition.
D : SATURATION - Intense competion. Market has ceased to grow.
E : DECLINE - New Technology appears which reduces demand.

Difficulties in applying the lifecycle concept

In reality, lifecycle patterns are far too variable in both shape and duration for any realistic predictions to be made. A second difficulty in applying the lifecycle concept lies in the inability of marketers to ascertain accurately where in the lifecycle a product actually is at any time. For example, a stabilization of sales may be a movement into maturity or simply a temporary plateau due to external causes. In fact, it is possible that the shape of the lifecycle is a result of an organization's marketing activity rather than an indication of environmental factors to which the organization should respond - in other words, it could lead to a self-fulfilling prophecy.

Another criticism of the concept is that the duration of the stages will depend upon whether it is a product class, form or brand which is being considered. For example, the lifecycle for holidays is probably quite flat, whereas those for particular formulations of holidays and for specific holiday operators' brands become progressively more cyclical.

4.3 NEW SERVICE

The Intangible nature of services means that it is often quite easy to produce slight variants of an existing service with the result that the term 'new service' can mean anything from a minor style change to a major innovation. Lovelock identifies five types of 'new' services:

- ***Style changes :*** These include changes in decor or logo - the revised design of telephone for example.
- ***Service improvements :*** These involve an actual change to a feature of the service already on offer to an established market - computerization of travel-agency information and booking procedures, for example.
- ***Service line extensions :*** These are additions to the existing service product range - new modes of study for an MBA course at a university, for example.
- ***New services :*** These are new services that are offered by an organization to its existing customers, although they may be currently available from its competitors - building societies offering current accounts, with cheque books, standing-order facilities, etc., for example.
- ***Major innovations*** : These are entirely new services for new markets - the provision of multi user 'voice mail' recording services, for example.

Table 4.2 : NEW SERVICE OPTIONS

Situation	*Resource*
1 Attempting to sell more existing services to existing clients	Existing capability, facilities, and market position
2 Attempting to sell existing services to new clients	Existing capabilities and facilities. No market resources
3 Attempting to sell new services to existing clients	Market resources, no existing capability or capability or facility resource
4 Attempting to sell new services in new markets	Nil

The difference between New Service product & improvement is shown in Table 4.3.

Table 4.3 : EXAMPLES OF SERVICE PRODUCT INNOVATIONS

Nature of Service Service	*New Service Product*	*Service Product Improvement*
Communications	Communication satellite	Free-standing public telephone
Educational	Three-year degrees	New Curricula
Financial	Bank credit cards	'Bank by mail'
Health	Treatment with lasers	Intensive care
Housing	Housing for the elderly	Hotel Swimming pool
Insurance	National health insurance	No-fault insurance
Legal	'Defend Yourself' kit	Legal services for the poor
Personal	Physical fitness	—
Recreational	Dual cinema	New play
Transportation	Unit train	Flight reservation system

4.4 SERVICE PRODUCT RANGE

Few service marketing organizations offer only one service. They usually offer a mix of services for use or purchase. The idea of the service product range concerns the set or mix of all service products offered by an organization.

The particular range of services offered will be developed in response to internal needs or to external influences. For example a leisure organization with highly seasonal patterns of usage may decide to add additional services to its range to help overcome these seasonal sales patterns. Or the same organization may add additional services to its range in response to expressed customers' wishes or as a reaction to competitors' actions.

A typical service product range has width and depth. Width refers to the number of different service product lines offered while depth refers to the assortment of items within each service product line. For its part a service product line is a group of service product items which share similar characteristics in terms of say; customers, end use, sales methods or price range. Table 4.5 illustrates the concepts of service product range, width, depth and service product line using simple customer-based categories for a local authority leisure centre. The basis of the width of the product range in the table could have been different. In this instance, for illustrative purposes, it is customer based but there is scope for more imaginative service product range bases which can be linked with market segments. Customer and user perceptions of product lines can often give service marketers useful insights into ways in which the service product mix should be extended or reduced or service product lines stretched or shortened.

In designing a service product range careful attention needs to be devoted to:

1 What the optimum range of service should be. There is no foolproof way to do this and most organizations rely on trial and error.

2 The positioning of the range of services provided against competitors' offerings.

3 The length and width of the range and the complementarity of separate service products within it; and the synergistic effects of range developments.

Table 4.5 : ILLUSTRATIVE SERVICE PRODUCT RANGE

← **WIDTH OF RANGE** →

Customer groups

SERVICES PRODUCT LINES — DEPTH (↕)

Infants	***Children***	***Mixed Adults***	***Single sex Adult Groups***	***Pensioners***
Creche	Swimming lesson	Badminton classes	Weight training	Exercise group
Socialisation groups	Football league	Squash coaching	Karate	Travel concessions
Mother and child classes	Tennis tournaments	Squash league	Slimming clubs	Social group
		Hockey teams		

4 In commercial services contexts, the profitability of the range of services. In most organizations the Pareto principle - the 80/20 principle - applies. 80% of profits come from 20% of customers and so on. However service marketers should remember that there is nothing immutable about the principle. It is not a natural law but one based upon empirical evidence. That does not necessarily make it a guiding principle for action.

Make or Buy Decision

A related decision faced by service marketing organizations is whether to invest in capital, people and training in order to develop additional service products through one's own efforts and resources or whether to buy in the resources of others. Thus a restaurant could buy in prepared foods or produce its own special dishes; a consultancy could train its own managers or buy in staff from outside; an advertising agency could buy in staff to provide additional specialist services like specialist photography or continue to sub-contract work to outsiders. The make or buy decision for service products, at its most general level, resembles the decision in relation to channel choice which revolves around the issue of cost versus control.

On a larger scale, make or buy decisions become a form of intra-service sector competition. Thus banks have broadened their range of services in recent years and this has now brought them into direct competition with other financial service organizations. They compete with insurance companies for some of their personal and pension scheme arrangements; they compete with building societies in the home loans market. Airlines own and operate their own hotels and terminals. Such examples illustrate some of the diversification growth which has occurred in the service sector.

4.5 NEW SERVICE DEVELOPMENT (NSD)

Idea Generation

Ideas may be generated in many ways. They can arise inside the organization and outside it; they can result from formal search procedures (e.g. marketing research) as well as informally: they may involve the organization in creating the means of delivering the new service product or they may involve the organization in obtaining rights to services product, like franchise. The sources of such ideas are many and have been illustrated in Figure 4.3.

Excluded from this figure are ideas generated through the internal creative process. The creative process of developing new ideas has intrigued marketers although the process itself still defies detailed understanding. This has led, in some cases, to the adoption of techniques, like 'synectics', brainstorming and lateral thinking to help improve the creative dimension of new product development.

Figure 4.3: EXTERNAL SOURCES OF NEW PRODUCT IDEAS

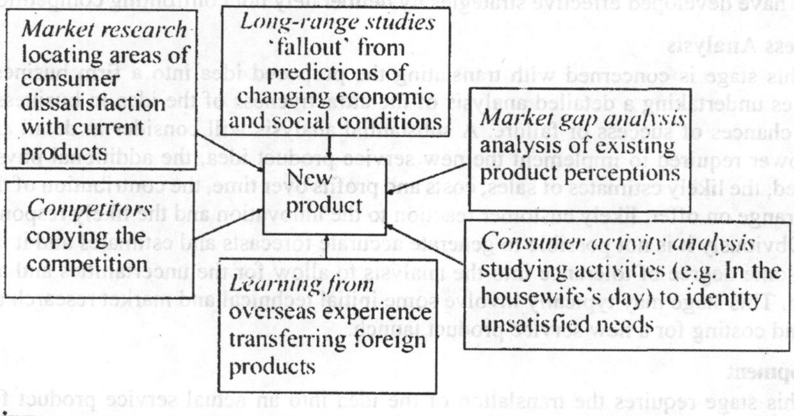

Idea Screening

This stage is concerned with checking out which ideas will justify the time, expense and managerial commitment of further research and study. Two features usually associated with the screening phase are:

1. The establishment or use of previously agreed evaluative criteria to enable the comparison of ideas generated (e.g. ideas compatible with the organization's objectives and resources);
2. The weighing, ranking and rating of the ideas against the criteria used.

Screening systems range from the highly sophisticated involving the collection and analysis on computers of a mass of data to simple checklists of a few factors considered to be vital.

Concept Development and Testing

Ideas surviving the screening process then have to be translated into product concepts. In the service product context this means concept development and concept testing.

(a) Concept Development

This phase is concerned with translating the service product idea, where the possible service product is defined in functional and objective terms, into a service product concept, the specific subjective consumer meaning the organization tries to build into the product idea. Thus a building society in attempting to sell the idea of regular saving to young, unmarried people might attempt to market the ideas on the basis that participants would be saving towards house purchase and might receive preferential treatment with a later mortgage application.

(b) Concept Testing

Concept testing is applicable in services contexts as well as in goods' contexts. Concept testing consists of taking the concepts developed after the stages of idea generation and idea screening and getting reactions to them from groups of target customers.

An associated stage of the development of the service product ideas is that of product positioning. Service product positioning is a concept increasingly widely referred to though it remains imprecisely defined, loosely used and difficult to measure. Essentially positioning is the visual presentation of the image of an organization's service product in relation either to competitive service products or to other service products in its own mix. The principle underlying this method of presentation is that it enables service product attributes to be compared with competitive offerings and with the customer's perceptions of products relative to his or her needs.

Comparison of the services and the perceptions of the occupations of persons who will use them reveals the existence of prestige and non-prestige services which give useful insights for developing a promotional programme.

Some services are best positioned directly against competition (e.g. tour operators). Other companies have developed effective strategies by deliberately not confronting competition directly.

Business Analysis

This stage is concerned with translating the proposed idea into a firm business proposal. It involves undertaking a detailed analysis of the attractiveness of the idea in business terms and its likely chances of success or failure. A substantial analysis will consider in detail aspects like the manpower required to implement the new service product idea, the additional physical resources required, the likely estimates of sales, costs and profits over time, the contribution of the new service to the range on offer, likely customer reaction to the innovation and the likely response of competitors. Obviously it is not possible to generate accurate forecasts and estimates and it is customary to build some degree of tolerance into the analysis to allow for the uncertainties and ambiguities involved. This stage may typically involve some initial technical and market research and initial timings and costing for a new service product launch.

Development

This stage requires the translation of the idea into an actual service product for the market. Typically this means that there will be an increase in investment in the project. Staff may have to be recruited or trained, facilities may have to be constructed, communications systems may need to be established. The tangible elements of the service product will be designed and tested. Unlike goods the development stage of new service product development involves attention to both the tangible elements of the service product and the service product delivery system.

Testing

Testing of new service products may not always be possible. Airlines may introduce a new class of service on a selected number of routes or a bank may make a new service available initially on a regional basis like automated cash dispensers. But some new service products do not have such an opportunity. They must be available and operate to designed levels of quality and performance from their introduction.

Commercialization

This stage represents or organization's commitment to a full-scale launch of the new service product. The scale of operation may be relatively modest like adding an additional service to an airline's routes or large scale involving the national launch of fast service footwear repair outlets operating on a concession basis. In undertaking the launch, Kotler suggests four basic decisions that apply:

(a) When to introduce the new service product;

(b) Where to launch the new service product, whether locally, regionally nationally or internationally;

(c) To whom to launch the new service product usually determined by earlier exploration in the new service product development process;

(d) How to launch the new service product. Unit trusts for example may offer a fixed price unit on initial investments for a certain time period.

With highly novel and innovative service products, organizations may be guided by the extensive literature and experience on innovation and diffusion. However like many areas of marketing most documented experience in this area has focussed upon tagibles rather than intangibles and innovation and diffusion knowledge in the service sector requires further empirical study.

A feature of new product development practices in recent years has been the growing experimentation and application of mathematical models

Example : The bank has tried to eliminate the possibility of product failure through testing wherever possible. Concept testing via direct consumer research and focus group' interviews are often used by research to determine the probable acceptability of the product. If the service involves a significant financial exposure, it is not unusual for the bank to conduct an actual market test. This avenue is being utilized more and more as a means of reducing failure, correcting product flaws and establishing proper market segments.

Although the product development area is responsible for the entire cycle, introduction often becomes a total marketing responsibility. During this phase the bank embarks on extremely complete sales and skills training programmes. It is not unusual to tie a product launch to an employee incentive campaign. Sales promotion efforts may link a premium campaign to the new product. Each affiliate has to opportunity to recommend a media programme which will most effectively sell the product in its community. This selection involves primarily the media mix, not the creative strategy. The bank recognizes the critical nature of the introduction phase and strives for maximum effectiveness by directing the right mixture of promotional tools at the right market.

4.6 NEW SERVICE PRODUCT FEATURES

The buyer's choice of a new service product may be influenced by features associated with it. These features may be seen as a fundamental part of the 'core' service by the consumer or as 'peripheral' to the core service. In tangible product marketing the brand, the colour, the design or the package may be important contributory factors to the consumer's purchase decision. Generally such elements are less conspicuous features in service product marketing but they may nevertheless be integral components of some forms of service product planning. The relevance of some of these features is described.

Service product Branding

'Branding, brand development and brand acceptance are usually not prominent in the marketing of services'.

Certainly branding is difficult because of the problems of maintaining consistency of quality in service settings. Example: In a study of brand loyalty in the context of the computer rental market it was found there was no one reason why customers terminated rental agreements or maintained or renewed their agreements. A combination of factors such as service speed, the quality of the computer system, a appearance of the staff appeared to be important. However it would seem that branding is not used much as it should be in services marketing. This is surprising for, given the intangible nature of services and the difficulty of distinguishing one service from another, branding provides a significant method for achieving some degree of service product differentiation.

Service Product Patents

The intangibility of services means that there are no patents. It is thus difficult to prevent competitors from copying service innovations though trade names can be protected. This means that innovations can have short life-cycles because they are easy to copy. Banks and airlines are examples where the absence of patent protection has brought large-scale copying of practices e.g. classes of air travel available.

Service Product Warranty

Warranties are usually related to product sales. However they can be an important element in the strategy of service marketers. In law a warranty is an undertaking on the vendor's part that the thing sold is the vendors and is fit for use or fulfills specified conditions. Such undertakings are of two kinds, implied and express. An implied warranty is one that exists through legislation and applies whether the vendor extends express warranties or not. An express warranty is one that is explicitly provided by the vendor. Express warranties have been used in the past for both sales promotion and vendor protection reasons.

Warranties can be of importance in marketing certain services. For example investment schemes which guarantee payments in spite of changes in external conditions can be a useful factor in marketing financial services. Also organizations which carry out warranties and go beyond what is legally required (e.g. airlines in their treatment of delayed passengers) can benefit in the longer term by retaining customers and building goodwill.

Service Product After-sale Service

After-sale service is usually associated with the sale of tangibles. However it too has relevance to services markets. For example, an airline can assist passengers to arrange hire cars and book hotels as part of their service; an insurance company can advise clients on changes they should make to their policies as their personal circumstances change; a stockbroker can assist a client to readjust a portfolio of shares; a dentist can provide a check-up some time after providing dental treatment.

4.7 FAILURE OF NEW SERVICE PRODUCTS

The lack of success of a new service offering is based upon management inability in handling four key decisions and the relationships between them.

The Service Concept

This has to be clearly defined. It must consider what customer benefits the service firm is intending to serve, the service attributes expressing the customer benefits, and ways and means the service is produced, distributed and consumed.

The Market Segment

The dimensions used to define the market segment must take account of the needs people have for a specific service and the trade-offs they are willing to make in terms of accessibility (e.g. time versus money).

The Organization-client Interface

The interface has to be organized as a network. Two key considerations are the participative behaviour expected from client and, with the development of large service networks, the control of interface complexity.

The Service Image

The service image is dependent not only on the use of the conventional mass media but also upon the way in which the whole image is created and sustained through clients interacting with the service organization and clients themselves spreading an image when sharing their experiences with others.

There must be coherence and cohesiveness within and between these four key elements.

In the context of bank services, the failure of many new bank services can be attributed to the failure of bank marketers to:

- Visualize new products from the perspective of the consumer;
- Engage in creative research for uncovering unfulfilled needs within various market segments;

- Effectively minimize the psychological discomfort associated with new products requiring substantive behavioural change of the consumer;
- Clearly and graphically communicate the benefits of new products to the market segments towards which they are directed.

What the evidence does confirm is that service products are as likely to fail in the marketplace as any others. Organizations concerned with their marketing may try to reduce the risks involved by utilizing the approach suggested to be of relevance for goods. This consists of adopting procedures to contain risk - as far as possible - in the new product development process.

4.8 ACHIEVING SUCCESS IN DEVELOPMENT OF NEW SERVICE PRODUCTS

Service firms are not, unfortunately, immune to the high failure rates that plague new manufactured products. A key question is the extent to which rigorously conducted and controlled development processes for new services will enhance their success rate or whether the real challenge lies in market launch. Three factors contributing most to success in order of importance are.

1. **Market synergy** - the new product fits well with the existing image of the firm, provides a superior advantage to competing products in terms of meeting customers' known needs, and receives strong support during and after the launch from the firm and its branches; further, the firm had a good understanding of its customers' purchase behaviour.
2. **Organizational factors** - there is strong inter-functional cooperation and coordination; development personnel are fully aware of why they were involved and of the importance of new products to the company.
3. **Market research factors**-detailed and scientifically designed market research studies are conducted early in the development process with a clear idea of the type of information to be obtained; a good definition of the product concept is developed before undertaking field surveys.

4.9 SERVICE PRODUCT ELIMINATION

In the previous section the relevance of systematic procedures for new service product development was emphasized. There is also a similar rationale for systematic procedures for service product elimination. The evidence for the existence of such elimination practices in the service sector is scanty.

The reasons for such unsystematic approaches are understandable:

- sheer sentimentality and vested interest;
- the hope that things will improve;
- lack of adequate data on which to base decisions;
- the disruptive consequences which may follow elimination;
- the inter-relationships that exist between sales of different service products.

But they are far outweighed by the benefits:

- improved profitability;
- time can be devoted to more successful service products;
- marginal service products tie up other resources like personnel and advertising budgets;
- weak service products may delay the search for new ones.

The elimination of service products of course is not easy and indeed organizations may adopt a number of strategies before doing so like selling overseas, optimizing profitability over whatever life remains or revitalizing the offering in some way. But these moves do not ultimately remove the need for systematic procedures to assist with decision making in this area. As Stanton says: 'Knowing when and how to abandon products successfully may be as important as knowing when and how to introduce new ones. Certainly management should develop a systematic procedure for phasing out its weak products.'

SHORT ANSWER QUESTIONS

1. Define the following:
   (a) Service product
   (b) Service level
   (c) Service form
   (d) Service offer
2. Can a service product be separated from the service delivery system?
3. How can success be achieved in the development of new service products?
4. Distinguish between 'core' services and 'peripheral' services.
5. What do you understand by the term 'life cycle'?
6. Why do some service products need elimination?
7. Is there any difficulty in applying the new service concept?
8. Why is service product branding difficult?
9. Outline the overlap in the 'product' element of the marketing mix between physical goods and services.
10. Give examples of some new service options.
11. How can success be achieved in the development of new services?

ESSAY QUESTIONS

1. What is the relationship between the 'customer benefit concept' and 'the service concept'?
2. What are the key components of a service offer?
3. What uncontrollable elements may influence a consumer's perceptions of a service product?
4. What is 'service product range'? What are the considerations?
5. What difficulties may arise in translating a 'service concept' into a 'service offer'?
6. What are the reasons for the failure of some new service products? Give examples.
7. What are the vectors in service product growth? What are the options in new services?
8. What are the various product strategies available to a service firm? What are the implications of each?
9. What is the relevance of the life cycle concept to service products?
10. Explain the process of new service development.

EXERCISE / ASSIGNMENTS

1. Choose any three service products. What are the service elements, forms and levels associated with them?
2. Trace the life cycle concept for the products of the following services, as experience in your place of residence:
   (a) Personal Care (Saloons, Body slimming, etc.)
   (b) Consultancy
   (c) Fast-food restaurants
   (d) Computer education
   (e) Travel agents.
3. What strategies would you adopt for the products of the following services? Give a detailed plan:
   (a) Web marketing
   (b) Paging
   (c) Tourism

   (d) Healthcare
   (e) Insurance.

4. Make a list of new service products as well as service product improvements for the following services:
   (a) Airlines
   (b) Education
   (c) Tele-communications
   (d) Repair services
   (e) Social services
   (f) Public utility services.

5

Service Location and Distribution

5.1 FLEXIBILITY

While service organizations often have a desire to centralize production in order to achieve economies of scale, consumers usually seek local access to services, often at a time which may not be economic for the producer to cater for. Service-location decisions therefore involve a trade-off between the needs of the producer and those of the consumer. This is in contrast to goods manufacturers, who can manufacture goods in one location where production is most economic, then ship them to where they are most needed.

Table 5.1 : LOCATIONAL FLEXIBILITY IN PRODUCTION AND CONSUMPTION OF INSEPARABLE SERVICES

Flexibility in consumption

LONG-TERM FLEXIBILITY IN PRODUCTION	*Low*	*High*
Low	Hospital Care	Tourist attractions
High	Banking	Hairdressing

The extreme case of inflexibility (Table 5.1) in production is provided by services where the whole purpose of the service is to be at one unique location - for example, tourism-related services based on a unique historic site by their very nature cannot be moved. A further group of services are locationally inflexible because they can only sensibly be produced in large-scale centralised production facilities. This can be the case where the necessary supporting equipment is expensive and offers opportunities for significate economies of scale. Where this equipment is also highly immobile, customers must come to a limited number of central service points to receive service. This is true with much of the specialized and expensive equipment needed for complex medical care, such as body scanners which tend to be provided at a small number of central locations. In cases where the equipment offers less scope for economies of scale and is more easily transported, service production can be distributed more widely.

Decisions on service location are also influenced by the extent to which consumers are willing or able to be flexible in where they consume a service. Inflexibility on the part of consumers can arise for a number of reasons:

a. Where a service is to be performed on a customer's possessions, those possessions may themselves be immovable, requiring the supplier to come to the customer (for example, building repairs).

b. Sometimes the customer may also be physically immobile (for example, physically disabled users of healthcare services).

c. For impulse purchases, or services where there are substantial competitive alternatives, customers are unlikely to be willing to travel far to seek out a service.

d. For specialist service, customers show more willingness to be flexible in where they are prepared to receive the service, compared to routine purchases for which they would be unwilling to travel.

It follows therefore that access strategies should be based on the identification of market segments made up of users with similar accessibility needs. Access strategies can then be developed which meet the needs of each segment :

a. ***Age*** frequently defines segments in terms of the level of access sought. For many elderly users of personal care services there is sometimes an unwillingness or an inability to leave home, making home availability of a service a sought attribute. For other groups, such as older teenagers, the very act of getting away from home to receive a service may be attractive. This could explain the current revived interest in going out to see a film at a cinema in the face of the competing alternatives provided by local video-rental shops or satellite television services.

b. Segmentation on the basis of an individual's ***economic status*** can be seen in the willingness of more affluent segments to pay premium prices in order to consume a service at a point and a time convenient to themselves rather than the service provider. Evidence of this is provided by home-delivery food services which target with high discretionary incomes.

c. ***Psychographic segmentation*** can be seen in the way groups of people seek out services that satisfy their life-style needs. As an example, some segments of the population are prepared to travel large distances to a restaurant whose design and ambience appeals to them.

d. The ***cultural background*** of some individuals can predispose them to seek a particular kind of accessibility. This can be seen in the reluctance of some groups to become involved in service-delivery methods which remove regular personal contact with the service provider. Insurance companies that collect premium from the homes of customers may give reassurance to some segments who have been brought up to distrust impersonal organizations, whereas a periodic visit to a bank or an annual payment by post may satisfy the needs of other segments.

e. Access strategies can be based on the ***type of benefit*** which users seek from a service. As an example, customers are often prepared to travel a considerable distance to a restaurant for a celebration meal, but would expect it to be easily accessible for a business lunch.

f. High ***frequency*** users of a service may place a greater premium on easy accessibility than casual ones.

g. In the case of business-to-business services, the ***level of access*** to a service can directly affect the customer's operating costs. A computer-repair company which makes its services available at buyers' offices avoids the costs which the latter would incur if it had to perform part of the service - delivery and collection - itself.

Location may vary in importance according to the nature of the service marketed. For a repair service conducted in the home, like emergency plumbing, then the location of the base of the performer of the service may be irrelevant in the customer decision - making process. On the other hand small-scale studies of university students' choice of bank suggest that convenience of location is a critical factor in the bank selection decision.

5.2 CLASSIFICATION BY LOCATION

(a) Location may be irrelevant.

(b) Services may be concentrated.

(c) Services may be dispersed.

Location may be Irrelevant

Location may be irrelevant for services like household repairs, car breakdown services and utilities. These services are performed where the customer is. Therefore location of any service facility is of less importance than for services performed in a specific location. What is critical about such services however is their 'accessibility' or 'availability' to the customer when service is required. In this sense then location refers not just to physical proximity: though this may be important for some organizations which develop branch offices to get nearer to clients (e.g. advertising agencies, architects). An important element in the design of such services then is the communications system which should permit speedy response to customer calls on the system. In setting and operating standards in these service organizations decisions are required on the level of service which is provided.

Services may be Concentrated

Many services are concentrated (e.g. software park). Here two factors-conditions of supply and tradition - act as centralizing forces. Reasons which encourage such concentration include the status associated with certain sites; low intensity of demand; customer willingness to be mobile; the historical development of complementary services in close proximity to core services and the unimportance of demand orientation.

Services may be Dispersed

Services which are dispersed locate in terms of market potential. The nature of demand and the characteristics of the service require dispersal into the market place. Sometimes institutions may be centralized (e.g. business consultants) but operations are dispersed (e.g. consultants visit specific customers).

These various patterns of service location are shown in Figure 5.1

The importance of location varies according to the type of service though a number of common questions should be considered by service marketers in making location decisions. These include :

Figure 5.1 : SERVICE LOCATION PATTERNS

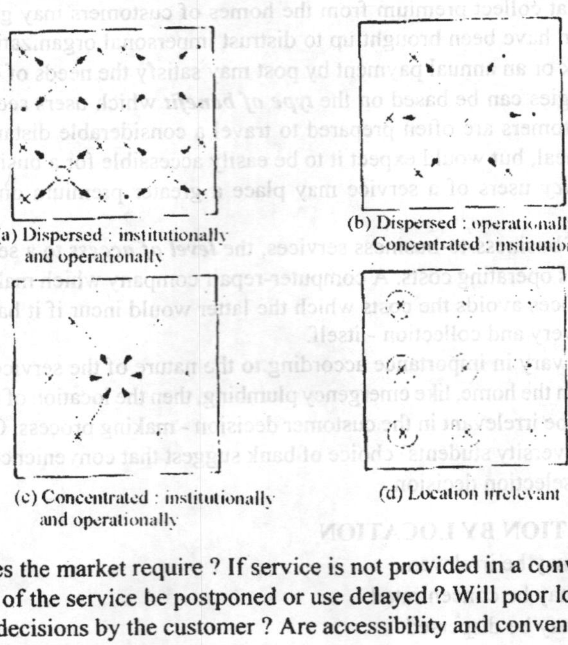

(a) Dispersed : institutionally and operationally

(b) Dispersed : operationally Concentrated : institutionally

(c) Concentrated : institutionally and operationally

(d) Location irrelevant

(a) What does the market require ? If service is not provided in a convenient location will purchase of the service be postponed or use delayed ? Will poor location lead to do-it-yourself decisions by the customer ? Are accessibility and convenience critical factors in service choice (e.g. bank choice)?

(b) What are the trends within the sector of service activity in which the service organization operates? Are competitors reaching out into markets (e.g. distance learning in education)? Could some competitive advantage be obtained by going against the norms operating in the sub-sector?

(c) How flexible is the service ? Is it technology based or people based ? How do these factors affect flexibility in location and relocation decisions ?

(d) Does the organization have an obligation to locate in convenient sites (e.g. public services like health care)?

(e) What new systems, procedures, processes and technology can be harnessed to overcome weaknesses of past location decisions (e.g. growth of banking by post)?

(f) How critical are complementary services to the location decision? Are customers seeking service systems or service clusters? Does the location of other service organizations reinforce any location decision taken (e.g. services can reinforce each other in attracting custom)?

5.3 ACCESSIBILITY THROUGH CO-PRODUCTION

Some service organizations choose to make their services available to consumers in combination with other goods and services with the collaboration of another producer. The outputs of the two organizations can be quite diverse. For example, a finance company could offer loan facilities in conjunction with customers buying hi-fi equipment. Other examples include a combined train fare and museum admission ticket and a combined hotel and travel offer.

On other occasions, a service can be made available in combination with similar services provided by potential competitors. The basis for doing this is that the combined value of the enlarged service offer will generate more business and ultimately be of benefit to all service providers involved. In this way, many regional travel tickets allow passengers to travel on the trains and buses of potentially competing operators, thereby making public transport as a whole a relatively attractive option. Similarly, banks benefit by sharing cash-dispenser networks. Those sharing gain a competitive advantage over a bank that chooses to go it alone with its own dedicated but smaller network.

5.4 SERVICE CHANNEL DEVELOPMENT

Independent Service Channels

Independent channels emerge to fulfill a specific need and are not necessarily associated with another product or service. Thus a consulting company or a travel agent not linked with any other company and operated separately from other firms are examples of independent service firms. Independent service firms may of course make use of other intermediaries (e.g. as in film distribution).

Combined Service Channels

Combined service channels on the other hand emerge when the service is integrated with a channel that distributes a product. Combined service channels can arise through :

(a) ***Combination by Acquisition*** - this is where services may be offered as part of a total product mix (e.g. finance for consumer durable purchases).

(b) ***Combination through Concessions*** - this is where services may be offered and operated within the facilities of another firm. The concessionaire pays rent, and perhaps some percentage of sales on the space occupied, to the firm granting the concession.

(c) ***Combination through a Tie in Agreement*** - this is where two or more independent companies come to some contractual agreement to cooperate in the marketing of a service. Thus finance companies and car dealers may operate tie-in agreements.

5.5 METHODS OF DISTRIBUTING SERVICES

A distribution channel for our purpose is the sequence of firms involved in moving a service from producer to consumer. The usual generalization made about service distribution is that direct sale is the most common method and that channels are short. Direct sale certainly is common in some services markets (e.g. professional services); but many service channels contain one or more intermediaries. Some of these intermediaries assume ownership risks; some perform roles that change ownership (e.g. purchasing); some perform roles that enable physical movement (e.g. transporting).

Direct Sale

Direct sale may be the chosen method of distribution for a service through choice or because of inseparability of service and provider. Where direct sale is selected through choice then the service marketer does so presumably to derive specific marketing advantages such as :

(a) Maintaining better 'control' over how the service is provided or performed. Loss of control may be a disadvantage of dealing through an intermediary;

(b) Obtaining distinguishable service product differentiation in what are otherwise standard and uniform markets through real personal service.

(c) Obtaining direct feedback from customers on their existing needs, how those needs are changing and their perceptions of competitors' market offerings.

Where direct sale is due to the inseparability of service and provider (e.g. as in legal services or certain kinds of household services) then the provider of the service may face problems. Among these are :

(a) Problems of expanding the business and coping with high workloads where the services of a particular individual may be in demand (e.g. a distinguished defence lawyer).

(b) Sometimes direct sale means limited geographic market coverage; particularly where a large personal element of service is involved and technology cannot be used, to any great extent, to bridge the gap between the service organization and its customers.

Direct sale may of course be accomplished by the customer going to the service provider (e.g. a hairdresser, tourists making use of an information centre) or by the provider going to the customer (e.g. a mobile bank; a plumber or a drain cleaning service). Many personal and business services are characterized by the direct channel between service organization and customer. Direct channels Are found in personal and business service fields like beauty shops, photographic studios, shoe repair shops, funeral service firms, consultants, security services and plant rental.

Sale via Intermediary (ies)

The most frequently used channel by service organization however is that which operates through intermediaries. Service channel structures vary considerably and some are now complex.

Many forms of intermediary are now common in services markets. They include :

(a) ***Agents.*** Common in markets like tourism, travel, hotels, transport, insurance, credit and employment and industrial services.

(b) ***Dealers.*** Intermediaries trained to perform or provide a service and franchised to sell it.

(c) ***Institutional middlemen.*** Arise in markets where services must be or are traditionally provided by intermediaries like the stock market or advertising.

(d) ***Wholesalers.*** Intermediaries in wholesale markets like merchant banks or laundry and dry cleaning services for industry.

(e) ***Retailers.*** Examples include photographic studios and shops providing dry cleaning services.

5.6 INNOVATIONS IN METHODS OF DISTRIBUTING SERVICES

There have been considerable innovations, in recent years, in methods of distributing services. This contrasts with views expressed some years ago that service marketer had lagged in using innovative marketing practices. Four examples are included here to illustrate the nature of some of these innovations. They cover new service developments and new service institutions. The examples are :

(a) the growth of rental services;

(b) the growth of franchising;

(c) the growth of service integration;

(d) quasi-retailing.

A. The Growth of Rental Services

In Industrial markets it is now possible to rent or lease items like cars, lorries, plant and equipment, aircraft, containers, office equipment of all kinds, uniforms, overalls, towels and so forth. In consumer markets too flats, homes, furniture and TV, sports goods, tents, tools, paintings, films, videos and social companions are amongst the range of items available for rental. A number of organizations traditionally involved in goods production have developed a service arm to their operations through renting and leasing their equipment and banks and finance houses play an important role in this market as third parties to many leasing and rental agreements.

Some products do not lend themselves to renting, particularly consumable items like food, medicines and oil. Also in many situations it is more beneficial to own a product - because it is more convenient to do so - or because financially the costs of renting are higher particularly when the residual value of an asset is taken into account.

There are however a number of advantages in renting for both the renter and the rentee. The importance and predominance of these will vary according to the nature of the market (e.g. consumer or industrial). For the renter some advantages are :

(a) Income obtainable after repair costs and maintenance and service charges may be higher than could be obtained by selling the product ;
(b) renting may enable the renter to tap markets that could not be reached otherwise because of capital costs involved;
(c) renting equipment may give the renter leverage in the sale of products associated with it (e.g. photocopiers and paper);
(d) rental arrangements can assist with the launch and distribution of new products and complement arrangements based on purchase and ownership by the customer.

For the rentee some advantages of rental arrangements include :

(a) Capital is not tied up in assets. Such capital can be used for other purchases.
(b) In industrial markets there may be tax advantages to renting or leasing rather than owning goods.
(c) Less capital outlay is required to enter business or markets where goods may be rented rather than acquired by purchase.
(d) New designs may become available to those who rent thus avoiding the risks in purchase of obsolescence and style change.
(e) In situations where seasonal demand or sporadic use only is made of a product (e.g. harvesting) then renting equipment may be a more sensible and economically sound strategy than ownership.
(f) The problems of service - maintenance, repair, breakdown - are usually the responsibility of others under many rental arrangements.
(g) Renting removes the risk of incorrect product selection and anxieties which may follow purchase.
(h) For many, renting or leasing is the mechanism which permits consumption and use which would not otherwise be possible (e.g. because of costs or practical problems of surveillance and maintenance as with holiday homes).

Consumption without ownership has great possibilities for expansion in consumer markets. Some of the more likely implications of trends in terms of its impact on marketing and business are:

(a) Increased investment in inventory for those leasing and renting. This will be coupled with lower stock turnover rates, greater demands for storage and facilities for maintenance, repair, renovation and repackaging of stock.
(b) The larger amount of inventory in turn requires different financing arrangements. This has led to financial institutions themselves assuming the ownership function within channels of distribution. Coupled with this though is that consumer credit requirements may be reduced as ownership is shifted elsewhere in the channel.

(c) New inventory concepts are required under conditions of leasing and renting (e.g. greater concern with 'occupancy rates' and 'capacity usage' rather than stockturn).

(d) Products rented and leased may need to be of better quality. Durability and ease of maintenance and repair are important characteristics where heavy and repeated use may occur.

(e) In addition it is suggested that leasing and renting in consumer markets affords an opportunity for salesmen to be 'consultants of consumption' occupying a greater advising role. Also there are opportunities for more 'flexible' pricing practices in situations in which goods are rented rather than owned, particularly over the life of the item in service.

B. The Growth of Franchising

Franchising is a growing phenomenon in those service industries where standardization of the service is possible. At a general level: 'a franchise is where one person grants rights to another to exploit an intellectual property right involving perhaps trade names, products, trade marks, equipment distribution'.

An illustrative list of some current types of business franchise operations is shown in Table 5.2.

Table 5.2 : ILLUSTRATIVE LIST OF BUSINESS FRANCHISE OPERATIONS

Accounting and tax services	Garments
Beauty Salons	Nursing Homes
Car rental services	Office Systems
Drain Cleaning Services	Pest Control
Employment Services	Restaurants
Fast food operations	Sales training services
Glass tinting	Travel Agencies
Hotels	Vending operations
Industrial Services	Weight control systems
Lawn and garden care	

It is likely to become of more importance in service marketing because of the benefits it affords. The franchiser gains :

(a) expansion possibilities in spite of capital or manpower limitations;

(b) motivated managers in multi-site operations because they are part owners of the business;

(c) a means of control over pricing, promotion, distribution and consistency of the service product offering;

(d) a source of revenue.

The franchisee gains :

(a) a chance to run his own business, usually with a tested service product concept;

(b) the backing of mass purchasing power;

(c) the backing of promotional support;

(d) the benefits of centralized management.

The customer gains :

(a) some assurance of service product quality particularly where the operation is established nationally.

C. The Growth of Service Integration

The growth of franchising outlined in the previous section is a manifestation of another phenomenon in the service sector - integration. Integrated corporate systems and integrated contractual systems are developing and beginning to dominate in certain fields. In travel and tourism the service systems link two or more service industries like airlines, hotels, motels, car rental, tour buses, restaurants, seat booking agencies, leisure and recreation sites, ski resorts, shipping lines and so on. Some large service organizations now control the complete 'package' offered to the tourist or holiday maker through control over horizontal and vertical service channel systems. Integration so often thought of only in manufacturing systems is an important feature of many modern service systems too.

D. Quasi-retailing

Quasi-retail outlets sell services rather than goods. They include :

Hairdressers	Estate agents	Amusement arcades
Undertakers	Building societies	Laundry
Travel agents	Employment agencies	Hotels
Ticket agents	Car hire agencies	Restaurants
Banks	Driving Schools	

Given that local authorities have an obligation to blend the mix of retail outlets in a commercial centre, questions are inevitably raised about the 'right' number, type and location of service outlets in shopping centres.

There is little evidence about the impact of quasi-retail outlets on the nature of centre as a whole. Some arguments against too great a number of such outlets in a centre include these :

(a) they can push up property values;

(b) they may create dead frontages which discourage window shopping;

(c) some service outlets may be closed on peak shopping days (e.g. banks on Sunday);

(d) some service outlets are bad neighbours (e.g. take-away food shops, amusement arcades);

(e) too many quasi-retail outlets in a centre can reduce the range of conventional retail store choice.

On the other hand arguments for encouraging quasi-retail outlet developments include these:

(a) many complement other retail business (e.g. users of facilities like banks and building societies may use shops selling goods on the same shopping trip);

(b) service outlets can have imaginative window displays to encourage window shopping.

5.7 INPUTS FOR LOCATION DECISIONS

It is clear that there is a whole range of inputs into the location decision. These are sourced within the organization, from the external environment and from professional agencies. Some of them are illustrated in Figure 5.2, which shows not only the source of these inputs to the decision, but also some of the relationships among the different sources. Thus the marketing department of the supermarket chain might approach a 'local' independent market research consultancy in an area being considered, for information concerning the locations and purchasing patterns of inhabitants (potential customers). The accounting/finance group within the organization will get information concerning land availabilities and costs from local estate agencies, and will approach central and local government departments for information about local financial incentives to develop in the particular area. The relative importance of the information and its impact on the decision will clearly vary from situation to situation. For the location of a theme park, weather will be a factor; for a hospital it might be proximity of patients, for a hotel, convenience for the city centre; for a mail order distribution centre, a good road network.

Figure 5.2 : SOME OF THE INVOLVEMENTS OF THE DIFFERENT FUNCTIONS AND AGENCIES IN THE LOCATION DECISION

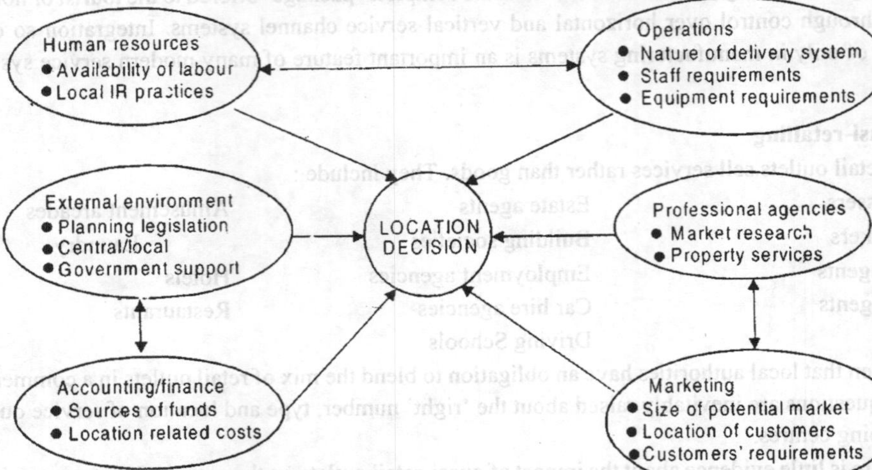

A Conceptual model of retail location drivers

Davies and Clarke present a model of some of the key factors which can be thought of as driving the retail location decision. This is shown in Figure 5.3. They divide the decision along a number of dimensions. One such dimension has convenience at one end, identifying with products which in some sense need replenishing ('consumable' goods, like petrol and perishable foods), and comparison at the other, where the consumer is likely to want to examine a range of products possibly sold at more than one outlet (e.g. durables like clothes and electrical equipment). They suggest that at the 'comparison' end of the spectrum behaviour is in some way leisure driven, while at the 'convenience' end time is an important factor. The second dimension relates to the size of the product, which can range from bulky to portable. This gives rise to four types of location; solus or free-standing outlets, retail parks, high street/town centre outlets, and parades of outlets in peripheral centres.

Figure 5.3 : A CONCEPTUAL MODEL OF RETAIL LOCATION DRIVERS

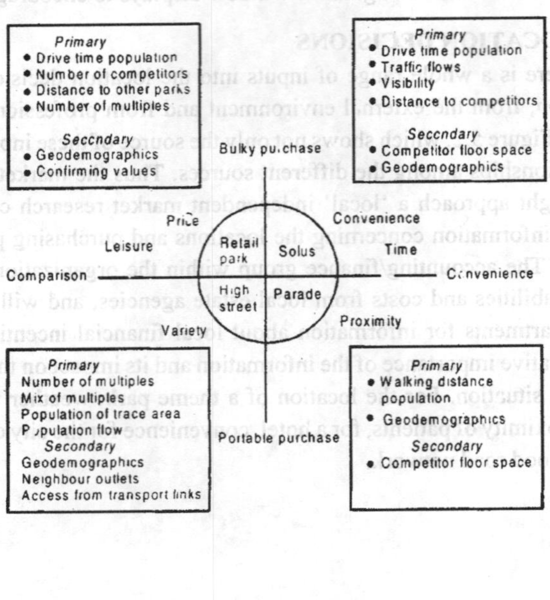

Figure 5.3 summarizes the key factors, split into primary and secondary, for each of these types of outlet. Thus for free-standing (solus) outlets (e.g. a store specializing in cane furniture for the whole house), ease of access is important, while the extent of the competition is less crucial. For shopping arcades (e.g. a fish and chip shop), the geodemographic profile of the local population is likely to be an important consideration in evaluating the performance of such an outlet. For an outlet in a retail park (e.g. a store selling domestic electrical equipment), the number of competitors, including the range of choice, is likely to be more important than the geodemographic profile of the local population. For the high street outlet (e.g. a chemist), the variety in other outlets is likely to be an important influence.

The rule of retail compatibility

The concepts of generative, shared and suscipient business is introduced to help explain the various relationships.

Generative business is that which an outlet generates through significant advertising or other related means. It is suggested that an organization that generates all of its own business needs an exceptional location.

Shared business is obtained by an outlet as a result of the 'traffic-generating' power of its neighbours. The tobacco shop in the busy shopping centre relies on this type of business. Indeed, the traffic-generating power of outlets is key to the concept of the 'anchor tenant' : big name retailers which will draw potential customers to a shopping area. The existence and location of these anchor tenants can be the key to the developing of retail parks and high street areas.

Suscipient business is when customers use an outlet even when their reasons for being in the area are other than for purchasing. An example is the 'boutiques' found on ferry-boats and at airports.

The rule of rental compatibility, as developed by Mason and Mayer, states that when two compatible business are located close to each other, there will be an increase in business volume which is proportional to :

- the extent of total customer interchange between them;
- the sum of the ratios of purposeful purchasing; and
- the ratio of the business volume of the smaller and larger store.

Thus,

$$IV = DI\,(TV_L + TV_S)\frac{TV_S}{TV_L}\left\{\frac{PP_L}{TV_L} + \frac{PP_S}{TV_S}\right\}$$

where

IV = increase in volume of purchases
DI = degree of interchange of customers between the outlets
TV_L = total volume of retail sales for the larger outlet
TV_S = total volume of retail sales for the smaller outlet
PP_L = volume of purposeful purchasing at the larger outlet.
PP_S = volume of purposeful purchasing at the smaller outlet

Reilly's law of retail gravity

Reilly's law purposes the limits of the attraction of one shopping centre in relation to its distance (in miles) from a second. As the analogy with gravitational forces suggests, as a consumer gets further from one shopping centre and closer to a second, the attraction of the first centre gets less. It is assumed that the populations of the communities in which the centres are based and the distance between the two centres are key factors in this relationship.

The law provides a formula for calculating that point at which a consumer is indifferent to the choice of shopping centre A or centre B. This point is found as follows :

$$\text{Distance of point of indifference from A} = \frac{\text{Distance from A to B}}{1+\sqrt{\dfrac{\text{Population of B}}{\text{Population of A}}}}$$

For illustration, suppose A has a population of 200,000 and B a population of 320,000 and that they are 15 miles apart. Reilly's law states that the point/line of indifference is at :

$$\frac{15}{1+\sqrt{\dfrac{320{,}000}{200{,}000}}} \text{ miles from A}$$

i.e. 6.62 miles from A, or :

$$\frac{15}{1+\sqrt{\dfrac{200{,}000}{320{,}000}}} \text{ miles from B}$$

i.e. 8.38 miles from B.

5.8 BASIC LOCATION MODELS

- Gravity models, sometimes also referred to as spatial interaction models.
- Regression analysis models.
- Checklists and analogs.

Gravity or spatial interaction models

These are based on the law of retail gravity developed by Reilly and described earlier. The basic principle behind these models is that movement of customers attracted to a particular retail outlet is inversely proportional to distance and directly proportional to the attraction of the outlet (frequently measured by its size).

Probably the most widely quoted model is that developed by Huff, Ghosh and Craigh which states that 'the probability of any individual choosing a particular retail store is equal to the ratio of the utility of that store to the sum of the utilities of all the other stores that the individual considers. In this context the utility is considered to be dependent on the size of the store and the distance between the individual customers and the stores. Expressing this relationship in mathematical terms :

$$P_{ij} = \frac{\dfrac{S_j}{D^{\beta}_{ij}}}{\sum_{k=1}^{n} \dfrac{S_k}{D^{\beta}_{ik}}}$$

where,

P_{ij}	is the probability that an individual in zone i (i=1,...m) will travel and shop in facility j (j=1,.. ,n)
S_j	is the size of shopping facility j
D_{ik}	is the distance or travel time between zone i and shopping facility k
m	is the number of zones
n	is the number of shopping facilities
β	is the parameter which has to be esumated empirically

Figure 5.4 : SITE SELECTION PROBLEM

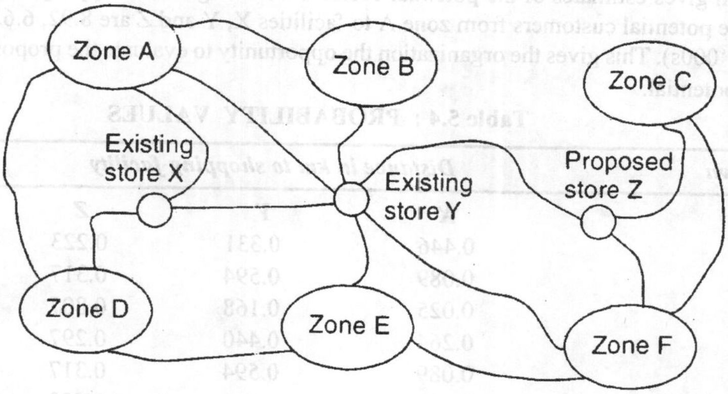

The parameter β reflects the influence of travelling time on various types of product purchase, and it is suggested that it might lie between 0.5 and 3.0 taking larger values for convenience goods and where distance has a major impact : for example, shopping for food.

The following example will illustrate the process.

Currently two major supermarkets located at X and Y provide a service for six small towns / zones (A, B, C, D, E and F). A national supermarket chain is considering opening a new store at location Z. These locations, together with some of the major roads, are shown in Figure 5.4.

Some data concerning the stores are presented in Table 5.3. This shows their travelling distances from the six towns; the floor area of the existing stores and that proposed for the new store, and the populations of the towns. Since distance has a significant, but not dominant impact and the stores are dealing largely in convenience foods, a value for β of 2 will be taken.

Table 5.3 : DATA FOR THE SITE SELECTION PROBLEM

Zone	*Population*	*Distance in km to shopping facility*		
		X	***Y***	***Z***
A	20000	10	15	20
B	30000	20	10	15
C	25000	20	10	5
D	40000	15	15	20
E	15000	20	10	15
F	20000	15	5	5
Floor area (sq. metres)		1500	2500	3000

The first step in the analysis is the calculation of the probabilities. The probability that an individual from town A will shop in facility X is given by :

$$\frac{\dfrac{1500}{10^2}}{\dfrac{1500}{10^2}+\dfrac{2500}{15^2}+\dfrac{3000}{20^2}} = 0.446$$

The remaining probabilities are shown in Table 5.4. It is then possible to explore in more detail the potential sales revenue. The starting point is the population (or households) in each town and the average expenditure per household. Simple multiplying the probability figures in Table 5.4 by the population gives estimates of the potential customers visiting each shopping facility. Thus, for example, the potential customers from zone A to facilities X, Y and Z are 8.92, 6.62 and 4.46 respectively (in '000s). This gives the organization the opportunity to evaluate the proposed site in terms of its sales potential.

Table 5.4 : PROBABILITY VALUES

From town	*Distance in km to shopping facility*		
	X	*Y*	*Z*
A	0.446	0.331	0.223
B	0.089	0.594	0.317
C	0.025	0.168	0.807
D	0.264	0.440	0.297
E	0.089	0.594	0.317
F	0.029	0.441	0.529

The model is perhaps best set up using a spreadsheet. It is then possible to investigate the alternative scenarios very quickly. A second proposed site can be considered simply by altering the appropriate distances from the six towns. Trade-offs between the extra sales generated at the shopping facility by increasing the sales area and the cost of this extra sales area can be evaluated.

Regression analysis models

Normally, regression models are used to predict store turnover, which is the dependent variable, considered to be a linear function of a number of independent variables which will be used as part of the forecasting process. Thus store turnover might be considered dependent on the sales area of the store, the number of competitors, the cost of parking, the population size in the area, and so on. The general form of this model is as follows :

$$Y = a_0 + a_1x_1 + a_2x_2 + a_3x_3 + ... + a_nx_n + \varepsilon$$

where,

y = the estimated turnover

x_i = the ith independent variable

a_i = a constant, the coefficient of the ith independent variable

a_0 = a constant

ε = an error term

It is likely that the set of independent variables and their relative importance will vary with store types.

These are shown in Table 5.5

Table 5.5 : FACTORS IN ASSESSING STORE LOCATION

Type of Store	*Location factors*
Department Stores	Competition Demographics Local economy Site size and characteristics
Variety Stores	Population size Presence of variety stores Site size Turnover threshold
Out-of-town warehouses	Accessibility Road layout

	Competition
	Population size
	Planning permission
	Site size
Grocery Superstores	Accessibility
	Road Layout
	Competition
	Population size by drive time
	Planning permission
Large and small high-street multiples	Location of key traders
	Prime pitch
	Pedestrian flow
	Population size
	Turnover
Convenience Stores	Site prominence
	Pedestrians and traffic flow
	Competition
Financial Outlets	Business Structure of area
	Planning permission
	Success of agencies

Checklists and analogs

Many organizations rely on checklists, analogs and intuition to support the solution to their location decision problems. In fact, intuition frequently has as its foundation the unstructured checklist. Their advantage is that they systematically take the analyst through what can be regarded as all of the key factors of potential importance.

A checklist is presented below in Table 5.6.

Table 5.6 : LOCATION CHECKLIST

Population	*Accessibility*	*Competition*	*Costs*
Population size	Pedestrian flow	Existing retail activity	Purchase price
Age profile	Pedestrian entry routes	- Direct competitors	Leasing terms
Household size	Public transport	- Indirect competitors	Site preparation
Income levels	- Types	- Anchor stores	Building restrictions
Income per capita	- Cost	- Cumulative attraction	Building costs
Occupation classifications	- Ease of use	- Compatibility	Development concessions
Main employees	- Potential	Existing retail specs	
Economic stability	Car ownership levels	- Selling areas	Rates payable
Unemployment levels	Road network	- Turnover estimates	Refurbishment needs
Seasonal fluctuations	Conditions	- Department/product analysis	Maintenance costs
Housing density	- Driving speeds		Security needs
Housing age/type	- Congestion	- Trade areas	Staff availability/ rates
Neighbourhood classification	- Restrictions	- Age of outlets	
House ownership levels	- Plans	- Standard of design	Delivery costs
Building/demolition plans	Parking	- Car parking	Promotional media/ costs
Life-style measures	- Capacity	Saturation index	
Cultural/ethnic groupings	- Convenience	Competitive potential	Turnover loss-other branches
Current shopping patterns	- Cost	- Outlet expansion	
	- Potential	- Refurbishment	
	Visibility	- Vacant sites	
	Access for staff	- Interception	
	Access for transport and deliveries	- Repositioning	
		- Competitor policy	

SHORT ANSWER QUESTIONS

1. Define the following:
   (a) Franchising
   (b) Reilly's law
   (c) Analog
   (d) Spatial interaction model.
2. What is quasi-retailing?
3. Why have rental services become more important in recent years?
4. Suggest three services for which the location of a service organisation is unimportant. Why?
5. How does 'perishability' of a service influence channel selection decisions?
6. What are the channels available for the distribution of services?
7. Give examples of services which are wholly dependent upon geographical location.
8. Who are institutional middlemen?
9. What are the advantages of rental agreements for a rentee?
10. How can the volume of increase in purchases be computed?
11. Mumbai has a population of 8,00,000 and Pune has a population of 4,23,000 and they are 150 km apart. What is the point of indifference for a customer?
12. What are checklists and analogs? Prepare a checklist for the location of:
    (a) Hotel (b) Bank (c) Hospital (d) Amusement Park.

ESSAY QUESTIONS

1. In what kinds of situations are services likely to be:
   (a) concentrated, and (b) dispersed?
2. Suggest suitable alternative channels of distribution for:
   (a) healthcare services
   (b) educational services.
3. Evaluate the importance of service location in a service industry where restrictions may apply on other elements of the marketing mix (eg. Professional services).
4. What are the innovations in the methods of distributing services?
5. What technological changes are likely to influence future channel choice decisions in service industries?
6. Outline the main factors which must be considered when making decisions about service location.
7. What are the advantages and limitations of franchising for franchisees?
8. Using the gravity model, compute the estimated sales potential for each of the proposed sites. Which site would be the ideal location for the service in each city?

Distance in km to shopping facility

	A	*B*	*C*
City X	15	15	20
City Y	20	10	15
City Z	20	10	05

The population of City X, Y and Z are 1 lakh, 76,000 and 82,000 respectively. The sizes of the proposed shopping facilities in City X, Y and Z are 10,000 ; 8,500 and 6,800 sq. feet respectively.

9. Enumerate the 'inputs' for location decisions.
10. What are the various models available for service locations? Discuss.

EXERCISE / ASSIGNMENTS

1. **Prepare an analog for determinants of location for the following services:**
   (a) Cinema Theatre
   (b) Auto repair
   (c) Warehousing
   (d) Real estate
   (e) Television broadcasting
   (f) Detectives.
2. **Prepare a comprehensive 'service package' for a family of four keen on travelling from Hyderabad to Kashmir via New Delhi.**
3. **Investigate the reasons that prompted the location of the following at a particular area (or particular point) in your neighbourhood:**
   (a) Any Pizza restaurant
   (b) Multinational Bank
   (c) Travel agent
   (d) Super Market
   (e) Educational Institution.

●●●

6

Pricing for Services

6.1 CHARACTERISTICS OF SERVICES AND PRICES

The characteristics of services may influences prices set in services markets. The influence of these characteristics will vary according to the type of service and market situation under consideration. They are however an added consideration when examining the traditional main forces influencing price; costs, competition and demand. Some impacts of these services characteristics include these five categories.

(a) Service perishability, the fact that service cannot be stored and that fluctuations in demand cannot be met as easily through using inventory, has price implications. Special price offers and price reductions to use up spare capacity may be used and marginal pricing may be more common place. This may happen in markets like airline travel and package holidays. Constant use of these forms of pricing may lead to increasing customer sophistication: buyers may deliberately hold off from purchasing certain services with the expectations that price reductions will occur. Sellers for their part may try to compensate for this effect by offering advantageous reductions on orders for services placed early. Again the holiday tour market exhibits some of these forces at work.

(b) Customers may be able to delay or postpone the performance or use of many services. Alternatively they may be able to perform certain services for themselves. These features can lead to keener competition amongst sellers of services. They can also encourage a greater degree of price stability in certain markets, in the short term.

(c) Intangibility has many price implications. First-time users may have great difficulty understanding what they get for their money but this may be influenced by the material content of the service product. The higher the material content , the more will prices set tend to be based on the costs and the greater the tendency towards more standard prices. The smaller the material content, the more customers orientated and the less standard will price be.

Service intangibility also means that services provided may be more easily varied than physical products. Thus service level, service quality and service quantity can be adjusted to meet particularly customer requirements. Prices may ultimately be determined by negotiation between buyer and seller.

(d) Where services are homogeneous (e.g. car washes, dry cleaners) then pricing may be highly competitive. On the other hand regulatory agencies may discourage price cutting through prescribed fees and charges (e.g. trade association or government agencies). The more unique a service then the greater the discretion of the seller to vary price according to what buyers in the market are prepared to pay. In such situations price may be used as a quality indicator and the reputation of the individual or organization offering the service may give considerable price leverage.

(e) The inseparability of service from the person providing it may place geographic limits or time limits on markets that can be served. Equally buyers of services may search for service provision within certain geographic or time zones. The degree of competition operating within these limits will influence prices charged.

6.2 PRICE TERMINOLOGIES

The terminology apropos price for various services differ as shown in Table 6.1

Table 6.1 : PRICE TERMINOLOGY FOR SELECTED SERVICES

Terminology	*Typical Service*
Admission	Theatre entry
Charge	Hairdressing
Commission	Stockbroking service
Dues	Union membership
Fare	Transport
Fee	Legal service
Honorarium	Guest speaker
Interest	Use of money
Premium	Insurance
Rate	Municipal services
Rent	Property usage
Retainer	Consultants' services
Salary / Wages	Employee services
Subscription	Membership
Tariff	Utilities
Toll	Road use
Tuition	Education

6.3 UNDERSTANDING THE COSTS OF SERVICE INCURRED BY CUSTOMERS

From a customer's standpoint, the monetary price charged by the supplier may be just the first of many costs associated with purchase and delivery of a service. Let's take a look at what's involved (as you do so, please consider your own experience in different service contexts).

Purchase price plus other financial costs of service

Customers often incur additional financial costs over and above the purchase price. Necessary incidental expenses may include travel to the service site, parking and purchase of other facilitating goods or services ranging from meals to baby-sitting. We'll call the total of all these expenses (including the price of the service itself) the financial costs of service. However, there's more to come, since the costs of service go beyond just financial outlays.

Non–financial costs of service for customers

In most situations, customers are likely to incur a variety of non-financial costs of service, representing the time, effort and discomfort associated with search, purchase and use. Customer involvement in production (which is particularly important in people-processing services and in self-service) means that customers incur such burdens as mental and physical effort, and exposure to unwanted sensory experiences – such as noise, heat and smells. Services that are high on experience and credence attributes may also create psychological costs, such as anxiety. Non- financial costs of service can be grouped into four distinct categories.

Figure 6.1 : COSTS OF SERVICE INCURRED BY CUSTOMERS

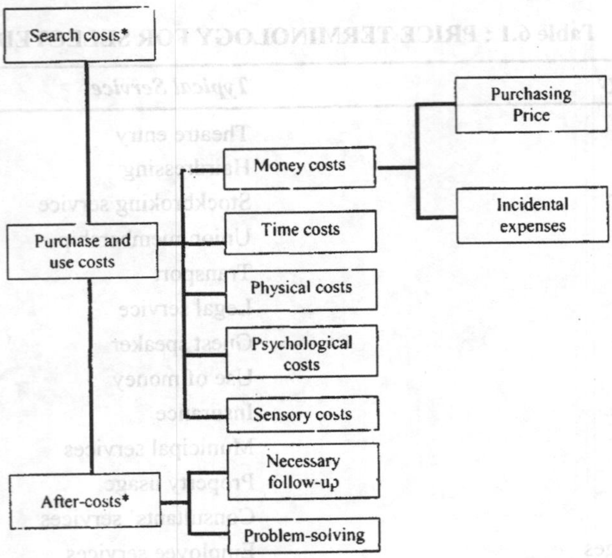

- Time costs of service are inherent in service delivery. There's an opportunity cost to customers for the time they are involved in the service delivery process, since they could spend that time in other ways. They could even be working to earn additional income. Internet users are often frustrated by the amount of time they waste trying to access a web site (not for nothing do people just joke about WWW as the World Wide Wait!)
- Physical costs of service (like fatigue, discomfort and occasionally even injury) may be incurred in obtaining services, especially if customers must come to the service factory and if delivery entails self-service.
- Psychological costs of service like mental effort, feelings of inadequacy, or fear are sometimes attached to evaluating service alternatives, making a selection, and then using a particular service.
- Sensory costs of service relate to unpleasant sensations affecting any of the five senses. In a service environment they may include putting up with noise, unpleasant smells, drafts, excessive heat or cold, uncomfortable seating (especially true in high-density aircraft seating configurations), visually unappealing environments and even unpleasant tastes.

As shown in Figure 6.1 the total costs of purchasing and using a service also include those associated with search activities. When you were looking at universities, how much money, time and effort did you spend before deciding where to apply? How much time and effort would you put into comparing alternative barbers or hairdressers if your existing one were to close? And there may be additional costs of service even after the initial service is completed. Thus a doctor may diagnose a medical problem for a patient and then prescribe a course of physical therapy and drugs that muse be continued for several months. On the other hand, service failures may force customers to waste time, money and effort trying to resolve the problem. The foundations underlying pricing strategy can be described as a tripod (Figure 6.2), with the three legs being named costs, competition, and value to the customer. The costs to be recovered set a floor to the price that may be charged for a specific product; the value of the product to the customer sets a ceiling; whereas the price charged by competitors for similar or substitute products may determine where, within the ceiling-to-floor range, the price level should actually be set.

Companies seeking to make a profit must recover the full costs associated with producing and marketing a service, and then add a sufficient margin to yield a satisfactory profit. An exception occurs in the case of "loss leaders," designed to attract customers who will also buy profitable products from the same organization. But even with such loss leaders, managers need to know the full costs associated with these products, so that the amount of promotional subsidy is fully understood.

Price may also play a role in communicating the quality of a service. In the absence of tangible clues, customers may associate higher prices with higher levels of performance on service attributes.

6.4 UNDERSTANDING VALUE

The term "value" is one that is rather loosely used. "What constitutes value – even in a single product category – appears to be highly personal and idiosyncratic. Four board expressions of value are (1) value is low price, (2) value is whatever I want in a product, (3) value is the quality I get for the price I pay, and (4) value is what I get for what I give.

Figure 6.2 : THE PRICING TRIPOD

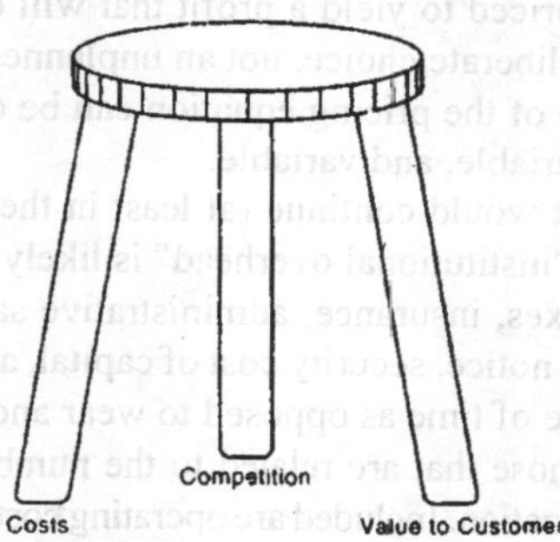

From this, it follows that the greater the positive difference between perceived benefits and perceived costs, he greater the net value. Economists use the term "consumer surplus" to define the difference between the price a customer actually pays and the greater amount he or she would have been willing to pay to obtain the desired benefits (or "utility") offered by the product in question.

If the perceived costs of using a service are less than the perceived benefits, then it will possess negative net value: Customers will probably describe the service as "poor value" and decline to purchase it.

A marketer can increase the net value of a product either by adding benefits or by cutting costs (or by a combination of the two). Of particular interest to service marketers are the opportunities to cut costs for customers by such means as:

- Reducing the amount of time involved in service purchase, delivery and consumption
- Minimizing unwanted mental effort or psychological stress involved in obtaining service
- Pruning out any unwanted physical effort that customers are required to undertake in order to obtain service
- Minimizing unpleasant sensory experiences through such means as creating more attractive visual environments, noise reduction, installing furnishings and equipment that are more comfortable to use, curtailing offensive smells, and ensuring that any foods, beverages, or medicines to be consumed taste nice. (Of course, these sensory problems can be solved completely in information-based services by eliminating the need for customers to visit the service factory.)

Cutting these types of costs significantly may even allow the marketer to increase the monetary price charged to the customer, while still offering what is perceived as "good value".

When customers evaluate competing services, they are basically comparing net values. However, perceptions are often highly inaccurate, so that customers may be making these comparisons based on very imperfect information. Further, perceptions of benefits and costs may vary widely from one customer to another, and even from one situation to another.

6.5 ESTABLISHING MONETARY PRICING OBJECTIVES

Underlying any decision on pricing strategy must be a clear understanding of the organization's objectives. There are three basic categories of pricing objectives open to a service organization: Revenue oriented (profit seeking or cost covering), operations oriented, and patronage oriented.

Alternative bases for pricing:

Revenue-Oriented Objectives

Private sector firms are profit-seeking organisations. Within certain limits, they attempt to maximise the surplus of income over expenditures. Managers responsible for public and non-profit service organisations, by contrast, are more likely to be concerned with breaking even or keeping the operating deficit within acceptable bounds. But although theirs is not-for-profit mission (and high prices may even be at variance with the organisational mission), they cannot afford to ignore the revenue implications or pricing strategy. In some instances, one or more elements in the product line may be to maximise patronage (where capacity is not a constraint), subject to achieving a certain minimum level of revenues priced to yield a profit that will cross-subsidize other products. Such cross-subsidies should be a deliberate choice, not an unplanned outcome of sloppy practice.

Determining the cost side of the pricing equation can be difficult. Let's look at three different types of costs : Fixed, semi-variable, and variable.

Fixed costs are those that would continue (at least in the short run) to be incurred even if no services were provided. This "institutional overhead" is likely to include such elements as building rent, depreciation, utilities, taxes, insurance, administrative salaries, wages of contract employees who cannot be laid off at short notice, security cost of capital, and whatever repairs and maintenance are necessitated by the passage of time as opposed to wear and tear from use.

Semi-variable costs are those that are related to the number of customers served or volume of services produced by the organization. Included are operating costs such as incremental utilities, cleaning at service delivery sites, and wages and salaries from one product to another, depending on the type of service provided, the number of people involved, and the extent of additional facilities required. Typically, Semi-variable costs rise in step-wise fashion. For instance it is not possible to add just one extra seat on a full flight; to accommodate and extra passenger means putting on a bigger aircraft or adding a backup aircraft. Adding more or larger equipment would involve extra labour costs, resulting in additional fuel consumption, and probably lead to increased maintenance expenditure.

Variable costs are those associated with making an additional sale-such as a new loan at a bank, a single seat in a train or theater, a room in a hotel, or one more repair job. In many services, such costs tend to be extremely low probably being close to zero in the typical train or theater (unless there is a tax on each ticket, or patrons receive free souvenirs, or users are particularly prone to littering or vandalism). By contrast, the incremental costs associated with selling food and beverage may form a significant percentage of the final selling price. Similarly, repairing a complex product such as a car may involve use of spare parts, oil, and electrical power. The fact that an organization has sold a service at a price that exceeds its variable cost then the contribution margin may be only a modest percentage of the final selling price.

Determination and allocation of costs is a difficult task that falls under the province of cost accounting (and may require the marketing manager to work closely with the firm's controller). It is particularly problematic in service operations because of the difficulties of deciding how to assign overhead costs. For instance, a hospital might assign overhead to its emergency unit on the basis of the percentage of total floor space it occupies, the percentage of employee hours or payroll it accounts for or the percentage of total patient contact hours involved. Each of these methods would probably yield a totally different fixed-cost allocation; one might make the emergency room appear a terrible financial drain, another make it seem a break-even operation, and a third make it look highly profitable.

Break-even analysis: Since managers need to known at what sales volume a service will be self-supporting, the fixed and Semi-variable costs attributed to that service must be related to the contribution per unit of sales. Dividing the fixed and Semi-variable costs of say, a theatrical performance by the unit contribution will tell us how many tickets we need to sell at that price to break even-that is to recover the costs of staging the show. The required sales volume can then be related to price sensitivity (will customers be willing to pay this much?), market size (is the market large enough to support this level of patronage?), and extent of competition (how strong an appeal do our competitors offer to potential customers?).

The value of break-even analysis is that it relates the demand characteristics of the market to the cost characteristics of the organization. It is particularly useful tool for deciding whether or not to make an addition to the organization product line and, if so, what price to charge.

Low costs per unit of service provide an enviable marketing advantage for any organization, giving it the option either of competing on price at levels that higher-cost competitors cannot afford to match or of charging market rate and earning larger profits than competing firms that have higher break-even points.

Operations-oriented objectives

Some organizations seek to match demand and supply so as to ensure optimal use of their productive capacity at any given time. Hotels, for instance, seek to fill their rooms, since an empty room is an unproductive asset. Similarly, professional asset. Similarly, repair shops try to keep their facilities, machines, and workers busy. When demand exceeds capacity, however, these organizations may try to increase profits and ration demand by raising prices.

Matching hotel demand to the number of rooms available may be achieved by pricing high at peak periods and pricing low to increase demand in off-periods, Repair shops may offer special deals at reduced rates when business is slack. The problem with matching demand to supply through price is that firms may be accused of price gouging when times are good. Some firms are reluctant to get a reputation for price discounting for fear that this be equated with a decline in quality.

Patronage-oriented objectives

Not all service organizations suffer form a short-term capacity constraint. New services, in particular, often have trouble attracting customers. Introductory price discounts may be used to stimulate trial, sometimes in conjunction with promotional activities such as contests and giveaways. Firms wishing to maximize their appeal among specific types of customers need to adopt pricing strategies that recognize a differential ability to pay among various market segments (as well as variations in preferences among customers for alternative levels of service).

In practice, pricing strategies cannot be developed with the single-minded aim of satisfying just one class of objectives. Realistically, each of the three perspectives noted earlier must be included, although the comparative importance of profits, operations, and customer preferences may vary from one situation to another.

6.6 PRICING RELATIVE TO DEMAND LEVELS

Service organizations may be eager to attract the largest possible number of customers or patrons, since high patronage not only ensures that the organization's resources are fully utilized but also increases public visibility. But customers often prefer to use services when they are not busy or crowded. (Sporting events and the performing arts are an exception, since a "full house" provides a more exciting and rewarding experience for both spectators and performers). Pricing to maximize use or attendance is not necessarily the same as pricing to maximize revenues. Much depends on the extent to which a change in price affects people's willingness to buy.

Price Elasticity

The concept of elasticity describes how sensitive demand is to changes in price. When price elasticity is at "unity" sales of a service rise (or fall) by the same percentage that price falls (or rises). When a small change in price has a big impact on sales, demand for that product is said to be price elastic. But when a change in price has little effect on sales, demand is described as price inelastic.

Most theaters and auditoriums do not have a single, fixed admission price for performances. Instead, the price varies according to (1) the location of the seats, (2) the time of the performance, (3) the projected cost of staging the performance, and (4) the anticipated appeal of the performance.

In establishing prices for different blocks of seats – a process known as scaling the house-it is important to identify what the demand for each price category will be, in order to determine the appropriate number of seats to offer at that price categories and immediate sellouts (and disappointed customers) in other categories. Management also needs to know theater-goers preferences for scheduling of performances – matinees versus evenings, the aim is managing demand over time to maximize either attendance, revenues, or a combination of the two (for example, maximizing revenues, subject to a minimum attendance goal per performance of 70 percent of all seats sold)

Many service businesses are increasingly concerned with yield management – that is, maximizing the revenue yield that can be derived from available capacity at any give time. Airlines and hotels have become particularly adept at varying their prices for what is essentially the same product in response to the price season. But there's a risk that pricing policies may become too complex. Jokes abound about travel agents having nervous breakdowns because they get a different quote every time they call the airline for a fare and because there are so many exclusions, conditions, and special offers.

Formulating pricing strategy

By now it should be clear that determining pricing strategies in a service organization requires making decisions on a range of different issues. These, in turn, must be based on both a clear understanding of the organization's objectives and sound information on a range of relevant inputs.

Six major issues related to monetary pricing decisions are:

How Much to Charge?

Realistic decisions on pricing are critical for the financial solvency of the organization. The pricing tripod model, discussed earlier (Figure 6.2) provides a useful point.

First, the manager must determine what the costs are and then whether the organization is trying to cover just the variable costs associated with delivering a specific service, whether it is seeking to recover a share of the fixed costs, too, or whether a target profit level is sought after covering all costs. This decision may depend on the availability of cross-subsidies from other profitable services to help recover all or part of these overheads. Determining the costs to be covered at different sales volumes and, as appropriate, the profit margin sought, sets a series of "floor" prices that must be charged at different volume levels if all costs are to be recovered and a desired profit achieved.

1. ***How Much Should Be Charged for this Service?***
   - What costs is the organization attempting to recover ? Is the organization trying to achieve a specific profit margin or return on investment by selling this service?
   - How sensitive are customers to different prices?
   - What prices are charged by competitors?
   - What discount(s) should be offered form basic prices?
   - Are psychological pricing points (e.g. Rs. 4.95 versus Rs. 5.00) customarily used?
2. ***What Should Be the Basis of Pricing?***
   - Execution of a specific task
   - Admission to a specific task
   - Units of time (hour, week, month, year)
   - Percentage commission on the value of the transaction
   - Physical resources consumed
   - Geographic distance covered
   - Weight or size of object serviced

- Should each service element be billed independently?
- Should a single price be charged for a bundled "package"?

3. Who Should Collect Payment?

- The organization that provides the service
- A specialist intermediary (travel or ticket agent, bank, retailer, et.,)
- How should the intermediary be compensated for this work- fee or percentage commission?

4. Where Should Payment Be Made?

- The location at which the services is delivered
- A convenient retail outlet or financial intermediary (e.g. bank)
- The purchaser's home (by mail or phone)

5. When Should Payment Be Made?

- Before or after delivery of the service
- At which times of day
- On which days of the week

6. How Should Payment Be Made?

- Cash (exact change or not?)
- Token (where can these be purchased?)
- Stored value card
- Check (how to verify?)
- Electronic funds transfer
- Charge card (credit or debit)
- Credit account with service provider
- Vouchers
- Third party payment (e.g., insurance company, government agency)

7. How Should Prices Be Communicated to the Target Market?

- Through what communication medium? (advertising, signage, electronic display, sales people, customer service personnel)
- What message content (how much emphasis should be placed on price?)

Second, the manager must assess consumer sensitivity to different prices, reflecting both the gross value of the service to prospective customers as well as their ability to pay. In pricing to recover fixed costs, it's very important to be able to make an accurate prediction of sales volumes at different price levels. This step sets a "ceiling" price for any given market segment.

The level of competitive prices provides a third input. The greater the number of similar competing alternatives that appeal to consumers, and the more widely available they are, the greater will be the pressure on the marketing manager to keep prices at or below those of the competition. The wider the gap between the floor and ceiling prices, the more room there is to maneouver. If a ceiling price is below that of the floor price, the manager has two choices. One is to recognize that the product is noncompetitive and either discontinue or modify it so that it becomes competitive at a higher price. The other is to seek third party funding to cover some of the costs, thus allowing the product to be sold at a lower price. This latter approach is commonly used for services delivered by public and nonprofit organizations in fields such as health, education, the arts, and urban transportation.

A strategy of discounting from basic prices should be approached cautiously, because it dilutes the average price received and reduces the contribution from each sale. Selective price discounting to specific market segments may offer important opportunities to tap new segments and fill capacity that would otherwise go unused. The challenge is to understand the price elasticities of different segments and to discourage high-paying segments form taking advantage of discounts designed to lure more price-sensitive consumers. The airlines, in particular, work hard to develop appropriate restrictions on the availability of discount fares (requiring, for instance, that travelers must stay over on Saturday night) to make it different for business travellers – whose fares are often being reimbursed by their employers-to travel cheaply. Discount fares, after all, are designed to attract pleasure travellers taking discretionary trips.

Next a specific price must be set. This raises the question of whether to price in round numbers or try to create the impression that prices are slightly lower than they really are. If competitors promote prices such Rs.3.95 and Rs. 5.95, a strategy of charging Rs. 4.00 or Rs. 6.00 may convey an image of prices somewhat higher than is really the case. On the other had, rounded prices offer convenience and simplicity - benefits that may be appreciated by both consumers and salespeople.

What Should Be the Basis for Pricing?

Deciding on the basis for pricing requires defining the unit of service consumption. Should it be based on completing a specific service task, such as cleaning a jacket or cutting a customer's hair? Should it be admission to a service performance, such as an educational program, or a movie , concert, or sports event? Should it be time based, as for using an hour of an attorney's time, occupying a hotel room for a night, renting a car for a week, subscribing to cable TV for a month, or paying for a semester's tuition at college? Should it be tied to value, as when an insurance company scales its premiums to reflect the amount of coverage provided or a realtor commission of the selling price of a house?

Some service prices are tied to consumption of physical resources, such as food, beverages, electricity, or gas. Rather than charging customers for renting a table and chairs, restaurants put a huge markup on the food and drink items consumed.

Transportation firms have traditionally charged by distance, with freight companies using a combination of weight or cubic volume and distance to set their rates. Such a policy has the virtue of consistency and reflects calculation of an average cost per mile (or kilometer). However, simplicity may suggest a flat rate, as with postal charges for first-class domestic letters below a certain weight. Or a zone rate for parcels that lumps geographic distances into broad clusters. Long-distance phone calls reflect a combination of distance and time, as with transportation, market analysis and competitive practices have largely eliminated strictly distance-based formulas.

Bundled prices offer the service firm a certain guaranteed revenue from each customer, while giving the latter a clear a clear idea in advance of how much the bill will be. Unbundled prices, unfortunately, lend themselves to unethical business practices. Rental car companies are a frequent offender in this respect, advertising a low rental rate and then arm-twisting the customer into paying for a variety of expensive extras. Some people joke, "the cars are cheap, the keys are extra!"

Who Should collect Payment?

The marketer must make it simple and convenient for the customer to obtain information, make reservations (for services), and offer payment. Sometimes an organization finds that this goal is best accomplished by delegating these tasks to intermediaries, thus freeing the organization to focus on service delivery. Examples include travel agents who make hotel and transportation bookings; ticket agents who sell seats for theaters, concert halls, and sports arenas; banks that sell monthly transit passes, and retailers who act as intermediaries for repair and maintenance work on products that they originally sold new. Although the service organization may have to pay a commission, the intermediary is usually able to offer customers greater convenience in terms of where, when and how the price should be paid. Even after paying commissions, the use of intermediaries often offers a net savings in administrative costs to the primary organization.

Where Should Payment Be Made?

Service organizations are not always conveniently located. Airports, theaters, and sports arenas, for instance, are often situated some distance form the areas where potential patrons live or work. When consumers purchase a service before using it, there are obvious benefits to using intermediaries that are more conveniently located, or allowing payment by mail. A growing number of organizations now accept telepLone reservations and sales by credit cards. Callers simply give their card numbers and have the charge billed directly to their accounts. Early experiments that allowed customers to use their credit cards to pay through the World Wide Web ran into security problems, but as these are resolved through more robust encryption, the Web will doubtless become a popular medium for purchasing an array of goods and services.

When Should Payment Be Made?

The two basic options are to ask customers to pay in advance of use (as with an admission charge, airline ticket, or purchase of postage stamps) or to bill them once service delivery has been completed, as with restaurant bills and repair charges Occasionally, a service provider may ask for an initial payment in advance of service delivery, with the balance being due later. This approach is quite common with expensive repair and maintenance jobs, when the firm-often a small business with limited working capital – must buy materials up front.

Asking customers to pay for service in advance of use means that the buyer is paying before the benefits are received. But there may be value to the customer as well as to the provider. Sometimes it's inconvenient to pay each time a regularly patronized service- such as the mail or public transportation – is used; to save time and effort, customers may prefer the convenience of buying a roll of stamps or a monthly transit pass. Performing arts organizations with limited funds and heavy up-front financing requirements often offer discounted subscription tickets in order to bring in money in advance. A different form of prepayment, involving the notion of insurance, is found in health maintenance organizations where members pay a fixed annual or monthly fee that entitles them to free (or minimally priced) care. In this instance, the benefit of peace of mind becomes available immediately.

How Should Payment Be Made?

There are a variety of different ways of paying for service. Cash may appear to be the simplest method, but it raises problems of security as well being inconvenient when exact change is required to operate machines. Tokens with a predefined value are often used to simplify the process of paying road and bridge tolls or transit fares. Accepting payment by cheque for all the smallest purchases is now fairly widespread and offers customer benefits, although it may require controls to discourage bad cheques.

Credit cards and bank cards are used for many types of purchases and are gaining acceptance around the world. Debit cards, first widely used in Europe and Australia, look like credit cards but act more like "plastic cheques" since the sum charged is debited promptly from the holder's account Electronic Point-of-sale terminals are connected directly to banking networks. As acceptance of credit and debit cards has become more universal, businesses that refuse to accept them may find themselves at a competitive disadvantage. Many business organizations offer customers the convenience of a credit account (which generates a membership relationship between the customer and the organization)

Other payment procedures include using vouchers as supplements to (or instead of cash, and directing the bill to a third party for payment (as often happens in health care). Vouchers are sometimes provided by social service agencies to groups such as elderly or low- income people. Such a policy achieves the same benefits as discounting, without the need to publicize an array of different prices and to require those who collect the money to act as police (a role for which they may be unsuited and untrained)

Now coming into broader usage are prepayment systems based on cards that store value on a magnetic strip or in a microchip embedded within the card In Japan, where credit is less widely available than in many other industrialized nations, prepayment cards were originally developed for telephone use, but are now finding a broadening array of applications for low-cost purchases that would otherwise require cash. Service firms that want to accept payment in this form must first install card readers.

Currently under testing in several countries are more sophisticated applications, involving partnerships between banks, retailers, and telephone companies. Together, these partners offer a smart card that serves as in "electronic wallet" customers can transfer funds to their cards form their bank accounts through the medium of a special telephone attachment. There is also provision to transfer funds from one card to another.

Growing interest in the Internet / World Wide Web as a medium for purchasing a variety of goods and services is leading many firms to work on development of fraud proof payment systems. One approach involves creation of prepaid "digital cash accounts" into which customers would deposit funds that could then be used to pay for purchases ordered over the Internet. A key issue for service marketers to remember in this and other contexts is that, for many transactions, the simplicity and speed with which payment is made may influence the customer's perception of overall service quality.

6.7 COMMUNICATING PRICES TO THE TARGET MARKETS

The final task, once each of the other issues has been addressed, is to decide how the organization's pricing policies can best be communicated to the target market(s). People need to know the price for some product offerings well in advance of purchase; they may also need to know how, where, and when that price is payable. This information must be presented in ways that are intelligible and unambiguous, so that customers will not be misled and question the ethical standards of the firm.

Managers must decide whether or not to include information on pricing in advertising for the service. It may be appropriate to relate the price to the costs of competing products or to alternative ways of spending one's money. Certainly, salespeople and customer service representatives should be able to give prompt, accurate responses to customer queries about pricing, payment, and credit. Good signage at retail points of sale will save staff members form having to answer basic questions on prices.

Price Tactics

Many of the tactical price techniques used to sell tangibles can be used to sell intangibles. In both cases the particular tactics used are dependent upon the kind of service involved, the target market and general conditions prevailing in that marketplace at the time (e.g.., supply shortages, therefore possible over-demand for service products Some of the frequently used pricing tactics in services markets are now considered. They are:

(a) differential or flexible pricing
(b) discrete pricing
(c) discount pricing
(d) diversionary pricing
(e) guarantee pricing
(f) high price maintenance pricing
(g) loss leader pricing
(h) offset pricing
(i) price lining.

Differential or flexible Pricing

Differential pricing is the practice of charging different prices according, for example, to customers' willingness to pay. It is used chiefly to :

(a) build primary demand particularly for non-peak time service use;
(b) even out fluctuations in demand which may occur in many services and to reduce the influence of 'perish ability' of a service.

Some forms of differential pricing include:

(a) price-time differentials (e.g. used in holiday, utilities and telephone services);

(b) customer ability to pay differentials (e.g. used in management consultancy; professional services; bank loan rates);

(c) service product type differentials (e.g. used for different models of telephone rental);

(d) place differential (e.g. used in hotel room pricing and in theatre seat pricing).

The ability to use differential pricing tactics is dependent upon a market being segmentable on a price basis, low chance of resale or reallocation of a service to another, and minimum customer resentment towards the practice.

Differential pricing seems to be one of the most common practices in the service sector. It is particularly used in those services where a bespoke price is quoted.

Some problems which can occur when differential pricing is used are :

(a) Customers may delay their purchases and wait for differentials to be exercised (e.g. holiday markets are increasingly experiencing this growing customer sophistication)

(b) Customer may come to expect discounts as a regular feature of service product offer where differential prices are used (see discount pricing)

For these reasons some service organizations deliberately resist differential pricing. Instead they use uniform price practices, charging the same price to all customers irrespective of time, place or ability to pay.

Discrete Pricing

Discrete pricing means setting the price so that it is pitched at a level that brings it within the competence of the decision-making unit which is sympathetic towards a particular service or organization . Practiced in a number of organizational markets for services like contract catering and plant maintenance it demands a clear knowledge of price limits within which decision makers have authority to work (e.g., purchasing officers may be able to order projects to a value of Rs.10,000 without further approval).

Discount Pricing

Discount pricing occurs in most markets. Discounts in services marketing serve two purposes.

(a) They are a payment or reward for services undertaken which enable service production and consumption to take place (e.g. fees paid to intermediates in financial markets)

(b) They are promotional devices to encourage actions like early payment, bulk purchase or off peak usage.

Examples of the former include commission payments to insurance brokers or unit trust advisers for services rendered, Examples of the latter include cash discounts offered by advertising agencies for prompt payment; quantity discounts offered by ferry operators for group travel; temporal discounts for off-peak daily use of a service (e.g. Rail discounts) or for use at a particular time of the week or season of the year, promotional discounts (e.g. short-term price reductions offered by a dry cleaning service or special offers made by a franchiser to a franchisee). These discounts may be on top of differential pricing practices that are operating in a market.

Most service organizations can offer special reductions or payments of these kinds. What is less well understood is that these payments erode the margins available to the service producer. Discounts have traditionally been regarded as tactical pricing adjustments. Increasingly though they are seen to have strategic importance. A new area of marketing, 'margin management' is emerging. It is concerned with the trade-off decisions which determine how the total channel margin should be split between intermediaries and customers involved in the process. It is as relevant to the marketing of services as it is to the marketing of goods.

Diversionary Pricing

This occurs where a low basic price may be quoted foe a service or parts of a service to develop an image of a low price structure. Restaurants may offer a basic meal at an attractive price to encourage custom though most diners may finish up eating from other higher priced menus; a garage may offer a reduced rate standard service in the expectation of picking up additional, higher priced repair work.

Guaranteed Pricing

This occurs where payment is made only if certain results are guaranteed. Employment agencies may only charge fees when clients obtain suitable employment; estate agents may only take commission if a property actually sells. It is an appropriate tactic for a service organization to use when:

(a) the specific promises inherent in a guarantee can be determined and assured;

(b) when high quality service operators are finding it difficult to compete in a competitive cut price competitive environment;

(c) the customer is seeking some clear assurance of results (e.g. rust proofing; guaranteed return on investments).

High Price Maintenance Pricing

This practice is used where consumers associate the price of service with its quality. In these circumstances some service organizations will deliberately pursue a high quality high price posture. Those organizations that have cultivated a particular market segment or established a particularly prestigious reputation may use this approach of using price as an index of quality.

Loss Leader Pricing

Loss leader pricing means charging a reduced price for the first order or contract in the hope of getting further business from a customer at better prices. It is an appropriate practice in those markets where:

(a) customers are dissatisfied with existing suppliers;

(b) buyers are relatively unsophisticated;

(c) market prices are competitive.

The chief disadvantage is that an initially low price may become a price ceiling. Customers may resist further price increases once that ceiling has been established. Nevertheless it is used in marketing consultancy and management education services.

Offset pricing

A practice similar to diversionary pricing in which a low basic price is quoted but 'extras' carry relatively higher charges. For example, a management consultant may quote a price for his time but exclude the extras associated with an assignment like travel and hotel costs.

Price lining

Price lining is where prices are not varied but the quality, quantity and level of service is to reflect cost changes. It is not normally recommended as a way of dealing with cost changes. It is more appropriate in circumstances where fixed set of charges can apply to a range of standard services. Leasing firms use price lining and dry cleaning establishments have recently introduced pricing practices which reflect lining. A problem with this practice is that quality, quantity and level of service product differentiation has to be relatively easy for customers to appreciate (e.g. as in airline travel on long haul flights). Price lining can therefore be difficult to implement in repair services. Studies have shown that customers do not expect to receive a lower quality repair service on lower cost products than higher cost products. The value of a repair is not necessarily related to the value of the product being repaired.

6.8 ADDITIONAL ASPECTS OF SERVICE PRICING

In addition to the tactical variations of price considered above there are other aspects of service pricing which should be noted. These are concerned with:

(a) price negotiation;

(b) competitive bidding;
(c) price awareness.

Price Negotiation

Price negotiation is a common feature of service pricing in a number of service industries. For example prices are negotiated in many professional services transactions. It is common practice too in consumer services like car repairs, foreign travel and financial assistance (e.g. bank loans). Certain specialized business services, like plant rentals, insurance and market research are also priced by negotiation.

Competitive Bidding

Some service contracts, particularly in organizational markets, may be awarded on the basis of competitive bidding or tenders. A bid is an offer price. It is based on expectations of how competitors will price their services. If a bidding company wants to gain a contract it will also need to consider its costs to determine the minimum price level at which it should bid. Currently a number of models are applied in bidding to take account of competitors' likely bids and they attempt to estimate expected profits at various bid prices. More sophisticated models take account of past bidding data in deriving bid prices.

One study which has examined the problems of competitive bidding from a buyer and a seller point of view identifies a number of disadvantages for both parties in service markets. From the seller's point of view the time, effort and cost involved, the possibility of ideas being borrowed and transferred to competitors and difficulties of knowing how bids are appraised are seen as arguments against their use. While for the buyer the time involved, problems with the timing of proposals and considerations regarding whether the specification is tight or flexible, also suggest that alternatives may be more satisfactory (e.g. rotate jobs among contacts).

Price Awareness

There is no evidence to suggest that price awareness is services markets is any different in its diversity from price awareness found in markets for goods. Low price awareness has been found in settings as diverse as professional services, freight transport and funerals. Where price awareness is low in a service market then two strategies are relevant for price makers:

(a) Exploit the low level of awareness through the price discretion it offers;
(b) Make the market aware of price levels thereby attaching competitive services (e.g. airline fares).

Price awareness studies are an example of where marketing research may be used in service markets. Prices adjustments may often be made once awareness studies have been conducted and there is evidence to suggest that the 'buy-response' method of analysis, used in many goods markets, may be suitable for services like dry cleaning services and travel agents.

6.9 PRICING STRATEGY

The factors that underlie pricing decisions have now been described. This section now analyses how these factors can be manipulated to give strategic direction to pricing policy so that organizational objectives can be met. The challenge here is to make pricing work as an effective element of the marketing mi, combining with the other mix elements to give a service provider a profitable market position. An effective strategy must identify how the role of price is to function as a service goes through different stages in its life, from the launch stage through growth to maturity.

This analysis of pricing strategy will consider first, the development of a strategy for new service launch, and second, price adjustments to established services. In practice, of course, it is often not easy to distinguish the two situations, as where an existing service is modified or relaunched.

New-service pricing strategy

In developing a price strategy for a new service, two key issues need to be addressed:

- What price position is sought for the service?

- How novel is the service offering?

The choice of price position cannot be separated from other elements of the marketing mix. For many consumer services, the price element can itself interact with the product-quality element of a positioning strategy. This can happen where consumers have difficulty in distinguishing between competing services before consumption, and the price charged is seen as an important indication of the quality of the service. Private consumers choosing a painter or decorator with no knowledge of their previous work record may be cautious about accepting the cheapest quotation. on the basis that it may reflect an inexperienced decorator with a poor record.

The novelty of a new service offering can be analysed in terms of whether it is completely new to the market or merely new to the company providing it but already available from other sources. In the case of completely new services the company will have some degree of monopoly power in its early years, as where one bank introduces a new ATM facility to a town which is the only such facility for many miles. On the other hand, the launch of a ' me too' service to compete with established services is likely to face heavy price competition from its launch stage. The distinction between innovative and copycat services is the basis of two distinct pricing strategies-'price skimming' and 'saturation pricing', which are now examined.

Price skimming

Most completely new product launches are aimed initially at the segment of users who can be labelled 'innovators' - consumers who have the resources and inclination to be trendsetters. This group includes the first people to buy innovative services such as telephone banking and portable telecommunications. Following these will be a group of early adopters, followed by a larger group often described as the 'early majority'. The subsequent 'late majority' group may take up the new services only when the product market itself has reached maturity. 'Laggards' are the last group to adopt a new service and only do so when the product has become a social norm and/or its price has fallen sufficiently.

Price – skimming strategies seek to gain the highest possible price from the early adopters. When sales to this segment appear to be approaching saturation level, the price level is lowered to appeal to the early adopter to be approaching saturation level, the price level is lowered to appeal to the early adopter segment that has a lower price threshold at which it is prepared to purchase the service. This process is repeated for the following adoption categories.

The art of effective pricing of innovative services is to identify who the early adopters are, how much they are prepared to pay and how long this price can be sustained before competitors come on the scene with imitation services at a lower price. A price-skimming strategy works by gradually lowering price to gain access to new segments and to protect market share against new market entrants. This pricing strategy is closely related to the concept of the product lifecycle. A typical price-skimming strategy showing price levels through time is shown in Figure 6.3 (a).

It can be argued that diffusion patterns for new industrial services are generally different from those for consumer services. There is less of a desire to be a trendsetter for its own sake and a greater rationality in purchase decisions, limiting the opportunities for price skimming to situations where commercial buyers can use innovative service inputs to gain an early competitive advantage.

Figure 6.3 : PRICING STRATEGIES COMPARED
(A) PRICE SKIMMING (B) SATURATION PRICING

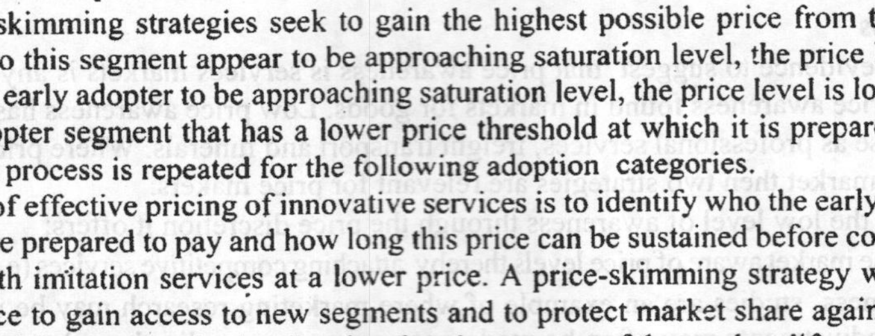

(a) (b)

For many innovative services, the trend of falling prices may be further enhanced by falling costs. Lower costs can occur due to economies of scale (for example the cost per customer of providing the technical support for a home-shopping service declines as fixed costs are spread over more volume of throughput) and also to the experience effect. The latter refers to the process by which costs fall as experience in production is gained. It is of particular strategic significance to service industries, since by pursuing a strategy to gain experience faster than its competitors, an organization lowers its cost base and has a greater scope for adopting an aggressive pricing strategy.

Saturation pricing

Many 'new' services are launched as copies of existing competitors' services. In the absence of unique product features, a low initial price can be used to encourage people who show little brand loyalty to switch service suppliers. Once an initial trial has been made a service provider would seek to develop increased loyalty from its customers, as a result of which they will be prepared to pay progressively higher prices. A saturation pricing strategy is shown diagrammatically in Figure 6.3 (b).

The success of saturation pricing strategy is dependent upon a sound understanding of the buying behaviour of the target market, in particular:

- ***The level of knowledge that consumers have about prices*** for some services, such as the rate of interest charged on credit cards, consumers typically have little idea of the charge they are currently paying, or indeed of the 'going rate' for such charges. Therefore any attempt to attract new customers on the basis of a differential price advantage may prove unsuccessful. Other incentives (for example, free gifts or money-off vouchers for reduced-prices holidays) may be more effective in inducing new business. Sometimes companies providing a diverse range of services may offer low prices on services where price comparisons are commonly made but charge higher ones on other related services where consumer knowledge is lower. Customers of solicitors may shop around for a standard service such as house conveyancing but may be more reluctant to do so when faced with a non-routine purchase such as civil litigation.

- ***The extent to which the service supplier can increase prices on the basis of perceived added value of the service offering***; the purpose of a low initial price is to encourage new users of a service to try a service and return later, paying progressively higher prices. If the new competitor's service is perceived to offer no better value than that of the existing supplier, the disloyalty which caused the initial switching could result in a switching back at a later date in response to tactical pricing. Worse still, a new service could be launched and experience teething troubles in its early days, doing nothing to generate a perception of added value.

- ***The extent to which the service supplier can turn a casually gained relationship into a long-term committed one***; incentives are frequently offered to lessen the attractiveness of switching away from a brand. This can take the form of a subscription rate for regular purchase of a service, or offering an ever-increasing range of services which together raise the cost to consumers of transferring their business elsewhere. Banks may offer easy transfers between various savings and investment accounts and, in doing so, aim to reduce the attractiveness of moving one element of the customer's business elsewhere.

In some cases where co-production of benefits among consumers in important, a high initial uptake may itself add value to the service offering. A telecommunications operator offering data-exchange facilities will be able to provide a more valuable service if large numbers of users are contracted to its system, offering more communications possibilities for potential new users. In the same way, airport landing slots becomes increasingly valuable to an airline operator as an airport becomes progressively busier, as each airline is able to offer a more comprehensive and valuable set of potential connections to customers. In both cases, a low initial price may be critical to gain entry to a market, while rising prices is consistent with increasing value to the users of the service.

6.10 PRICING AND MARKETING STRATEGY

Integrated marketing strategies imply that the various elements of the marketing mix are formulated and implemented with the objectives of those strategies clearly in mind. Pricing decisions are no exception to the principle. In setting price objectives for services a number of factors must be considered. The more significant of these are :

(a) the planed market position for the service product;
(b) the stage of the life – cycle of the service product ;
(c) elasticity of demand ;
(d) the competitive situation;
(e) the strategic role of price.

The planned Market Position for the Service Product

Market position means the place the service product is intended to take up and does take up in the customer's eyes and in comparison with competitors. It refers to the customer's perceptual positioning of the service product: in other words how the service product is 'seen' in relation to others available. Clearly price is an important element in the marketing mix influencing this position. Tangible products may occupy a particular position by virtue of their physical characteristics (e.g. a grade of industrial steel tubing). Services, on the other hand, are more often 'positioned' on the basis of their intangible attributes.

The Stages of the life – Cycle of the Service Product

The price of the service product will also relate to its life – Cycle. For example in introducing a new service an organization could opt to set low prices to penetrate markets and gain rapid market share Alternatively an organization could opt to charge high prices to make as much profit as possible in a short time (skimming policy). This strategy is only possible if there is no immediate competition and a high level of buyer need urgency (e.g. windscreen replacement services).

Elasticity of Demand

The discretion a service organization has to determine its pricing objectives will be influenced by elasticity of demand in the market. Elasticity of demand refers to the responsiveness of demand to changes in price. In some markets demand is much influenced by price changes (e.g. urban bus services) in others this is less so. Clearly it is vital for a service organization to understand how elastic or inelastic demand for its services is in response to price change. For example, if a service company reduces its prices and demand is elastic then the effect would be to reduce margins with no compensating increase in demand. Elasticity may impose limitations on certain price options.

The Competitive Situation

The strength of competition in the market influences a service organization's discretion over its prices. In situations where there is little differentiation between service products and where competition is intense (e.g. a seaside resort during a poor tourist season) then price discretion is limited. Competition of course has number of dimensions apart from inter-brand or inter-type competition. In transport services, for example, there is competition between different modes of transport (e.g. rail versus road), different brands, as well as alternative uses of the potential customers' time and money (e.g. not to travel at all). Nevertheless a degree of price uniformity will be established in those markets with little differentiation between service products and strong levels of competition. In other settings tradition and custom may influence prices charged (e.g. Advertising agencies commission system).

The Strategic Role of Price

Pricing policies have a strategic role aimed at achieving organizational objectives. Thus the pricing decision on any particular service product should fit in with strategic objectives. For example, a new holiday company intent upon establishing itself in the package holiday market might use a deliberate policy of low prices to obtain substantial market share although this could mean unprofitable trading for some time. Maximum sales would be won through penetration pricing as a deliberate policy. Any pricing strategy must of course fit in with the way in which other elements of the marketing mix are manipulated to attain strategic ends.

Price as an Indicator of Service Quality

One of the intriguing aspects of pricing is that buyers are likely to use price as an indicator of both service costs and service quality – price is at once an attraction variable and a repellent. Customers' use of price as an indicator of quality depends on several factors, one of which is the other information available to them. When service cues to quality are readily accessible, when brand names provide evidence of a company's reputation, or when level of advertising communicates the company's belief in the brand, customers may prefer to use those cues instead of price. In other situations, however, such as when quality is hard to detect or when quality or price varies a great deal within a class of services, consumers may believe that price is the best indicator of quality Many of these conditions typify situations that face consumers when purchasing services. Another factor that increases the dependence on price as a quality indicator is the risk associated with the service purchase. In high-risk situations, many of which involve credence services such as medical treatment or management consulting, the customer will look to price as a surrogate for quality.

Because customers depend on price as a cue to quality and because price sets expectations of quality, service prices must be determined carefully. In addition to being chosen to cover costs or match competitors, prices must be chosen to convey the appropriate quality signal. Pricing too low can lead to inaccurate inferences about the quality of the service. Pricing too high can set expectations that may be difficult to match in service delivery.

Because goods are dominated by search properties, price is not used to judge quality as often as it is in services, where experience and credence properties dominate. Thus, services marketer must be aware of the signals that price conveys about its offerings.

SHORT ANSWER QUESTIONS

1. Define the following terms:
   (a) Value
   (b) Fixed Costs
   (c) Semi-variable costs
   (d) Variable costs
   (e) Contribution margin
   (f) Price elasticity
   (g) Price skimming
   (h) Saturation pricing
2. What is the relationship between product lifecycle theory and pricing strategy?
3. Using examples, compare the advantages and disadvantages of cost-plus and marginal-cost pricing.
4. How can prices be fixed for services?
5. What are the various price terminologies used for services?
6. Can price discrimination be used as a marketing tool by service industries?
7. What prices do users 'pay' for services?
8. Why is pricing of services difficult?
9. Why is cost-based pricing particularly problematic in service industries?
10. In what ways does competition-based pricing work in favour of many service providers? In what circumstances, does it not?
11. Compare and contrast the strategic and functional role of pricing.
12. Explain the concept of yield management in a service setting.

❖❖❖

13. Which approach to pricing (cost-based, competition-based, or demand-based) is the most fair to customers? Why?
14. Is it possible to use all the three approaches simultaneously when pricing services? If yes, describe a service that is priced this way.
15. How is price communicated to target markets?
16. What are the strategies to be adopted by price makers when price awareness is low?

ESSAY QUESTIONS

1. Examine the role that is likely to be played by pricing for a local authority-owned leisure centre.
2. Comment on the importance of price-quality relationships in services marketing.
3. How do financial cost differ from non-financial costs of service? Discuss.
4. Explain the importance of demand elasticity in the pricing of services.
5. 'Pricing of services is more flexible than pricing of goods'. Discuss.
6. What problems are involved in preparing a competitive bid for a service like market research?
7. Comment on the roles of 'regulation' and 'tradition' in the pricing of services.
8. From a customer perspective, what serves to define value in the following services:
   (a) a hairdressing salon ?
   (b) a legal firm specialising in business and taxation law?
   (c) A nightclub?
9. Describe the non-monetary costs involved in the following services:
   (a) having a will prepared
   (b) getting an automobile loan
   (c) belonging to a health club
   (d) having allergies diagnosed and treated
   (e) attending an executive education class
   (f) buying life insurance.
10. Write short notes on any three of the following:
    (a) Price lining
    (b) Guarantee pricing
    (c) Discrete pricing
    (d) Saturation pricing
    (e) Loss leader pricing.
11. What are the major issues related to monetary pricing decisions? Explain with examples.

EXERCISE / ASSIGNMENTS

1. Give examples to illustrate situations where price competitiveness may be largely absent in service markets.
2. Analyse the product mix of a diverse service organisation and identify the pricing strategies used to increase total revenue.
3. Using a service company of your choice, analyse how price discrimination is practiced between different groups of customers.
4. Illustrate the ways in which different kinds of discounts may be used in service pricing.
5. List 5 services for which you have no reference price. Now put yourself in the role of the service providers for two of those services and develop pricing strategies. Be sure to include in your description which of the value definitions you believe customers will possess and what types of strategies would be appropriate given those definitions.
6. Consider that you are the owner of a new private college and can prepare a value / price package that is appealing to students. Describe your approach. How does it differ from existing offerings?

●●●

7

Promoting Services

7.1 INTRODUCTION

This chapter deals with the promotion of service products. Here promotion includes the following.

(a) **Advertising** - defined as any paid form of non-personal presentation and promotion of services by an identified individual or organization.

(b) **Personal selling** - defined as the personal presentation of services in a conversation with one or more prospective purchasers for the purpose of making sales.

(c) **Publicity** -defined as the non-personal stimulation of demand for a service by obtaining commercially significant news about it in any medium or obtaining favourable presentation of it in any medium that is not paid for by the service sponsor.

(d) **Sales promotion** - marketing activities other than advertising, personal selling or publicity that stimulate customer purchasing and use and enhance dealer effectiveness (e.g. competitions, coupons).

These four types of promotion are the traditional marketer-dominated ways of influencing sales for service products. Between them they offer the organization a wide range of possibilities for promoting services in the marketplace. Astutely used they can be most effective tools of communication and influence. However two important qualifications should be noted. First, service organizations promote themselves and their service products in other ways than the four forms considered here. Though this chapter deals with 'personal salesmen' as part of 'promotion', in many services markets the 'selling' of services and the 'performance' of services cannot be separated. Indeed there may not be a separate sales force as such. So this separation of the 'selling role' may be unrealistic in practice. The comments about people in this chapter should be seen alongside the 'other service personnel' who can influence promotional effort. Also physical evidence will influence customer response to service products.

Second, there is increasing research evidence that in some kinds of services markets these marketer dominated ways of influencing sales for service products may not necessarily be the most effective. For example, a study covering eight different types of retail services (dry cleaning, hairdressing, car loan finance, dentistry, photography, carpet shampoo, car repair, gynecological services) showed that customers of retail services do not reply on the more traditional information sources. Instead, they prefer to use more personal sources of information from friends and other contacts. Also location is a key factor in the final purchase decision. The importance of personal recommendations has been confirmed in the life insurance market too. Customers in this market have been shown to rely heavily on the opinions and influences of others through word of mouth communication.

7.2 PROMOTIONAL OBJECTIVES

The general purposes of promotion in services marketing are much the same as in other kinds of marketing to :

(a) build awareness and interest in the service product and the service organization;

(b) differentiate the service offer and the service organization from competitors;

(c) communicate and portray the benefits of the services available;

(d) build and maintain the overall image and reputation of the service organization;

(e) persuade customers to buy or use the service.

Ultimately the purpose of any promotional effort is to sell the service product through informing, persuading and reminding. Clearly these general objectives vary according to the nature of each service industry and service product. For example, the kinds of promotional objectives that are considered to be relevant in the *transport and distribution* business include :

(a) creating awareness of the firm's service among potential users;

(b) generating detailed knowledge of the firm's product and service including details of cost-benefit relationship, price and other pertinent information;

(c) improving the firm's image among existing and potential users so as to improve the firm's target group towards being more receptive to the new service which will be launched in the near future;

(d) eliminating perceived misconceptions;

(e) advising existing and potential customers of special offers or modifications of the service;

(f) advising the marketplace of new channels.

Clearly the specific objective for any particular service in any service product/market situation will vary. So too will use made of the elements of the promotion mix.

Table 7.1 summarizes a wide array of possible objectives relating to customers, intermediaries, and competitors.

Table 7.1 : POSSIBLE OBJECTIVES OF CONSUMER PROMOTIONS FOR SERVICES

1. ***Objectives Targeted at Customers***

- Increase awareness of a new or existing service
- Encourage trial of a service
- Encourage nonusers to :
  - Attend a demonstration of the service
  - Make trial use of an existing service
  - Apply to join or subscribe to a service in which admission, acceptance, or installation of technical hookups is a prerequisite to receive the service
- Persuade existing customers to :
  - Continue purchasing the service and not terminate use of the service or switch to a competing alternative
  - Increase their purchase frequency of the service
  - Commit to purchasing the service for an extended time period (thus taking the consumer out of the market for competing alternatives)
- Change the timing of customer demand for the service
- Reinforce advertising for the service and draw audience attention to it
- Obtain market research information about how, when, and where the service is purchased and used
- Promote the service as part of a broader product line (or link it to sales of a complementary service marketed by another organization)
- Encourage customers to change the way in which they interact with the service delivery system, such as
  - Perform tasks themselves (self-service)
  - Use a new technology, e.g., the Web

2. ***Objectives Targeted at Intermediaries***
   - Persuade intermediaries to deliver a new or relaunched service
   - Persuade existing intermediaries to provide additional push for the service, including point-of-sale merchandising
   - Insulate intermediaries from consumer price negotiation at the point of purchase
   - Insulate intermediaries from any temporary sales reduction that might result from a price increase
3. ***Objectives Targeted at Competition***
   - Move offensively or defensively on a temporary basis against one or more competitors

7.3 DIFFERENCE IN PROMOTING SERVICES

The promotion of goods and services has many similarities. Thus we do not need to discriminate between the two when considering matters like:

the role of promotion in marketing;
the problem of creating effective promotions;
the managerial problems involved in executing promotional efforts;
the broad methods and media available for promotional efforts;
the institutions available to assist with promotions.

These similarities however tend to obscure some of the differences that exist between promoting goods and services. These differences are of two kinds due to the characteristics of (a) service industries; (b) services.

(i) Differences due to the Characteristics of Service Industries

Service industries are very heterogeneous. This makes it problematic to identify differences that apply in all cases. The factors listed here are then indicative of some of the reasons why there may be variation between goods and services promotion. They have relevance in some cases but not necessarily in all cases.

a. Lack of Marketing Orientation

Some service industries are product oriented They are unaware of the possibilities that the practice of marketing would offer in their industries. They see themselves as producers of services and got as organizations serving customer needs. Managers are untrained, unskilled and unaware of the role that promotion could play within marketing.

b. Professional and Ethical Constraints

There may be professional and ethical constraints placed upon the use of certain marketing and promotional methods. Tradition and custom may prevent the use of certain forms of promotion. They may be regarded as 'inappropriate' by the industry or to be in 'bad taste'.

c. Small Scale of Many Service Operations

Many service operations may be small in scale (e.g. one man business). They may not regard themselves as large enough to warrant expenditure on marketing in general and promotions in particular.

d. Nature of Competition and Market Conditions

Many service organizations may not need to promote their services extensively because of their inability to cope with present work loads. They do not see that even in this situation promotional effort may have a longer term role to play in maintaining a secure market position.

e. Limited View of Promotion Methods Available

Service organizations may have a limited view of the very wide range of promotional methods available. They may only consider mass advertising and personal selling and ignore the scores of other methods which may be appropriate, are just as effective and may be less costly.

f. The Nature of the Service

The nature of the service may itself limit the use of certain promotional devices on any large scale. For example, advertising agencies rarely use mass media advertising. The kind of service, the traditions in the particular service industry, the limitations of some methods of promotion for certain kinds of services may constrain the use of promotions.

(ii) Differences Due to the Characteristics of Services

These differences are to do with :

(a) consumer attitudes;

(b) needs and motives for purpose;

(c) buying process.

a. Consumer Attitudes

Consumer attitudes are a key influence upon purchase decisions. With services intangibility is an important quality in marketing them. Consumers are more likely to rely upon subjective impressions of the service and of the performer or seller of the service when purchasing. This reliance on subjective impressions may be of less importance in the purchase of tangible goods. Two dimensions of consumer attitudes towards service sellers and service industries on which services are different from goods are

(a) service are perceived as being more personal than goods;

(b) consumers are sometimes less satisfied with purchases of services.

b. Needs and Motives for Purchase

Needs and motives for the purchase of goods and services are much the same. The same kinds of needs are satisfied whether through the purchase of tangibles or intangibles. However, one need that is important - in both situations-is the desire for personal attention. Satisfying this need for personal attention is one way in which service sellers can differentiate their service products from competitors. Though in some services like plant and computer maintenance , need for personal attention may be less important than other factors.

c. Buying Process

Difference between goods and services are more noticeable in the buying process. Some service purchase are regarded as riskier partly because it may be more difficult for buyers to evaluate quality and value. Also consumers are more likely to be influenced by others, such as friends and neighbours who have experiences of purchase and use. This more dominant role for personal influence in the buying process has implications for services marketing. In particular the needs to develop a professional relationship between service suppliers and their customers; and the need for promotional efforts to build upon word of mouth communication.

7.4 SELECTION CRITERIA

Careful thought should be given to deciding whether or not a specific type of promotion can contribute usefully to marketing strategy. Each situation must be examined on its merits. In particular, alternative promotional techniques should be considered against the following criteria:

- Overall marketing objectives
- Nature of the service
- Characteristics of target consumers
- Nature and attitudes of intermediaries (if any)
- Activities of competitors
- Cost effectiveness
- Integration with other marketing elements
- Requirements for effective implementation
- Measurement issues
- Legal considerations

1. Objectives

- **Is the promotion consistent with overall marketing objectives for the service?**
- **Is the promotion versatile, capable of effectively reaching several groups (such as both new and existing users) and fulfilling several objectives (such as stimulating switching and multiple purchases) simultaneously?**
- **Does the promotion have appeal to consumers, to intermediaries, and to contact personnel?**
- **Can the promotion function efficiently as a national promotion and/or as local promotion in selection market areas? For example, coupon drops can be arranged in an individual market area, but sweepstakes or contests must generally be national.**

2. The Service

- **Is the service a planned or an impulse purchase? If the latter, does the promotion make an impact at the point of service delivery ?**
- **Is the product frequently or infrequently purchased? (If the promotion offer requires multiple purchases, slippage will be greater to the extent that the product is less frequently purchased.)**
- **Are the characteristics of the product appropriate for this promotional approach ?**

3. The Consumer

- **Are target consumers accustomed to this promotional technique for this service? If not, might they perceive it as inappropriate?**
- **Does the promotion reduce perceived purchase risk?**
- **Are the terms of the promotion simple and easy to understand?**
- **Does the promotion offer an immediate or delayed reward to the consumer?**
- **How much consumer effort is required to take advantage of the promotional offer ?**
- **Are the terms of the promotion flexible, offering options to the consumer ?**

4. The Intermediaries

- **How much incremental effort is required of intermediaries to successfully implement the promotion ?**
- **Does the promotion offer a direct sales benefit to intermediaries?**
- **How much flexibility does the promotion offer intermediaries in terms of timing and execution?**
- **Does the promotion permit intermediaries to appear to be the source of the offer?**
- **Does the promotion lend itself to creative and exciting point-of-sale displays?**

5. Competition

- **Are competitive products currently using this promotion technique ?**
- **How rapidly can a competitor respond with a similar or superior promotion?**

6. Cost Effectiveness

- **What is the maximum expected liability for the promotion ?**
- **Can the terms of the promotional offer be designed to minimize liability? (For example, the number of purchase proofs required for a refund offer can be increased such that slippage increases and actual costs decrease.)**
- **How well can costs for the promotion be forecast? Is it vulnerable to the activities of ad hoc intermediaries (such as coupon brokers) such that forecast costs may be greatly exceeded ?**
- **Will the promotion tie up capital, for example, in an inventory of premium merchandise?**
- **Are the expenses for the promotion incurred on a pay-as-you-go (coupons) or investment (sweepstakes) basis?**
- **Is this promotion vulnerable to waste and abuse through such activities as pilferage and non-redemption?**
- **Can the promotion be designed to minimize the number of consumers who can take advantage of the offer more than once?**

7. **Integration**
   - Can the promotion be integrated easily with other elements of the communications mix, including advertising, personal selling, and point-of-sale displays?
   - Can the promotion reinforce the service advertising theme and contribute to franchise building?
   - Can the promotion be integrated with other promotional activities to create a dramatic event?
   - Can the promotion be used easily in line promotions involving several services as well as in single service promotions?
   - Is the promotion part of a successful marketing tradition for this service category?
8. **Implementation**
   - How much incremental effort is required of management and the sales force to successfully implement the promotion?
   - Does the sales force expect the promotion to facilitate its selling task?
   - To what extent are the services of outside agencies required to implement the promotion?
   - Does management control the costs and timing of delivering the offer ?
   - Does management have prior experience with this type of promotion?
   - How much lead time is required for implementation ?
9. **Measurement**
   - What measures are available to gauge response to the promotion and how valuable are they ?
   - Can the impact be inexpensively measured and compared to the impact of other promotions both of the same and of different types?
   - Is response concentrated in a short time period after the promotion is launched, or are there significant lag effects which may reduce the accuracy and increase the expense of measurement?
10. **Legal and Ethical**
   - Are there legal or ethical constraints on the design and use of this type of promotion?
   - Can this type of promotion be implemented nationally, or are there local laws which require adaptation of the offer in each state?

7.5 DEVELOPING THE PROMOTIONAL MIX

The promotion mix refers to the combination of channels that an organization uses to communicate with its target markets. Communication is received by audiences from two principal sources-those within an organization and external sources. The latter includes word-of-mouth recommendation from friends, editorials in the press, etc. which, it has already been noted, may have high credibility in the service-evaluation process. Sources originating within an organization can be

Figure 7.1 : THE MARKETING COMMUNICATIONS MIX FOR SERVICES

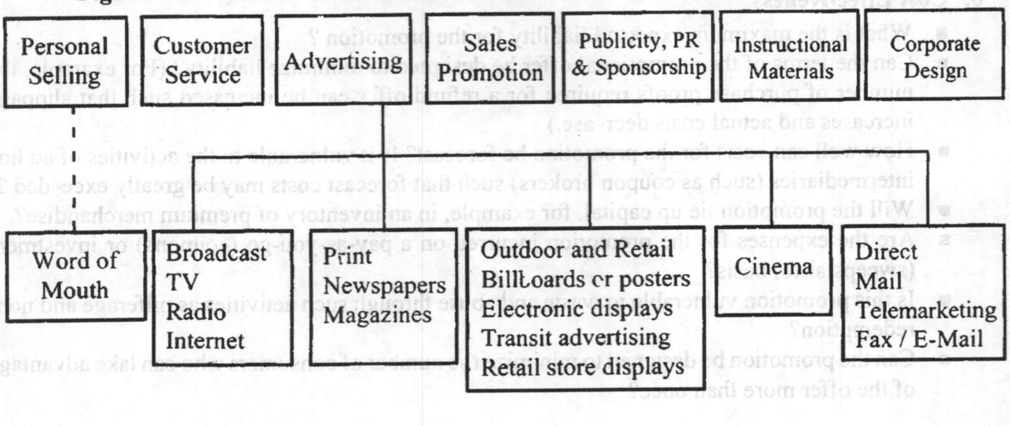

divided into those from the traditional marketing function (which can be divided into personal two-way channels such as personal selling and impersonal one-way channels such as advertising), and those from frontline production resources. Because services normally involve consumers in the production process, the promotion mix has to be considered more broadly than is the case with manufactured goods. Frontline operations staff and service outlets become a valuable channel of communication. The elements of the services promotion mix are illustrated in Figure 7.1.

Personal selling involves interpersonal encounters on a face-to-face (or in tele-marketing, voice-to-voice) basis. This proximity allows the sales representative to tailor the message to fit the customer's needs and concerns. During a sales call, which may take place in person or by phone, communication flows in both directions, allowing the sales rep to learn more about the customer. Questions and objections can be met and answered.

In addition to a field sales force (which often targets its efforts at institutional customers and intermediaries rather than at individual consumers), most service firms have personnel whose jobs bring them into contact with customers either face to face or by telephone. Professionals in firms such as accounting and management consulting are required to bring in new clients as well as to build lasting relationships with existing ones.

A broad array of paid advertising media are available to marketers to act as communication channels. Broadcast advertising has traditionally taken place through television and radio, but exciting new opportunities exist through the new channels offered by the Internet and World Wide Web.

Print advertising is usually defined as paid message inserted in newspapers and magazines; however, printed messages of a much larger format may appear on outdoor media such as billboards and posters as well as on public transportation vehicles. Electronic displays have the potential to create striking presentations that include moving images and changing colors. Another form of advertising, often linked to sales promotion, consists of retail displays in store windows. Finally, there is direct marketing, in the form of mail, tele-marketing, and fax or E-mail. This last-mentioned group offers the potential for personalized messages sent to highly targeted micro-segments, including one-to-one communications.

A promotion can be thought of as a communication attached to an incentive, which often takes the form of a price reduction. The term "promotion" is derived from the Latin word meaning "to move forward". And that's precisely what promotions are designed to do: To advance sales (especially during periods when demand would otherwise be weak), to speed the introduction of new services, to accelerate acceptance of new service delivery systems, and generally to get customers to act faster than they would in the absence of any promotional incentive. Promotions aren't limited to customers; they can also be used to motivate employees (internal marketing) and to stimulate intermediaries (distribution strategy).

Another key communications element for service business is corporate design, which refers to the consistent use of distinctive colours, symbols, lettering, and layout on such tangible elements as signage, retail storefronts, vehicles, uniforms, and stationery to provide a unifying and recognizable theme linking all the firm's operations.

Service delivery sites (such as hotels, hospitals, or banks) often stand in prominent locations offering exposure to a broad audience. Memorable architecture and attractive signing can convey a variety of important messages from overall image to highlighting a particular competitive advantage.

The promotional role of employees

An important role is played by frontline operational personnel as 'part-time marketers'. It has also been noted that the activities of such staff can be important in creating an image of an organizations which can live on to influence target customers' perceptions.

Staff who have frontline encounters with customers should be trained to treat encounters as promotional opportunities. Without appropriate training and explanation of expectations, a call for such employees to promote their service can be little more than rhetoric. Training might seek to develop a number of skills in frontline staff:

An ability to spot cross-selling possibilities can call for empathy on the part of frontline staff. A bank clerk who sees a customer repeatedly using a service that is not adequately fulfilling his or her needs could be trained to cross-sell another service which better meets the customer's requirements. Training should make such employees aware of the services available and give them skills in effectively approaching customers and referring them to appropriate personnel.

Many operational staff have quite clearly defined sales roles. For example, waiters may be expected to encourage customers to spend more on their visit to a restaurant.

The general manner of staffs' interaction with customers is important in encouraging customers to return and to tell their friends about their good experience. Again, training should emphasize those behaviours that have a positive effect on customers' evaluation of their encounter.

Staff can directly facilitate future business by encouraging customers to book a repeat service or by giving them literature to pass on to friends.

The promotional role of service outlets

From the outside, service outlets can be seen as billboards capable of conveying messages about the services that take place within them. They are therefore powerful tools in appealing to both customers and non-customers. The general appearance of an outlet can promote the image of a service organization-a brightly coloured and clean exterior can transmit a message that the organization is fast, efficient and well run. Outlets can be used to display advertising posters which, in heavily trafficked locations, can result in valuable exposure.

7.6 GUIDELINES FOR IMPROVING THE PROMOTION OF SERVICES

The differences between goods and services can have some implication for promotional effort. This section gives general guideline which may be appropriate for service organisations in attempting to improve the effectiveness of their promotion mix. Each element of this mix is examined.

Advertising

(a) should not contain explicit or implicit criticisms of the professional services of others.
(b) should be factual and not be likely to mislead;
(c) should not refer to fee levels but must include a statement to the effect that the fee basis will be discussed before an assignment is accepted;
(d) should not make claim to any particular expertise and should be restricted to all or any of the following : accountancy, auditing, book keeping, trusts, personal and/or corporate taxation and advisory services related to the foregoing;
(e) should be of a style and content appropriate to the profession.

We are likely to see many more service organizations lifting their restrictions on advertising in the next few years. We are also likely to see wider use of advertising by many kinds of services who may not have used it in the past (e.g. medicine). Given that service advertising may become more widespread and faced with the inherent problems posed by the characteristics of services what measures can service advertisers take?

There are a number of guidelines that advertisers of services can use to ensure more effective impact.

(a) Use Clear, Unambiguous Messages

A major difficulty with service advertising is that of communicating the range, depth, quality and level of services provided in simple written or illustrated form. Some service advertising can use pictures or symbols to help convey the advertising message. Other services however may have to present more detailed explanations of their services (e.g. professional services). This can lead to 'wordy' advertising which may interfere with advertising effectiveness. Advertising agencies face considerable creative problems in developing clear and simple message which neatly encapsulate the richness and dimensions of many service offerings.

(b) Emphasize the Benefits of Services

Attention getting and influential advertising should emphasize the benefits of services advertised rather than their technical details. The emphasis on benefits is in accord with the marketing concept and its concern with fulfilling customer needs. It is important though that benefits stressed should be in line with benefits sought. The benefit appeals used should therefore be based on a clear understanding of customer needs to ensure maximum favourable impact.

(c) Only Promise what can be Delivered

The promise of benefits which can be obtained through service use should not be unrealistic, raise excessive expectations in customers and be incapable of delivery by the service organization. Service organisations must be able to fulfil advertising promises.

(d) Advertise to Employces

Employees are particularly important in many people-intensive services and in many services where the interaction between service employees and customers is central to customer satisfaction. This means that employees are a potential audience for service advertising: 'When the performances of people are what customer buy the advertiser needs to be concerned not only with encouraging customers to buy, but also with encouraging employees to perform.

(e) Obtain and Maintain Customer Cooperation in the Service Production Process

Service marketers face two challenges in their service advertising. The first, common to goods and service advertising, is how to obtain and maintain customer patronage as users of the services in question. The second, unique to many services, is how to obtain and maintain customer collaboration and cooperation in the service production process.

Well-conceived advertising will thus sometimes focus on how to obtain and maintain the compliance and cooperation of the customer in service production.

(f) Build on Word-of-mouth Communications

In the introduction to this chapter it was indicated non-marketer-dominated sources may be more influential in determining service organization and service product choice. One strong influence is word-of-mouth communication; service advertisers should therefore build upon this form of communication.

(g) Provide Tangible Clues

Service advertisers should use tangible clues wherever possible to strengthen their promotional efforts. It is interesting that much tangible product advertising emphasizes abstract, intangible associations in its appeals. On the other hand, services are already abstract and to add further intangible associations to an already abstract concept could be counter-productive:

(h) Develop Continuity in Advertising

Service organizations can help overcome two disadvantages they may face-intangibility and service product differentiation-through using consistent and continuous symbols, themes, formats or images in their advertising.

(i) Remove Post-purchase Anxiety

Consumers of goods and services are subject to doubts about the soundness of their purchases. With goods some tangible object is available for post-purchase evaluation, with services this may not be so. In service marketing more effort must usually be spent in reassuring the buyer of the soundness of choice and in encouraging customers to tell others about the benefits derived from service purchase and use. Advertising is one means of doing this.

Five **roles** for services advertising are:

(a) ***Creating the company's world in the mind of the customer*.**

This involves describing the world in which the company operates; its activities; what is special about its services; the values of the company.

(b) ***Building an appropriate personality for the company*.**

This involves long-term efforts to shape the customer's ideas and expectations about the company and its services and to get the customer to feel favourably towards the company.

(c) ***Identifying the company with the customer*.**

This involves getting customers to identify strongly with the service company. The company image and service should be relevant to the needs, values and attitudes of its customers.

(d) ***Influencing company personnel on how they deal with customers*.**

Services advertising has two audiences - customers and company personnel. Services advertising needs to represent and reflect company employees' views, and be understood by them if they are to support company marketing effort.

(e) ***Helping to open doors for sales representatives*.**

Services advertising should form a favourable backdrop against which company sales representatives can operate. Favourable customer predispositions towards a company and its services can help sales representatives calling on prospects.

7.7 THE ROLE OF SALES PROMOTION

Sales promotion contributes in a number of ways to achieving overall promotional objectives. While it can be used merely to gain attention for a service, it is more likely to be employed as an incentive incorporating an offer which represents value to the target audience. It can also act as an invitation to engage in a transaction now rather than later. Sales promotion usually attracts brand switchers but is unlikely to turn them into loyal brand users without the use of other elements of the promotion mix.

Sales-promotion planning

As in the case of advertising, effective sales promotion involves an on-going process with a number of stages.

Establishment of objectives: Sales-promotion objectives vary according to the target market. If the target is the customer, objectives could include the encouragement of increased usage or the building of trial among non-users or other brand users. For intermediaries, objectives could be to encourage off-season sales or offsetting competitive promotions. Sales-promotion activity could also be aimed at internal personnel, making up part of the reward system

Selection of promotional tools: Promotional objectives form the basis for selecting the most appropriate sales-promotion tools. The cost and effectiveness of each tool must be assessed with regard to achieving these objectives in respect of each target market. The tools available to the service marketer are described in more detail in the next section.

Planning the sales-promotion programme: The major decisions that need to be made when designing the sales-promotion programme relate to the timing of the promotion and how long this tool is to be used. Also important are the size of incentive, rules for eligibility and, of course, the overall budget for the promotion.

Pre-testing: This needs to be undertaken to ensure that potentially expensive problems are discovered before the full launch of a promotion. Testing in selected market segments can highlight problems of ambiguity, response rates and give an indication of cost effectiveness.

Implementation: The programme for implementation must include two important time factors. First, it must indicate the 'lead time'- the time necessary to bring the programme up to the point where the incentive is made available to the public. Second, the 'sell in time' which is the period of time from the date of release to when approximately 90-95 per cent of incentive material has been received by potential customers.

Evaluation: The performance of the promotion needs to be assessed against the objectives set. If objectives are specific and quantifiable, measurement would seem to be easy. However, extraneous factors could account for the apparent success of many sales-promotion activities. For example, competitive actions or seasonal variations may have influenced customers' decision making. It can also be extremely difficult to separate out the effects of sales-promotion activity from other promotional activity-or indeed from other marketing-mix changes.

7.8 SALES-PROMOTION TOOLS

A wide and ever-increasing range of sales-promotion tools is employed by service organizations. Some of the more commonly used tools aimed at the final consumer include the following:

Free samples / visits / consultations: These encourage trial of a service and can be valuable where consumers are loyal to an existing service supplier. It could, for example, be used by a video film-rental chain to entice potential customers into their branch so that they can learn something about the nature of the service on offer. In the case of new services that are perceived as being expensive and of poor value to a consumer, they can encourage trial - this has been used by satellite television companies, for example. Taken to extremes, the excessive offering of free samples can demean the value of the service on offer and of the service provider. Customers may become reluctant to pay for a service which they have seen being given away freely.

Money-off price incentives: These are used to stimulate demand during slack periods where price is considered to be a key element in customers' purchased activity. Price incentives can be used tactically to counteract temporary increases in competitor activity. They can also be employed to stimulate sales of a new service shortly after launch. Price incentives tend to be expensive to the service provider, as the incentive is given to customers regardless of its motivational effect on individual customers. A leisure park reducing its prices for all is unable to extract the full price from those customers who may have otherwise been willing to pay that price. There is also a danger that price incentives can become built into consumers' expectations and their removal may result in a fall in business.

Coupons / vouchers: These allow holders to obtain a discount off a future purchase and can be targeted at quite specific groups of users or potential users. To encourage trial by potential new users, vouchers can be distributed to non-users who fit a specified profile. In this way, the operator of a plaza might arrange for vouchers to be given to customers of a cooperating hairdressing salon. To encourage repeat usage, vouchers can be given as a loyalty bonus. Voucher offers tend to be much more cost effective than straight price incentives because of their ability to segment markets. In this way, a leisure park operator is able to recognize that a visitor from overseas may see the full price as being only a small part of their total holiday cost and representing good value, while a local family might need an incentive to make more frequent visits to the park. Coupons usually take one of three forms: a straight price cut; a discount or fee waiver for one or more patrons accompanying the original purchaser; or a free or discounted enhancement of the basic service (such as free waxing with each car wash). Traditionally, coupons were printed in newspapers and magazines or sent by direct mail. Today, however, they are often sold in books which provide purchasers with the opportunity to use the services of a wide array of restaurants and cafes, laundry and dry cleaning establishments, garages, cinemas and other suppliers. With the advent of electronic scanning in shops, many of these promotional offers are now implemented electronically.

Gift offers: These allow an organization to augment its service offer with an additional gift which can satisfy a number of objectives. In order to promote initial enquiry and to give tangible cues of the service company's offering and image, many firms-especially in the financial services sector-offer a gift for merely enquiring about their service. Items offered by insurance companies for merely requesting a quotation often include pocket calculators and pens. A gift can also be used to bring about immediate action-for example, a free clock radio if a policy is taken out within a specified period. For existing customers, gifts can be used to develop and reward loyalty. Sometimes, a company may charge for a gift, making the sales-promotion self-financing. The gift could also carry a message that makes the service tangible to the user and others. In this way, some petrol retailers and football clubs-among others-sell ranges of promotional clothing, paid for by a combination of vouchers and cash.

Competitions: The inclusion of a competition in a service offer adds to the value of the total offer. Instead of simply buying an insurance policy, customers buy the policy plus a dream of winning a prize to which they attach significance. Competitions can be used both to create trial among non-users and to retain loyalty among existing users (for example, a competition for which a number of proofs of purpose are necessary to enter). Prize promotions introduce an element of chance, like a lottery or sweepstakes. They can be used effectively to add involvement and excitement to the service experience and are generally designed to encourage increased use of the service. Fast-food restaurants, video rental outlets and service stations sometimes offer lottery-like promotions tied to special events giving all purchasers tickets with scratch-off award categories. TV stations may offer listeners the chance to claim instant cash and other prizes if they call within a prescribed time after the announcement is broadcast.

Short-term discounts: Price cuts that are promoted as being available for only a limited time period, such as any form of 'sale' designed to boost business during slack periods. Another example is 'charter memberships' in health and fitness clubs which are sold at decreasing rates of discount prior to opening the club; such strategies help to build a base of customers quickly and improve initial cash flow.

Sign-up rebates: May be offered by 'membership' service organizations that charge a preliminary sign-up fee for applying, joining or making connections to a network. Examples include application fees for education institutions, joining fees at many private clubs and installation fees for connections to pay TV systems. To attract new members or subscribers, these fees may be waived or alternatively credited towards payment of future usage fees.

Short-term increases in sales commission: These, together with sales bonuses, can be used to stimulate sales during slack periods or to develop loyalty from intermediaries in the face of competitor activity.

Point-of-sale material: To stimulate additional sales, a service principal can provide a range of incentives to help intermediaries. Examples include tour operators who agree to send a representative to a travel agency to provide additional information and reassurance for customers, or to host a film evening for the agency's clients.

Cooperative advertising: A service principal often agrees to subscribe to local advertising by an intermediary, often in conjunction with a significant event-for example, the opening of a new outlet by the intermediary or the launch of a new service.

In service settings, there are a number of guidelines which may be used for service selling.

(a) Develop Personal Relationships with Customers

Good personal contacts between employees and customers can lead to mutual satisfaction. The image of personal attention and personal interest that a service organization may try to convey through its advertising programmes has to be supported by real personal interest and attention in the marketplace. However, a high level of personal interest and attention is not without its problems. First it can be expensive to implement. Secondly, more staff may need to be employed with increased risks of more variability in staffing performance. Thirdly, there are organizational implications. A service organisation intent on giving high levels of personal attention has to be organized and resourced to do so (e.g. backup facilities, detailed knowledge of customer service levels required). Fourthly, personal attention usually takes place at the expense of standardization.

(b) Adopt a Professional Orientation

The customer in most service transactions must have confidence in the sellers' ability to deliver the expected results. A professional approach to business can assist this process. Selling services means people have to be thoroughly competent in their jobs as sellers (e.g. sound knowledge of services available). They must also be perceived by customers to act and sound like professionals. The sellers' appearance, actions, behaviour and attitudes must conform with customers' views of how 'professional' sales people are expected to conduct themselves.

(c) Use Indirect Selling

Three general forms of indirect selling:

1. Create derived demand by measures like promoting and selling related goods and services and helping customers use existing services more effectively and efficiently.
2. Use referees, testimonials and opinion leaders in the customer choice process
3. Self selling

(d) Build and Maintain a Favourable Image

Effective marketing depends upon the creation and maintenance of a favourable image. People and organisations will develop and have images anyway. What marketing activities (e.g. advertising, public relations) try to ensure is that the image develops in a way consistent with how the individual or organization would like to be seen; and in a way which is congruent with customer perceptions of what that image should be. The impressions that customers and non-customers have of an organization and its staff will greatly influence their patronage decisions.

Image building and maintenance is an important element in service marketing because high levels of intangibility in a service mean reliance must be placed in reputation and subjective impressions of the service. Second non-marketer sources of influence (e.g. word-of-mouth) are important in service selling and the image formed.

(e) Sell Services not Service

In selling core services, organizations can benefits from having a range of support services surrounding the core services. These make it easier, more convenient and less troublesome for the customer to purchase. Package holidays provide a convenient example of how a range of services can be rolled into one straightforward purchase from the customer's viewpoint. Insurance companies, airlines, banks and retail organizations have extended the range of services offered (e.g. financial arrangements). All these supplementary services can strengthen the impetus to purchase the core service (e.g. travel, risk reduction, credit).

(f) Make Purchase Easy

Service products may be conceptually difficult for customers to understand. This may be because the customer is making an infrequent purchase (e.g. buying a house). It may also be that in certain circumstances the customer is under great emotional strain (e.g. using the services of a funeral director). In these circumstances professional service sellers will make it easy for the customer to purchase. It implies looking after all arrangements in a professional way while keeping the customer informed of progress in the performance of the service. Minimal demands are imposed on the customer.

7.9 DIRECT MARKETING

The key elements of a direct marketing system are the following :

- An accurate record of the names of existing customers, former customers and prospective customers classified into different groups.
- A system for recording the results of communications with targets. From this, the effectiveness of particular messages and the responsiveness of different target groups can be assessed.
- A means of measuring and recording actual purchase behaviour.
- A system to follow up with continuing communication where appropriate.

The two most common forms of direct marketing used by service organizations are tele-marketing and direct mail.

Tele-marketing

Tele-marketing involves two-way communication by telephone- 'outbound' Tele-marketing occurs where suppliers take the initiative and 'inbound' where customers act in response to another stimulus, such as a newspaper advertisement.

The effectiveness of Tele-marketing can be assessed by measuring the cost per telephone call, the cost per telephone hour and the number and quality of enquiries received. Furthermore, by asking questions of inquirers, the source of particularly effective supporting advertisements can be identified. It can often be possible to measure the cost effectiveness of Tele-marketing in terms of the value of sales generated, especially, where there is little extraneous media advertising which could itself have explained sales success.

Direct mail

Direct mail describes the way in which an organization distributes printed material aimed at specifically targeted potential customers with a view to carrying on direct interchange between the two parties. Its use is becoming increasingly popular among service industries and a number of important advantages which it has over the other promotional tools can be identified :

- It can be used very selectively to target quite specific groups of potential private or business customers.
- The sales message can be personalized to needs of individual recipients.
- Direct mail offers a very versatile and creative medium and is flexible in the range of materials that can be used.
- It can be timed effectively to fit in with the overall marketing strategy and is quick to produce.
- It is also quick in terms of producing results.

7.10 PUBLIC RELATIONS

Public relations is an indirect promotional tool whose role is to establish and enhance a positive image of an organization and its services among its various publics. It is defined as 'the deliberate, planned and sustained effort to establish and maintain mutual understanding between an organisation and its public'. It seeks to persuade people that a company is an attractive organization with which to relate or do business, which is important for services as it has already been noted that services are evaluated very subjectively and often rely on word-of-mouth recommendation. Public relations facilitates this process of subjective evaluation and recommendation. Some of the important elements used within this promotion mix are as follows:

Press releases: The creation and dissemination of press releases is often referred to as 'publicity' 'activity of securing editorial space, as divorced from paid space, in all media read, viewed or heard by a company's customers or prospects, for the specific purpose of assisting in the meeting of sales goals'

Lobbying: Professional lobbyists are often employed in an effort to inform and hence influence key decision makers who may be critical in allowing elements of a marketing plan to be implemented.

Education and training: In an effort to develop a better understanding-and hence liking-of an organization and its services, many service organizations aim education and training programmes at important target groups. In this way, banks frequently supply schools and colleges with educational material that will predispose its recipients to their brand when they come to open a bank account.

Exhibitions: Most companies attend exhibitions not with the intention of making an immediate sale but to create an awareness of their organization that will result in a sale over the longer term. Exhibitions offer the chance for potential customers to talk face to face with representatives of the organization and the physical layout of the exhibition stand can give valuable tangible evidence about the nature of the service on offer. Exhibitions are used for both consumer and business-to-business services.

In-house journals: Many service organizations have developed their own magazines which are given to customers or potential customers. By adopting a news-based magazine format, the message becomes more credible than if it were presented as a pure advertisement.

Special events: In order to attract media attention, organizations sometimes arrange an event which is in itself newsworthy and will create awareness of the organization.

Sponsorship: Increasingly used by services companies to provide a 'backbone' for events.

Preparing the publicity strategy

As with all aspects of the communication mix, publicity will achieve maximum effectiveness if a clear plan is formulated which identifies objectives, has a clear strategy and implementation programme and effective monitoring.

- Publicity objectives typically include the desire to raise awareness of a new service launch or to identify the organization with a desired image.
- Planning involves identifying items that should be brought to the attention of a wider audience by means of publicity.
- Implementing the plan requires a great deal of care and may involve carefully building up mutual trust with important media editors.
- Evaluation is difficult as publicity is usually used in conjunction with other promotional tools. It is easier to evaluate if publicity is used before other tools. There are, however, a number publicity response measures that can be employed. For example, 'exposures' relate to the number of times news about the company has been carried by the media. However, this does not give any indication of how many people actually saw or heard the information. Alternatively, surveys of awareness, comprehension and attitudes before and after publicity could be undertaken and these may give some indication of the response to publicity.

7.11 THE ROLE OF MARKETING COMMUNICATION

The tasks performed by marketing communication (Figure 7.2) are to:

- ***Inform and educate*** prospective customers about an organization and the relevant features of the goods and services that it offers.
- ***Persuade*** target customers that a specific service product offers the best solution to their needs, relative to the offerings of competing firms.
- ***Remind*** customers and prospects of product availability and motivate them to act.
- ***Maintain contact*** with existing customers, providing updates and further education on how to obtain the best results from the firm's products in the light of each customer's documented usage behaviour.

The key differences between products and services should be taken into account in considering service communication as follows:

- ***Simultaneous production and consumption***. The layout, shop facia, and the appearance and manner of the staff are critical communication variables.
- ***Intangibility***. Service providers should attempt to reduce the risk to the consumer of buying an intangible product by providing tangible clues about the service offering. These clues comes from all aspects of corporate communication.
- ***Heterogeneity***. This, too, leads to greater perceived risk. Again communications can help to reduce this factor. It may be appropriate to communicate a service guarantee or promise or to demonstrate how well-trained your staff are.
- ***Perishability***. Many promotional tools, e.g. advertising, sales promotion, and direct marketing, have a role to play in shaping demand. This is one of the most challenging aspects of service management and arises from the fact that services cannot be inventoried.

Flowing from this there are five key aspects of communication for the service marketer:

- The role of personal selling
- The targeting of employees in external communications
- The management of expectations
- The provision of tangible clues
- Word-of-mouth communications

Figure 7.2 : THE COMMUNICATION PROCESS

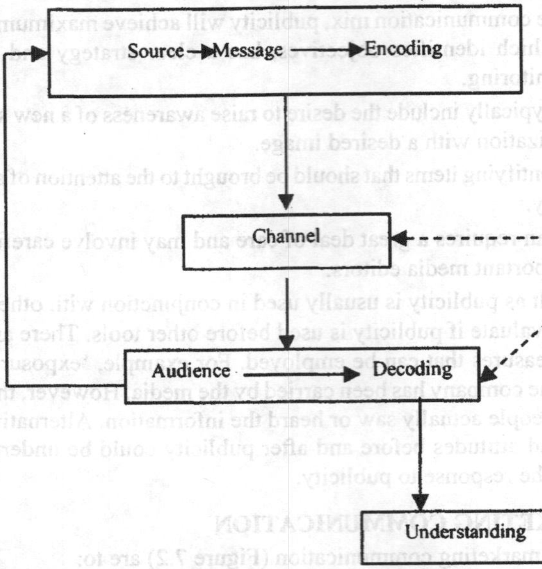

7.12 TARGET AUDIENCE

The target audience of a communication must be clearly defined and this can be done in a number of ways:

- The most traditional method of defining audiences is in terms of social, economic, demographic and geographical characteristics. In this way, audiences are characterized using parameters such as age, sex, social class, area of residence, etc.
- Audience can be defined in terms of the level of involvement of potential recipients of the communication. For example, a distinction can be made between those people who are merely aware of the existence of a service, those who are interested in possibly purchasing it and those who wish to purchase the service.
- An audience can be identified on the basis of target customer's usage frequency (for example, regular users of an airline are likely to respond to communications in a way different from occasional users).
- Similarly, audiences can differ in the benefits that they seek from a category of service. Railways aim different messages at leisure users who may seek benefits such as meeting distant friends, compared to business users for whom speed and reliability may be of greatest importance.
- In the case of services supplied to corporate buyers, audiences can be defined in terms of the type and size of business and its geographical location. More importantly, the key decision makers and influencers must be identified and used in identifying the audience. For example, for many corporate travel services, secretaries can be important in choosing between competing services rather than the actual service user, and therefore be included in a definition of the target audience.

People differ in their readiness to try new products and a number of attempts have been made to classify the population in terms of their level of risk taking.

This has led to a classification of markets into the following adopter categories (Figure 7.3):

- Innovators
- Early adopters
- Early majority
- Late majority
- Laggards

Figure 7.3 : ADOPTION CATEGORIES

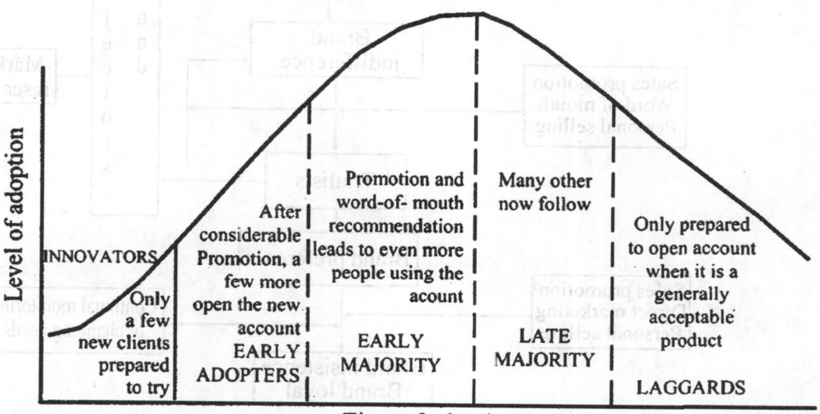

7.13 BRANDING SERVICES-TRENDS

- There is an increasing proliferation of brands within service sectors. Service markets are becoming more competitive.
- It has been shows to be up to five times cheaper to retain current customers than to attract new ones.
- Product/service life cycles are becoming shorter. NPD/NSD thus assumes a greater importance. The risks of product launches are reduced in the context of umbrella branding.
- The service itself may offer no unique tangible benefit - this can be added by development of brand imagery.

7.14 BRAND IMAGE DEVELOPMENT

Brand rejection occurs when your communications message is not motivating. It may not be motivating to those who are not target consumers. That is not a problem. What is more worrying is when the rejectors are in your target.

Consumers who are brand indifferent need more motivation. In many cases this arises because the service has not been experienced. Sales promotion techniques aimed at including trial should be considered (Figure 7.4).

Brand insistence/loyalty is every marketer's dream. How do you get there?

- Encourage repeat purchase using sales promotion. This makes consumers familiar with your service which in turn diminishes risk.
- Keep your current customer satisfied by developing and sustaining unique service advantages. As Dobree and Page state, " Branding is one key method of addressing the problem of competitive advantage. Branding is often the best way of sustaining a competitive advantage. A competitive advantage built solely on functional benefits is much easier for competitors".
- Introduce penalties so that the cost of changing brands is high. Financial institutions practise

Figure 7.4 : BRAND IMAGE DEVELOPMENT

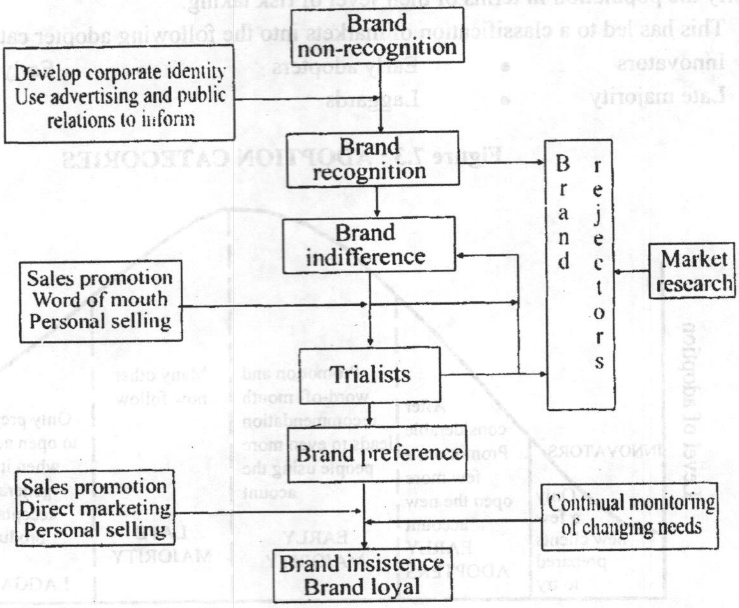

this to good effect. If you decide to move to a company that offers a higher rate of interest, then the original lending company will charge you a penalty for doing this. This financial penalty will often mean that there is no longer any pecuniary advantage from making the change.

7.15 SETTING ADVERTISING OBJECTIVES

One approach to the setting of advertising objectives and strategy is to consider the four variables (Table 7.2) that are used to describe the difference between services and products.

Table 7.2 : SETTING ADVERTISING OBJECTIVES TO ADDRESS SERVICE VARIABLES

Service variable	*Advertising objective*
Intangibility	Provision of tangible clues Reduce risk Provide reassurance
Heterogeneity	Customization Reduce risk Provide Reassurance
Inseparability	Staff focus: selection, training etc. Customer empathy
Perishability	Use advertising to manage demand (price offers)

Another approach to the setting of objectives is to seek answers to the following questions at the beginning of the development process:

- What is it that motivates consumers to use my service?

- Was it credible to communicate to them in this context?
- Can I deliver what I promise?

In other words, in developing the communication the advertiser has to consider 'What, to Whom, How, When, and Where?

Advertising exposure: The number of advertising exposures of a particular communication is determined by two factors: cover/reach and frequency. 'Cover' or 'Reach' is the percentage of a particular target audience reached by a medium or a whole campaign, while 'frequency' is the number of times a particular target audience has an 'opportunity to see/hear' (OTS/OTH) and advertising message. The combination of these two factors results in an index of advertising exposure which is usually stated in terms of 'Gross Rating Points' (GRPs). For example, if an objective is to reach 50 per cent of the target audience three times a year, this would be stated as a GRP of 150 (i.e. 50 x 3).

Advertising impact: Although impact is usually more closely related to the message than the medium, different media vehicles can produce different levels of impact of an identical message. Where a service organisations links a powerful tangible image to its service offering (e.g. McDonald's use of the Ronald McDonald character) the impact will be greatest with a visual medium that has movement and colour.

Wearout: The concept of advertising exposure assumes that all advertising insertions have equal value. However, the effect of additional insertions may in fact decline, resulting in diminishing returns for each unit of expenditure. There is usually a 'threshold' level of advertising beneath which little audience response occurs. Once over this threshold, audience response tends to increase quite rapidly through a 'generation' phase until eventually a saturation point is reached. Any further advertising leads to a negative or declining response, i.e. 'wearout'. Generally, wearout is more a function of the message, but if wearout for the same message does vary between media, this should be taken into account when choosing between media. Wearout may be alleviated by broadening the variety of media being used (although this is likely to increase marginal costs) or, alternatively, by incorporating a more 'creative' approach in the message.

Cost: The cost of using different media varies markedly, and while a medium which at first appears to be expensive may in fact be good value in terms of achieving promotional objectives, a sound basis for measuring cost is needed. There are generally two related cost criteria:

Cost per Gross Rating Point: This is usually used for broadcast media and is the cost of a set of commercials divided by the Gross Rating Points.

Cost per Thousand: This is used for print media to calculate the cost of getting the message seen by one thousand members of the target market.

These measures can be used to make cost comparisons between different media vehicles. However, a true comparison needs to take into consideration the different degrees of effectiveness each medium has. In other words, the strength of the media vehicle needs to be considered, as does the location, duration, timing and-where relevant-size of the advertisement plus a variety of more complex factors. These are all combined to form 'media weights' which are used in comparing the effectiveness of different media. Cost effectiveness therefore, is calculated using the following formula.

$$\text{Cost effectiveness} = \frac{\text{Readers/viewers in target} \times \text{Media weight}}{\text{Cost}}$$

Determining the advertising budget

Advertising expenditure could become a drain on an organizations' resources if no conscious attempt is made to determine an appropriate budget and to ensure that expenditure is kept within it. A number of methods are commonly used to determine an advertising budget:

What can be afforded: This is largely a subjective assessment and pays little attention to the long-term promotional needs of a service. It regards advertising as a luxury which can be afforded in good times, to be cut back during lean ones. In reality, this approach is used by many smaller service companies to whom advertising spending is seen as the first and easy short-term target for reducing expenditure in bad times.

Percentage of Sales: By this method, advertising expenditure rises or falls to reflect changes in sales. In fact, sales are likely to be influenced by advertising rather than vice versa, and this method is likely to accentuate any given situation. If sales are declining during a recession, more advertising may be required to induce sales, but this method of determining the budget implies a cut in advertising expenditure.

Comparative Parity: Advertising expenditure is determined by the amount spent by competitors. Many market sectors see periodic outbursts of promotional expenditure, often accompanying a change in some other element of firms' marketing mix.

Residual: This is the least satisfactory approach and merely assigns to the advertising budget what is left after all other costs have been covered. It may bear no relationship whatever to promotional objectives.

Objective and Task: This approach starts by clearly defining promotional objectives. Tasks are then set which relate to specific targets. In this way, advertising is seen as a necessary-even though possibly risky-investment in a brand, ranking in importance with other more obvious costs such as production and salaries. This is the most rational approach to setting a promotional budget.

Figure 7.5 : ADVERTISING STRATEGY

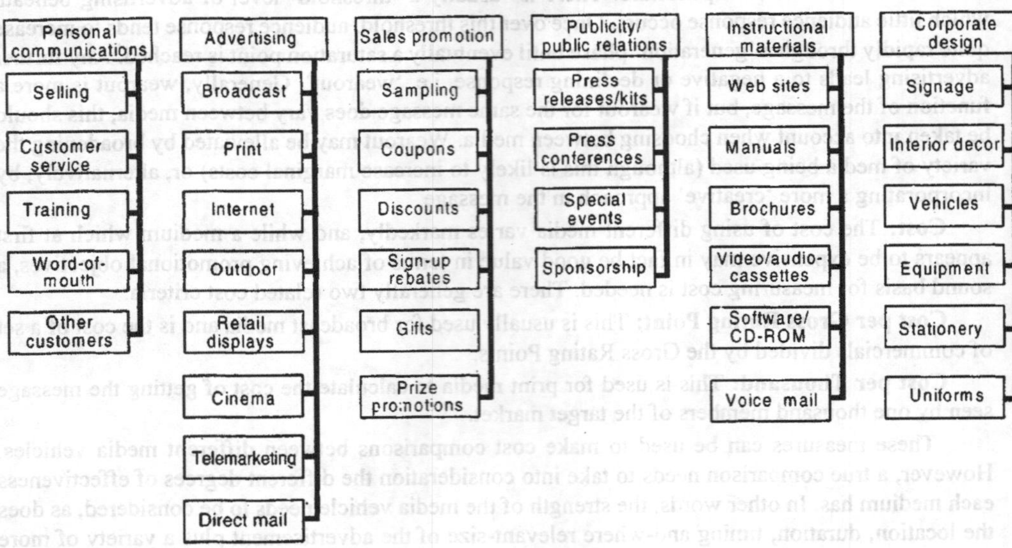

It can be seen from Figure 7.5 that various strategies are available for Advertising

7.16 AUDIENCE RESPONSE

The communicator will be seeking any one or more of three audience responses to the communication:

- ***Cognitive responses:*** The message should be considered and understood
- ***Affective responses:*** The message should lead to some change in attitude
- ***Behavioural responses:*** Finally, the message should achieve some change in behaviour (a purchase decision)

A model of buyer states is shown in Table 7.3.

Table 7.3 : MODELS OF BUYER STATES

Domain	*AIDA model*	*Hierarchy of effects model*	*Innovation-adoption model*
Cognitive	Awareness	Awareness Knowledge	Awareness
Affective	Interest Desire	Liking Preference	Interest Evaluation
Behavioural	Action	Conviction Purchase	Trial Adoption

The Message

Messages can be classified into a number of types, according to their dominant themes. The following are common focal points for them:

- ***The nature and characteristics*** of the organization and the service on offer. For example, the television advertisements for Cathay Pacific Airlines emphasize the high quality of their inflight service.
- ***Advantages over the competition:*** A campaign during the early 1990s emphasized the relative spaciousness and high standards of its seating compared to its airline competitors.
- ***Adaptability to buyers needs:*** Many insurance companies stress the extent to which their policies have been designed with the requirements of particular age segments of the population in mind.
- ***Experience of others:*** In this way, testimonials of previous satisfied customers are used to demonstrate the benefits resulting from use and the dependability of the service provider.

Noise

Noise factors can be divided into two major types:

Those that relate to the individual, i.e., psychological factors.

Those that relate to other groups of people, i.e. sociological factors.

Psychological factors: No two individuals are the same in terms of their psychological makeup. Each person undergoes different experiences influencing their personalities, their perceptions of the world, their motives for action and their attitudes towards people will interpret communications differently.

An individual's experience of a service or service organization is an important influence on how messages about that service are interpreted. Both positive and negative experiences predispose an individual to decode messages in a particular way. Also, the personality of specific members of an audience can significantly influence interpretation of a message. For example, an extrovert may interpret a message differently from an introvert. Similarly, an individual's motives can influence how a message is decoded.

Sociological factors: In addition to possessing inherent personal characteristic which influence behaviour, individuals are affected by the presence of other people around them. The conditioning process brought about by the existence of these groups of people can be analysed in terms of past experience-they are extremely enduring and very influential in determining how a message is perceived. For example, an individual may have a negative attitude towards a particular bank as a result of having previously been refused overdraft facilities by that bank. This negative attitude is likely to distort the individual's interpretation of any marketing communication from the bank. In this context, therefore, the communication should involve an attempt to shift attitude as well as merely to inform.

7.17 GUIDELINES FOR SERVICE ADVERTISING

One is to recognize that service is a performance rather than an object. Advertising, they say, should not only encourage customers to buy the service but should also target employees as a second audience, motivating them to deliver high quality service. To this end, service firms should try to use their own employees-rather than professional models-in their print and broadcast advertisements.

Tangible clues should include not only employees but also physical facilities such as service delivery sites. Animal motifs are also popular physical symbols for some service providers.

Another guideline is to capitalize on word-of-mouth advertising by trying to stimulate this highly credible form of communication. They also urge service advertisers to seek continuity over time through the use of recognizable symbols, spokesperson, slogans, trademarks, and music. It's essential to promise what's possible, so as to foster realistic expectations.

The potential gaps in advertising perceptions between decision makers and employees is shown in Table 7.4. The perceptions differ in a sense that:

(a) Advertisements are perceived as inaccurate.

(b) Advertisements are perceived as value incongruent.

(c) Advertisements are perceived as ineffective.

Table 7.4 : POTENTIAL GAPS IN ADVERTISING PERCEPTIONS BETWEEN DECISION MAKERS AND EMPLOYEES

Advertisements Are Perceived as Inaccurate: Potential Sources of Problem	*Potential Solutions*
• Decision makers do not have a complete understanding of products/services and may overpromise or even underpromise.	Research advertising accuracy with employees, particularly those who make products, deliver service, or otherwise interact with customers.
• Advertisements designed to picture the organization's culture in an ideal way for the target market might be viewed by employees as untrue.	Research employee perceptions of organizational culture; keep claims in some reasonable range or make advertising part of internal change effort.
• Decision makers do not understand employees' self-roles or view discrepancies from roles as more minor than do employees.	Research role perceptions of any portrayed employee groups. Either include rank-and-file employees or communicate the effectiveness of the approach taken with target markets.
• Employees overreact to minor inaccuracies because they do not understand the creative strategy.	Explain how the creative approach will be effective with the target market.
Advertisements Are Perceived as Value Incongruent: Potential Sources of Problem	**Potential Solutions**
• Decision makers believe the primary value-related complaint will be about advertising spending.	Research how employees really feel. Most believe that advertising is important in a competitive environment.
• Decision makers do not believe employees understand the company's target market. Employees do know about target markets but still object to advertisements that are value incongruent.	Create advertisements that are effective with target audiences without being value-incongruent with a significant portion of employees. Some employees will be neutral about value-incongruent advertisements when

	they believe the advertisements will be liked by the target market.
• Decision makers do not know that employees often are called on to defend or explain company advertising to extra organizational networks.	Give employees adequate information to influence their personal networks positively and to make them feel like insiders.

Advertisements Are Perceived as Ineffective:

Potential Sources of Problem	Potential Solutions
Employees do not understand advertising goals other than sales	Explain the relationship of other goals to sales. Also, explain how new advertisements will gain attention and comprehension, are well targeted, and are credible and/or authentic. Employees associate these characteristics with effective advertising.
Employees do not receive information about the outcomes associated with a campaign and thus tend to evaluate effectiveness globally by comparing current advertisements with especially well-liked previous company advertisements and those of competitors.	Use campaign introductions to discuss business and advertising strategy and goals in internal communications. Frame new campaign introductions by describing how new advertisements share characteristics with previous well-liked advertisements.
Some advertisements are not effective	During pretesting, include employees who are members of the target audience and/or employees who have frequent contact with customers.

SHORT ANSWER QUESTIONS

1. Is word-of-mouth publicity important for services?
2. What are the objectives of promotion?
3. What do you understand by corporate identity?
4. How can the image of police department be developed?
5. "Tradition and custom may prevent the use of certain forms of promotion". Do you agree?
6. Define the following:
   (a) Cost per thousand
   (b) Residual approach
   (c) Cost per GRP
   (d) Sign-up rebates
   (e) Cost effectiveness
   (f) Laggards
   (g) OTS and OTH
   (h) Wearout
7. What are the key elements of a direct marketing system?
8. What is tele-marketing?
9. What are the sales promotion activities aimed at intermediaries?
10. When are advertisements perceived as 'value incongruent' and 'ineffective'?
11. What are the criteria in the selection of media?

12. "Promise only what can be delivered". Comment.
13. Identify the methods of external communication to the customers.
14. What is the role of services advertising?

ESSAY QUESTIONS

1. What kind of advertising objectives need to be set for the following services:
   (a) Banking
   (b) Transportation
   (c) Charities
   (d) Hotels
   (e) Post & Courier.
2. How are markets classified based on adopter categories?
3. What are the tools of sales promotion? Explain with examples for any two services.
4. How can public relations be fostered? Do all services require public relations? Why? Why not?
5. What are the methods of determining advertising budgets?
6. What is the need of service marketing communication? What could be its objectives?
7. Suggest potential solutions for potential gaps in advertising perceptions.
8. "Service organisations may have a limited view of the very wide range of promotional methods available". Discuss.
9. How does promoting services differ from promotion of goods?
10. How can the promotion of services be improved? Are there any guidelines for the same?

EXERCISE / ASSIGNMENTS

1. Prepare the promotional strategies and objectives for the following services:
   (a) Newly opened hospital
   (b) Chinese food joint
   (c) Film festival
   (d) Financial services
   (e) Multi-storeyed housing complex.
2. List the possible innovative sales promotion tools that could be utilized for the following services:
   (a) Garden care
   (b) Laundry
   (c) Theatre bookings
   (d) Community park
   (e) Marriage halls.

8

The Service Process

8.1 INTRODUCTION

Customers of service organization obtain benefits and satisfactions from the services themselves and from how those services are delivered. The way in which service systems operate is crucial. Service systems which operate efficiently and effectively can give marketing management considerable marketing leverage and promotional advantage. It is clear that a smooth running service operation offers competitive advantages, particularly where differentiation between service products may be minimal.

In service systems the marketing implications of operational performance are so important that the two functions have to co-operate. In services, marketing must be just as involved with the operational aspects of performance as operations managers; that is, with the 'how' and the 'process' of service delivery.

Operations management is not just concerned with manufacturing.

Here we define operations as the means by which resource inputs are combined, reformed, transformed or separated to create useful outputs (goods and services). Operations management is concerned with planning, organizing and controlling this resource conversion process which is illustrated in Figure 8.1. The concept of 'useful' is important; for the purpose of the process is to add 'utility' or 'value' over and above the costs incurred in obtaining system inputs and in undertaking the transformation process.

Figure 8.1 : OPERATIONS SYSTEM

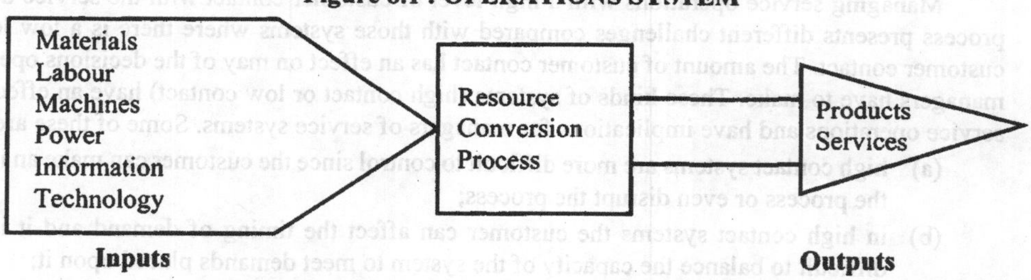

8.2 CLASSIFICATION OF SERVICES OPERATING SYSTEMS

Services operating systems may be classified in a number of ways. Two considered here for illustrative purposes are according to :

(a) the type of process;

(b) the degree of contact.

A. The type of process

Three types of processes of relevance to service organization are :

(a) line operations;

(b) job shop operations

(c) intermittent operations

Line Operations

In a line operation there is an arranged sequence of operations or activities undertaken. The service is produced by following this sequence. In manufacturing, an assembly line for domestic appliances typifies this type of process; in services, a self-service restaurant typifies this process. In the latter people move through a sequence of stages although there is no reason why customers should not remain stationary and receive a sequence of services. The high degree of inter-relationship between different elements of a line operation mean that performance overall is limited by performance at the weakest link in the system and hold-ups can arise (e.g. a slow check-out operator in a self-service cafeteria). Also it tends to be a relatively inflexible type of process although tasks in the process can be specialized and made routine giving more speedy performance. This process is most suitable in service organizations with high volumes of fairly continuous demand for relatively standard kinds of service.

Job Shop Operations

A job shop operation produces a variety of services using different combinations and sequences of activities. The services can be tailored to meet varying customer needs and to provide a bespoke service. Restaurants and professional services are examples of job shop operations. While flexibility is a key advantage of this type of system it may suffer from being more difficult to schedule, from being more difficult to substitute capital for labour in the system and from being more difficult to calculate the capacity of the system.

Intermittent Operations

Intermittent operations refer to service projects which are one off or only infrequently repeated. Examples include the construction of new service facilities, the design of an advertising campaign, the installation of a large computer or the making of a major film. The scale of such projects makes their management a complex task. Such projects provide an appropriate field for the ready transfer of many project control and scheduling techniques like Critical Path Analysis. The scale and infrequency of these projects make them different in kind from line and job shop operations.

B. The Degree of Contact

Managing service operations with a high level of customer contact with the service delivery process presents different challenges compared with those systems where there is a low level of customer contact. The amount of customer contact has an effect on may of the decisions operations managers have to make. These kinds of systems (high contact or low contact) have an effect upon service operations and have implications for managers of service systems. Some of these are:

(a) high contact systems are more difficult to control since the customer can make an input to the process or even disrupt the process;

(b) in high contact systems the customer can affect the timing of demand and it is more difficult to balance the capacity of the system to meet demands placed upon it;

(c) workers in high contact systems can have a great influence upon the customers' view of the service provided;

(d) in high contact systems production scheduling is more difficult;

(e) it may be more difficult to rationalize high contact systems (e.g. by substituting technology);

(f) it may be beneficial to separate high contact and low contact elements of a service system and encourage staff specialization in these different functions because of the varying skills required.

Both of the schemes outlined are useful ways of classifying service systems for operational purposes. Both however imply that the sequence of operations involved in the service process can be made explicit to enable the systems to be categorized according to degree of contact. One step that service managers can take to understand their process of service delivery is to flow chart the system and the interactions with customers within that system.

8.3 POLICIES AND FLOWCHARTING

Flow charting offers a number of advantages including:

(a) Providing a visual representation of the service system. It shows what activities take place and how they relate to each other;

(b) identifying possible bottlenecks in the process and estimating capacity required at each stage;

(c) identifying the steps in which the customers is involved in the process;

(d) identifying information requirements at each stage of the process.

Some of the key questions service managers need to consider in developing policy for service organizations emerge from this kind of analysis. They include:

What steps are involved in the process?

Are they arranged logically?

Can some steps be eliminated or combined?

Are the capacities of each step balanced?

Where are customers involved in the process?

Can unnecessary customer contact be reduced or eliminated?

Can technology be used to speed up the process?

Can some steps in the process be transferred elsewhere?

A fundamental decision in managing a service operation is what level of capacity will be provided. Too much may make the operation uneconomic; too little can cause bottlenecks in service delivery, customer resentment because of inefficiency and lost business. In some systems it is not easy to identify when peak loads will occur or to transfer them when they do (e.g. holiday resorts during a fine spring weekend). In manufacturing systems inventory acts as a buffer between the system and demands placed upon it. Most service systems do not have the luxury of such a buffer 'stock of service'. A constant difficulty then for many service operations is the balancing of supply and demand.

8.4 BALANCING SUPPLY AND DEMAND

Some ways of balancing supply and demand are shown in Table 8.1.

Table 8.1 : ACTIONS TO BALANCE SUPPLY AND DEMAND IN SERVICE SYSTEMS

Supply Side	*Demand Side*
1. Inventory wherever possible (e.g. spare capacity, people, etc.)	1. Have customers wait in favourable environments
2. Schedule workers according to demand (e.g. shift working, part-time employees)	2. Schedule customers (e.g. appointment systems)
3. Subcontract work to other service organizations	3. Provide substitute goods or services (e.g. automatic tellers)
4. Have peak-time efficiency routines (e.g. only do essential jobs)	4. Diversity demands (e.g. enter counter seasonal markets)
5. Increase customer participation in the production process (e.g. self-service)	5. Turn customers away during peak demand period (e.g. differential pricing)
6. Share services/facilities with other service organizations	6. Use marketing to shift demand (e.g. advertising campaigns)
7. Improve the service system (e.g. use technology where possible)	7. Change customer expectations of service (e.g. through usage)

8.5 CHANGE

Seven steps to help achieve the successful implementation of operations management changes are given below

(a) Develop customer trust

The willingness of customers to accept change may be a functions the organization's perceived trustworthiness.

(b) Understand customer habits

This will assist in successful presentation of the rationale for any changes.

(c) Pretest new procedures and equipment

Get an assessment of customer understanding and their reactions through field tests.

(d) Understand the determinants of consumer behaviour

Understand why customers behave the way that they do.

(e) Teach consumers how to use service innovations

Customers may be resistant to change particularly mechanization, and may need training and reassurance.

(f) Promote the benefits and stimulate trial

Acceptance is frequently a function of perceived customer benefits.

If these are not apparent it is important that they should be promoted.

(g) Monitor and evaluate performance

An integral part of service system change is continuing monitoring, evaluation and modification.

8.6 ORGANIZATIONAL CONFLICT IN SERVICE SYSTEMS

Four general sources of inter-functional conflict between marketing and operations when a service firm is introducing a service innovation are:

(a) **Different motivations for change**

Different functions may have varying motives for change (e.g. operations may be excited by a technical development, marketing by the possibility of increasing market share).

(b) **Revenue versus cost orientation**

Operations managers tend to be concerned with efficiency and cost reduction, marketing mangers with opportunities for increasing sales and revenue.

(c) **Different time horizons**

Marketing may adopt a short-term orientation focusing on current concerns, operations a longer-term orientation to bring in new technology and operating procedures.

(d) **Perceived fit of the new service with existing operations**

A new service product introduced by marketing may be incompatible and not fit existing operating systems.

Some ways in which service organizations try to overcome inter-functional conflict include:

(a) **Inter-functional transfers**

Moving staff between different functions by job rotation.

(b) **Task forces**

Task forces may be formed to integrate functional viewpoints and resolve inter-functional conflicts.

(c) **New tasks and new people**

Redirecting existing staff and bringing in people from other parts of the business or from outside.

(d) **Developing a marketing orientation at the field level.**

Field level managers can be encouraged to be more consumer-oriented by:

1 **Decentralizing revenue responsibility**
Cost-based evaluations can be transformed into revenue-based evaluations.

2 **Internal marketing**
Winning co-operation and acceptance of service innovations requires internal marketing as well as external marketing.

3 **Control by procedures manuals**
Consumer-orientated procedures and controls can be developed and laid down in procedures manuals.

8.7 THE SYSTEMS CONCEPT IN SERVICES

The systems concept is widely used in operations management to model the fundamental nature of the conversion process in manufacturing (i.e. there is a logical sequence with inputs of raw materials passing through a conversion process in which technologies are applied, value is added and finished goods are produced). However applying this model is more difficult in some service systems because distinctions between inputs, conversions and outputs is less clear. For example, the transactional nature of many services may mean that certain steps are missed out or repeated. Also 'unintended conversions' may take place (e.g. a client may decide to run his own training programme after talking to a business school). Part of the problem is that it may not be as easy to seal off the technical core of a service system as in a manufacturing system, because tasks to be undertaken and workflow may be more uncertain. While some service systems may try to develop less open-ended systems through careful customer selection and socialization and through routinizing the conversion process; there is a danger that customer satisfaction may decrease as the service process moves towards a more closed system of operation. The system concept has already been explained in detail in chapter one (Section 1.6)

8.8 PURCHASE PROCESS

The purchase process for services comprising three stages, namely, Pre-purchase stage, Service encounter stage, and post-purchase stage is outlined by means of a flowchart in Figure 8.2

8.9 PROCESS OF VISION

High-performance service companies have gained their status in large measure by turning the strategic service vision inward: by targeting important groups of employees as well as customers. In the head offices of these organizations, questions such as those listed in Table 8.2 are heard often. In asking them, management shows it's aware that the health of the enterprise depends on the degree to which core groups of employees subscribe to and share a common set of values and are served by the company's activities.

The basic elements start with the service concept designed with employees' needs in mind. The operating strategy is to meet these needs in a superior fashion at the lowest cost, a result often achieved through the design of the service delivery system. The integrative elements include positioning of a service concept, which it is hoped will lead to low labour turnover, low training costs, and the opportunity to develop shared goals and values.

Table 8.2 summarises the externally oriented strategic service vision while Table 8.3 summarises the internally oriented strategic service vision.

Figure 8.2 : THE PURCHASE PROCESS FOR SERVICES

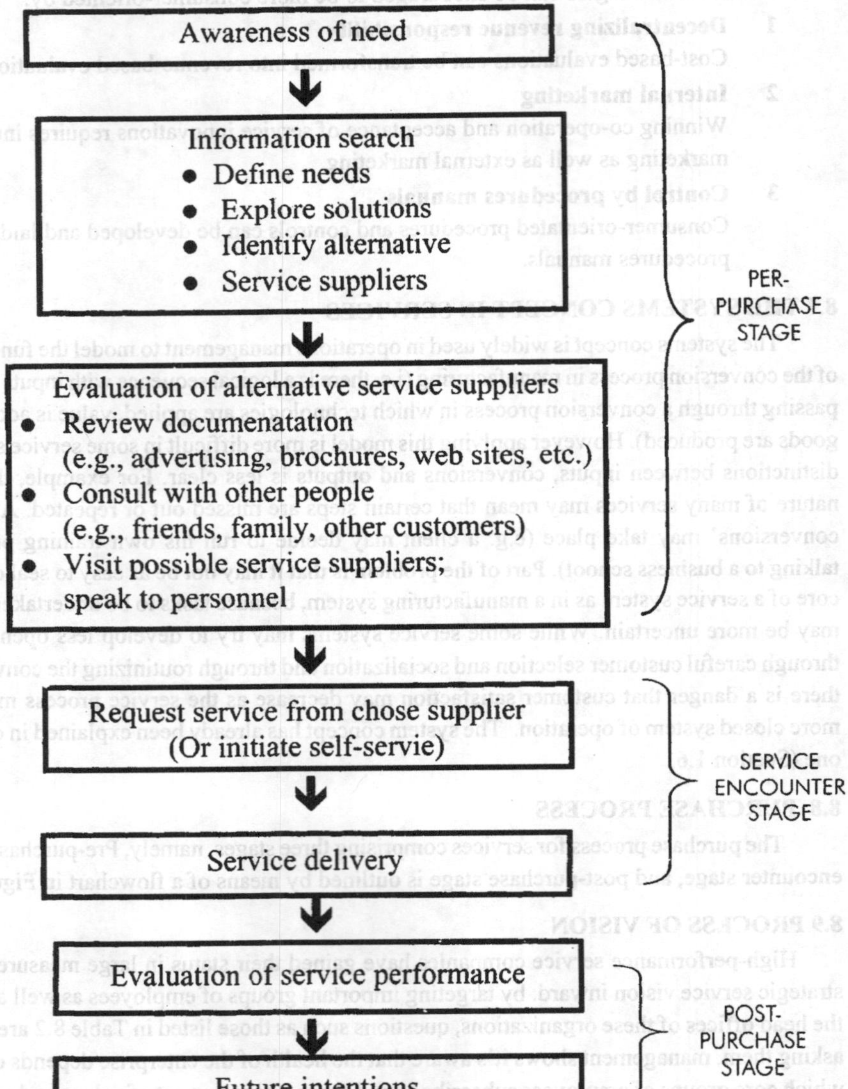

8.10 FACILITATING PROCESS

The facilitator firm is defined by its ability to acquire market information and expertise (which are not the same), and to bring these to bear in matching the needs of buyers and sellers in order to complete a transaction. To review the management tasks this imposes on the firm, a conceptual model is shown in Figure 8.3.

Figure 8.3 : THE FACILITATING PROCESS

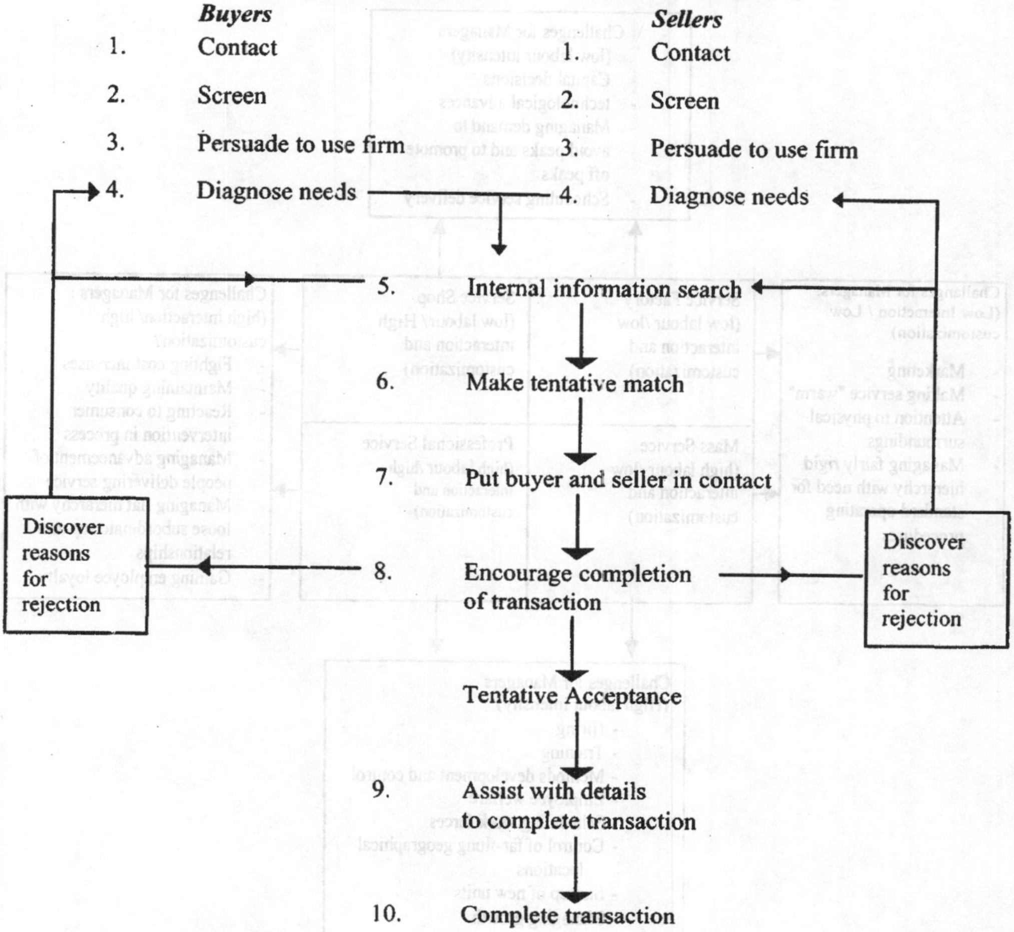

8.11 CHALLENGES FOR SERVICE MANAGERS

Different managerial challenges (Figure 8.4) surface when we consider the distinctions made between high and low levels of consumer interaction and customisation. When the degree of interaction and customisation is low (e.g. airlines, retail stores, commercial banks), the service business faces a stiff marketing challenge. Such a business firm must try to make the service it provides warm, even though it does not give all the personal attention that a customer might want. This means that attention to physical surroundings becomes important. In addition, with a low degree of interaction and with little customisation, standard operating procedures can be instituted safely. In this type of service, the hierarchy of the operation itself tends to be the classic pyramid with a broad base of workers and many layers of management. Furthermore, the relationships between levels in the pyramid tend to be fairly rigid.

Figure 8.4 : CHALLENGES FOR SERVICE MANAGERS

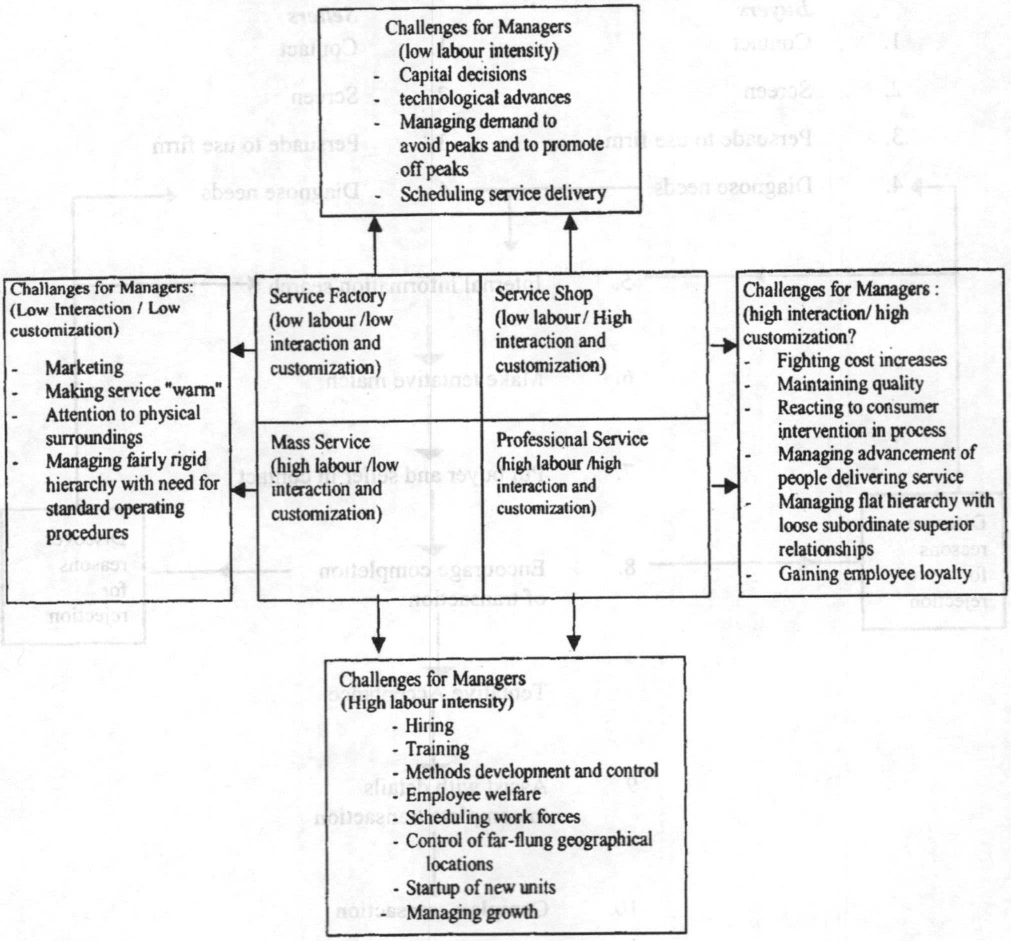

As the service takes on a higher degree of interaction and customisation (e.g. professional associations, hospitals, repair services), management must deal with higher costs and more talented labour. Managing costs effectively - either by keeping them down or by passing them on to customers - becomes a significant challenge. Maintaining quality and responding to consumer intervention are also important. In addition, talented employees demand attention and expect advancement in the organisation. In effect, what this all means for many service businesses with high interaction and customisation is that the hierarchy of control tends to be flat unlike the classic pyramid.

As Figure 8.4 demonstrates, the high versus low differentiation made for labour intensity and the degree of consumer interaction and customisation yield distinct combinations of management challenges for four service types.

The operational and marketing perspectives on operational issues are presented in Table 8.4. For each operational issue, the typical operations goals and the common marketing concerns is shown.

Table 8. 2 : EXTERNALLY ORIENTED STRATEGIC SERVICE VISION

Target market segments	Positioning	Service Concept	Value-cost leveraging	Operating strategy	Strategy-systems integration	Service delivery system
What are common characteristics of important market segments? What dimensions can be used to segment the market? Demo-graphic? Psycho-graphic? How important are various segments? What needs does each have? How well are these needs being served? In what manner? By whom?	How does the service concept propose to meet customer needs? How do competitors meet these needs? How is the proposed service differentiated from competition? How important are these differences? What is good service? Does the proposed service concept provide it? What efforts are required to bring customer expectations and service capabilities into alignment?	What are important elements of the service to be provided, stated in terms of results produced for customers? How are these elements supposed to be perceived by the target market segmen? By the market in general? By employees as a whole? How do cutomers perceive the service concept? What efforts does this suggest in terms of the manner in which the service is: Designed? Delivered? Marketed?	To what extent are differences between perceived value and cost of service maximized by: Standardization of certain elements? Customization of certain elements? Emphasizing easily leveraged services? Management of supply and demand? Control of quality through Rewards? Appeal to pride? Visibility and supervision? Peer group control? Involving the customer? Effective use of data?	What are important elements of the strategy? Operations? Financing? Marketing? Organization? Human resources? Control? On which will the most effort be concentrated? Where will investments be made? How will quality and cost be controlled? Measured? Incentives? Rewards? What results will be expected versus competition in terms of : Quality of service? Cost profile? Productivity? Morale and loyalty of servers?	To what extent are the strategy and delivery system internally consistent? Can needs of the strategy be met by the delivery system? It not, what changes must be made in The operating strategy? The service delivery system? To what extent does the coordination of operating strategy and service delivery system ensure: High quality? High productivity? Low cost? High morale and loyalty of servers?	What are Important features of the service delivery system, including: The role of people? Technology? Equipment? Layout? Procedures? What capacity does it provide? Normally? At peak levels? To what extent does it: Help ensure quality standards? Differentiate the service from competition? Provide barriers to entry by competitors?

☐ Basic elements ☐ Integrative element

Table 8. 3 : INTERNALLY ORIENTED STRATEGIC SERVICE VISION

Target employee Segments	Positioning	Service Concept	Value-cost leveraging	Operating strategy	Strategy-systems integration	Service delivery system
What are common characteristics of important employee groups?	How does the service concept propose to meet employee needs?	What are important elements of the service to be provided, stated in terms of results produced for employees and the company?	To what extent are differences between returns to employees and the level of effort they put forth maximised by: The design of service concept? The design of the elements of the operating strategy? Job design? The leveraging of scarce skills with a support system? The management of supply and demand?	How important is direct human contact in the provision of the service?	To what extent are the strategy and delivery system for serving important employee groups internally consistent?	What are Important features of the service delivery system, including; The role of people? Technology? Equipment? Layout? Procedures?
What dimensions can be used to describe these employee groups? Demo-graphic? Psycho-graphic?	How do competitors meet such needs?	How are these elements supposed to be perceived by the targeted employee group?	Control of quality through Rewards? Appeal to pride? Visibility? Supervision? Peer group control?	To what extent have employees been involved in the design of the service concept and operating strategy?	To what extent does the intergration of operating strategy and services delivery system ensure: High quality? High productivity? Low cost? High morale and "bond-ing" of the target employee group?	What does it require of target employee groups? Normally? At peak periods of activity?
How important are each of these groups to the delivery of the services?	How are relationships with employees differentiated from those between compertitors and their employees?	How are these elements perceived?		How desirable is it to: Increase employee satisfaction? Increase employee productivity?		To what extent does it help employ-ees: Meet quality standards? Differentiate their service from competitors? Achieve expectations about the quality of their work life?
What needs does each group have?	How important are these differences?	What further efforts does this suggest in terms of the manner in which the service is: Designed? Delivered?		What incentives are provided for : Quality? Productivity? Cost?		
How well are these needs being served?	What is "good service" to employees?			How does the strategy address employee needs for: Selection? Assignment? Develop-ment?		
	Does the proposed service concept provide it?					
	What efforts are required to bring employee expectations and service capabilities into align-ment?					

Basic elements   Integrative element

Table 8.4 : OPERATIONS AND MARKETING PERSPECTIVES ON OPERATIONAL ISSUES

Operational	*Typical Operations Goals*	*Common Marketing Concerns*
Productivity improvement	Reduce unit cost of production	Strategies may cause decline in service quality
Make-versus buy decisions	Trade off control against comparative advantage and cost savings	"Make" decisions may result in lower quality and lack of market coverage; "buy" decisions may transfer control to unresponsive suppliers and hurt the firms' image
Facilities location	Reduce costs; provide convenient access for suppliers and employees	Customers may find location unattractive and inaccessible
Standardization	Keep costs low and quality consistent; simplify opera tions tasks; recruit low-cost employees	Consumers may seek variety, prefer customization to match segmented needs
Batch versus unit processing	Seek economies of scale, consistency, efficient use of capacity	Customers may be forced to wait, feel "one of a crowd," be turned off by other customers
Facilities layout and	Control costs; improve design efficiency by ensuring proximity of operationally related tasks, enhance safety and security	Customers may be confused, shunted around unnecessarily find facility unattractive and inconvenient.
Job design	Minimize error, waste, and fraud; make efficient use of technology, simplify tasks for standardization	Operationally oriented employees with narrow roles may be unrespon sive to customer needs
Learning curves	Apply experience to reduce time and costs per unit of output	Faster service is not necessarily better service; cost saving may not be passed on as lower prices
Management of capacity	Keep costs down by avoiding wasteful underutilization	Service may be unavailable when needed; quality may be of resources be compromised during high-demand periods
Quality control	Ensure that service execution conforms to predefined standards	Operational definitions of quality may not reflect customer needs, preferences.
Management of queues	Optimize use of available capacity by planning for average throughput; maintain customer order, discipline	Customers may be bored and frustrated during wait, see firm as unresponsive

8.12 BREAKTHROUGH SERVICES

The Tables in Appendix, namely Table A.1 to Table A.13, deal with the processes of creating breakthrough services, developing a vision of the service business, building customer loyalty, focussing and positioning a service, determining the true cost of poor quality, developing devices for achieving total customer satisfaction, managing for quality and productivity gains, managing demand and supply, management of networks, managing information technology, mobilising people, organising work and envisioning future breakthroughs.

8.13 PROCESS IMPROVEMENT

Improving a process involves various elements like leaders, team memberships, time commitment, charters, resources, risks and drivers. The examples for such elements is shown in Table 8.5. Also, these examples have been contrasted with the corresponding concepts of re-engineering.

Table 8.5 : PROCESS IMPROVEMENT VERSUS RE-ENGINEERING

	Process Improvement	*Re-engineering*
Leader	Senior executive or manager working part-time	Full-time senior executive with authority and experience
Team Membership	Cross-functional, cross-level Management, workers,	Cross-functional, cross-level Management, workers, customers, customers, suppliers suppliers
Time Commitment	2 - 4 hrs per week	Full time
Charter	make incremental impro vements to the process	Redesign the process to provide new outputs and / or meet new performance requirements
Duration	Forever	Until new process is up and running successfully
Resources	No additional resources Minimal funds allocated as needed	Potential high investment Precommitted budget
Disruption	Low and gradual	Potentially high
Risk	Low	High
Driver	Customer	Critical need for new function and / or performance
Key Words	Improve	Replace

8.14 THE SELF-REINFORCING SERVICE CYCLE

The various concepts described in the previous sections of this chapter can be summarised by means of a system as shown in Figure 8.5.

One portion of the figure deals with the customer while the other deals with the service provided. If there is greater conformance with expertations, the value of the service will increase. This would inturn lead to increased volume which would lead to lowering of cost of service. As a consequence, there would be increased margen and scope for greater investment. Investments in the various functional areas of management would result in higher server satisfaction and improved results.

These sub-processes are inter-linked to form a self - reinforcing service cycle.

Figure 8.5 : THE SELF-REINFORCING SERVICE CYCLE

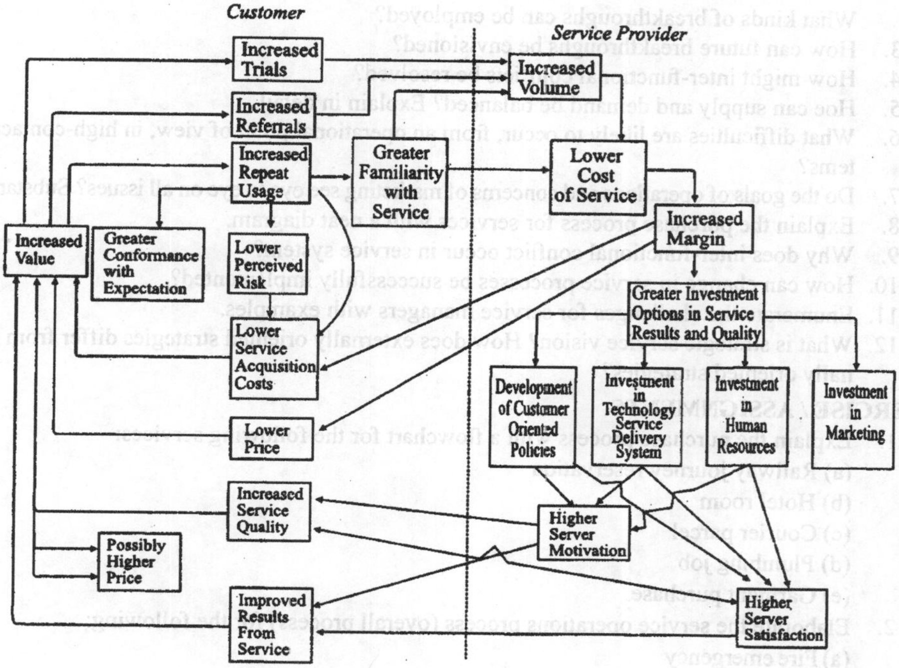

SHORT A NSWER QUESTIONS

1. Describe two ways in which service systems may be classified.
2. What are the types of processes relevant to service organisations?
3. What are the benefits of flowcharting in a service system?
4. How do people influence service processes?
5. What are 'breakthrough' services? How can they be created?
6. How are networks managed in services?
7. "Service systems are more open than closed". Discuss.
8. Explain a service operations system with diagram.
9. "Information technology needs a different type of handling as far as services are concerned". Comment.
10. How are costs of service processes ascertained?
11. How does process improvement differ from re-engineering?
12. Do service processes need a vision? Why? What are the related issues?
13. Do processes in service operations differ from manufacturing processes?
14. How do service processes 'position' the marketing the mix elements?
15. What role does quality play in services? How are gains in productivity ensured?
16. How can personal development and empowerment of people be achieved in services?
17. What are the steps in the facilitating process?

ESSAY QUESTIONS

1. Why should marketing be involved in operational aspects of service system performance?
2. "The ultimate aim of service processes are to enable customer satisfaction and delight". What kinds of breakthroughs can be employed?
3. How can future breakthroughs be envisioned?
4. How might inter-functional conflicts be resolved?
5. Hoe can supply and demand be balanced? Explain in detail.
6. What difficulties are likely to occur, from an operational point of view, in high-contact systems?
7. Do the goals of operations and concerns of marketing see eye to eye on all issues? Substantiate.
8. Explain the purchase process for services with a neat diagram.
9. Why does inter-functional conflict occur in service system?
10. How can change in service processes be successfully implemented?
11. Enumerate the challenges for service managers with examples.
12. What is strategic service vision? How does externally oriented strategies differ from internally oriented strategies?

EXERCISE / ASSIGNMENTS

1. Explain the purchase process with a flowchart for the following services:
   (a) Railway journey reservation
   (b) Hotel room
   (c) Courier parcel
   (d) Plumbing job
   (e) Garment purchase.
2. Elaborate the service operations process (overall process) for the following:
   (a) Fire emergency
   (b) Drinking water supply
   (c) Town planning
   (d) Power restoration
   (e) Legal opinion.

●●●

9

Physical Evidence

9.1 ELEMENTS

Services being intangible, customers often rely on tangible cues, or physical evidence, to evaluate the service before its purchase and to assess their satisfaction with the service during and after consumption.

General elements of physical evidence are shown in Table 9.1. They include all aspects of the organization's physical facility (the servicescape) as well as other forms of tangible communication. Elements of the servicescape that affect customers include both exterior attributes (such as parking, landscape) and interior attributes (such as design, layout, equipment, decor). Physical evidence examples from different service contexts are given in Table 9.2. It is apparent that some services communicate heavily through physical evidence (e.g. hospitals, resorts, child care), while others provide limited physical evidence (e.g. insurance, express mail).

Table 9.1 : ELEMENTS OF PHYSICAL EVIDENCE

Servicescape	***Other tangibles***
Facility exterior	Business cards
Exterior Design	Stationery
Signage	Billing statements
Parking	Reports
Landscape	Employee dress
Surrounding environment	Uniforms, Brochures
Facility Interior	
Interior design	
Equipment	
Signage	
Layout	
Air quality/temperature	

Table 9.2 : EXAMPLES OF PHYSICAL EVIDENCE FROM THE CUSTOMERS POINT OF VIEW

Service	***Physical Evidence***	
	Servicescape	***Other Tangibles***
Insurance	Not applicable	Policy itself Billing statements Periodic updates Company Brochure

Hospitals	Building exterior Parking Signs Waiting areas Admissions office Patient care room Medical equipment Recovery room	Letters/Cards Uniforms Reports/stationery Billing statements
Airline	Airline gate area Airplane exterior Airplane interior (decor, seats, air quality)	Tickets Food Uniforms
Express mail	Not applicable	Packaging Trucks Uniforms Computers
Child Care Centre	Building exterior Parking Signs and layout Hallways, rooms Equipment Decor, air quality	Brochures Billing statements Food

9.2 ROLE OF SERVICE EVIDENCE

A distinction is made in services marketing between two kinds of physical evidence :

(a) Peripheral evidence;

(b) Essential evidence.

Peripheral Evidence

Peripheral evidence is actually possessed as part of the purchase of a service. It has however little or no independent value. Thus a bank chequebook is of no value unless backed by the funds transfer and storage service it represents. An admission ticket for a cinema equally has no independent value. It merely confirms the service. It is not a surrogate for it. Peripheral evidence 'adds to' the value of essential evidence only as far as the customer values these symbols of service. The hotel rooms of many large international hotel groups contain much peripheral evidence like directories, town guides, pens, notepads, welcome gifts, drink packs, soaps and so on. These representations of service must be designed and developed with customer needs in mind. They often provide an important set of complementary items to the essential core service sought by customers.

Essential Evidence

Essential evidence, unlike peripheral evidence, cannot be possessed by the customer. Nevertheless essential evidence may be so important in its influence on service purchase it may be considered as an element in its own right. The overall appearance and layout of a hotel; the 'feel' of a bank branch; the type of vehicle rented by a car rental company; the type of aircraft used by a carrier are all examples of physical evidence.

Managing the Evidence

Service organizations with competing service products may use physical evidence to differentiate their service products in the marketplace and give their service products a competitive advantage. A physical product like a car or a camera can be augmented through the use of both tangible and intangible elements. A car can be given additional tangible features like a sliding roof or stereophonic radio equipment; a camera can be given additional tangible features like control devices which enable use in a wide variety of light conditions. A car may be sold with a long life anti-rust warranty or cost-free service for the first year of ownership; a camera with a long-life warranty or free lens insurance. Tangible and intangible elements may be used to augment the essential product offer. In fact organizations marketing tangible dominant products frequently use intangible, abstract elements as part of their communications strategy.

Service marketing organizations also try to use tangible clues to strengthen the meaning of their intangible products.

Make the Service more Tangible

The bank credit card is an example of the tangible representation of the service, 'credit'. The use of a credit card means :

(a) The service can be separated from the seller;

(b) intermediaries can be used in distribution thereby expanding the geographic area in which the service marketer can operate ;

(c) the service product of one bank can be differentiated from the service product of another bank (e.g. through colour, graphics and brand names like Visa).

(d) the card acts as a symbol of status as well as providing a line of credit.

Make the Service Easier to Grasp Mentally

There are two ways in which a service can be made easier to grasp mentally.

(a) Associate the service with a tangible object which is more easily perceived by the customer.

This approach may be used in advertising messages where the intangible nature of service is transferred into tangible objects representing that service. These may have more significance and meaning for customers. It is easier for the customer to grasp what their service means compared with competitors. With this approach it is obviously vital to :

(a) use tangible objects that are considered important by the customer and which are sought as part of the service. Using objects that customers do not value may be counter-productive.

(b) ensure that the 'promise' implied by these tangible objects in fact is delivered when the service is used. That is, the quality of the goods must live up to the reputation implied by the promise.

If these conditions are not met then incorrect, meaningless and damaging associations can be created.

(b) Focus on the Buyer-seller Relationship

This approach focuses on the relationship between the buyer and the seller. The customer is encouraged to identify with a person or group of people in the service organization instead of the intangible services themselves. Advertising agencies use account executives; market research agencies assemble client teams; the Bank uses 'personal' bankers. All encourage a focus on people performing services rather than upon the services themselves.

However before a service organisation can translate intangibles into more concrete clues it must ensure that it :

(a) knows precisely its target audience and the effect being sought by the use of such devices.

(b) has defined the unique selling points which should be incorporated into the service and which meet the needs of the target market.

9.3 ROLES OF THE SERVICESCAPE

The servicescape can play many roles simultaneously. An examination of the variety of roles and how they interact makes clear how strategically important it is to provide appropriate physical evidence of the service.

Package

Similar to a tangible product's package, the servicescape and other elements of physical evidence essentially "wrap" the service and convey an external image of what is "inside" to consumers. The servicescape is the outward appearance of the organization and thus can be critical in forming initial impressions or setting up customer expectations - it is a visual metaphor for the intangible service. This packaging role is particularly important in creating expectations for new customers and for newly established service organizations that are trying to build a particular image. The physical surroundings offer an organization the opportunity to convey an image in a way not unlike the way an individual chooses to "dress for success".

Facilitator

The servicescape can also serve as a ***facilitator*** in aiding the performances of persons in the environment. How the setting is designed can enhance or inhibit the efficient flow of activities in the service setting, making it easier or harder for customers and employees to accomplish their goals. A well-designed, functional facility can make the service a pleasure to experience from the customer's point of view and a pleasure to perform from the employee's. On the other hand, poor and inefficient design may frustrate both customers and employees.

Socializer

The design of the servicescape aids in the socialization of both employees and customers in the sense that it helps to convey expected roles, behaviours, and relationships. For example, a new employee in a professional services firm would come to understand her position in the hierarchy partially through noting her office assignment, the quality of her office furnishings, and her location relative to others in the organization. The design of the facility can also suggest to customers what their role is relative to employees, what parts of the servicescape they are welcome in and which are for employees only, how they should behave while in the environment, and what types of interactions are encouraged.

Differentiator

The design of the physical facility can differentiate a firm from its competitors and signal the market segment the service is intended for. Given its power as a differentiator, changes in the physical environment can be used to reposition a firm and/or to attract new market segments. In shopping malls the colours used in decor and displays and type of music wafting from a store signal the intended market segment. The design of a physical setting can also differentiate one area of a service organization from another. This is commonly the case in the hotel industry where one large hotel may have several levels of dining possibilities, each signed by differences in design.

While it is useful from a strategic point of view to think about the multiple roles of the servicescape and how they interact, making actual decisions about servicescape design requires an understanding of why the effects occur and how to manage them.

Figure 9.1 represents a comprehensive stimulus-organism - response model that recognizes complex dimensions of the environment, impacts on multiple parties (customers, employees, and their interactions), multiple types of internal responses (cognitive, emotional and physiological), and a variety of individual and social behaviours that can result.

9.4 BEHAVIOURS IN THE SERVICESCAPE

Individual Behaviors

Environmental psychologists suggest that individuals react to places with two general, and opposite, forms of behavior: approach and avoidance. Approach behaviours include all positive behaviours that might be directed at a particular place, such as desire to stay, explore, work, and affiliate. Avoidance behaviors reflect the opposite-a desire not to stay, to explore, to work, or to affiliate.

In addition to attracting or deterring entry, the servicescape can actually influence the degree of success consumers and employees experience in executing their plans once inside. Each individual comes to a particular service organization with a goal or purpose that may be aided or hindered by the setting.

Figure 9.1 : A FRAMEWORK FOR UNDERSTANDING ENVIRONMENT-USER RELATIONSHIPS IN SERVICE ORGANISATIONS

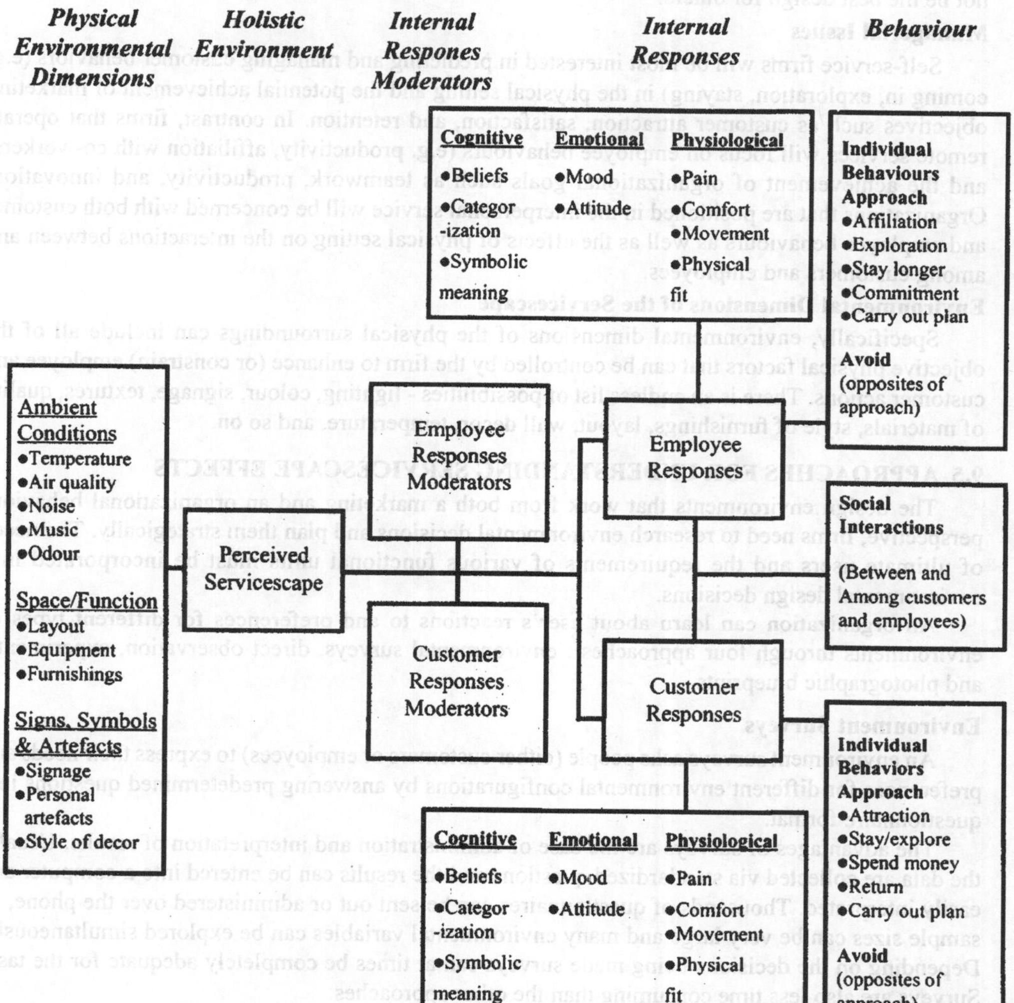

Clearly firms will want to encourage approach behaviours and the ability of customers and employees to carry out their plans and at the same time discourage avoidance behaviors.

Social Interactions

In addition to its effects on their individual behaviours, the servicescape influences the nature and quality of customer and employee interactions, most directly in interpersonal services. In many service situations, a firm may want to ensure a particular progression of events (a "standard script") and limit the duration of the service. Environmental variables such as physical proximity, seating

arrangements, size, and flexibility can define the possibilities and limits of social episodes such as those occurring between customers and employees, or customers and other customers.

Behaviours such as small-group interaction, friendship formation, participation, aggression, withdrawal and helping have all been shown to be influenced by environmental conditions.

One of the challenges in designing environments to enhance individual approach behaviours and encourage the appropriate social interactions is that the best design for one person or group may not be the best design for others.

Managerial Issues

Self-service firms will be most interested in predicting and managing customer behaviors (e.g. coming in, exploration, staying) in the physical setting and the potential achievement of marketing objectives such as customer attraction, satisfaction, and retention. In contrast, firms that operate remote services will focus on employee behaviours (e.g. productivity, affiliation with co-workers) and the achievement of organizational goals such as teamwork, productivity, and innovation. Organizations that are positioned in the interpersonal service will be concerned with both customer and employee behaviours as well as the effects of physical setting on the interactions between and among customers and employees.

Environmental Dimensions of the Servicescape

Specifically, environmental dimensions of the physical surroundings can include all of the objective physical factors that can be controlled by the firm to enhance (or constrain) employee and customer actions. There is an endless list of possibilities - lighting, colour, signage, textures, quality of materials, style of furnishings, layout, wall decor, temperature, and so on.

9.5 APPROACHES FOR UNDERSTANDING SERVICESCAPE EFFECTS

The design environments that work from both a marketing and an organizational behaviour perspective, firms need to research environmental decisions and plan them strategically. The needs of ultimate users and the requirements of various functional units must be incorporated into environmental design decisions.

An organization can learn about user's reactions to and preferences for different types of environments through four approaches : environmental surveys, direct observation, experiments, and photographic blueprints.

Environment Surveys

An environment surveys asks people (either customers or employees) to express their needs and preferences for different environmental configurations by answering predetermined questions in a questionnaire format.

The advantages of surveys are the ease of administration and interpretation of results. Usually the data are collected via standardized questions and the results can be entered into a computer and easily interpreted. Thousands of questionnaires can be sent out or administered over the phone, so sample sizes can be very large and many environmental variables can be explored simultaneously. Depending on the decisions being made surveys can at times be completely adequate for the task. Surveys are also less time consuming than the other approaches.

The primary disadvantage of an environmental survey is that sometimes the results may be less valid than results from other methods - that is, the answers to the survey questions may not truly reflect how people feel or how they will behave. This can occur when the dimensions of the servicescape affect people subconsciously or through complex interrelationships of dimensions, and people cannot accurately express these effects through paper and pencil surveys.

Direct Observation

Using observation methods, trained observers make detailed accounts of environmental conditions and dimensions, and observing and recording the reactions and behaviours of customers and employees in the servicescape.

The advantages of direct observation, when done by highly trained and skilled observers, are the depth of information acquired and its accuracy. The inter-relationship of elements of the environment and the reactions and interactions of participants in the environment can be unobtrusively recorded, increasing the validity of the findings beyond what is typically found in a standardized survey.

Direct observation can also be useful when there is a very specific servicescape question that needs answering.

The disadvantages of direct observation are primarily related to time and costs. First, the researchers who observe the servicescape must be highly trained and skilled in ethnographic methods, which makes data collection expensive. Second, they must be allowed to observe for some period of time, and the interpretation of their detailed records can be very labour intensive. Unlike the survey method, the data cannot as a rule be entered into a computer and analyzed with nice, clean quantitative results.

Experiments

Experimental methods are one of the best ways to assess specific customer and employee reactions to environmental changes or alternatives when it is important to know their true reactions and preferences. Experiments involve exposing groups of customers to different environmental configurations and measuring their reactions.

The advantages of experiments lie primarily in the validity of the results; that is, if the experiment is carefully done, you can believe and rely on the results. Because environmental dimensions often affect people subconsciously and the multitude of dimensions interact to form a composite impression, it is difficult to get accurate responses to questions about the environment in the absence of actual experience. By controlling the environmental conditions experimentally and then measuring consumers' responses, there is a certainty that the environment and not something else actually was the cause of the internal response or the behaviour. Further, different dimensions can be varied systematically to assess the independent impact of factors such as music, colour, layout. The interactions among the dimensions can also be assessed systematically. Experiments also overcome the disadvantage of surveys in which people respond to questions in one way but actually behave differently in the real situation.

As with direct observation methods, the disadvantages of experiments relate primarily to costs and time.

Photographic Blueprints

A photographic blueprint essentially provides a visualization of the service at each customer action step. The visual can be a slide, a photograph, or the entire service process as videotaped from the customer's point of view. By combining a service blueprint with photos, managers and other service employees can see the evidence of service from the customer's point of view. The photographic blueprint can provide a powerful analytic tool to begin assessing the service process.

Photographic blueprints are extremely useful in providing clear and logical documentation of the physical evidence as it currently exists in a given service situation. Before changes can be made, the current state of physical evidence should be made apparent to all concerned. The photos and/or videotapes give more depth to the process blueprint and the blueprint forces a certain logic on the analysis of the physical evidence. The photographic blueprint can give a vivid picture of how things are. The main disadvantage of a photographic blueprint is that it is just a starting point. In and of itself it doesn't answer any questions, but many questions can be asked of it. In and of itself it doesn't give clues as to customer and employee preferences and needs; it could, however, be used as a catalyst for gathering customer and employee opinions.

Ilumination

Natural light is usually the most comfortable source of light. Strip lighting, particularly when it flickers, can cause actual discomfort for some people, whether customers or employees. In some cases it can even cause migraines. Unfortunately, the amount of natural light varies with the time of day and weather conditions. Glare from sunlight on screens can also cause problems.

Table 9.3 : EXAMPLES OF SUITABLE LIGHTING LEVELS IN WORKROOMS

Type of Work	*Examples*	*Recommended lighting (lx)*
General	Storeroom	80-170
Moderately precise	Packing : despatch; works laboratory; simple assembly winding thick wire onto spools; work on carpenter's bench; turning; boring; milling; locksmith's work	200-250 250-300
Fine work	Reading; writing; book-keeping; laboratory technician; assembly of fine equipment; winding fine wire; woodworking by machine; fine work on tool-making jig	500-700
Very fine to precision work	Technical drawing; colour proofing; adjusting and testing electrical equipment; assembling delicate electronics; watchmaking; invisible mending	1000-2000

On a functional level, different illumination levels are needed to perform tasks, depending on the level of detailed attention required. An example of inappropriate lighting is the lighting in the suite facilities of many hotels. Good light is needed for putting make-up on or shaving, and yet frequently the lighting provided is very poor. The actual measure of light now in use is the lux (lx) which is equal to 1 lumen (lm) per square meter, the lumen being a unit of luminous flux. Light used to be measured in footcandles, where 1 footcandle is approximately equal to 10 lux. Table 9.3 gives an indication of the different levels of illumination needed to perform various tasks.

Lighting can also contribute to the creation of atmosphere. Low levels of lighting are associated with romantic settings. Strobe lighting is often used in nightclubs to excite and arouse. Well-lit passages will feel safer than those which are poorly lit. Light bulbs which have failed and not been replaced create an ill-kept, inefficient image.

Colour

Colour and illumination are often used in conjunction. A colour at different levels of illumination may look quite different. The effect of neighbouring colours also changes the impact of a colour : some clash and have a disturbing or arousing effect; others complement and have a more soothing or calming effect. Greens and blues are 'cool' colours, often used for quiet or rest areas. 'Warm' colours are reds, oranges and yellows. Some examples of the use of colours are presented here.

Purple : Regarded as disturbing and psychologically 'difficult'. In a Swedish study it was the most disliked colour in terms of environmental settings.

Red: The colour of fire and passion, suggesting activity, energy, joy. It is used by interior designers to increase comfort levels in unheated spaces and is also regarded (along with pink) as good for restaurants, especially the fast-food variety. One study showed that red-stimulated diners tend to eat more quickly and move on for the next person.

Orange : Although researchers have claimed that an orange environment improves social behaviour, cheers the spirit and lessens hostility and irritability, it is seldom used by professional designers.

Yellow: Conflicting evidence here which on the one hand suggests its ideal stimulative effect where concentration is required. However, if it is used too strongly, those in its environment are likely to get 'stressed up'.

Green: Symbolizes the natural world and is widely believed to be a calming hue. Ideal for areas where relaxation is required and along with blue is found to enhance our appetite; thus good for dining areas.

Blue: Symbolizes authority and implies truth, prudence and wisdom - ideal for banks and building societies. It is considered as having a calming effect which makes it ideally suited for hospital cardiac units.

Temperature and Humidity

Temperature and humidity affect the comfort of customers. This can be difficult to control in situations where the number of customers in the system fluctuates. For example, a crowded train or theatre may become unbearably hot because there are so many customers in the system. The converse of this is the lecture theatre where the air-conditioning is fine when the theatre is full of students, but when half-empty leaves students huddling in their coats. The negative impact on perceptions of the service can be quite severe.

The level of activity undertaken during the service will also be relevant: the higher the level of exercise, the lower will be the requirement for heat. Table 9.4 gives recommended room temperatures for various activities in a work context and Table 9.5 examines the effect on work of deviations from a comfortable working temperature.

Table 9.4 : RECOMMENDED ROOM TEMPERATURES FOR VARIOUS ACTIVITIES

Type of Work	*Room temperature (°C)*
Sedentary mental	21
Sedentary light manual	19
Standing light manual	18
Standing heavy manual	17
Severe work	15-16

Table 9.5 : EFFECTS OF DEVIATIONS FROM A COMFORTABLE WORKING TEMPERATURE

20°C	Comfortable Temperature	Maximum efficiency
↓	* Discomfort :	Mental Problems
	Increased Irritability ; loss of concentration; loss of efficiency in mental tasks	
	* Increase of errors : loss of efficiency in skilled tasks; more accidents	Psycho-physiological problems
	* Loss of performance of heavy work; disturbed water and salt balances; heavy stresses on heart and circulation; intense fatigue and threat of exhaustion	Physiological problems
35-40°C	Limit of tolerance of high temperature	

Noise

Background noise often interferes with concentration and can make learning difficult. The unit of measurement of sound is the decibel and this is related to the physical unit of sound pressure called the micropascal. The minium sound that a human ear can hear is 20 micropascals, and this is equivalent to 1 decibel. The relationship between micropascals and decibels is logarithmic, so that each time sound pressure in micropascals is multiplied by 10, 20 decibels are added to the decibel level. Bearing in mind the fact that a logarithmic scale applies to decibels, Table 9.6 gives an indication of noise levels in decibels for various activities. The generally recommended maximum level to which workers should be exposed over a working day is 90 decibels.

Table 9.6 : NOISE LEVELS FOR VARIOUS ACTIVITIES

Noise	*Decibels (db)*
Quiet speech	40
Light traffic at 25 metres	50
Large busy office	60
Busy street, heavy traffic	70
Pneumatic drill at 20 metres	80
Textile factory	90
Circular saw - close work	100
Riveting machine - close work	110
Jet aircraft taking off at 100 metres	120

The perception of noise varies between individuals. Some people are just better than others at 'screening out' noise, and may be oblivious to the loud music from next door. The maker of the noise is often either oblivious to the noise (e.g. a typist) or enjoys the noise (e.g. a pianist). In a hospital ward, the potential problem of noise is recognized and all patients have earphones to listen to whatever they wish to hear on the radio without walkmans. The problem with the latter is that, although some consideration has been shown, the background rhythm is frequently still audible to the other passengers, which is often highly infuriating. Lack of control over the source of the noise is in itself stressful. Circumstances may also affect sensitivity to noise. Students writing examinations may find the rustling of papers highly distracting, when normally they would not even notice the noise. Some factors affecting the level of annoyance caused by noise are summarized here.

1. The louder the noise, and the higher the pitch, the greater the annoyance.
2. Intermittent and unfamiliar noises intrude on the consciousness more than continuous or familiar sounds
3. Previous experience of exposure to noise can influence perceptions of sounds; for example, the sound of a dentist's drill, or a similar sound, can arouse anxiety.
4. Non-participation in the creation of the noise increases the likelihood of annoyance. This effect will be influenced by the degree of dislike of the sound (e.g. the type of music), by the attitude towards the person creating the sound, and by the inability to control the source of the noise.
5. The situation in which the noise is experienced. If a person is trying to get to sleep, or concentrate on a difficult task, a noise which would otherwise be acceptable, or not even noticed, may become extremely annoying.

Smell

The smell of freshly baked bread or freshly ground coffee has a very positive appeal to many people. In contrast, many people find the smell of cigarette smoking obnoxious. Once again, however, the service provider must recognize that all customers will perceive odours in different ways. Smoking, in particular, causes problems. In some countries, smoking in public places is prohibited. This is fine for the non-smoker, but for the 10-cigarettes-a-day smoker, having to refrain from smoking on a flight lasting two hours or more can be very uncomfortable, particularly if he or she is anxious about flying.

The implication of this is that more has to be spent on ventilation to minimize the effect on non-smokers if some customers are to be allowed to smoke. Segregation is one way of trying to minimize the impact. The problem with this is that smoke drifts, and many non-smokers will notice when a cigarette has been lit even if at the opposite side of the room. The smell of smoke also lingers well after the smoker has gone. Hotel bedrooms which have been occupied by smokers previously can be unacceptable to non-smokers. Probably the best answer to this problem is to have totally separate rooms for smokers. However, the actual solution will depend upon the mix of customers and the country in which the service is being provided.

Signs, Symbols and Artefacts

There are two aspects to signs, symbols and artefacts. First, they may help customers to orient themselves within the service environment, and second, they provide cues about the service being provided.

In terms of orientation, signs indicate where customers should go; for example, in hospitals, signs usually indicate where out-patients should report. They may also be used to instruct customers; for example, in a laundry signs may be used to instruct the customer how to use the washing machine. The effect on the customer's perception of the service can often be negatively affected by the lack of signs, or by ambiguous signs. Getting lost in the railway station and missing a train can be extremely annoying, and of course it is always when the passenger is short of time that clear, prominent signs which are essential in such circumstances are non-existent !

Signs often represent the first encounter that a new customer has with the organization, and influence those 'first impressions' which are so very important. Being able to find the way quickly and without trouble encourages a positive frame of mind.

Various design aspects of signs are important, and they will affect the visibility, legibility and intelligibility of the message. The orientation of the signs will also have an impact on their ease of use.

Visibility of signs refers to their positioning in such that they can easily be seen.

Legibility refers to the clarity of the message on the sign.

Intelligibility refers to the sense of the message. The sign itself may be perfectly visible and the shapes distinct, but can the customer understand the message ?

In services, some customers may be illiterate. Symbols can overcome the language and literary problems, but are sometimes themselves unclear.

Symbols and artefacts may also act as cues. As service is intangible, and often there is an expertise gap between the service provider and the customer (e.g. doctor and patient), it is often difficult for the customer to judge the proficiency of the 'expert'. Certificates on walls are a visible cue or symbol of achievement and many provide reassurance to the customer. Similarly, an office lined with bookshelves suggests knowledge, while original oil paintings may indicate success. The style of the decor generally can create an impression of cheap, cheerful and fun, or sedate, serious and expensive, etc. Inappropriate use of artefacts can create the wrong impression completely : leopard skins hung on the office wall would hardly be appropriate in an organization trying to project an image of concern for wildlife and the future of the environment generally.

Artefacts such as paintings, plants and sculptures can also be used in conjunction with the spatial layout to create a type of landmark along a corridor, helping navigation around a building with a symmetrical layout. In such buildings, it is sometimes difficult to tell the difference between floors or corridors. A distinctive plant in the north-west corner of the fifth floor, for example, provides a point of reference when trying to get one's bearings.

Spatial layout

Ease of access, good visibility, proximity of linked services and so on will help to make a customer feel in control of the process. If a customer is lost, stress levels rise. Unless the whole point of the exercise is to create a sense of mystery and excitement, as in a maze in a theme park perhaps, then one of the main objectives for the design of the layout of the facilities should be to facilitate ease of use for the customer.

Personal Space

Linked with spatial layout is the concept of personal space. Every person needs space around them to feel comfortable. If other people enter this space, stress levels will rise. Personal space comprises four zones, each with an increasingly large distance from the individual. Figure 9.2

illustrates these four zones. Only very close friends can be admitted to zone A without causing psychological discomfort, which in turn may lead to stress and associated physical effects, such as sweating. Zone B is reserved for friends, and zone C for business-type encounters. The limit of zone C represents the closest that strangers can approach without causing discomfort. Zone D extends to that distance within which the presence of others is noted.

Figure 9.2 : PERSONAL SPACE ZONES

A Intimate distance
B Personal distance

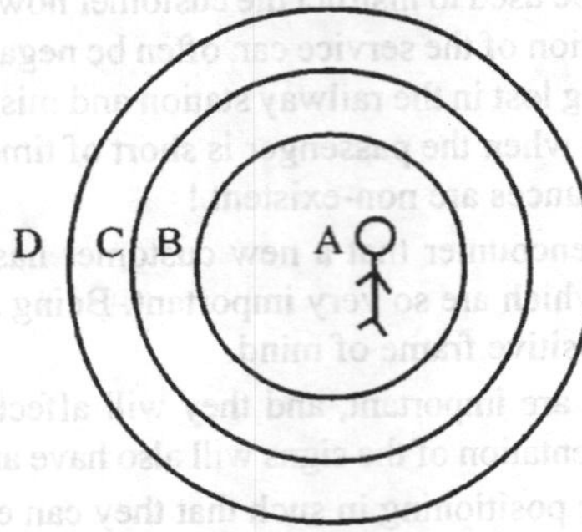

C Social distance
D Public distance

The size of the zones varies among people, and in particular among people of different cultures. Touching is much more acceptable in some cultures than in others, which clearly necessitates close proximity. Other variables which affect the size of the different zones are age, personality, gender and status of the individuals involved.

The implications of this for the design of the service are to recognize that expecting customers to share their 'space' with others will lead to increased stress levels and is likely to have a negative impact on their perception of the service received, or at least make them feel uncomfortable. This can be used to some advantage if the aim is to encourage customers to vacate tables quickly, as in a fast-food restaurant, or when the aim is to arouse, as in exciting/scary experiences. However, if the aim is to create a relaxing atmosphere, crowding must be avoided.

Body Language

One of the ways to try and standardize the service provided is to prepare 'scripts' for employees to follow. These may be quite detailed or simply provide an outline. For example, telephone sales operators are often trained to follow a script, with the exact opening lines and follow-up questions being predefined. In fast-food restaurants, the opening and closing lines that the server has to use may be prescribed. However, 'Have a nice day' can become an irritant to customers who perceive the phone lines as always engaged and inaudible. The reason why customers often feel that the words spoken are not meant is because the accompanying body language is conveying another message.

Body language, which includes facial expression and bodily positioning, conveys emotion or attitude. Spoken language conveys information, although the way something is said can also convey emotion. Greeting a customer or thanking a customer without making eye contact or smiling will not have the effect that management would like the lines to have. It is relatively easy to tell employees to learn a script, but it is far more difficult to foster the desired body language.

Training is needed here, but as such interpersonal behaviour is a skill, it cannot be learnt without practice and feedback. This form of training is time consuming and costly. More often than not, it is not provided, as front-line serving staff are frequently part time or temporary, and such an investment is not perceived to be justified.

9.6 GUIDELINES FOR PHYSICAL EVIDENCE STRATEGY

Given the relative intangibility of most services, the strategy for managing physical evidence of service is critical. And customers will react to the company's evidence whether or not an evidence strategy exists.

The guidelines for effective strategy are :

Recognize the Strategic Impact of Physical Evidence

For an evidence strategy to be effective it must be linked clearly to the organization's overall goals and vision. Thus, planners must know what those goals are and then determine how the evidence strategy can support them. At a minimum, the basic service concept must be defined, the target markets (both internal and external) identified, and the firm's broad vision of its future known. Because many evidence decisions are relatively permanent and costly (particularly servicescape decisions), they must be planned and executed deliberately.

Map the Physical Evidence of Service

Everyone should be able to see the service process and the existing elements of physical evidence. An effective way to depict service evidence is through the service map, or blueprint. From the map one can read the actions involved in service delivery, the complexity of the process, the points of human interaction that provide evidence opportunities, and the tangible representations present at each step. To make the map even more useful, photographs or videotape of the process can be added to develop a photographic blueprint, as described earlier in this chapter.

Clarify Roles of the Servicescape

Sometimes the servicescape may have no role in service delivery or marketing from the customer's point of view. This is essentially the case for telecommunication services or express mail services. Clarifying the roles played by the servicescape in a particular situation will aid in identifying opportunities and deciding just who needs to be consulted in making facility design decisions.

Assess and Identify Physical Evidence Opportunities

Once the current forms of evidence and the roles of the servicescape are understood, possible changes and improvements can be identified. A strategy might be developed to provide more evidence of service to show customers exactly what they are paying for. Or the pricing or the facility design would need to be changed, depending on the restaurant's overall strategy.

Be Prepared to Update and Modernize the Evidence

Some aspects of the evidence, particularly the servicescape, require frequent or at least periodic updating and modernizing. Even if the vision, goals, and objectives of the company don't change, time itself takes a toll on physical evidence, necessitating change and modernization. There is clearly an element of fashion involved, and over time different colours, designs, and styles may come to communicate different messages. Organizations obviously understand this when it comes to advertising strategy, but sometimes they overlook other elements of physical evidence.

Work Cross-functionally

In presenting itself to the consumer, a service firm is concerned with communicating a desired image, with sending consistent and compatible messages through all forms of evidence, and with providing the type of service evidence the target customers want and can understand.

A multifunction team approach to physical evidence strategy is often necessary, particularly for making decisions about the servicescape. It has been said that "Facility planning and management... is a problem-solving activity that lies on the boundaries between architecture, interior space planning and product design, organizational (and consumer) behavior, planning and environmental psychology".

SHORT ANSWER QUESTIONS

1. What is physical evidence in services?
2. What are photographic blueprints?

3. What do you understand by the term 'servicescape'?
4. Differentiate between peripheral and essential evidence.
5. What are the advantages and disadvantages of environment surveys?
6. "Smelling and Hearing (Noise or otherwise) are different sensory activities yet are an integral part of the physical evidence environment". What is their significance in services?

ESSAY QUESTIONS

1. What are the elements of physical evidence?
2. Enumerate the guidelines for effective physical evidence strategy.
3. What are the various approaches for understanding servicescape effects?
4. How do signs, symbols and artefacts provide good orientation in the service environment? Give examples.
5. "Often words spoken do not seem to be meant due to accompanying body language". Discuss.
6. What roles do servicescape play towards physical evidence of the service?
7. Do colour, illumination levels and temperature have any effects on service operations? What are the recommendations/

EXERCISE / ASSIGNMENTS

1. Prepare the servicescape and other tangible elements for the following services:
   (a) Shopping complex
   (b) Beach resort
   (c) Public library
   (d) Museum
   (e) Internet.
2. Investigate the reasons and motives that helped in designing the following service environments in your locality:
   (a) Restaurant
   (b) Petrol bunk
   (c) Amusement parks
   (d) Travel agent
   (e) Electronic goods repair shop.

●●●

10 People and Services

10.1 SERVICE PERSONNEL

Service personnel are those people who provide an organization's services for customers.

Service personnel are important in all organizations. However, they are particularly important in those situations where, in the absence of clues from tangible products, the customer will form an impression of the organization from the behaviour and attitudes of its staff.

Service personnel include operators, bus drivers, lift attendants, librarians, clerks in banks, chefs , receptionists and counter clerks in hotels or hire car companies, security guards, telephonists, repair and servicing personnel and waiters. These people may perform a 'production' or 'operational' role but may also have a customer contact role in service organizations. Their behaviour may be as important in influencing the perceived quality of a service as the behaviour of formal sales staff. It is crucial therefore that these service personnel perform their jobs effectively and efficiently; also that the service organization's measures of effectiveness and efficiency include a strong element of customer orientation among its staff.

10.2 CUSTOMERS

Another factor which may influence the marketing of services is the relationships between customers. A customer's perception of the quality of a service may be formed and influenced by other customers as well as by service organization personnel. Customers may talk to other customers about service organizations. Or where groups of customers 'receive' a service at the same time (e.g. a package tour) the enjoyment of the service may be shaped by the behaviour of other customers. In services marketing, management may play a role in 'quality controlling' the interactions between customers and in influencing the relationship that takes place between them. Relationships between customers are, of course, just one dimension of their behaviour as participants in the service production process and in the service consumption process.

It was observed that : 'the selling of a services and the rendering of the service can seldom be separated'. Examples of situations where the service cannot be separated from the person providing the service include window cleaning, dentistry and hairdressing. It is only with mechanized and automated services that people play little part in service transactions (e.g. automatic photograph booths ; vending machines).

Human beings therefore may play a unique role in the marketing and the production of services. This has important implications for the marketing function since it is clear that the human service representatives constitute an important element of any service marketing strategy and are an element in any service marketing mix.

What distinguishes service organizations from industrial good companions is that the customer may come into contact with people whose primary role is to perform a service rather than to market a service.

Service personnel include those members of the organizations from industrial good companies is that the customer may come into contact with people whose primary role is to perform a service rather than to market a service.

Service personnel include those members of the organization who are in contact with customer (contact personnel) and those members of the service organization who are not in contact with customers. Some of these staff may be visible to the customer during purchase and consumption of a service. Some may not. Figure 10.1 illustrates the kinds of occupations falling into these categories.

Figure 10.1 : ORGANIZATION PERSONNEL INVOLVED IN SERVICE PRODUCT PERFORMANCE AND DELIVERY

	Contact with client	Non-contact with client
Visible to client	Waitress Service engineer	Cook in restaurant Computer operator
Not visible to client	Telephone operator Airline pilot	Maintenance worker Accountant

10.3 SERVICE PERSONNEL QUALITY

The type of service a customer receives can be viewed as consisting of two elements :

(a) technical quality ;

(b) functional quality.

Technical Quality

Technical quality refers to 'what' the customer receives in his interactions with service organizations : the bedrooms in a hotel ; the meal in a restaurant; the transport service of a distribution company. It may be capable of objective measurement as with any product and it forms an important element in any customer's evaluation of a service.

Functional Quality

Functional quality refers to 'how' the technical elements of the service are transferred. Two important components of how the technical elements of service are provided are the process and the people involved in operating the system. Functional quality may be less capable of object measurement. It nevertheless forms an important element in any customer's evaluation of a services.

The relationship between technical quality and functional quality is shown in Figure 10.2. This also shows how both contribute to the image of the organization.

Figure 10.2 : MANAGING THE PERCEIVED SERVICE QUALITY

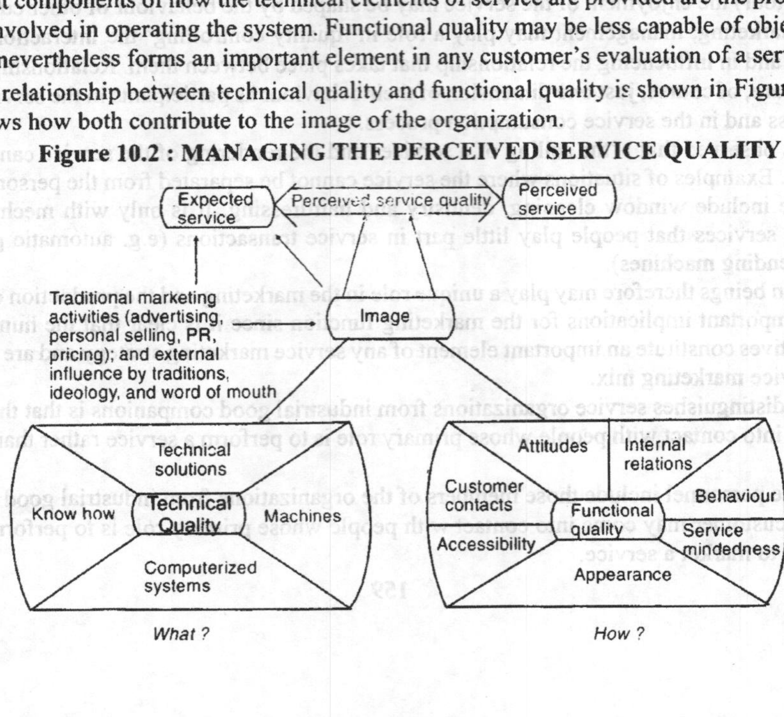

The components of the system are :

- attitudes of employees;
- behaviour of employees;
- the relationship between them;
- the importance of employees who have contact with customers;
- the appearance of service personnel;
- the general 'accessibility' of services to customers;
- the general service mindedness of personnel.

10.4 MAINTAINING AND IMPROVING SERVICE PERSONNEL QUALITY AND PERFORMANCE.

There are a number of ways in which a service organization can maintain and improve the quality of personnel and their performance. Four are examined here. They are :

(a) careful selection and training of service personnel;

(b) internal marketing ;

(c) using practices to obtain consistent behaviour ;

(d) ensuring consistent appearance.

These ideas are intended only to illustrate some of the measures service organizations may take. In practice there is often overlap between actions and practices in each category and a number of other possibilities may be considered.

A. Careful Selection and Training of Service Personnel

The clear implication of the importance of personal contact to many services is that recruitment, selection, training and development programmes have to be tailored to the needs of the services being provided. There should be a clear understanding of the job by service personnel. This involves drawing up detailed job specifications. Also the qualities required in the people undertaking customer contact jobs should be defined. Service jobs traditionally can be classified according to the type of educational requirements, previous experience required, social skills required and so forth. One recent suggestion is that service sector employees should be divided according to the communication demands placed upon them by customers. The nature and type of communication may be an important determinant of employee qualities sought. Finally attention needs to be given to how the job will be controlled and organized.

B. Internal Marketing

What the internal marketing concept (Table 10.1) does is to re-emphasize the importance of marketing to people who serve external customers. Internal marketing means applying the philosophy who serve the external customers so that (i) the best possible people can be employed and retained and (ii) they will do the best possible work.

This interpretation implies that employees are viewed as internal customers and jobs are internal products which have to be designed to better meet the needs of customers. If the organization offers employees better, more satisfying jobs then it increases its ability to be a more effective service organization.

Internal marketing is of crucial importance since staff may be reluctant to sell a service product which they do not find acceptable. This point can be illustrated by the attitude of some staff to the banks' new charging policies for credits collected for other banks. During the introduction of these policies, some staff would not accept the directive to charge customers for using the service partly due to certain long-established customer relationships. The policy had to be modified and ended in an authority to charge only when 'feasible'.

Table 10.1 : THE INTERNAL MARKETING CONCEPT

Internal marketing Overall objective:	To get a motivated and customer-conscious personnel.
Strategic level Objective :	To create an internal environment which supports customer – consciousness and sales mindedness among the personnel. -Supporting management methods; -Supporting personnel policy; -Supporting internal training policy; -Supporting planning and control procedures.
Tactical level Objective :	To sell services, supporting services (used as means of competition), campaigns and single marketing efforts to the employees. - the personnel is the first market of the service company : the employees must understand why they are expected to perform in a certain manner, or in a certain situation actively support, for example, a given service or supporting service; the employees must accept the services and other activities of the company in order to be expected to support them in their in their contact with the consumers ; a service must be fully developed and internally accepted before it is launched ; the internal information channels must work ; personal selling is needed internally, too.

C. Using Practices to Other Consistent Behaviour

A third problem for the service organization lies in achieving consistency of behaviour among staff. The behaviour of the consumer will affect the behaviour of the human representatives of the firm and the quality of the service provided may vary since it depends very much on the individual who offers it. For example, the branches of a bank may offer identical services to their customers ; but the success of individual cashiers in 'producing' these services can vary widely. Achieving consistency of human effort is an important goal of many service organizations. Clearly it is important for service organizations to establish set procedures for some of their services to ensure they are performed in a consistent way. There are dangers though that such practices can become too mechanistic. Most organizations have to strike a balance between too much rigidity in their systems and too much flexibility. Procedures have to be flexible enough to tolerate the ambiguity of customer variety.

An outline of one service company's recent campaign plan to improve its service to customers, including training of existing staff, is show below.

Customer Services Campaign Plan

1. Communication with Management and Staff

There is a need for staff to concentrate their efforts in work to their highest level of competence and this depends to a great extent in involvement in corporate objectives. To this end it is necessary to produce a planned, professional approach to staff communication. This requires an investigation into the appropriate medium to be used.

2. Training

Customer service training is vital but it is prerequisite that arbitrary nominations are not made for any such course.

It is necessary therefore to identify units where customer service training is appropriate and take the action required in programming courses and staff lists. It should also be made clear to staff nominated that the whole point of any course is to increase standards of customer service.

3. Management / Staff Relationships

The other facet besides involving staff in company policies is to make people feel wanted and show that the company is interested in their problems. This requires on the part of management and supervisors the necessity to get amongst the staff on the "shop floor".

4. Customer Service Improvement

An important part of this campaign involves making improvements. This can take the form of either changing a procedure/introducing a new service or can be attitude development. We should therefore identify many of the limitations and obstacles with which we confront our customers and have a plan to remove them.

5. Link Major Changes to Customer Service

It will be difficult to get commitment to a customer service campaign if staff do not see evidence of effort to remove some of the production inadequacies which frustrate them. There must be, therefore, a means of passing on to all personnel, information on the effects that a change has been made, however small.

6. Rewards for Outstanding Individual Performance

This should be a major feature of the campaign and ranges from a supervisor saying "well done", to a special Customer Service Awards Scheme. Therefore we have to establish a policy among all section heads towards the recognition of individual performance. A method of reward scheme, possibly in the form of free tickets, should be considered, with a committee appointed to consider nominations.

D. Ensuring Consistent Appearance

Bearing in mind the characteristic of intangibility of many services, the appearance of the establishment and its personnel are often the only tangible aspects of a service organization. Therefore 'the consumer can be expected to choose a service supplier whose place of business and sales personnel clearly suggest the quality of service desired for the satisfaction of his needs. One way in which organizations attempt to create an image and suggest quality of service is through the appearance of service personnel.

The appearance of service personnel can be controlled by service management. One way in which this may be accomplished is through the use of 'uniforms' and styles of dress. Waiters in hotels, airline stewardesses, motoring centre repairmen may all be required to adopt certain formal styles of dress. The degree of formality may range from the issue of a top coat to a complete uniform including accessories. Further standardization of appearance may be accomplished by recruiting service personnel with specific characteristics (e.g. of a certain height or age range). Also the service organization may provide facilities to encourage personal care like hairdressing and beauty parlours. Even when a service organization does not require the wearing of a formal uniform for protective or promotional purposes, an 'acceptable' style of dress may be deliberately encouraged (e.g. amongst bankers and stockbrokers). Equally 'unacceptable' dress styles may be discouraged. Such uniforms help create standards of 'uniformity' and thus are an important input to the overall image of a service organization, where uniformity is required. Where uniformity is not required, service organizations may encourage varying styles of non-conforming dress to cultivate an unconventional image of variety (e.g. as in advertising agencies).

10.5 PERSONNEL AUDIT

The service personnel audit is one way of ensuring standards are set and maintained. It is a systematic, critical and unbiased review of service personnel practices. In any service organization it forms part of the marketing audit. Basically the service audit aims to take stock of the organization's total service with the goal of supporting effective marketing practices and correcting faulty behaviour.

Service organizations may use a range of methods to monitor performance. Practices will vary according to the kind of service organization and numbers of service personnel involved. Five common practices are described here. They are :

(a) sales related systems;

(b) complaint systems;

(c) suggestion systems ;

(d) audit visits ;

(e) customer satisfaction surveys.

A. Sales – related Systems

Many organizations rely on sales related systems – sales growth, market share, profitability, repeat purchase – as measures of customer and employee satisfaction. These types of measure are clearly important but can give misleading feedback particularly when there is a little competition, where demand is rising naturally or where there is a good deal of customer inertia (e.g. to change bank accounts). Nevertheless as a surrogate measure they can provide a general indirect indication of performance.

B. Complaint Systems

Service organizations should make it easy for customers to complain. Many organizations fail to give enough attention to establishing easy and simple mechanisms to ensure that customer problems and complaints get heard and acted upon. Customers who are not given an opportunity to complain might reduce their business and do damage to the organization through the 'word of mouth' influence they have on exiting or potential customers.

C. Suggestion Schemes

Suggestion schemes can be used to solicit customer and employee views of how a service organization performs. When tied to a reward system they can be a valuable source of ideas for service, system and organizational improvement.

D. Audit Visits

Audit visits may vary from routine, structured and announced to non-routine, unstructured and unannounced. The kinds of audit-routine used will be influenced by the nature of the service organization and the types of markets it serves. Some service organizations monitor telephone switch board staff through asking a series of complex questions and enquiries. Another way to audit personnel is to use mystery 'shoppers' who are : 'generally trained, experience interviewers and observers who have been briefed in advance about what to expect and look for, and who operate under semi-controlled conditions'.

E. Customer Satisfaction Surveys

Many service organizations use periodic surveys of customer satisfaction to check out what past customers like and dislike about services offered. Airlines, garages, management training centres and hotels have all used such surveys in the past. Many hotels for example leave questionnaires in their bedrooms and invite guests to give their comments on standards of food, accommodation, service and so on.

All of the above of course are ways of checking out whether or not a service organization services customers well. They help identify areas for improvement and corrective action.

10.6 CUSTOMERS AS PRODUCERS OF SERVICES

If the customers assume a more active role in the service production and delivery process, they effectively remove some of the labour tasks from the serving organisations.

The first implication is seen in the service delivery system. This is the process in which the customer may participate. Since it may be impossible to separate the customer from the production process, for example in personal and medical services, the service provider must either go to the market or bring the market to the service facility. Thus, each service facility may have a limited geographic area from which to draw customers : 'the close production marketing interface requires that the service delivery system must be located within the market and therefore sized for the specific market.

Hence, the multi - site nature of many service operations and the managerial challenges of looking after multi-site operations (e.g. achieving uniform service standards).

The second implication, resulting from the importance of the customer in the production process for services, is that : 'service systems with high customer contact are more difficult to control and more difficult to rationalise than with low customer contact'.

Examples of high-contact services include restaurants, personal services and schools. The customer can, in high-contact systems, affect the service in terms of time of demand and quality of service. Also the high degree of producer-customer interaction in the production of a service is a 'mixed blessing', since while problems of uncertainty about time and quality exist as a result of the customer's participation in the system, customers are also ' a source of productive capacity'. Customers therefore play an active role in shaping the service offering either adversely (by causing queues in a bank perhaps) or by improving quality (providing the atmosphere in a restaurant). The customer can make an input to or cause disruption in the production process.

The third implications is in respect of the range of roles the customer may now be required to play in service production. When an individual sets out to obtain a service he or she is first of all a buyer, getting something for which he or she or a third party must usually pay. But the customer is also involved in other relationships, for example as a worker and co-producer, giving time and effort without which the service could not be produced. The participation of the customer in the division of labour involved in the production of the service means that there is interdependence between buyer and seller of the service.

10.7 CUSTOMERS AS USERS OF SERVICES

An understanding of how customers behave and what factors influence their choice is clearly of vital importance to marketing success.

Much of this knowledge has been summarized, organized and presented in the form of various models of buyer behavior.

The models of consumer behaviour are of value for a number of reasons:

(a) They provide a framework for presenting knowledge on consumer behaviour. They enable us to present ideas in a simple and economic way; in particular to show relationships between variables thought to influence choice.

(b) They help identify inadequacies and weakness in knowledge of consumer behaviour and point to areas for future research and development.

10.8 THE SASSER, OLSEN AND WYCKOFF CONSUMER MODEL

This model attempts to indicate how a market segment of consumers with similar needs and behaviour makes judgements about services.

The consumer is shown to have a set of needs (e.g. for substantive service such as a hotel room, for control over choice, for trust in the service performer). These needs are translated into a set of desired attributes. Some may be clear to the consumer ; others will be more vague and will be clarified by the service organization's suggestions. Over time however the consumer forms a model of what is desired. These desired attributes include factors like :

- Security (e.g. reliability of service);
- Consistency (e.g. reliability of reactions);
- attitude (e.g. interpersonal reactions);
- completeness (e.g. array of services provided);
- condition (e.g. 'atmosphere' of service environment);
- availability (e.g. ease of access in time or space);
- timing (e.g. length of time required for service).

10.9 THE FISK CONSUMPTION/EVALUATION PROCESS MODEL

This model attempts to describe the consumption / evaluation process for services. The model is shown in Figure 10.3 and is divided into three stages. Pre-consumption, Consumption and Post-consumption.

Figure 10.3 : CONSUMPTION/EVALUATION PROCESS FOR SERVICES

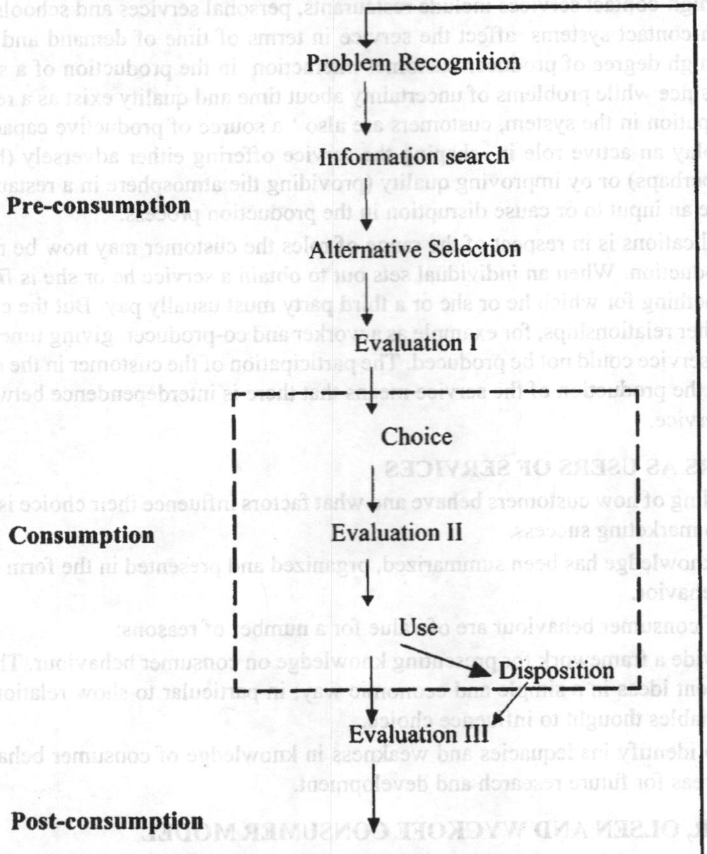

The pre-consumption stage incorporate the events and actions that typically precede consumption behaviour (i.e. problem recognition, information search, the selection of alternative solutions). Evaluation I is an attempt to identify the 'best' solution.

Table 10. 2 : THE EVOLUTION AND TRANSFORMATION OF CUSTOMERS

	Customers as a Passive Audience			*Customers as Active Players*
	Persuading predeter mined groups of buyers	***Transacting with individual buyers***	***Lifetime bonds with individual customers***	***Customers as cocreators of value***
Time frame	***1970s, early 1980s***	***Late 1980s and early 1990s***	***1990s***	***Beyond 2000***
Nature of business exchange and role of cutomers	Customers are seen as passive buyers with a predetermined role of consumption			Customers are part of enhanced network; they cocreate and extract business value. They are collaborators, codevelopers and competitors.
Managerial mind-set	The customers in an average statistic; group of buyers are predeter mined by the company.	The customer is an individual statistic in a transaction.	The customer is a person - cultivate trust and relationships.	The customer is not only an individual but also part of an emergent social and cultural fabric.
Company's interaction with customers, and development of products and services	Traditional market research and inquiries; products and services are created without much feedback.	Shift from selling to helping customers via help desks, call centers, and customer service programs; identify problems from customers, then redesign products feedback.	Providing for customers through observation of users; identify solutions from lead users, and reconfigure products and services based on of customers.	Customers are codevelopers of personalized experiences. Companies and lead customers have joint roles in education, shaping expectations, and cocreating products and services.
Purpose and flow of communication	Gain access to and target predetermined groups of buyers. One-way communication.	Database marketing; two-way communication.	Relationship marketing; two-way communication and access.	Active dialogue with customers to shape expectations and create buzz. Multilevel access and communication.

The consumption stage is where the consumer acts by choosing the 'best' service. Evaluation II is a function of Evaluation I and Choice behaviour. Evaluation I forms expectations about the service while the choice and any experience associated with choice may still lead to service use or attempts to reduce dissatisfaction (e.g. complaints, non-payment). Use concludes the consumption phase of the process.

Following service use Evaluation III occurs which is a function of Evaluation I, Evaluation II and Use. If the consumer is satisfied then repurchase motivation will occur ; if not then repurchase motivation will not occur and dissatisfaction may lead to complaining behaviour.

10.10 THE EVOLUTION AND TRANSFORMATION OF CUSTOMERS

Some industries have already gone further than others in drawing on the competencies of customers. Consider the software industry, in which companies have moved from testing products in usability laboratories to testing them in customer environments. For example, more than 650,000 customers tested a beta version of Microsoft's Windows 2000 and shared with the software giant their ideas for changing some of the product's features. Many of those customers were even prepared to pay Microsoft a fee to do this. Working with the beta software helped many of those customers understand how windows 2000 could create value for their own businesses. The beta tests also helped clear the glitches from early versions of the software. The value of the collective R & D investment by Micorsoft's customers in codeveloping Windows was estimated at more than $ 500 million worth of time, effort, and fees.

The notion of the customer as a source of competence is starting to appear in less obvious industries, too. Take medicine. Andy Grove, Chairman of Intel, in 1995 was diagnosed with prostrate cancer. He researched the causes of the disease and, with his doctors, developed a unique treatment plan. Now, you may expect someone like Grove to take his treatment into his own hands, but the point is that he is hardly alone. The availability of medical information on the Internet, in magazines such as *Time, Newsweek, and Reader's digest,* on TV, and in local newspapers is helping more and more patients enter into a dialogue with their doctors. The more knowledgeable they become, the more likely these customers are to shape their health care regimen. Doctors may resent the consumer's exercise of his or her knowledge, but they would do well to learn how to co-opt.

harnessing the competencies of the consumer is not an easy task. It's complicated enough for a large company like Ford to understand its internal competence base, let alone the competencies of each of its top 100 suppliers. Just imagine how difficult it will be for Ford's managers to understand the competence base of the millions of heterogeneous individuals who are the automaker's customers. But that's the challenge. At a minimum, managers must come to grips with four fundamental realities in harnessing customer competence. They have to engage their customers in an active, explicit, and ongoing dialogue; they have to mobilize communities of customers; they have to manage customer diversity; and they have to cocreate personalized experiences with customers. Table 10.2 maps their evolution through three stages and along several key dimensions.

SHORT ANSWER QUESTIONS

1. Who are service personnel?
2. "Selling of services and the rendering of the service can seldom be separated". Substantiate.
3. "Consumers form a model of what they desire". What did Sasser and others espouse in their model?
4. "The appearance of service personnel can be controlled by service management". How is this possible?
5. How is service quality influenced by people?

ESSAY QUESTIONS

1. Explain the consumption / evaluation process with the help of a model.
2. What is personnel audit? What are the related issues?
3. How can perceived service quality be managed? What are the factors involved?
4. Explain the dual role of customers as producers and users of services.
5. Describe Fisk's consumption / evaluation process model.
6. What is the 'internal' marketing concept? Outline its objectives.
7. How has the role of customers evolved over the last three decades? Explain the transformation.
8. Device a customer service campaign plan for any service of your choice.

EXERCISE / ASSIGNMENT

1. Use Fisk's model to delineate the consumption / evaluation process for the following services / service providers:
   (a) Credit Cards
   (b) Hotels
   (c) Banks
   (d) Doctors
   (e) Beauty parlours.
2. Construct the client visibility-contact matrix for the following services:
   (a) Counsellor
   (b) Railway engine driver
   (c) Municipality workers
   (d) Postman
   (e) Detectives
   (f) Factory worker
   (g) Cinema actors
   (h) Policeman.

●●●

11

Internal Versus External Marketing

11.1 SIX MARKETS FRAME WORK

Six markets, namely, customer, referral, supplier, employee, influencer & internal, are shown in Figure 11.1.

Figure 11.1 : THE SIX MARKETS MODEL : A BROADENED VIEW OF SERVICES

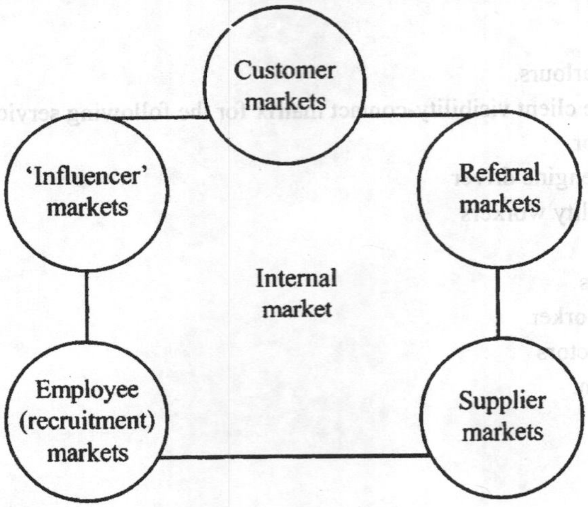

Customer markets

There is no doubt that the primary focus of marketing was and remains on the customer. More recently there has been a changing emphasis in the focus of marketing from transactional marketing that emphasizes the individual sale to relationship marketing which emphasizes long-term lasting relationships.

Our experience, and those of other practitioners and researchers, suggests that the greater part of most companies' marketing activity is directed at seeking new customers. While a focus on gaining new customers is necessary to the development of all businesses it is also essential to ensure that ongoing marketing activity is directed at existing customers. By placing too much focus on marketing activities directed at new customers, companies often experience the 'leaking bucket' effect.

Referral Markets

The referral markets are referred to under various names within different industry sectors, including: intermediaries, connectors, multipliers, third-party markets, agencies, networks and referral sources. In most industries they have to things in common, they are becoming more important and there are more of them.

In the case of the bank, these include insurance companies, property brokers, accountants, solicitors, surveyors and valuers, other banks, as well as existing customers and internal referrals. The present and likely future importance of these referral source should be identified and a specific plan developed to determine the appropriate levels of marketing resources that should be devoted to each of them. While a highly focused pilot scheme can sometimes suggest where the greatest benefit can be obtained it should be emphasized that the development of these relationships takes time and all the benefits of such marketing activity may not be realized for some time.

Supplier markets

There is mounting evidence of a movement from the traditional adversarial relationship between suppliers and their customers towards a new form of relationship based on cooperation. This emphasizes a long term very close relationship and a win-win philosophy rather than the win-lose philosophy inherent in adversarial relationships.

In the past, firms have typically focused on trying to extract the best price from suppliers, but the unknown costs of this has often been variability in supply or quality, or both. Many firms see this as a process of playing one supplier off against another. This approach is slowly being revised and is being replaced with a more enlightened approach whereby suppliers are viewed as collaborators and recognition is being made that there is a need to establish greater partnership in the marketing channel between companies and their suppliers.

This new attitude to supplier market is described by a number of labels such as 'co-makership' (Philips), the 'vendorship partnership' (AT & T), 'co-marketing' and 'relationship marketing'

Employee markets

Increasingly, companies are finding strong competition in their efforts to attract a sufficient number of suitably motivated and trained employees into their ranks. Many firms are today learning that the limiting factor to their success is far more predicated on the availability of satisfactorily skilled people to work in their organizations than the availability of other resources such as capital or raw materials.

The reducing pool of available labour will create special problems for customer service delivery in the years ahead. Despite recognizing this problem many firms have not responded to this problem by development of a plan aimed at improving their competitive edge in employee markets.

While in times of high unemployment some companies will have adequate personnel resources at the clerical and blue collar levels the demographics of young people and graduates argue this will be a critical area for relationship marketing over the next decade.

'Influencer' markets

Examples of where marketing activity may need to be directed include finance markets, regulatory markets and the government. These can be described as 'influencer' markets – additional markets which, depending on their circumstances, may need to be addressed. Such things are of particular importance for companies who sell equipment of an infrastructural character, such as nuclear reactors, telephone systems and defence products. These are products which may impact on the country's economic performance, employment levels or financial status or may be important from a political point of view. Companies involved in such sensitive fields as defence may well recognize the importance of these target markets but may well not have formulated detailed and coherent marketing strategies to gain maximum advantage from these relationships. Such plans are essential to sustained success in such markets. These plans, whether described internally as public relations or marketing, will benefit from the application of a strategic marketing approach.

Internal markets

In the past decade the term internal marketing has emerged in many companies to describe the application of marketing internally within the firm. This seems to be an area where practice appears ahead of theory.

11.2 EXTERNAL VERSUS INTERNAL MARKETING

The concept of internal marketing differs from the concept of external marketing in a variety of ways as shown in Table 11.1.

Table 11.1 : EXTERNAL VERSUS INTERNAL MARKETING

EXTERNAL MARKETING	INTERNAL MARKETING
1. Interaction between company (Management) and customers	1. Interaction between company (management) and employees
2. Customer play a greater role in influencing operations	2. Management takes a lead role to finish tasks and direct employees
3. Company makes promises to the customers regarding their services	3. Enables the employees to fulfill the promises made during external marketing
4. Customers benefit through service offered	4. Employees benefit through compensation system
5. Increases customer satisfaction or delight	5. Increases job satisfaction of employees
6. Market research is applied	6. Research is through appraisal and feedback system
7. Needs of customers are highly fluctuating	7. Needs of employees are less fluctuating
8. Promotional aspects include advertising, word-of-mouth, publications, etc.	8. Promotional aspects include transfers, wages / salary increase, awards, recognition, etc.
9. Quality cultural and social factors,. standard of living, needs and wants of customer are important	9. Values, attitudes, beliefs and personalities are important determinants
10. Good public relations is needed	10. Counselling and disciplinary action is needed
11. Requires feedback and control	11. Requires vision and planning
12. "Relationship" is the key word	12. "Partnership" is the key word
13. Constrained by trends, fashions and money power	13. Constrained by available resources and other institutional factors
14. Demand - Supply inequilibrium cannot be tolerated	14. Demand - Supply inequilibrium can be tolerated
15. Operational level in focus	15. Strategic and tactical levels in focus
16. Retention of customers is critical	16. Retention of employees is critical
17. Target group are customers (buyers, suppliers, consultants, government, institutions, etc.)	17. Target group are employees
18. Incentives are through discounts, premiums, gifts, contests, etc.	18. Incentives are in addition to salary eg. Financial and non-financial

11.3 MARKET ANALYSIS AND SEGMENTATION

When a critical review of any market is undertaken it soon becomes clear that the notion of a single market for a given product or service is of limited use. All markets are made up of market segments and even if the product supplied is identical from a physical point of view, a consideration should be made of how the total offer can be differentiated from competitive offers. Many companies following a market aggregation strategy, (i.e. not recognizing market segments) are increasingly considering means of appealing to different segments. Thus companies, such as McDonalds, offer different product ranges in different countries, banks recognize the value of different delivery systems for standard products, and manufacturers of 'commodity' products are seeking differentiation through customer service.

The process of market segmentation is one of dividing a total market up into a series of submarkets (or market segments). The marketing segmentation approach is concerned with first considering the alternative bases for segmentation; second, choosing specific segments (or a single segment) within that base and finally determining appropriate service levels for these segments. Three criteria are commonly used in selecting target segments. Market segments should be :

(i) Accessible - it should be possible to communicate with segment markets with a minimum of overlap with other segments and distribution channels should be available to reach them.

(ii) Measurable - it should be possible to measure or estimate the size of the segment and to quantify the impact of varying marketing mix strategies on that segment.

(iii) Size - the segment should be sufficiently large, to make it financially worthwhile to service.

Seven broad bases have traditionally been used in market segmentation.

a. Geographic segmentation

An approach whereby customers are differentiated on the basis of where they are located. Thus a customer may be segmented into urban, suburban or rural groups. A common geographic segmentation may divide customers into areas on the basis of pincodes which might also represent different groups in terms of relative wealth, socio-economic and other factors.

b. Demographic and socioeconomic segmentation

Demographic and socio-economic segmentation is based on a wide range of factors including age, gender, family size income, education, social class and ethnic origins. It is thus helpful in indicating the profile of people who purchase a company's product or services.

c. Psychographic segmentation

Psychographic segmentation involves an analysis of lifestyle characteristics, attitudes and personality. Recent research in several countries suggests that the population can be divided into between ten and fifteen groups, each having an identifiable set of lifestyle, attitude and personality characteristics.

d. Benefit segmentation

Benefit segmentation involves grouping customers together on the basis of the benefits they are seeking from a product. For example, purchasers of motor cars seek widely varying benefits. For example, they may seek fuel economy, size, bootspace, performance, reliability or prestige.

e. Usage segmentation

Usage segmentation, a very important variable for many products, usually divides consumers into heavy users, medium users, occasional users or non-users of the product being considered. Marketers are often concerned with the heavy-user segment who consume many times the amount of the product compared with occasional users.

f. Loyalty segmentation

Loyalty segmentation is concerned with identifying the relative loyalty a customer has to a particular product or brand. Customers can be divided into groups who are very loyal, moderately loyal and unloyal. These groups are then examined in an attempt to identify any common characteristics they have so the product can be targeted at prospectively loyal customers.

g. Occasion segmentation

Occasion segmentation recognizes that customers may vary in their usage of a product or brand depending on the situation. For example, a better drinker may drink light beer with his workmates before driving home, a conventional beer in his home and a premium or imported beer at a special dinner in a licensed restaurant.

These are the more common forms of segmentation. However, there are obviously many other ways in which markets may be segmented.

Segmentation by service

One area of potential which has received relatively little attention is the consideration of how customers respond to varying service offerings. In a sense this may be considered as a subset of benefit segmentation , it is of sufficient importance to be addressed separately. The various elements of customer service that can be offered, and possible differentiation in terms of service levels within these elements, represent considerable opportunity to design service packages appropriate to different market segments.

Segmenting markets by service involves addressing these issues:

- Can groupings of customers be identified with similar service requirements?
- Can we differentiate our service offering?
- Do all our products require the same level of service?

11.4 PLANNING PROCESS

In outline the marketing planning process comprises the following steps:

- Gathering information on the external environment and the organization internally; Identifying the major strengths and weaknesses of the organization and opportunities and thi eats externally (SWOT);
- Formulating basic assumptions about key determinants of marketing success;
- Laying down market objectives for the organization, based on the information gathered, the SWOT analysis and the assumptions made and formulating strategies;
- Devising detailed plans and programmes to accomplish objectives;
- Measuring progress towards achievement of objectives, reviewing and amending the plan as necessary.

Figure 11.2 : illustrates this process showing the main steps involved.

Developing a Marketing Plan

Planning is a method for achieving an end. If a service business wishes to survive and prosper in a competitive environment, it needs to establish a set of marketing goals that explicitly recognizes where the organization is now, where it would like to be, and how it proposes to get from here to there. Table 11.2 summarizes the key elements in a marketing plan, beginning with an analysis of the current situation and identification of problems and opportunities.

Figure 11.2 : THE MARKETING PLANNING PROCESS

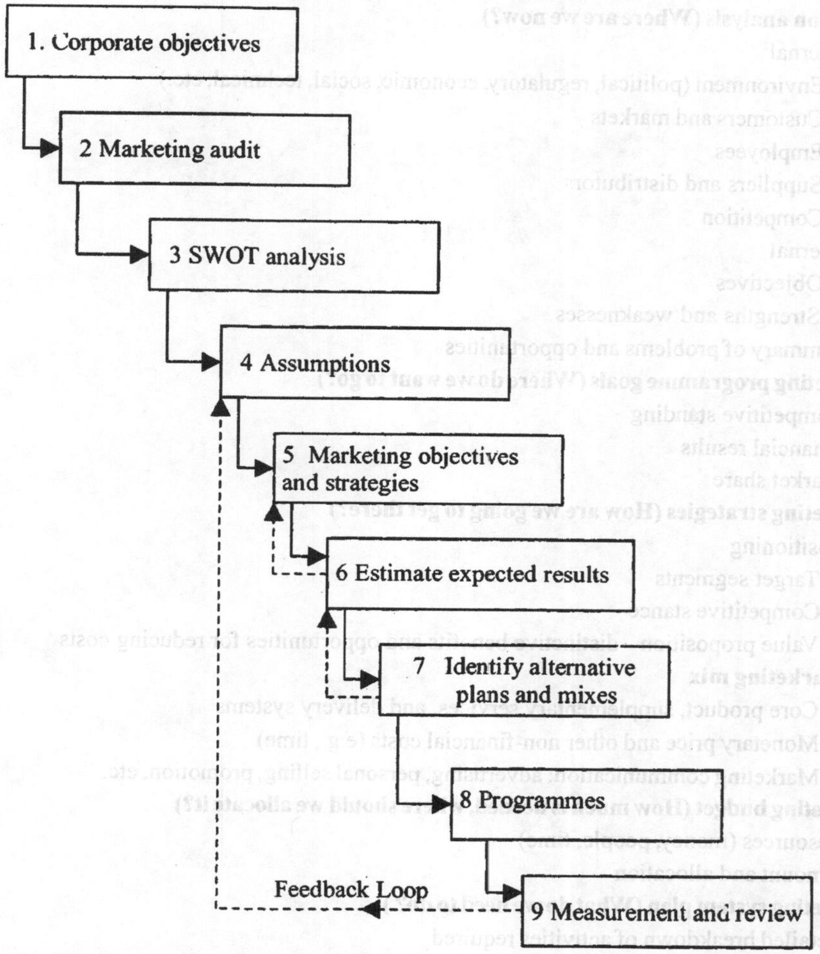

A good marketing plan does more than identify goals and strategies that are based on facts and current assumptions; it also provides a plan of action for accomplishing the mission, using existing or readily available resources. Among the requirements for effective implementation are:

- Establishment of the necessary organization
- Definition of responsibilities in terms of who should do what at specific points in time
- Procedures and control systems that allow the general manager (and subordinates) to delegate authority without losing strategic control
- Provision for continuity of execution over the full operating period of the plan, avoiding ad hoc decisions, yet allowing enough flexibility for contingencies
- Coordination of many different but related activities over an extended time period
- Good communication between mangers so that all know what each is trying to achieve and how he or she intends to accomplish specific tasks

Table 11.2 : MARKETING PLAN FORMAT

Situation analysis (Where are we now?)

- External
  - Environment (political, regulatory, economic, social, technical, etc.)
  - Customers and markets
  - Employees
  - Suppliers and distributors
  - Competition
- Internal
  - Objectives
  - Strengths and weaknesses
- Summary of problems and opportunities

Marketing programme goals (Where do we want to go?)

- Competitive standing
- Financial results
- Market share

Marketing strategies (How are we going to get there?)

- Positioning
  - Target segments
  - Competitive stance
  - Value proposition - distinctive benefits and opportunities for reducing costs
- **Marketing mix**
  - Core product, supplementary services, and delivery systems
  - Monetary price and other non-financial costs (e.g., time)
  - Marketing communication: advertising, personal selling, promotion, etc.

Marketing budget (How much is needed, where should we allocate it?)

- Resources (money, people, time)
- Amount and allocation

Marketing system plan (What do we need to do?)

- Detailed breakdown of activities required
- Responsibility by name
- Activity schedule in milestone format
- Tangible and intangible results expected from each activity

Monitoring system (Are we moving toward our destination?)

- Ongoing situation analysis
- Intermediate and final measures of performance
- Variances between goals and performance triggering course correction actions

11.5 RETHINKING THE CUSTOMER SERVICE FUNCTION

At many forward-looking firms, the customer-service department has evolved into a management function that is now independent of operations and sales at lower levels in the organization but still works in close collaboration with each (Figure 11.3). In this organizational model, customer service has taken over certain routine tasks and simple problem -solving efforts from both sales and operations, leaving each of these departments to focus on those tasks that they are uniquely qualified to perform.

Figure 11.3 : ROLE OF THE CUSTOMER SERVICE FUNCTION

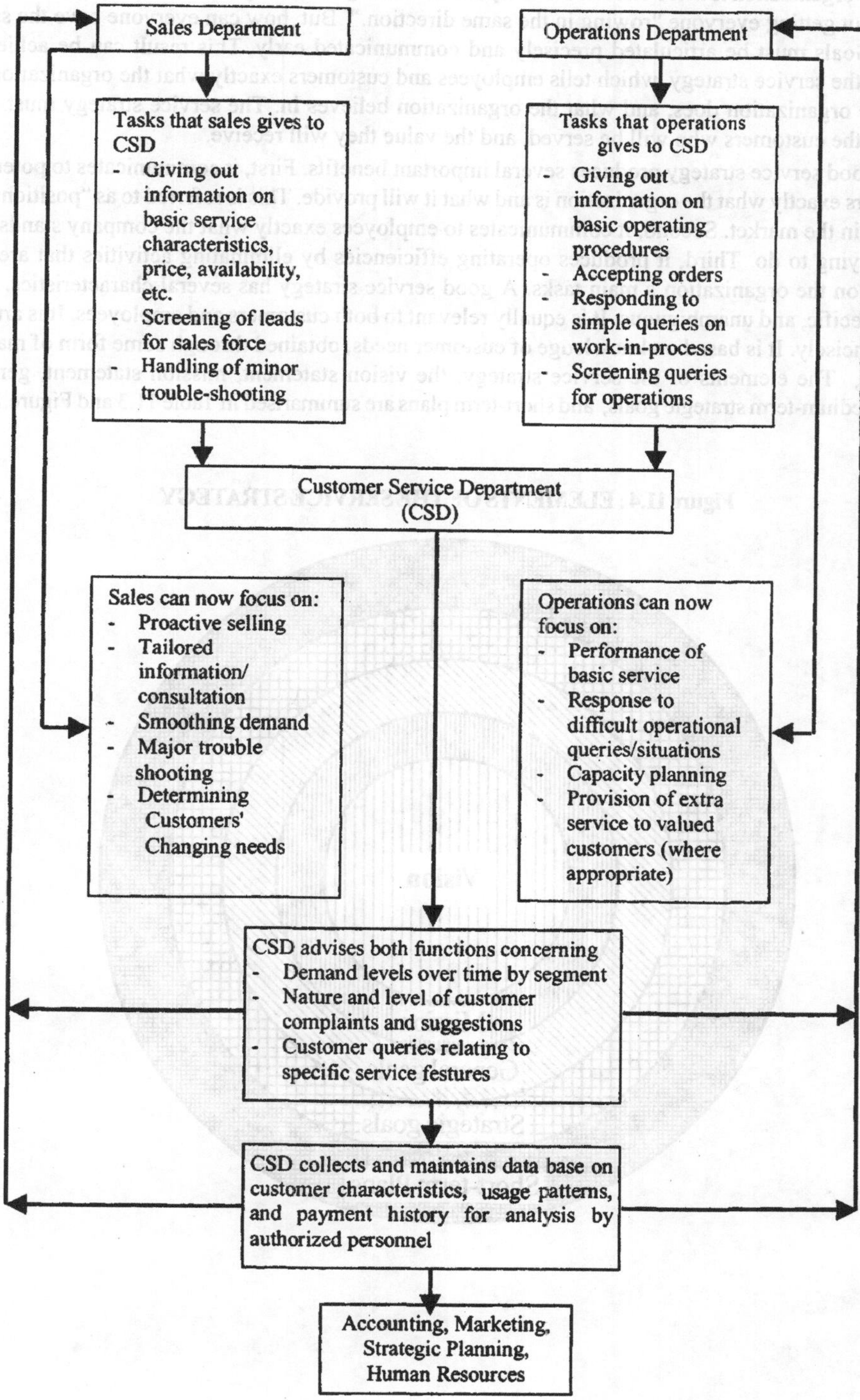

11.6 THE SERVICE STRATEGY-FOCUSING & POSITIONING

Any organization is more effective if everyone is working to accomplish the same goals. We often hear about getting everyone "rowing in the same direction." But how can everyone have the same goals? Goals must be articulated precisely and communicated early. This result can be achieved through the service strategy, which tells employees and customers exactly what the organization is, what the organization does, and what the organization believes in. The service strategy must also identify the customers who will be served, and the value they will receive.

A good service strategy produces several important benefits. First, it communicates to potential customers exactly what the organization is and what it will provide. This is referred to as "positioning" the firm in the market. Second, it communicates to employees exactly what the company stands for, and is trying to do. Third, it produces operating efficiencies by eliminating activities that are not focused on the organization's main tasks. A good service strategy has several characteristics. It is clear, specific, and unambiguous. It is equally relevant to both customers and employees. It is articulated concisely. It is based on knowledge of customer needs, obtained through some form of market research, The elements of the service strategy: the vision statement, mission statement, general goals, medium-term strategic goals, and short-term plans are summarised in Table 11.3 and Figure 11.4.

Figure 11.4 : ELEMENTS OF THE SERVICE STRATEGY

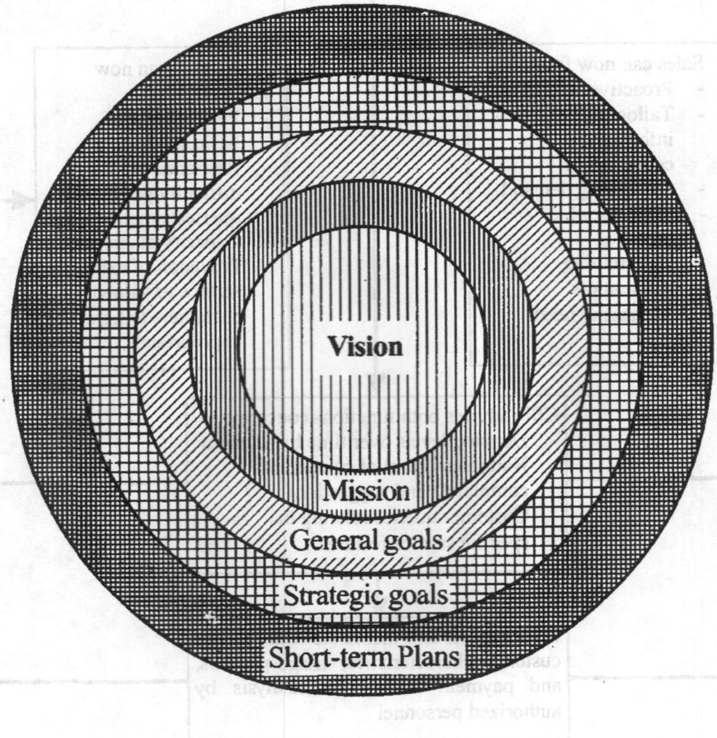

Table 11.3 : VISION, MISSION, GOALS, AND PLANS (WITH SOME EXAMPLES)

(1) Vision	To be the leading supplier of cricket bats in the world
Mission	To provide high quality cricket bats, at a reasonable price, to schools, clubs, and recreational players.
General Goal Example	To be the leading supplier of bats to cricket teams
Strategic Goal Example	Devise a high-quality bat
Short-Term plan Example	Determine what players want in a bat
(2) Vision	To be a "landmark restaurant" in Bangalore
Mission	To provide excellent food and the most efficient and professional service in town at a moderate to high price.
General Goal Example	To achieve higher ratings on service satisfaction (rated by "mystery shoppers") than those of the major competitors
Strategic Goal Example	Ensure that the waiters and waitresses are thoroughly trained
Short-Term plan Example	Have each new waiter or waitress serve on apprenticeship under the supervision of an experienced" mentor"

Four focus strategies

The extent of a company's focus can be described on two different dimensions - market focus and service focus. Market focus is the extent to which a firm serves few or many markets, while service focus describes the extent to which a firm offers few or many services. These two dimensions define the four basic focus strategies shown in Figure 11.5.

Figure 11.5 : BASIC FOCUS STRATEGIES FOR SERVICES

Number of markets served	**Breadth of service offerings:** Narrow	Wide
Many	Service focused	Unfocused (Everything for everyone)
Few	Fully focused (Service and market focused)	Market focused

A fully-focused organization provides a very limited range of services (perhaps just a single core product) to a narrow and specific market segment. A market - focused company concentrates on a .... segment but has a wide range of services. Service-focused firms offer a narrow range of services to a fairly broad market.

Finally, many service providers fall into the unfocused category because they try to serve broad markets and provide a wide range of services.

STEPS IN DEVELOPING A POSITIONING STRATEGY

Competitive strategy is often narrowly focused at direct competitors - firms that market products that offer customers a similar way of achieving the same benefits (e.g., in the case of education, another college offering similar classes). However, there may also be a serious threat from generic competitors, which offer customers a different way of achieving similar benefits (for instance, distance learning via broadcast programmes or self-study through use of books, CDs and videotapes both offer generic competition to conventional university classes).

The research and analysis that underlie development of an effective positioning strategy are designed to highlight both opportunities and threats to the firm in the competitive marketplace, including the presence of generic competitors. Figure 11.6 identifies the basic steps involved in identifying a suitable market position and developing a strategy to reach it.

Figure 11.6 : DEVELOPING A MARKET POSITIONING STRATEGY

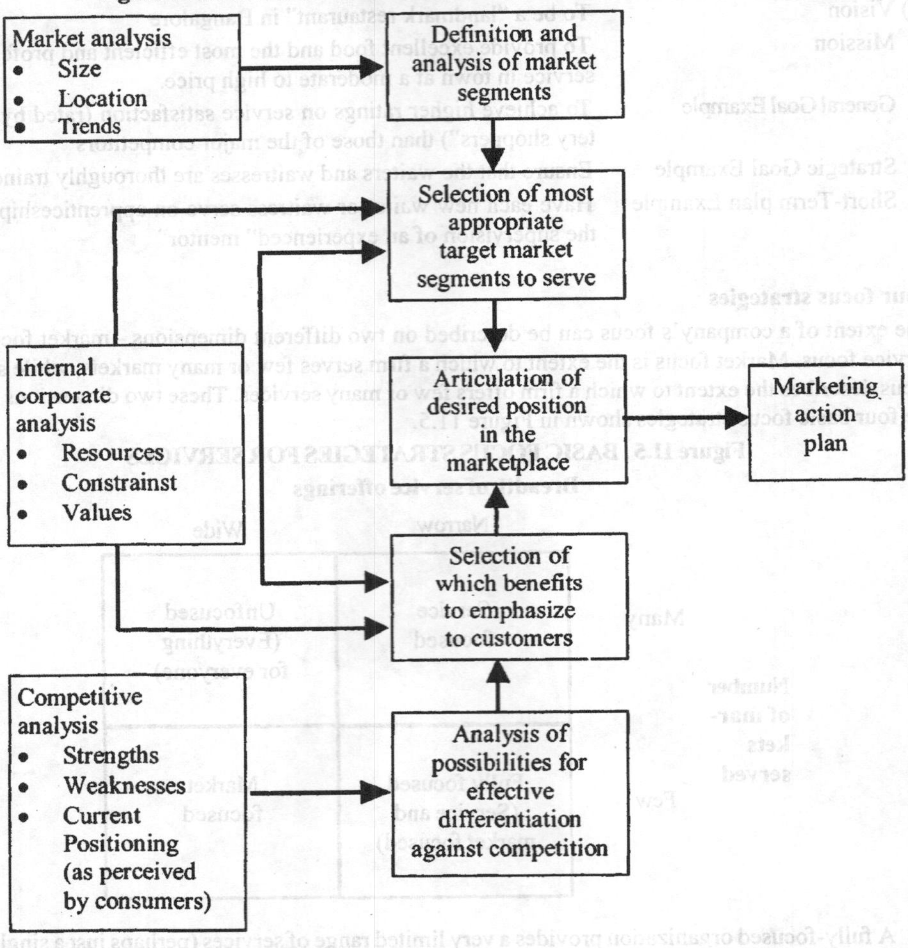

11.7 STRUCTURAL ALTERNATIVES AND CHANGE

Table 11.4 shows some changes that a mid-priced family restaurant might consider to alter complexity and divergence for competitive purposes. Any prospective change or mix of changes to determine which mix is most likely to provide the maximum competitive differentiation.

Though processes are intangible, the means by which services are rendered are very real. There are only two, people (both providers and consumers) and facilitating goods. Any shift in overall complexity or divergence, or the introduction of any new process design, must be implemented with a clear understanding of the potential impact on these 'producers' of the process.

Table 11.4 : STRUCTURAL ALTERNATIVES

Lower complexity/divergence	*Current process*	*Higher complexity/divergence*
No reservations	Take reservation	Specific table selection
Self-seating. Menu on blackboard	Seat guests, give menus	Recite menu: Describe specials
Eliminate	Serve water and bread	Assortment of hot breads
Customer fills in form	Take orders	Taken personally to table
	Prepare orders	
Pre-prepared: no choice	Salad (4 choices)	Individually prepared at table
Limit to four choices	(15 choices)	Expand to 20 choices: Add flaming dishes; Bone fish at table; Prepare sauces at table
Sunday bar: Self-service	Dessert (6 choices)	Expand to 12 choices
Coffee, tea, milk only	Beverage (6 choices)	Add exotic coffee; Wine list, Liquors
Serve salad, Bill and beverage together	Serve orders	Separate course service
Cash only : Pay when leaving	Collect payment	Choice of payment. Including house accounts; serve mints.

SHORT ANSWER QUESTIONS

1. In what situations does a service company need marketing research?
2. What are the marketing problems and opportunities of a product-management structure for an insurance company?
3. In what ways is marketing information such a valuable resource to service organizations?
4. Explain some focus strategies.
5. What is meant by positioning?
6. What is the 'marketing concept'? How is a marketing plan developed?
7. How does market segmentation for products differ from that of services?
8. If service organization are close to their customers, why do they need to use marketing research?
9. How can marketing planning contribute towards corporate planning within the services sector?
10. What are the different types of markets? Give examples.
11. What is the connection between positioning, market segmentation and customer choice behaviour?
12. What are the consequences for a company of not having a clear position in the market?
13. How important is it to have a structured approach to marketing planning?

14. List some key research areas for service firms.
15. What factors should be taken into consideration by a travel agency in seeking to position its chain of outlets?
16. List some major marketing research agencies in India.

ESSAY QUESTIONS

1. Why should research objectives be established before marketing research can be conducted?
2. Why are both qualitative and quantitative research methods needed in a services marketing research programme?
3. Do you agree with the idea that a marketing department can actually be a barrier to the successful development of a marketing orientation within service organizations? Give examples.
4. What are 'cultural typologies'? Explain with examples.
5. Comment on the difficulties marketers have in differentiating their services from those of competitors.
6. Examine the strategic alternatives open to a restaurant chain seeking to expand and suggest a framework within which strategic alternatives may be evaluated.
7. What kinds of information could be gleaned from research on intermediate customers? What would intermediate customers know that service providers might not?

EXERCISE / ASSIGNMENTS

1. What reasons can you give for companies' lack of use of research information? How might you motivate managers to use the information to a greater extent? How might you motivate frontline workers to use the information?
2. Create a perceptual map showing the competitive positions of different companies for the following service industries:

   (a) Fast-food restaurants (b) Supermarkets (c) Theatres.
3. Choose a local services organization to interview about marketing research. Find out what the firm's objectives are and the types of marketing research it currently uses. Using the information in this chapter, think about the effectiveness of its marketing research. What are the strengths and weaknesses?
4. Suggest steps that could be taken by the following service organizations to make its marketing management more responsive to customers' needs:

   (a) Telecommunications (b) Charities (c) Consultants (d) Education (e) Government departments.
5. Suppose you manage a grocery store.

   (a) Design a sampling plan for conducting a customer satisfaction survey.

   (b) Plan and defend an appropriate mode of data collection.

   (c) Determine the relevant business processes.

   (d) Write a re-purchase intention question and overall satisfaction question.

   (e) Write an overall process question.
6. Identify the most likely marketing research objectives for the following services:

   (a) College (b) Hotel (c) Tourist spot (d) Courier.

● ● ●

12 Service Design

12.1 INTRODUCTION

Customers' requirements for what is needed from the service and the performance standards that the service needs to satisfy form the specifications for the design. The design consists of four related components (Figure 12.1). Service product design refers to the design of the physical attributes of the service. The meal served at a restaurant, subscription options for home cable television service, or the banking transactions that are available through an automatic teller machine are examples of such attributes. Since providing these attributes may involve the assembly of raw materials or developing software, the design of these attributes is analogous to designing a physical product.

Service facility design refers to the design of the physical layout of the facilities where the service is delivered - for example, a restaurant interior or a car rental office. Customers' perceptions of the quality of the service are influenced by attributes such as the cleanliness, spaciousness, lighting, and layout of the environment where the service takes place. In addition to these "front room" (i.e., visible to the customer) facilities, back-room facilities (invisible to the customer) such as a restaurant kitchen or an airport baggage handling building also need to be designed. The efficiency of service operations depends on the configuration of these facilities.

Figure 12.1 : DESIGN AND DELIVERY COMPONENTS

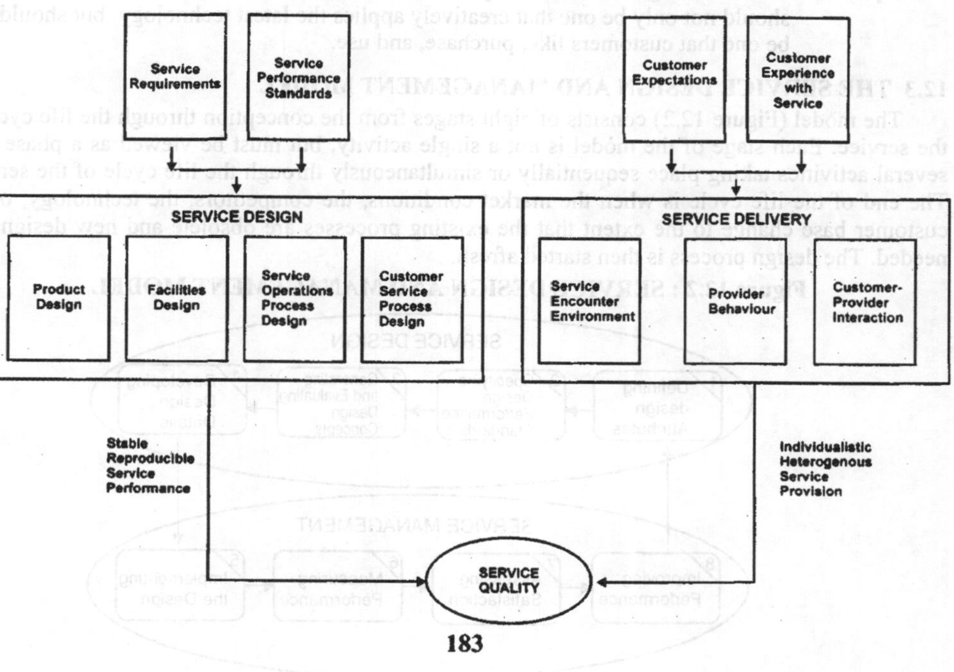

Service operations process design refers to the activities that are needed to deliver or maintain a service. Examples are the steps needed to rent a car (collect license, collect credit card, validate payment option, check car availability, print contract, obtain customer signature, deliver car keys and contract), or to deliver a meal to a customer. The activities that make up the operations processes are those required for the service to deliver its output. By contrast, the activities comprising the customer service process design pertain to the interactions between the customer and the service provider. For example, in the car rental example described above, in addition to the operational steps, the representative may greet the customer on arrival, refer to him by name, ask him for his preference of cars, and bid him farewell on departure. The customer service and service operations activities together make up the car rental process. The quality of the service experience depends on the performance of both types of activities. These activities therefore need to be designed together.

12.2 DESIGN METHODOLOGY

A real design exercise involves the complex interactions of a variety of technical and non-technical factors that affect the quality of the design. In order to design a product that can be competitive in the market, it is imperative to employ a methodology that integrates the engineering aspects of the design with the marketing and management principles that are required to ensure the commercial viability of the product. Such a methodology is referred to as total design.

Five principles need to be followed in order to adopt a total design methodology:

Principle 1 : Involve the customer in all stages of the design process.

Principle 2 : Derive the specifications of the design from these customers and not from previous designs or internal organizational criteria.

Principle 3 : Derive the technical aspects of the design from these customer provided specifications. In other words, the technology should be a derivative of the customer needs and not the other way around.

Principle 4 : Design the service using a multi-function team with representatives from all relevant organizations.

Principle 5 : Test the design in the marketplace, and not in the laboratory. A successful design should not only be one that creatively applies the latest technology, but should also be one that customers like, purchase, and use.

12.3 THE SERVICE DESIGN AND MANAGEMENT MODEL

The model (Figure 12.2) consists of eight stages from the conception through the life cycle of the service. Each stage of the model is not a single activity, but must be viewed as a phase with several activities taking place sequentially or simultaneously through the life cycle of the service. The end of the life cycle is when the market conditions, the competitors, the technology, or the customer base change to the extent that the existing processes are obsolete and new designs are needed. The design process is then started afresh.

Figure 12.2 : SERVICE DESIGN AND MANAGEMENT MODEL

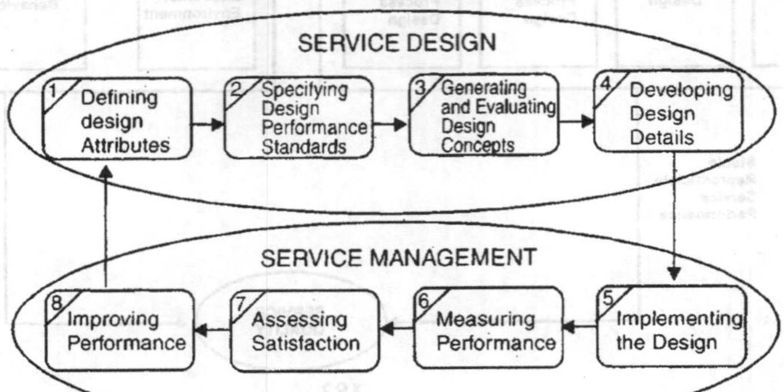

This does not imply that new design activity should only be begun at the end of the life of a service. Rather, the design of new processes should be an ongoing activity, and new designs should be phased in smoothly before the old designs lose their effectiveness. If is too late to introduce new designs after customers complain or switch to the competition's service. The development and introduction of new services and enhanced processes should be an integral part of the service management strategy of the firm.

12.4 OVERVIEW OF MODEL STAGES

Stage 1 : Defining design attributes

- Identify the key customers of the service.
- Determine the needs that customers expect the service to fulfill.
- Prioritize the needs in order of importance.
- Specify the attributes required by a service that meets these needs.
- Create quantitative measures for design attributes.
- Establish the relationships between needs and attributes.
- Determine the most important attributes.

Stage 2 : Specifying performance standards

- Identify the customers' desired performance level for each attribute.
- Analyze the performance of the competitors.
- Determine the relationship between performance and satisfaction.
- Specify design performance standards for each attribute.

Stage 3 : Generating and evaluating design concept

- Define the key functions needed to provide the service.
- Assemble these functions into processes.
- Document these processes using flow charts.
- Create alternate design concepts for the service.
- Evaluate and select a concept for detailed design.

Stage 4 : Developing design details

- Partition concept into process-level design components.
- Generate design alternatives for each component.
- Predict performance of each design alternative.
- Evaluate and select alternatives for each component.
- Evaluate and select design for implementation.
- Test performance of overall service design.
- Make any necessary modifications to the design.
- Specify detailed functional requirements.

Stage 5 : Implementing the design

- Develop implementation project plan.
- Develop a service construction plan.
- Develop a pilot and testing plan.
- Develop a communications plan.
- Develop a rollout and transition plan.
- Develop a service management plan.
- Implement all the plans.

Stage 6 : Measuring performance

- Select key attributes to be analyzed.
- Measure performance of attributes relative to standards.
- Measure capability of attributes.

- Measure efficiency of key processes.
- Develop reporting and analysis procedures.
- Identify attributes whose performance does not meet standards.
- Analyze the root cause of poor performance.
- Perform any corrective active, if necessary.

Stage 7 : Assessing satisfaction

- Measure customers' satisfaction with performance of service.
- Measure satisfaction relative to customers' expectations.
- Measure satisfaction relative to the competition.
- Validate these results against those from Stage 2.

Stage 8 : Improving performance

- Estimate relationship between financial objectives and overall satisfaction.
- Set strategic satisfaction targets.
- Estimate relationship between satisfaction and attribute performance.
- Select one or more attributes for improvement, and set targets.
- Estimate relationship between service - level and process - level attributes.
- Select process - level improvement alternatives.
- Evaluate the benefits and costs of different improvement alternatives.
- Select and implement optimal process improvement initiatives.

12.5 BLUEPRINTING

Blueprinting (also called "flowcharting") is a technique that helps to understand the totality of a service as a process, so that "fail points," those stages of the service that have a high statistical probability of generating problems, can be identified, understood, and possibly redesigned. The blueprint is an objective, graphical depiction of the service.

The rationale behind service blueprinting (Figure 12.3) was developed by Lynn Shostack.

Shostack identified the key steps in preparing the service blueprint as follows:

1. Identify the activities involved in delivering the service and present these in a diagrammatic form. The level of detail will depend on the complexity and nature of the service.
2. Identify the fail points. These are stages where things might go wrong. The actions necessary to correct these must be determined, and systems and procedures developed to reduce the likelihood of them occurring in the first instance.
3. Set standards against which the performance of the various steps might be measured. Frequently, this is the time taken.
4. Analyze the profitability of the service delivered, in terms of the number of customers served during a period of time.

Figure 12.3 : SERVICE BLUEPRINT COMPONENTS

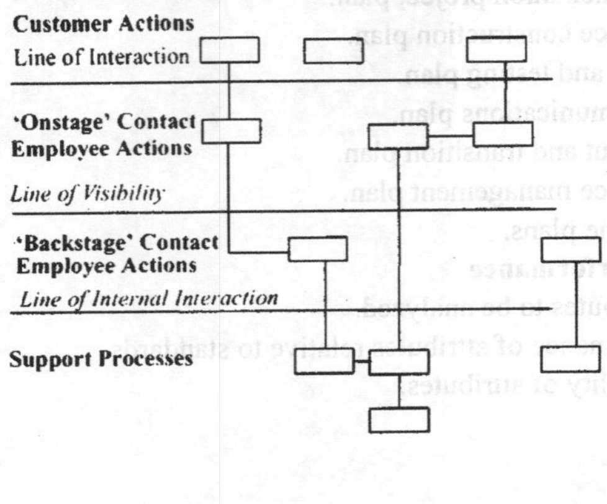

Those activities that the contact employee performs that are visible to the customer are the "onstage" employee actions. In the legal services setting, the actions of the attorney (the contact employee) that are visible to the client are, for example, the initial interview, intermediate meetings, and final delivery of legal documents.

Those contact employee actions that occur behind the scenes to support the onstage activities are the 'backstage" contact employee actions. In the example, anything the attorney does behind the scenes to prepare for the meetings or to prepare the final documents will appear in this section of the blueprint, together with phone call contacts the customer has with the attorney or other frontline staff in the firm.

The support processes section of the blueprint covers the internal services, steps, and interactions that take place to support the contact employees in delivering the service. Again in the legal example, any service support activities such as legal research by staff, preparation of documents, and secretarial support to set up meetings will be shown in the support processes area of the blueprint.

One of the most significant differences in service blueprints compared with other types of process flow diagrams is the inclusion of customers and their view of the service process. In fact, in designing effective service blueprints it is recommended that the diagramming start with the customer's view of the process and work backward into the delivery system. The boxes shown within each action area depict steps performed or experienced by the actors at that level.

The four key action areas are separated by three horizontal lines. First is the line of interaction, representing direct interactions between the customer and the organization. Anytime a vertical line crosses the horizontal line of interaction, a direct contact between the customer and the organization, or a service encounter, has occurred. The next horizontal line is the critically important line of visibility. This line separates all service activities that are visible to the customer from those that are not visible. In reading blue prints it is immediately obvious whether the consumer is provided with much visible evidence of the service simply by analyzing how much of the service occurs above the line of visibility versus the activities carried out below the line. This line also separates what the contact employees do onstage from what they do backstage. For example, in a medical examination situation, the doctor would perform the actual exam and answer the patient's questions above the line of visibility of onstage, while she might read the patent's chart in advance and dictate notes following the exam below the line of visibility, or backstage. The third line is the line of internal interaction, which separates contact employee activities from those of other service support activities and people. Vertical lines cutting across the line of internal interaction represent internal service encounters.

12.6 BUILDING A SERVICE BLUEPRINT

1. Identify the process to be blueprinted.
   Basic business concept
   A service (within a family of services)
   A specific service component
2. Map the process from the customer's point of view.
3. Draw the line of interaction.
4. Draw the line of visibility
5. Map the process from the customer contact person's point of view, distinguishing on-stage from backstage actions.
6. Draw the line of internal interaction.
7. Link customer and contact person activities to needed support functions.
8. Add evidence of service at each customer action step.

Consider as an illustration the operations of a small restaurant (the service blueprint is shown in Figure12.4). Customers arrive and check whether a table is available. They can either have a drink in

Figure 12.4 : SERVICE BLUEPRINT FOR RESTAURANT SERVICE

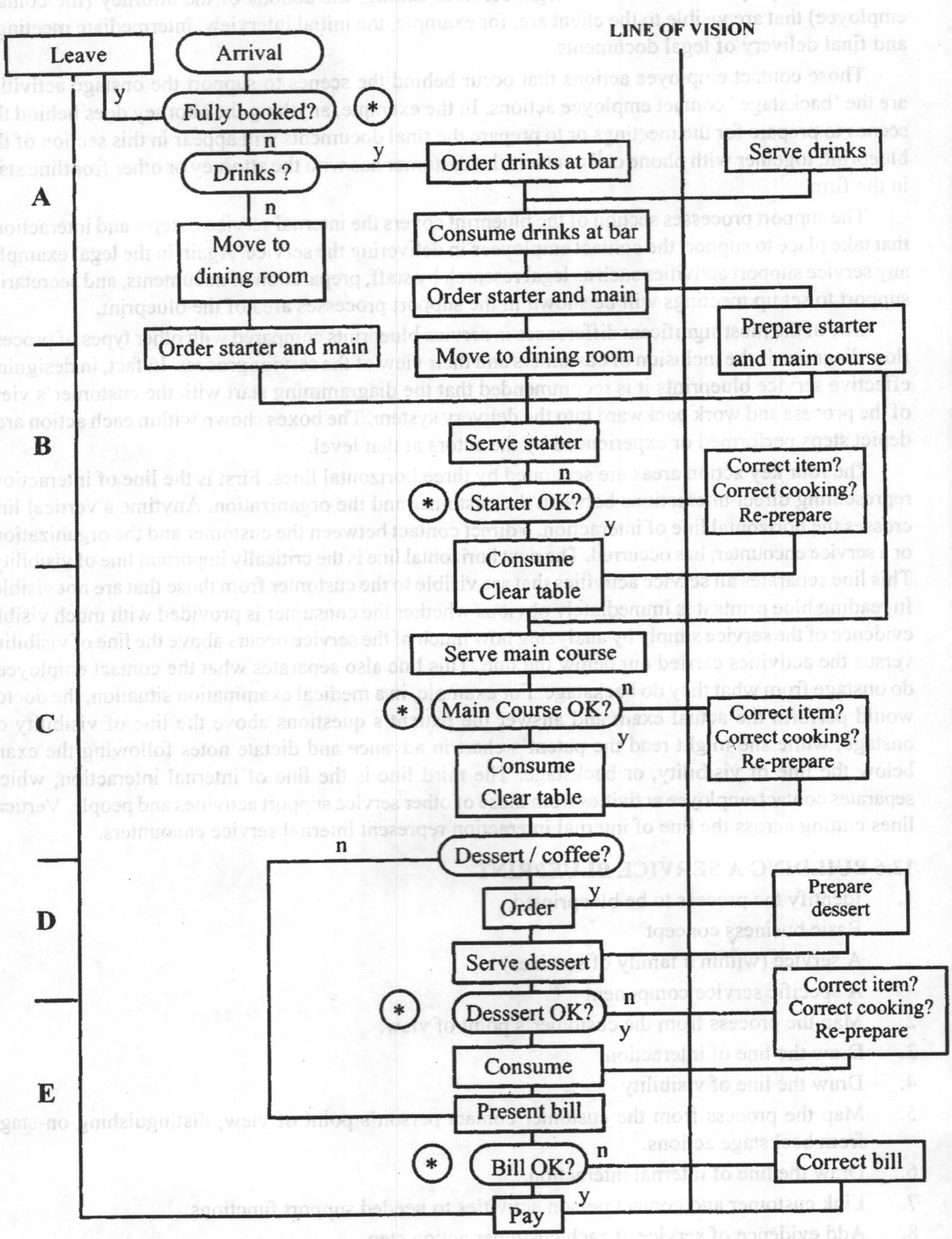

* Show fail points

the bar area and choose their dishes, or go straight through to the restaurant / eating area and order at the table. Decision are shown in rounded boxes (the convention in computer flow charts is the use of a diamond). The line of vision is between the restaurant / bar and the preparation areas, and the interaction between customer and server. One of the first fail points, marked with an asterisk, is if the starter is unsatisfactory It might 'fail' because it is the incorrect dish or it has been incorrectly cooked. 'Foolproofing' systems to minimize the occurrence of this could include the use of standardized terms for menu items, explanations of cooking styles (rare, medium rare, rose for meat - what do these actually mean?), standard recipes for consistency, procedures to ensure food is ready just as the customer is ready to eat it (or at least ensuring that it can be kept at the correct temperature without drying up or spoiling) and so on. This then repeats for the serving and consumption of the main course. Customers may or may not then take dessert and coffee. The service finishes with the presentation of the bill, and the final fail point. Again, formal procedures in recording the dishes selected, reconciling information from the bar and so on reduce the likelihood of errors here.

Figure 12.4 also shows the estimated duration of the various stages :

A	5-20 minutes
B	15-30 minutes.
C	20-40 minutes.
D	0-30 minutes.
E	2-5 minutes.

Thus the entire meal may take between 42 and 125 minutes. Clearly, if desirable these could be broken down into more detail. The variations will be determined in part by the customers (how many drinks do they have at the bar before the meal? How fast do they eat? And in part by the ratio of staff to clients. However, care is needed (in terms of the design of the system) to ensure the customers are not kept waiting for undue lengths of time, or do not feel that they are being rushed through. Procedures need to be developed to ensure this. The times can be useful as guidelines (how fast can we serve the business group in a hurry?), and to determine profitability (how many diners can be served in one evening with existing staffing levels?)

Consider the application and value of blueprinting for a car repair service. The perspective is that of a customer using it for the first time (Figures 12.5, 12.6 and 12.7). Prior to making the initial contact with the garage (phoning for appointment and arrival at the garage) the customer will have formed some expectations from, for example, word-of-mouth and advertising. The telephone call and particularly arrival at the garage will go some way towards confirming or contradicting the customer's expectations, and are in fact more powerful tools once he has made contact. The customer will use various pieces of evidence (telephone response time and manner, attitudes and appearance of proprietor/employees, equipment and layout etc.) as clues to the likely quality of service. Making assumptions about service quality from the type of evidence mentioned above is understandable but has the potential to mislead. The seemingly chaotic, untidy garage manned by employees covered in oil and possessing little by way of modern equipment may be perceived as likely to render a poor service. Yet the opposite may be nearer the truth.

The diagnosis represents an encounter point where the customer may, for example, describe symptoms to assist in determining the problem. It is critical in the sense that promises made to the customer and the resource implications of the job are determined on the basis of the diagnosis. If the diagnosis is subsequently found to be incorrect, relationships with the customer may be impaired. After the initial diagnosis the customer will depart, without ever seeing the repair section.

Where the organization draws the line of visibility, distinguishing the front office from the back office, is of some significance for service organizations. The nature of the service and how it is delivered offers guidance on where to draw the line, e.g. a hairdresser's operation will be predominantly front office while a credit card company operates a very large percentage of its service in the back office. Other services like a restaurant may feel ambivalent about where to draw the line separating the front and back office.

In making the distinction a service organization needs to address the following questions.

- How much of the service does the customer need to witness/experience?
- Will greater involvement lead to more understanding and favourable impressions, i.e. improved effectiveness.
- What effect will there be on efficiency if the customer is allowed greater access to the service process?

Figure 12.5 : BLUEPRINTS FOR AN AUTO DEALER'S SERVICE

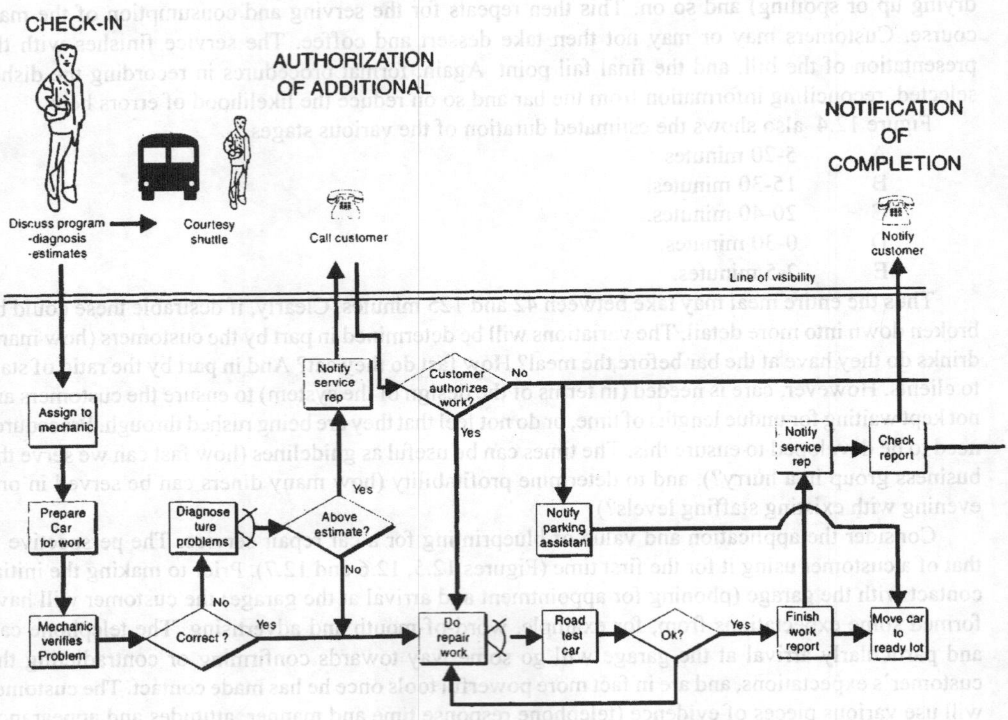

12.7 BENEFITS OF SERVICE BLUEPRINTING

1. Provides an overview so employees can relate "what I do" to the service viewed as an integrated whole, thus reinforcing a customer-oriented focus among employees.
2. Identifies fail points, that is, weak links of the chain of service activities, which points can be the target of continuous quality improvement.
3. Line of interaction between external customers and employees illuminates the customer's role and demonstrates where the customer experiences quality, thus contributing to informed service design.
4. Line of visibility promotes a conscious decision on what customers should see and which employees will be in contact with customers, thus facilitating rational service design.
5. Line of internal interaction clarifies interfaces across departmental lines, with their inherent interdependencies, thus strengthening continuous quality improvement.
6. Stimulates strategic discussions by illuminating the elements and connections that constitute the service. Those who participate in strategic sessions tend to exaggerate the significance

Figure 12.6 : CONTINUATION OF FIGURE 12.5

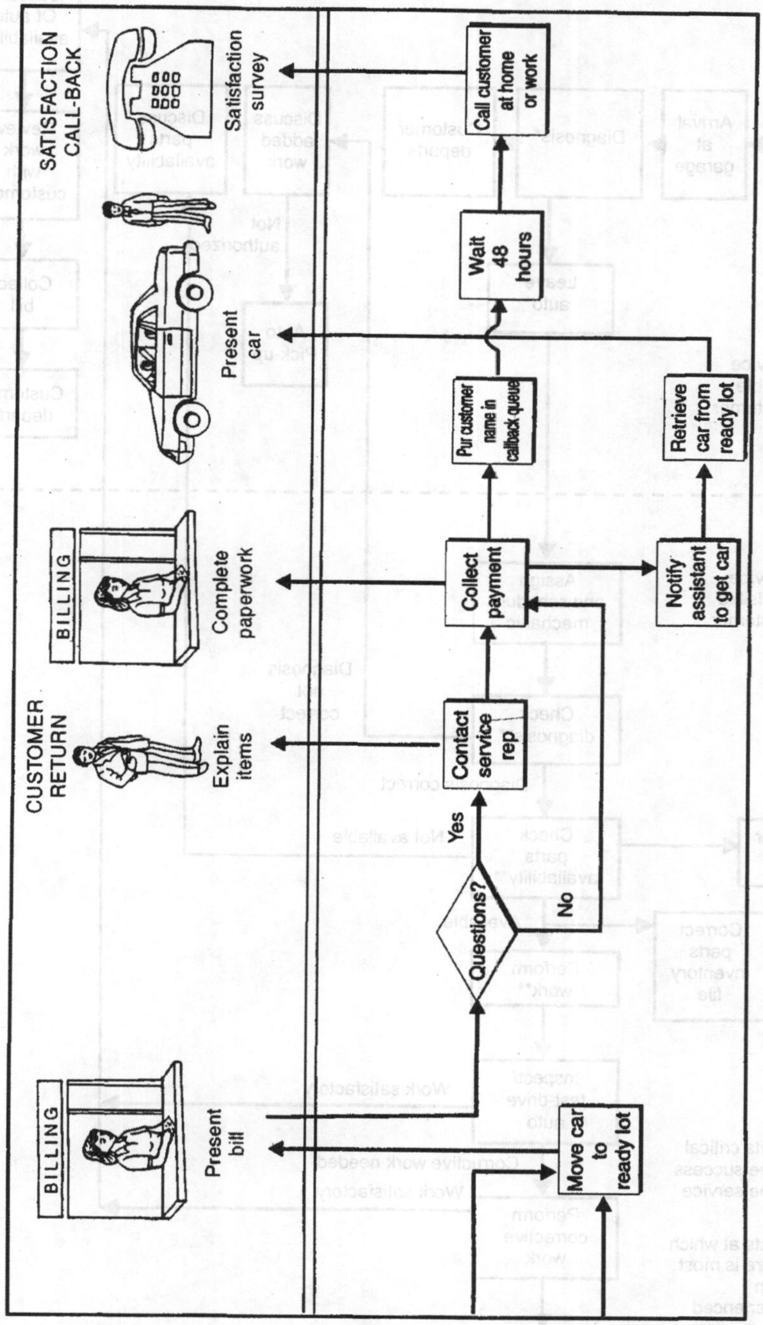

Figure 12.7 : FLOWCHART OF AUTO DEALER'S SERVICE BLUEPRINT

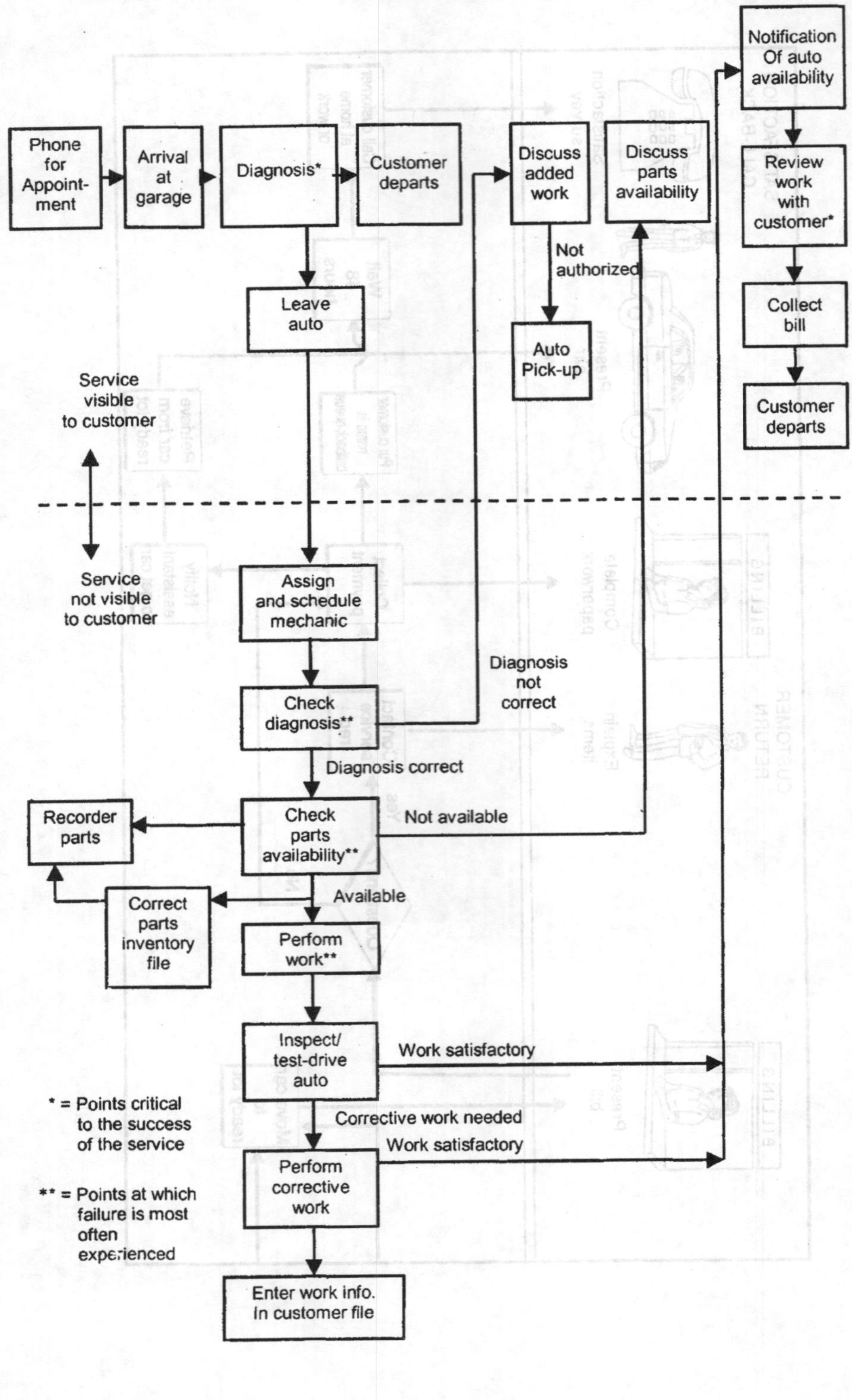

of their own special function and perspective unless a common ground for an integrated view of the service is provided.

7. Provides a basis for identifying and assessing cost, revenue, and capital invested in each element of the service.
8. Constitutes a rational basis for both external and internal marketing. For example, the service map makes it easier for an advertising agency or an in house promotion team to overview a service and select essential messages for communication.
9. Facilitates top-down, bottom-up approach to quality improvement. It enables mangers to identify, channel, and support quality improvement efforts of grass roots employees working on both frontline and support teams. Employee work teams can create service maps and thus more clearly apply and communicate their experience and suggestions for improvements

12.8 SERVICE MAPPING

Service maps build on blueprints and provide two additional features to add to management information.

- They pay greater attention to customer interaction with the service organization
  Clear diagrammatic distinctions are made between actions of customers and of service contact personnel. In effect, more detail is provided on the frontstage activities in blueprints such as Figure 12.8.
- Additional vertical layers to the diagram are drawn in service maps to provide a visual representation of the structure of the service.
- In particular, the backstage activities are divided into those provided by frontline employees, support staff and management services.

In a service map (Figure 12.8), therefore, the horizontal axis denotes the process, going from left to right, and the vertical axis denotes the structure of the service provided. The larger the service organisation, the greater the need to make clear the structure in order that the service logic is understood by all employees.

In the blueprinting examples, one horizontal line divides the frontstage from the backstage. It is commonly known as the line of visibility. In service maps, the organisation structure, denoted on the vertical axis, is made clearer through more dividing lines. There are four lines in total :

1. the line of interaction
   This denotes the distinction between the customers' and frontline employee's parts in the service encounter.
2. the line of visibility.
   Note here, that whilst much of the work of frontline employees is concerned with the service encounter, which is above the line of visibility, some of their work is carried out below the line of visibility, that is, out of sight of the customers.
3. the line of internal interaction
   This denotes the division between the frontline employees and the operations support staff. Such internal interactions normally occur out of sight of customers.
4. the line of implementation
   This denotes the division between operations support staff and general management services. If may be the case that the latter are located physically at a distance from the former and are not therefore directly involved with implementing the service.

Figure 12.8 : SERVICE MAP

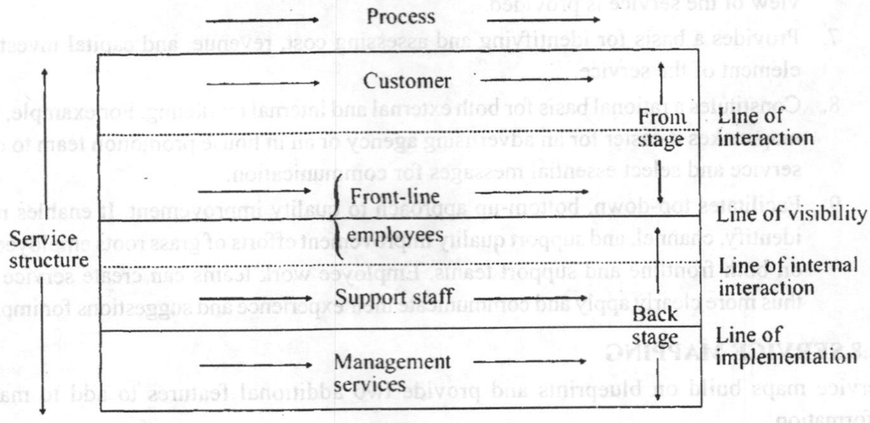

12.9 SERVICE FAILURES

Whatever the diagrammatic form of a service design - whether it be a blueprint, a specific service map or a concept service map - one of the main aim will be to identify the potential points in the process which may result in a service failure. It is probably inevitable that on some occasion either the customer or the server will make some mistake. If these occasions can be anticipated, and the mistake prevented from turning into a service 'defect' and hence a service failure, then the effect spent in service design may be justified. Once points of potential service failures have been identified, fail-safes can be designed to reduce the risk of human mistakes turning into actual service failures.

Customer errors can be classified as relating to preparation for the service encounter, the encounter itself, or to the resolution of the encounter.

- Preparation errors may result from the failure of customers to bring the necessary materials to the encounter, or to understand their roles in the service encounter.
- Encounter errors include failure of customers to remember steps in the service process, to follow the system flow or to specify desires or follow instructions.
- Resolution errors include failure of customers to signal service failures, learn from experience, adjust expectations or execute appropriate post-encounter actions.

12.10 DESIGN ELEMENTS

In designing any service, eleven key factors should be taken into account

CUSTOMER CONTACT

- How much contact will the customer have with the service and what will the nature of that contact be?

SERVICE MIX

What service will be provided in terms of breadth and depth? Breadth equals the number of items in each line; for example, a local authority sports and leisure service may offer the following service lines (breadth): outdoor sports, indoor sports, adventure sports and leisure activities. Within the last mentioned might be art galleries, theatres, museums and parks (depth).

LOCATION OF SERVICE CONSUMPTION

- Will the customer come to a service facility (Single or multi-site) or will the service come to the customer (at home or mobile)?

DESIGN OF SERVICE FACILITY AND ACCESSORIES

- What should the layout, furnishing, colour, etc. of the facility be?
- What design discussions need to be made in respect of staff (uniforms), vehicles (colour, logo), and non-personal communication (letter headings, signs, brochures etc.)?

TECHNOLOGY

- What will be the balance between technology and people, e.g. how will it apply to the employee's work and the customer's usage of the service?
- Will the technology be predominantly hard, e.g. automation or soft, e.g. pre-planned systems - pre-packaged tours?

EMPLOYEES

- How many will be required?
- What will the ratio be between back office employees and front-office employees?
- How many supervisors will be required to control frontline employees?
- What skills will be needed and how will they be acquired?
- How flexible will employees need to be?

ORGANIZATION STRUCTURE

- How many layers in the organization are desirable?
- How should the finance, operations, personnel and marketing functions be organized?

INFORMATION

- What information is desirable for running the organization and how easily will it be acquired?
- How will it be stored?
- How accessible will it be and who will have access?

DEMAND AND SUPPLY MANAGEMENT

- How much knowledge is there about demand patterns and levels?
- What strategies are known for influencing demand?
- How flexible is capacity for meeting demand fluctuations, e.g. work schedules, sub contracting, reservation systems, stock control?

PROCEDURES

- Will the service be mainly standardized or customized?
- How complex will the service be?

CONTROL

- What systems will be in place and what techniques will be available for ensuring the smooth running of the operation and the provision of quality output e.g. critical path analysis, forecasting methods, flow charts, queueing theory application? Such considerations are shown in Table 12.1.

Table 12.1 : MAJOR DESIGN CONSIDERATIONS IN HIGH-AND LOW-CONTACT SYSTEMS

Decision	*High-contact system*	*Low-contact system*
Facility location	Operations must be near the customer	Operations may be placed near supply, transport or labour
Facility layout	Facility should accommodate the customer's physical and psychological needs and expectations	Facility should enhance production
Product design	Environment as well as the physical product define the nature of the service	Customer is not in the service environment so the product can be defined by fewer attributes

Process design	Stages of production process have a direct, immediate effect on the Customer	Customer is not involved in majority of processing steps
Scheduling	Customer is in the production schedule and must be accommodated	Customer is concerned mainly with completion dates
Production planning	Orders cannot be stored, so smooth production flow will result in loss of business.	Both backlogging and production smoothing are possible
Worker skills	Direct workforce comprises a major part of the service production and so must be able to interact well with the public	Direct workforce need only have technical skills
Quality control	Quality standards are often in the eye of the beholder and hence variable	Quality standards are generally measurable and hence fixed
Time standards	Service time depends on customer needs, and therefore time standards are inherently loose	Work is performed on customer surrogates (e.g. forms), thus time standards can be tight
Wage payment	Variable output requires time-based wage systems.	'Fixable' output permits output-based wage systems
Capacity planning	To avoid lost sales, capacity must be be set to match peak demand	Storable output permits capacity at some average demand level
Forecasting	Forecasts are short-term, time oriented	Forecasts are long-term, output oriented

12.11 QUALITY FUNCTION DEPLOYMENT

While blueprints help to ensure that service processes run smoothly and that all contract points with the customer are well through out, further research is usually necessary to ensure that the service meets customer needs. A complicating factor in the design of quality services is the imperfect relationship between the technical design elements of a service and customer who are dissatisfied with some level of a service. For example, how much faster does restaurant service have to be before it is noticed as better? What does a bank have to do to improve customer perceptions that it "listens to their needs"? What elements of office decor will contribute most to an atmosphere that supports perceptions of "professionalism" and "competence"? How can we find the proper balance between providing quick response to waiting customers and taking sufficient time with the customer currently being served? Quality Function Deployment (QFD) was developed to help designers find the links between customer needs and design elements.

QFD was developed in Japan in the 1960s and was fist used at Mitsubishi's Kobe shipyard in 1972. It was subsequently adopted by Toyota and its suppliers where it began to receive worldwide notice. It has been in use in the United States, primarily by manufacturers of automobiles, electronic equipment, and other products. Its used in the service sector has been less extensive but it offers benefits there as well. The purpose of QFD is to translate customers' vague statements into actionable design specifications. It also provides an objective, structured forum in which people from various functions of the design and production process can communicate their needs and opinions on the structure of the service. QFD is an approach, not a rigidly designed set of procedures. But although firms must adapt the methods of QFD to suit their own particular needs, certain common tools are employed by all users of QFD.

The central tool of QFD analysis is a diagram called the House of Quality. The general layout of such a diagram is shown in Figure 12.9. The figure actually shows a small portion of a diagram for

Figure 12.9 : HOUSE OF QUALITY

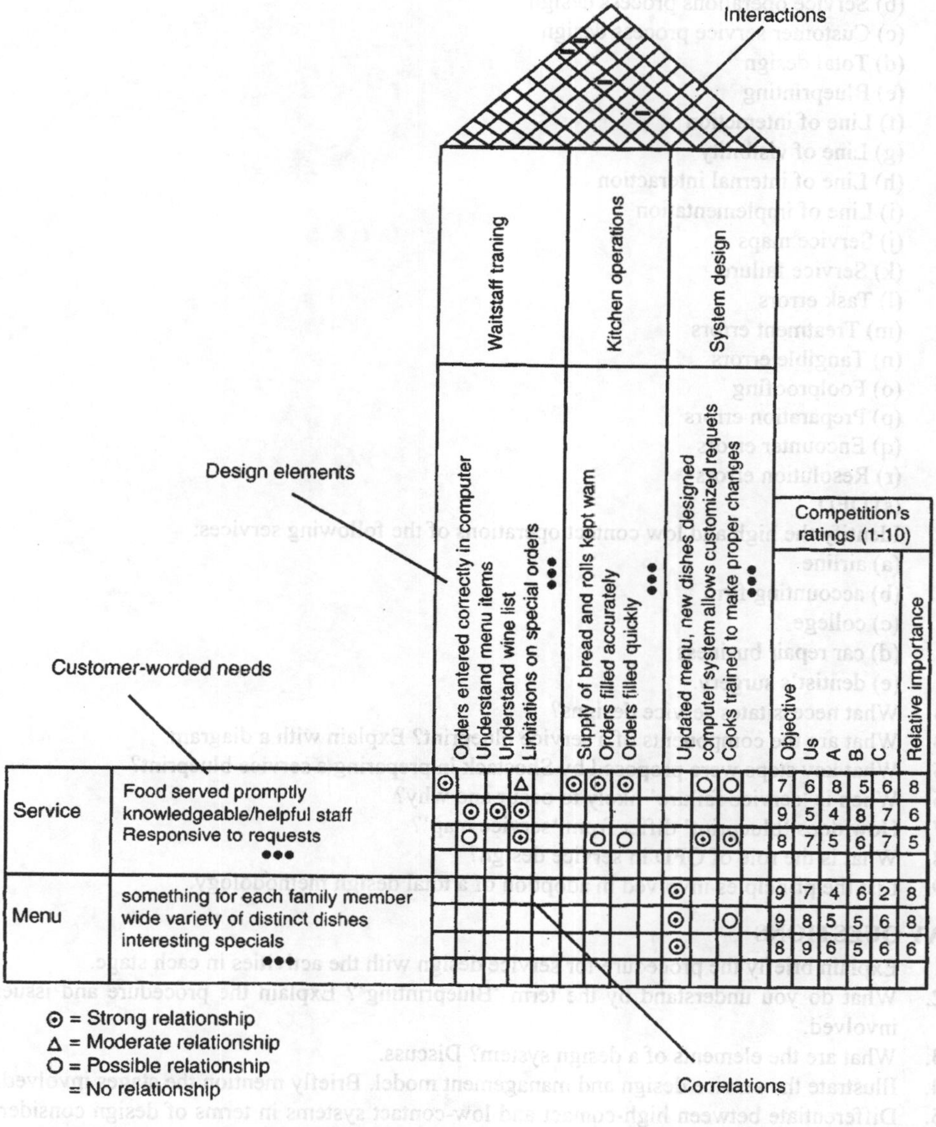

the design of a new chain restaurant. The central part of the diagram is a matrix whose rows correspond to the list of customer needs developed and organized into a hierarchical structure. In this case, we see portions of two major categories of customer needs, Service and Variety. The column labels are the technical components of the service design, also organized in a hierarchical fashion. Components of several categories, staff training, kitchen operations, and menu design are shown. Entries in the matrix are symbols or numbers that indicate the strength of the effect that a design component (column) is likely to have on customer perceptions of a particular need (row).

SHORT ANSWER QUESTIONS

1. Define the following terms:
   (a) Service facility design
   (b) Service operations process design
   (c) Customer service process design
   (d) Total design
   (e) Blueprinting
   (f) Line of interaction
   (g) Line of visibility
   (h) Line of internal interaction
   (i) Line of implementation
   (j) Service maps
   (k) Service failure
   (l) Task errors
   (m) Treatment errors
   (n) Tangible errors
   (o) Foolproofing
   (p) Preparation errors
   (q) Encounter errors
   (r) Resolution errors
   (s) QFD
2. Identify the high and low contact operations of the following services:
   (a) airline
   (b) accounting firm
   (c) college
   (d) car repair business
   (e) dentist's surgery.
3. What necessitates service designs?
4. What are the components of a service blueprint? Explain with a diagram.
5. What key steps were proposed by Shostack in preparing a service blueprint?
6. When is 'service failure' likely to occur and why?
7. How does 'blueprint' differ from 'service map'?
8. What is the role of QFD in service design?
9. List the principles involved in adoption of a total design methodology.

ESSAY QUESTIONS

1. Explain briefly the procedure for service design with the activities in each stage.
2. What do you understand by the term 'Blueprinting'? Explain the procedure and issues involved.
3. What are the elements of a design system? Discuss.
4. Illustrate the service design and management model. Briefly mention the stages involved.
5. Differentiate between high-contact and low-contact systems in terms of design considerations.
6. Draw the service blueprint for the following services:
   - airlines
   - fast-food restaurant
   - lodge
   - courier
   - cinema
7. Enumerate the benefits of service blueprinting.

EXERCISE / ASSIGNMENTS

1. Is it possible for a service organisation to substitute technology for people or use a self-service design and sill keep a high customer focus? Explain and support your answer with examples.
2. Develop a blueprint for a service of your own choice. On completion consider:
   - whether all steps are really necessary
   - the extent to which standardisation is possible, and advisable, throughout the process.
   - The location of critical or pressure points and points where failure is likely to occur
   - Measures of performance at each step.
3. The four operating systems (service factory, mass service, service shop and professional service) face different challenges and problems. Explain and discuss what you think they are.

13

Service Demand and Supply

13.1 THE MANAGEMENT OF CUSTOMER DEMAND

The task of managing markets and ensuring a good fit between supply and demand is usually very much more complex for services than for goods. Because goods manufacturers are able to separate production from consumption, they have the ability to hold stocks of goods that can be moved to even out regional imbalances in supply and demand. Stocks can also be built up to cater for any peaks in demand, for example, umbrella manufacturers can work during the summer months making umbrellas to store to meet the sudden surge in demand each monsoon. Those umbrellas not sold in that monsoon can be sold later in the year at a lower clearance price, or put back into stock for the following year.

Many of the strategies for managing supply and demand which are open to goods manufacturers are not available to services producers. The perishability and inseparability of the service offer means that it is not sufficient to match supply and demand over the longer term within a broadly defined geographical market. Instead, supply and demand must be matched temporally and spatially. An excess of production capacity in one time period cannot be transferred to another period when there is a shortage, nor can excess demand in one area normally be met by excess supply located in another.

The concept of demand can in itself be ambiguous, with economists and marketers adopting somewhat varying definitions of demand. It is therefore useful to begin by identifying possible demand conditions that a service organization may face. Eight different demand situations are:

- ***Negative demand*** occurs where most or all segments in a market possess negative feelings towards a service, to the extent that they may even be prepared to pay to avoid receiving that service. Many medical services are perceived as unpleasant and are purchased only in distress, even though there may be benefit to individuals from receiving regular preventive treatments. The task of marketing management in this situation is to identify the cause of negative feelings and to counter these with positive marketing programmes. In the case of dentists, the introduction of relaxing interior design for surgeries, background music, friendly personnel and a promotion campaign to stress both the pleasantness of modern surgeries and the valuable long-term health benefits may overcome the problems of negative demand.
- ***No demand*** occurs where a product is perceived by certain segments as being of no value. In the financial services sector, young people often see savings and pensions policies as being of no value to themselves. The task of marketing management seeking to create demand in such segments is to reformulate the product offering and promotional methods used so that the product's benefits are more readily comprehended by the target segments.
- ***Latent demand*** occurs where an underlying need for a service exists but there is no product that can satisfy this need at an affordable price to consumers. The task of marketing management becomes one of identifying methods by which new services either could be developed, or are made available at a price that would allow latent demand to be turned into actual demand. Within the travel market, a latent demand for leisure travel to Australia exists, prevented from

being actual demand by the high cost of airfares. The development of more fuel-efficient wide-bodied aircraft and the gradual liberalizing of air-licensing thereby turning some of this latent demand into actual demand.

- ***Faltering demand*** is characterised by a steady fall in sales which is more than a temporary downturn. The task of management is to identify the causes of this downturn and to develop a strategy for reviving demand. Corner shops have often found themselves facing a faltering demand, which has sometimes been successfully transformed by the introduction of longer opening hours and by refocusing the range of goods sold.
- ***Irregular demand*** is characterized by a very uneven distribution of demand through time. The inability to store services from one period of low demand to another of high demand means that this pattern of demand poses major problems for many service industries. It can be overcome by a combination of demand management designed to reduce the irregularity of demand and supply management aimed at meeting demand as closely as practical.
- ***Full demand*** exists where demand is currently at a desirable level and one which allows the organization to meet its objectives. A hotel in a historic city with no scope for further physical expansion may have an occupancy rate that is difficult or impractical to improve. The management task moves away from increasing the volume of demand to improving its quality-by concentrating on high-value activities aimed at high-spending segments, for example.
- ***Overfull demand*** occurs where there is excess demand for a service on a permanent basis. A pop group may find that tickets for all its concerts are sold out very quickly and could be sold many times over. The marketing management task is to stifle demand in a manner which does not cause long-term harm (for example, stifling demand by high prices alone may build up an exploitative image which may be harmful in the future should demand need to be stimulated once more). It also involves increasing supply where this is possible and substitutes for concerts, such as video recordings).
- ***Unwholesome demand*** occurs where an organization receives demand for a service which it would prefer not to have. It may be forced to meet the demand because of legal requirements (for example, the Post Office cannot refuse to deliver letters for customers who are very expensive to service) or because of long-standing commitment to supply service to a customer (a medical insurance company which agreed to automatically renew premiums each year regardless of changes in the customer's state of health will consider renewal requests from sick customers to be a form of unwholesome demand). Marketing management's task here is to try to eliminate new demand through - among other things - reduced promotional activity and higher prices.

13.2 STRATEGIES FOR MANAGING DEMAND

At any given point in time, a fixed - capacity service organization may be faced with one of four conditions (see Figure 13.1)

- Demand exceeds maximum available capacity with the result that potential business may be lost.
- Demand exceeds the optimum capacity level; no one is turned away, but all customers are likely to perceive a deterioration in the quality of service delivered.
- Demand and supply are well balanced at the level of optimum capacity.
- Demand is below optimum capacity and productive resources are underutilized; this poses the risk (in some instances) that customers may find the experience disappointing or have doubts about the viability of the service.

Figure 13.1 : IMPLICATIONS OF VARIATIONS IN DEMAND RELATIVE TO CAPACITY

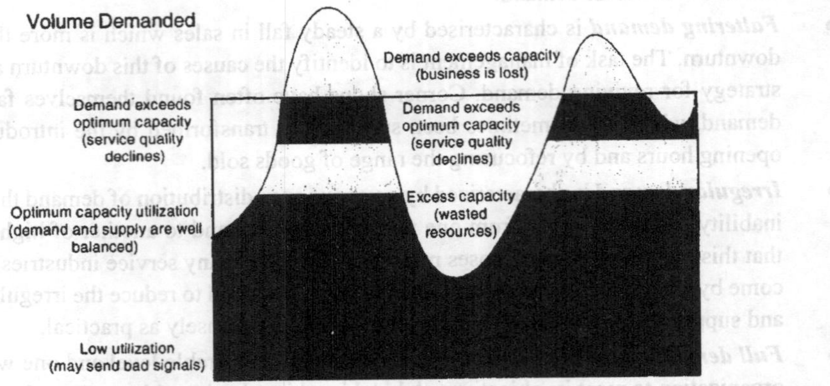

There is a distinction between ***maximum capacity*** and ***optimum capacity***. When demand exceeds maximum available capacity, some potential customers may be turned away and their business lost for ever, but when demand is operating between optimum and maximum capacity, there's a risk all customers being served at that time may start to receive inferior service. In such conditions, service managers need to employ what they call a coping strategy to control the fall in service standards and thus prevent customer dissatisfaction.

Sometimes optimum and maximum capacities are one and the same. At a live theatre or sports performance, a full house is desirable, since it stimulates the players and creates a sense of excitement and audience participation. The net result? A more satisfying experience for all. But with most other services, you probably feel that you get better service if the facility is not operating at full capacity. The quality of restaurant service, for instance, often deteriorates when every table is occupied, because the staff are rushed and there's a greater likelihood of errors or delays.

Optimizing the use of capacity requires looking at the mix of business obtained as well as at the total volume. Some market segments may be more desirable than other because the customers fit particularly well with the organization's mission, reinforce the ambiance that the service organization is trying to create, have needs that match the professional skills and interests of staff members, or pay higher rates and are more profitable. Marketing managers should examine the components of overall demand and seek to stimulate or discourage demand from particular segments on a selective basis. Of course, if a firm wants to attract new business during its low season, it may have to choose between accepting customers from a segment that fits less well with its mission or foregoing the revenues that they might bring.

There are five common approaches to managing demand. The first, which has the virtue of simplicity but little else, involves taking no action and leaving demand to find its won levels. Eventually customers learn from experience or word of mouth when they can expect to stand in line to use the service and when it will be available without delay. The trouble is they may also learn to find a competitor who is more responsive.

More interventionist approaches involve influencing the level of demand at any given time, by taking active steps to reduce demand in peak periods and to increase demand when there is excess capacity.

Two more approaches both involve inventorying demand until capacity becomes available. You can accomplish this either by introducing a reservations system, that promises customers access to capacity at specified times, or by creating formalized queuing systems (or by combination of the two).

Table 13.1 links these five approaches to the three basic situations of insufficient capacity relative to demand, sufficient capacity, and excess capacity,

Table 13.1 : ALTERNATIVE DEMAND MANAGEMENT STRATEGIES FOR DIFFERENT CAPACITY SITUATIONS

Approach Used to Manage Demand	*Capacity Situation Relative to Demand*		
	Insufficient Capacity (Excess Demand)	*Sufficient Capacity* (Satisfactory Demand)*	*Excess Capacity (Insufficient Demand)*
Take up action	Unorganized queuing results. (May irritate Customers and discourage future use.)	Capacity is fully utilized. (But is this the most profitable mix of business?)	Capacity is wasted. (Customers may have a disappointing experience for services like theater.)
Reduce demand	Pricing higher will increase profits. Communication can be employed to encourage usage in other time slots. (Can this effort be focused on less profitable / desirable segments?)	Take no action	Take no action
Increase demand	Take no action, unless opportunities exist to stimulate (and give priority to) more profitable segments.	Take no action, unless opportunities exist to stimulate (and give priority to) more profitable segments.	Price lower selectively (try to avoid cannibaliz ing existing business; ensure all relevant costs are covered). Use communications and variation in products / distribution (but recognize extra costs, if any, and make sure appropriate trade-offs are made between profit ability and usage levels).
Inventory demand by reservation system	Consider priority system for most desirable segments. Make other customers shift (a) to outside peak period or (b) to futur peak.	Try to ensure most profitable mix of business.	Clarify that space is available and that no reservations are needed.
Investory demand by formalized queuing	Consider override for most desirable segments. Seek to keep waiting customers occupied and comfortable. Try to predict wait period accurately	Try to avoid bottleneck delays.	Not applicable.

* "Sufficient capacity" may be defined as maximum available capacity or optimum capacity, depending on the situation.

13.3 UNDERSTANDING THE PATTERNS AND DETERMINANTS OF DEMAND

The search for demand management strategies starts with an understanding of what factors govern demand for a specific service at a given point in time. Managers should address the following questions:

1. **Does the level of demand for the service follow a predictable cycle? If so, is the cycle duration:**
   - One day (varies by hour)
   - One week (varies by day)
   - One month (varies by day or by week)
   - One year (varies by month or by season; or reflects annually occurring public holidays)
   - Some other period.
2. **What are the underlying causes of these cyclical variations?**
   - Employment schedules
   - Billing and tax payment / refund cycles
   - Wage and salary payment dates
   - School hours and vacations
   - Seasonal changes in climate
   - Occurrence of public or religious holidays
   - Natural cycles, such as cyclones.
3. **Do demand levels seem to change randomly? If so, could the underlying causes be:**
   - Day-to-day changes in the weather (consider how rain and cold affect the use of indoor and outdoor recreational or entertainment services).
   - Health events whose occurrence cannot be pin-pointed exactly (heart attacks and births affect the demand for hospital services).
   - Accidents, acts of nature and certain criminal activities (these require fast response not only from fire, police, and ambulance but also from disaster recovery specialists and insurance firms).
4. **Can demand for a particular service over time be disaggregated by market segment to reflect such components as:**
   - Use patterns by a particular type of customer or for a particular purpose?
   - Variations in the net profitability of each completed transaction?

Random fluctuations are usually caused by factors beyond management's control. But analysis will sometimes reveal that a predictable demand cycle for one segment is concealed within a broader, seemingly random pattern. The fact illustrates the importance of breaking down demand on a segment – by-segment basis.

For instance, a repair and maintenance shop that services industrial electrical equipment may already know that a certain proportion of its work consists of regularly scheduled contracts to perform preventive maintenance. The balance may come from "walk-in" business and emergency repairs. Although it might seem hard to predict or control the timing and volume of such work, further analysis could show that walk-in-business was more prevalent on some days of the week than others and that emergency repairs were frequently requested following damage sustained during thunderstorms (which tend to be seasonal in nature and can often be forecast a day or two in advance).

Keeping good records of each transaction helps enormously when it comes to analyzing demand patterns based on past experience. Computer-based services, such as telecommunications, can track customer consumption patterns by date and time of day automatically. When relevant, it's also useful to record weather conditions and other special factors (a strike, an accident, a big convention in town, a price change, launch of a competing service, etc.) that might have influenced demand.

Most periodic cycles influencing demand for a particular service vary in length from 1 day to 12 months. In many instances, multiple cycles may operate simultaneously. For example, demand levels for public transport may vary by time of day, day of week, and season of year. The demand for service during the peak period on a Monday in summer may be different from the level during the peak period on a Saturday in winter, reflecting day-of-week and seasonal variations jointly.

Figure 13.2 shows how the combination of 4 time-of-day periods (morning peak, mid-days, afternoon peak, evening/night), 2 day of week period (weekday, weekend), and 3 seasonal periods (peak, shoulder, off-peak) can be combined to create 24 different demand periods. In theory, each of these might have its own distinct demand level (at a given price) and customer profiles (with resulting differences in needs and expectations). But in practice, analysis might show close similarities between many of the periods. Such a finding would make it possible to collapse the framework into a total of perhaps three to six cells, each requiring a distinct marketing treatment to optimize the use of available capacity and obtain the most desirable customer mix.

13.4 DISAGGREGATING DEMAND BY MARKET SEGMENT

Can marketing efforts smooth out random fluctuations in demand? The answer is generally no, since these fluctuations are usually caused by factors beyond the service organization's control. But detailed market analysis may sometimes reveal that a predictable demand cycle for one segment is concealed within a border, seemingly random pattern. As already mentioned a repair and maintenance shop may know that a certain proportion of its work consists of regularly scheduled contractual business, representing preventive maintenance. The balance may come from "walk-in" business and emergency repairs, and it may be hard to predict or control the timing and volume of such work.

Figure 13.2 : IDENTIFYING VARIATIONS IN DEMAND BY TIME PERIOD

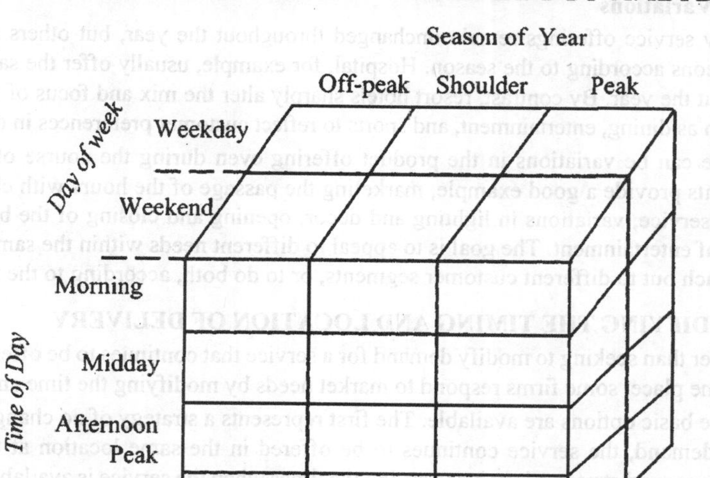

The ease with which total demand can be disaggregated depends on the nature of the records kept by the service organization. If each customer transaction is recorded separately, and backed up by detailed notes (as in hospital visit or accountant's audit) when each customer's identity is known and itemized monthly bills are sent, managers can gain some immediate insights into usage patterns. Some services - such as telephone - even have the ability to track subscriber consumption patterns by time of day although the service is being used, it is often possible to make informed judgements about the volume of sales generated by different user groups.

Analysis may also show that part of the demand for a particular service is undesirable, for instance, calls to emergency services to rescue cats from trees. Discouraging undesirable demand through marketing campaigns or screening procedures will not, of course, eliminate random fluctuations in the remaining demand. But is may bring the peaks of that demand within the service capacity of the organization.

No strategy for smoothing is likely to succeed unless it is based on an understanding of why customers from a specific market segment choose to use the service when they do. For example, most hotels find it difficult to convince business travelers to remain on Saturday nights since few executives do business over the weekend.

Instead, hotel managers should consider promoting use of their facilities for other purposes at weekends, such as conferences or pleasure travel. Similarly, attempts to get commuters on public transport to shift their travel to off-peak periods will probably fail, since the timing of most commute travel is determined by people's employment hours. Instead, marketing efforts should be directed at employers to persuade them to adopt flexitime or staggered working hours.

13.5 USING MARKETING MIX ELEMENTS TO SHAPE DEMAND

All the elements of the marketing mix have a role to play in stimulating demand during periods of excess capacity and in decreasing it (demarketing) during periods of insufficient capacity. Price is often the first variable to be proposed for bringing demand and supply into balance, but changes in product, distribution strategy, and communication efforts can also play an important role. Although each element is discussed separately, effective demand management efforts often require changes in two or more elements jointly.

Product Variations

Many service offerings remain unchanged throughout the year, but others undergo significant modifications according to the season. Hospital, for example, usually offer the same array of service throughout the year. By contrast, resort hotels sharply alter the mix and focus of their peripheral services such as dining, entertainment, and sports to reflect customer preferences in different seasons.

There can be variations in the product offering even during the course of a 24-hour period. Restaurants provide a good example, marketing the passage of the hours with changing menus and levels of service, variations in lighting and decor, opening and closing of the bar, and presence or absence of entertainment. The goal is to appeal to different needs within the same group of customers, to reach out to different customer segments, or to do both, according to the time of day.

13.6 MODIFYING THE TIMING AND LOCATION OF DELIVERY

Rather than seeking to modify demand for a service that continues to be offered at the same time in the same place, some firms respond to market needs by modifying the time and place of delivery.

Three basic options are available. The first represents a strategy of no change: regardless of the level of demand, the service continues to be offered in the same location at the same times. By contrast, a second strategy involves varying the times when the service is available to reflect changes in customer preference by day of week, by season, and so forth. Theaters often offer matinees at weekends when people have leisure time throughout the day; during the summer in hot climates, banks may close for two hours at midday while people take a siesta, but remain open later in the evening when other commercial establishments are still active.

A third strategy involves offering the service to customers at a new location. One approach is to operate mobile units that take the service to customers, rather than requiring them to visit fixed -site service locations. Travelling libraries and vans equipped with primary care medical facilities are two examples that might be copied by other service businesses. A cleaning and repair firm that wishes to generate business during low demand periods might offer free pickup and delivery of portable items that need servicing.

Alternatively, service firms whose productive assets are mobile may choose to follow the market when that, too, is mobile. For instance, some car rental firms establish seasonal branch offices in resort communities. In these new locations, they often change the schedule of service hours (as well as certain product features) to conform to local needs and preferences.

13.7 PRICING STRATEGIES

For price to be effective as a demand management tool, the marketing manager must have some sense of the shape and slope of a product's demand curve (i.e., how the quantity of service demanded responds to increases or decreases in the price per unit) at a particular point in time.

Figure 13.3 : VARIATIONS IN DEMAND CURVES BY TIME PERIOD

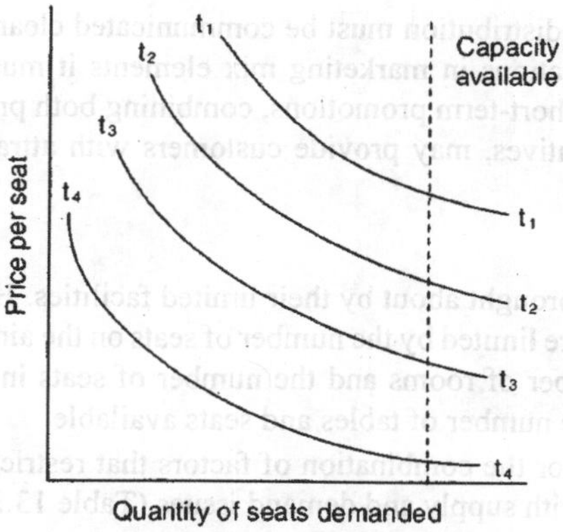

Key : t_1 = Peak hour, weekday, high season
t_2 = Peak hour, weekday, low season
t_3 = Peak hour, weekend, high season
t_4 = Off-peak hour, weekend, low season

Figure 13.4 : DIFFERING DEMAND CURVES FOR DIFFERENT SEGMENTS IN TWO TIME PERIODS

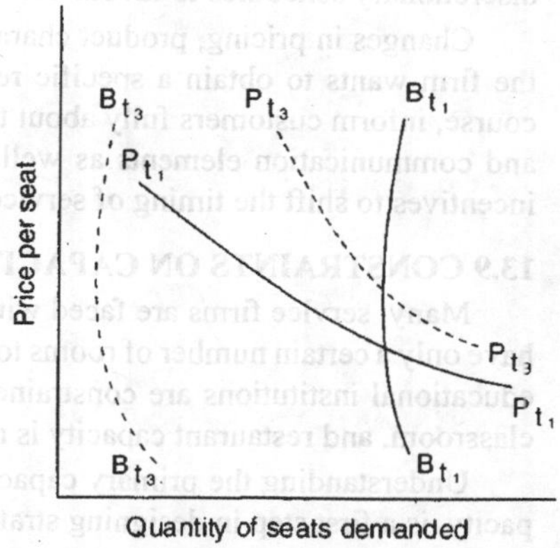

Key : B = Business travelers
P = Pleasure travelers
t_1 = Peak hour, weekday, high season
t_3 = Peak hour, weekend, high season

It's important to determine whether the aggregate demand curve for a specific service varies sharply from one time period to another (Figure 13.3). If so, significantly different pricing schemes may be needed to fill capacity in each time period. To complicate matters further, there may be separate demand curves for different segments within each time period (Figure 13.4) reflecting variation between segments in the need for the service or inability to pay. One of the most difficult tasks facing service marketers is to determine the nature of all these different demand curves. Research, trial and error, and analysis of parallel situations in other locations or in comparable services are all ways of obtaining an understanding of the situation.

Many service businesses explicitly recognize the existence of different demand curves for different segments during the same time period by establishing distinct classes of service, each priced at levels appropriate to the demand curve of a particular segment. In essence, each segment receives a variation of the basic product, with value being added to the core service in order to appeal to the higher paying segments. For instance, top-of -the-line service in airlines offers travelers larger seats, free drinks, and better food; in computer service bureaus, product enhancement takes the form of faster turnaround and more specialized analytical procedures and reports.

In each case, the objective is to maximize the revenues received from each segment. However, when capacity is constrained, the goal in a profit-seeking business should be to ensure that as much capacity as possible is utilized by the most profitable segments. For this reason, various usage conditions may have to be set to discourage versions of the product. Airlines, for instance, may insist the excursion tickets be purchased 21 days in advance and that ticket holders remain at their destinations for at least one week before returning - conditions that are too constraining for most business travellers.

13.8 COMMUNICATION EFFORTS

Even if the other variables of the marketing mix remain unchanged, communication efforts alone may be able to help smooth demand. Signing, advertising, and sales messages can remind customers of peak periods and encourage them to travel at uncrowded , off-peak times when service is, perhaps, faster or more comfortable. Examples include postal service requests to "Mail Early for Christmas," public transport messages urging non-commuters -such as shoppers or tourists - to avoid the rush hours, and communications from sales reps for industrial maintenance firms advising customers of periods when preventive maintenance work can be done quickly. In addition, management can ask service personnel (or intermediaries such as travel agents) to encourage customers with discretionary schedules to favour off -peaks periods.

Changes in pricing, product characteristics, and distribution must be communicated clearly. If the firm wants to obtain a specific response to variations in marketing mix elements it must, of course, inform customers fully about their options. Short-term promotions, combining both pricing and communication elements as well as other incentives, may provide customers with attractive incentives to shift the timing of service usage.

13.9 CONSTRAINTS ON CAPACITY

Many service firms are faced with restrictions brought about by their limited facilities. Hotels have only a certain number of rooms to sell, airlines are limited by the number of seats on the aircraft, educational institutions are constrained by the number of rooms and the number of seats in each classroom, and restaurant capacity is restricted to the number of tables and seats available.

Understanding the primary capacity constraint, or the combination of factors that restricts capacity, is a first step in designing strategies to deal with supply and demand issues (Table 13.2)

Table 13.2 : WHAT IS THE CONSTRAINT ON CAPACITY?

Nature of the constraint	*Types of service**
Time	Legal Consulting Accounting Medical
Labour	Law firm Accounting firm Consulting firm Health clinic
Equipment	Delivery services Telecommunication Utilities Health club
Facilities	Hotels Restaurants Hospitals Airlines Schools Theaters Churches

* The examples illustrate the most common capacity constraint for each type of service. In reality, any of the service organizations listed can be operating under multiple constraints. For example, a law firm may be operating under constrained labour capacity (too few attorneys) and facilities constraints (not enough office space) at the same time.

13.10 MEASURING AND MANAGING CAPACITY

What do we mean by productive capacity? The term refers to the resources or assets that a firm can employ to create goods and services. In a service context, productive capacity can take at least five potential forms.

1. **Physical facilities designed to contain customers** and used for delivering people-processing services or mental stimulus processing services. Examples include hospital clinics, hotels, passenger aircraft, buses, restaurants, swimming pools, cinemas, concert halls and college classrooms. In these situations, the primary capacity constraint is likely to be defined in terms of such furnishings as beds, rooms, seats, tables or desks. In some cases, local regulations may set an upper limit to the number of people allowed in the interest of health or fire safety.
2. **Physical facilities designed for storing or processing goods** that either belong to customers or are being offered to them for sale. Examples include supermarket shelves, pipelines, warehouses, car parks, freight containers or railway freight cars.
3. **Physical equipment used to process people, possessions or information** may embrace a huge range of items and be very situation-specific - machinery, telephones, hair dryers, computers, diagnostic equipment, airport security detectors, toll gates on roads and bridges, cooking ovens, bank ATMs, repair tools and cash registers are among the many items whose absence in sufficient numbers for a given level of demand can bring service to a crawl (or a complete stop).
4. **Labour**, a key element of productive capacity in all high-contact services and many low-contact ones, may be used for both physical and mental work. Staffing levels for personnel, from restaurant waiters and waitresses to nurses to telephone operators, must be sufficient to meet anticipated demand - otherwise customers will be kept waiting or service rushed. Professional services are especially dependent on highly skilled staff to create high value-added, information-based output. Abraham Lincoln captured it well when he remarked that "A lawyer's time and expertise are his stock in trade".
5. **Infrastructure**. Many organizations, are dependent on access to sufficient capacity on the public or private infrastructure to be able to deliver quality service to their own customers. Capacity problems of this nature may include busy telephone circuits, electrical power failures (or black outs caused by reduced voltage) congested air ways that lead to air traffic restrictions, and traffic jams on major roads.

13.11 MEASURING CAPACITY

Measures of capacity utilization include : the number of hours (or percentage of total available time) that facilities, labour and equipment are productively employed in revenue operation, and the percentage of available space (e.g., seats, cubic freight capacity, telecommunications bandwidth) that is actually utilized in revenue operations. Human beings tend to be far more variable than equipment in their ability to sustain consistent levels of output over time. One tired or poorly trained employee staffing a single station in an assembly-line operation like a cafeteria restaurant can slow the entire service to crawl. In a well-planned, well-managed service operation, the capacity of the facility, supporting equipment and service personnel will be in balance. Similarly, sequential operations will be designed to minimize the likelihood of bottlenecks at any point in the process. In practice, it's difficult to achieve this ideal all the time.

13.12 STRETCHING AND SHRINKING THE LEVEL OF CAPACITY

Some capacity is elastic in its ability to absorb extra demand. A carriage on the Kolkata Underground or Metro, for instance, may offer 40 seats and allow standing room for another 60 passengers with adequate handrail and floor space for all. Yet at rush hours, when there have been delays on the line, perhaps 200 'standees' can be accommodated under sardine-like conditions. Service personnel may be able to work at high levels of efficiency for short periods of time, but would quickly tire and begin providing inferior service if they had to work at such a pace all day long..

Even where capacity appears fixed, as when it's based on the number of seats, there may still be busy times. Some airlines, for instance, increase the capacity of their aircraft by slightly reducing legroom throughout the cabin and cramming in another couple of rows. Similarly a restaur ant may add extra tables and chairs. Upper limits to such practices are often set by safety standards or by the capacity of supporting services, such as the kitchen.

Another strategy for stretching capacity is to use the facilities for longer periods, Examples of this include restaurants that open for early dinners and late suppers, extend their schedules from, say 14 to 18 hours a day. Alternatively, the average amount of time that customers (or their possessions) spend in process may be reduced. Sometimes this is achieved by minimizing slack time, as when the bill is presented promptly to group of diners relaxing at the table after a meal. In other instances, it may be achieved by cutting back the level of service - say, offering a simpler menu at busy times of day.

13.13 CHASING DEMAND

Another strategy, known as ' chase demand' involves tailoring capacity to match variations in demand. Possible ways to adjust capacity as needed include:

- **Schedule downtime during periods of low demand**. The ensure that 100 per cent of capacity is available during peak periods, repairs and renovations should be conducted when demand is expected to be low, and employee holidays should be taken then.
- **Use part-time employees.** Many organizations hire extra workers during their business periods. Examples include postal workers and retail shop assistant at Christmas time, extra staff within tax preparation service at the end of the financial year and additional hotel employees during holiday periods and major conferences.
- **Rent or share extra facilities and equipment**. To limit investment in fixed assets, a service business may be able to rent extra space or machines at peak times. Firms with complementary demand patterns may enter into formal sharing agreements.
- **Cross-train employees.** Even when the service delivery system appears to be operating at full capacity, certain physical elements - and their attendant employees may be underutilized. If employees can be cross-trained to perform a variety of tasks, they can be shifted to bottleneck points as needed, thereby increasing total system capacity. In supermarkets, for instance, the manager may call on stockers to operate cash registers when checkout queues start to get too long. Likewise during slow periods, the cashiers may be asked to help stock shelves.

13.14 CREATING FLEXIBLE CAPACITY

Sometimes, the problems lies not in the overall capacity but in the mix that's available to service the needs of different market segments. For instance, on a given flight, an airline may have too few seats in economy even though there are empty places in the business class cabin; or a hotel may find itself short of suites one day when there are standard rooms still available. One solution lies in designing physical facilities to be flexible. Some hotels build rooms with connecting doors. With the door between two rooms locked, the hotel can sell two bedrooms ; with the door unlocked and one of the bedrooms converted into a sitting room, the hotel can now offer a suite.

13.15 MATCHING CAPACITY TO DEMAND

Management must analyze these components of capacity, particularly at periods of maximum demand to determine which ones are causing service bottlenecks (Table 13.3) A technique called blueprinting, can be used to identify critical stages. Those points that are constraining capacity should then be altered to provide the level of service desired.

Strategies for Capacity Flexibility The amount of flexibility a firm should build into its capacity is a strategic decision, which is determined by the types of service offered, costs, labour availability and other factors. At one extreme is a level-capacity strategy, in which the firm designs its systems to provide a constant level of capacity and absorbs the costs when demand is far above or far below that level. At the other extreme is the strategy to meet current needs. A given firm's optimal level of flexibility to match capacity to demand will fall somewhere between those two extremes.

A firm should tend toward a level-capacity strategy, particularly in its personnel policies, when employees are required to have high skill levels and to work with minimal supervision and must exercise personal discretion in dealing with customers. Such jobs typically have high recruitment and training costs, so low turnover is essential. These may also require long lead times to change facility or equipment capacity, and these changes can only be made in large, discrete increments. This strategy is also more acceptable if operations are automated to the extent that the marginal cost of dealing with additional customers is low.

Table 13.3 : USING THE MARKETING MIX TO MATCH DEMAND AND CAPACITY

	When Demand is Too High	*When Demand is Too Low*
Price	Raise prices, in general or to certain segments Use price promotions to shift demand to off-peak times	Lower prices, in general or to certain segments Offer price promotions
Promotion product/process	Encourage off-peak usage Schedule less reservations Alter process to allow more customer involvement Standardize or simplify to increase productivity and production Capacity use waiting lines	Encourage trial Add new services to use slack capacity and attract new users
Distribution	Extend hours add additional sites, if possible	Make hours more convenient Offer more convenient locations
People	Train more people to perform parts of process Keep part-timers available Segment customers by time-sensitivity and encourage less sensitive to come at off-peak times	Keep inappropriate segments from mixing together

A chase strategy is more appropriate for firms with labour-intensive operations requiring low-skilled employees who require little training and where part-time employees can be quickly brought in. High labour turnover is actually an advantage in this case, because capacity can be quickly reduced without incurring layoff costs.

Customer Involvement Another source of additional capacity is the customer himself or herself. By converting certain operations to self-service, the firm's own personnel can be diverted to other functions. Buffets and salad bars at restaurants are a common example. Discount investment brokers who leave researching of investment alternatives to the customer, have been remarkably successful, now accounting for more than 30% of the broker business. In general, requiring customers to provide their own service must be reflected in lower prices or they tend to feel they are being cheated. Self-service firms also lose a certain measure of control over service quality when customers are asked to perform key steps, so managers must be careful to transfer only easily accomplished tasks to their patrons.

Other Methods to Alter Capacity In addition to adjusting the various components of capacity listed above, services have developed other ways to increase capacity. One is to use subcontractors to bolster service capacity. This can give the firm access to highly-trained employees for short periods of time. Similarly, the firm may be able to rent facilities and equipment on short notice.

13.16 CAPACITY MANAGEMENT STRATEGIES

In some environments it is important that the services can be 'guaranteed'. Examples, are the emergency services (fire, police, ambulance) and also the so-called utilities (gas, electricity and water). For these, it is not unusual to maintain excess capacity, and to develop contingency plans to handle the extremely high levels of demand which can occur very infrequently. Non-urgent, routine tasks are in part used to absorb the excess capacity. This might include maintaining equipment, training and providing advisory service. Within the fire service, plans are drawn up whereby one fire station can have back-up provided by a neighbouring station if levels of demand' (fires or other emergencies) are at an extremely high level.

It is sometimes possible to offer an alternative service when capacity limitations are reached within one area. Illustrations are the air passenger upgraded from tourist to club/business class be-

Figure 13.5 : DIFFERENT CAPACITY MANAGEMENT STRATAGIES

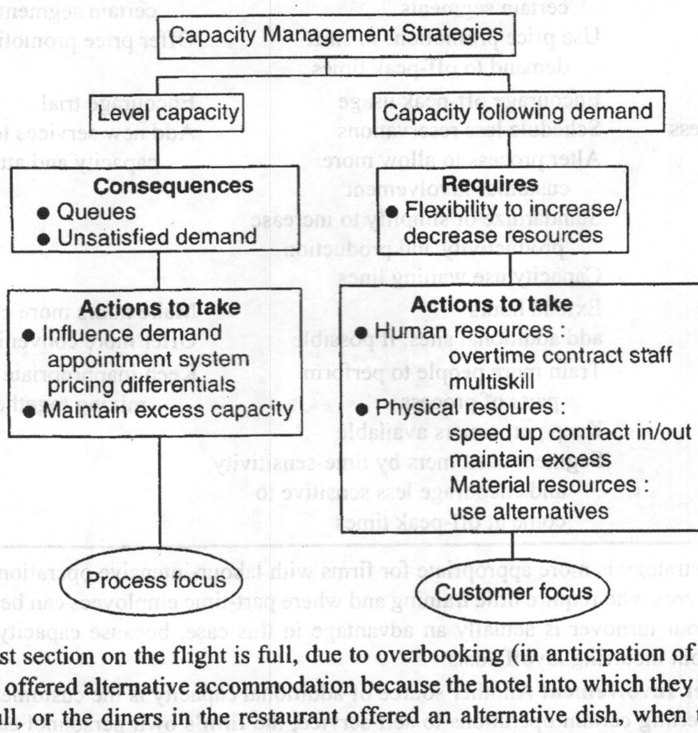

cause the tourist section on the flight is full, due to overbooking (in anticipation of no-shows), the holidaymakers offered alternative accommodation because the hotel into which they were originally booked was full, or the diners in the restaurant offered an alternative dish, when the one chosen originally was finished. This process has to be handled with care as it can change customers' expectations of the services (the passenger might always expect champagne during the flight!) and it can cause problems with other customer (the other passengers who paid the full club-class fare). On occasions, it is possible to alter the service : for example, at a fairground the rides will tend to be shorter at the weekend and in the evenings as demand gets higher. Again, this can have an impact on the perceived quality of the services.

Two key parameters are the demand from customers and the time required to provide the service. A number of possibilities are available to influence or attempt to manage demand. The most common is the appointment or reservation system. However, this does have the disadvantage that, depending on the consequences, a proportion of customers might not turn up for any given appointment, As a result, organizations can be encouraged to overbook appointments, which can result in either delaying or changing the service. During periods of non-peak demand, different prices are often used to stimulate During periods of non-peak demand, different pricing policies are often used to stimulate demand (weekend break offers in hotels, early bird meals in restaurants, happy hours in bars, saver tickets on the rail service). Some of these strategies are summarized in Figure 13.5.

13.17 QUEUING SITUATIONS

With the frequent necessity of the presence of the customer in service situations and the inability to hold or make for stocks, queues have an important role to play in service delivery systems and in the management of capacity. There are a number of key parameters in queuing situations: these include the arrival pattern of customers, the service times, the number of servers, the queuing configuration and the queue discipline. These are the parameters which the organization can consider controlling in attempting to manage capacity. In the previous section, some of the alternatives in terms of managing demand were discussed.

Example

A small fast-food restaurant has a single service position operated by one person. Studies have shown that customers arrive on average every 4 minutes (at the rate of 15 per hour), and that when a customer arrives does not depend on when the previous customer arrived (normally called random or negative exponential arrivals). It currently takes the server an average of 3 minutes to serve each customer (a rate of 20 per hour), and there is considerable variation in this time.

In general, if the arrival rate per hour is l and the service rate per hour is m, then the utilization:

$$u = \frac{l}{m}$$

It can be shown that the average waiting time :

where s is the average service time in minutes.

Applying these results to the example (given that the arrival intervals and service times are negative exponential) :

$$u = \frac{15}{20} = 0.75 \text{ (OR 75\% UTILIZATION)}$$

It is worth noting that, unless the arrival rate is less than the service rate ($l < m$), the queue will get longer and longer.

The average length of time that a customer will have to wait can be calculated as :

$$W = \frac{0.75}{1 - 0.75} \text{ x 3 minutes} = 9 \text{ minutes.}$$

Figure 13.6 : RELATIONSHIP BETWEEN WAITING TIME AND UTILIZATION

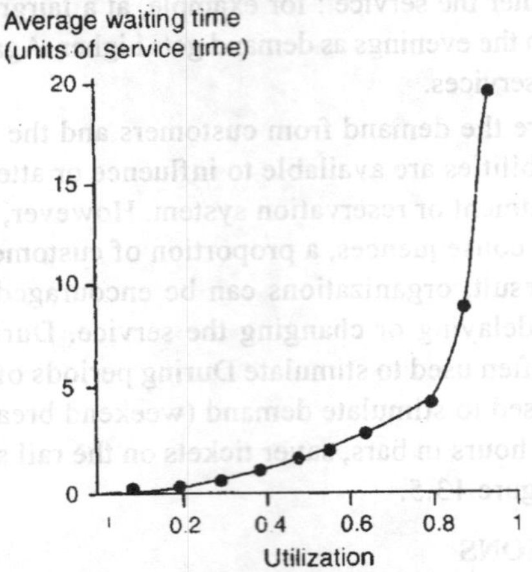

It might be felt that this is unacceptably long, Several options might be possible. The first might be to purchase a more sophisticated cash register which will speed up the payment process and reduce the average service time to $2\frac{1}{2}$ minutes. The effect of this can be evaluated as follows :

$$l = 15, \text{ but } m = 24 \text{ so } u = \frac{15}{24} = 0.625$$

$$\text{and } W = \frac{0.625}{1 - 0.625} \times 2.5 \text{ minutes} = 4.2 \text{ minutes}$$

It is interesting to note the relationship between utilization and the average waiting time. This is shown in Figure 13.6 for the single-server queue with negative exponential arrivals and service time. As the organization aims for high levels of utilization, this is at the expense of longer customer waiting times; equally, as shorter waiting times are offered, lower utilization of resources results.

A second option open to the fast-food restaurant would be to employee a second server, and again it would be useful to examine the impact on the average waiting time. Typically, the decisions open to an organization can be generalized from the above example and frequently expressed in cost terms. This involves balancing the costs associated with customers waiting (customer's lost time, space and so on) and the costs of providing the service (which typically increase as the waiting time decreases). As resources are increased, the cost of providing the services increases, but the cost of waiting reduces. The challenge for management is to determine the resource level which minimizes the total of these two costs.

13.18 SCHEDULING AND PLANNING

Scheduling and planning are generally carried out over a relatively short timescale, typically hours, days or weeks, depending on the environment, at the level of detail of the smallest (or at least a smaller) unit of resource. A variety of different terms are used to describe the process in different services. In education, 'timetabling' is commonly used, work rostra are frequently referred to, and the term 'work scheduling' is sometimes employed. It is important to distinguish between the method used to present the plan and the process by which the plan is produced, although the presentation method can significantly assist the planning process. Normally underlying this is a figure which

shows what the resources, or group of resources, are doing against a timescale. This can be viewed from the perspective on a customer.

Time tables can be used to show what a particular group of students were doing (first-year undergraduates in business studies), or a member (or group) of staff. Clearly, the information in this final option becomes more difficult to interpret, as the number of student groups and staff members gets large. This form of presentation could easily be adapted to cover a range of situations : for example, staffing the different areas in a fast-food restaurant.

When the focus is on the customer, and the 'processing time' can vary considerably, then a form of bar chart can be used to represent the manner in which the customers are being served. Figure 13.7 shows a bar chart for patients arriving (at random) to see one of three physicians. They join a common queue and wait to see the first one who becomes free.

Figure 13.7 : SIMPLE BAR CHART

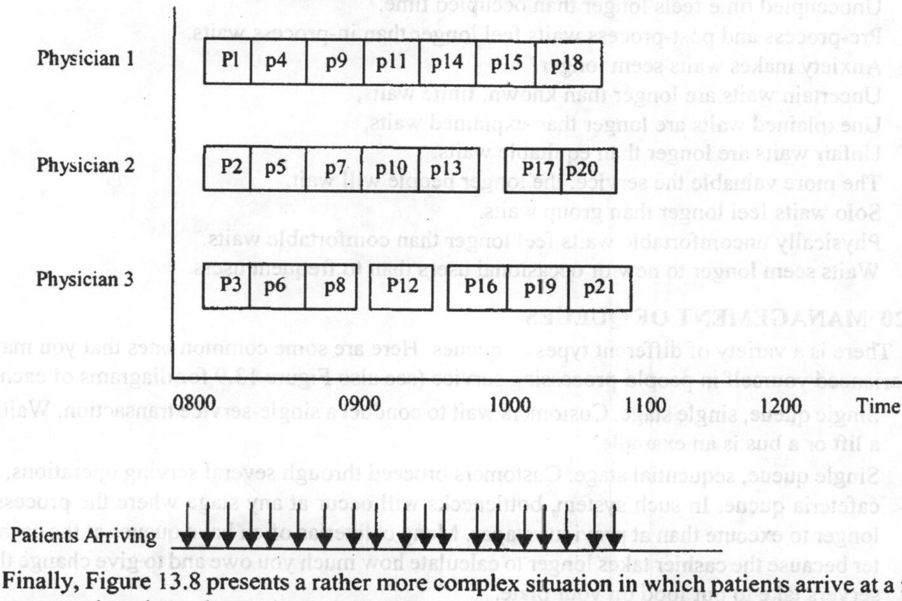

Finally, Figure 13.8 presents a rather more complex situation in which patients arrive at a medical centre, and go through a variety of procedures after reception. The first patient sees to physician, and has an X-ray : the second sees the physician, then visits the drug dispensary, and finally sees the nurse; the third goes to see the nurse for some treatment; the fourth sees the physician and then goes to the dispensary, and so on.

Figure 13.8 : COMPLEX BAR CHART

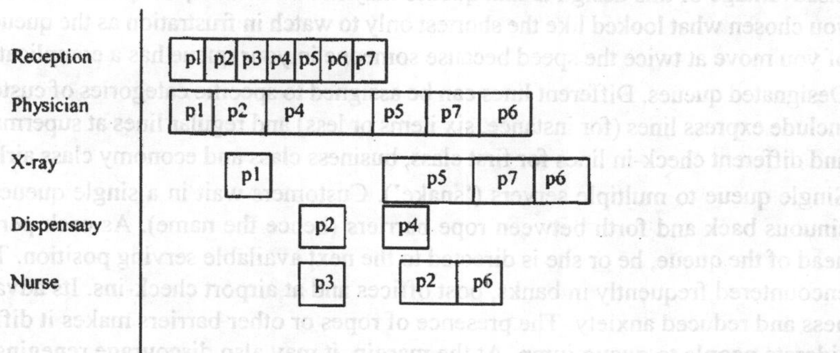

Most scheduling takes place 'forwards' in time, from when the customer is likely to enter the system, or from when the resource is available. However, there are some situations where planning 'backwards' can be appropriate. This tends to be the case when a particular task is due for completion by a particular time and a number of activities are to be completed sequentially before this can be achieved. An example could be planning a meal (purchasing the ingredients preparing them, cooking them and finally serving for a reception at 7.00 p.m.).

13.19 THE PSYCHOLOGY OF WAITING TIME

The noted philosopher William James observed : "Boredom results from being attentive to the passage of time itself". Based on this observation, David Maister formulated eight principles about waiting time. Adding two additional principles gives us a total of ten, summarized in Table 13.4

Table 13.4 : TEN PROPOSITIONS ON THE PSYCHOLOGY OF WAITING LINES

1. Unoccupied time feels longer than occupied time.
2. Pre-process and post-process waits feel longer than in-process waits.
3. Anxiety makes waits seem longer.
4. Uncertain waits are longer than known, finite waits,
5. Unexplained waits are longer than explained waits,
6. Unfair waits are longer than equitable waits.
7. The more valuable the service, the longer people will wait.
8. Solo waits feel longer than group waits.
9. Physically uncomfortable waits feel longer than comfortable waits.
10. Waits seem longer to new or occasional users than to frequent users.

13.20 MANAGEMENT OF QUEUES

There is a variety of different types of queues. Here are some common ones that you may have experienced yourself in people-processing service (see also Figure 13.9 for diagrams of each type).

- Single queue, single stage. Customers wait to conduct a single-service transaction. Waiting for a lift or a bus is an example.
- Single queue, sequential stage. Customers proceed through several serving operations, as in a cafeteria queue. In such system, bottlenecks will occur at any stage where the process takes longer to execute than at previous stages. Many cafeterias often have queues at the cash register because the cashier takes longer to calculate how much you owe and to give change than the servers take to put food on your plate.
- Parallel queues to multiple servers (single or sequential stages). This system offers more than one serving station, allowing customers to select one of several queues in which to wait. Fast-food restaurants usually have several serving queues in operation at busy times of day, with each offering the full menu. A parallel system can have either a single stage or multiple stages. The disadvantage of this design is that queues may not move at equal speed. How many times have you chosen what looked like the shortest only to watch in frustration as the queues on either side of you move at twice the speed because someone in your queue has a complicated transaction?
- Designated queues. Different lines can be assigned to specific categories of customer. Examples include express lines (for instance, six items or less) and regular lines at supermarket checkouts, and different check-in lines for first class, business class and economy class airline passengers.
- Single queue to multiple servers ('snake'). Customers wait in a single queue, often winding sinuous back and forth between rope barriers (hence the name). As each person reaches the head of the queue, he or she is directed to the next available serving position. This approach is encountered frequently in banks, post offices and at airport check-ins. Its advantages are fairness and reduced anxiety. The presence of ropes or other barriers makes it difficult for inconsiderate people to queue-jump. At the margin, it may also discourage reneging.

Figure 13.9 : ALTERNATIVE QUEUE CONFIGURATIONS

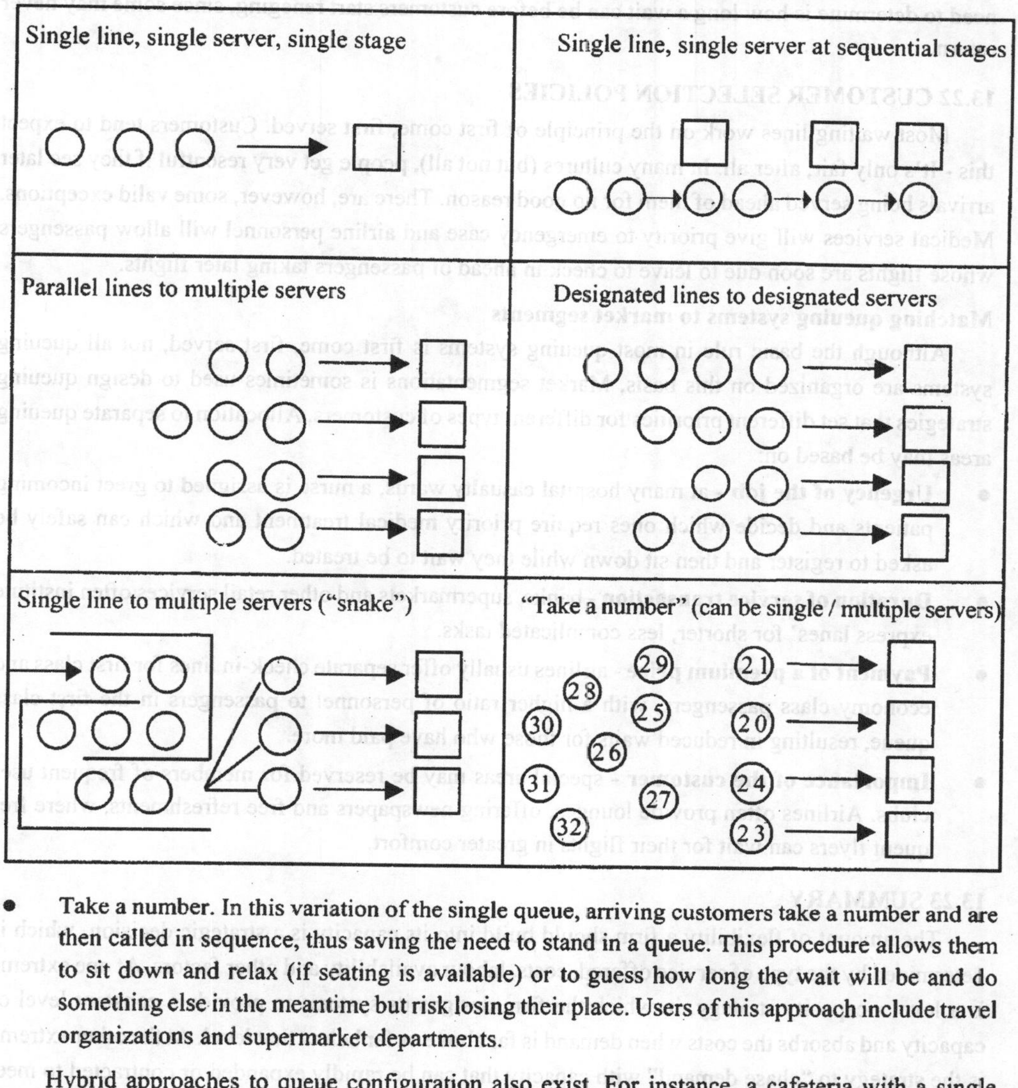

- Take a number. In this variation of the single queue, arriving customers take a number and are then called in sequence, thus saving the need to stand in a queue. This procedure allows them to sit down and relax (if seating is available) or to guess how long the wait will be and do something else in the meantime but risk losing their place. Users of this approach include travel organizations and supermarket departments.

Hybrid approaches to queue configuration also exist. For instance, a cafeteria with a single serving queue might offer two cash register stations at the final stage Similarly, patients at a small medical clinic might visit a single receptionist for registration, proceed sequentially through multiple channels for testing, diagnosis and treatment, and conclude by returning to a single queue at the receptionist's desk to book a follow-up appointment.

13.21 RENEGING

You know the situation (perhaps all too well!). The queue is not that long, but it's moving at a snail's pace. The person at the front of the queue has been there for at least five minutes and his problem seems nowhere near solution. There are two other people ahead of you and you have an uneasy feeling that their transactions are not going to be brief either. Looking at your watch for the third time, you realize that you only have a few minutes until your next appointment. Frustrated, you turn and leave. In the language of queue management, you have reneged. One of the things planners need to determine is how long a wait can be before customers start reneging, since some may never return.

13.22 CUSTOMER SELECTION POLICIES

Most waiting lines work on the principle of first come, first served. Customers tend to expect this - It's only fair, after all. In many cultures (but not all), people get very resentful if they see later arrivals being served ahead of them for no good reason. There are, however, some valid exceptions. Medical services will give priority to emergency case and airline personnel will allow passengers whose flights are soon due to leave to check in ahead of passengers taking later flights.

Matching queuing systems to market segments

Although the basic rule in most queuing systems is first come, first served, not all queuing systems are organized on this basis, Market segmentations is sometimes used to design queuing strategies that set different priorities for different types of customers. Allocation to separate queuing areas may be based on:

- **Urgency of the job** - at many hospital casualty wards, a nurse is assigned to greet incoming patients and decide which ones require priority medical treatment and which can safely be asked to register and then sit down while they wait to be treated.
- **Duration of service transaction** - banks, supermarkets and other retail services often institute express lanes' for shorter, less complicated tasks.
- **Payment of a premium price** - airlines usually offer separate check-in lines for first class and economy class passengers, with a higher ratio of personnel to passengers in the first class queue, resulting in reduced waits for those who have paid more.
- **Importance of the customer** - special areas may be reserved for members of frequent user clubs. Airlines often provide lounges, offering newspapers and free refreshments, where frequent flyers can wait for their flights in greater comfort.

13.23 SUMMARY

The amount of flexibility a firm should build into its capacity is a strategic decision, which is determined by the type of service offered, costs, labour availability and other factors. At one extreme is a level - capacity strategy, in which the firm designs its systems to provide a constant level of capacity and absorbs the costs when demand is far above or far below that level. At the other extreme is the strategy to "chase demand" with capacity that can be rapidly expanded or contracted to meet current needs. A given firm's optional level of flexibility to match, capacity to demand will fall somewhere between those two extremes. Figure 13.10 shows the strategies for matching supply of and demand for services. *(See Fig. next page)*

Figure 13.10 : STRATEGIES FOR MATCHING SUPPLY OF AND DEMAND FOR SERVICES

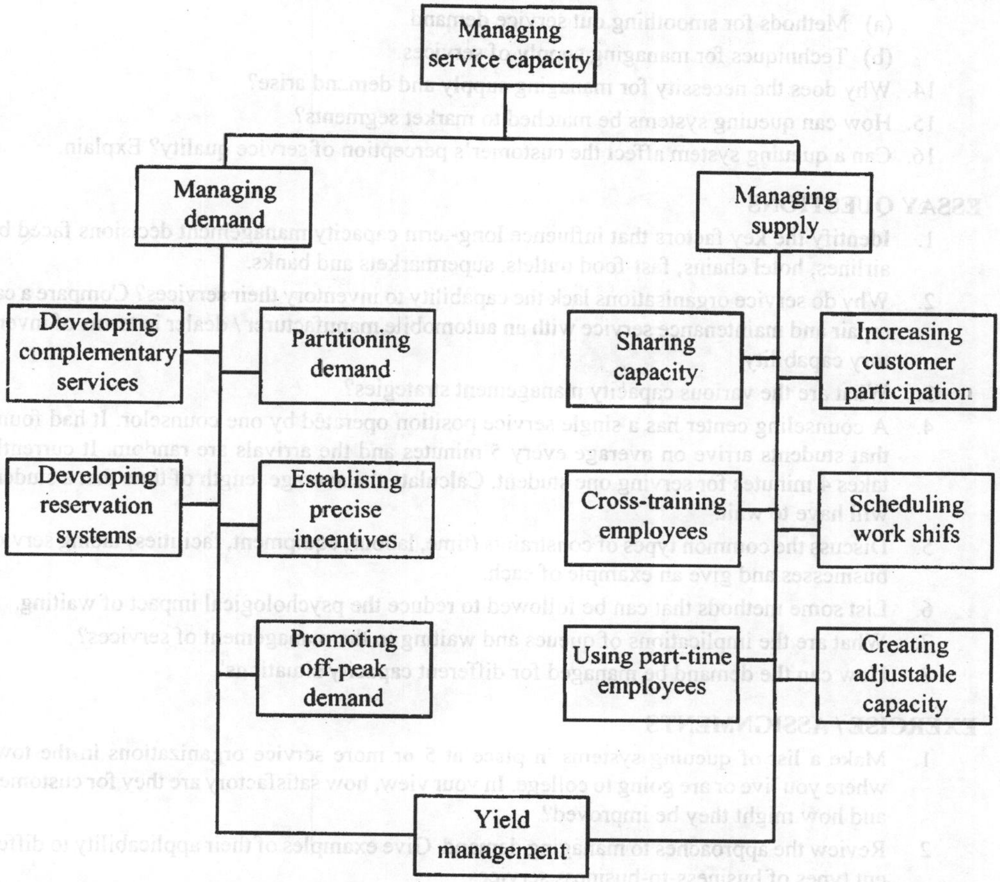

SHORT ANSWER QUESTIONS

1. Why is capacity management particularly significant in a service setting?
2. What is 'chasing demand'?
3. Distinguish between optimum and maximum capacity. What are their respective implications for customers, employees and managers?
4. What are the various types of demand situations?
5. Define capacity in relation to all the service elements offered to customers by (a) a hotel, (b) an airline, (c) a restaurant, and, (d) management consulting firm.
6. What are the strategies for managing demand?
7. Describe two basic strategies for matching supply and demand and give atleast two specific examples for each.
8. What are waiting line strategies?
9. Choose a capacity-constrained service industry and identify the options that are available to increase its elasticity of supply.
10. What are the various queue configurations? Explain with illustrations.
11. Explain some strategies for matching supply of and demand for services.

12. What are the challenges involved in the management of demand and supply of services?
13. Write short notes on:
    (a) Methods for smoothing out service demand
    (b) Techniques for managing supply of services.
14. Why does the necessity for managing supply and demand arise?
15. How can queuing systems be matched to market segments?
16. Can a queuing system affect the customer's perception of service quality? Explain.

ESSAY QUESTIONS

1. Identify the key factors that influence long-term capacity management decisions faced by airlines, hotel chains, fast-food outlets, supermarkets and banks.
2. Why do service organisations lack the capability to inventory their services? Compare a car repair and maintenance service with an automobile manufacturer / dealer in terms of inventory capability.
3. What are the various capacity management strategies?
4. A counseling center has a single service position operated by one counselor. It had found that students arrive on average every 5 minutes and the arrivals are random. It currently takes 4 minutes for serving one student. Calculate the average length of time that a student will have to wait.
5. Discuss the common types of constraints (time, labour, equipment, facilities) facing service businesses and give an example of each.
6. List some methods that can be followed to reduce the psychological impact of waiting.
7. What are the implications of queues and waiting to the management of services?
8. How can the demand be managed for different capacity situations?

EXERCISE / ASSIGNMENTS

1. Make a list of queuing systems in place at 5 or more service organizations in the town where you live or are going to college. In your view, how satisfactory are they for customers and how might they be improved?
2. Review the approaches to managing demand. Give examples of their applicability to different types of business-to-business services.
3. Discuss the scenario (excess demand, demand exceeds optimum capacity, demand and supply are balanced, excess capacity) in the context of a cricket club selling seats for its games. What are the challenges for management under each scenario?

●●●

14

The Service Delivery

14.1 THE SERVICE SETTING

The setting and surroundings in which a service is delivered can be vital. It shapes expectations since it is the first tangible clue that the consumer is given about potential service delivery.

The control by the designer of corporate elements that form interior spaces can impact on the success of that delivery in a variety of ways. It can influence the client's or customer's perception of the particular service sector and can enhance the function, appropriateness and ambience of the activity.

It is important to regard design in terms of the possibilities it has to offer marketing. Every situation is unique and a 'painting by numbers' approach to design is inappropriate.

On viewing and subsequently entering a bank, hotel, restaurant, or solicitor's office, customers will have reflected consciously or subconsciously on some or all of the following :

- What does the exterior say about what is on offer inside?
- Does it communicate, clearly, anything about the nature of the service?
- What does the interior communicate in terms of atmosphere?
- What mood/feeling is evoked?
- How is one expected to behave?

Many service providers have not given elaborate consideration to how the design of the service setting may affect consumer feelings and responses. Unfortunately, there are no ten commandments which would determine how a service setting should or should not be designed. From the customers' view point it is still very much a matter of taste coupled with perceptions of what is appropriate. Nevertheless, just as companies want to know how and why customers respond to packaging, price, product, advertising, service organizations should develop understanding of customer responses to layout, furnishings, colour, light etc. Research should focus on overall impressions and feelings (Table 14.1) followed by an investigation of specific environmental ones.

The atmospheres displayed in Table 14.1 generate an expected response. The wider questions are :

Table 14.1 : ATMOSPHERE AND FEELINGS

Environmental atmosphere generated	Reaction in terms of Customer feelings
Elegance	Status
Professionalism	Trust, Security
Welcoming	Happiness, enjoyment
Welcoming	Depressed, gloomy
Forbidding	Anxious
Warmth	Comfort
Lively	Inviting

- Does the environmental design always bring about the appropriate response?
- What is meant by 'elegance, professionalism, welcoming etc.'?
- What aspects of the environment convey such atmospheres?
- How should a solicitor's office, hairdresser, hospital, advertising agency, social security office appear?
- Are there limits (in a cultural rather than physical sense) on design options for particular services?
- If there are limits, how severe should they be?

Specific environmental cues should be subjected to user evaluation. Research must reveal:

- What is important/unimportant
- What is liked/disliked
- How various aspects are rated on a scale of excellent through to poor.

Users' attitudes and perceptions can be gathered by open-ended discussion and / or measurement of scales. The following list is a sample of the kind of topics that could be covered:

- How adequate is the space? Does it lead to overcrowding and is this desirable or stressful?
- What is the effect of the layout on safety?
- How appropriate is the layout for the activity involved?
- Is the temperature comfortable or uncomfortable?
- Is the noise unobtrusive or uncomfortable?
- Is the lighting adequate?

The primary objective would be the determination of relationships between environmental conditions and behavioural outcomes.

Drawing on developments in decision-making in which customer were responding to more than simply the tangible product or service, Kotler proposed that atmospheres be regarded as an important marketing tool. He suggests that, 'In many areas of marketing in the future, marketing planners will use spatial aesthetics as consciously and skilfully as they now use price, advertising, personal selling, public relations and other tools of marketing'. He maintains the atmosphere of a place affects purchase behaviour in three ways:

1. As an attention-creating medium - use of colours, noise etc. to make it stand out.
2. As a message-creating medium - communicating with the intended audience, level of concern for customers etc.
3. As an effect-creating medium - use of colours, sounds etc. to create or heighten an appetite for certain goods, services or experiences.

When planning the design of a service setting, service providers should have in mind a framework that will assist debate over the impact of the physical surroundings. They should consider this design in terms of the three headings in Figure 14.1.

Environmental stimuli

- ambience - temperature, air quality, noise, music, odour
- space - layout, equipment, furnishings
- sings, symbols, artefacts - e.g. style of decor, personal objects displayed.

Beliefs and feelings

- Cognitive - beliefs
- Emotional - mood, likes/dislikes, attitudes
- Physiological - pain, comfort, ease of movement

Figure 14.1 : A SERVICE SETTING FRAMEWORK FOR UNDERSTANDING BEHAVIOUR AND RELATIONSHIP

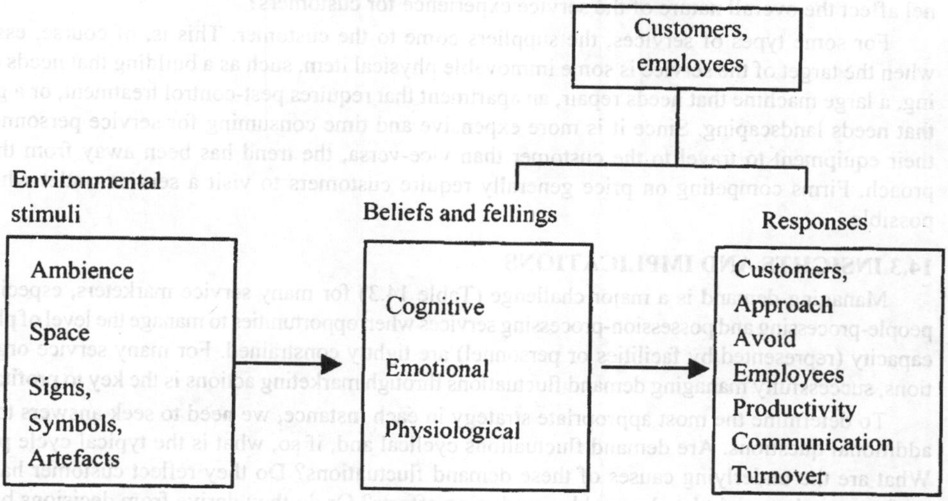

Responses

- Approach - willingness to stay, explore, interact and subsequently return
- Avoid - avoid interactions, a wish to get out and not return.

14.2 NATURE OF SERVICE DELIVERY

How and where service is delivered (Table 14.2) forms the basis of distribution strategy. It also affects the nature of customers' service experiences including the encounters they have with specific service personnel - and impacts the costs they incur in obtaining service.

The convenience of service factory locations and operational schedules may assume great importance when a customer has to be physically present - either throughout service delivery or even just to initiate and terminate the transaction. Managers should be asking themselves: Is our service offered at times and in locations convenient for customers? How much time must customers spend in actually receiving service, and how much in traveling to and from the facility, obtaining information, waiting in line, and paying for service? What financial costs involved in travel?

Table 14.2 : METHOD OF SERVICE DELIVERY

Nature of Interaction Between Customer and Service Organization	Availability of Service Outlets	
	Single Site	Multiple Sites
Customer goes to service organization	Theater Barbershop	Bus service Fast - food chain
Service organization comes to customers	Garden care service Pest control service Taxi	
Customer and service organization transact at arm's length (mail or electronic communications)	Credit card company Local TV station	Broadcast network Telephone company

How much physical and mental effort is required? How appealing are our retail facilities relative to competing alternatives? And how does the combination of facilities, equipment and personnel affect the overall nature of the service experience for customers?

For some types of services, the suppliers come to the customer. This is, of course, essential when the target of the service is some immovable physical item, such as a building that needs cleaning, a large machine that needs repair, an apartment that requires pest-control treatment, or a garden that needs landscaping. Since it is more expensive and time consuming for service personnel and their equipment to travel to the customer than vice-versa, the trend has been away from this approach. Firms competing on price generally require customers to visit a service outlet wherever possible.

14.3 INSIGHTS AND IMPLICATIONS

Managing demand is a major challenge (Table 14.3) for many service marketeıs, especially in people-processing and possession-processing services when opportunities to manage the level of physical capacity (represented by facilities or personnel) are tightly constrained. For many service organizations, successfully managing demand fluctuations through marketing actions is the key to profitability.

To determine the most appropriate strategy in each instance, we need to seek answers to some additional questions. Are demand fluctuations cyclical and, if so, what is the typical cycle period? What are the underlying causes of these demand fluctuations? Do they reflect customer habits or preferences that might be changed by marketing efforts? Or do they derive from decisions by third parties, such as employers and school setting working and classroom hours? Alternatively, are variations in demand caused by more random events, such as weather conditions and health emergencies?

Table 14.3 : WHAT IS THE NATURE OF DEMAND FOR THE SERVICE RELATIVE TO SUPPLY ?

Extent to Which Supply Is Constrained	*Extent of Demand Fluctuations Over Time* *Wide*	*Narrow*
Peak demand can usually be met without a major delay	1. Electricity Natural gas Telephone Hospital maternity unit	2. Insurance Legal services Banking Laundry and dry cleaning
Peak demand regularly exceeds capacity	4. Accounting and tax preparation Passenger transportations Hotels, Restaurants Theaters	3. (Services similar to those in cell above, but which have insufficient capacity for their base base level of business).

One way of smoothing the ups and downs of demand is through strategies that encourage customers to change their plans voluntarily, such as offering special discount prices or added product value during periods of low demand. Another approaches to ration demand through a reservation or queuing system, which basically inventories demand rather than supply. Alternatively, to generate demand in periods of excess capacity, new business development efforts might be targeted at prospective customers with a countercyclical demand pattern. For instance, an accounting firm with a surfeit of work at the end of each calendar year might seek new customers whose financial year ended on June 30 or September 30.

Figure 14.2 : UNDERSTANDING THE CHARACTERISTICS OF THE SERVICE

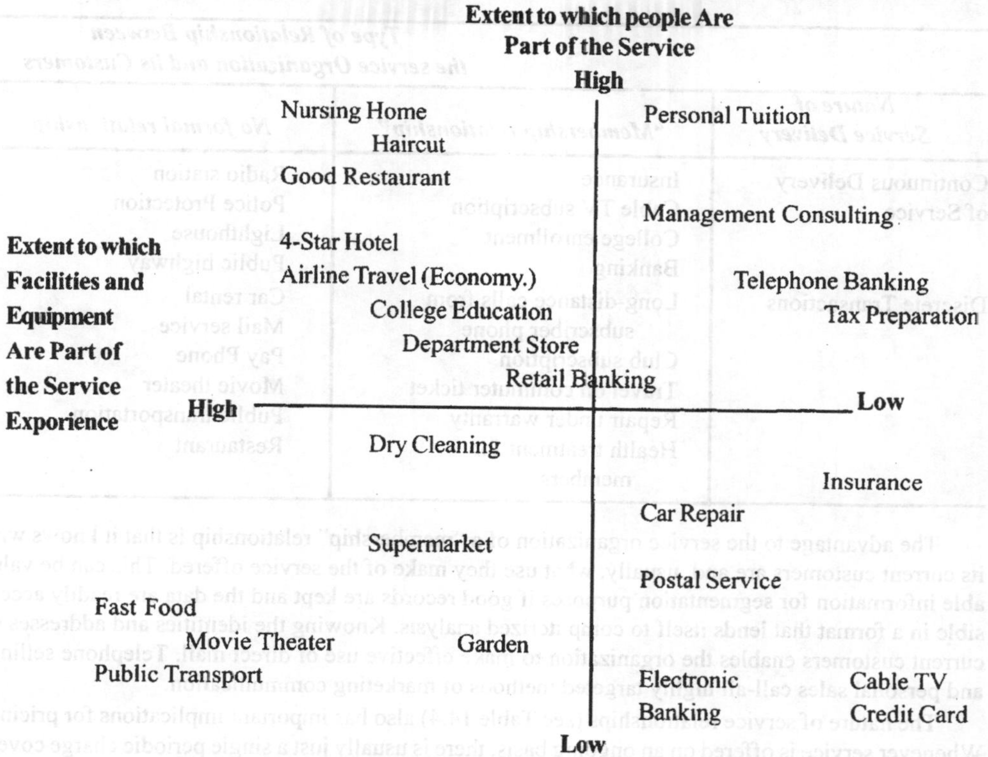

The greater the degree of physical involvement by the customer in the service process, the more likely service personnel, equipment, and facilities are to form an important part of the service experience. In choosing between competing suppliers, customers may base their choice criteria as much on their appraisal of these elements as on their evaluation of the actual service output.

The classification scheme presented in Figure 14.2 can help marketers zero in on what types of attributes are dominant in the service package, so that they can then look for insights from other service businesses with a similar facilities/people emphasis, for instance, a hospital might usefully look to well-run hotels for marketing insights, or a public accounting firm might consider the marketing strategies employed by a successful management consulting firm. Alternatively, this type of analysis might show that services provided by the same industry-such as highway motels and resort hotels, or electronic banking and conventional, branch-based retail banking-prove to have little in common as far as their relative emphasis on facility and people attributes are concerned. The implication here is that the marketing strategies used by one type of service in an industry may not be generalizable to other services offered by that same industry.

Service businesses that are high on people attributes tend to be more difficult to manage than those that are primarily equipment-based. Of particular concern to marketers is the fact that consistency of product execution is harder to achieve through people than through machines. Some service businesses, like retail banking, are switching from labour-intensive distribution systems, such as services delivered by bank tellers, to self-service systems in which customers operate equipment such as bank tellers, to self-service systems in which customers operate equipment such as automated teller machines (ATMs). As shown in Figure 14.2, a change in the nature of delivery procedures may alter the characteristics of the service product, thus shifting its position within the matrix. Unless customer service personnel are available to provide assistance, a user who is having difficulties with an ATM must either contact an anonymous person at the other end of telephone or ask a fellow customer for help.

Table 14.4 : RELATIONSHIPS WITH CUSTOMERS

Nature of Service Delivery	Type of Relationship Between the service Organization and its Customers	
	"Membership relationship"	*No formal relationship*
Continuous Delivery of Service	Insurance Cable TV subscription College enrollment Banking	Radio station Police Protection Lighthouse Public highway
Discrete Transactions	Long-distance calls from subscriber phone Club subscription Travel on commuter ticket Repair under warranty Health treatment for members	Car rental Mail service Pay Phone Movie theater Public transportation Restaurant

The advantage to the service organization of a "membership" relationship is that it knows who its current customers are and, usually, what use they make of the service offered. This can be valuable information for segmentation purposes if good records are kept and the data are readily accessible in a format that lends itself to computerized analysis. Knowing the identities and addresses of current customers enables the organization to make effective use of direct mail. Telephone selling, and personal sales call-all highly targeted methods of marketing communication.

The nature of service relationships (see Table 14.4) also has important implications for pricing. Whenever service is offered on an ongoing basis, there is usually just a single periodic charge covering all contracted service. Most insurance policies fall in this category, as do tuition and board fees at a residential college. The big advantage of this package approach is its simplicity. Some memberships, however, entail a series of separate and identifiable transactions with the price paid being tied explicitly to the number and type of such transactions. While more complex to administer, such an approach is fairer to customers (whose usage patterns may vary widely) and may discourage wasteful use of what are perceived as "free" service. In such instances, "members may be offered advantages over casual users-for instance, discount rates (telephone subscribers pay less for long-distance calls made from their own phones than do pay phone users) or advance notification and priority reservations (club subscriptions).

As shown in Table 14.5 customization can proceed along at least two dimensions (1) how much the characteristics of the service and its delivery system lend themselves to customization and (2) how much judgement customer-contact personnel are able to exercise in defining the nature of the service received by individual customers.

Table 14.5 : CUSTOMIZATION AND JUDGEMENT IN SERVICE DELIVERY

Extent to which Customer-Contact Personnel Exercise Judgement in Meeting Individual Customer Needs	Extent to which service characteristics are characterized	
	High	*Low*
High	Legal services Health care/surgery	Education (large classes) Preventive health programs

	Architectural design Real estate agency Taxi service Beautician Plumber Education (tutorials)	
Low	Telephone service Hotel services Retail banking (excluding major loans) Good restaurant	Public transportation Routine appliance repair Fast-food restaurant Movie theater Spectator sports

To a much greater degree than in the manufacturing sector, service products are "customer-made". Yet customization has its costs. Service management often represents an ongoing struggle between the desires of marketing managers to add value and the goals of operations managers to reduce costs through standardization. Resolving such disputes-a task that may require arbitration by the general manager - requires a good understanding of consumer choice criteria, particularly as these relate to price-value trade-offs and competitive positioning strategy. At the present time, most senior managers in service businesses have come up through the operations route; hence, participation in executive education programmes may be needed to give them the necessary perspective on marketing to make balanced decisions.

When customers are required by the nature of the service process to visit the service site-as in people-processing services-or choose to do so in other types of services (such as traditional retail banking offices), they may be asked to participate actively in the process of service creation, delivery, and consumption. The service delivery system consists of the visible elements (or "front stage") of the service operations system and may include service facilities, equipment, personnel, and even other customers. The design of this physical environment - what Bitner has called the Servicescape - is often an important determinant of customer satisfaction and may play a substantive role in differentiating one service provider from another. In the case of services delivered at arm's length, the physical delivery system may be replaced by an electronic one, thus radically changing the nature of the service experience.

14.4 DESIGNING AND DELIVERING SERVICES

All service organization face choices concerning the types of products to offer and the operational procedures to use in creating them. Figure 14.3 shows the key steps involved in planning, creating, and delivering services. The task begins at the corporate level with a statement of institution objectives and an appraisal of current or obtainable resources. From market and competitive analysis, marketing opportunities can be identified. Positioning statement can be developed for each service that the firm plans to offer to one or more specific market segments, indicating the characteristics that distinguish it form the competition in meaningful ways.

This positioning strategy must then be related to a statement of the operating assets needed for execution. Can the organization afford to allocate the necessary physical facilities, equipment, information and communication technology, and human resources needed to support a given positioning strategy? Alternatively, could the firm leverage its own resources by using off-balance sheet assets obtained by developing partnerships with intermediaries or even with customers themselves? Does the positioning strategy promise sufficient profits to yield an acceptable return on the assets employed after deducting all relevant costs?

The next step in the process involves establishing a service marketing concept, to clarify the benefits offered to customers and the costs that they will incur in return. This marketing concept considers both core and supplementary services, reliability levels for these services, and where and

Figure 14.3 : PLANNING, CREATING, AND DELIVERING SERVICES

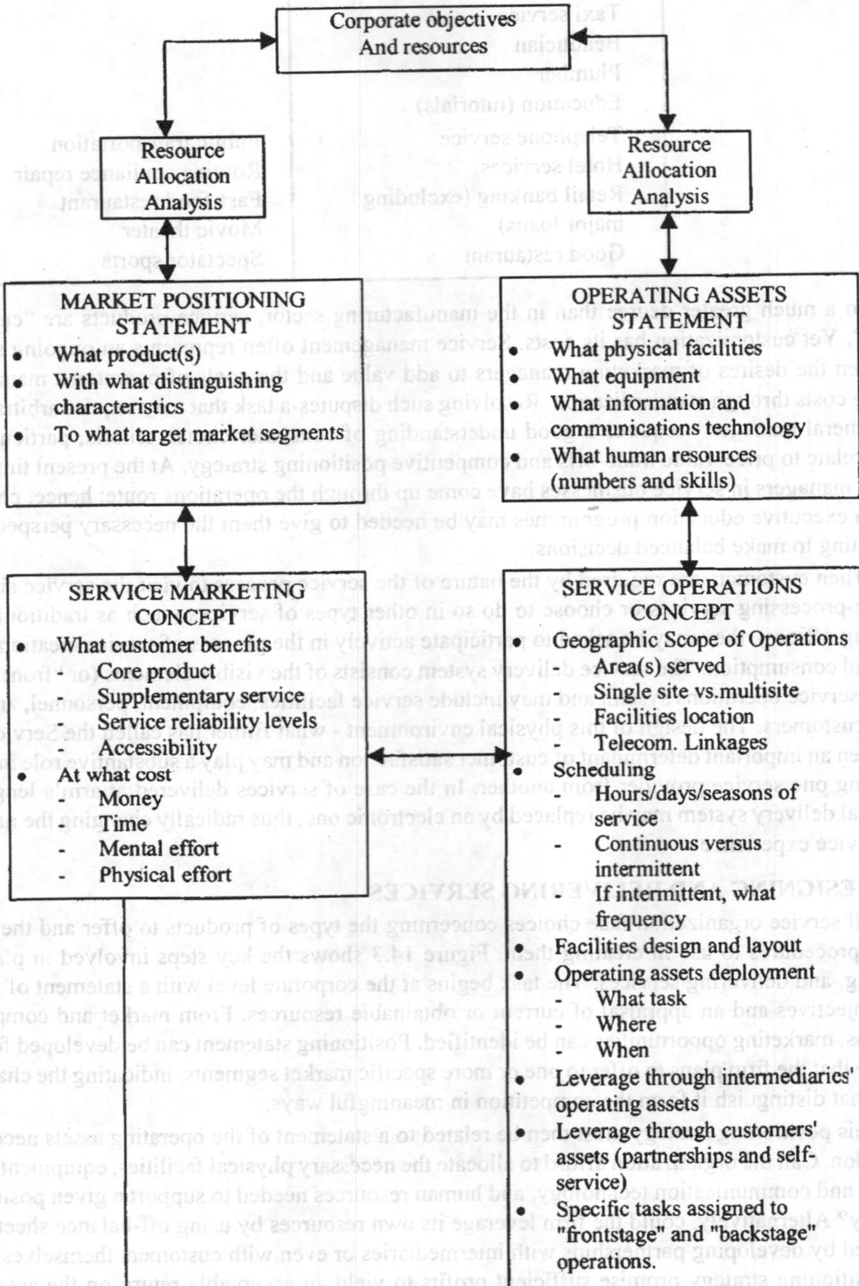

when customers will be able to have access to them. Costs include money, time, mental effort, and physical effort.

A parallel step is to establish a service operations concept, which stipulates the geographic scope and scheduling of operations, describes facilities design and layout, and indicates how and when operating assets should be deployed to perform specific tasks. The operations concept also addresses opportunities for leveraging through intermediaries or the customers themselves. Finally, it clarifies which tasks will be assigned to front stage and which to backstage operations.

These two concepts interact with a set of choices that management must make in configuring the service delivery process (Figure 14.4).

- What should be the sequencing of the various steps in the service delivery process? Where (location) and when (scheduling) should these steps take place?
- Should service elements be bundled or unbundled for delivery purposes (for instance, should a service firm take responsibility for all elements or delegate certain supplementary services, such as information and reservations, to an intermediary?)
- What should be the nature of the service process at each step? Should customers be served in batches or individually, or should they serve themselves?

FIGURE 14.4 : SERVICE DELIVERY AND EVALUATION

Service marketing concept | Service operations concept

SERVICE DELIVERY PROCESS

- Sequencing of service delivery steps - what steps, in what order, where, when, and how quickly?
- Extent of delegation
  Should the firm take responsibility for all steps or delegate some to intermediaries?
- Nature of contact between customers and provider
  Customer comes to provider
  Provider comes to customer
  Arm's length transactions
- Nature of process
  Customers served in batches
  Customers served individually
  Customers serve themselves (self-service)
- Protocol for allocating limited capacity
  Reservations procedures
  Queuing procedures
- Imagery and atmosphere
  Employee scripts and protocols
  Variations in decor, lighting, and music

PERFORMANCE EVALUATION

- By customers
- By managers
- By employees

- What should be the serving protocol: Should the firm operate a reservations system or work on a first come, first served basis, with queuing as necessary? Alternatively, should a priority system be established for certain types of customers?
- What imagery and atmosphere should the service delivery environment (or servicescape) strive to create? For a high-contact service, this concerns decisions on (1) facility design and layout, (2) staff uniforms, appearance and attitudes, (3) the type of furnishings and equipment installed, and (4) the use of music, lighting, and decor. The characteristics of the area surrounding the chosen location will also contribute to the customers' overall experience.

Finally comes performance evaluations. Customer satisfaction will be based largely on how users perceive service performance relative to their expectations. The firm, by contrast, may use more formal approaches, measuring performance on certain characteristics against predefined standards and seeking employee inputs-assuming that management is sufficiently disciplined.

Falling prices, greater affluence, and new easy-to-use technologies also allow individual and corporate users to replace service professional in a variety of other fields. Thus, washing machines and dryers for home use replace laundry services for many types of clothes. Today, anyone who already owns a computer loaded with presentation graphics software can now purchase an inexpensive color printer to make color illustrations or overhead transparency charts and word-slides-something that would have required services of a skilled (and expensive) graphics artist in the past. Telephone answering machines have cut deeply into the business of telephone answering service. But now, in a new technological development, answering machines them selves face competition from the automated voice-mail services offered by telephone companies.

As the wheel of progress turns, customers may continue to change the way in which they obtain the valued benefits they seek. The telephone created the need for answering services among busy people, many of whom solved this need first from services, then from manufactured goods, and most recently from services again.

14.5 STRATEGIES FOR EFFECTIVE SERVICE DELIVERY THROUGH INTERMEDIARIES

Three categories of intermediary management strategies: control strategies, empowerment strategies, and partnering strategies are discussed below:

Control Strategies

In this category, the service principal believes that intermediaries will perform best when it creates standards both for revenues and service performance, measures results, and compensates or rewards on the basis of performance level. To use these strategies the principal must be the most powerful participant in the channel, possessing unique service with strong consumer demand or loyalty, or other forms of economic power.

(a) **Measurement** : Some franchisers maintain control of the service quality delivered by their franchisees by ongoing measurement programmes that feed data back to the principal. Virtually all automobile dealers' sales and service performance is monitored regularly by the manufacturer, which creates the measurement programme, administers it, and maintains control of the information. The company survey customers at key points in the service encounter sequence : after sale, thirty days out, ninety days out, and after a year. The manufacturer designs the instruments (some of them with the assistance of dealer councils) and obtains the customer feedback directly. On the basis of this information, the manufacturer rewards and recognizes both individuals and dealerships that perform well and can potentially punish those that perform poorly. The obvious advantage to this approach is that the manufacturer retains control: however, the trust and goodwill between manufacturers and dealers can easily be eroded if dealers feel that the measurement is used to control and punish.

(b) **Review:** Some franchisers control through terminations, non-renewals, quotas, and restrictive supplier sources. Expansion and encroachment are two of the tactics being used today. Another means by which franchisers exert control over franchisees is through quotas and sales goals, typically by offering price breaks after a certain volume is attained.

Empowerment Strategies

Empowerment strategies, where the service principal allows greater flexibility to intermediaries based on the belief that their talents are best revealed in participation rather than acquiescence, are useful when the service principal is new or lacks sufficient power to govern the channel using control strategies. In empowerment strategies, the principal provides information, research, or processes to help intermediaries perform well in service.

(a) **Help the intermediary develop customer-oriented service processes.** Individual intermediaries rarely have the funds to sponsor their own customer research studies or re-engineering efforts. One way for a company to improve intermediary performance is to conduct research or standard-setting studies relating to service performance, then provide them as a service to intermediaries.

(b) **Provide Needed Support Systems.** In airlines and hotels, as well as other travel and ticketing service, the service principal's reservation system is an important support system. Holiday Inn has a franchise service delivery system that adds value to the Holiday Inn franchise and differentiates it from competitors.

(c) **Develop Intermediaries to Deliver Service Quality.** In this strategy, the service originator invests in training or other forms of development to improve the skills and knowledge of intermediaries and their employees.

(d) **Change to a Cooperative Management Structure.** Companies use the technique of empowerment to manage and motivate franchisees. They develop worker teams in their outlets to hire, discipline, and handle financial tasks such as deposits and audits.

Partnering strategies

The group of strategies with the highest potential for effectiveness involves partnering with intermediaries to learn together about end-customers, set specifications, improve delivery, and communicate honestly. This approach capitalizes on the skills and strengths of both principal and intermediary and engenders a sense of trust that improves the relationship.

(a) **Alignment of Goals.** One of the most successful approaches to partnering involves aligning company and intermediary goals early in the process. Both the service principal and the intermediary has individual goals that they strive to achieve. If channel members can see that they benefit the ultimate consumer of services and in the process optimize their own revenues and profit, they begin the relationship with a target in mind.

(b) **Consultation and Cooperation.** This strategy is not as dramatic as setting joint goals, but it does result in intermediaries participating in the decision-making process. In this approach, which could involve virtually any topic, from compensation to service quality to the service environment, the principal makes a point of consulting intermediaries and asking for their opinions and views before establishing a policy.

14.6 AGENTS AND BROKERS

In common terminology, an agent is an intermediary who acts on behalf of a service principal (such as a brokerage firm or a popular sports figure) and is authorized to make agreements between customers and those principals. Agents and brokers do not take title to services but instead deliver the rights to them. They have legal authority to market services as well as to perform other marketing functions on behalf of producers. The two forms of intermediaries perform many of the same functions but are distinct from each other in some ways.

Types of Agents

Selling agents, have contractual authority to sell a service principal's output (which can be anything from an athlete's time to insurance or financial service), usually because the principal is not interested, feels unqualified, or lacks the resources to do so. Because they know the market better than the service principal, they are typically entrusted with influence over prices, terms, and conditions of sale. Unlike a sale force, the selling agent normally has no territorial limits but represents the service principal in all areas.

Purchasing agents also have long-term relationships with buyers, evaluating and making information to clients as well as obtaining the best services and prices available. Purchasing agents are frequently hired by companies and individuals to find art, antiques, and rare jewelry.

Facilitating agents help with the marketing process by adding expertise or support such as financial services, risk taking, or transportation.

Types of Brokers

Brokers bring buyers and sellers together while assisting in negotiation. They are paid by the party who hired them, rarely become involved in financing or assuming risk, and are not long-term representatives of buyers or sellers. The most familiar examples are real-estate brokers, insurance brokers, and security brokers.

Benefits and challenges in using agents and brokers are summarized in Table 14.6

Table 14.6 : SUMMARY OF BENEFITS AND CHALLENGES IN DISTRIBUTING SERVICES THROUGH AGENTS AND BROKERS

Benefits	*Challenges*
Reduced selling and distribution costs Intermediary's possession of special skills and knowledge Wide representation Knowledge of local markets Customer choice	Loss of control over pricing the other aspects of marketing Representation of multiple service principals

Challenges of Delivering Service through Agents and Brokers

Loss of control over Pricing and Other Aspects of Marketing

As representatives of service principals and experts on customer markets, agents and brokers are typically empowered to negotiate price, configure services, and otherwise alter the marketing of a principal's service. This issue could be particularly important-and possibly detrimental when a service provider depends on a particular (high) price to convey a level of service quality. If the price can be changed, it might reach a level that undermines the quality image. In addition, the agent has the flexibility to give different prices to different customers. As long as the customers are geographically dispersed, this will not create a problem for the service principal; however, if buyers compare prices and realize they were given different prices, they may perceive the service principal as unfair or unethical.

Representation of Multiple Service Principals

When independent agents represent multiple suppliers they offer customer choice. From the perspective of the service principal, however, customer choice means that the agent represents - and in many cases advocates - a competitive service offering. This is the same challenge a manufacturer confronts when distributing products in a retail store. Only in rare cases are its products the only one in a given category on the retail floor. In a service context, consider the use of independent insurance agents. These agents carry a range of insurance products from different companies, serving as a surrogate service retail store for customers. When they find a customer who needs insurance, they sell from their portfolio the offering that best match customers' requirements.

14.7 ELECTRONIC CHANNELS

Electronic channels are the only service distributors that do not require direct human interaction. What they do require is some pre-designed service (almost always information, education, or entertainment) and an electronic vehicle to deliver it. We are all familiar with telephone and television channels, and other electronic vehicles are currently being developed. Video dial tone (VDT) is the term used by telecommunications companies to describe full-motion video that is delivered on a switched basis. Some of the newer ways in which sound, video, and information are transported directly to service customers are through the Internet, satellites, and computers. And the consumer and business services that will be made possible through these vehicles include movies on demand, interactive news and music, banking and financial service, multimedia libraries and data bases, distance learning, desktop video conferencing, remote health service, and interactive network based games.

The more a service relies on technology and/or equipment for service production, and the less it relies on face-to-face contact with service providers, the less the service is characterized by inseparability and non-standardization. Using electronic channels overcomes some of the problems associated with service inseparability and allows a form of standardization not previously possible in most services.

Table 14.7 : BENEFITS AND CHALLENGES IN ELECTRONIC DISTRIBUTION OF SERVICES

Benefits	*Challenges*
Quality control	Lack of control of electronic environment
Low cost	Inability to customize
Customer convenience	Customer Involvement
Potential for wide distribution	Security
Customer choice	

14.8 CHALLENGES IN DISTRIBUTING SERVICES THROUGH ELECTRONIC CHANNELS

Lack of Control of the Electronic Environment. It did not take long for the Internet to face the challenges of unregulated media. As soon as the network became popular, pornographic and other controversial material started to appear. When a service's advertising or information appears in proximity to such material, the result can be a negative spillover effect.

Inability to Customize. Some of you have experienced learning basic college courses through large, video-transmitted courses. If you consider what you missed in learning that way compared with learning directly from a professor, you will understand this challenge. In mass sections, you cannot interact directly with the professor, ask questions, raise points for clarification, or experience the connection that you receive in person. In electronic classes-as in video conferences that are springing up in many businesses-the quality of the service can also be impeded by the way the audience reacts (or doesn't react) in those situations. People talk among themselves, leave, laugh, and criticize, among other behaviors.

Customization can be achieved in these channels. IN college courses, small groups of students can be led by teaching assistants to discuss the electronic lecture. Call-in questions can simulate direct interaction. Two-way video can control the behavior of receivers. In advertising on the Internet and other electronic channels, it is conjectured that personalized advertising will ultimately be developed because customers will be in control. Consumers will actively seek pertinent advertising, so marketers must develop ways to make their advertising compelling. Ad resources will shift toward supplying information the customer wants to know, rather than pitching what the company wants to sell.

Customer Involvement May times the customer produces the service herself using the technology. Unless the technology is highly user-friendly, customers may be reluctant to try it or to continue using it if it requires ongoing education.

Security One issue confronting marketers using electronic channels is security of information, particularly financial information. Many marketers who advertise on the Internet will not accept credit-card orders because of potential security problems in the transactions.

The value delivery system

The value delivery sequence consists of three key steps - choose the value, provide the value and communicate the value (Figure 14.5).

Choose the value. It can be argued that customers select products and services because they believe they offer superior value. The prerequisite here is an understanding of changing customer needs in terms of the forces driving demand as well as customer economics and the buying process and also understanding how well the competition serves those needs particularly in terms of the products, the service and price charged.

Figure 14.5 : THE VALUE DELIVERY SYSTEM

(A) THE PHYSICAL PROCESS SEQUENCE

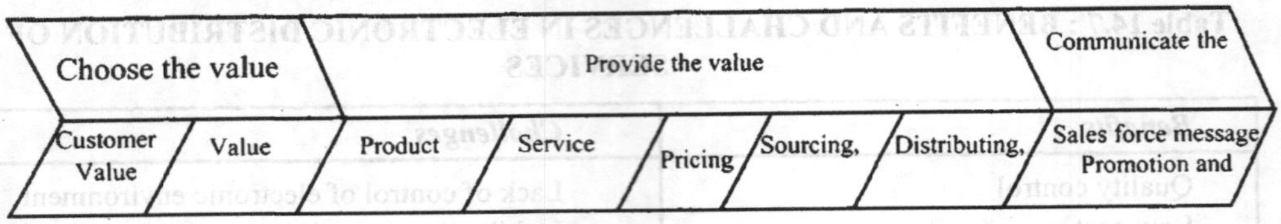

(B) THE VALUE DELIVERY SEQUENCE

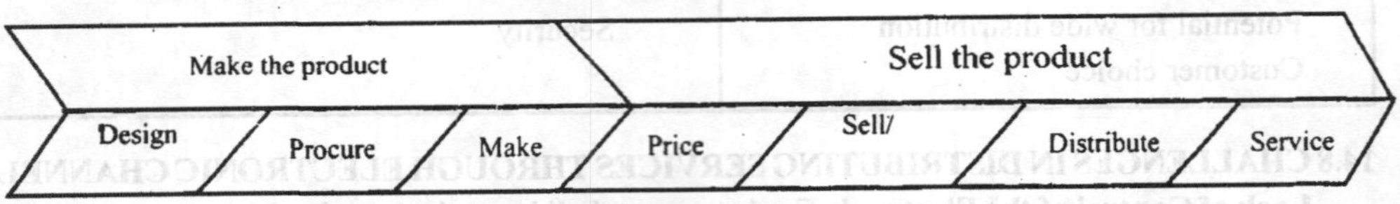

Provide the value. The second stage, providing the value, is concerned with developing a product/service package that creates clear and superior value. This involves a focus on things such as product quality and performance, service cost and responsiveness, manufacturing cost and flexibility, channel structure and performance, and price structure.

Communicate the value. This involves the various aspects of promotional activity needed to persuade customers that the values are better than those offered by competitors. It involves not only the issues of organising sales promotion, advertising and the sales force, but also of providing outstanding service in a way that is continually recognized by the target audience.

14.9 FLOW CHARTING THE SERVICE DELIVERY SYSTEM

In the same way that manufacturing systems can be analysed and modelled to improve operating performance, so too can the service delivery system.

A basic starting point in the process is what has come to be known as the service 'blueprint'. Essentially this is a flow chart or systems analysis of the entire process for the delivery of each aspect of the service package. Shostack describes the procedures involved in blueprinting:

- The first step in blueprinting is to diagram all the components of a service so that the service can be clearly and objectively seen.
- The next important task in blueprinting is the identification of fail points - that is, the areas most likely to cause execution or consistency problems.
- Setting execution standards is the third critical part of the blueprint. These represent the main

quality targets for the service. Execution standards not only define the costs of a service, they also define the performance criteria and tolerances for the completion of each service step.

Finally, the manager must identify all of the evidence of the service that is available to the customer. Each item that is visible to the customer represents an encounter point, during which interaction with the service will occur.

The aim of flow charting is to break the flow of activities within a defined process down into logical steps and sequences. The flowchart itself is a diagram which shows a series of events that occur from beginning to end, keeping in mind of course that the end of one process (output) is the beginning of another (input). The flow chart is made up of symbols that help identify what type of action occurs at each step of the process. Inevitably variability is built into the process due to the effects of human judgement, random unpredictability or assignable causes.

Building up a flow chart requires a basic tool kit, which is nothing more than a set of symbols for describing key steps in any work process (see Figure 14.6).

Figure 14.6 : WHAT IS A FLOW CHART ?

A flow chart is a diagram which shows a series of events that occur in a process from beginning to end, made up of symbols that help to identify what type of action occurs at each step in the process. The table defines each symbol used to draw a flow chart.

Activity	*Description*
	Inspection A checking function.
	Operation Indicates the main steps in a process. It involves the addition of information to a paper or a handling operation, such as stapling, folding, sorting, collating, assembling, filing and so on.
	Delay This symbol means that there is a time delay in the process.
	Combined activity When two activities are performed at the same time, or at the same work station.
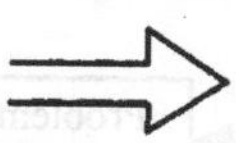	Travel Travelling occurs when something is moved from one place to another.
	Storage / filing This symbol is used when a form or document is filled or stored for a period of time

14.10 CUSTOMER RESPONSE TO SERVICE FAILURES

What options are open to customers when they experience a service failure? Figure14.7 depicts the courses of action available. This model suggests at least four major courses of action :

- Do nothing
- Complain is some form to the service firm.
- Take action through a third party (consumer advocacy group, consumer affairs or regulatory agencies, civil or criminal courts).
- Abandon this supplier and discourage other people from using the service (negative word-of-mouth).

Following through the sequence of possible reactions, we can see a variety of end-results, leaving the customer anything from furious to delighted. The risk of defection is high, especially when there are a variety of competing alternatives.

14.11 SERVICE RECOVERY FOLLOWING CUSTOMER COMPLAINTS

Service recovery is an umbrella term for systematic efforts by a firm to correct a problem following a service failure and retain a customer's goodwill. Service recovery efforts play a crucial role in achieving (or restoring) customer satisfactions (Figure 14.8) in every organization, things may occur that have a negative impact on its relationships with customers. The true test of a firm's commitment to satisfaction and service quality isn't in the advertising promises or the decor and ambience of its offices, but in the way it responds when things go wrong for the customer (unfortunately, firms don't always react in ways that match their advertised promises). Effective service recovery requires thoughtful procedures for resolving problems and handling disgruntled customers. It is critical for firms to have effective recovery strategies, because even a single service problem can destroy a customer's confidence in a firm under the following conditions:

The failure is totally outrageous (for instance, blatant dishonesty on the part of the supplier).

The problem fits a pattern of failure rather than being an isolated incident.

The recovery efforts are weak, serving to compound the original problem rather than correct it.

Figure 14.7 : COURSES OF ACTION OPEN TO A DISSATISFIED CUSTOMER

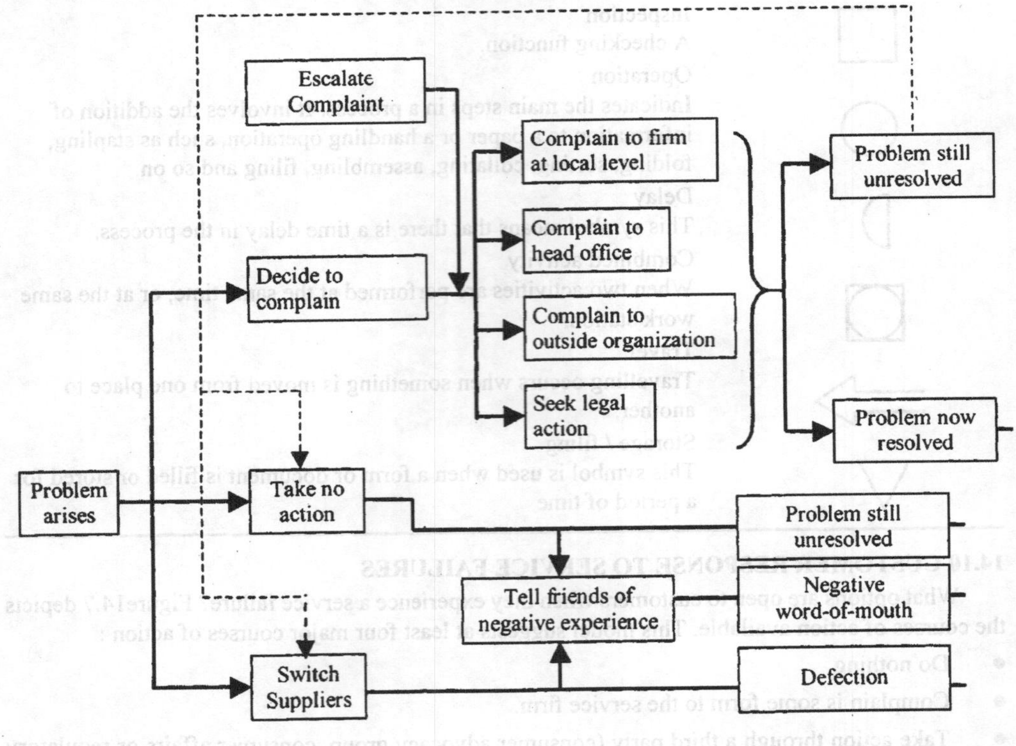

Figure 14.8 : COMPONENTS OF AN EFFECTIVE SERVICE RECOVERY SYSTEM

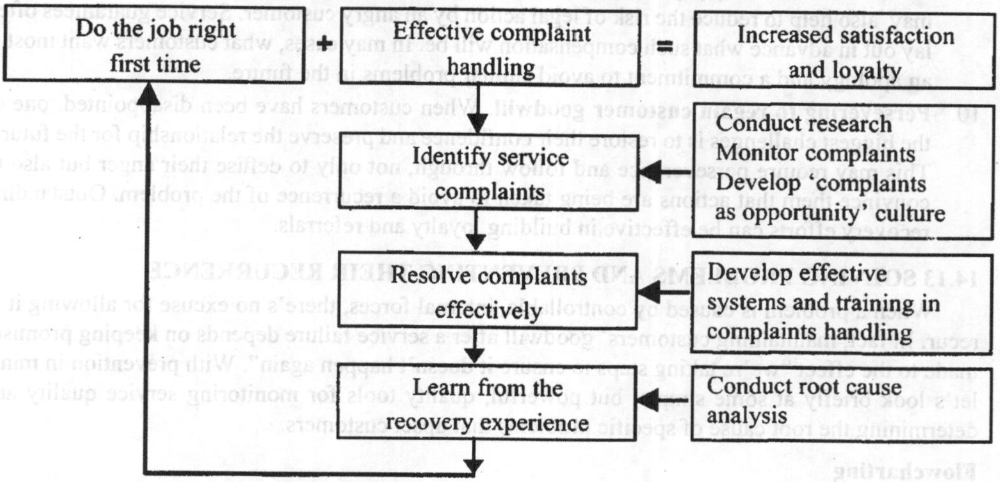

14.12 GUIDELINES FOR EFFECTIVE PROBLEM RESOLUTION

1. **Act fast.** If the complaint is made during service delivery, then time is of essence to achieve a full recovery. When complaints are made after the fact, many companies have established policies of responding within 24 hours, or sooner. Even when full resolution is likely to take longer, fast acknowledgment remains very important.
2. **Admit mistakes but don't be defensive.** Acting defensively may suggest that the organization has something to hide or is reluctant to fully explore the situation.
3. **Show that you understand and problem from each customer's point of view.** Seeing situations through the customers' eyes is the only way to understand what they think has gone wrong and why they are upset. Service personnel should avoid jumping to conclusions with their own interpretations.
4. **Don't argue with customers.** The goal should be to gather facts to reach a mutually acceptable solution, not to win a debating contest or prove that the customer is an idiot. Arguing gets in the way of listening and seldom defuses anger.
5. **Acknowledge the customer's feelings**, either tacitly or explicitly ("I can understand why you're upset"). This action helps to build rapport, the first step in rebuilding a bruised relationship.
6. **Give customers the benefit of the doubt.** Not all customers are truthful and not all complaints justified. But customers should be treated as though they have a valid complaint until clear evidence to the contrary emerges. If a lot of money is at stake (as in insurance claims or potential lawsuits) careful investigation is warranted; if the amount concerned is small, then it may not be worth haggling over a refund or other compensation - but it's still a good idea to check records to see if there is a past history of dubious complaints by the same customer.
7. **Clarify the steps needed to solve the problem.** When instant solutions aren't possible, telling customers how the organization plans to proceed shows that corrective action is being taken. It also sets expectations as to the time frame (so don't over promise!).
8. **Keep customers informed of progress.** Nobody likes being left in the dark. Uncertainty breeds anxiety and stress. People tend to be more accepting of disruptions if they know what is going on and receive periodic progress reports.
9. **Consider compensation.** When customers did not receive the service outcomes that they paid for, or suffered serious inconvenience and/or loss of time and money because the service failed,

then either a monetary payment of offer of equivalent service in kind is appropriate; such action may also help to reduce the risk of legal action by an angry customer. Service guarantees often lay out in advance what such compensation will be. In may cases, what customers want most is an apology and a commitment to avoid similar problems in the future.

10. **Persevering to regain customer goodwill.** When customers have been disappointed, one of the biggest challenges is to restore their confidence and preserve the relationship for the future. This may require perseverance and follow through, not only to defuse their anger but also to convince them that actions are being taken to avoid a recurrence of the problem. Outstanding recovery efforts can be effective in building loyalty and referrals.

14.13 SOLVING PROBLEMS AND PREVENTING THEIR RECURRENCE

When a problem is caused by controllable, internal forces, there's no excuse for allowing it to recur. In fact, maintaining customers' goodwill after a service failure depends on keeping promises made to the effect "we're taking steps to ensure it doesn't happen again". With prevention in mind, let's look briefly at some simple, but powerful, quality tools for monitoring service quality and determining the root cause of specific problems that upset customers.

Flowcharting

Once managers understand the underlying processes behind service delivery, it's easier to identify potential fail points which represent weak links in the chain. Knowing what can go wrong (and where) is an important first step in preventing service quality problems.

Control charts

These charts offer a simple method of displaying performance over time against specific quality criteria. Since they are visual, trends are easily identified. Figure 14.9 shows an airline's performance on the important criterion of on-time departures, suggesting that this issue needs to be addressed by management, since performance is erratic and not very satisfactory. Of course, control charts are only as good as the data on which they are based.

Figure 14.9 : CONTROL CHART

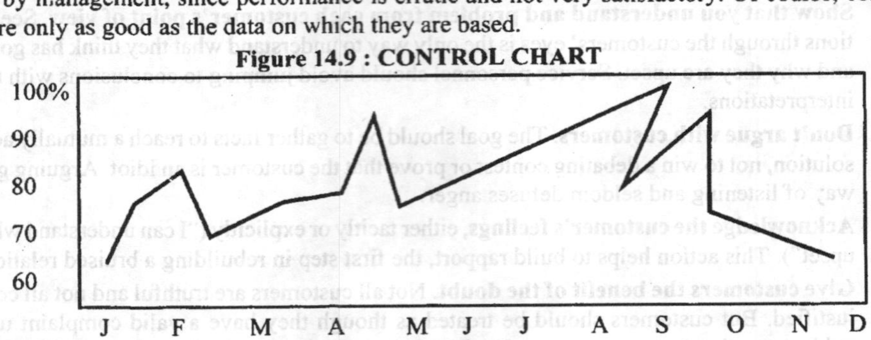

The fishbone chart

Cause-and-effect analysis employs a technique first developed by the Japanese quality expert, Kaoru Ishikawa. Groups of managers and staff brainstorm all the possible factors that might cause a specific problem. The resulting factors are then categorized into one of five groupings - Equipment, Manpower (or People), Material, Procedures, and Other - on a cause and effect chart, popularly known as a fishbone chart because of its shape. This technique has been used for many years in manufacturing and, more recently, in services (Figure 14.10)

Pareto analysis. Pareto analysis (named after the Italian economist who first developed it) seeks to identify the principal causes of observed outcomes. This type of analysis underlies the so-called 80/20 rule, because if often reveals that around 80% of the value of one variable (in this instance, number of service failures) is accounted for by only 20% of the causal variable (i.e. number of possible causes).

Figure 14.10 : CAUSE AND EFFECT CHART FOR AIRLINE DEPARTURE DELAYS

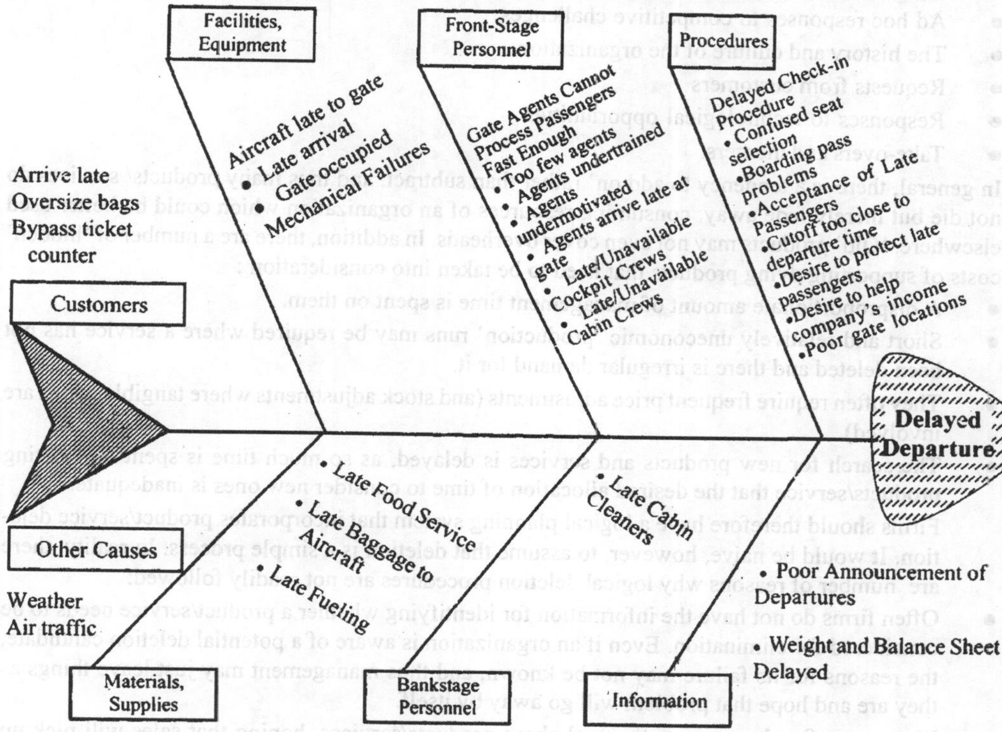

14.14 A NEW QUALITY GOAL : ZERO DEFECTIONS

Quality failures weaken brand loyalty. When disappointed customers have a choice of service suppliers, they may decide to abandon the one that has let them down in favor of a competitor. Reichheld and Sasser popularized the zero defections, which they describe as keeping every customer the company can profitably serve. When customers have a membership relationship with an organization, their use of the service can be tracked on an individual account basis. Declining usage - say, less frequent visits to a hotel chain for a business traveller, reduced purchases from a retail store, fewer checking transactions at a bank - are often a good predictor of potential defection. Intervention at this point (with a view to restoring brand loyalty) is preferable to waiting until the customer ceases all activity or formally closes an account. Not only does a rising defection rate indicate that something is already wrong with quality (or that competitors offer better value), it also signals a probable profit slump ahead.

14.15 SERVICE DELETION

Good product management depends upon reliable marketing information to show when a product is failing to achieve its objectives. As well as maintaining successful services and investing in new ones, service organizations must also have the courage to eliminate services that are no longer likely to be of benefit to the organization as a whole. This implies a need for the following:

1. Establishment of targets for each service
2. Periodic reviews of each service's performance
3. Modification of existing services when necessary
4. Elimination of services where necessary
5. Development of new services.

In reality, an organization's portfolio of products/services is often the result of a number of factors:

- Ad hoc responses to competitive challenges
- The history and culture of the organization
- Requests from customers
- Responses to technological opportunities
- Take-overs and mergers.

In general, there is a tendency to add on' rather than subtract, and thus many products/ services do not die but merely fade away, consuming resources of an organization which could be better used elsewhere. 'Old' products may not even cover overheads. In addition, there are a number of 'hidden' costs of supporting dying products that need to be taken into consideration :

- A disproportionate amount of management time is spent on them.
- Short and relatively uneconomic 'production' runs may be required where a service has not been deleted and there is irregular demand for it.
- They often require frequent price adjustments (and stock adjustments where tangible goods are involved).
- The search for new products and services is delayed, as so much time is spent on existing products/service that the desired allocation of time to consider new ones is inadequate.

  Firms should therefore have a logical planning system that incorporates product/service deletion. It would be naive, however, to assume that deletion is a simple process. In reality, there are number of reasons why logical deletion procedures are not readily followed:

- Often firms do not have the information for identifying whether a product/service needs to be considered for elimination. Even if an organization is aware of a potential deletion candidate, the reasons for its failure may not be known, and thus management may just leave things as they are and hope that problem will go away by itself.
- Managers often become sentimental about products/services, hoping that sales will pick up when the market improves. Sometimes, particular elements of marketing strategy will be blamed for lack of success and thus there is the belief that a change in advertising or pricing, for example, will improve the situation.
- Within organizations there may be political difficulties in seeking to delete a service. Some individuals will have vested interests in a service and may fight elimination efforts. In fact, staff may hide the true facts of a service's performance to ensure that deletion is not considered at all.
- Finally, there is sometimes the fear that the sales of other products and services are tied into the product/service being deleted. For example, a car dealer who closes down its new car sales department may subsequently lose business in its servicing and repairs department. Furthermore, some candidates for elimination may be sold to a small number of important customers, leading to fears that deletion would cause all of their business to go elsewhere.

Table 14.8 : PRODUCT - RETENTION INDEX

Factor	*Factor (FWi) weighting*	*Product / service ranking (SRi)*
Future market potential for Product/service?		
How much could be gained from modification?		

How much could be gained from marketing strategy modification?	
How much useful executive time could be released by abandoning product / service	
How good are the firm's alternative opportunities?	
How much is the product/service contributing beyond its direct costs?	
How much is the product/service contributing to the sale of other product/services?	
Total	

The product/service retention index SRI = the sum of (FWi x SRi)

In fact, many companies tackle product/service elimination in a piecemeal fashion, only considering the matter once a service is seen to be losing money, or when there is some crisis leading to a cutback. There is clearly a need for a systematic approach. At regular intervals, every product/service should be reviewed in terms of its sales, profitability, average cost, market share, competitor share, competitor prices, etc.

Having acquired the relevant information, an organization can identify 'weak' elements of the overall product / service mix.

One possible method of deciding which products to eliminate is the development and implementation of a product/service-retention index. This can include a number of factors, each of these being individually weighted according to the importance attached to them by a particular firm. Each service is then ranked according to each factor, the product-retention index thus being equal to the sum of the products of the weighted index. An illustration of a product retention index in shown in Table 14.8.

Two of the product-retention factors relate to potential modification approaches in terms of either the service itself or of the whole marketing strategy, non-deletion alternatives for poorly performing services includes :

1. Modifying the product or service. Here the emphasis is on modifying the features so that any new benefits fit with the needs and wants of the market.
2. Increasing the price. This may be a sensible strategy if there is a primary market for the product/service from which demand is fairly inelastic.
3. Decreasing the price. This is a useful approach if the existing demand curve is elastic.
4. Increasing promotional expenditure. This assumes that sales of the service are sufficiently responsive to this increased promotion.
5. Decreasing promotional expenditure. If sales are now concentrated in a small primary market, promotional saving can be made.

6. Revising the promotional mix. This may come about as a result of a re-evaluation of the original promotional programme.
7. Increasing salesforce effort so that the service can be more competitive.
8. Decreasing salesforce effort if sales are concentrated in a primary market.
9. Changing the physical distribution system, where there is a significant tangible element to the service offer.
11. Additional marketing research effort may indicate new markets or additional uses for the product or service. Additionally, information relating to why success has declined may also be forthcoming.
12. Licensing agreements to another firm may be a possibility.

If any of the non-deletion alternatives are chosen the firm must decide how such options are to be implemented in terms of timing and size of any changes to the marketing mix. If, on the other hand, deletion is the chosen alternative, decisions must be made as to how this is to be implemented. This is not always a simple task and a number of options can be identified:

1. **Ruthlessly eliminate 'overnight'.** The potential problem here is that there are still likely to be customers of the service. How will they respond? Will they take their business to competitors? Will they take their business for other services in the mix with them.
2. **Increase the price and let demand fade away.** This could mean that the firm makes good profits on the service while demand lasts.
3. **Reduce promotion or even stop it altogether.** Again this could increase profitability while demand lasts.

Whichever decision is made, an organisation has to consider the timing of such a decision. There are a number of areas that a firm planning to delete the service needs to consider.

1. **Notification of consumers.** A firm has everything to gain and little to lose by informing consumers of the service that deletion is imminent. Such a policy at least allows people time to make alternative arrangements and this may also have the added advantage of promoting the firm's caring image.
2. **Resources Management** should move freed-up resources, particularly labour, to other appropriate service as soon as is possible. This not only eliminates the possibility of idle resources and layoffs of manpower but is also an important part of internal marketing which is so important for services firms.
3. **Legal implications** Service elimination may bring with it legal liabilities. In the case of suppliers an organization may be committed to take supplies regardless of a deletion strategy (for example a holiday tour operator may be contractually committed to buying aircraft seats for the remainder of a season). In the case of customers, it may not be possible to delete services provided under a long-term contract until that contract comes to an end. This can be particularly important for the financial services sector, where mortgages and pension plans usually allow no facility for a unilateral withdrawal of supply by the service producer, even though a pension policy may still have over 30 year to run.

SHORT ANSWER QUESTIONS

1. In what ways does a travel agent assist tour operators in the process of making holidays available to customers?
2. In what situations is a service principal likely to prefer dealing directly with its customers, rather than through intermediaries?
3. What are the determinants of effective service delivery?
4. What are the main differences between agents and brokers?
5. What marketing and management challenges are raised by the use of intermediaries in a service setting?

6. In what ways do customers and employees benefit from productivity enhancement and improvement in a service setting?
7. What is 'product retention index'?
8. When is service deletion necessitated?
9. What is a fishbone chart? What is its relevance to service delivery?
10. What are the challenges and benefits of electronic distribution of services?
11. How do customers respond to service failures?
12. What do you understand by 'value delivery'?

ESSAY QUESTIONS

1. What are the most important factors influencing the location decision for a proposed new gymnasium?
2. Explain a service delivery system.
3. Of what value are modeling techniques in deciding on retail store location?
4. List services that are sold through selling agents. Why is the use of agents the chosen method of distribution for these services? Could any of these services be distributed through other ways?
5. How is service recovery effected? What are the components and issues involved?
6. Identify services that are in the following stages of the life cycle: introduction, growth, maturity, saturation and decline. What do you think could have been done to forestall decline?
7. By what methods could a bank obtain ideas for new-service developments?
8. Develop a flowchart to depict the delivery of the following services:
   (a) Hotel catering (b) Banking (c) Public relations in a supermarket (d) Police action.
9. How are service delivery problems analysed and prevented?
10. Identify the factors that might influence an airline's decision whether or not to delete a loss-making route.
11. Enumerate the strategies for effective service delivery through intermediaries.
12. In what specific ways does the distribution of services differ from the distribution of goods?
13. Develop a franchising plan for a service concept or idea that you believe could be successful.
14. Identify the factors that might influence an airline's decision whether or not to delete a loss-making route.

EXERCISE / ASSIGNMENT

1. Using examples, contrast the role of 'push' and 'pull' methods of making services available within the service sector.
2. Analyse the potential problems and opportunities for a dry-cleaning company seeking to expand through franchising.
3. Use the elements of a franchise agreement (of any service) to describe the plan in detail. In your opinion, what would franchisees pay to become an affiliate of the franchiser?
4. Visit a franchisee and discuss the pros and cons of the arrangement from his or her perspective.
5. Select a service industry of your choice or with which you are familiar. How do service principals in that industry distribute their services? Also, develop possible approaches to manage intermediaries.
6. Select a service organisation with which you are reasonably familiar, and construct what you believe to be a flowchart, representative of its service operations system. What appear to you to be 'moments-of-truth', that is, critical points within the service delivery process, likely to have a significant bearing on customers' perceptions and sense of satisfaction, and why? How would you go about managing these?

15 Service Quality

15.1 INTRODUCTION

It is widely acknowledged that efforts to define and measure the quality of tangible products, as distinct from services, have proved more successful. The characteristics of services have made the determination of what constitutes quality that much more difficult and thereby its measurement less than complete. To increase our understanding and to enable practical steps to be taken two things need to be present:

- Specification of the determinants of service quality
- Measurable quality standards set.

Achievement in these two areas will vary depending on whether the focus is:

- A low contact or a high contact service, e.g., a fast-food outlet versus an education course.
- Process or output.

Determining the process and output quality of a fast-food restaurant is arguably more straightforward than an education course.

Whatever the service, it is useful to bear in mind the following questions when it comes to quality :

- What is the service supposed to do?
- What does the service actually do?

Quality then refers to the extent to which a service is what it claims to be and does what it claims to do. It must not be confused with grade. For example the quality of a library cannot be judged in an abstract way by, say, counting the number of Shakespeare volumes possessed and subtracting the number of other novels. Instead the prime aspect of quality is whether the library provides people with what they want - It is a good library if it does and a bad library if it does not.

$$\text{Service quality} = \frac{\text{Perceived performance}}{\text{Desired expectation}} \times 100$$

15.2 THE IMPACT OF SERVICE QUALITY

Quality needs to be understood and managed throughout a service organization. Four areas in particular may serve as an arena within which the question of quality can be addressed (Figure 15.1)

Service encounter - the customer interacts with animate (the service employees) and inanimate objects (the physical evidence, e.g., an information sign).

- How knowledgeable and courteous is the service employee?
- How effective is the sign in terms of visibility, information provided, positioning?
- How can the customer contribute to the quality of the encounter?
- What contribution do script theory and role theory make?

Figure 15.1 : THE IMPACT OF QUALITY

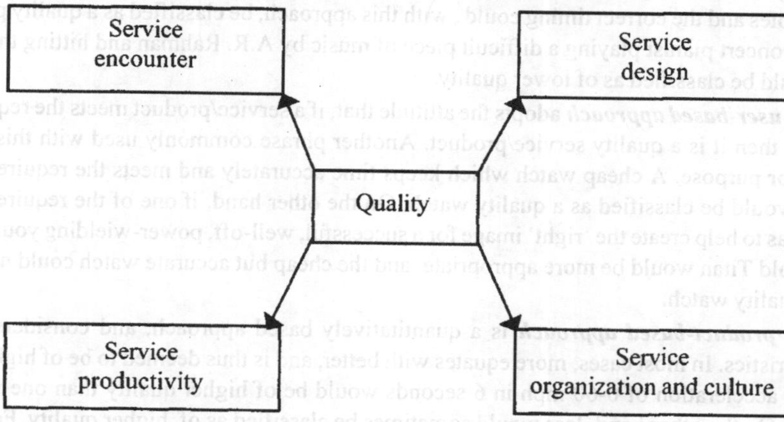

Service design - the customer goes through a process to obtain a service.

- How well designed is the process?
- Is there a blueprint/flowchart of the process?
- To what extent is there flexibility in the system?
- Does the process require customization of standardization?

Service productivity - there is a relationship between the quantity and quality of goods or services produced and the quality of resources used to produce them.

- What are the possible relationships between changes in quality and changes in quantity? i.e., if quantity increases (number of patients seen by a general practitioner) what effect could that have on the quality of service?
- What role should the customer play in the productivity equation?

Service organization and culture - the culture of an organization and the way it is organized can affect the quality of service.

- How do the various organization cultures (power, role, achievement and support) act as a key to understanding the kind of service produced?
- What characteristics/features of an organization enable it to respond positively to customer needs and deliver a quality service?

15.3 APPROACHES TO SERVICE QUALITY

The word 'quality' has different meanings and can be used in different ways. Garvin (1984) identified five categories or approaches to the concept of quality :

- The transcendent approach
- The manufacturing - based approach
- The user - based approach
- The product-based approach.
- The value-based approach

The ***transcendent approach*** follows the Pocket Oxford Dictionary's definition. ' degree of excellence, relative nature. 'Quality in this sense in innate excellence. It reflects the 'best' there is. So, for example, a five-star hotel would be classed as a quality hotel, as opposed to a one-star, family-run hotel.

The ***manufacturing-based approach*** relates to conformance with design or specification. A quality service or product would be one which was free of errors, where an error would be defined as non-compliance with specification. The performance of a child playing a simple piece of music with no wrong notes and the correct timing could , with this approach, be classified as a quality performance, while a concert pianist playing a difficult piece of music by A.R. Rahman and hitting the odd wrong note, could be classified as of lower quality.

The ***user-based approach*** adopts the attitude that, if a service/product meets the requirements of the user, then it is a quality service/product. Another phrase commonly used with this approach is fitness for purpose. A cheap watch which keeps time accurately and meets the requirements of the wearer would be classified as a quality watch. On the other hand, if one of the requirements of the watch was to help create the 'right' image for a successful, well-off, power-wielding young executive, then a gold Titan would be more appropriate, and the cheap but accurate watch could not be considered a quality watch.

The ***product-based approach*** is a quantitatively based approach, and considers measurable characteristics. In most cases, more equates with better, and is thus deemed to be of higher quality. A car with acceleration of 0-60 mph in 6 seconds would be of higher quality than one which took 8 seconds. On the other hand, less would sometimes be classified as of higher quality. For example, a dentist who took only 5 minutes, as compared with 10 minutes, to complete a filling would be considered as providing a higher-quality service!

The ***value -based approach*** is based on customs and traditions. If the service conforms to traditional beliefs and emotions, it is perceived to be of high value.

15.4 THE TEN ORIGINAL DIMENSIONS OF SERVICE QUALITY

The dimension of service quality are listed below and Table 15.1 gives example of how these are used by customers to evaluate service quality.

1. ***Tangibles***
   The physical appearance of the facilities, staff, buildings, etc., e.g. Does the equipment appear modern? How clean is the waitress's apron?
2. ***Reliability***
   The ability to reproduce the same level of service again and again e.g. Is feedback regarding student progress always given? Are messages always passed on?
3. ***Responsiveness***
   The speed with which queries etc. and dealt with. e.g. Are letters replied to by return of post, or does it take a month? Is feedback on assignments given within a week in time for students to assimilate the information, or does the feedback come too late, after the examination has been taken?
4. ***Communication***
   The clarity and understandability of the information given to the client, e.g. Does the doctor take the time to explain in terms the patient can understand, what is going to happen next? Does the solicitor explain clearly what the legal jargon means?
5. ***Credibility***
   The trustworthiness of the service provider. e.g. Does the newspaper reporter report all the facts or only those which support his/her argument? Does the financial adviser present all the options or only those which earn him/her the most commission?
6. ***Security***
   The physical safety of the customer or privacy of client information. e.g. Are the medical records of patients kept confidential? Are the stands in the football ground strong enough to support the weight of all the supporters?
7. ***Competence***
   The actual technical expertise of the service provider, e.g. Is the doctor really qualified to perform

heart surgery? Does the financial adviser have sufficient knowledge of all the relevant tax regulations?

8. *Courtesy*

The attitude of the service provider and manner adopted by the server, e.g.. Is the receptionist friendly, helpful and polite? Does the doctor treat the patient as an inferior being?

9. *Understanding*

How well the provider of the service understands the client's needs e.g Does the bank recognize that most clients cannot get to the bank in working hours? Are there mirrors positioned in the hotel bathrooms which allow guests to see the back of their hair?

10 *Access*

How easy is it to reach the service provider, geographically or by phone, e.g Are there car parking facilities close to the solicitor's office? Does it always take five attempts to get the solicitor on the phone?

Table 15.1 : GENERIC DIMENSIONS USED BY CUSTOMERS TO EVALUATE SERVICE QUALITY

Dimension	*Definition*	*Examples of Questions That Customers Might Raise*
Credibility	Trustworthiness, believability honesty of the service provider	- Does the hospital have a good reputation? - Does my stockbroker refrain from pressuring me ?
Security	Freedom from danger, risk, or doubt	- Does the repair firm guarantee its work? - Is it safe for me to use the bank's ATMs at night? - Is my credit card protected against unauthorised use? - Can I be sure that my insurance policy provides complete coverage?
Access	Approachability and ease of contact	- How easy is it for me to talk to a supervisor when I have a problem? - Does the airline have a 24- hour toll-free phone number? - Is the hotel conveniently located?
Communication	Listening to customers and keeping them informed in language they can understand	- When I have a complaint, is the manager willing to listen to me? - Does my doctor avoid using technical jargon? - Does the electrician call when unable to keep a scheduled appointment?
Understanding the customer	Making the effort to know customers and needs	- Does someone in the hotel recognize me as a regular customer? - Does my stockbroker try to determine my specific financial objectives? - Is the moving company willing to accommodate my schedule?
Tangibles	Appearance of physical facilities, equipment, personnel, and commu nication materials	- Are the hotel's facilities attractive? - Is my accountant dressed appropriately? - Is my bank statement easy to understand?

Responsiveness	Willingness to help customers and provide prompt service	- When there's problem, does the firm resolve it quickly ? - Is my stockbroker willing to answer my questions? - Is the cable TV company willing to give me a specific time when the installer will show up?
Competence	Possession of the skills and knowledge required to perform the service	- Can the bank teller process my transaction without fumbling around? - When I call my travel agent is she able to obtain the information I need? - Does the dentist appear to know what he is doing?
Courtesy	Politeness, respect, consideration, and friendliness of contact personnel	- Does the flight attendant have a pleasant demeanour? - Are the telephone operators consistently polite when answering my calls? - Does the plumber take off his muddy shoes before stepping on my carpet?

15.5 A MODEL OF SERVICE QUALITY

To enhance knowledge of service quality and encourage investigation of the key issues, a model has been developed (Figure 15.2)

Its key features are:

1. The identification of key attributes of service quality from a management and consumer perspective.
2. Highlighting the gaps between consumers and service providers with particular reference to perceptions and expectations.
3. Understanding the implications for service management of closing the gaps.

15.6 SERVICE GAPS

Gap 1 - this is the overall gap between service provider and consumer. It sates that many organizations just do not understand what consumers expect in a service.

Gap 2 -service organization often experience great difficulty in even meeting far less exceeding consumer expectations. This is invariably attributed to a number of factors - absence of total management commitment to service quality, lack of resources, and excessive demand.

Gap 3 - even when formal standards or specifications for maintaining service quality are in existence, the delivery of quality service is by no means certain. The main reason given is that the performance of customer contact personnel can be so variable.

Gap 4 - advertising other forms of communication by a service organization can affect consumer expectations. The danger is that promises made are not kept. Many service organizations use the brochure or prospectus (some very glossy) for communication with potential customers. It should be a statement of what the customer will receive, not an attractive set of promises that cannot be delivered.

Gap 5 - this gap represents the key challenge, to ensure good service quality the provider must meet or exceed customer expectations. Perceived service quality is the result of the consumer's comparison of expected service with perceived service delivery.

15.7 PRESCRIPTIONS FOR CLOSING SERVICE GAPS

Gap 1 Prescription : Learn What Customers Expect

Get a better understanding of customer expectations through research, complaint analysis, customer panels, etc.,

Figure 15.2 : MODEL OF SERVICE QUALITY

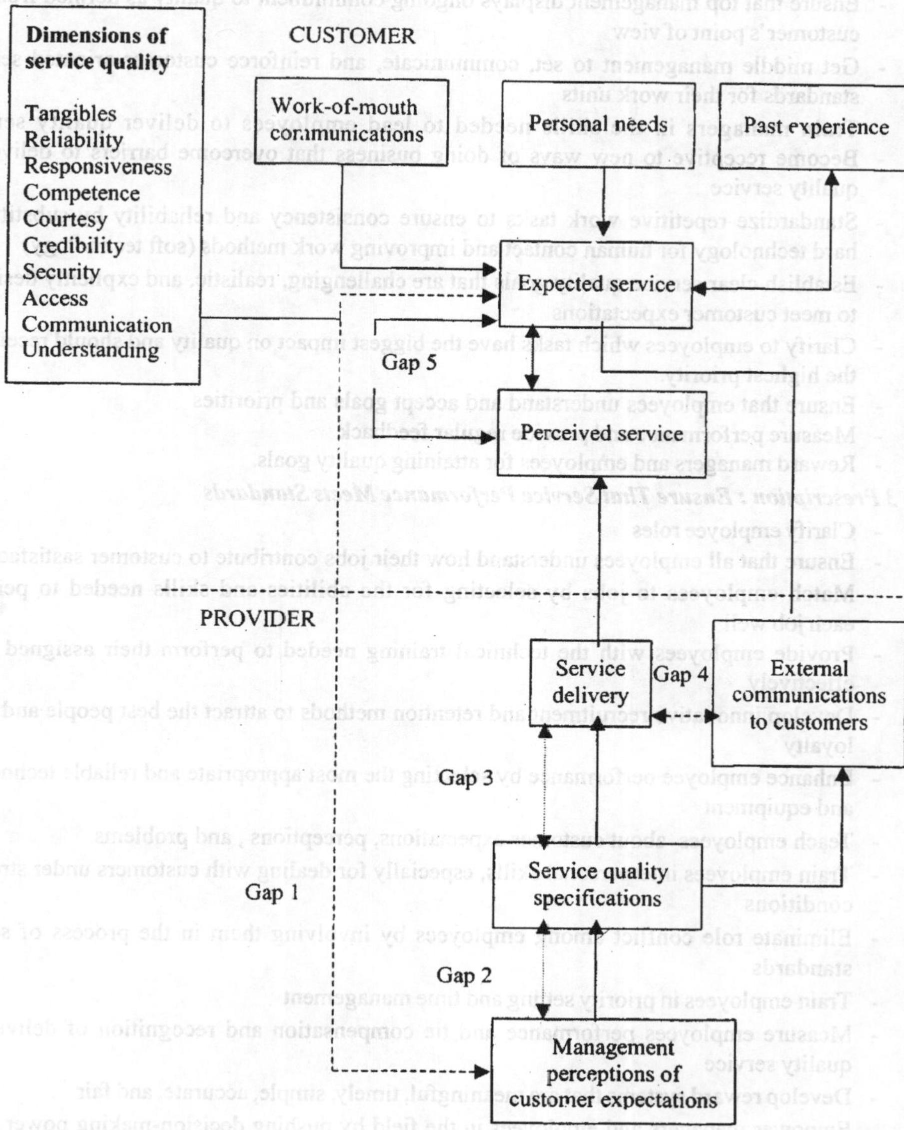

- Increase direct interactions between managers and customers to improve understanding
- Improve upward communication from contact personnel to management and reduce the number of levels between the two
- Turn information and insights into action

Gap 2 Prescription : Establish the Right Service Quality Standards

- Ensure that top management displays ongoing commitment to quality as defined from the customer's point of view
- Get middle management to set, communicate, and reinforce customer-oriented service standards for their work units
- Train managers in the skills needed to lead employees to deliver quality service
- Become receptive to new ways of doing business that overcome barriers to delivering quality service
- Standardize repetitive work tasks to ensure consistency and reliability by substituting hard technology for human contact and improving work methods (soft technology)
- Establish clear service quality goals that are challenging, realistic, and explicitly designed to meet customer expectations
- Clarify to employees which tasks have the biggest impact on quality and should receive the highest priority.
- Ensure that employees understand and accept goals and priorities
- Measure performance and provide regular feedback
- Reward managers and employees for attaining quality goals.

Gap 3 Prescription : Ensure That Service Performance Meets Standards

- Clarify employee roles
- Ensure that all employees understand how their jobs contribute to customer sastisfaction
- Match employees to jobs by selecting for the abilities and skills needed to perform each job well
- Provide employees with the technical training needed to perform their assigned tasks effectively
- Develop innovative recruitment and retention methods to attract the best people and build loyalty
- Enhance employee performance by selecting the most appropriate and reliable technology and equipment
- Teach employees about customer expectations, perceptions , and problems
- Train employees interpersonal skills, especially for dealing with customers under stressful conditions
- Eliminate role conflict among employees by involving them in the process of setting standards
- Train employees in priority setting and time management
- Measure employees performance and tie compensation and recognition of delivery of quality service
- Develop reward systems that are meaningful, timely, simple, accurate, and fair
- Empower managers and employees in the field by pushing decision-making power down the organization: allow them greater discretion in the methods they use to reach goals
- Ensure that employees working at internal support jobs provide good service to customer contact personnel
- Build teamwork so that employees work well together, and use team rewards as incentives

- Treat customers as "partial employees" clarify their roles in service delivery, train and motivate them to perform well in their roles as coproducers

Gap 4 Prescription : Ensure That Delivery Matches Promises

- Seek inputs from operations personnel when new advertising programmes are being created
- Develop advertising that features real employees performing their jobs
- Allow service providers to preview advertisements before customers are exposed to them
- Get sales staff to involve operations staff in face-to-face meetings with customers
- Develop internal education, motivational, and advertising campaigns to strengthen links between marketing, operations, and human resource departments
- Ensure that consistent standards of service are delivered across multiple locations
- Ensure that advertising content accurately reflects those service characteristics that are most important to customers in their encounters with the organization
- Manage customers' expectations by letting them know what is and is not possible - and the reasons why
- Identify and explain uncontrollable reasons for shortcomings in service performance
- Offer customers different levels of service at different prices, explaining the differences between these levels.

15.8 QUALITY TRAPS

In managing change, most of what needs to be done is invisible from the outside, hidden from sight. The part that is clearly visible can be wrongly interpreted as the whole of the action. This is what we mean by a 'quality trap'. Here are seven common quality traps.

Trap one

"We will cascade our commitment down to the troops. That should do it'

Internal marketing messages are going to be rejected by many staff unless the communications have a coherent logic which fits the evidence of their past experience. Just as with advertising, internal marketing communications work best when they are designed to 'preach to the converted.' Message making is a difficult job when it attempts to get people to change their minds. Messages work best when they reinforce how people already feel and think.

Trap two

'We must invest in more training'

The most common mistake is to jump directly into intensive training. In marketing terms the questions that should be asked (and often are not) are:

- Who is my target audience?
- What are their expectations?
- What knowledge do they need now?
- What skills do they need now?
- How can we monitor the learning process?

The investment in training is wasted if too much training is provided for too many people too soon. These issues concern scale. On the other hand, training in skills is necessary so that individuals can adjust to changing work contexts. This kind of learning has been called single loop learning', especially where the intention is that organizational performance remains stable within organizational norms. The strategic issue, however, concerns scope. The pathway to continuous quality improvement challenges the patterns of operations and they very organizational norms which have previously defined effective performance. This second kind of learning is called 'double loop learning.

Trap three

'We intend to build a strong culture as a priority'

Just as the culture of a nation is shaped and sustained by deeply held values and beliefs, so too in the world in business, changing the 'culture' of a particular company is a task of great subtlety. It is possible, for example, to change surface appearances without changing the culture at all, by changing the marketing artefacts such as logo, signage, mission statements, 'corporate wardrobe', and the design of the stationery. Giving a company a superficial change of identity, in itself, will have no significant or lasting cultural impact.

Trap four

'We want to get everybody involved'

Getting everybody involved sounds fine. It is a question of time-scale. Many companies give the impression of wanting to get it over and done with. People in organizations are so focused on the daily problems to be sorted out and on the downside risk of not doing so, they end up shutting out messages which signal opportunities and possibilities all around them. There is often virtue in starting small. In that way commitment can be built, confirmed by action programmes and the results broadcast across the organization. This provides a signal to other that the commitment has integrity.

Trap five

'We will introduce quality circles and see what happens'

A quality circle is a volunteer group of work-force members who have undergone training for the purpose of solving work-related problems. The circle concept evolved in Japan in the early 1960s as a support for the quality management techniques which had been introduced there by Deming and Juran in 1950 and 1954 respectively. Historically, circles are an adjunct to a more broadly based quality management approach. Quality circles differ from other participative groups such as quality improvement teams or diagnostic review groups in that they are always volunteer-based and usually select their own problems for diagnosis.

Difficulties arise when circles are unsupported by management and they do not have access to valid customer data which guide the choice of problems for diagnosis.

Trap six

'We can't improve service unless we set standards'

Only the customer can 'set' service standards. Therefore, how the customers' standards are signalled and interpreted by the company is the central issue. It is no good setting operational standards which have no meaning to the customer.

Trap seven

'Our bottom line tells us when we are succeeding'

There is no one solitary way of measuring the score and what is useful is a range of external and internal feedback mechanisms which enable a 'fix' on quality.

Quality improvement can actually reduce the cost of quality. It is a question of eliminating waste in resources and time without reducing value to the customer.

15.9 CAUSES OF SERVICE QUALITY PROBLEMS

Several reasons have been put forward as explanations of poor service quality:

Inseparability of production and consumption and labour intensity

The provision of service, as distinct from the manufacture of goods, occurs in the presence of customers. Inevitably as with any human encounter, problems do arise. The service employee may exhibit poor presentational skills, conduct himself improperly and dress inappropriately. All of these and more may influence the customer's perception of service quality. The intensive involvement of humans in service delivery will always have the potential to pose problems for quality.

Inadequate services to intermediate or internal customers

The frontline employee is by definition at the 'sharp-end' of the service delivery system. To execute the service effectively, the employee requires proper support from further back in the organization (Figure 15.3)

Figure 15.3 : IMPORTANCE OF EMPLOYEE SUPPORT IN THE EXECUTION OF EFFECTIVE SERVICE

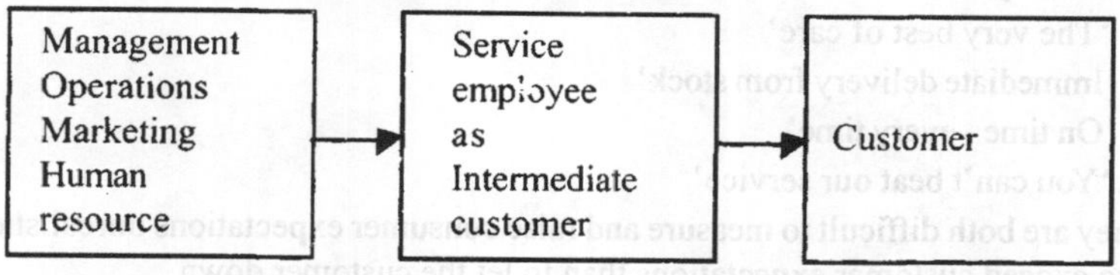

The support will emanate from the main management functions (operations, marketing and human resource) and involve:

1. Equipment e.g tools, materials, uniforms`
2. Skills training
3. Information e.g. of a new service launch's operating procedures.

Communication gaps

Good communication is the life-blood of a healthy organization, and its contact with customers. However, it is a problems of some magnitude and manifests itself in the followings ways:

1. Failure to deliver promises made
2. Failure to keep a customer informed
3. Failure to communicate in a manner the customer can understand
4. Failure to listen.

Viewing customers as statistics

For a service organization there are often compelling reasons for offering a standardized service, not least of which are the efficiencies to be gained from treating a large number of customers in a standardized manner. For the customer, this approach to service delivery is often welcomed. By contrast, customization of the service seeks to recognize the particular needs of individual customers. Service organizations should be sensitive to how their customers feel about how they are treated. A remark made by a student perhaps exemplifies the issue. He said, 'In my two years at college, not once did a lecturer recognize me by name'.

Short-run view of the business

Organizations take a short run view of the business when it comes to performance evaluation. Management are frequently required to meet targets on a yearly basis. The obsession inevitably becomes one of cost reduction and productivity increases to meet a profit target. This is understandable but detrimental to building a quality service in the longer term.

15.10 HOW TO IMPROVE SERVICE QUALITY

Improving service quality is certainly not a simple, straightforward exercise. It will have implications for the whole culture of the organization. Some ideas put forward are worthy of consideration:

Identifying primary quality determinants

Knowing what determines quality is, of course, crucial. However, consumers and producers of services do not necessarily perceive service quality on common dimensions and even when they do hold common dimensions, they evaluate them differently.

Managing customer expectations

To attract custom, organizations are often tempted to raise customer expectations. Companies make promises to consumers on aspects of their business that they think the customer will value in order to give the organization a competitive advantage. However care must be exercised in making promises to customers. For example, consider the following sample taken from the Yellow Pages Directory:

- 'Nobody does it better'
- 'The very best of care'
- 'Immediate delivery from stock'
- 'On time - every time'
- 'You can't beat our service'

They are both difficult to measure and raise consumer expectations unrealistically. As a rule it is better to exceed customer expectations than to let the customer down.

Managing evidence

The 'evidence' from the viewpoint of a service organization includes many things and consumers look to these as an indicator of what the service might be like (pre-service expectation) and what, in fact, the service was like after using it (post-service evaluation).

Physical and human evidence play a significant part in image formation. Retailers are interested in several aspects relating to architecture and design for promoting an image. Similarly, atmosphere influences image. The term 'atmospherics' has been coined to define the conscious design of space to influence buyers. The atmosphere influences the buyers' expectations and perceptions of the service. For example lawyers' offices and banks are designed to communicate confidence.

Various factors such as colours, music, furnishing, space etc. can evoke a variety of feelings about the service organization, e.g. friendliness, austerity, sobriety, authority, rationality, stability, flexibility. The physical aspects of a service will allow us to make sense of it and we expect the physical signs to be in tune with the nature of the service. Incongruity can make us uncertain and uncomfortable.

Educating consumers about the service

Helping the customer to understand the service would appear to be a sine qua non for dispensing a quality service. However, for many services, e.g. garage repair business, professional services, the challenge can be a daunting one and one that perhaps they are not willing to confront. Equally, the willingness of the customer 'to be educated' requires evaluation along with their capacity to assimilate the nature of the service being delivered.

Developing a quality culture

Quality is not delivered in a vacuum but through an organization with all its imperfections. Commitment to quality must pervade the whole organization. A number of institutional factors can either help or hinder the provision of quality service. They are:

1. Human - job descriptions, selection, training, rewards, career path.
2. Organization/structure - integration/coordination of functions and reporting structure
3. Measurement - complaint and customer satisfaction tracking and performance evaluation.
4. Systems support - technical, computers, databases.
5. Services - value added, range and quality, standards or performance, satisfying needs and expectations.
6. Programmes - complaint management, sales/promotional tools, management tools.
7. Communication (internal) - policies and procedures, feedback within the organization.
8. Communication (external) - consumer education, creation of expectations, image.

Automating quality

The variability in quality service emanating from human inadequacy can be avoided through automation. Before such a decision is made, research needs to establish which parts of the service require the human touch and which require automation. The danger is that automation takes over for reasons other than automation.

Following up the service

Organizations need to continuously monitor their performance by contacting customers to determine their view of the service delivered.

More recently, organizations have been asked to consider five imperatives for improving service quality:

1. Define a clear service role and standard for service employees and communicate and reinforce these standards.
2. Compete for talent - allocate people to jobs according to ability and aptitude and give them more flexibility and control to do the job. The problem with this is that many service jobs are by nature narrow in scope and perceived as 'dead end'.
3. Emphasize service teams - getting people to work as a team is an attractive proposition and potentially very effective for delivering quality. However, entrenched attitudes (negative) to work and strong personalities can quite easily prevent the development of a team spirit. The action (or inaction) of management is crucial here. Good employees need to see management doing something about the members of the team who are simply not pulling their weight.
4. Go for reliability - at the heart of excellent service is reliability and it is argued that nothing less than 100 percent reliability is acceptable.
5. Be great at problem resolution - service organizations cannot avoid things going wrong for a customer but it is their reaction to this that is critical. Their response can make things better or very much worse. Customers need to feel that actions are being taken to try to resolve the problem. For large service organizations client dissatisfaction of attempts at problem resolution is a real issue.

Quality leadership curve (Figure 15.4) model enables you to set your expectations on the journey to quality, to act strategically, and to watch for problems and opportunities on the way. There are a series of leadership steps, or more correctly transitions, towards the quality goal. Each phase has its own special characteristics and there is likely to be some degree of 'turbulence' before breaking through from one phase to the next.

Quality leadership could be any company's strategic intent, when success is measured against customer expectations, within defined target markets. Just what this might entail will always be vague at the outset. Commitment to a precise goal at an early stage could lead to an incorrect choice. 'Quality leadership' is a qualitative target. Having said that, there are steps to take, and these will involve transitions in the way things are normally done. This is a process of 'learning by doing'. These steps can be logically planned to advantage, individual projects set up and completed, and motivational and organizational structures put in place. All this can be achieved in terms of commitment to a superordinate quality leadership goal.

15.11 SERVICE-QUALITY INFORMATION SYSTEM

To improve service, companies must use multiple research approaches among different customer groups to ensure that they are hearing what customers are saying and responding to their suggestions.

The quality of listening has an impact on the quality of service. Firms intent on improving service need to listen continuously to three types of customers: external customers who has experienced the firm's service; competitors' customers who the firm would like to make its own; and internal customers (employees) who depend on internal services to provide their own services. Without the voices of these groups guiding investment in service improvement, all companies can hope for are marginal gains.

FIGURE 15.4: QUALITY LEADERSHIP CURVE

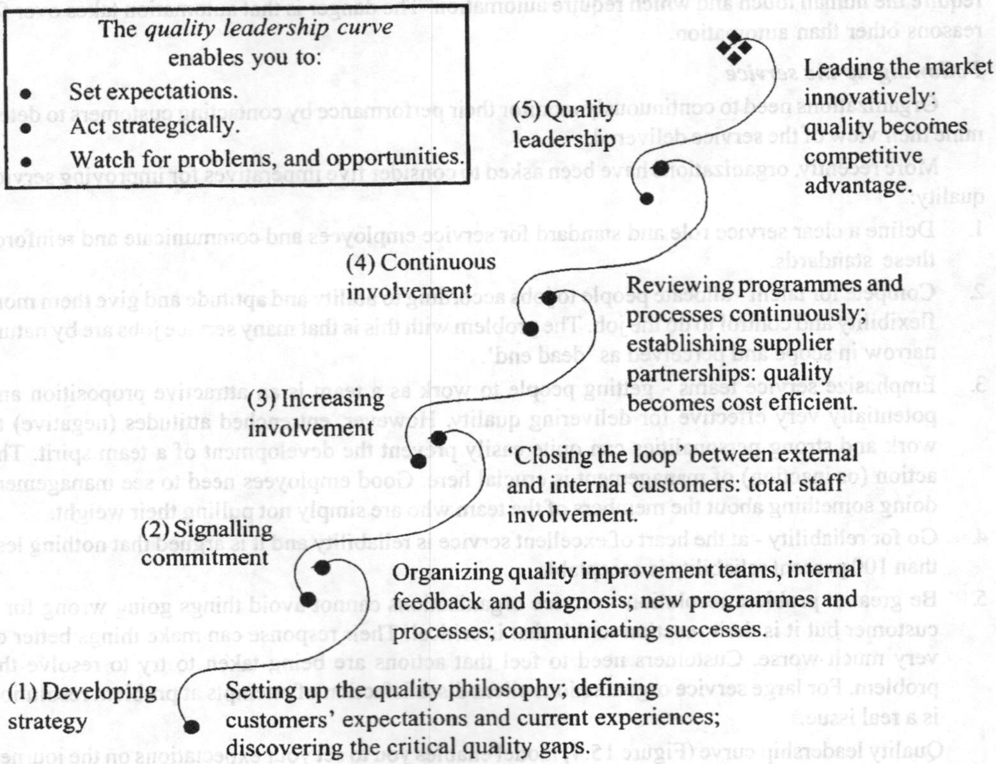

Systematic listening

A service-quality information system uses multiple research approaches to systematically capture, organize, and disseminate service-quality information to support decision-making. Continuously generated data flow into databases that decision-makers can use on both a regular scheduled and as needed basis.

The use of multiple research approaches is necessary because each approach has limitations as well as strengths. Combining approaches enables a firm to tap the strengths of each and compensate for weaknesses. Continuous data collection and dissemination informs and educates decision-makers about the patterns of change - for example, customers' shifting service priorities and declining or improving performance in the company's or the competitors' service.

An effective service-quality information system offers a company's executives a larger view of service quality along with a composite of many smaller pictures. It teaches decision-makers which service attributes are important to customers and prospects, what parts of the firm's service system are working well or breaking down, and which service investments are paying off. A service-quality information system helps to focus service improvement planning and resource allocation. It can help sustain managers' motivation for service improvement by comparing the service performance of various units in the organization and linking compensation to these results. And it can be the basis for an effective first-line employee reward system by identifying the most effective service providers. Figure 15.5 shows the principal benefits of a service-quality information system.

Figure 15.5 : PRINCIPAL BENEFITS OF AN EFFECTIVE SERVICE -QUALITY INFORMATION SYSTEM

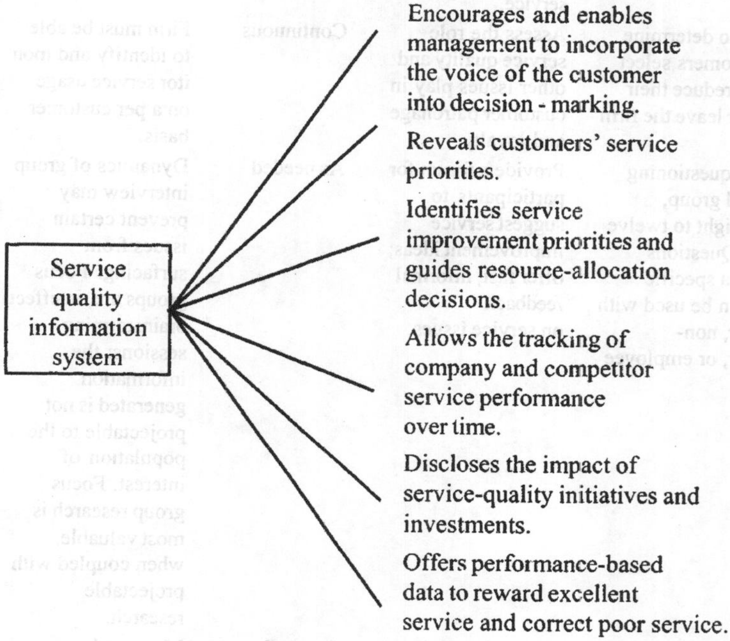

Approaches to service research

A company can choose from many possible research approaches to build a service-quality information system (Table 15.2). A firm would not use all approaches in the table in the same system; too much information obscures the most meaningful insights and may intimidate intended users. Conversely, incomplete information injects needless guessing into decision-making or, worse, paints a false picture. The nature of the service, the firm's service strategy, and the needs of the information users determine which service-quality research approaches to use.

Table 15.2 : RESEARCH APPROACHES FOR BUILDING SERVICE-QUALITY INFORMATION SYSTEMS

Type	*Description*	*Purpose*	*Frequency*	*Limitations*
Transactional survey	Service satisfaction survey of customers following a service encounter.	Obtain customer feedback while service experience is still fresh; act on feedback quickly if negative patterns develop.	Continuous	Focuses on customers' most recent experience rather than their overall assessment. Non-customers are excluded
Mystery shopping	Researchers become 'customers' to experience and evaluate the quality of service delivered.	Measure individual employee service behaviours for use in coaching, training, peformance evalua-tion, recognition and rewards; identify systemic strengths	Quarterly	Subjective evalua-tions: researchers may be more 'judge mental' than custo mers would be; expense limits repetitions; potential to hurt

		and weaknesses in customer-contact service.		employee morale if improperly used.
New, declining and lost customer surveys	Surveys to determine why customers select the firm, reduce their buying or leave the firm	Assess the role service quality and other issues play in customer patronage and loyalty.	Continuous	Firm must be able to identify and mon itor service usage on a per customer basis.
Focus group interviews	Directed questioning of a small group, usually eight to twelve people. Questions focus on a specific topic. Can be used with customer, non-customer, or employee group.	Provide a forum for participants to suggest service improvement ideas; offer fast, informal feedback on service issues.	As needed	Dynamics of group interview may prevent certain issues from surfacing. Focus groups are, in effect brainstorming sessions; the information generated is not projectable to the population of interest. Focus group research is most valuable when coupled with projectable research.
Customer advisory panels	A group of customer recruited periodically to provide the firm with feedback and advice on service performance and other issues. Data are obtained in meetings, over the telephone, through mail questionnaires or via other means. Employee panels also can be formed	Obtain in-depth, timely feedback and suggestions about service quality from experienced customers who cooperate because of 'membership' nature of the panel.	Quarterly	May not be projectable to entire customer base. Excludes non-customers. Panelists may assume role of 'expert' and become less representative of customer base.
Service reviews	Periodic visits with customers (or a class of customers) to discuss and assess the service relationship. Should be a formal process with a common set of questions, capture of responses in a database, and follow-up communication with customers.	Identify customer expectations and perceptions of the company's service performance and improvement priorities in a fact-to-face conversation. A view of the future not just a study of the past. Opportunity to include multiple decision - makers and decision - influencers in the discussions.	Annually or semi-annually	Time consuming and expensive. Most appropriate for firms marketing complex services on an ongoing, relationship basis.

Customer complaint, comment, and inquiry capture	**System to retain, categorize, track and distribute customer complaints and other communications with the company.**	**Identify most common types of service failure for corrective action. Identify through customer communications opportunities to improve service or otherwise strengthen customer relationship.**	**Continuous**	**Dissatisfied customers frequently do not complain directly to the company. Analysis of customer complaints and comments offers only a partial picture of the state of service.**
Total market surveys	**Surveys that measure customer's overall assessment of a company's service. Research includes both external customers and competitors' customers, i.e., the total market.**	**Assess company's service performance compared to competitors; identify service-improvement priorities; track service improvement over time.**	**Semiannually or quarterly**	**Measures customers' overall service assessments but does not capture assessments of specific service encounters.**
Employee field reporting	**Formal process for gathering, categorizing and distributing field employee intelligence about service issues.**	**Captue and share at the management level intelligence about customers service expectations and perceptions gathered in the field.**	**Continuous to monthly**	**Some employees will be more conscientious and efficent reporters than others. Employees may be unwilling to provide negative information to mangement.**
Employee surveys	**Surveys concerning the service employees provide and receive, and the quality of their work lives.**	**Measure internal service quality; identify employee perceived obstacles to improved service; track employee morale and attitudes. Employee surveys help answer 'why' service performance is what it is.**	**Quarterly**	**The strength of employee surveys is also a weakness; employees view service delivery from their own vantage point, subject to their own biases. Employees cna offer valuable insights into the root causes of service problems but are not always objective or correct in their interpretations.**
Service operating data	**A system to retain, categorize, track and distribute key service performance operating data, such as services response times, service failure rates and service delivery costs**	**Monitor service performance indicators and take action.**	**Continuous**	

15.12 SERVQUAL INSTRUMENT

The revised (1991) version of the Servqual questionnaire is presented in Tables 15.3 and 15.4. The first section of the questionnaire asks questions relating to expectations of the service. The second section repeats the same questions, but instead of eliciting responses about expectations, the perceptions of actual service received are sought. A final section seeks information regarding relative importance of the dimensions.

Table 15.3 : SERVQUAL QUESTIONNAIRE (EXPECTATIONS)

Expectations section

Directions : Based on your experiences as a customer of telephone repair services, please think about the kind of telephone company that would deliver excellent quality of repair service. Think about the kind of telephone company with which you would be pleased to do business. Please show the extent to which you think such a telephone company would possess the features described by each statement. If you feel a feature is not at all essential for excellent telephone companies such as the one your have in mind, circle the number '1'. If you feel a feature is absolutely essential for excellent telephone companies, circle '7'. If your feelings are less strong, circle one of the numbers in the middle. there are no right or wrong answers - all we are interested in is a number that truly reflects your feelings regarding telphone companies that would deliver excellent quality of service.

Note : Each of the statements was accompanied by a 7-point scale anchored at the end by the labels 'Strongly Disagree' (=1) and 'Strongly Agree' (=7). Intermediate scale points were not labelled. Also the headings (Tangibles, reliability, etc), shown here to indicate which statements fall under each dimension, were not included in the actual questionnaire.

Tangibles

E1. Excellent telephone companies will have modern-looking equipment.

E2. The physical facilities at excellent telephone companies will be visually appealing.

E3. Employees of excellent telephone companies will be neat-appealing.

E4. Materials associated with the service (such as pamphlets or statements) will be visually appealing in an excellent telphone company.

Reliability

E5. When excellent telephone companies promise to do something by a certin time, they will do it.

E6. When customers have a problem, excellent telephone companies will show a sincere interest in solving it.

E7. Excellent telephone companies will perform the service right the first time.

E8. Excellent telephone companies will provide their service at the time they promise to do so.

E9. Excellent telephone companies will insist on error-free records.

Responsiveness

E10. Employees of excellent telephone companies will tell customers exactly when service will be performed.

E11. Employees of excellent telephone companies will give prompt service to customers.

E12. Employees of excellent telephone companies will always be willing to help customers.

E13. Employees of excellent companies will never be too busy to respond to customer requests.

Assurance

E14. The behaviour of employees of excellent telephone companies will instill confidence in customers.

E15. Customers of excellent telephone companies will feel safe in their transactions.

E16. Employees of excellent telephone companies will be consistently courteous with customers.

E17. Employees of excellent telephone companies will have the knowledge to answer customer questions.

Empathy

E18. Excellent telephone companies will give customers individual attention.

E19. Excellent telephone companies will have operating hours convenient to all their customers.

E20. Excellent telephone companies will have employees who give customers personal attention.

E21. Excellent telephone companies will have the customers' best interests at heart.

E22. The employees of excellent telephone companies will understand the specific needs of their customers.

Table 15.4 : SERVQUAL QESTIONNAIRE (PERCEPTIONS)

Perceptions section

Directions : The following set of statements relate to your feelings about XYZ Telephone Company's repair service. For each statement, please show the extent to which you believe XYZ has the feature described by the statement, Once again, circling a '1' means that you strongly disagree that XYZ had that feature, and circling a '7' means that you strongly agree. You may cicle any of the numbers in the middle to show how strong you feelings are. There are no right or wrong ansers - all we are interested in is a number that best shows your perceptions about XYZ's repair service.

Tangibles

P1. XYZ has modern-looking equipment.

P2. XYZ's physical facilities are visually appealing.

P3. XYZ's employees are neat-appearing.

P4. Materials associated with the service (such as pamphlets or statements) are visually appealing at XYZ.

Reliability

P5. When XYZ promises to do something by a certain time, it does so.

P6. When you have a problem, XYZ shows a sincere interest in solving it.

P7. XYZ performs the service right the first time.

P8. XYZ provides its services at the time it promises to do so.

P9. XYZ insists on error-free records.

Responsiveness

P10. Employees of XYZ tell you exactly when services will be performed.

P11. Employees of XYZ give you prompt service.

P12. Employees of XYZ are always willing to help you.

P13. Employees of XYZ are never too busy to respond to your requests.

Assurance

P14. The behaviour of employees of XYZ instils confidence in customers.

P15. You feel safe in your transactions with XYZ.

P16. Employees at XYZ are consistently courteous with you.

P17. Employees of XYZ have the knowledge to answer your questions.

Empathy

P18. XYZ gives you individual attention

P19. XYZ has operations hours convenient to all its customers.

P20. XYZ has your best interests at heart.

P22. Employees of XYZ understand your specific needs.

Point-allocation question

Directions : Listed below are five features pertaining to telephone companies and the repair

services they offer. We would like to know how important each of these features is to you when you evaluate a telephone company's quality of repair service. Please allocate a total of 100 points among the five features according to how important each feature is. The more important a feature is to you, the more points you should allocated to it. Please ensure that the points you allocate to the five featurese add up to 100.

1.	**The appearance of the telephone company's physical facilities, equipment, personnel and communications materials.**	**_______ Points**
2.	**The ability of the telphone company to perform the promised service dependably and accurately**	**_______ Points**
3.	**The willingness of the telephone company to help customers and provide prompt service**	**_______ Points**
4.	**The knowledge and courtesy of the telephone companys employees and their ability to convey trust and confidence**	**_______ Points**
5.	**The caring, individualized attention the telephone company provides its customers**	**_______ Points**
	Total points allocated	**100 Points**

15.13 BENCHMARKING

Benchmarking is part of the process of continuous improvement. It is defined as measureing that of the strongest competition in order to establish 'best practice'. Benchmarking can be applied at three levels. Internal benchmarking can be carried out in the larger orgnization by way of comparisons between operations units. Thus the supermarket chain might benchmark operations across stores, a financial institution across branches, different hospitals under the same health authority, different college under the same education authority. Clearly of paramount importance is how performance is measured, and this has a clear link to the strategy of the organization.

At a second level, competitive benchmarking can be used. This is probably the most frequently quoted use where comparisons are made with directly competitive orgnizations. This can be achieved relatively easily in some service environments because of the necessity for the customer to participate in the process. As a hotel owner, it is possible to 'sample' the service of a competitor simply by 'posing' as a guest. Often, however, this is done in an informal manner. A comparative impression is gained of the service without examining the different facets in a structured way and attempting to measure them.

The third approach is functional or generic benchmarking, which compares specific functions, such as distribution and after-sales service. The advantage here is that information is sometimes easier to obtain then when comparisons are being made with competitors.

Care has to be taken in selecting the dimensions and scales to be used for performance measurement, and in ensuring that due account is taken of all relevant factors. This process is shown in Figure 15.6.

Some of the benefits realised through benchmarking include:

1. **The best practices from any industry may be creatively incorporated into a company's opera tions. Thus, benchmarking should not be aimed solely at direct competitors and, in fact, it would be mistake to do so.**
2. **Benchmarking is motivating. It provides targets that have been achieved by others.**
3. **Resistance to change may be lessened if ideas for improvement come from other industries.**
4. **Technical breakthroughs from other industries that may be useful can be identified early.**
5. **Benchmarking broadens people's experience base and increases knowledge.**

Figure 15.6 : THE BENCHMARKING PROCESS

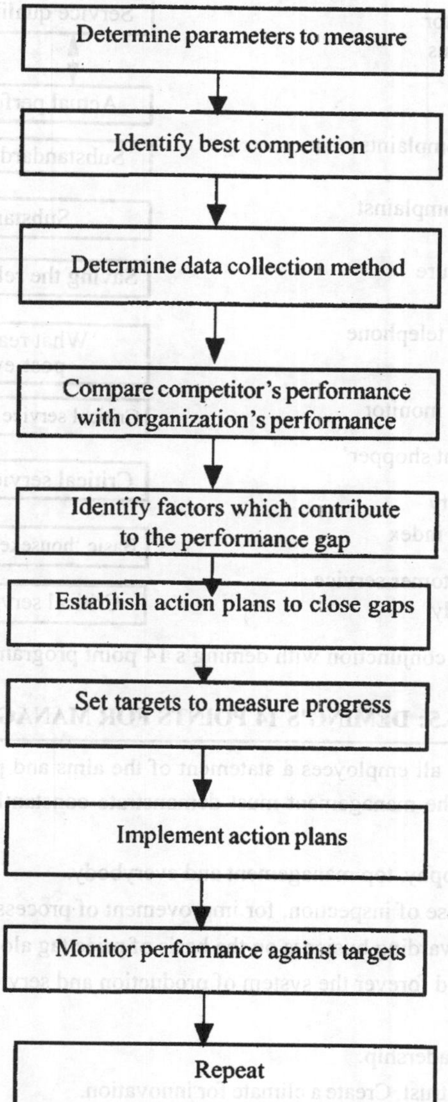

15.14 FEEDBACK AND MEASUREMENT SYSTEM

A model service quality feedback and measurement system is presented in Figure 15.7. The elements of the system include reward systems, service standards, analysis of complaints, interviews, surveys, monitoring, indices, research studies and risk analysis.

Figure 15.7 : SERVICE QUALITY MANAGEMENT FEEDBACK AND MEASUREMENT SYSTEM

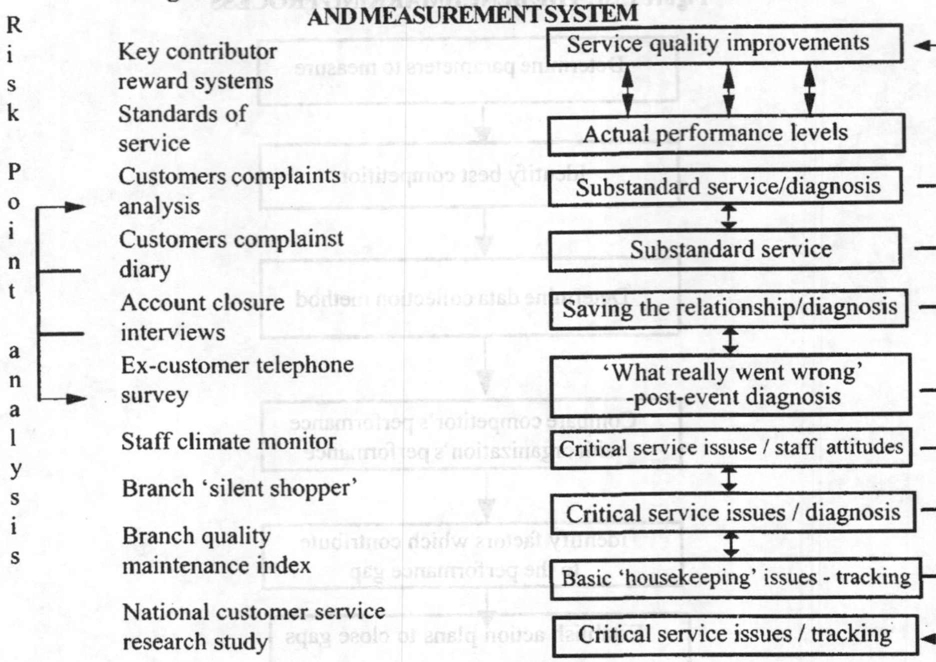

This model can be used in conjunction with deming's 14 point programme (Table 15.5) to manage service quality effectively.

Table 15.5 : DEMING'S 14 POINTS FOR MANAGEMENT

1. Create and publish to all employees a statement of the aims and purposes of the company or other organization. The management must demonstrate constantly their commitment to this statement.
2. Learn the new philosophy, top management and everybody.
3. Understand the purpose of inspection, for improvement of processes and reduction of cost.
4. End the practice of awarding business on the basis of price tag alone.
5. Improve constanly and forever the system of production and service.
6. Instiute training.
7. Teach and institute leadership.
8. Drive out fear. Create trust. Create a climate for innovation.
9. Optimize toward the aims and purposes of the company the efforts of teams, groups, staff areas.
10. Eliminate exhortations for the workforce.
11. (a) Eliminate numerical quotas for production. Instead, learn and institute methods for improvement. (b) Eliminate MBO (management by objective). Instead, learn the capabilities of processes and how to improve them.
12. Remove barriers that rob people of pride of workmanship.
13. Encourage education and self-improvement for everyone
14. Take action to accomplish the transforemation

15.15 THE COSTS OF QUALITY

The traditional view encompassed categories like rework, warranties and system auditing (Figure 15.8). The breakthrough manager's view now considers categories like internal costs, external costs, quality maintenance costs, prevention costs and costs of recovery. The internal costs refer to rework costs , facility downtime, loss of morale, higher employee turnover, loss of employee productivity and incremental marketing, while external costs comprise verifiable and non-verifiable costs. Verifiable costs, inturn, comprise warranties and guarantees, future profit stream from lost customers. Non-verifiable costs include customer out-of-pocket expenses, customer time and customer emotional costs. Appraisal, inspection, testing and system auditing costs fall under quality maintenance costs. The prevention costs comprise recruiting, selection, training, vendor selection, development of new technology, policies and procedures and facility design. The other costs comprise costs due to service recovery.

Figure 15.8 : TWO VIEWS OF COST OF QUALITY

The traditional View

Rework (back office)

Warranties

System auditing

The breakthrough Manager's View

Internal Costs
- Rework (back office)
- Facility downtime
- Loss of morale
- Higher employee turnover
- Loss of employee productivity
- Incremental marketing (lost vs. new customers)

External Costs

Verifiable
- Warranties and guarantees
- Future profit stream from lost customers

Nonverifiable
- Customer out-of-pocket expenses
- Customer time
- Customer emotional costs

Quality Maintenance Costs

Appraisal
- Inspection
- Testing
- System auditing

Prevention
- Recruiting
- Selection
- Training
- Vendor selection
- Development of new technology
- Policies and procedures
- Facility design

Recovery

15.16 QUALITY DELIVERY PROCESS

There are ten steps in the quality delivery process, as follows:

1. Create mission statement - a mission statement is a sentence that defines the work group's activities. It is focussed on the end objective rather than the means of achieving it.
2. Determine the outputs of the work group and check that they fulfil the mission.
3. Identify the customer(s), both internal and external, who receive the outputs.
4. For each output, define agreed customer requirements which must be met in order to achieve customer satisfaction.
5. Develop the work group's output specification fro each output.
6. Determine the group's work processes, including the identification of inputs, which will; deliver the outputs to the customer(s) at the lowest internal cost.
7. Identify the measurements of each output which will compare the 'actual' quality level delivered with the output specification.
8. Identify any problem caused by a measured 'shortfall' to target (or identify an 'opportunity' to exceed target at no additional cost; or an 'opportunity' to meet customer requirements at a lower internal cost).
9. Establish a project team to solve the identified problem which will improve the 'actual' quality level delivered to the customer (or capture the 'opportunity' in step 7).
10. Measure customer satisfaction against the agreed customer requirements.

15.17 TEN REASONS TO BELIEVE IN QUALITY

1. Would you like to improve your long-term profitability?
2. Would you like to eliminate those nasty incidents which cause the customer not to come back but tell his friends (other customers) what happened instead?
3. Would you like your service to stand out from the rest?
4. Your customers want it; your competitors may already be doing it...wouldn't you be better being ahead of the game?
5. Would you like a sharper, leaner, more flexible organisation?
6. When you have set a clear business strategy, would you like the organisation to follow it, quickly and decisively?
7. Would you like a better return from your projects and restructuring endeavours?
8. Would you like your organisation to be one which everyone is proud to work for?
9. Would you like to better yourself...be a better manager, achieve more, have greater prospects?
10. Would you like to create a better way of doing business, to adapt, to innovate, to improve continuously...and do it faster than others?

THEN DO BELIEVE IN QUALITY !

SHORT ANSWER QUESTIONS

1. Discuss the reasons why quality has become an increasingly important issue in services marketing.
2. Giving examples, distinguish between the concepts of 'functional' and 'technical' quality.
3. Define quality? Can it be measured quantitatively?
4. What are the various costs associated with quality?
5. What are the determinants of quality?
6. In what way can the personnel input to services be managed in order to achieve more consistent quality standards?
7. List the causes of poor service quality.
8. List the benefits of a service quality information system.
9. What do you understand by Benchmarking?

10. What were the prescriptions of Deming apropos quality?
11. What are the benefits associated with quality?
12. What are the main ingredients of a quality system?
13. Is quality always quantifiable? Justify your answer.
14. What role do service encounters play in service quality?
15. "Service quality depends to a large extent on people". Comment.
16. What is a quality leadership curve? What does it espouse?
17. How would you develop a quality culture?
18. Illustrate the model of service quality.
19. What factors would impact the quality of service offered to students.
20. What are the applications of benchmarking?

ESSAY QUESTIONS

1. In what ways can an airline attempt to measure the quality of its services?
2. What are the various approaches to service quality? Give examples.
3. Explain the process of Benchmarking.
4. Explain the model of service quality? What are the gaps?
5. How can the various gaps of service quality be closed?
6. How are feedback and measurement systems designed?
7. Enumerate the various "service traps"? How can these traps be avoided?
8. How can service quality be improved? Elucidate.
9. What is a service quality information system? What are its components and determinants?
10. What is SERVQUAL? What is its application?
11. List out the information required to maintain an information system for providing quality services in the following:

    (a) Hospitals (b) Banks (c) Hotels (d) Financial (e) Educational.

EXERCISE / ASSIGNMENT

1. Using a public sector organization of your choice, give examples of the methods by which the organization can seek to manage service quality.
2. Critically assess the usefulness of the SERVQUAL technique for measuring quality in an industry of your choice.
3. Enumerate the dimensions used by customers of the following services to evaluate quality:

    (a) Health care (b) Counselling (c) Telecommunications (d) Education (e) Banking.
4. Develop a SERVQUAL for any three services of your choice. Test the same and make modifications based on recommendations.

●●●

16

Service Performance and Measurement

16.1 MEASURES FOR SERVICE MONITORING AND IMPROVEMENT

To ensure that the right information is accurately collected and available when needed, the service management term's first priority should be to set up processes for regularly collecting quantitative measures of the performance of the service. Figure 16.1 shows the complete set of measures that are needed to monitor and manage the service and their relationships. The questions that the measures help to answer are also listed in the figure.

In Figure 16.1, service performance measures evaluate the current performance of the service and ensure that it is continuing to reliably meet the design specifications. Customer measures indicate the impact of service performance on the customers. Financial measures are indicators of the financial health of the organization.

Figure 16.1 : MEASURES FOR SERVICE MONITORING AND IMPROVEMENT

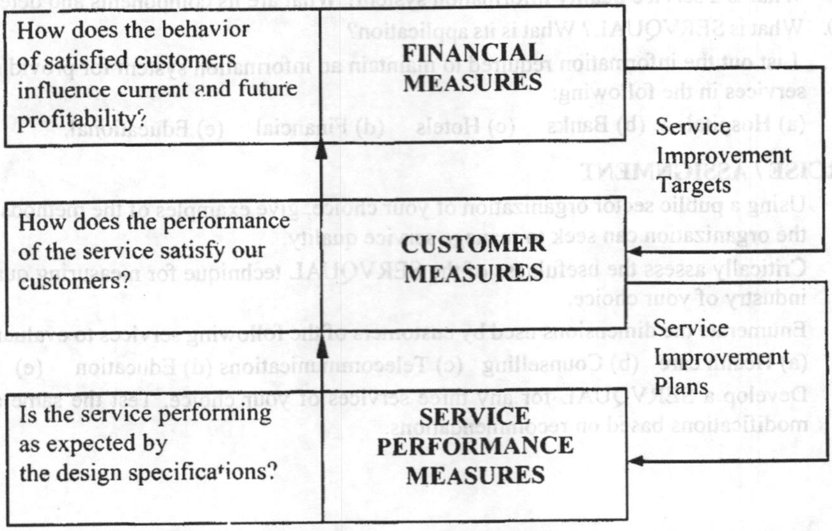

The correlation between the financial and customer measures determines the revenue generating potential of the service. This correlation can indicate the increase in customer satisfaction needed to achieve a specified market share gain or a strategic financial objective, which can then be used to set service improvement targets or new performance standards. The relationship between service performance measures and the customer measures determines the operational improvements that can achieve the required increase in customer satisfaction. This is used to make improvement plans that specify how the current design should be improved.

16.2 PERFORMANCE MONITORING AND STABILIZATION PROCEDURE

At regular intervals (weekly or monthly, and in some cases hourly or daily), the service management team should collect and analyze service performance data. This procedure should follow the steps listed below.

Step 1 : Select the design attributes to be analyzed

Step 2 : Measure the performance effectiveness of each selected attribute

Step 3 : Measure the capability of each selected attribute

Step 4 : Measure the efficiency of key processes

Step 5 : Identify attributes whose performance does not conform to standards or shows unusual change.

Step 6: Analyze the attributes identified in Step 5 in detail to determine the cause for poor performance or for unusual change in performance.

Step 7 : Decide whether any corrective action is necessary, and if so, what steps need to be taken.

Step 8 : Take the corrective action.

Before we move on, it is important to explain the term changes in performance. Many teams take this to automatically imply that only changes in a negative direction are worthy of further analysis. Improvement in performance is often treated as good news and ignored.

16.3 NEED FOR ACCURATE DATA

What is the key determinant of the service management team's ability to successfully execute the eight steps described above ? Note that three steps begin with words "measure" and one step contains the word "analysis". It is impossible to underestimate the importance of quantitative analysis using current and accurate data. This requires the following:

Metrics must be correctly defined to ensure that the *right information* is available.

Data collection procedures must be implemented and tested so that *accurate information* is available.

Aggregation, reporting, and distribution processes should be designed so that the information is available to the team in a *timely* manner.

Team members should be trained in *interpreting* analysis results, charts, and diagrams.

The data should be stored in a system that allows easy access to *historical performance information*.

Designing a system and / or a process to satisfy these requirements, called a *performance management system*, should be the first activity of the service management team. This activity should be begun while the service is being implemented so that the system is in place when the service goes into operation. In practice, however, many teams responsible for managing a newly designed service do not take the time to develop a complete and integrated performance management system. This is usually because the teams are assembled several months (or years) after the service is in operation, by which time it is difficult to replace the dozens of local reports and data collection techniques that are already in place. Many service management teams believe they base their decisions on quantitative data, but very often the metrics used are inaccurate or incomplete, and present an erroneous picture of the performance of the service. Incorrect data is sometimes more detrimental than no data at all, since misleading or even counter-intuitive results obtained may be unquestionably accepted just because they are presented as the output of quantitative analysis.

16.4 SERVICE PERFORMANCE METRICS

Recall from steps 2, 3 and 4 of the performance monitoring and stabilization procedure that effectiveness, capability and efficiency are the three characteristics of performance measured by the service management team. The metrics that are used to measure these characteristics are correspondingly called ***effectiveness** metrics, **capability** metrics, and **volume and efficiency** metrics.*

Effectiveness metrics

Consider the following metrics:

- Percent of orders delivered within 5 hours
- Number of bills produced with no errors
- Number of customers rating service provider "exceptionally reliable"

How are these three metrics similar? Each metric measures the performance of an attribute *relative to a target or a standard*. For the first metric, the target is 5 hours. For the second, the standard is zero errors. For the third, the standard is the "exceptionally reliable" rating. Each metric measures the extent to which the performance of the service meets its standard. These kinds of metrics therefore measure the effectiveness of the performance of the attribute.

Table 16.1 presents an example for a restaurant.

Table 16.1 : EFFECTIVENESS METRICS FOR A RESTAURANT

Service attribute	*Effectiveness metric*
Degree of friendliness of greeting	% of customers rating attribute "Exceptional"
Degree of friendliness of meal service	% of customers rating attribute "Exceptional"
Degree of responsiveness of meal service	% of customers rating attribute "Exceptional"
Degree of friendliness of leave-taking	% of customers rating attribute "Exceptional"
Time between seating and menu delivery	% of customers with menu delivery interval less than 5 minutes
Degree of knowledge about menu	% of customers rating attribute "Exceptional"
Degree of order-taking patience	% of customers rating attribute "Exceptional"
Time between ordering and meal delivery	% of customers served between 10 and 11.5 minutes
Percent of bills produced without error	% of bills produced without errors
Percent of bills settled without error	% of bills settled without errors
Degree of effectiveness in problem resolution	% of customers rating attribute "Excellent"

Capability metrics

How can we measure the capability of the attributes of a service? The capability of a process is its intrinsic ability to reliably meet the performance standards. The capability of a process is its intrinsic ability to reliably meet the performance standards. The capability therefore depends on the *shape* and *spread* of the performance distribution of he attribute. The average performance and the variability of performance (measured by the standard deviation) are two obvious metrics of these characteristics. In general, any descriptive statistic of the performance of a service attribute is a potential capability metric. Depending on the application, minimum values, maximum values, ranges, medians, quartiles, etc., can all be used to measure the extent of variability of performance.

Table 16.2 shows the capability metrics for the attributes of the restaurant.

Table 16.2 : CAPABILITY METRICS FOR A RESTAURANT

Service attribute	Capability metric
Degree of friendliness of greeting	Mean, standard deviation of performance rating
Degree of friendliness of meal service	Mean, standard deviation of performance rating
Degree of responsiveness of meal service	Mean, standard deviation of performance rating
Degree of friendliness of leave-taking	Mean, standard deviation of performance rating
Time between seating and menu delivery	Mean, standard deviation of menu delivery interval
Time between menu delivery and ordering	Mean, standard deviation of ordering interval
Degree of knowledge about menu	Mean, standard deviation of performance rating
Degree of order-taking patience	Mean, standard deviation of performance testing
Time between ordering and meal delivery	Mean, standard deviation of meal delivery interval
Percent of bills produced without error	Mean, standard deviation of production error rate
Percent of bills settled without error ment	Mean, standard deviation of settle-error rate
Degree of effectiveness in problem resolution	Mean, standard deviation of performance rating

Efficiency metrics

The cost of delivering the service and the resources utilized in delivery are measured by the *efficiency metrics*. The amount of resources needed to deliver the required level of service through the operating range should be specified by the design. If the service operations are stable, we should expect that the utilization of resources and the costs of delivering the service are consistent with the levels predicted during the evaluation of the design. On the other hand, if the actual volume of units processed is larger than the design operating range, or there is a greater amount of rework than expected, then the costs of delivering service will be greater.

The following are some common examples of *efficiency metrics* :

Average utilization level of human or machine resources
Average percentage or reworked items (as a percentage of the total number of items)
Average time spent in rework for each process (as a percentage of total cycle time)
Average amount of material wasted
Average number of overtime hours (by process)
Average ratio of overhead time to productive time (by process)
Average absentee rate
Average system availability rate

When used in conjunction with the effectiveness and capability metrics, the efficiency metrics identify areas where the service might be improved to provide the required performance level at a lower cost, or indicate where additional resources are needed to sustain current levels of performance

16.5 DESIGN AND COLLECTION OF THE RIGHT DATA

Factors affecting the collection of accurate data

The regular availability of accurate data is the single most critical determinant of the team's ability to effectively manage and improve the service. All too often, however, teams have to deal with insufficient or incorrect information, and in many cases, with no information at all. Some of the factors that impede the collection of accurate data are these:

1. No well-defined process for data collection.
2. Manual data collection procedures.
3. Inadequate training.
4. Data collection not integrated with work activities.
5. Measurements drive the wrong behavior.

Designing effective data collection procedures

The following are guidelines for designing effective data collection procedures:

1. Select a few, critical items for measurement.
2. Sample, if necessary.
3. Automate, if possible.
4. Avoid paper forms for data collection.
5. Develop easy data access and reporting capabilities.
6. Decentralize data analysis.
7. Make data collection part of job function.
8. Openly communicate the objective of data collection.

16.6 ROUTINE AND AD HOC ANALYSIS

Two kinds of analyses are typically needed to gain insights into service performance data. They are *routine analysis* and *ad hoc analysis*. Routine analysis, as its name suggests, refers to the regular, systematic analysis that is performed in every reporting period to evaluate the performance of the service on the effectiveness, capability, and efficiency metrics. Ad hoc analysis is the detailed diagnostic testing that is needed to investigate the reasons for unexpected performance changes. The nature and complexity of ad hoc analysis will differ from situation to situation.

Routine analysis activities should be planned so that they can be performed with the least amount of effort. Many teams are so consumed by the effort needed to produce results every month that little time is left over for interpretation or ad hoc analysis. Yet ad hoc analysis should be the primary focus of the service management team, because it is through the details of this analysis that the most important insights about service performance can be obtained. On the other hand, routine analysis procedures should be repeatable, documented, and decentralized.

Repeatable means that it should be possible to follow the same analysis steps in every time period. Some teams change their metrics every few months, making it very difficult to obtain a comprehensive picture of the performance of the service over time. As far as possible, analysis procedures must be left unchanged for at least twelve months so that trends can be studied. The procedures for routine analysis should be *documented* so that all individuals performing the analysis will follows the same steps in the same sequence. Proper documentation also assists in the training of new personnel. To the extent possible, the most repetitive tasks of routine analysis should be automated so that they can be regularly reproduced with little intervention. *Decentralization* means that almost all the routine analysis (and as much of the ad hoc analysis as appropriate) should be performed close to where the work is done.

Procedures for sharing analysis results

If the service delivery is distributed across several geographic areas, or if different subprocesses are managed by different organizations, then agreements must be developed that detail how the analysis results will be sent to the service management team, and in what format. Typically, results from the various organizations should be consolidated and aggregated by the service management team. Any ad hoc analysis that is necessary may either be performed by the team, or by the appropriate responsible organisation. The service management team may also perform spot checks or audits of the departmental and regional results from time to time.

When all ad hoc analyses are complete, the team should develop a list of interventions that may be required to stabilize the performance of one or more processes, and should then pass these back to the appropriate organizations for implementation. In general, the analysis procedures must be designed to provide the service management team access to all the information that it needs without requiring it to perform large amounts of data analysis on its own. The procedures must also ensure that all regions and departments for managing various service components are equally involved in providing inputs and recommendations to the service management team.

Analysis tools

Results can be displayed either as number in tables or in graphical form. With the large number of graphical tools now available for desktop computers, it is easy to produce results in the form of charts of graphs. The advantage of graphical or visual displays is that large amounts of information can be conveniently presented in a manner that can be readily assimilated. The disadvantage of these displays is that they can be manipulated to give the viewer a biased or erroneous first impression of the data. For example, the scale of a graph can be adjusted so that small differences between data points are magnified, leading a viewer to believe that large differences are being presented. Even if the data are not manipulated on purpose, careless or incompetent presentation can result in viewers reaching undesired conclusions. The presenters of graphical data must therefore take care to make sure that the display method chosen is the most appropriate for representing the information, and that visual biases are minimized.

We now briefly describe four versatile methods of graphically displaying data that can be used in a wide variety of applications: **histograms, run charts, scatter plots, and control charts**. These methods allow us to visually answer the following common questions asked during any data analysis:

How are the data distributed?

How variable is the performance?

How have the results changed over time?

What factors affect the observed results?

How stable is the performance around the standards?

How close is the performance to the standards?

Histograms

A histogram is a bar chart that shows the number of times each value of a variable occurs in a sample of observations. The tabulation of the number of occurrences of each value is called a frequency distribution, and a histogram is a graphical representation of this distribution. The variables can either be discrete (i.e., taking ordinal values such as 1,2, 3) or continuous. Histograms of discrete variables are also referred to as a bar chart. Continuous variables such as cycle time are segmented into groups, and the number of observations in each group is charted. The midpoint of each group is usually used as representative value for the group, though any other value may be used as well. The histogram is a visual picture of the shape of the distribution of the data. Some questions that can be answered from a histogram include the following:

Is the distribution symmetrical?

Are there long tails (i.e., large numbers of values at either end of the scale?)

Are there multiple peaks?

How wide is the spread in the data (i.e., does the variable take on many values or a few?)

Special versions of histograms are useful for specific applications. A **Pareto chart** is a histogram where the bars are ordered from the largest frequency to the smallest. This chart can be used to identify the critical few factors that contribute the most to the variability in the data. Pareto charts are useful in analyzing the major causes for defects, in identifying the activities contributing to the greatest costs, or in determining the factors that have the largest impact on consumer satisfaction. A special case of a bar chart is a **clustered or stacked bar** chart that can be used to compare a variable across multiple discrete dimensions.

Run Chart

A run chart is a graph that shows the performance of a variable over time. These plots serve the following purposes:

To identify cyclic performance patterns or seasonal variations.

To determine historical trends in performance.

To evaluate the effect of service improvements on performance.

To identify the time lag between service improvements and changes in performance.

To determine wear or experience effects that cause performance to drift over time

To assess the gap between the desired and actual performance over time.

Scatter plot

A scatter plot shows the relationship between two variables such as defect rate and employee experience, or the time taken to complete a service transaction and customer satisfaction. The scatter plot shows the following:

Whether a relationship exists between two variables.

The shape of the relationship (i.e. linear, curved).

The amount of random variability in the relationship between two variables.

Whether this variability differs for different values of the two variables.

A scatter plot is a graph, with the values of the **dependent variable** (whose value is predicted) on the y-axis and those of the **predictor** or **independent variable** (which predicts the value of the dependent variable) on the x-axis. Each point on the graph represents a pair of values of the dependent and predictor variables.

The slope of a scatter plot shows the extent of the average relationship between two variables. If the slope is flat, no relationship exists. The amount of scatter in the plot (i.e., whether the y values are fairly close for each value of x, or whether they form a "cloud") shows the extent of random variability in the data, and is a measure of the strength of the relationship between the two variables. A scatter plot is often a useful first step before estimating a regression equation, because it gives an indication of the nature, strength, and shape of the relationship between two variables.

The scatter plot can also be used to validate assumptions made during the design of a service. Suppose a design team is trying to develop a performance function for a particular service attribute for which the exact functional form is unknown. Suppose the design team approximates the function using a mixture of experience and judgment. After the service is in operation, a scatter plot can be used to validate the assumed functional form. The service management team can collect data on the performance of the attributes at various levels of operating characteristics. The design may need to be modified if the actual performance function is significantly different from what was assumed.

Control chart

A control chart is a graphical tool which is part of a methodology known as "statistical process control (SPC)". This methodology is used to measure the variability of manufacturing and service processes with a view to determining whether this variability is attributable to systematic or random causes.

A control chart compares the performance of a continuous or discrete variable against statistically computed "control limits". The idea of control limits stems from the fact that the performance of any service attribute is inherently variable because of a variety of random causes that cannot be identified or controlled. This random variability should be the only source of variability in a service that has been designed to produce a stable average performance level that is robust to changes within a given operating range. Moreover, this variability should remain within limits specified by the design. A control chart tests the stability of performance throughout the operation of the service. If the performance is normally distributed, then from the properties of the normal distribution, we would also expect that 99.7% of the performance values will lie randomly within three standard deviations of the average value. If these expectations are met by the collected data, the service performance is said to be in control. The performance values represented by three standard deviations are referred to as the control limits.

The procedure for plotting a control chart consists of two steps: calibration and control. In the calibration step, the mean and variability of the data are calculated from historical process performance data and the control limits are determined. As mentioned above, the control limits are the performance values at three standard deviations on either side of the mean. Various methods exist for estimating the standard deviation of the data. A transformation of the range of the observations, which is the difference between the maximum and minimum value, is a commonly used estimate.

In the control step, current observations of process performance are regularly plotted on the calibrated control chart. If the process is under control, we would expect over 99% of the points on the chart to lie between the upper and lower control limits We would also expect the points to be randomly distributed, i.e., no unusual patterns should be seen in the data. Standard tests exist to check for unusual patterns through visual inspection.

Report distribution

After the data analysis is completed, the results and the suggested actions must be shared with those responsible for their implementation. The results may also be sent to senior management. The results need not be presented at the same level of detail for everyone in the organization. For senior management, it is enough to present a short and succinct summary that lists the current and past performance of key indicators, actions to be taken, and their predicted effect on future performance and details of their process should be provided (for example, effectiveness and capability by work location, region, order, or customer type). For managers of a work location, a summary of overall performance must be supplemented with details of their own work location. The idea should be to provide all the key stake holders with an overview of the performance of all components of the service, and to provide specific details to those in charge. The information needed at various levels of the organization is presented in Table 16.3

Table 16.3 : PERFORMANCE INFORMATION REQUIRED AT EACH ORGANIZATION LEVEL

Organisation level	*Information required*
Senior management	Financial measures summary. Customer satisfaction summary. Service effectiveness and efficiency summary. Performance and market predictions.
Service management team level	Financial measures summary. Customer satisfaction summary. Service performance (effectiveness, efficiency, and capability) summary.

	Root cause analysis of performance discrepancies. Service stabilization activities
Process / attribute level	Customer satisfaction summary. Service performance summary. Attribute specific performance details Subprocess / activity specific performance details. Investigation / analysis of performance discrepancies. Exception analysis.
Work location level	Customer satisfaction summary. Service performance summary. Work location specific customer satisfaction details. Work location specific service performance details. Resolution of customer complaints at work location. Benchmarks / comparisons of work location costs and performance. Other work location specific details.
Work group level	Customer satisfaction summary. Service performance summary. Work location specific customer satisfaction details. Work location specific service performance details. Resolution of customer complaints. List of defective orders and their resolution. List of employees absent, on disability, in training, etc.

16.7 MONITORING SERVICE PERFORMANCE-RESTAURANT EXAMPLE

Eight steps of the performance monitoring and stabilization procedure to measure and analyze the performance of the service are :

Step 1 : Select the design attributes to be analyzed

Step 2 : Measure the performance effectiveness of each selected attribute.

Step 3: Measure the capability of each selected attribute

Step 4: Measure the efficiency of key processes.

Step 5 : Identify attributes whose performance does not conform to standards or shows unusual change.

Step 6 : Analyze the attributes identified in Step 5 in detail to determine the cause for poor performance or for unusual change in performance

Step 7 : Decide whether any corrective action is necessary, and if so, what steps need to be taken.

Step 8 : Take the corrective action.

In this section, we can see how these eight steps can be used to analyze the performance of the order-taking process of a restaurant.

Step 1 : Select the design attributes to be measured

In order to reduce the amount of data needed and the analysis effort required, performance measurements should be restricted to a few key attributes for each process. These attributes should be selected based on their importance specified in the QFD matrix, or based on the slopes of their performance/ satisfaction functions. In our example, since only three attributes are defined for the order-taking process, we will select all three attributes (promptness, patience, and knowledge) for analysis.

Step 2 : Measure the performance effectiveness of each attribute

Please refer section 16.4 on effectiveness metrics and section 16.5 on data collection.

Step 3 : Measure the capability of each selected attribute

For the three attributes, the average performance and the variability of performance are chosen as measures of capability. For the promptness attributes, the variability is measured by the mean and standard deviation of the order-taking cycle time. The patience and knowledge attributes are measured on a discrete scale of 1 through 6, with 6 corresponding to exceptional performance. For variables measured on discrete scales, the maximum and minimum rating (or range) is a better indicator of variability than the standard deviation. Table 16.4 shows the capability metrics for the three attributes of the order-taking process.

Table 16.4 : CAPABILITY OF ORDER-TAKING PROCESS RESTAURANT

Metric	*Average*	*Variability*	*No. of observations*
Promptness (mins.)	4 minutes	Std.dev. = 0.65 min.	2110
Patience (rating)	5.9	Minimum rating = 5 Maximum rating =6	1876
Knowledge (rating)	5.99	Minimum rating =5 Maximum rating =6	1876

Step 4 : Measure the efficiency of key processes

Two measures of efficiency are used. The first is the average utilization of the waiters, which is a measure of resource productivity (and therefore of cost). The second is the percentage of customers who need to reorder items because their first choice was unavailable. This is a measure of rework and of the cost of quality of the process. We will see how each of these measures is calculated:

1. Average utilization

A sample of the data required for calculating this measure is shown in Table 16.5 for an average waiter station consisting of four tables. Depending on the evening, either four or five waiters work at the station.

The available minutes in Table 16.5 measure the capacity of the waiter station. Assuming a 5-hour (600-minute) dinner period, the total capacity is given by the number of waiters available for the evening multiplied by 300 minutes. The available minutes are 1200 when four waiters are assigned and 1500 when five waiters are assigned.

The active minutes measure the total time during the course of the evening that the waiters at the station are busy. It is assumed that a waiter is busy if a table is occupied. The active time is therefore calculated by tracking the number of minutes during the course of the evening when each table at the waiter station is occupied and adding up this time across the four tables. The utilization is given by the number of active minutes divided by the available minutes.

Table 16.5 : SAMPLE DATA FOR COLLECTING WAITER UTILIZATION

Date	*No. of waiters*	*Available minutes*	*Active minutes*	*Utilization*
April 1	4	1200	876	0.73
April 2	5	1500	1145	0.76
April 3	5	1500	1200	0.80
April 4	4	1200	864	0.72
April 5	4	1200	852	0.71
April 6	4	1200	756	0.63
April 7	4	1200	696	0.58

Table 16.6 : EFFICIENCY MEASURES FOR THE ORDER-TAKING SUBPROCESS

Metric	*Actual value*	*Design value*
Waiter utilization	0.70	0.75
% customers reordering	13%	15%

The service management team should collect a sample of data similar to Table 16.5 at various points during the month. It may not be necessary to track every waiter station every day; rather, tracking a few selected waiter stations several days a month (making sure that a least one data point is collected for every day of the week) and averaging these results should provide an adequate estimate of the average efficiency.

2. Percentage of customers reordering

This measure is specific to the order-taking process and is an indicator of the rework in the process. If the initial order is not available, the customer needs to place another order. This metric can be automatically measured by the ordering system, which tracks each instance when this takes place.

Table 16.6 shows these two efficiency measures.

Step 5: Identify attributes whose performance fails to conform to standards or shows unusual change

The analysis described in this step is conducted in three parts:

A. Effectiveness analysis

B. Capability analysis

C. Efficiency analysis

In effectiveness analysis, the effectiveness metrics are examined to identify attributes that do not meet the performance standards, or those that meet them marginally. For these attributes, we use the run chart of the effectiveness metrics to check whether the poor performance has been encountered in the past.

In capability analysis, capability metrics are examined, of selected attributes that may contribute to the poor performance of the attributes identified during the effectiveness analysis. Both current and historical measures are examined.

In efficiency analysis, the efficiency metrics are examined, of selected attributes that may contribute to the poor performance of the attributes identified during the effectiveness and capability analyses.

Step 6 : Analyze the attributes identified in Step 5 to determine the cause of poor performance or of unusual change in performance

In this step, we test the hypotheses posed in the previous step through more detailed analysis. Once again, the proposed analysis in this step is carried out in three parts:

A. Exception analysis
B. Subprocess analysis
C. Root cause analysis

In exception analysis, we check whether any unexpected performance changes in a given reporting period can be attributed to any unique, uncontrollable causes or special circumstances. This is usually done by examining exception reports that provide details about each service encounter that did not meet the performance standard. In some applications, these exception reports may be generated by sorting on special codes that may have to be entered into a tracking system if there was a problem with a service encounter. If exception reports are not available, the service management team may examine a sample of service encounters in detail (for example, by looking at records of each transaction) to determine whether any unique patterns can be discerned.

The objective of subprocess analysis is to isolate the source of a performance problem to a particular subprocess or function. This analysis replicates the process-level analysis at the subprocess level. For each process attribute whose performance needs to be examined, the process / subprocess matrix is used to identify the relevant subprocesses that affect the performance of that attribute. The effectiveness, capability, and efficiency of these subprocesses are analyzed to identify areas of poor performance. This analysis is repeated at the function level if necessary, until the source of the problem is clearly identified.

Finally, once the source of the problem is established and cannot be attributed to a special or unique circumstance, root cause analysis is performed to diagnose the reason for the problem. The objective of this analysis is not to settle on the first apparently obvious, superficial reason, but to follow the casual chain all the way until the primary, fundamental source of the problem has been determined. Attempting to solve the problem at this level is more likely to produce a long-term solution than a temporary "quick fix" that attacks only the symptoms.

16.8 DETERMINANTS

Figure 16.2 : FACTORS WHICH DETERMINE THE PERFORMANCE MEASUREMENT SYSTEM

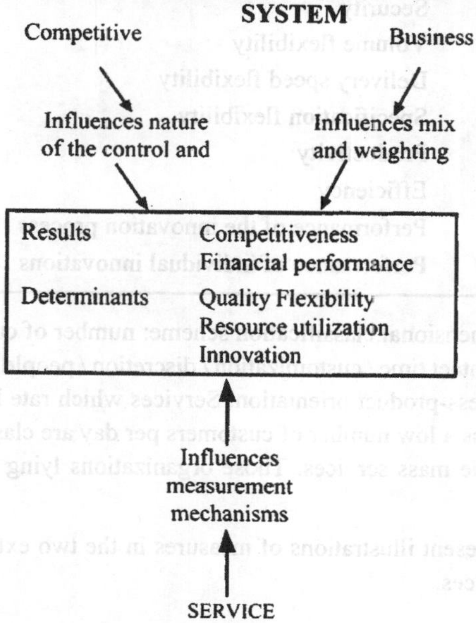

Fitzgerald suggests an approach which links types of measure, to dimensions of performance, to either results or determinants, which are linked in turn to the factors which determines the desired results and determinants. This is illustrated in Table 16.7 and Figure 16.2.

Table 16.7 : PERFORMANCE MEASUREMENT ACROSS SIX DIMENSIONS

Dimensions of Performance	*Type of measure*
Results	
Competitiveness	Relative market share and position Sales growth
	Measure of the customer base
Financial performance	Profitability
	Liquidity
	Capital structure
	Market ratios
Determinants	
Quality of service	Reliability
	Responsiveness
	Aesthetics/appearance
	Cleanliness / tidiness
	Comfort
	Friendliness
	Communication
	Courtesy
	Competence
	Access
	Availability
	Security
Flexibility	Volume flexibility
	Delivery speed flexibility
	Specification flexibility
Resource utilization	Productivity
	Efficiency
Innovation	Performance of the innovation process
	Performance of individual innovations

Fitzgerald uses a two-dimensional classification scheme: number of customers processed by a typical unit per day, versus contact time / customization / discretion / people equipment focus / front-back office orientation / process-product orientation. Services which rate highly on contact time / customization, etc. and process a low number of customers per day are classed as professional services. At the other extreme lie mass services. Those organizations lying in between the two are labelled service shops.

Tables 16.8 and 16.9 present illustrations of measures in the two extreme situations: professional services and mass services.

Table 16.8 : PERFORMANCE MEASUREMENT IN PROFESSIONAL SERVICES

Key issue	*Performance dimension*	*Examples of measures*
Ability to win new customers Customer loyalty.	Competitiveness	% success in tendering % repeat business Market share relative to key competitors
Control of staff costs Trading of labour hours to individual jobs to aid pricing decisions.	Financial performance	Staff costs Debtor and creditor days Value of work in progress Profit per service
Relationship building between customer and individual staff. Negotiation of project specification with customer. Measurement of customer satisfaction; Use of unstructured, informal methods.	Quality	Investment in training % non-chargeable: chargeable hours Adherence to project specification and delivery promise Customer satisfaction with various aspects of service
Management of short-term volume, specification and delivery speed flexibility. Provision of flexibility through job scheduling, multi-skilling, job rotation and staff discretion in dealing with customers.	Flexibility	% orders lost due to late delivery Staff skill mix % hours bought in from other offices Customer satisfaction with delivery speed
Control of front office staff time.	Resource utilization Ration of supervisors to staff	Ration of hours chargeable to client and non-chargeable hours
Measurement of the success of the innovation process and the innovation itself	Innovation	Number of new services New service introduction lead times % training spend invested in new services

Table 16.9 : PERFORMANCE MEASUREMENT IN MASS SERVICES

Key issues	*Performance dimension*	*Examples of measures*
Ability to win new customers Customer loyalty	Competitiveness	No. of customers Market share Comparison of competitor prices and product ranges
Asset Turnover Control of labour and capital costs Costs difficult to trace to services due to high degree of cost allocation Profit per service difficult to measure	Financial Performance	Return on net assets Working capital Profit per market segment
Relationship between customer and organisation Setting of clear customer expectations Measurement of customer satisfaction: use of formal, structured, sample-based methods	Quality	Equipment availability Product range Customer processing time Customer satisfaction with various aspects of service
Building volume, delivery speed and specification flexibility into the service design in the long term Use of level capacity starategies. Employment of part-time and floating staff. Use of price and promotion strategies to smooth demand.	Flexibility	Monitoring of queue length. No. of part time and floating staff. Customer satisfaction service availability
Utilisation of facilities, equipment and staff.	Resource utilisation	Costs per customer Revenue per customer Occupation ratios (e.g. % hotel rooms occupied)
Measurement of the success of the innovation process and the innovation itself.	Innovation	% new: existing products and services R & D costs

16.9 DEVELOPING AN OPTIMAL PROCESS IMPROVEMENT STRATEGY

The basic steps needed to implement any service improvement plan are:

Generation of improvement alternatives

Evaluation of alternatives

Selection of alternatives

Implementation of alternatives

For a well-designed service, the objective of strategic process improvements should not be to improve the process performance to meet some rigidly defined target, but instead should be to enhance the service level to the point where profitability is maximized. The process improvement targets are useful guidelines because they reflect the strategic growth objectives of the firm, but the benefits of achieving these targets should always be compared to the cost and effort required to achieve them. If the costs are too high, then the targets must be reduced to the level at which the greatest net benefit can be achieved. Increasing customer satisfaction through service improvements to enhance market share or revenue is a viable option only if the costs of these improvements are low enough to increase the firm's profitability. If the estimataed costs of meeting the improvements targets are higher than the projected revenue increase, then it may be more profitable to implement only part of the improvements, or to do nothing at all. A sensitivity analysis should be performed for each process to determine if "do nothing" or partial improvement is more effective than meeting the performance target. The improvement level that maximizes the returns should be selected.

This kind of sensitivity analysis is not appropriate when designing the service. This is because there is a base level of performance (specified by the design standards) that needs to be achieved in the design stage, and partial achievement of this level is not an acceptable option.

Sensitivity analysis of service improvement initiatives

How do we perform sensitivity analysis of service improvement initiatives? The foundation for such an analysis lies in the calculation of the costs and benefits of the improvement effort. The analysis itself is relatively simple if costs and benefits are calculated at a detailed functional level. All the activities that need to be performed for the processes to be improved should be listed in detail. These should include both the activities that will be carried out once (such as training or software development) and those that will be carried out regularly as a result of process changes. The evaluation of costs and benefits should then be done at the level of these activities.

Performing a sensitivity analysis involves the following activities:

1. Identify the benefits and costs of achieving the service improvement target (total improvement).
2. Determine the benefits of doing nothing.
3. Determine the benefits and costs of various partial improvements. This is relatively simple if the costs and benefits are defined at the activity level, since the partial improvements can then be defined as the partial completion of the activities.
4. Compute the net benefits (i.e. benefits - cost) value for each level of improvement.
5. Plot a net benefit curve for each level of improvement.
6. Selecte the improvement level with the highest net benefit for implementation.

Benefits arising from service improvements are typically realized from two sources:

Increase in satisfaction resulting from improvements in performance

Reduction in costs due to increases operating efficiency

These typical costs are associated with process improvements:

Costs of implementing the improvement effort.

Incremental operating costs due to the process improvements.

Sensitivity analysis - restaurant example:

(a) Process activities

(b) Process improvement targets

(c) Proposed process improvements

(d) Benefits of proposed improvements

(e) Costs of proposed improvements

(f) Sensitivity analysis

(a) **Process activities** : The first step is to list the activities of the greeting and seating process(performed by the host) :

1. Greeting the customer upon arrival
2. Escorting the customer to his or her table
3. Signalling the assigned waiter to explain the ordering system

(b) **Process improvment target** : The target is a 10% increase in the average friendliness rating as a result of the improvements.

(c) **Proposed process improvements** : In order to determine how best to improve the process, the restaurant can conduct a special survey of customers. Customers who participated in the survey may indicate that they are generally satisfied with the friendliness level, but that some additional improvements are needed to make the performance of the process exceed their expecctations. Based on the results of the survey, the following improvement options are proposed.

Option 1 : Ten hours of role -playing training for the hosts to teach poise, pace, and communication skills. The objectives of this training are the following :

Increased eye contact between the host and the customer

Better-quality interaction ("improved conversation skills")

Option 2: A change in the process that requires the host to explain the ordering system (instead of the waiter). The objective of this change is to encourage a more relaxed interction between the hosts and the guests, and to allows guests to get started with the ordering process before the waiter arrives.

(d) **Benefits of proposed improvements** : Three benefits are predicted as a result of the improvement. The first two result in increased satisfaction, and the third in increaased efficiency. The benefits are these :

1. Better-quality interaction as a result of the training
2. More time for relaxed interaction between the host and guests resulting from the process change
3. Increase in waiter capacity (since the host now peforms one of the tasks previously performed by a waiter).

These benefits are quantified using experience and judgment. For example, past experienced with the role-playing training have shown that 10-hour session produces the required 10% increase in the average performance ratings. The increase in watier capacity is calculated by computing the time normally taken by a waiter to explain the ordering system to a customer and multiplying this time by the number of customers in a month. This is the total amount of additional waiter time that is now available every month.

(e) **Costs of proposed improvements:** Three costs are predicted:

1. Training delivery costs (one time)
2. Cost of resources to plan and implement improvement (one time)
3. Cost of hiring additional hosts to make up for extra time spent with guests (ongoing)

The cost of hiring new hosts is calculated in the same way that the cost savings for the waiter were calculated above. The additional time spent by a host with each customer is multiplied by the number of customers in a month. The costs for various modules of the training package are obtained from the vendor. The cost of resources to plan and implement the improvement is calculated as a function of the time that is spent on this effort by various members of the organization who are involved in implementing this effort.

(f) **Sensitivity analysis** : A seperate sensitivity analysis should be performed for each proposed improvement option (i.e., training and process change). We will begin with option 2(process change that requires host to explain ordering system).

First consider the cost side for this option. The service management team discovers that the costs of hiring and training new hosts almost exactly balances the savings due to the additional waiter capacity that is generated by the process change. In fact, it seems feasible to retrain the surplus waiters as additional hosts, with minimal training costs and no additional hiring costs. Therefore, no additional costs will be incurred in implementing the process change.

On the benefit side, the process change provides the benefit of increased customer satisfaction resulting from the additional time spent by the host with the customer. Option 2 therefore results in a constant positive net benefit. Clearly, there can be no argument about implementing this change.

The sensitivity analysis is therefore only necessary for option 1 (special training for hosts). To perform the sensitivity analysis, we calculate the costs and benefits associated with various levels of partial training (i.e., less than 10 hours). This will reduce costs, but also benefits. If the cost or benefit function is nonlinear, then a partial solution may produce a higher net benefit than a total implementation. The costs and benefits of a 90% implementation (9-hour training), 80% implementation (8-hour training), and so on are calculated. Costs are computed at the rate of Rs. 10,000 per hour, and are assumed to decrease linearly up to Rs. 50,000, which is the base cost of the training program up to 5 hours. Benefits are quantified as the expected increase in average performance ratings as a result of the training. The models linking performance and financial measures are used to translate the expected service improvements into rupees of revenue.

The results of the sensitivity analysis are shown in Figure 16.3. The y-axis in Figure 16.3 shows both the net and the total benefits, expressed in units of thousands of rupees per month of additional revenue. The x-axis shows the number of hours of training provided. When no training is provided, the costs are zero, and so are the benefits. As more hours are spent on training, the benefits increase. However, since the minimum cost of training is at least Rs. 50,000, there is no reason to coniser training that is less than 5 hours in duration. As can be seen from Figure 16.3, 5 hours of training produces a slightly larger net benefit than the do-nothing operation. Increased expenditure in training beyond this amount produces increasing returns, but a dimishing rate, as is indicated by the flattening slope of the total benefits curve. This means an expenditure of Rs. 90,000 or Rs. 1,00,000 does not result in significantly greater satisfaction than a Rs. 60,000 to Rs. 70,000 expense. The optimal training expenditure is therefore somewhat more than Rs. 50,000, but somewhat less than Rs. 1,00,000. Figure 16.3 shows that maximum returns are obtained for an expenditure of Rs. 70,000, which translates into 7 hours of training.

In summary, the sensitivity analysis leads to the following optimal improvement recommendation for the greeting and seating process of the restaurant:

(a) Spend 8 hours in training waiters and hosts on advanced communication skills.

(b) Transfer the task of explaining the ordering system from the waiter to the host.

Figure 16.3 : SENSITIVITY ANALYSIS OF THE IMPACT OF TRAINING ON RESTAURANT REVENUE

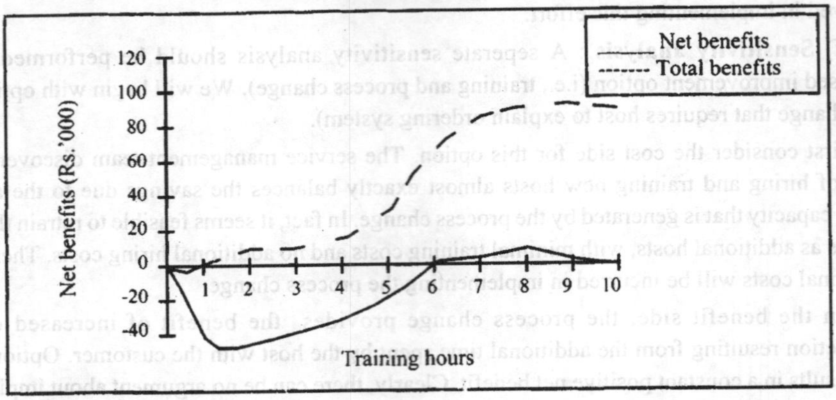

SHORT ANSWER QUESTIONS

1. What is sensitivity analysis?
2. What are the options for process improvements?
3. What is 'performance measurement'?
4. How does resource utilization differ from financial performance in terms of measurement?
5. Hoe does run chart differ from scatter plot?
6. Give examples of efficiency metrics.
7. What are histograms and control charts?
8. Differentiate between routine and ad hoc analysis.
9. How do effectiveness metrics differ from efficiency metrics?

ESSAY QUESTIONS

1. "The performance of service delivery systems is frequently judged in terms of efficiency and productivity". Discuss.
2. what are the measures for service monitoring and measurement?
3. What are 'capability metrics'? Give examples for (a) Airlines and (b) Financial services.
4. How does performance measurement for mass services differ from that of professional services?
5. Is data collection important for measurement? How is the right data collected?
6. What are the types of measures for quality of service?
7. How are processes measured for their efficiency?
8. What are the information required for measuring performance at different organizational levels?

EXERCISE / ASSIGNMENTS

1. Enumerate the effectiveness, efficiency and capability metrics for the following services: (a) Civil services (b) Professional services (c) Personal care.
2. How will you measure the efficiency of the following?
   (a) Enquiry service
   (b) Charities
   (c) Police
   (d) Education
   (e) Green services (environment care).

●●●

17

Service Mix Scenario (7 Ps)

17.1 ROLE OF SERVICE MIX

The role of the marketing mix for products and services is shown in Figures 22.1 and 22.2 respectively. As already discussed, the service industries have an extended marketing mix. This mix comprises price, place, promotion, product, people, process and physical evidence. Each service has its own characteristics and the mix therefore differs in many aspects. The seven Ps for the following services have been summarised : (1) Roadways (2) Railways (3) Postak and Courier (4) Fire Control (5) Civil Aviation (6) Electricity (7) Telecommunications (8) Health Care (9) Tourism (10) Hotel (11) Travel (12) Consultancy (13) Education (14) Insurance (15) Personal Care (16) Professional Institution (17) Advertising Agency (18) Banking (19) Entertainment (20) Web Marketing (21) Green Marketing. The list is not exhaustive and the reader can add on to the examples mentioned for each P.

17.2 SERVICE : ROADWAYS (PUBLIC UTILITY SERVICES)

a.	**Product**	:	Tar roads, Medians, Pavements
b.	**Place**	:	Cities, Towns, Villages, Forests, Toll gates
c.	**Price**	:	Materials, Wages, Salaries, Surveys
d.	**Promotion**	:	Publicity, Word-of-Mouth Promotion, Public Relations
e.	**Phy. Evid**	:	Signs, Milestones, Road roller, Tar, White and Yellow Lines, Zebra Crossing Lamp posts, Speed breakers,
f.	**People**	:	Committees, Govt. departments, Traffic, Police, Engineers, Labour
g.	**Process**	:	Digging, Laying, Repairs, Rolling, Purchasing, Planning, Contracting, Surveying.

17.3 SERVICE : RAILWAYS (PUBLIC UTILITY SERVICES)

a.	**Product**	:	Coaches, Locomotives, Tracks, Signals, Platforms, Bridges, Tickets
b.	**Place**	:	Stations
c.	**Price**	:	Travel class, Distance travelled, Luggage
d.	**Promotion**	:	Advertising, Publicity, Sales promotion, Word-of-Mouth Promotion, Public Relations, Broadcasting
e.	**Phy. Evid**	:	Tracks, Fish plates, Signals, Crossing, Stations, Stalls, Trains
f.	**People**	:	Drivers, Guards, Maintenance staff, Railway Police, Station Master, Ticket collectors
g.	**Process**	:	Routing, Ticketing, Repair, Track laying, Signalling, Coach manufacturing, Transporting

17.4 SERVICE : POSTAL AND COURIER (PUBLIC UTILITY SERVICES)

a.	**Product**	:	Letters, Cards, Stamps, Savings schemes, Post boxes, Mail bags
b.	**Place**	:	Post offices, Post Box, Collection centers, Door receipts
c.	**Price**	:	Distance, Weight, Nationality, Speed, Size
d.	**Promotion**	:	Advertising, Publicity, Sales promotion, Word-of-Mouth Promotion, Public Relations
e.	**Phy. Evid**	:	Letters, Packets, Parcels, Documents, Receipts, Proof of delivery (POD), Post box, Mail van, Stamps, Seals, Pincodes, Addresses, Consignment slips
f.	**People**	:	Government servants, Private operaters, Postmen, Delivery boys, Booking staff, Logistics staff
g.	**Process**	:	Enquiries, Booking, Transportation, Delivery, Documentation

17.5 SERVICE : FIRE CONTROL (PUBLIC UTILITY SERVICES)

a.	**Product**	:	Fire Engines, Clothing, Helmets
b.	**Place**	:	Wherever fires erupt eg. Houses, Offices, Forests, etc.
c.	**Price**	:	Free service for public which is indirectly collected through taxes
d.	**Promotion**	:	Advertising, Publicity, Word-of-Mouth Promotion, Public Relations
e.	**Phy. Evid**	:	Fire engines, First aid kits, Hoses, Water, Fire-proof clothing, Cranes, Fire stations
f.	**People**	:	Truma care personnel, Drivers, Fire - Fighters
g.	**Process**	:	Training, Fire fighting, Medical aid, Counselling, Safety education

17.6 SERVICE : CIVIL AVIATION (PUBLIC UTILITY SERVICES)

a.	**Product**	:	Aeroplanes, Tickets, Magazines, Skyshopping
b.	**Place**	:	Airports (Restricted areas)
c.	**Price**	:	Distance travelled, Travel class, Schemes
d.	**Promotion**	:	Advertising, Publicity, Sales promotion, Word-of-Mouth Promotion, Telemarketing, Public Relations, Broadcasting
e.	**Phy. Evid**	:	Aeroplanes, Airports, Tarmacs, Radars, Control Towers, Aerobridges, Terminals, Passengers, Cargo, Conveyors, Ladders
f.	**People**	:	Pilots, Cabin crew, Caterers, Administrative staff, Technicians, Engineers Security, Helpers, Customs personnel
g.	**Process**	:	Ticketing, Boarding, Transporting, Hospitality, Bookings, Announcements, Displaying information, Public Relations, Protocols, Communications, Legal procedures, Selling, Traffic control, Logistics Management

17.7 SERVICE : ELECTRICITY (PUBLIC UTILITY SERVICES)

a.	**Product**	:	Meters, Transformers, Switch boards, Distribution towers and lines, Energy, Fuses
b.	**Place**	:	Homes, Offices, Factories, Commerical Establishments, Manufacturing, Agriculture, Services, Medical centers
c.	**Price**	:	Industrial consumption, Domestic consumption, Subsidies
d.	**Promotion**	:	Advertising, Publicity, Word-of-Mouth Promotion, Public Relations
e.	**Phy. Evid**	:	Transmission towers, Grids, Transformers, Meters, Fuses, Lines, Generating stations, Meter reading cards, Bills

f.	**People**	:	Electricity boards, Technicians, Administrative staff
g.	**Process**	:	Resource assimilation, Generation, Supply, Metering, Billing, Collections, Vigilance, Repairs Emergency calls, Installations

17.8 SERVICE : TELECOMMUNICATIONS (PUBLIC UTILITY SERVICES)

a.	**Product**	:	Telephone, Telegraph, Fax, Internet, Intranet, Telex
b.	**Place**	:	Telecom Centres, Home, Workplace, Private operators
c.	**Price**	:	Distance, Time of the day, Duration, Service charge
d.	**Promotion**	:	Advertising, Publicity, Sales promotion, Word-of-Mouth Promotion, Personal selling, Telemarketing, Public Relations, Broadcasting
e.	**Phy. Evid**	:	Directories, Telecom equipments, Bills, Yellow colour display boards, Electronic meter display, Tone, Modem
f.	**People**	:	Operators, Service personnel
g.	**Process**	:	Machine operation, Billing, Collections

17.9 SERVICE : HEALTH CARE

a.	**Product**	:	Diagnostic equipments, Surgical equipments, First-aid kits, Medicines
b.	**Place**	:	Clinic, Hospital, Camps
c.	**Price**	:	Length of stay, Level of illness, Frequency of visits, Use of equipments, Tests required, Type of room, Specialists
d.	**Promotion**	:	Advertising, Publicity, Word-of-Mouth Promotion, Public Relations
e.	**Phy. Evid**	:	Hospitals, Intensive Care, Wards, Medical Shops, Diagnostic and Surgical equipments, Clinics, Ambulance, Mortuary, Out-patient wards, Emergency wards
f.	**People**	:	Doctors, Nurses, Lab Technicians, Support staff, Paramedics, Pharmacists, Security, Dieticiants, Specialists
g.	**Process**	:	Physical examinations, Testing, Medicines, Immunisation, Surgery, First-Aid, Recording, Catering, Laundry

17.10 SERVICE : TOURISM (HOSPITALITY SERVICES)

a.	**Product**	:	Accommodation - Five star, Four star, Three star, Two-star, One-star; Cottages, Pubs, Restaurants, Shops, Attractions
b.	**Place**	:	Heritage sites, Monuments, Parks, Lakes, Hill stations, Beaches, Resorts, Theme parks, Palaces, Places of worship, Buildings, Scenic spots
c.	**Price**	:	Distance travelled, Entry fee, Accommodation, Food, Drinks, Guides
d.	**Promotion**	:	Advertising, Publicity, Sales promotion, Word-of-Mouth Promotion, Personal selling, Telemarketing, Public Relations, Broadcasting
e.	**Phy. Evid**	:	Mouments, Historic Placces, Leisure centres, Healing locations
f.	**People**	:	Tour operators, Government, Travel agents, Tourists, Guides, Hawkers
g.	**Process**	:	Training, Guiding, Explaining, Preserving, Documenting

17.11 SERVICE : HOTEL (HOSPITALITY SERVICES)

a.	**Product**	:	Reception, Area, Rooms, Entertainment, Shopping, Personal care, Communication and transport, Medical, Restaurants, Bars, Lounges, Swimming Pools, Parks
b.	**Place**	:	Near Airports, Bus stands, Stations, Ports, Tourist spots, Shopping areas, Places of worship

c.	**Price**	:	Occupancy period, Star category, Room capacity, Air-conditioning, Location, Room service, Taxes
d.	**Promotion**	:	Advertising, Publicity, Sales promotion, Word-of-Mouth Promotion, Telemarketing, Public Relations, Broadcasting
e.	**Phy. Evid**	:	Tariff cards, Menu cards, Interior decoration, Furnishing, House keeping, Display boards, Lighting, Valets, Banquet halls, Swimming pools, Gardens, Halls
f.	**People**	:	Receiption staff, House keeping staff, Banquet staff, Bell boys, Waiters, Chefs, Maintenance staff, Administrative staff
g.	**Process**	:	House keeping, Food preparation, Check-in, Check-out, Foreign exchnange, Room service, Secretarial services, Meeting arrangements, Functions, Maintenance, Landscaping

17.12 SERVICE : TRAVEL (HOSPITALITY SERVICES)

a.	**Product**	:	Luxury, Express, Point to point, Ordinary service, Light & Heavy vehicles
b.	**Place**	:	Tourist places, Business, Establishments, Personal visits, Airports, Stations, Meeting venues
c.	**Price**	:	Kilometres travelled, Hours travelled, Flat rates, Driver tips, Fuel consumed, Interior facilities provided, Seating capacity, Luggage
d.	**Promotion**	:	Advertising, Publicity, Sales promotion, Word-of-Mouth Promotion, Personal selling, Telemarketing, Public Relations, Mobile displays
e.	**Phy. Evid**	:	Vehicles, Booking offices, Tariffs, Brochures, Mobile Displays
f.	**People**	:	Drivers, Maintenance staff, Booking staff, P.R.Os, Liaison officers
g.	**Process**	:	Bookings, Vehicle purchase, Maintenance, Marketing, Billing, Collections, Public relations, Documentation

17.13 SERVICE : CONSULTANCY (PROFESSIONAL SERVICES)

a.	**Product**	:	Legal, Technical, Financial, Medical, Managerial, Organisational
b.	**Place**	:	Branch offices, Site offices, Through media, Through representative
c.	**Price**	:	Degree of problem, Research involved, Time period, No. of staff
d.	**Promotion**	:	Advertising, Publicity, Sales promotion, Word-of-Mouth Promotion, Personal selling, Telemarketing, Public Relations, Broadcasting
e.	**Phy. Evid**	:	Offices, Brochures, Tapes, Logo
f.	**People**	:	Experts, Administrative staff, Data entry operators, Researchers, Counsellors, Trainers
g.	**Process**	:	Training, Counseling, Visiting, Information processing, Analysis, Report preparations, Auditing

17.14 SERVICE : EDUCATION

a.	**Product**	:	Kinder garden or elementar y education, Primary education, Secondary education, Higher education, Distance education, Adult education, Special education, Vocational education, Research
b.	**Place**	:	Schools, Colleges, Universities, Coaching centers, Home (Distance education), Laboratories, Libraries
c.	**Price**	:	Facilities, Stationery, Publishing, Faculty, Administration, Buildings and equipments

d.	**Promotion**	:	Advertisements, Word-of-mouth, Social service, Community welfare, innovations, Ranks and awards
e.	**Phy. Evid**	:	Classrooms, Playgrounds, Books, Geometrical tools, Labs, Uniforms, Identity Cards, Certificates, Computers, Calculators, Drawing equipments, Audio-visul aids, Buses
f.	**People**	:	Faculty, Non-teaching staff, Lab technicians, Administrative staff
g.	**Process**	:	Applications, Admissions, Teaching, Examinations, Evaluations, Counselling, Training, Development

17.15 SERVICE : INSURANCE (FINANCIAL SERVICES)

a.	**Product**	:	Policies- Whole life, Ordinary, Limited Payment, Convertible, Anticipated, Endowment, Term, Diminishing, Marriage, Education, Renewable, Marine, Fire, Cargo, Building, Vehicle, Theft, Medicare, Mortgage, Redemption, Salary saving, Annuities, Underwriting, Debentures, Shares, Bonds, Group insurance, Consultancy, Engineering, Export Risk, Accident
b.	**Place**	:	Branches, Office, Home
c.	**Price**	:	Premium, Rate of death, Rate of interest, Expenses incurred
d.	**Promotion**	:	Advertising, Publicity, Sales promotion, Word-of-Mouth Promotion, Personal selling, Telemarketing, Public Relations, Broadcasting
e.	**Phy. Evid**	:	Brochures, Leaflets, Environment, People, Currency, Client, Interior Decoration
f.	**People**	:	Brokers, Agents, Company staff
g.	**Process**	:	Applications, Verification, Sanction, Receipts

17.16 SERVICE : PERSONAL CARE

a.	**Product**	:	Beauty parlours, Garment making, Shoemaking, Hair Dressing, Physical Fitness, Dental care, Nutrition and hygiene, Yoga
b.	**Place**	:	City, Street, Hospital, Health Centers
c.	**Price**	:	Local Currency, Based on services rendered
d.	**Promotion**	:	Advertising, Discount offered, Self satisfaction, Quick service, 24 Hours facility, Proper Care
e.	**Phy. Evid**	:	License, Registration, Cleanliness, Surroundings and Good Atmosphere
f.	**People**	:	Hair Cutter, Sweeper, Doctors
g.	**Process**	:	Good service environment, People, Service at the time of need

17.17 SERVICE : PROFESSIONAL INSTITUTION (PROFESSIONAL SERVICES)

a.	**Product**	:	Specialised services, Printed materials
b.	**Place**	:	Offices, Home, Via telecom media, At desired spot in emergency situations
c.	**Price**	:	Hourly rates, Fixed fee, Tenders
d.	**Promotion**	:	Advertising, Publicity, Sales promotion, Word-of-Mouth Promotion, Personal selling, Public Relations, Broadcasting
e.	**Phy. Evid**	:	Uniforms, Logo, Code of conduct, Branch offices, Brochures, Videos, Signage
f.	**People**	:	Experts in different areas, Administrative staff, Liaison officers, Consultants
g.	**Process**	:	Client development, Updating information, Staff development, Staff training, Enquiries handling, Counselling, Reviewing, Analysis, Planning, Control

17.18 SERVICE : ADVERTISING AGENCY (PROFESSIONAL SERVICES)

a.	**Product**	:	Media compaigns, Layouts, Accounts, Videos, Audio tapes
b.	**Place**	:	Agency office, Client's office, Other meeting venues
c.	**Price**	:	Media involved, Target audience, Time, No of persons, Physical work, Compensation method adopted, Budgets
d.	**Promotion**	:	Advertising, Publicity, Sales promotion, Word-of-Mouth Promotion, Personal selling, Telemarketing, Public Relations, Broadcasting
e.	**Phy. Evid**	:	Photographs, Brochures, Printouts, Printed or published Material, Logo, Trademarks, Brand Names
f.	**People**	:	Editors, Copywriters, Creative thinkers, Artists, Technicians, Marketers, Administrative staff, Psychologists, Consultants, Media personnel
g.	**Process**	:	Account handling, Copywriting, Layouts, Typography, Photosetting, Drawing, Media planning, Shooting, Recording, Distributing, Researching, Producing, Marketing, Budgeting

17.19 SERVICE : BANKING (FINANCIAL SERVICES)

a.	**Product**	:	Deposits, Letters of credit, Foreign Currency, Consultancy, Merchant Banking, Project and investment counselling, Advances, Loans, Bill Discounting, Guarantees, Credit Cards, Remittances, Collections, Trusteeship, Standing Instructions
b.	**Place**	:	Branches, Branch and off - site ATMs, Online Banking
c.	**Price**	:	Interest, Commission, Dividends, Shares, Bonds, Non-Performing Assets (NPA)
d.	**Promotion**	:	Advertising, Publicity, Sales promotion, Word-of-mouth promotion, Personal selling, Telemarketing, Public relations
e.	**Phy. Evid**	:	Staff, Cheque books, Currency, Receipts, Application Forms, Counters, ATMs, Credit Cards, Record Books
f.	**People**	:	Staff, Agents, Auditors, Board of Directors, Banking service recruitment board (BSRB), Reserve bank of India (RBI), Trade unions
g.	**Process**	:	Convassing, Applications, Verifications, Sanctioning, Delivering, Inspection, Documenting

17.20 SERVICE : ENTERTAINMENT (FILM MARKEING)

a.	**Product**	:	Cameras, Filters, Lights, Reflectors, Light meter, Clap board, Film, Console, Cables, Liquids, Make-up kits, Animators, Tapes
b.	**Place**	:	Studios, Movie theatres, Dubbing theatres, Recording theatres, Film Cities, Public places, Labs
c.	**Price**	:	Salary, Wages, Signing amount, Location, Shooting period, Equipments, Rentals, Costumes, Special effects, Avertising
d.	**Promotion**	:	Advertising, Publicity, Sales promotion, Word-of-Mouth Promotion, Personal selling, Telemarketing, Public Relations, Broadcasting
e.	**Phy. Evid**	:	Vans, Generators, Lights, Studios, Theatres, Film Cities, Reels, Equipments, Tickets, Hoardings, Crowds, Copyrights
f.	**People**	:	Art director, Artists, Audiographers, Designers, Choreographers, Suppliers, Technicians, Directors, Distributors, Editors, Financiers,

			Assistants, Mediators, Musicians, P.R.Os, Singers, Photographers, Producers, Engineers, Fans, Stuntment, Lyricists, Writers
g.	**Process**	:	Editing, Directing, Choreography, Stunts, Music, Production, Financing, Scripting, Processing, Printing, Developing, Recording, Dubbing, Exhibiting, Distributing, Acting, Mixing, Animating, Casting, Screenplays

17.21 SERVICE: WEB MARKETING

a.	**Product**	:	Communications medium (intagible), website
b.	**Place**	:	Service provider's centre, Home PC, Office PC
c.	**Price**	:	No. of hours, No. of days, Schemes, Design involved, Promotion
d.	**Promotion**	:	Internet, Posters, Pamphlets, Print Media
e.	**Phy. Evid**	:	E-mail, Pop-up windows, Banners, Spam (Junk e-mail), Monitors or other visual display units
f.	**People**	:	Suppliers, Shareholders, Employees, Government, Intermediaries, Professionals, Community, Media
g.	**Process**	:	Create content, Design the look and feel, Programme, Choose a host, Buy or License content, Update context, E-commerce system, Website, Promotion, Maximise traffic, Receive feedback, Research

17.22 SERVICE: GREEN MARKETING

a.	**Product**	:	Healthcare, Pollution abatement equipment, Bucket of earthworms to improve soil quality of garden
b.	**Place**	:	Natural environments
c.	**Price**	:	Enviornment friendly raw materials, Cleaner process and technology, Complying with new green law, Preparing for ecological disasters or clean-ups, Insurance premium, Green taxation,
d.	**Promotion**	:	Advertising, Publicity, Word-of-Mouth Promotion, Public Relations, Broadcasting
e.	**Phy. Evid**	:	Raw materials, Energy efficiency, Waste, Pollution, Packaging, Lifespan, Re-usability, Recyclability, Effect on Consumer Behaviour, Socio-economic impact
f.	**People**	:	Environmentalists, Activits, scientists, Conservationists, Technicians, Educationsists
g.	**Process**	:	Preserving, Educating, Documenting, Appealing, Canvassing, Researching, Experimenting, Developing

Figure 17.1 : ROLE OF MARKETING IN A TRADITIONAL PRODUCT SECTOR FIRM

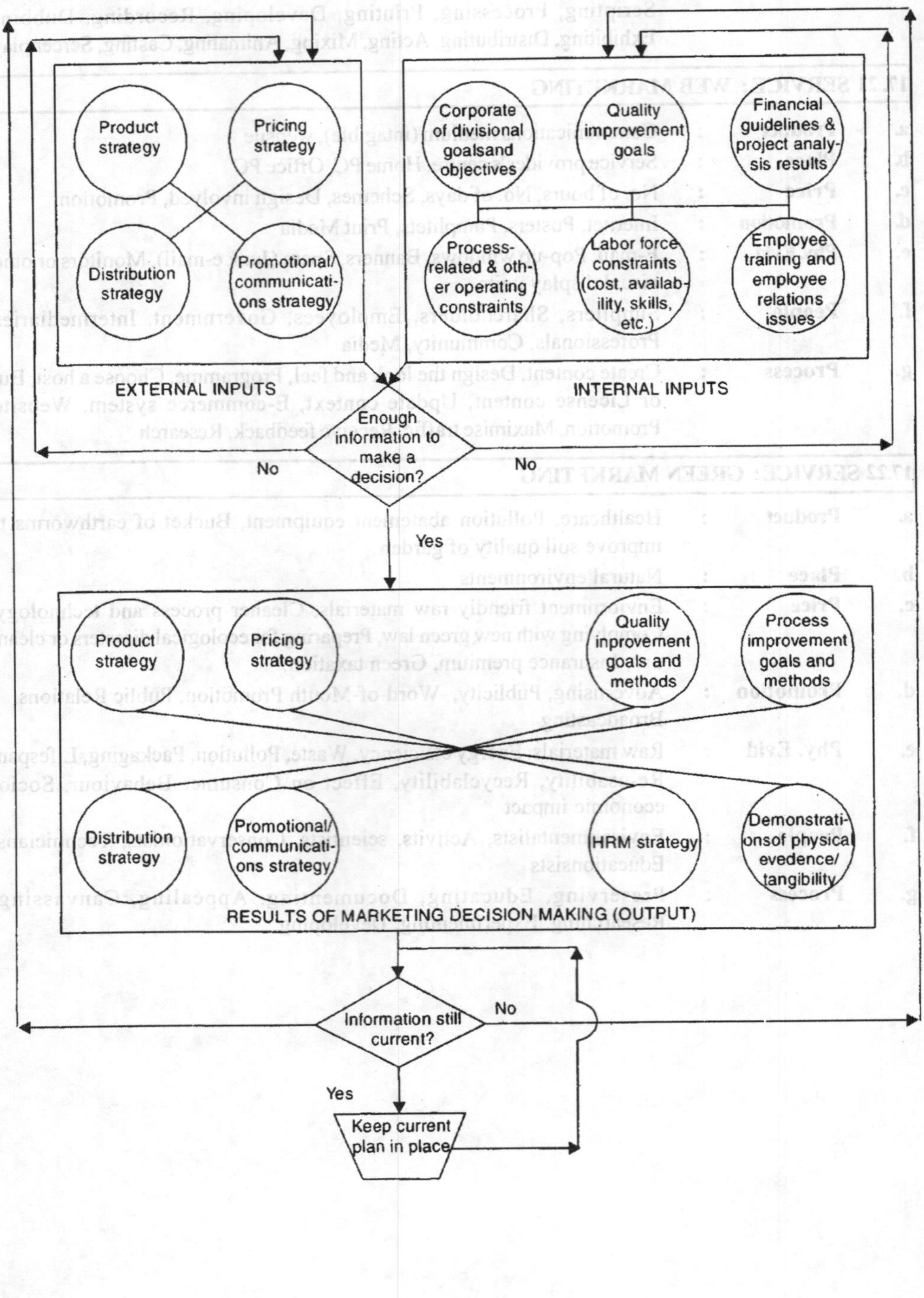

Figure 17.2 : ROLE OF MARKETING IN THE SERVICE SECTOR

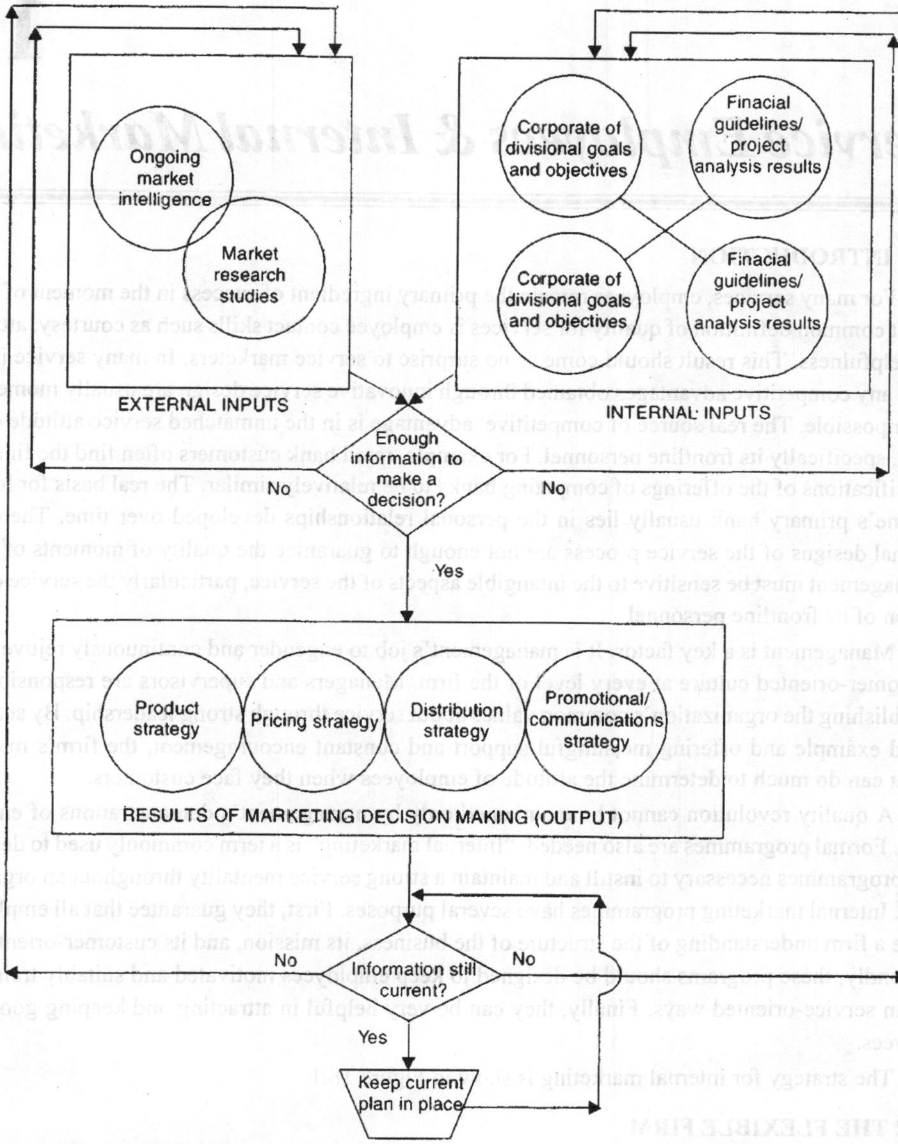

EXERCISE / ASSIGNMENT

For each of the services mentioned in this chapter, compile the Indian and Foreign Market Scenario. Some of the sub-headings could be :

1. **Major Players.**
2. **Industry Statistics**
3. **SCOT analysis**
4. **USP**
5. **Future Prospects**
6. **Varuious Environments (Demographic, Economic, Social, Legal, etc.)**

● ● ●

18

Service Employees & Internal Marketing

18.1 INTRODUCTION

For many services, employees remain the primary ingredient of success in the moment of truth. Most common definition of quality for services is employee contact skills such as courtesy, attitude, or helpfulness. This result should come as no surprise to service marketers. In many service industries any competitive advantages obtained through innovative service design are usually momentary or impossible. The real source of competitive advantage is in the unmatched service attitude of the firm, specifically its frontline personnel. For example, retail bank customers often find the financial specifications of the offerings of competing banks to be relatively similar. The real basis for loyalty to one's primary bank usually lies in the personal relationships developed over time. Therefore, formal designs of the service process are not enough to guarantee the quality of moments of truth. Management must be sensitive to the intangible aspects of the service, particularly the service orientation of its frontline personnel.

Management is a key factor. It is management's job to engender and continuously rejuvenate a customer-oriented culture at every level of the firm. Managers and supervisors are responsible for establishing the organization's common values about service through strong leadership. By setting a good example and offering meaningful support and constant encouragement, the firm's management can do much to determine the attitude of employees when they face customers.

A quality revolution cannot be maintained only by management's demonstrations of enthusiasm. Formal programmes are also needed. "Internal marketing" is a term commonly used to describe the programmes necessary to instill and maintain a strong service mentality throughout an organization. Internal marketing programmes have several purposes. First, they guarantee that all employees have a firm understanding of the structure of the business, its mission, and its customer-orientation. Secondly, these programs should be designed to keep employees motivated and suitably trained to act in service-oriented ways. Finally, they can be very helpful in attracting and keeping good employees.

The strategy for internal marketing is show in Figure 18.1.

18.2 THE FLEXIBLE FIRM

The demand for many services can be highly variable, with peaks and troughs which can be daily, weekly, annual, seasonal, cyclical or unpredictable in pattern. A number of methods of managing demand have been suggested in previous chapters, including differential pricing to encourage off-peak consumption and reformulating the service offer to provide added benefits during off-peak periods. On the supply side, great importance is attached to the flexible management of service personnel in such a way that they can respond rapidly to meet changes in the volume of service demand.

Figure 18.1 : STRATEGY FOR INTERNAL MARKETING

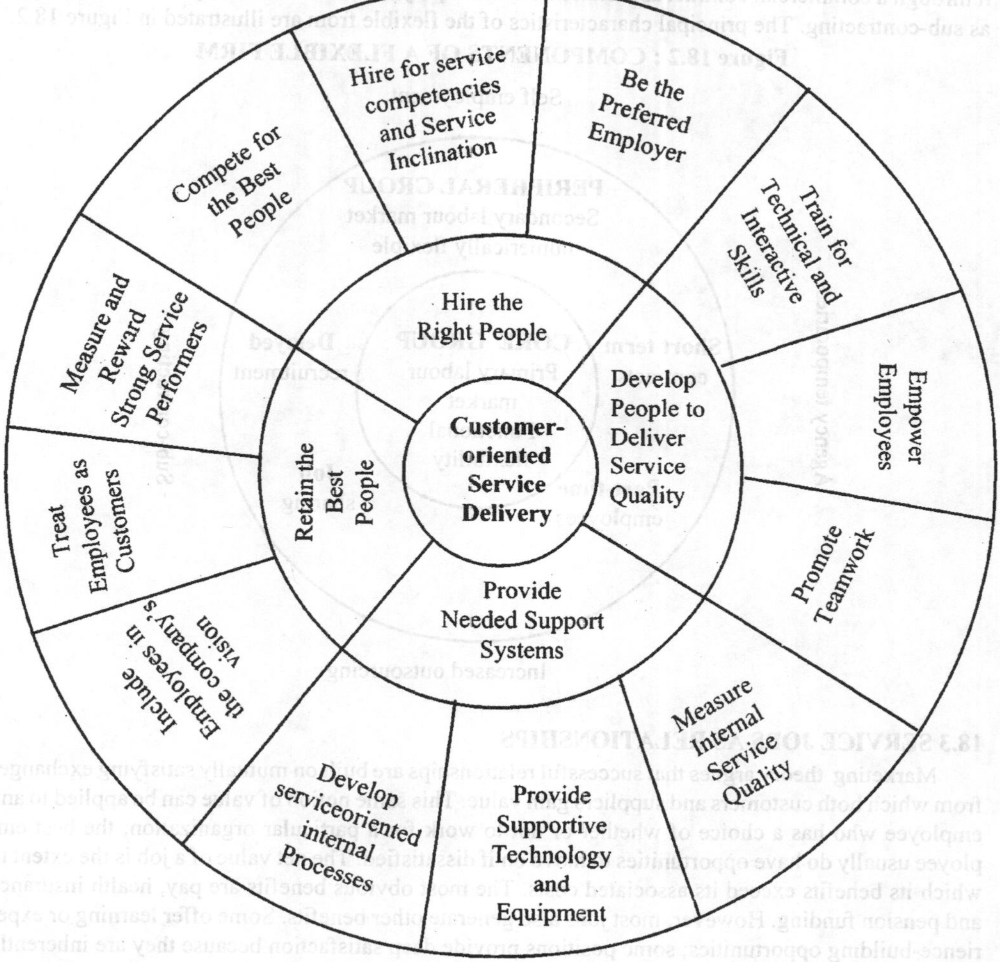

As well as being able to achieve short-term flexibility, service organizations must also have the flexibility over the longer term to shift their human resources from areas in decline to those where there is a prospect of future growth. For example, in order to retain its profitability a bank must have the ability to move personnel away form relatively static activities such as cash handling and current-account cheques handling towards the more profitable growth area of financial services.

Flexibility within a service organization can be achieved by segmenting the workforce into core and peripheral components. Core workers have greater job security and have defined career opportunities within an internal labour market. In return for this job security core workers may have to accept 'functional flexibility', whereby they become responsible for a variety of job tasks. As part of a HRM approach, the work output of this group is intensified. For this to be successful, employees require effective training and motivation which, in turn, has to be sustained by effective participation methods.

Peripheral employees, on the other had, have lesser job security and limited career opportunity. They are 'numerically flexible' while financial flexibility is brought about through the process of 'distancing'. In this situation a firm may utilize the service and skills of specialist labour but acquire it through a commercial contract as distinct from an employment contract. This process is referred to as sub-contracting. The principal characteristics of the flexible from are illustrated in Figure 18.2.

Figure 18.2 : COMPONENTS OF A FLEXIBLE FIRM

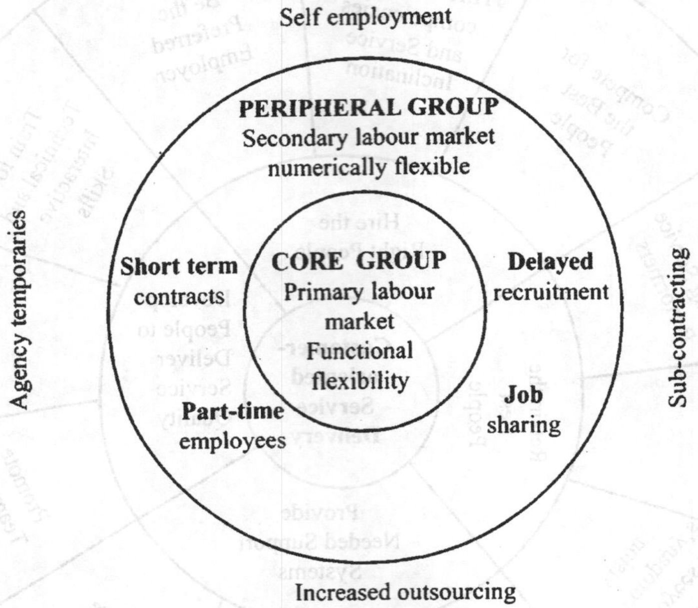

18.3 SERVICE JOBS AS RELATIONSHIPS

Marketing theory argues that successful relationships are built on mutually satisfying exchanges from which both customers and suppliers gain value. This same notion of value can be applied to any employee who has a choice of whether or not to work for a particular organization; the best employee usually do have opportunities to move on if dissatisfied. The net value of a job is the extent to which its benefits exceed its associated costs. The most obvious benefits are pay, health insurance and pension funding. However, most jobs also generate other benefits. Some offer learning or experience-building opportunities; some positions provide deep satisfaction because they are inherently interesting or provide a sense of accomplishment; still others provide companionship, a valued chance to meet other people, a sense of dignity and self-worth, opportunities to travel and the chance to make a social contribution.

But working in any job has its costs, too, beginning with the time spent on the job and travelling to and from work. Most jobs also entail some monetary costs, ranging from special clothes to commuting and childcare. Stress can be a psychological and physical cost in a demanding job. Unpleasant working conditions may involve exposure to noise, smells and temperature extremes. And, of course, some jobs require intense physical or mental effort. It can be helpful for HR managers to view employees as customers who may leave if dissatisfied. Measuring employee satisfaction can help to identify what workers see as the benefits of their job and what as drawbacks. Decisions to change the nature of the service operation frequently affect employees, too. The perceived value of their jobs may go up or down as a result. But not everybody has the same priorities and concerns - there is segmentation among employees as well as among customers. Part of the HR challenge is to match round pegs to round holes of the right diameter.

Frontstage service jobs add another dimension : frequent customer contact sometimes but not always involving extended relationships with the same customers. Depending on the employee's personality, such encounters may be seen in the abstract as a benefit to enjoy or a cost to be borne. In reality, good training, good support and satisfied customers should increase the pleasure (or diminish the pain), while the reverse will also be true.

Job design cannot be restricted to ensuring that the firm gets its money's worth out of employees. It must also consider the design of the working environment, and whether or not employees have the tools and facilities they need to deliver excellent service. Smart human resource managers know that if a job is changed through redesign, it will become more or less attractive to certain types of employees - and they can usually predict which one. To an increasing degree, health and safety legislation is requiring changes in the workplace to eliminate physical and even psychological hazards, but only management can create a positive working climate - and that takes a long time. Reducing the negative aspects of the job and improving its positive ones may make it easier for firms to recruit and retain the best available employees, without having to pay premium salaries and increase the emphasis on conventional 'benefits'. Employees who enjoy their work are more likely than unhappy ones to give good service to customers.

18.4 CYCLES OF FAILURE, MEDIOCRITY AND SUCCESS

All too often, bad working environments translate into dreadful service, with employees treating customers they way their managers treat them. Businesses with high employee turnover are frequently stuck in what has been termed the 'Cycle of Failure' Others, which offer job security but little scope for personal initiative, may suffer from an equally undesirable 'Cycle of Mediocrity' However, there is potential for both vicious and virtuous cycles in service employment, with the latter being termed the 'Cycle of Success.

18.5 THE CYCLE OF FAILURE

In many service industries the search for productivity is pursued with a vengeance. One solution takes the form of simplifying work routines and hiring workers as cheaply as possible to perform repetitive work tasks that require little or no training. The cycle of failure captures the implications of such a strategy, with its two concentric but interactive cycles : one involving failures with employees; the second, with customers.

The employee cycle of failure (Figure 18.3) begins with a narrow design of jobs to accommodate low skill levels, emphasis on rules rather than service and the use of technology to control quality. A strategy of low wages is accompanied by minimal effort on selection or training. The consequences include bored employees who lack the ability to respond to customer problems, become dissatisfied and develop a poor service attitude. The outcomes for the firm are low service quality and high employee turnover. Because of weak profit margins, the cycle repeats itself with hiring of more low-paid employees to work in this unrewarding atmosphere.

The customer cycle of failure begins with repeated emphasis on attracting new customers who become dissatisfied with employee performance and the lack of continuity implicit in continually changing faces. These customers fail to develop any loyalty to the supplier and turn over as rapidly as the staff thus requiring an endless search for new customers to maintain sales volume.

The departure of discontented customers is especially worrying in light of what we now know about the great profitability of a loyal customer base. For conscientious managers, it should be deeply disturbing to contemplate the social implications of an enormous pool of nomadic service employees moving from one low-paying employer to the next and experiencing a stream of personal failures in part because of the unwillingness of these employers to invest in efforts to break the cycle.

Managers have offered a veritable litany of excuses and justifications of excuses and justifications for perpetuating this cycle :

- 'You just can't get good people nowadays'

Figure 18.3 : THE CYCLE OF FAILURE

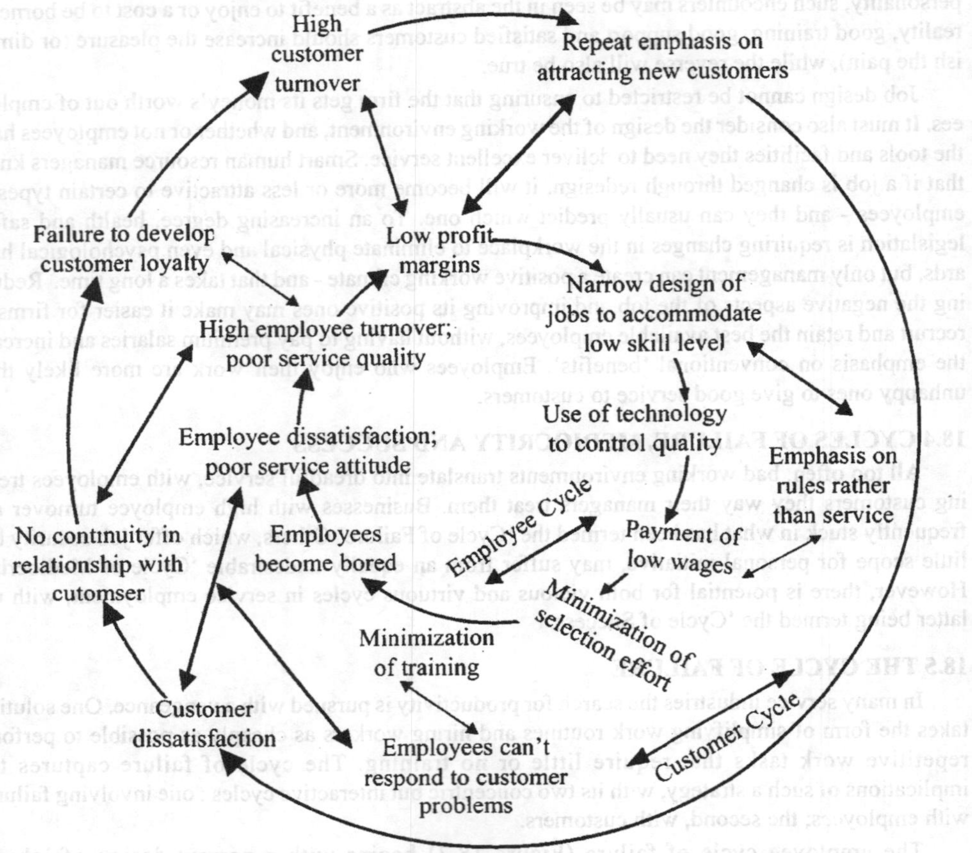

- 'People just don't want to work today'
- 'To get good people would cost too much and you can't pass on these cost increases to customers'
- 'It's not worth training our frontline people when they leave you so quickly.'
- 'High turnover is simply an inevitable part of our business. You've got to learn to live with it'.

Too many managers make short-sighted assumptions about the financial implications of low pay/high turnover human resource strategies. Part of the problem is failure to measure all relevant costs. Often omitted are three key cost variables; the cost of constant recruiting, hiring and training (which is as much a time cost for managers as a financial cost), the lower productivity of inexperienced new workers, and the costs of constantly attracting new customers (requiring extensive advertising and promotional discounts). Also ignored are two revenue variables: future revenue streams that might have continued for years but are lost when unhappy customers take their business elsewhere and potential income from prospective customers who are deterred by negative word-of-mouth. Finally, there are less easily quantifiable costs such as disruptions to service while a job remains unfilled and loss of the departing employee's knowledge of the business (and its customers).

18.6 THE CYCLE OF MEDIOCRITY

Another vicious employment cycle is the 'Cycle of Mediocrity' (Figure 18.4). It's most likely to be found in large, bureaucratic organizations - often typified by state monopolies, industrial cartels or regulated oligopolies - where there is little incentive to improve performance and where fear of entrenched unions may discourage management from adopting more innovative labour practices.

In such environments (which today are in decline), service delivery standards tend to be prescribed by rigid rule-books, oriented towards standardized service, operational efficiencies and prevention of both employee fraud and favouritism towards specific customers. Employees often expect to spend their entire working lives with the organization. Job responsibilities tend to be narrowly and unimaginatively defined, tightly categorized by grade and scope of responsibilities, and further rigidified by union rules. Salary increases and promotions are based on longevity, with successful performance in a job being measured by absence of mistakes, rather than by high productivity or outstanding customer service. Training, such as it is, focuses on learning the rules and the technical aspects of the job, not on improving human interactions with customers and fellow-workers. Since there are minimal allowances for flexibility or employee initiative, jobs tend to be boring and repetitive. However, in contrast to cycle of failure jobs, most positions provide adequate pay and often good benefits, combined with high security - thus making employees reluctant to leave. This lack of mobility is compounded by an absence of marketable skills that would be valued by organizations in other fields of endeavour.

Figure 18.4 : THE CYCLE OF MEDIOCRITY

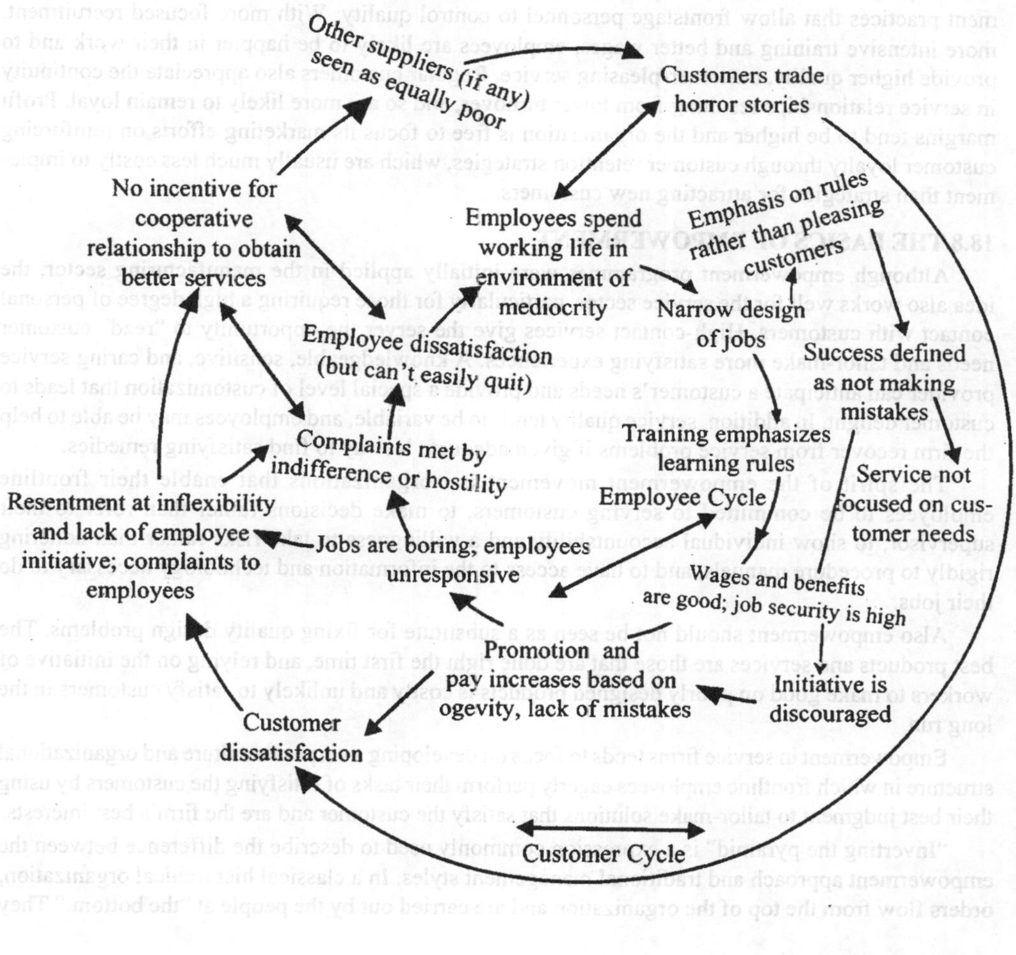

Customers find such organizations frustrating to deal with. Faced with bureaucratic hassles, lack of service flexibility and unwillingness of employees to make an effort to serve them better on grounds such as 'That's not may job', users of the service may become resentful. What happens when there is nowhere else for customers to go either because the service provider holds a monopoly or because all other available players are perceived as being as bad or worse? We shouldn't be surprised if dissatisfied customers display hostility towards service employees who, feeling trapped in their jobs and powerless to improve the situation, protect themselves through such mechanisms as withdrawal into indifference, playing overtly by the rule-book or countering rudeness with rudeness. The net result? A vicious cycle of mediocrity in which unhappy customers continually complain to sullen employees (and also to other customers) about poor service and bad attitudes, generating ever greater defensiveness and lack of caring on the part of the staff. Under such circumstances, there is little incentive for customers to cooperate with the organization to achieve better service.

18.7 THE CYCLE OF SUCCESS

Some firms reject the assumptions underlying the cycles of failure or mediocrity. Instead, they take a long-term view of financial performance, seeking to prosper by investing in their people in order to create a 'cycle of success' (Figure 18.5). As with failure or mediocrity, success applies to both employees and customers. Broadened job designs are accompanied by training and empowerment practices that allow frontstage personnel to control quality. With more focused recruitment, more intensive training and better wages, employees are likely to be happier in their work and to provide higher quality, customer-pleasing service. Regular customers also appreciate the continuity in service relationships resulting from lower turnover, and so are more likely to remain loyal. Profit margins tend to be higher and the organization is free to focus its marketing efforts on reinforcing customer loyalty through customer retention strategies, which are usually much less costly to implement than strategies for attracting new customers.

18.8 THE BASICS OF EMPOWERMENT

Although empowerment programmes were initially applied in the manufacturing sector, the idea also works well for the service sector, particularly for those requiring a high degree of personal contact with customers. High-contact services give the server the opportunity to "read" customer needs and tailor-make more satisfying experiences. A knowledgeable, sensitive, and caring service provider can anticipate a customer's needs and provide a special level of customization that leads to customer delight. In addition, service quality tends to be variable, and employees may be able to help the firm recover from service problems if given adequate leeway to find satisfying remedies.

The spirit of the empowerment movement is : organizations that enable their frontline employees to be committed to serving customers, to make decisions rather than refer to their supervisor, to show individual accountability and a willingness to take risks rather than adhering rigidly to procedure manuals, and to have access to the information and technology necessary to do their jobs.

Also empowerment should not be seen as a substitute for fixing quality design problems. The best products and services are those that are done right the first time, and relying on the initiative of workers to make good on poorly designed products is costly and unlikely to satisfy customers in the long run.

Empowerment in service firms tends to focus on developing a corporate culture and organizational structure in which frontline employees eagerly perform their tasks of satisfying the customers by using their best judgment to tailor-make solutions that satisfy the customer and are the firm's best interests.

"Inverting the pyramid" is a expression commonly used to describe the difference between the empowerment approach and traditional management styles. In a classical hierarchical organization, orders flow from the top of the organization and are carried out by the people at "the bottom." They have little discretion in changing services because the expertise, and therefore decision-making authority, is considered to reside at the top of the organization. In an empowered organization, the hierarchy (often drawn as a pyramid) has been inverted. Serving customers is considered to be the most important function in the organization, and the people on the font line who provide it are considered to be the most important people. They need training to do their jobs, but once educated in their jobs and the organization's goals they are given the authority to do what is necessary to serve the customer. The role of management in this structure is that of facilitator to support the service providers with necessary resources, including information, training and other tools necessary to do the best possible job of satisfying the customers.

Figure 18.5 : THE CYCLE OF SUCCESS

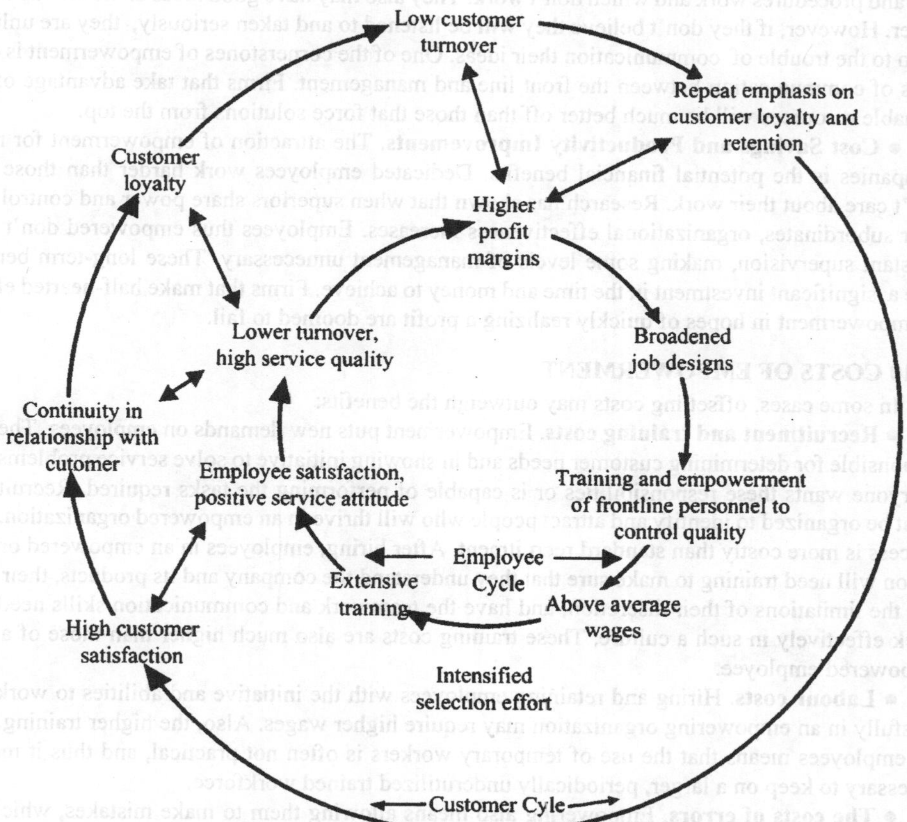

18.9 BENEFITS OF EMPOWERMENT

Several types of benefits accrue from successfuly empowering the workforce:

• **Greater employee satisfaction.** Proponents of empowerment insist that employees want to make a difference and to feel respected. People want to have a sense of control so that they can take personal pride of accomplishment in the results of their hard work. Noble ambition, but what's in it for the company? Actually, plenty. In addition to the fact that such employees are likely to be more productive and provide much more satisfying service for customers, enormous cost savings can be realized from lower absenteeism and less employee turnover. In industries where the costs of hiring and training service workers are high, this can have a substantial effect on profits.

• **Greater customer satisfaction**. Employees who identify with their company's goals are more likely to provide attentive, personable service.

If employees have the authority to respond quickly to a customer's special needs, they can heighten customer satisfaction or avert problems, by customizing the moment of truth to delight the customer the first time. However, when problems do occur, the ability to fix problems on the sport can turn a potentially angry customer into a loyal one. Reduced employee turnover can also be a source of improved customer satisfaction. For example, many retail banking customers prefer to develop personal relationships with bank employees whom they can seek out for advice or call to resolve problems. Banks with high employee turnover tend to alienate such customers.

• **Good ideas for improvement**. Frontline service workers know from experience which policies and procedures work and which don't work. They also may have good ideas on how to do things better. However, if they don't believe they will be listened to and taken seriously, they are unlikely to go to the trouble of communication their ideas. One of the cornerstones of empowerment is open lines of communication between the front line and management. Firms that take advantage of this valuable resources will be much better off than those that force solutions from the top.

• **Cost Savings and Productivity Improvements**. The attraction of empowerment for many companies is the potential financial benefits. Dedicated employees work harder than those who don't care about their work. Research has shown that when superiors share power and control with their subordinates, organizational effectiveness increases. Employees thus empowered don't need constant supervision, making some levels of management unnecessary. These long-term benefits take a significant investment in the time and money to achieve. Firms that make half-hearted efforts at empowerment in hopes of quickly realizing a profit are doomed to fail.

18.10 COSTS OF EMPOWERMENT

In some cases, offsetting costs may outweigh the benefits:

• **Recruitment and training costs**. Empowerment puts new demands on employees. They are responsible for determining customer needs and in showing initiative to solve service problems. Not everyone wants these responsibilities or is capable of performing the tasks required. Recruitment must be organized to identify and attract people who will thrive in an empowered organization. This process is more costly than standard recruitment. After hiring, employees in an empowered organization will need training to make sure that they understand the company and its products, their roles and the limitations of their discretion, and have the teamwork and communication skills needed to work effectively in such a culture. These training costs are also much higher than those of a non-empowered employee.

• **Labour costs**. Hiring and retaining employees with the initiative and abilities to work successfully in an empowering organization may require higher wages. Also, the higher training costs for employees means that the use of temporary workers is often not practical, and thus it may be necessary to keep on a larger, periodically underutilized trained workforce.

• **The costs of errors**. Empowering also means allowing them to make mistakes, which can also be costly. For example, employees may be overly generous to aggrieved customers when helping the organization to recover from mistakes.

Empowering employees requires that the firm absorb such mistakes as learning experiences, rather than use them as grounds to "punish the guilty." It is the role of training to reduce the occurrence of such errors of judgment in the future.

• **Service inefficiencies and inequities**. The reduction of standardization and increase in employee discretion that empowerment brings can also lead to ill will and claims of unfairness if customers feel that some servers are more generous or helpful or accommodating than others. The person at the airline ticket counter receiving extra time to accommodate a special request to reroute his flight may be delighted by the attentive and resourceful agent. The long line of people waiting behind him for service may be less enthusiastic. There are times when customers prefer a machine-like system that moves high volumes of customers efficiently. In these circumstances, customers will accept limited options as the trade-off for smoothly run operations. Once the planning process has decided upon the proper service level for the firm's strategic positioning the limits of employee discretion must be clearly taught in training sessions.

• **Role stress on employees.** When workers are empowered, middle managers must make the transformation from being a supervisor of frontline workers to a facilitator, motivator, and coach of frontline workers. This can become a very difficult, even threatening change for many managers. Frontline workers also feel stress, as they must now learn to make judgment between alternatives that satisfy customers versus those that protect the company's profits.

18.11 DEGREES OF EMPLOYEE INVOLVEMENT

For employees to be empowered they must feel they have a role in the success of the organization. However, employee involvement in the organization is not an all-or-nothing proposition. Different levels of employee involvement may be appropriate for different industries and corporate cultures. Lawler identified three different levels of employee involvement that a firm can adopt as it leaves behind the controlling, production line view of employees. The lowest level he called suggestion involvement, where the employee's ability to affect the business is limited to that of quality circles or formal suggestion programmes. Their day-to-day jobs are not affected directly by these programmes, but the employers do have the ability to provide some input about their circumstances. The second level is job involvement, in which job enrichment and teamwork are used to give employees a wider range of meaningful tasks and to achieve a greater sense of achievement and satisfaction. While frontline workers' jobs are richer at this level, senior management need not change its behavior to engender this transformation in the organization. Finally, in high-involvement organizations, employees at all levels are fully involved in the quality effort, share information, work on teams to solve problems and share in the success of the company. The number of organisations successfully achieving this ideal is small. The costs and efforts involved are enormous, and there aren't many managers with experience in this very innovative approach.

Should every company empower its workers, and if so, how much? There is no clear-cut answer to this question, but some characteristics of business make it more or less a candidate for empowerment. Bowen and Lawler suggested five contingencies or dimensions, depicted in Table 18.1, on which firms vary that can be used to determine the appropriateness of employee empowerment in a specific organization. They are described in the following paragraphs.

Basic business strategy. For low-cost, high-volume business empowerment may be impractical and may actually get in the way of what customers want and will pay for. For example, the core concept of a concession stand at a busy stadium is the delivery of a limited menu of products quickly, customers do not expect to be able to receive specialized orders, and would not tolerate the time spent delivering such services to others. Employees are expected to exchange products for cash as fast as possible, and have no need for much discretion in satisfying customers beyond providing items on the menu, However, the more a firm provides differentiation, customization and personalized service, the greater the need to empower frontline workers.

Table 18.1 BOWEN AND LAWLER'S DIMENSIONS AFFECTING THE NEED TO EMPOWER WORKERS

Dimension	*Empowerment important?*	
	Yes	*No*
Basic business strategy	Customized for individual customers	High-volume, low-cost; standardization
Ties to customers	Long-term relationship	Infrequent transactions
Technology	High personal component	Highly automated
Business environment	Unpredictable	Highly predictable
Employee attitudes	Risk takers, challenge Seekers, ambitious	Risk-averse employees, no initiative or ambition for challenge

Ties to customers. The more the firm must establish a long-term relationship with its customers, as opposed to engaging in short, infrequent transactions, the greater the value from empowering employees. Concession stands at tourist resorts can perhaps afford to be brusque with customers. The tellers at a neighborhood bank branch cannot.

Technology. To the extent that technology removes or replaces human interaction in the service delivery, empowerment in the usual sense becomes less necessary. However, other means to keep these employees enthusiastic about their jobs are still required. For example, at many organizations automated, menu-driven telephone answering systems are taking over most of the duties of the human operators. And yet, there always remains the need to have operators available to deal with exceptions and problems. As the opportunities to interact with and serve customers become reduced to overseeing the operations of a machine, employee morale can fall, and jobs must be redesigned to offer stimulation and a sense of pride.

Business environment. Unpredictable environments often require frontline employees with the discretion and ingenuity to respond to unanticipated situations. A stockbroker who is bound to offering a fixed set of investment opportunities under any economic conditions would not keep many customers. Empowerment is essential for business that require innovation to survive. Stable situations make empowerment much less necessary because they allow management to design ideal responses to anticipated situations in advance.

The people in the organization. Not all managers are able to function in a participative atmosphere, and not all employees are looking for responsibility and personal growth. Providing exceptional service often requires that an employee make an extra effort to listen and understand the customer's problem, to seek solutions, and to step outside the basic job description to complete the task. Not everyone has the ambition to make this effort or is willing to risk possible reprimands from superiors for going too far. Barring a complete replacement of its workforce, a firm must adopt an empowerment level that is comfortable for its employees.

Other conditions that advise against empowerment are those where turnover is high and pay is low, because the cost of training simply isn't worth it. There are also industries where government regulations or technical requirements severely limit the breadth of employee discretion, such as accounting practices or the management of nuclear power plants.

To decide on the level of empowerment that is appropriate for a particular firm, one should weigh each of these five contingencies, and any other compelling data, to determine the net effect.

18.12 MOTIVATING EMPOWERED EMPLOYEES

The models of empowerment that focus on delegation of authority generally assume that employees will be self-motivated to use this newly obtained power. What are the psychological components of empowerment?

Building self-Confidence

In their model of employee motivation Conger and Kanungo point out that delegating authority to employees may be necessary to empower them, but it doesn't guarantee that they will have the will or incentive to use it. They propose that empowerment should be thought of as a "motivational" construct, the act of giving a person a sense of power. They defined empowerment as a process of psychologically enabling employees by creating conditions that give them a greater feeling of self-confidence and a greater belief in the power of their actions to make a difference. Employees must be convinced that they are not victims. To achieve this state of affairs, management must act to strengthen employees' beliefs in their ability to accomplish meaningful tasks (self-efficacy).

Research in the areas of expectancy theory and self-efficacy theory has shown that a person's motivation to work harder at a task depends on separate expectations about two stages of task completion, as in Figure 18.6 (1) the self-efficacy expectation, a belief that the effort will provide an acceptable level of performance ("I am able to do the job required.") and (2) the outcome expectation, a belief that the performance level will be sufficient to yield the desired outcome (Doing this will make a difference). Conger and Kanungo's definition of empowerment is concerned with building up the first stage, self-efficacy expectation.

Figure 18.6 : THE TWO-STAGE EXPECTANCY MODEL OF MOTIVATION

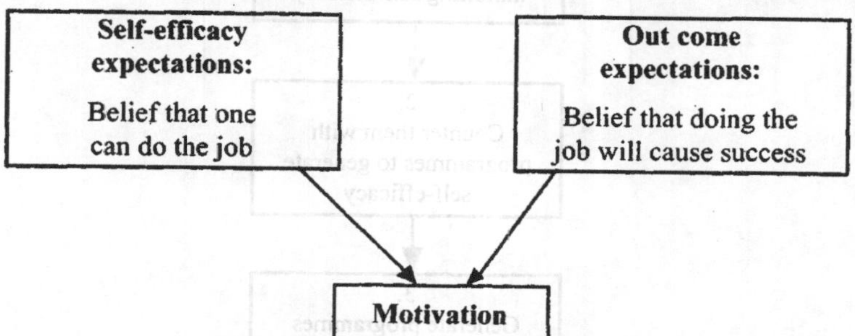

Separating the influences on motivation into these two expectations implies that a person's self-confidence is not necessarily linked to outcomes. So employees can feel good about themselves and the efforts they are making, even if the business results of their actions are not favourable. This has important implications for motivating employees. If managers continue to build up their employees' expectations for their own abilities, the employees will continue to take on challenges and show initiative even under trying circumstances. Once employees believe they are doing a good job, they will be likely to continue to deliver quality work, even if sales fall or other potentially discouraging events occur.

Using this self-efficacy definition, Conger and Kanungo propose that the process of empowerment must go through five stages, as shown in Figure 18.7. In the first stage, managers must identify the feelings of powerlessness among employees, specifically those conditions that make employees feel that they have no control over their own situations and that their efforts cannot change how the firm operates. These factors can include formal organizational structures and policies; management styles of superiors; reward systems that do not recognize effort, innovation, or initiative; and the specific nature of the jobs. Such inhibitors must be addressed before employees will be self-motivated enough to extend themselves to performing high-quality work

The second stage of the empowerment programme involves the firm's taking actions that will promote feelings of self-efficacy among employees. Providing participative decision-making opportunities, training programmes to build up skills, improving communication programmes, decentralizing the control of resources, and instituting reward systems that encourage innovation are all recommended here, as before, But so are programmes that explicitly encourage and express confidence in employees, that design more interesting, meaningful jobs, and set challenging but attainable goals.

The third stage of this empowerment process is the development of feedback programmes to inform employees of their self-efficacy. The most effective feedback programmes let employees discover their own abilities. They start by assigning employees to easy tasks and then slowly increase task difficulty, thereby guaranteeing that employees will experience early success and realize their increasing potential. Other forms of feedback are also useful, but less effective, such as formal recognition programmes and the informal encouragement and support of supervisors. In addition, management must also be prepared to contend with the emotional stress that these change can generate in the workforce. Providing a supportive, trusting environment has also been shown to improve self-efficacy.

Ideally, the final two steps in the process are the achievement of strengthened feelings of self-efficacy among employees, followed by heightened levels of effort and persistence in accomplishing tasks.

Figure 18.7 : CONGER AND KANUGO'S STAGES OF EMPLOYEE EMPOWERMENT

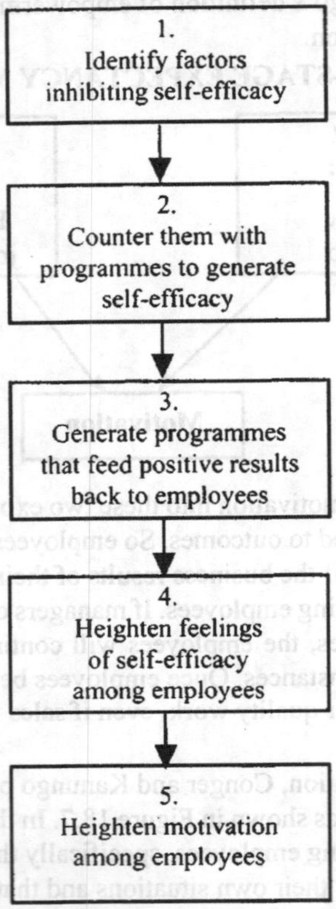

18.13 ENTHUSIASM FOR THE WORK

Thomas and Velthouse pursued the approach of Conger and Kanungo by digging more deeply into the determinants of employee motivation. After all, self-confidence alone isn't enough to ensure that a person will make the effort to do a good job. Their research asked the question, what energizes people to purses particular tasks? Their definition of empowerment is "intrinsic task motivation", a person's intrinsic commitment to do a good job motivated by the "pull" of the task, not the "push" of management. Their model of motivation also has important implications for management's role in implementing empowerment programmes.

The core of the Thomas and Velthouse model, seen in Figure 18.8 is a cycle of three events that can either build or reduce motivation among employees.The core determinant of whether a person will be motivated to make an effort is task assessment, or judgments about a particular task being considered. These judgments cover four dimensions of the task: will it produce the desired effect? Does the person believe that he or she has the skills necessary to do the task? Is the task meaningful enough to care about? Does the person have a choice? Many scholars consider this last component, choice, to be an essential component of intrinsic motivation. Of course, choice is primarily what is offered to employees by the definitions of empowerment that emphasize participatory management, perspectives to assess the task come in part from environmental events, or observations of the results of previous actions, training, communication with other employees, and so forth. Task assessments directly affect the person's behaviour.

Figure 18.8 : THE THOMAS AND VELTHOUSE MODEL

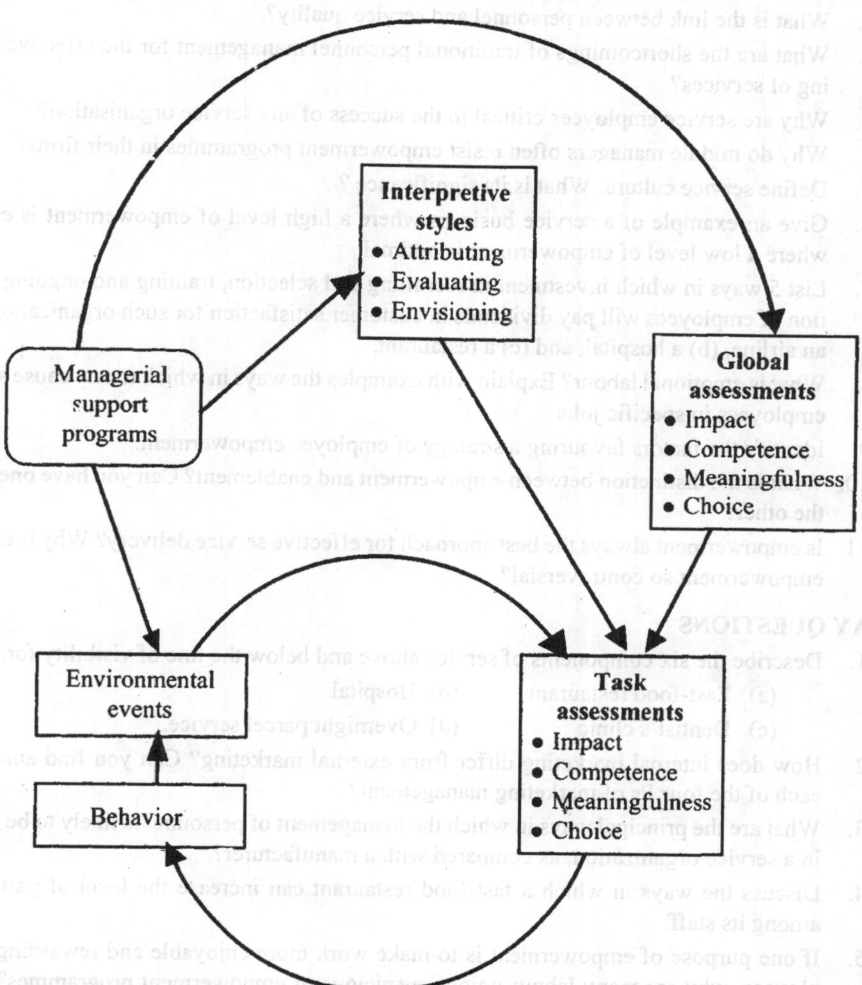

18.14 SERVICE CULTURE

Corporate culture has been defined as "the pattern of shared values and beliefs that given the members of an organization meaning and provide them with the rules for behaviour in the organization. "Culture has been defined more informally as "what we do around here" or "organizational glue" or "central themes". A customers-oriented, service -oriented organization will have at its heart a "service culture" defined as "a culture where an appreciation for good service exists, and where giving good service to internal as well as ultimate, external customers is considered a natural way of life and one of the most important norms by everyone". This is a very rich definition with many implications for employee behaviours. First, a service culture exists if there is an "appreciation for good service". This doesn't' mean that the company has an advertising campaign that stresses the importance of service, but that "in that underneath sort of way" people know that good service is appreciated and valued. A second important point in this definition is that good service is given to internal as well as external customers. It is not enough to promise excellent service to final customers; all people within the organization deserve the same kind of service. Finally, in a service culture good service is "a way of life" and it comes naturally because it is the important norm of the organization.

SHORT ANSWER QUESTIONS

1. What is the link between personnel and service quality?
2. What are the shortcomings of traditional personnel management for the effective marketing of services?
3. Why are service employees critical to the success of any service organisation?
4. Why do middle managers often resist empowerment programmes in their firms?
5. Define service culture. What is its significance ?
6. Give an example of a service business where a high level of empowerment is essential; where a low level of empowerment is optimal.
7. List 5 ways in which investment in recruiting and selection, training and ongoing motivation of employees will pay dividends in customer satisfaction for such organizations as (a) an airline, (b) a hospital, and (c) a restaurant.
8. What is emotional labour? Explain with examples the ways in which it may cause stress for employees in specific jobs.
9. Identify the factors favouring a strategy of employee empowerment.
10. What is the distinction between empowerment and enablement? Can you have one without the other?
11. Is empowerment always the best approach for effective service delivery? Why is employee empowerment so controversial?

ESSAY QUESTIONS

1. Describe the six components of service above and below the line of visibility for:
   (a) Fast-food restaurant (b) Hospital
   (c) Dentist's clinic (d) Overnight parcel service.
2. How does internal marketing differ from external marketing? Can you find analogies to each of the four Ps of marketing management?.
3. What are the principal ways in which the management of personnel is likely to be different in a service organization, as compared with a manufacturer?
4. Discuss the ways in which a fast-food restaurant can increase the level of participation among its staff.
5. If one purpose of empowerment is to make work more enjoyable and rewarding for employees, why are many labour unions suspicious of empowerment programmes? Do you think they have a point?
6. What are some of the benefits a company receives from empowering its workers? What costs and risks must it incur?
7. What insight about employee motivation do Conger and Kanungo provide by separating the concepts of self-efficacy expectation and outcome expectation?
8. What are the components of the principal recurring cycle in the Thomas-Velthouse model? What can managers do to begin a cycle of positive reinforcement of the cycle?
9. What can a marketing perspective bring to the practice of human resource management?

EXERCISE / ASSIGNMENT

1. Using an industry with which you are familiar, identify methods by which the effects of variability of the personnel inputs can be minimised in order to produce a consistent standard of output.

2. **Using examples, show how Human Resource Management policies can help to overcome the problems associated with peaked patterns of demand.**
3. **Make a list of new duties a manager assumes in a newly empowered organization.**
4. **What important ethical issues do you see facing human resource managers in high contact service organisations?**
5. **Design a blueprint for the drive-through window operation of a typical fast-food restaurant. In your experience, are there any fail points? How would you redesign your blueprint to reduce the probability of these service failures?**
6. **Choose one or more of the human resource strategy themes (hire the right people, develop people to deliver quality service, provide needed support systems, retain the best people). Interview a manager in a service organisation of your choice regarding his or her current practices within the theme you have chosen. Describe the current practices and recommend any appropriate changes for improving them.**

●●●

19

Customer Management and Service Guarantees

19.1 CUSTOMER SERVICE

One of the most fundamental concepts in analyzing service operations is the distinction between the "front stage" and the "backstage". Frontage procedures are those experienced by the consumer. In the case of low-contact services such procedures represent a very small proportion of the service firms' total activities. For instance, the extent of personal contact between customers and credit card companies is limited to receiving and paying a monthly statement, and an occasional letter or telephone call if problems arise. Tasks such as review of credit card applications, credit checks, and processing of credit card slips, all take place behind the scenes.

By contrast, in a high-contact service such as a hotel the customer is exposed to the physical facilities and is likely to have service encounters with numerous hotel personnel, ranging from telephone reservation agent to doorman, from bellboy to receptionist, and from restaurant server to housekeeper. Customer service takes different forms, according to the degree of contact, but it's important wherever it occurs.

Customer service involves task-oriented activities, other than proactive selling, that involve interactions with customers in person, by telecommunications, or by mail. This function should be designed, performed, and communicated with two goals in mind : Customer satisfaction and operational efficiency".

19.2 MANAGEMENT PROCESS

1. Conducting ongoing research to determine customer needs, wants, and satisfaction levels concerning each of their service encounters.
2. Identifying the key sources of customer satisfaction (or dissatisfaction) and relating them to current service elements
3. Setting service-level standards for each element with reference to how they relate to each other
4. Designing jobs and technological systems to meet these standards
5. Periodically revising standards and delivery systems in the light of changing customer preferences, technological innovation, and competitive activities.

19.3 CREATING THE PETALS OF THE FLOWER OF SERVICE

Customer service is basically an umbrella term for delivering the various types of supplementary services that surround the core product like the petals of a flower. The array of jobs that fall under the customer service umbrella is quite broad. Figure 19.1 highlights some of the jobs that go with specific petals of the Flower of Service. In terms of job assignments, customer service may involve people who:

- Provide information and technical advice in their capacity as members of the sales support staff
- Take orders and reservations over the phone and pass them along to those individuals responsible for order fulfillment

- Communicate with customers following receipt of orders or reservations to provide information on availability, advise on shipping dates or reservation details, confirm shipment or trace missing orders
- Greet customers on arrival at a service facility, offer refreshments, and attend to other needs

Figure 19.1: EXAMPLES OF JOBS PROVIDING SPECIFIC SUPPLEMENTARY SERVICES

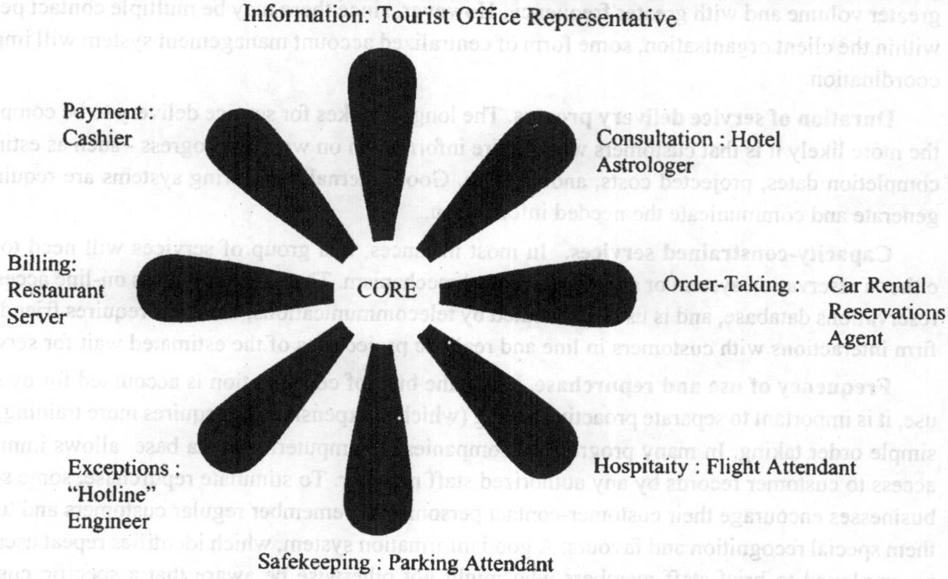

- Take responsibility for customers' cars, bags, coats, or other possessions while they are at a service facility
- Maintain contact with customers while supervising assembly or completion of special or customized orders
- Schedule transportation and expedite deliveries to customers
- Handle installation and repairs
- Attend to special requests, resolve problems, handle complaints
- Compile billing information, send out bills, accept payment, pursue delinquent payers, make refunds

19.4 FACTORS SHAPING THE CUSTOMER SERVICE FUNCTION

The nature of the customer-contact function inevitably varies by industry, service category, and type of organization. Among the factors that serve to shape the tasks performed and the place of customer service within the organization are the following:

Presence or absence of intermediaries. Some customer-contact tasks are often more efficiently performed by intermediaries. Usually these relate to initial contacts by customers prior to delivery of the core service. Examples include travel agents and the ticket agencies that provide information and advice, make reservations, and collect payment. Some smaller hotel chains contract out their toll-free telephone reservations service to a specialist firm. Although this strategy weakens the control of he firm over performance of key customer-contact tasks, it may result in better service at a lower cost.

High-contact versus low-contact. The more involvement the customer has with a service firm, the greater the number of customer-contact points ("moments of truth") and the more likely these are to take place in locations far distant from the head office. This situation poses a greater risk of mistakes or poor service and is thus more complex to manage. By contrast, low-contact services entail few interactions with customers, with contacts usually limited to mail or telecommunication contact with personnel in a central office, where management controls can be much tighter.

Institutional versus individual purchases. Greater variability may be introduced into customer-service activities directed at the general public (who are often infrequent users of a particular service) than when working with institutional customers. The latter tend to purchase in greater volume and with greater frequency. However, since there may be multiple contact persons within the client organisation, some form of centralized account management system will improve coordination.

Duration of service delivery process. The longer it takes for service delivery to be completed, the more likely it is that customers will require information on work in progress - such as estimated completion dates, projected costs, and so forth. Good internal monitoring systems are required to generate and communicate the needed information.

Capacity-constrained services. In most instances, this group of services will need to offer either a reservation system or a queuing-control mechanism. The former requires on-line access to a reservations database, and is usually handled by telecommunications; the latter requires friendly but firm interactions with customers in line and realistic projections of the estimated wait for service.

Frequency of use and repurchase. When the bulk of consumption is accounted for by repeat use, it is important to separate proactive selling (which is expensive and requires more training) from simple order taking. In many progressive companies, a computerized data base allows immediate access to customer records by any authorized staff member. To stimulate repurchase, some service businesses encourage their customer-contact personnel to remember regular customers and to offer them special recognition and favours. A good information system, which identifies repeat users, can be employed to brief staff members who might not otherwise be aware that a specific customer merited special treatment.

Level of complexity. Some services are simple for customers to use and easy for the operations department to deliver. Other services are more complex, with the result that inexperienced users require assistance. A related problem in complex services is that there are more things that can go wrong. So these services require customer-contact personnel who can provide information and help to educate the customer. They also require contingency plans for problem resolution, necessitating careful training of personnel on what actions to take when a particular problem arises. Superior performance by service personnel in service recovery (which may include providing an acceptable alternative) can create a very favourable impression in customers' minds, distinguishing an excellent organization from mediocre competitors.

Degree of risk. Service managers must understand the consequences of service failure for their customers. Contingency planning is often required by government regulation when personal safety is a factor. Other consequences for customers may range from personal inconvenience to monetary loss. The higher the probability of a service failure and the more serious the consequences, the more important it is to employ mature, well-trained contact personnel who not only behave calmly and tactfully when faced by upset customers, but also can work to resolve the problem as quickly as possible.

Assignment of Tasks to Customer Service

The array of tasks standing under the umbrella of customer service is quite broad. An important question for any organization is : Which specific tasks should be assigned to the formal customer service function?

Figure 19.2 : THE CUSTOMER CONTACT MATRIX

	INBOUND COMMUNICATIONS	***OUTBOUND COMMUNICATIONS***
SELLING ACTIONS	Order taking reservations	Personal or phone solicitation Advertising support
NON-SELLING ACTIONS	Requests for information and advice Complaint handling and problem solving Receipt of payments	Market research Confirmations and appointment reminders Post-use follow-up Billing and collections

Potential tasks can be divided in to selling-related and counselling activities, and also into customer-initiated and firm-initiated interactions (Figure 19.2) Although customer-service personnel can become involved in selling-related activities, this should normally be seen as an adjunct to their work, not its principal focus.

19.5 CUSTOMER PARTICIPATION

The level of customer participation low, medium, high - varies across services, as shown in Table 19.1. In some cases, all that is required is the customer's physical presence (low level of participation), with the employees of the firm doing all of the service production work, as in the case of a symphony concert. Symphony-goers must be present to receive the entertainment service, but little else is required once they are seated. In other cases, consumer inputs are required to aid the service organization in creating the service (moderate level of participation). Inputs can include information, effort, or physical possessions.

Table 19.1 LEVELS OF CUSTOMER PARTICIPATION ACROSS DIFFERENT SERVICES

Low : Consumer presence reqd. during service delivery	Moderate : Consumer inputs required for service creation	High :Consumers co-create the service product
Products are standardized.	Consumer inputs customize a standard service.	Active consumer participation guides the customized service.
Service is provided regardless of any individual purchase.	Provision of service requires consumer purchase.	Service cannot be created apart from the customer's purchase and active participation.
Payment may be the only required consumer input.	Consumer inputs (information, materials) are necessary for an adequate outcome, but the service firm provides the service.	Consumer inputs are mandatory and co-create the outcome.
Examples:	***Examples:***	***Examples:***
Airline travel	Haircut	Marriage counseling
Concert	Tax preparation	Personal training
Fast-food restaurant	Annual physical exam	Dissertation advising
	Full service restaurant	Weight-reduction programme

19.6 THE CUSTOMER MIX

The process of managing multiple and sometimes conflicting segments is known as compatibility management, broadly defined as a "process of first attracting homogeneous consumers to the service environment, then actively managing both the physical environment and customer-to-customer encounters in such a way as to enhance satisfying encounters and minimize dissatisfying encounters". Compatibility management will be critically important for some businesses (e.g. health clubs, public transportation, hospitals) and less important for others. Table 19.2 lists seven interrelated characteristics of service businesses that will increase the importance of compatibility management.

To manage multiple (and sometimes conflicting) segments, organizations rely on a variety of strategies. Attracting maximally homogeneous groups of customers through careful positioning and segmentation strategies is one approach. This is the strategy used by famous hotel companies, for which upscale travelers are the primary target segment. The hotel is positioned to communicate that message to the market place, and customers self-select into the hotel. However, even in that context there are potential conflicts, for example when the hotel is simultaneously hosting a large business convention and serving individual business travellers. A second strategy is often used in such cases. Compatible customers are grouped together physically so that the segments are less likely to interact directly with each other.

Table 19.2 : CHARACTERISTICS OF SERVICE THAT INCREASE THE IMPORTANCE OF COMPATIBLE SEGMENTS

Characteristic	*Explanation*	*Examples*
Customers are in close physical proximity to each other.	Customers will more often notice each other and be influenced by each other's behaviour when they are in close physical proximity.	Airplane flights Entertainment events Sports events
There is verbal interaction among customers.	Conversation (or lack thereof) can be a component of both satisfying and dissatisfying encounters with fellow patrons.	Full service restaurants Cocktail lounges Educational settings
Customers are engaged in numerous and varied activities.	When a service facility supports varied activities all going on at the same time, the activities themselves may not be compatible	Libraries Health clubs Resort hotels
The service environment attracts a heterogeneous customer mix.	Many service environments, particularly those open to the public, will attract a variety of customer segments	Public parks Public transportation Open-enrollment colleges
The core service is compatibility.	The core service is to arrange compatible relationships between customers	Matrimonial services Weight-loss groups Mental health support groups.
Customers must occasionally wait for the service.	Waiting in line for service can be monotonous or anxiety producing. The boredom or stress can be magnified or lessened by other customers depending on their compatibility.	Medical clinics Tourist attractions Restaurants

Customers are expected to share time, space, or service utensils with each other.	The need to share space, time, and other service factors is common in many services, but may become a problem if segments are not comfortable with sharing or with each other of when the need to share is intensified due to capacity constraints.	Golf courses Hospitals Retirement communities Airplanes

19.7 PRINCIPLES OF COMPLAINT MANAGEMENT

How does one go about solving the root of the problem? Managerial experience suggests several principles of successful complaint management. These are:

1. Communication links from the front line to the information system
2. Immediate advocacy
3. Authority to settle complaints
4. Responsiveness
5. Not further inconveniencing the customer

Communications links are invaluable in resolving complaints. For example, through a travel agent one executive had arranged for a rental car at a good rate (Rs. 500 per day). When he arrived at his destination, he went to the rental counter and asked for his car. The attendant said, "Fine, that will be Rs. 600 per day." The executive pointed out that he had agreed to Rs. 500 per day. At this point the attendant resorted to her secret weapon, the communication links to the customer database. She was able to show the executive that the travel agent had made an error, and exactly how and when the error occurred. This got the rental car company completely off the hook. The problem was between the executive and his travel agent.

Pizza Hut delivery provides another example of using communication links. Whenever a customer places a telephone order, Pizza Hut calls up a computer database, sorted by phone number. The data base includes such informations as address, directions, and even previous orders.

Immediate advocacy is another important principle. This means that someone from the company is immediately on the customer's side, working to bring about a successful resolution to the complaint. This is not the same as immediate resolution of the problem. Some problems take a long time to solve. However, someone in the company should always represent the complaining customer's interests.

Another key principle is the authority to settle complaints. The more service oriented the advanced economies become, the more decentralized complaint resolution becomes. For this reason, and because speed of resolution is important, authority to settle complaints is usually best handled at the front line. For example, Airlines give its ticket agents and gate agents broad authority to do just about anything (within reason) to solve a customer's problems. Taking a problem up through channels would simply be too slow. A key to successful delegation of authority is "employee empowerment".

Related to this principle is responsiveness, which means that the complaint will be resolved quickly. If the complaint can't be resolved quickly, the company must at least communicate this fact to the customer quickly, and indicate exactly what is being done to address the problem.

The final principle of successful complaint management is don't further inconvenience the customer. Whenever the organization has made a mistake, it is the organization's sole responsibility to make things right. When this principle is violated, the results can sometimes be comical.

19.8 PROBLEM IMPACT TREE ANALYSIS

Figure 19.3 shows the branches of the problem impact tree. Each branch represents the possible outcomes of a customer contact. Either the customer experiences no problem (good), or experiences a problem (bad). If the customer does experience a problem doesn't complain, then there is no opportunity to resolve the problem. If the customer complains, then the problem is either resolved successfully by the company (good) or not (bad).

Figure 19.3 : THE PROBLEM IMPACT TREE

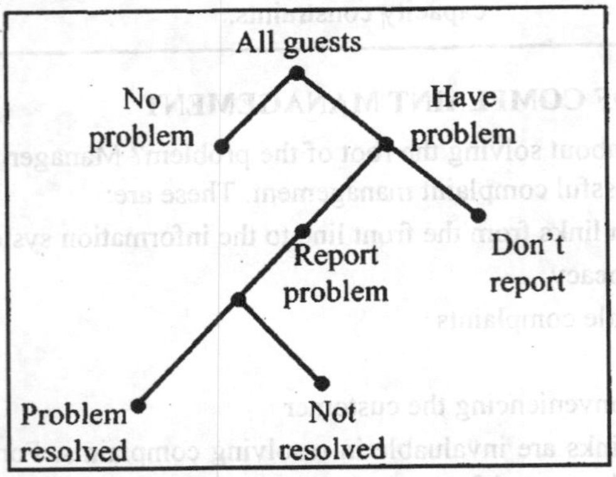

A problem impact tree analysis is conducted quarterly for all hotels. The hotels routinely collect data that may be used to determine how many people fall into each category. This technique involves sending out mail questionnaires to a large sample of customers shortly after these customers have checked out of the hotel. The hotel asks, as part of a general customer survey, whether the customer had experienced a problem or not, and, if so, whether or not it was reported, and whether or not it was satisfactorily resolved. Example percentages are given in Figure 19.4. We see that in this instance 75% of all guests had no problem. Of the 25% who did, only half complained, and 70% of complaints were successfully resolved. From these numbers we can make several useful observations. First, a very high percentage of people with problems do not complain, which removes any possibility of resolving the problem. Also, only 70% of complaints result in successful resolution, which may indicate that problem resolution is not particularly successful.

A further indication of the importance of problem resolution is the large differences in summary measures, such as satisfaction and repurchase intention. Figure 19.5 shows the percentage of people responding in the top two boxes of a five-point customer satisfaction scale, and Figure 19.6 shows the percentage who say they intend to repurchase. We see that if there is no problem, then 95% are satisfied and 95% intend to return. This is very good. On the other hand, among customers who experience a problem but don't report it, only 75% are satisfied and only 80% intend to return. This is a big drop out.

What happens if the customer complains? If the customer complains, and the complaint is resolved, then 90% are satisfied and 90% intend to return. This is almost as good as not having a problem in the first place! On the other hand if a complaint is not resolved, then satisfaction and repurchase plummet. Only 50% are satisfied, and only 60% intend to repurchase. The conclusion is that if a complaint is made, it is very important to resolve it successfully.

Figure 19.4 : COMPLAINT MANAGEMENT RESOLUTION PERFORMANCE

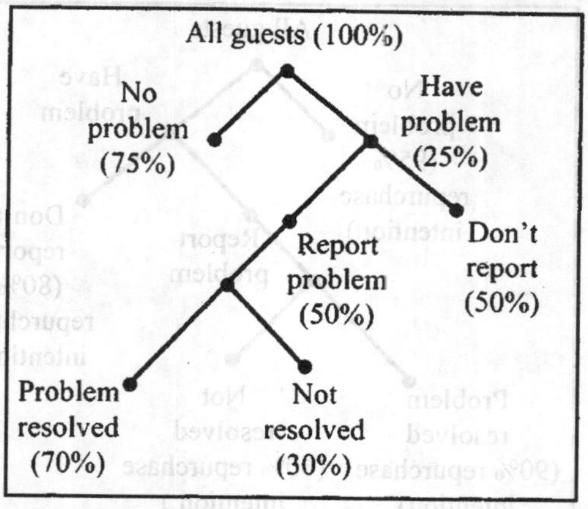

Figure 19.5 : COMPLAINT MANAGEMENT AND CUSTOMER SATISFACTION

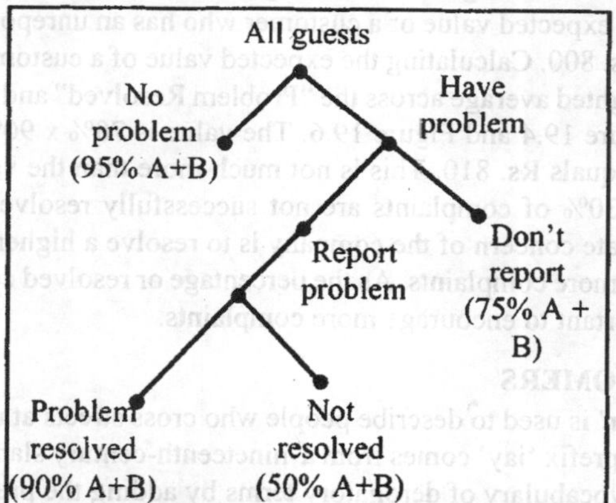

We can use the problem impact tree to analyze the value of complaint resolution outcomes, by incorporating the lifetime value of the customer Let us suppose that the lifetime value of a returning customer, in terms of the net present value of future profits, and ignoring word-of-mouth effects (to make things simple), is Rs. 1,000, and suppose that the numbers in Figures 19.4 and 19.6 apply. What is the value of avoiding a problem in the first place? The left most branch ("No Problem") has a 95% repurchase rate. Multiplying this by Rs. 1,000 gives an expected value of Rs. 950 for a customer in this branch. Now we need to find the repurchase rate for the other side of the tree. This is obtained as a weighted average of the three possible outcomes.

The calculation is: Average retention rate = (0.5 x 0.7 x 0.9) + (0.5 x 0.3 x 0.6) + (0.5 x 0.8) = 80.5%

Then the expected value of the right side of the tree is 80.5% x Rs. 1000 = Rs. 805. This is Rs. 145 less than the expected value if there is no problem. Thus it is worth Rs. 145 per customer for the company to avoid a problem in the first place. This is quite a lot.

We might also consider the value of resolving a problem, given that a complaint has been made. The expected value of the "Problem Resolved" branch is 90% x Rs. 1000 = Rs. 900, and the expected value of the "Not Resolved" branch is 60% x Rs. 1000 = Rs. 600. Notice that it is worth Rs. 900 - Rs. 600 = Rs. 300 to resolve a problem. The company can profit by pampering a complaining customer quite a bit, based solely on the value of future repurchases. Of course, if we factor in the word-of-mouth effect, the numbers get even more impressive.

Figure 19.6 : COMPLAINT MANAGEMENT AND REPURCHASE INTENTIONS

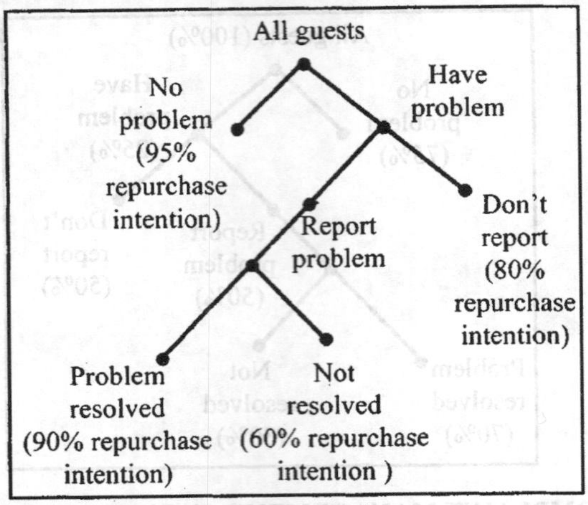

Another issue is how much we gain from having a customer report a problem. From Figure 19.6 it is easy to calculate the expected value of a customer who has an unreported problem. The value is 80% x Rs. 1000 = Rs. Rs. 800. Calculating the expected value of a customer who has a problem and reports it involves a weighted average across the "Problem Resolved" and "Not Resolved" branches, using the number in figure 19.4 and Figure 19.6. The value is 70% x 90% x Rs. 1,000 plus 30% x 60% x Rs. 100, which equals Rs. 810. This is not much more than the value of non-reporting customer, mostly because 30% of complaints are not successfully resolved. From these numbers it appears that the immediate concern of the company is to resolve a higher percentage of complaints rather than encouraging more complaints. As the percentage or resolved complaints increases, it will then become more important to encourage more complaints.

19.9 ABUSIVE CUSTOMERS

The term 'jaywalker' is used to describe people who cross streets at unauthorized places or in a dangerous manner. The prefix 'jay' comes from a nineteenth-century slang term for a stupid person. We can create a whole vocabulary of derogatory terms by adding the prefix 'jay' to existing nouns and verbs. How about 'jay customer', for example, to denote someone who 'jay uses' a service or 'jay consumes' a product (and then 'jay disposes' of it afterwards)? Or 'jay employees' who deliver poor service and abuse customers? Or even 'jay managers'?

We define a jay customer as one who acts in a thoughtless or abusive way, causing problems for the organization, its employees and other customers. Every service encounters its share of jay customers. But management opinions on this topic seem to polarize around two opposing views of the situation. One is denial: 'the customer can do no wrong'. The other view sees the marketplace of customers as positively overpopulated with nasty people (and even nastier corporate purchasers) who simply cannot be trusted to behave in ways that self-respecting suppliers should expect and require.

Since defining the problem is the first step in resolving it, let's start by considering the different types (or segments) of jay customers who prey upon suppliers of both goods and services.

The thief

This jay customer has no intention of paying and sets out to steal goods and services (or to pay less than full price by such devices as switching price tickets, or contesting bills on baseless grounds). Shoplifting is a major problem in retail stores. What retailers euphemistically call 'shrinkage' is estimated to cost enormous amounts of money each year, which simply gets passed back to honest customers through slightly higher prices. Certain services lend themselves to clever schemes for avoiding payment. For those with a technical bent, it is sometimes possible to bypass electricity meters, access telephone lines free of charge, or circumvent normal cable TV feeds. Customers who succeed in travelling free on public transportation, sneaking into cinemas or not paying for restaurant meals are a constant problem for managers in those industries. Both individual and corporate buyers have been known to use fraudulent forms of payment such as stolen credit cards or to issue cheques that are intended to bounce. Managers need to devise procedures for protecting themselves against thieves, while avoiding the risk of harassing or inconveniencing the overwhelming percentage of honest customers.

The rule breaker

Just as highways need safety regulations (including 'Don't Jaywalk'), many service businesses find it necessary to establish rules of behaviour for employees and customers. Some of these rules are imposed by government departments for reasons of health and safety. Air travel is perhaps the best example; there can be few other environments outside prison where healthy, mentally competent, adult customers are quite so constrained (albeit with good reason). In addition to enforcing government regulations, suppliers often lay down their own set of rules to facilitate the smooth functioning of the operation, avoid unreasonable demands being placed on employees, prevent misuse of products and facilities, protect themselves legally and discourage individual customers from behaving in ways that would detract from the quality of other people's service experiences.

There are risks attached to making lots of rules. They can make an organization appear bureaucratic and overbearing. And they can transform employees, whose orientation should be service to customers, into police officers who see (or are told to see) their most important task as enforcing all the rules. A third problem is that there will always be some customers who break the rules anyway - either inadvertently or deliberately.

The belligerent

You've probably seen him (or her) in a store, at the airport, in a hotel or restaurant. Red in the face and shouting angrily, or perhaps icily calm and voicing insults, threats and obscenities. Things don't always work as they should: machines break down, service is clumsy, customers are ignored, a flight is delayed, an order is delivered incorrectly, staff are unhelpful, a promise is broken. Or perhaps the customer in question is going through a difficult period in his or her personal life. Service personnel are often abused, even when they are not to blame. If an employee lacks authority to resolve the problem, that may make the belligerent madder still, even to the point of physical attack. Drunkenness and drug abuse add extra layers of complication. Organizations that care about their employees go to great efforts to develop skills in dealing with these difficult situations. Training exercise that involve role playing help employees to develop the self-confidence and assertiveness that they need to stand up to upset customers. Employees also need to learn how to defuse anger, calm anxiety and comfort distress (particularly when there is good reason for the customer to be upset with the organization's performance).

But what is an employee to do when an aggressive customer brushes off attempts to defuse the situation? In a public environment, one priority should be to move the person away from other customers. Sometimes supervisors may have to arbitrate disputed between customers and staff members; at other times, they need to stand behind the employee's actions. If an employee has been physically assaulted by a customer, then it may be necessary to summon security officers or the police. Some firms try to conceal such events, fearing bad publicity, but others feel obliged to make a public stand on behalf of their employees.

Telephone rudeness poses a different challenge. Service personnel have been known to hang up on angry customers, but that action doesn't resolve the problem. Bank customers, for instance, tend to get upset when learning that cheques have been returned because they are overdrawn (they've broken the rules) or that a request for a loan has been denied).

The vandal

It's astonishing the level of physical abuse to which service facilities and equipment can be subjected. Soft drinks are poured into a bank's cash machines; graffiti are scrawled on both interior and exterior surfaces; cigarettes burn holes in carpets, table cloths and bed covers; bus seats are slashed and hotel furniture broken; telephone handsets are ripped off; customers' cars are vandalized; glass is smashed and fabrics torn. The list is endless. Not all of the damage is done by customers, of course, Much exterior vandalism is done by bored youths. And disgruntled employees have been known to commit sabotage. But much of the problem does originate with wrongly behaved, paying customers. Alcohol and drugs are sometimes the cause, psychological problems may contribute and plain carelessness plays a role. And there are occasions when unhappy customers, feeling mistreated by the service provider, try to get their own back. Finally, there are those charming people with a constant urge to carve their name on something, so that posterity may remember their visit.

The best cure is prevention. Improved security can discourage some vandals, Good lighting helps, as does open design of public areas. Consultants can suggest pleasing yet vandal-resistant surfaces, protective coverings for equipment and rugged furnishings. Better education of customers on how to use equipment properly (rather than fighting with it) and warnings about fragile objects can reduce the likelihood of careless handling. And then there are economic sanctions: security deposits or signed agreements in which customers agree to pay for any damage that they cause.

Figure 19.7 : EFFECTIVE COMPLAINTS HANDLING PROCESS

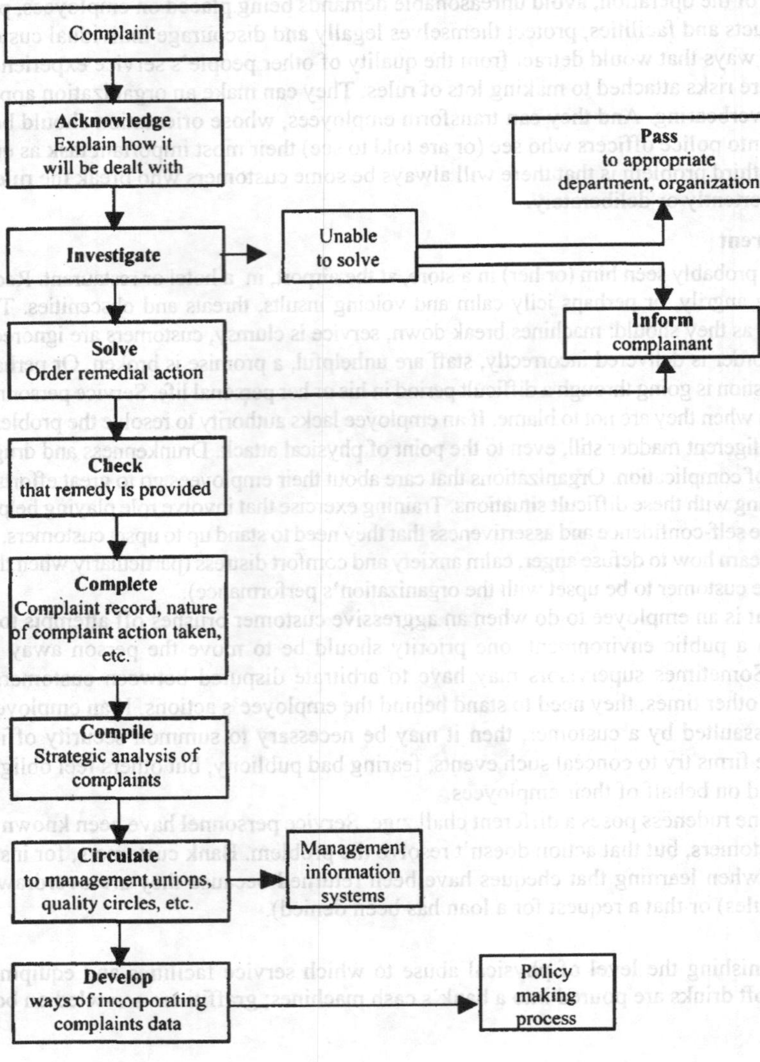

The deadbeat

Leaving aside those who never intended to pay in the first place (the term for them is 'thief'), there are many reasons why customers end up as delinquent accounts who fail to pay what is due for the service they have received. But once again, prevention is better than cure. A growing number of service businesses insist on pre-payment, any form of ticket sale being a good example. Direct marketing organizations ask for your credit card number as they take your order. The next best thing is to present the customer with a bill immediately on completion of service. If the bill is to be sent by mail, it's a good idea to send it quickly, while the service is still fresh in the customer's mind.

Not every apparent delinquent is a hopeless deadbeat. Perhaps there's good reason for the delay, perhaps acceptable payment arrangement can be worked out.

The process for handling complaints is shown as a flowchart in Figure 19.7

19.10 MATCHING SERVICE DELIVERY AND PROMISES

The approaches for matching service delivery and promises are shown in Figure 19.8

Figure 19.8 : APPROACHES FOR MATCHING SERVICE DELIVERY AND PROMISES

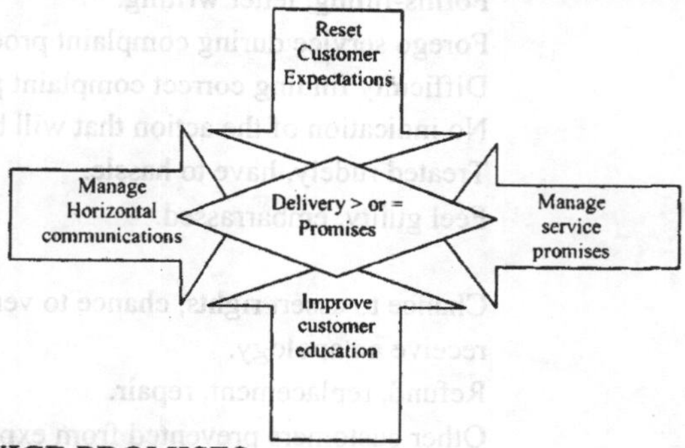

19.11 MANAGING SERVICE PROMISES

In manufacturing physical goods, the departments that make promises and those that deliver them can operate independently. Goods can be fully designed and produced and then turned over to marketing for promotion and sale. In services, however, the sales and marketing departments make promises about what other employees in the organization with fulfill. Because what employees do cannot be standardized the way physical goods produced mechanically can be, greater coordination and management of promises are required. Successful services advertising and personal selling become the responsibility of both marketing and operations: Marketing must accurately but beguilingly reflect what happens in actual service encounters and operations must deliver what is promised in advertising. If advertising or personal selling sets up unrealistic expectations for customers, the actual encounter will disappoint the customer. In a similar way, operations must cooperate with advertising to carry out themes of courtesy, responsiveness, and reliability that are presented in advertising, Interdependence exists. making cooperation and communication between these two functions critical.

Figure 19.9 shows specific strategies that are effective in managing promises.

Figure 19.9 : APPROACHES FOR MANAGING SERVICE PROMISES

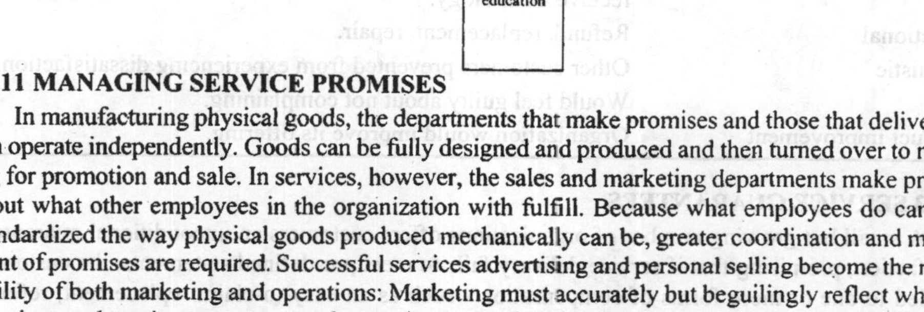

19.12 COSTS AND BENEFITS

If consumers expect to achieve something by complaining then they are much more likely to complain. Some psychologists would go even further, by suggesting that even if there is no possibility of rectifying the situation, it is still best to express anger, in order to accept the dissatisfaction.

The average consumer would probably not take this advice too seriously no matter how beneficial it may be to him psychologically. He is much more likely to weigh up all the costs and benefits associated with complaining. His emotional well-being will be only one factor. If he perceives the benefits to outweigh the costs, then he will complain. Table 19.3 lists the factors that help fashion the costs and benefits of complaining.

Table 19.3 : THE COSTS AND BENEFITS OF COMPLAINING

Costs	
Inconvenience	Special trip to complain.
	Forms-filling, letter writing.
	Forego service during complaint process.
Uncertainty	Difficulty finding correct complaint procedure.
	No indication of the action that will be taken.
Unpleasant	Treated rudely, have to hassle.
	Feel guilty, embarrassed.
Benefits	
Emotional	Chance to assert rights, chance to vent anger, receive an apology.
Functional	Refund, replacement, repair.
Altruistic	Other customers prevented from experiencing dissatisfaction.
	Would feel guilty about not complaining.
Product improvement	Organization would improve its offering.

19.13 SERVICE GUARANTEES

A small but growing number of organizations offers customers an unconditional guarantee of satisfaction, promising that if service delivery fails to meet pre-defined statements, the customer is entitled to one or more forms of compensation - such as an easy-to-claim replacement, refund or credit. These service guarantees are powerful tools for both promoting and achieving service quality for the following reasons:

1. Guarantees force firms to focus on what their customers want and expect in each clement of the service.
2. Guarantees set clear standards, telling customers and employees alike what the company stands for. Payouts to compensate customers for poor service cause managers to take guarantees seriously, because they highlight the financial costs of quality failures.
3. Guarantees require the development of systems for generating meaningful customer feedback and acting on it.
4. Guarantees force service organizations to understand why they fail and encourage them to identify and overcome potential failure points.
5. Guarantees build 'marketing muscle' by reducing the risk of the purchase decision and building long-term loyalty.

The provision of guarantees

In addition to handling complaints effectively, the service provider may also decide to offer consumers a guarantee. To invoke a guarantee, a customer generally has to begin by making a complaint, and so all the principles of efficient complaint handling still apply.

The function of the guarantee is that it reduces risk to consumers both before and after purchase. Pizza Hut guarantees its customers their pizzas in 30 minutes or they get their money back (and the late pizza besides!). In this situation, customers know that once they have placed their order the delivery of their food is imminent. They also know what to expect if it does not appear.

Figure 19.10 : TANGIBILITY AND THE PROVISION OF GUARANTEES

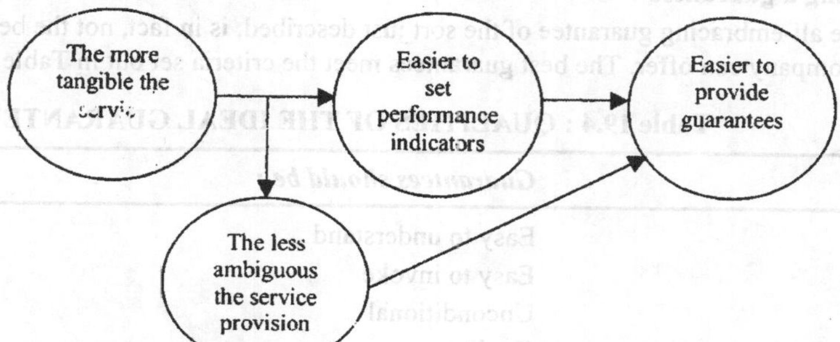

In reducing risk, the guarantee often diminishes much of the ambiguity often associated with service provision. However, ambiguity often arises from the intangible nature of the service, and the more intangible the service, the more difficult it is to provide guarantees (Figure 19.10).

For example, it is easy for a cobbler to guarantee to repair shoes in 24 hours or to provide his service free of charge. The smart cobbler should rarely find himself working for nothing. If he expects to turn round all those in a 24 hour period, then once he has taken on all that he can manage in this time, he can just refuse to accept any more under the conditions of the guarantee.

It is more difficult for a tutor to guarantee the results of his students. There are many intangible aspects of such a service, and not all of these are under the control of the tutor. This is not to say that those responsible for providing services with some intangibility should not provide guarantees. Too often those who provide the more intangible services shelter behind the shield of difficulty when it comes to the provision of guarantees. These companies will often regard a sincere apology as sufficient acknowledgment of a complaint.

However, is an apology enough for the consumer who goes through all the trouble of complaining? Even those offering intangible services can offer something a bit more tangible than an apology when it comes to compensating the aggrieved customer. This also applies when the situation giving cause for complaint cannot be retracted or rectified at a later date, e.g. if a retailer refuses to accept payment by credit card because the credit card company has mistakenly refused to authorize the customer's use of the card, the customer will be embarrassed. No matter what the credit card company now does it cannot retract that situation. Sending the customer a bunch of flowers will probably be greeted with more enthusiasm than wordy apology, and may stand a greater chance of effecting service recovery.

Many companies operating in such industries, particularly where the market is competitive, use guarantees as a positioning tool. They use it as a means of differentiating themselves from the competition, e.g. when one company offered 'No surcharges guaranteed' it was the first tour operator to do this. However, the uniqueness of this benefit was short-lived. Like so many service developments, it was easily copied. Note also that this particular guarantee only applied to one aspect of the service.

Sometimes companies adopt a more all-embracing approach. Instead of providing a specific guarantee, they guarantee total customer satisfaction. We can probably all think of services that provide 'satisfaction guaranteed'. Whether or not we believe them is another matter. Many such companies attach no meaning to these statements. Using them merely as a form of words intended to convey a quality service.

Other more reputable companies that provide this sort of guarantee, probably suffer as a result. They genuinely mean that they will do everything in their power to make customers satisfied. The principle is part of the company's philosophy, and employees are aware of the importance that is attached to satisfying the customer. The customer however, may well remain sceptical.

Designing a guarantee

The all-embracing guarantee of the sort just described, is in fact, not the best type of guarantee that a company can offer. The best guarantees meet the criteria set out in Table 19.4.

Table 19.4 : QUALITIES OF THE IDEAL GUARANTEE

Guarantees should be :
Easy to understand
Easy to invoke
Unconditional
Credible
Focused on customer needs
Meaningful (significant penalty or payout)
Provide clear performance standards

Easy to understand

The guarantee should be as short and simple as possible. It should be written in clear, plain English to help prevent any ambiguity from creeping in. The ideal is to think of an advertising end line; normally only one sentence in length, and with the intention of being highly memorable.

Easy to invoke

Companies are often fearful of making guarantees easy to invoke because they are frightened of the potential cost. They can see the benefits of offering guarantees to customers, but cannot see what benefits are to be gained by making them easy to invoke.

Most builders that install damp proof courses provide guarantees. However, they are so difficult to invoke that they are of little benefit to the customer. In order to invoke his guarantee, the dissatisfied customer must first pay for a site inspection. The company who carried out defective work insist that their company carries out this inspection. Their opinion is hardly likely to be unbiased. To save costs, they generally find some explanation for the damp that exempts them from liability. Therefore to invoke his guarantee, the customer has to go to further expense. He will expect the process to take some time, and will expect to have to wrangle in order to achieve any sort of satisfactory outcome. It is not an easy guarantee to invoke.

Unconditional

For the same reasons that it is important to make it easy for dissatisfied customers to complain, it is best to make the guarantee as unconditional as possible. This type of guarantee communicates to staff and customers that the service provider believes in the quality of their offering. Naturally, it is only sensible to offer such a guarantee if the service is a quality one.

Credible

To provide a guarantee that customers regard as incredible casts doubts on everything that the company does. Driving schools that guarantee learner drivers will pass first time are making unbelievable promises. The learner will know that there are many factors affecting whether or not they pass the driving test that are outside the control of the instructor, e.g. the nerves of the learner, or the mood of the test instructor. A table of pass rates relative to other driving schools would probably prove more credible, and would serve the main purpose of providing a guaranteed risk reduction.

Focused on customer needs

A guarantees should be guaranteeing aspects of service that are important to customers. It should not be focusing on what the company regards as important, or on what the company thinks customers regard as important.

The enlightened service provider should have identified those aspects of his service that are critically important to customers, not only to aid the design of a guarantee, but also to enable him to design a quality service.

Meaningful (with significant penalties or payouts)

The guarantee is not meaningful if the penalties that accrue to the provider, or the levels of compensation paid to the customer are insignificant. In both these cases there is little incentive for the company to improve its service offering. Most dissatisfied customers will not take the trouble to complain. Even if they did, the company would not suffer high payout costs and so is less likely to work on service improvement.

WHY A GUARANTEE WORKS

A satisfaction guarantee may appear to be primarily altruistic, but in fact it has positive effect on the bottom line in several important ways, both indirectly and directly. Indirectly, the guarantee creates more employee sensitivity to the issue of quality. This generates a higher level of quality, which in turn generates greater customer retention as well as increased customer attraction through positive word of mouth (Figure 19.11). The direct effects include successful advertising through use of the guarantee and improved retention of those successfully invoking the guarantee.

WHEN IS A GUARANTEE NOT A GOOD IDEA?

Although the advantages of a satisfaction guarantee are considerable, a guarantee is not for every company. There are several reasons why a guarantee can backfire. For example, a firm may be top quality to the point that a guarantee is essentially implied. The recognized quality leader in an industry whose employees are broadly empowered to solve customer problems might not need a satisfaction guarantee. That is because the company already acts as if it has a guarantee anyway, and the customers know it.

For other companies, low quality makes a guarantee impossible. Suppose half of the customers demanded their money back. How would the company stay in business? The only way poor-service providers can have a guarantee is if it is written in legal terms to the extent that nobody can actually invoke it, or is written so vaguely that it does not promise anything, signs which proudly proclaim "100% satisfaction guaranteed!" or, even better, "110% satisfaction guaranteed!!" What does the customer do with such a proclamation? Nothing is promised. If you can want to have fun some time, the next time you see such a sign, tell a service provider that you are only 85% satisfied and would like to invoke the guarantee. They will assume that you are joking.

Figure 19.11: INDIRECT BENEFITS OF A SATISFACTION GUARANTEE

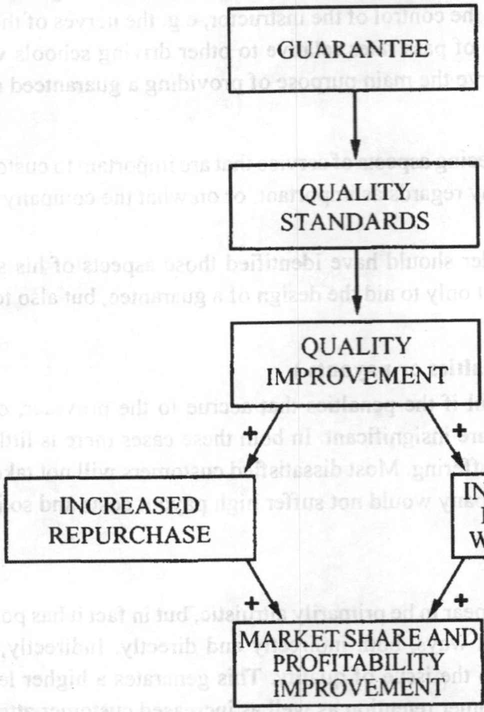

Sometimes low quality is not a problem, but service delivery is still erratic because of uncontrollable variables. Suppose, for example, the Mumbai airport wanted to guarantee air passengers that their planes would leave on time. That would not be feasible, because many of the variables that might cause late departure (fog, rain, airline mechanical problems, etc.) are beyond the airport's control. If the airport wanted to guarantee satisfaction, it could guarantee things that were within its control, such as adequate parking and clean rest rooms.

For some companies, a guarantee would not be possible because of excessive cheating. Nevertheless, in some circumstances this may be a problem. Consider, for example, what would happen if a satisfaction guarantee was offered by a prison. Imagine something like, "If you are not completely satisfied with your cell and food, we don't expect you to stay." Under those circumstances the incentive to cheat would be too great!

19.14 DESIGNING CUSTOMER SERVICE SYSTEMS & AUDITS

Whether a company is designing customer service systems for consumer affairs departments, catalog fulfillment operations, financial institutions, or a host of other applications, planners still have to address the same key issues:

Creation of an overall service delivery model. The model (which describes how the system works, must meet two central customer requirements for good service : Speed and quality. Time is money for many customers, both corporate users and individuals. They do not relish being kept waiting and in some cases, the consequences of delay may be quite severe. At the same time, customers expect reliable, courteous, customized service that solves their problems with a minimum of hassle.

Call management and administration. The mechanics of answering, routing and tracking calls tend to involve both telecommunications and database management; increasingly, the most powerful approaches explicitly link the two. Procedures should ensure that the system works well for customers, employees, and distributors or other intermediaries.

Access to data and applications. The information a firm needs to complete a transaction with a customer often resides in more than one database and may run on different hardware platforms. To deliver good service and simultaneously achieve operational efficiency, customer service reps need instant, easy access to all relevant sources and applications.

Adapting to change. Procedures and equipment do not exist in a vacuum. Firms have to integrate new systems with existing ones and must plan to accommodate future changes, including some that are not yet commercially available. Unless systems are carefully planned in advance, installing even modest upgrades can be an awesome task. (Programmers joke irreverently that the reason God was able to create the world in only seven days was that God didn't have to deal with an installed base.

The outline format for a customer service audit is shown in Table 19.5.

Table 19.5 : OUTLINE FORMAT FOR A CUSTOMER SERVICE AUDIT

1. ***Identify customer-contact tasks (other than sales), such as:***
   Information, advice
   Order-taking, reservations
   Core service delivery tasks (plus hospitality and safekeeping of customers' possessions)
   Billing and receipt of payment
   Problem solving, complaint handling
2. ***Review standard procedures for each task***
   Written standards (procedures manual) for each task
   Oral/written instructions (ad hoc)
   Availability (hours/days, locations)
   Interactions with other personnel
3. ***Identify performance goals by task***
   Specific quantitative goals
   Qualitative goals
   Contribution to related activities
   Contribution to long-term success of system
4. ***Specify measures of performance by task***
   Money based
   Time based
   Management/supervisor evaluations
   Customer evaluations
5. ***Review and evaluate personnel elements***
   Recruiting/selection criteria and practices
   Nature, content of training
   Job definition, career path (if any)
   Interactions with other employees
   Nature of supervision, quality control
   Evaluation procedures
   Corrective actions available
   Employee attitudes, motivation
   Hours, extent of paid/unpaid overtime
6. ***Identify and evaluate support systems***
   Instruction manuals, brochures, form letters
   Office facilities, furnishings, layout
   Office equipment (phones, fax, computers, word processors, etc.)
   Vehicles and equipment for repair/maintenance
   Radio or cellular telephone communications
   Record-keeping materials (for example, log books, laptop computers, and bar code scanners

SHORT ANSWER QUESTIONS

1. Explain the courses of action open to a dissatisfied consumer.
2. What do you understand by customer participation?
3. Describe the factors that may inhibit a dissatisfied consumer from complaining.
4. Think about the last time you experienced a less than satisfactory service experience. Did you complain? If you did not complain, explain why not.
5. When was the last time you were delighted with an organizations' response to your complaint. Describe in detail what happened. Why do you think you were delighted?
6. How are customer service audits designed?
7. What are the costs and benefits of complaining?
8. Evaluate the service guarantee of hotels. What do you see as its main advantages and disadvantages?
9. Identify some of the measures that can be used to encourage long-term relationships with customers.
10. What does segmentation have to do with capacity utilization? For what types of services is it a relevant issue?
11. Do guarantees always work? Why? Why not?
12. Explain the process for handling complaints effectively.
13. What are the arguments for spending money to keep existing customers loyal?
14. What are the principles of complaint management?

ESSAY QUESTIONS

1. Discuss the general importance of customers in the successful delivery of service using your own personal examples.
2. How are service promises managed?
3. What are the types of abusive customers? How can they be tackled?
4. What are the characteristics of service that increase the importance of compatible segments?
5. Use the elements of the drama metaphor (actors, audience, setting) to describe airline services. What insights can you gain by thinking of the service in this way?
6. What is problem impact tree analysis? Explain the methodology.
7. What is a service guarantee? What are its qualities? Give examples of ideal guarantees.
8. Describe a time when your satisfaction in a particular situation was increased because of something another customer did. Could (or does) the organization do anything to ensure that this happens routinely? What do they do? Should they try to make this routine occurrence?
9. Describe a time when your satisfaction in a particular situation was decreased because of something another customer did. Could the organization have done anything to manage this situation more effectively? What?
10. Evaluate the strengths and weaknesses of frequent user programmes in different service industries.
11. Make a case 'both for and against the statement that the 'customer is always right'.
12. Apply the principles of service recovery at the managerial level to a service organization with which you are familiar. Describe how this organization follows/does not follow these guidelines. What impact do you see this as having on their customers' loyalty?
13. Review the methods used by banks to keep customers loyal. Which of these might be adapted for use in other types of service business?
14. Select a people-processing service business, then pick two types of jay customer and develop strategies designed (a) to discourage these people from using your service in the first place,

(b) if they have already begun to cause problems, to prevent them from causing distress to other customers and/or to employees, and (c) to minimize financial loss to your organization.

EXERCISE / ASSIGNMENT

1. Visit a service establishment where customers can influence each other (i.e., theme park, entertainment establishment, resort, shopping mall, restaurant, airline, school, hospital). Observe (or interview) customers and record cases of positive and negative customer influence. Discuss how you would manage the situation to increase overall customer satisfaction.
2. Interview some one regarding his or here decision to outsource a service, for example, legal services, payroll, maintenance in a company; cleaning, child care, pet care, in a household. Use the criteria for internal versus external exchange described in the text to analyze the decisions to outsource.
3. Think of a service where a high level of customer participation is necessary for the service to be successful (e.g., health club, educational setting, weight loss, golf lessons). Interview a service provider in such an organization to find out what strategies the provider uses to encourage effective customer participation.
4. Think of specific services you have experienced that fall within each of the three levels of customer in each case. How did your involvement vary across the three types of service situations?
5. Discuss the customers' role as a productive resource for the firm. Describe a time when you played this role. What did you do and how did you feel? Did the firm help you to perform your role effectively? How?
6. Discuss the customers' role as a contributor to service quality, satisfaction, and value. Describe a time when you played this role. What did you do and how did you feel? Did the firm help you to perform your role effectively? How?
7. Discuss the customers' role as a potential competitor. Describe a time when you chose to provide a service for yourself rather than pay someone to provide the service for you. Why did you decide to perform the service yourself? What could have changed your mind, causing you to contract with someone else to provide the service?

●●●

20

Customer Retention and Relationship Marketing

20.1 INTRODUCTION

The major objective of 'relationship marketing' is to turn new customers into regularly purchasing clients, and then to progressively move them through being strong supporters of the company and its product, to finally being active and vocal advocates for the company.

The development of a closer, long-term relationship with customers is particularly important in certain types of service operation; namely when the service cannot be provided completely on one occasion, for instance, certain treatments at the dentist which require several visits, or a problem with a car which requires more than one visit to the mechanic. Similarly, if the service itself is highly intangible, the existence of a stronger relationship can be an important influence on a customer's decision to pay for the services of one provider in preference to another. If there is little tangible evidence available to assess the quality of the service on offer, customers frequently turn to the provider they have used before, whom they feel they can trust.

20.2 THE EVOLUTION OF RELATIONSHIP MARKETING

The formal study of marketing has focused on an evolving range of marketing sectors over the past few decades as shown in Figure 20.1.

Figure 20.1 : THE CHANGING FOCUS OF MARKETING

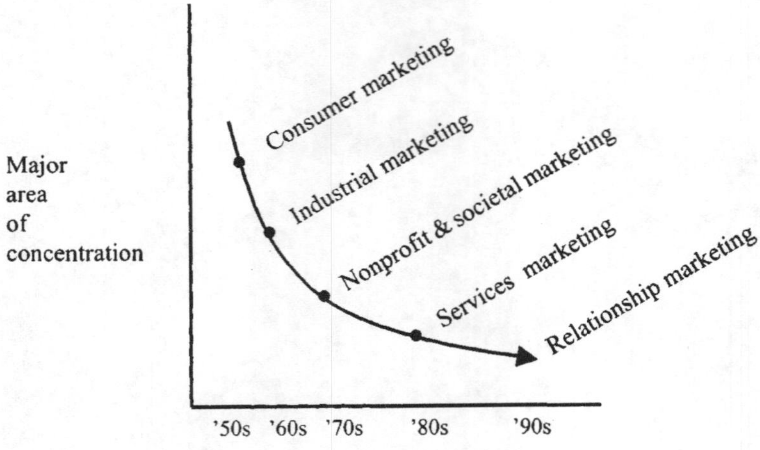

In the 1950s, marketing interest was primarily focused on consumer goods. In the 1960s, increased attention also started to be directed towards industrial markets. In the 1970s, considerable academic effort was placed on the area of non-profit or societal marketing. In the 1980s, attention started to be directed at the services sector, an area of marketing that had received remarkably little attention in view of its importance in the overall economy. In the 1990s, we believe that relationship marketing is the area that will receive increasing attention. This involves two major considerations. First, at a macro level, the recognition that marketing impacts on a wide range of areas including customer markets, employee markets, supply markets, internal markets, referral markets and influencer markets such as the governmental and financial markets; and second, at the micro level, the recognition that the nature of inter-relations with customers is changing. The emphasis is moving from a transaction focus to a relationship focus. These changes are characterized in Table 20.1.

Table 20.1 : TRANSACTION VERSUS RELATIONSHIP MARKETING

Transaction marketing	Relationship marketing
Focus on single sale	Focus on customer retention
Orientation on product features	Orientation on product benefits
Short time-scale	Long time-scale
Little emphasis on customer service	High customer service emphasis
Limited customer commitment	High customer commitment
Moderate customer contact	High customer contact
Quality is primarily a concern of production	Quality is the concern of all

Figure 20.2 : THE TRANSITION TO RELATIONSHIP MARKETING

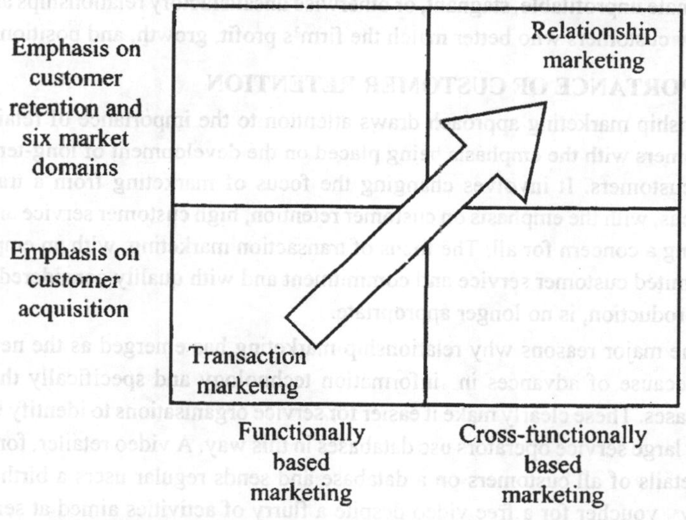

The transition from transaction marketing to relationship marketing (Figure 20.2) includes:

- A move from functionally-based marketing to cross -functionally based marketing
- A shift from marketing activities which have emphasis on customer acquisition to marketing activities which emphasise customer retention.
- An approach which addresses a total of six markets, not just the traditional customer market.

20.3 DEGREE OF RELATIONSHIP BUILDING

Kotler has identified five different levels of relationship marketing at which a firm may choose to operate.

(a) **Basic** : No lasting relationship is really established. The transaction is made and both parties go their own ways.

(b) **Reactive** : The seller offers to respond if the buyer has any problems.

(c) **Accountable** : The seller contacts the buyer after the sale to find out how the product has been received and whether it could have been better.

(d) **Proactive** : The seller calls the customer from time to time with updates on improvements to the product and other services to make the product's consumption more satisfying.

(e) **Partnership** : Both parties work together to find solutions to mutual problems and opportunities for mutual success. This arrangement is generally limited to business -to-business marketing.

20.4 PATHWAYS TO GROWTH

Service businesses can grow in one or more of the following ways:

1. Attract new customers.
2. Encourage existing customers to purchase more units of service
3. Encourage existing customers to purchase higher value services (for instance, travel first class rather than economy).
4. Reduce the extent of turnover -or "churn" -resulting from desirable customers withdrawing their patronage (a particular problem in easily terminated - subscription services such as cable television).
5. Terminate unprofitable, stagnant, or otherwise unsatisfactory relationships and replace them by new customers who better match the firm's profit, growth, and positioning goals.

20.5 THE IMPORTANCE OF CUSTOMER RETENTION

A relationship marketing approach draws attention to the importance of retaining as well as attracting customers with the emphasis being placed on the development of long-term relationships with existing customers. It involves changing the focus of marketing from a transactional to a relationship focus, with the emphasis on customer retention, high customer service and commitment, and quality being a concern for all. The focus of transaction marketing, with an emphasis on single transactions, limited customer service and commitment and with quality considered to be primarily a concern for production, is no longer appropriate.

One of the major reasons why relationship marketing has emerged as the new paradigm for marketing is because of advances in information technology and specifically the generation of customer databases. These clearly make it easier for service organisations to identify loyal customers. Both small and large service operators use databases in this way. A video retailer, for example, holds membership details of all customers on a database and sends regular users a birthday card with a complementary voucher for a free video despite a flurry of activities aimed at serving customers better, only a few companies have achieved meaningful, measurable improvements in customer loyalty. It would appear that although companies seem to agree that customer loyalty is a good thing, not so many are prepared to make loyalty retention measures an integral part of their strategy.

20.6 THE ENHANCEMENT OF INTERNAL AND EXTERNAL RELATIONSHIPS

Relationship marketing implies consideration of not just better relationships with customer markets, but also the development and enhancement of relationships with supplier, recruitment, internal, referral and influence markets.

Relationships with Suppliers

As far as relationships with suppliers are concerned, there is clear evidence that organisations are moving away from a traditionally adversial relationship to one based on mutual support and cooperation. There is increasing awareness of the benefits to be gained by working together to meet the needs of the final consumer. The specific relationship developed between the organisation and its suppliers has been termed 'co-makership'. In the relationship, the buyer recognises that fact that supplies are very much a part of the final products, and that working together with suppliers can increase the benefits to both parties. Benefits in this context have been found to include shorter delivery lead times, lower stock levels, fewer quality problems and faster implementation of design changes. Strategies aimed at improving relationships with suppliers also form part of what has been referred to in the service marketing literature as 'reverse marketing'.

Relationships with Recruitment Markets

Relationship marketing also involves having a closer relationship with those who supply human resources to the organisation, that is, recruitment markets. Service organisations need to cultivate long-term relationships with the suppliers of such employees to ensure that they receive both the right quantity and quality of employees.

Relationships with Internal Markets

Employees need to feel that they have formed a long-term relationship with the service provider and have a shared understanding of the mission of the organisation. Human resource strategies need to focus on internal markets and specifically on employee retention. The longer employees stay with the company, the more familiar they become with the business, the more they learn, and the more valuable they can be.

Relationships with Referral Markets

Specific strategies need to be devised to reward the referral sources that generate the most business. Although, traditionally, satisfied customers are the key referral source for service organisations, other sources might include suppliers, other agencies dealing with the company, for instance, banks, and in some cases even competitors.

Relationships with Influence Markets

Influence markets can also affect the strength of the relationship the organisation has with its customers like legislative bodies, political groups, and trade and consumer associations.

Alignment between Marketing, Customer Service and Quality

A relationship marketing orientation involves a closer alignment between three crucial areas, marketing, customer service and quality. Measures aimed at improving customer service levels have often been taken in isolation from quality initiatives. A true relationship marketing orientation would require all three areas to be linked together.

20.7 THE RELATIONSHIP CHAIN

Combining the relationship concept of marketing with the need for a cross-functional, coordinated focus on customers , leads us to the idea of the relationship management chain ('the relationship chain'- Figure 20.3).

Figure 20.3 : THE RELATIONSHIP MANAGEMENT CHAIN

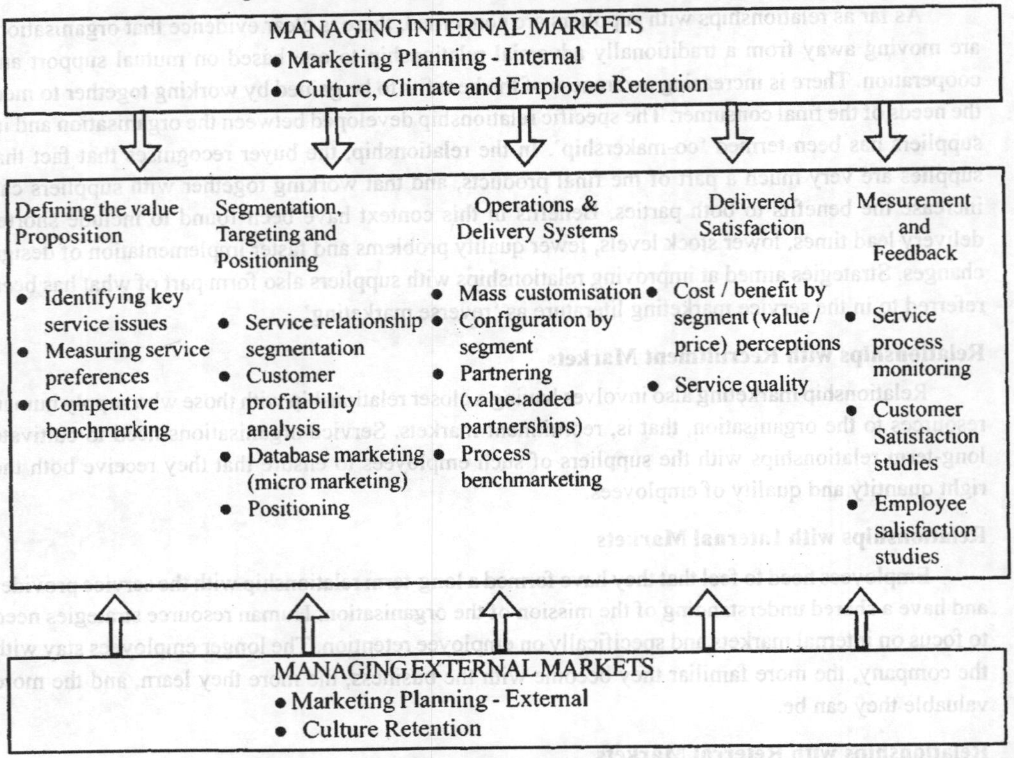

Relationship marketing is concerned with a much broader view of marketing in order to provide the best value proposition - in terms of both the product and service - it is necessary to consider a wider range of markets. A company should also consider developing marketing plans for supplier markets, referral markets, influence markets, recruitment markets and internal markets.

20.8 STRATEGIES

Service organizations use a number of strategies (framework shown in Figure 20.4) to move their customers through the stages of relationship development.

- The possibility of relationships developing can occur only where the parties are aware of each other and of their mutual desire to enter into exchange transactions. At this stage, the parties may have diverging views about the possibility of forming a long-term relationship. The supplier must be able to offer potential customers reasons why they should show disloyalty to their existing supplier. In some cases, low introductory prices are offered by service organizations which provide a sufficient incentive for disloyal customers of other companies to switch supplier.

  Non-price-related means of gaining attention include advertising and direct mail aimed at the market segments with whom relationships are sought. Over time, the supplier would seek to build value into the relationship so that customers would have little incentive for seeking lower-prices solutions elsewhere. Inevitably, sellers face risks in adopting segments of the population who are likely to show most disloyalty by withdrawing from the relationship at the point when it is just beginning to become profitable to the supplier.
- On entering into a relationship, buyers and sellers make a series of promises to each other. In the early stages of a relationship, suppliers' promises result in expectations being held by buyers

as to the standard of service that will actually be delivered. Many studies on service quality have highlighted the way in which the gap between expected and actual service performance determine customers' perception of quality. Quality in perceived service delivery is a prerequisite for a quality relationship being developed.

- At the first encounter, many service organizations record information about customers that will be useful in assessing their future needs. From an initial encounter, a travel agent can judge the type of service that a customer prefers and gradually refine this profile as subsequent transactions are undertaken. This can be used to build up a database from which customers are kept in touch with new-service developments of specific interest to them.

Figure 20.4 : RELATIONSHIP STRATEGY FRAMEWORK

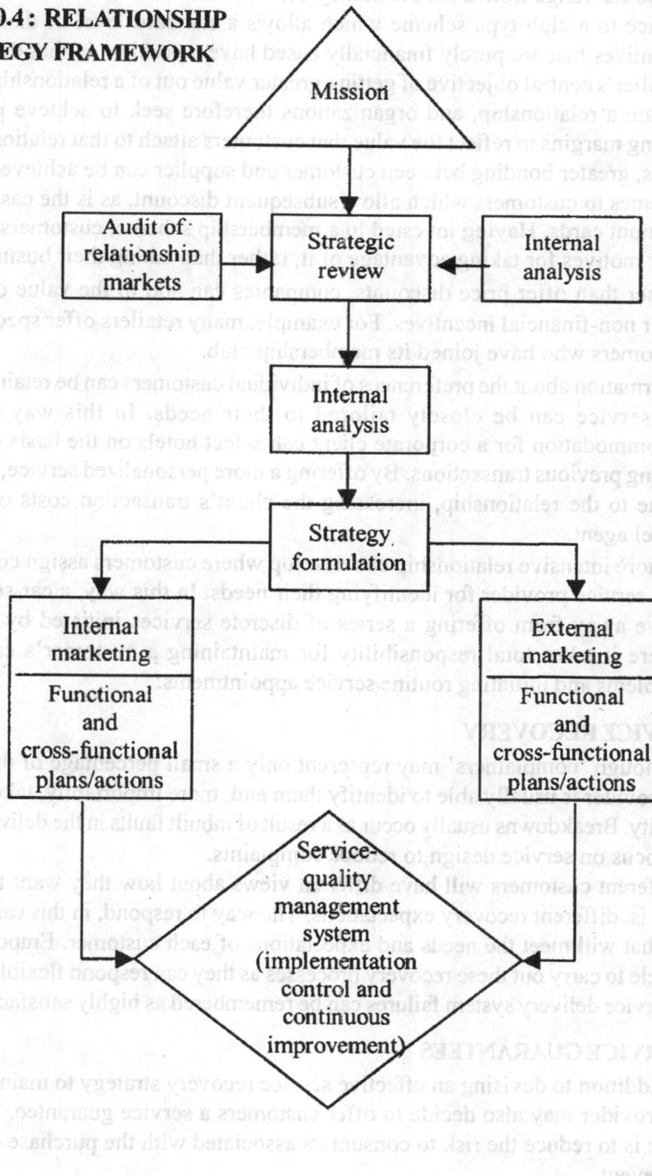

- At a relatively simple level, incentives for frequent users can help to develop short to medium-term loyalty-many airlines, for example, reward frequent business passengers with free or reduced-price leisure tickets.
- A strategy used by some companies is to create relationships by turning discrete service delivery into continuous delivery. In this way, bus companies offer season tickets valid at all times, which avoids customers having to make a choice-where it is available-between competing bus operators.
- Financial incentives are often given to customers as a reward for maintaining their relationship. These can range from a simple money-off voucher valid for a reduction in the price of a future service to a club type scheme which allows a standard level of discount for club members. Incentives that are purely financially based have a problem in that they can defeat the service supplier's central objective of getting greater value out of a relationship. It is often expensive to initiate a relationship, and organizations therefore seek to achieve profits at later stages by raising margins to reflect the value that customers attach to that relationship. However, in some cases, greater bonding between customer and supplier can be achieved by selling membership schemes to customers which allow subsequent discount, as is the case with a number of store discount cards. Having invested in a membership scheme, customers are likely to rationtalize their motives for taking advantage of it, rather than taking their business elsewhere.
- Rather than offer price discounts, companies can add to the value of relationship by giving other non-financial incentives. For example, many retailers offer special preview evenings for customers who have joined its membership club.
- Information about the preferences of individual customers can be retained so that future requests for service can be closely tailored to their needs. In this way a travel agent booking accommodation for a corporate client can select hotels on the basis of preferences expressed during previous transactions. By offering a more personalized service, the travel agent is adding value to the relationship, increasing the client's transaction costs of transferring to another travel agent.
- A more intensive relationship can develop where customers assign considerable responsibility to a service provider for identifying their needs. In this way, a car-service station attempts to move away from offering a series of discrete services initiated by customers to a situation where it takes total responsibility for maintaining a customer's car, including diagnosing problems and initiating routine service appointments.

20.9 SERVICE RECOVERY

Although 'complainers' may represent only a small percentage of dissatisfied customers, the service provider is usually able to identify them and, more importantly, take some action to maintain their loyalty. Breakdowns usually occur as a result of inbuilt faults in the delivery system. Organisations need to focus on service design to reduce complaints.

Different customers will have different views about how they want their problems to be dealt with, that is, different recovery expectations. The way to respond, in this case, is to design a recovery strategy that will meet the needs and expectations of each customer. Empowered employees are the best vehicle to carry out these recovery processes as they can respond flexibly as, and when, a problem arises. Service delivery system failures can be remembered as highly satisfactory if handled properly.

20.10 SERVICE GUARANTEES

In addition to devising an effective service recovery strategy to maintain customer loyalty, the service provider may also decide to offer customers a service guarantee. The basic function of the guarantee is to reduce the risk to consumers associated with the purchase decision, both before and after the event.

Guarantees can be given for many of the more tangible components of the service and are often used not only to reassure customers about the quality of the service they are likely to receive, but also to differentiate the service provided by one operator from another.

Service guarantee will be highest when one or more of the following conditions exist:

- The price of the service is high or perceived to be high by customers.
- The customer's personal reputation could be affected if the service goes wrong.
- The customer does not really understand whether the service has been carried out properly or not, that is, they do not have the relevant expertise to make a judgement.
- The negative consequence of service failure are high.
- The success of the company depends on frequent customer repurchases.
- The company's business is affected deeply by word of mouth.

20.11 THE 7-S FRAMEWORK

The 7-s framework of Mckinsey has been adopted here wherein strategy, shared values, style, structure, skills, staffing and systems are integrated to evolve a comprehensive system.

Strategy

- Integrated plan for development of marketing orientation
- Formalized definitions of markets and mission
- Detailed specification of marketing objectives
- Commitment to implementation

Shared values

- 'We will become a fully customer-driven organization'
- 'Customer come first'
- 'Marketing expenditures are an investment'
- 'Service is paramount'

Style

- Top management support for marketing through symbolic actions and commitment of time to marketing and customer-related activities.
- Open communications between all functional groups and marketing staff
- Recognition and reward of customer/market-oriented behaviour

Structure

- Simple structure based on markets/geography
- Key account sales structure to service most important customers
- Decentralized marketing staff to provide close and fast support to customers.
- Staff rotation of non-marketing staff through customer contact positions

Skills/Staffing

- Recruitment of an adequate number of people with requisite marketing skills
- Marketing training programs and facilities
- Knowledge of market
- Analytical skills in segmenting markets and identifying decision making units (DMU's)

Systems

- Customer intelligence reports
- Competitor intelligence reports
- Marketing planning and control systems
- Remuneration and performance appraisal systems geared to support marketing orientation

- Financial reporting systems reflecting product line contribution and profitability

The above framework is shown in Figure 20.5.

Figure 20.5 : THE 7-S FRAMEWORK

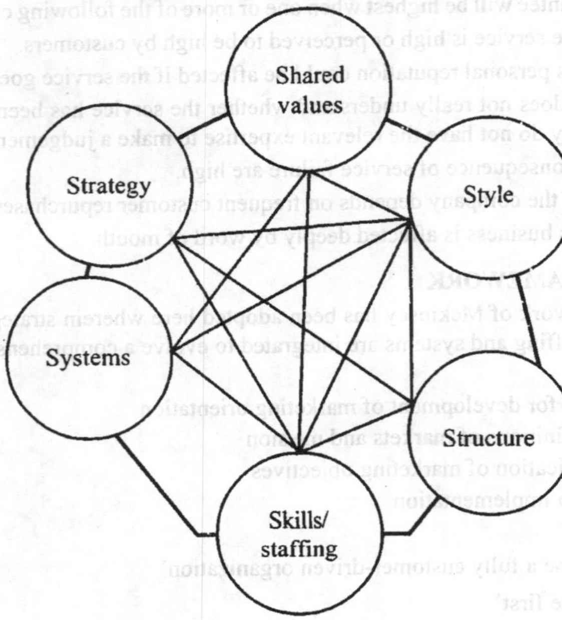

20.12 DETERMINING THE VALUE OF A CUSTOMER

A measure of customer value is called Customer Return on Assets (CRA). The basic idea is to measure the profitability of relationships with individual customers, something often overlooked by accounting systems that tend to focus more on product performance. Systems that measure revenue only, combined with a dedication to high service levels at any cost, are likely to lead to terrible misallocations of effort by the sales force and other customer relations personnel. Relationship managers should also be tracking the costs of maintaining relationships. These costs can be traced to individual accounts and include sales costs, service costs, and other costs related to serving the particular account (Table 20.2).

Table 20.2 : THE COMPUTATION OF CUSTOMER RETURN ON ASSETS

	Amount	Percent of Sales
Revenue	Rs. 542,893	100
less:		
a. Cost of labor (sales, equipment, materials)+	291,018	54
b. Reserves for damaged and returned merchandise+	7,573	1
c. Discounts and allowances	36,287	7
	334,878	62
= Gross margin	208,015	48

less:

a. Selling cost +	27,145	5
b. Promotion cost+	86,863	16
c. Product development cost+	5,423	1
d. Direct warehousing cost+	4,859	1
e. Customer freight cost+	3,435	1
f. Post-sale service cost+	55,144	10
	182,869	34
= Customer contribution to overhead [208,015-182,869]	25,146	5
divided by:		
a. Accounts receivable+	90,577	17
b. Inventory (finished goods)	11,531	2
	102,108	19
= Customer return on assets (CRA):	25,146 / 102,108 = **24.6%**	

20.13 LIFETIME VALUE OF A CUSTOMER

"If companies knew how much it really costs to lose a customer, they would be able to make accurate evaluations of investments designed to retain customers. Unfortunately, today's accounting systems do not capture the value of a loyal customer." One way of documenting the rupee value of loyal customers is to estimate the increased value of profits that accrue for each additional customer who remains loyal to the company rather than defecting to the competition.

Example : It is estimated that a 20-person office has approximately Rs. 75,000 per month in business with Professional Couriers. Assuming a 10-year average lifetime for a customer in the express mail industry, the value of the firm to Professional Couriers becomes:

Rs. 75,000/month x 12 months/year x 10 years = Rs. 90,00,000

Going even further, it can be estimated that in this industry a happy customer will create at least one new customer via word of mouth:

Rs. 90,00,000 x 2 new customers = Rs. 180,00,000

Thus the value of the company's business for Professional Couriers is about Rs. 180,00,000.

It can also be estimated that the average Professional Courier delivery person stops at 40 business houses each day:

Rs. 180,00,00/company x 40 companies = Rs. 720 million portfolio of lifetime business for the company.

Thus the average employee at Professional Couriers is managing Rs. 720 million portfolio of lifetime business for the Company.

Figure 20.6 shows a ladder wherein the customer moves from being a prospect to a partner in view of the fact that relationships foster customer loyalty.

Figure 20.6 : THE RELATIONSHIP MARKETING LADDER OF CUSTOMERS LOYALTY

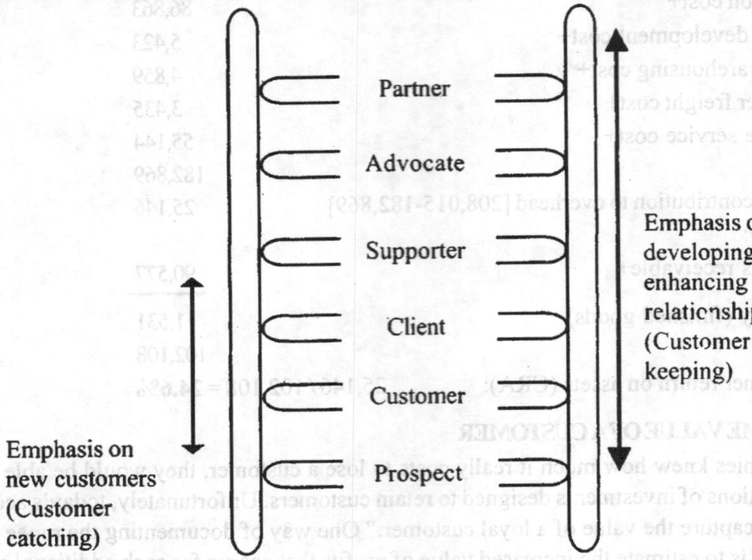

20.14 CUSTOMER RELATIONSHIP MANAGEMENT STRATEGIES

Two types of strategies, namely, solicited feedback and operations feedback are used to improve the activites of the organization. Various type of research are employed including customer expectation research, performance research, direct customer feedback research and process managnient reseach. The sources of data comprise customer satisfier survey, customer value tree, contact survey, benchmarking, commendations, suggestions, complaints, non-contact association, call monitoring, customer retention, ERC feedback, customer contact standards, customer contact monitoring and call type trend. The customers opinions and complaints must be listened to, both for short-term and long-term development. The short-term measures relate to modification of existing policies / procedures and standards. The long-term measures relate to integration of customer feedback into the strategic planning and product / service development process. The feedback mechanism should be continuous.

Figure 20.7 depicts the process of customer relationship management strategies.

The customer focus framework comprises four stages : Building of a shared vision, Designing to achieve high performance, Implementing change and Driving continuous improvement. The sixteen steps are shown in Figure 20.8.

20.15 TYPES OF RELATIONSHIP MARKETING (30 Rs)

The various types of relationships that exist in today's dynamic and complex world can be categorised broadly as:

(*a*) ***Classic*** market relationships,

(*b*) ***Special*** market relationships,

(*c*) ***Mega*** relationships and

(*d*) ***Nano*** relationships.

Figure 20.7 : CUSTOMER RELATIONSHIP MANAGEMENT STRATEGIES

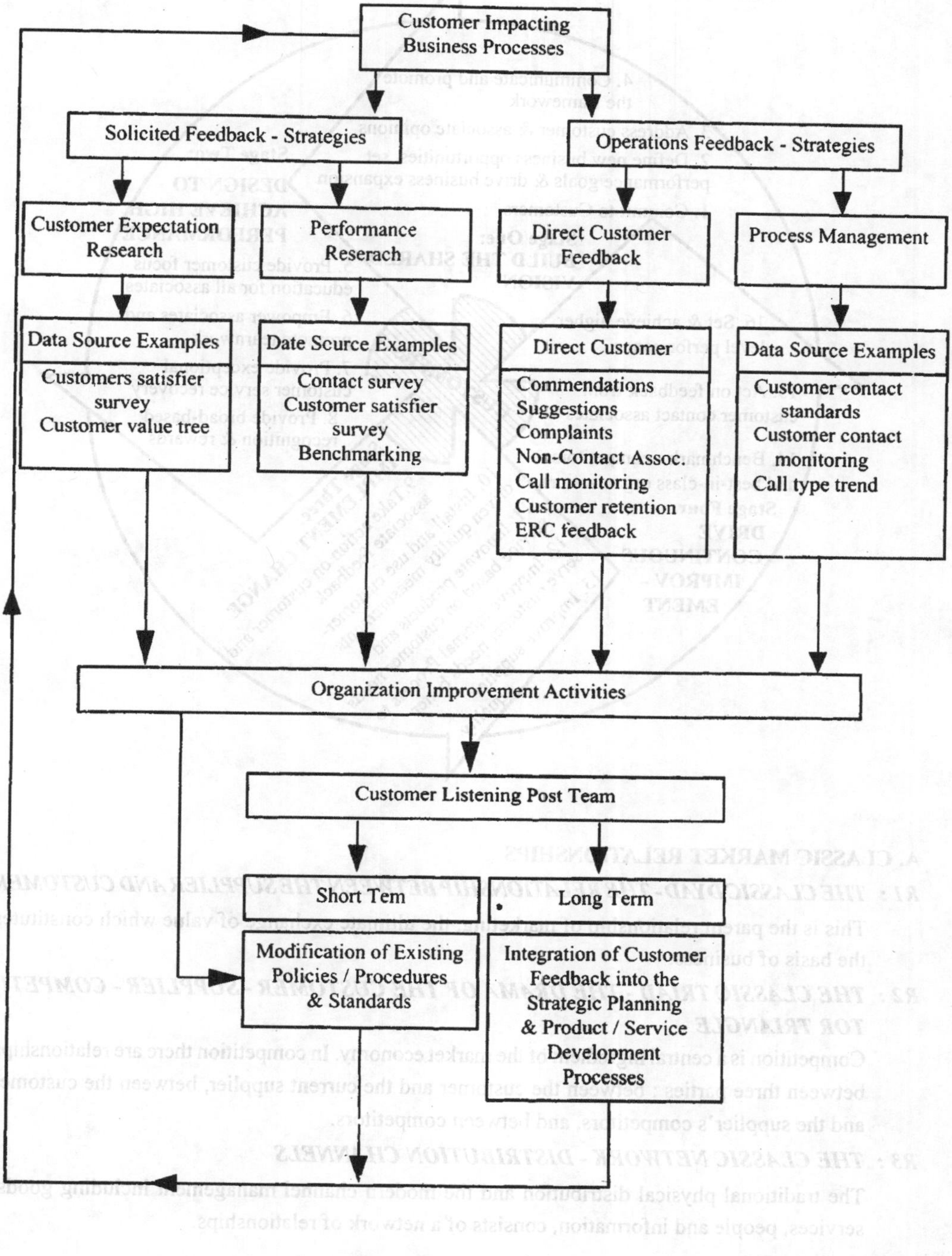

Figure 20.8 : THE CUSTOMER FOCUS FRAMEWORK

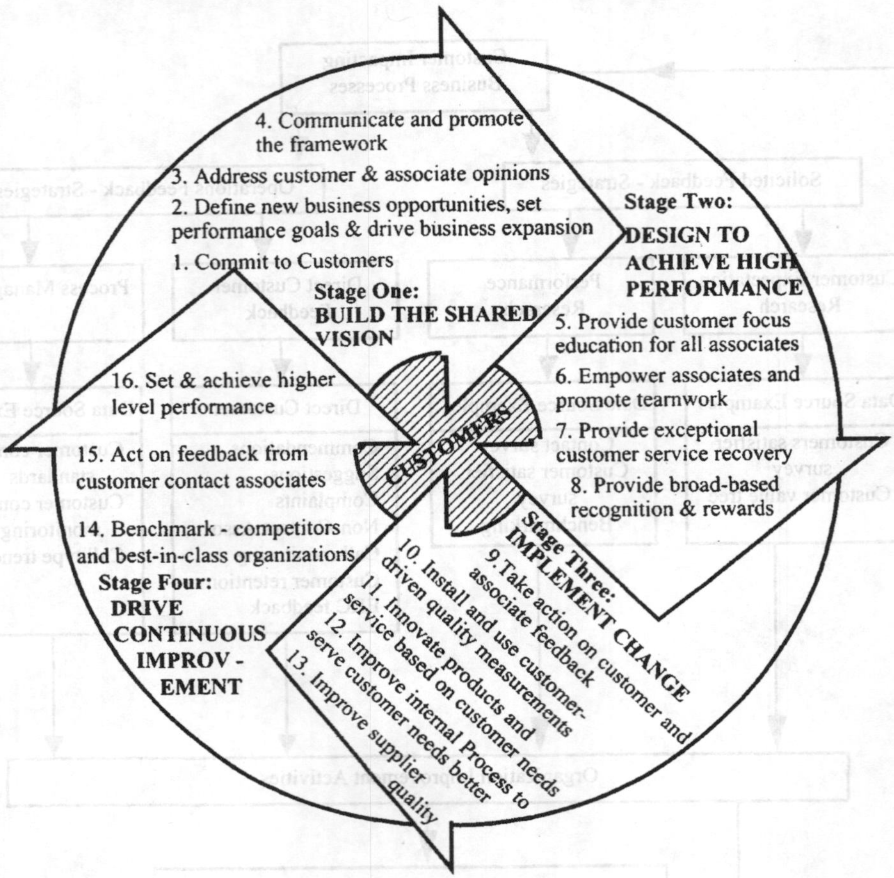

A. CLASSIC MARKET RELATIONSHIPS

R1 : THE CLASSIC DYAD - THE RELATIONSHIP BETWEEN THE SUPPLIER AND CUSTOMER

This is the parent relationship of marketing, the ultimate exchange of value which constitutes the basis of business.

R2 : THE CLASSIC TRIAD - THE DRAMA OF THE CUSTOMER - SUPPLIER - COMPETITOR TRIANGLE

Competition is a central ingredient of the market economy. In competition there are relationships between three parties : between the customer and the current supplier, between the customer and the supplier's competitors, and between competitors.

R3 : THE CLASSIC NETWORK - DISTRIBUTION CHANNELS

The traditional physical distribution and the modern channel management including goods, services, people and information, consists of a network of relationships.

B. SPECIAL MARKET RELATIONSHIPS

R4 : RELATIONSHIPS VIA FULL-TIME MARKETERS (FTMs) AND PART-TIME MARKETERS (PTMs)

Those who work in the marketing and sales departments - the FTMs - are professional relationship makers. All others, who perform other main functions but yet influence customer relationships directly or indirectly, are PTMs. There are also contributing FTMs and PTMs outside the organization.

R5 : THE SERVICE ENCOUNTER - INTERACTION BETWEEN THE CUSTOMER AND THE SERVICE PROVIDER

Production and delivery of services involve the customer in an interactive relationship with the service provider, often referred to as the moment of truth.

R6 : THE MANY- HEADED CUSTOMER AND THE MANY-HEADED SUPPLIER

Marketing to other organizations - industrial marketing or business marketing - often means contacts between many individuals from the supplier's and the customer's organization.

R7 : THE RELATIONSHIP TO THE CUSTOMER'S CUSTOMER

A condition for success is often the understanding of the customer's customer; and what suppliers can do to help their customers become successful.

R8 : THE CLOSE VERSUS THE DISTANT RELATIONSHIP

In mass marketing, the closeness of the customer is lost and the relationship becomes distant, based on surveys, statistics and written reports.

R9 : THE RELATIONSHIP TO THE DISSATISFIED CUSTOMER

The dissatisfied customer perceives a special type of relationship, more intense than the normal situation, and often badly managed by the provider. The way of handling a complaint - the recovery - can determine the quality of the future relationship.

R10 : THE MONOPOLY RELATIONSHIP : THE CUSTOMER OR SUPPLIERS AS PRISONERS

When competition is inhibited; the customer may be at the mercy of the supplier - or the other way round. One of then becomes the prisoner.

R11 : THE CUSTOMER AS 'MEMBER'

In order to create a long-term sustaining relationship, it has become increasingly common to enlist customers as members of various loyalty programmes.

R12 : THE ELECTRONIC RELATIONSHIP

Information technology - telecom, computers, TV - are elements of all types of marketing today and they now form new types of relationships.

R13 : PARA-SOCIAL RELATIONSHIPS - RELATIONSHIPS TO SYMBOLS AND OBJECTS

Relationships do not only exist concerning people and physical phenomena, but also to mental images and symbols such as brand names and corporate identities.

R14 : THE NON - COMMERCIAL RELATIONSHIP

This is a relationship between the public sector and citizens / customer, but it also includes voluntary organizations and other activities outside of the profit-based and monetarised economy, such as those performed in families.

R15 : THE GREEN RELATIONSHIP

Environmental and health issues has slowly but gradually increased in importance and are creating a new type of customer relationship through legislation, the voice of opinion-leading customers, changing behaviour of consumers and an extension of the customer-supplier relationships to encompass a recycling process.

R16 : THE LAW-BASED RELATIONSHIP

A relationship to a customer is sometimes founded primarily on legal contracts and the threat of litigation.

R17 : THE CRIMINAL NETWORK

Organised crime is built on tight and often impermeable networks guided by an illegal business mission. They exist around the world and are apparently growing but are not observed in marketing theory. These networks can disturb the functioning of a whole market or industry.

C. MEGA RELATIONSHIPS

R18 : PERSONAL AND SOCIAL NETWORKS

Personal and social networks often determine business networks. In some cultures even, business is solely conducted between friends and friends-of-friends.

R19 : MEGA MARKETING - THE REAL 'CUSTOMER' IS NOT ALWAYS FOUND IN THE MARKETPLACE

In certain instances, relationships must be sought with governments, legislators, influential individuals and others in order to make marketing feasible on an operational level.

R20 : ALLIANCES CHANGE THE MARKET MECHANISMS

Alliances mean closer relationships and collaborations between companies. Thus competition is partly curbed, but collaboration is necessary to make the market economy work.

R21 : THE KNOWLEDGE RELATIONSHIPS

Knowledge can be the most strategic and critical resource and 'knowledge acquisition' is often the rationale for alliances.

R22 : MEGA ALLIANCES CHANGE THE BASIC CONDITIONS FOR MARKETING

SAARC (South-Asian Association for Regional Cooperation) and ASEAN (Association of South-East Asian Nations) are examples of alliances above the single company and industry. They exist on a government and supranational levels.

R23 : THE MASS MEDIA RELATIONSHIP

The media can be supportive or damaging to marketing and they are particularly influential in forming public opinion. The relationship to media is crucial for the way media will handle an issue.

D. NANO RELATIONSHIPS

R24 : MARKET MECHANISMS ARE BROUGHT INSIDE THE COMPANY

By introducing profit centers in an organization, a market inside the company is created and internal as well as external relationships of a new kind emerge.

R25 : INTERNAL CUSTOMER RELATIONSHIP

The dependency between the different tiers and departments in a company is seen as a process consisting of the relationships between internal customers and internal suppliers.

R26 : QUALITY PROVIDING A RELATIONSHIP BETWEEN OPERATIONS MANAGEMENT AND MARKETING

The modern quality concept has built a bridge between design, manufacturing and other technology- based activities and marketing. It considers the company's internal relationships as well as its relationships to the customers.

R27 : INTERNAL MARKETING : RELATIONSHIPS WITH THE 'EMPLOYEE MARKET'

Internal marketing can be seen as a part of relationship marketing as it gives indirect and necessary support to the relationships with external customers.

R28 : THE TWO-DIMENSIONAL MATRIX RELATIONSHIP

Organisational matrices are frequent in large corporations, and above all, they are found in the relationships between product management and sales.

R29 : THE RELATIONSHIP TO EXTERNAL PROVIDERS OF MARKETING SERVICES

External providers reinforce the marketing function by supplying a series of services, such as those offered by advertising agencies and market research institutes, but also in the area of sales and distribution.

R30 : THE OWNER AND FINANCIER RELATIONSHIP

Owners and other financiers partly determine the conditions under which a marketing function can operate. The relationship to them influences the marketing strategy.

SHORT ANSWER QUESTIONS

1. What is the significance of customer retention?
2. List the degrees of relationship building.
3. What are the markets that are related to building customer relationships?
4. How doe service businesses grow?
5. What is the need for relationships? How do they alter service quality?
6. How will you estimate the life-time value of a customer. Explain with an example.
7. Discuss the concept of service recovery.
8. How is customer retention achieved?
9. What do you understand by relationship marketing?
10. Briefly explain the '6 markets' framework.
11. List the various types of relationships in service industries.
12. When is there said to a 'customer focus'?
13. How can relationships be built?

ESSAY QUESTIONS

1. How did the concept of relationship marketing emerge?
2. Explain the relationship management chain.
3. How will you determine the value of a customer. Give examples.
4. Write short notes on:
   (a) Classic market relationships
   (b) Special market relationships
   (c) Mega relationships
   (d) Nano relationships.

5. Develop a framework that focuses on the customer. What are the issues involved?
6. How are feedback and measurement systems employed? What are the related strategies?
7. What constitutes the relationship strategy framework? Explain its dimensions.
8. Enumerate the customer relationship management strategies?
9. Apply the 7-S framework for fostering relationships.
10. How can internal and external relationships be enhanced?
11. How does transaction marketing differ from relationship marketing?
12. How is satisfaction 'delivered'? What are the related strategies?
13. What are the conditions for highly valued service guarantees?
14. Enumerate relationships which have a negative shade? How can such relationships be curbed?
15. What are the ingredients that foster a good relationship chain?
16. Enumerate the special market relationships. Give examples from current happenings.
17. How do nano relationships differ from mega relationships?
18. Explain the relationship marketing ladder of customer loyalty? How can such loyalty be built?
19. What is CRA? What is its significance in terms of quality and profitability?
20. How can customer relationships be facilitated on the internet and other telecommunications media?

EXERCISE / ASSIGNMENT

1. Develop a plan to promote electronic relationships. What would be the likely obstacles?
2. How is the relationship chain linked to productivity? What category of relationships would you suggest for the following services?
   (a) Hotel (b) Tourism (c) Civil aviation (d) Post and Telegraph (e) Charities (f) Public utility.
3. Prepare a questionnaire for a IT industry which centres on various aspects of relationship building? Suggest measures for improvement based on the findings of the study.
4. Take any three services in your neighbourhood. Ascertain the gaps in relationships. Suggest suitable strategies to improve the relationships.
5. Study any service organisation of your choice. Trace its history in terms of customer retention and relationship building. Use illustrations.
6. Devise campaign plans that help in establishing relationships on a one-to-one basis.
7. Suggest innovative methods of creating and sustaining relationships in the service industries.

●●●

21

Service Leadership

21.1 INTRODUCTION

Companies that are viewed as leaders in a particular service industry - set the standards for service quality, recognize for initiating important innovations, and define the terms on which other companies seek to compete.

Realistically, it's very difficult for a firm to achieve and maintain leadership in an industry if it lacks human leaders.

The qualities that are often ascribed to leaders in general include vision, charisma, persistence, high expectations, expertise, empathy, persuasiveness and integrity.

Personnel-related activities in a modern service corporation can be subsumed under four broad policy areas.

1. ***Human resource flow*** is concerned with ensuring that the right number of people and mix of competencies are available to meet the firm's long-term strategic requirements. Issues include recruitment, training, career development and promotions.
2. ***Work systems*** involve all tasks associated with arranging people, information, facilities and technology to create (or support) the service produced by the organization.
3. ***Reward systems*** send powerful messages to all employees as to what kind of organization management seeks to create and maintain, especially as to desired attitudes and behaviour. Not all rewards are financial in nature; recognition may be a powerful motivator.
4. ***Employee influence*** relates to employee inputs concerning business goals, pay, working conditions, career progression, employment security and the design and implementation of work tasks. The movement towards greater empowerment of employees represents a shift in the nature and extent of employee influence.

21.2 THE THREE IMPERATIVES

Changing traditional organizational perspectives doesn't come readily to managers who have been comfortable with established approaches. It's easy for them to become obsessed with their own function, forgetting that all areas of the company must pull together to create a customer-driven organization. Achieving the necessary coordination and synergy requires that top management establish clear imperatives for each function (Figure 21.1).

Each imperative should relate to customers and define how the function in question contributes to the overall mission. Although a firm will need to phrase each imperative in ways that are specific to its own business, we can express them generically as follows:

The marketing imperative

The firm will target specific types of customers whom it is well equipped to serve, and then create ongoing relationships with them by delivering a carefully defined product package of all actions and reactions' that they desire to purchase. Customers will recognize this package as being one of consistent quality that delivers solutions to their needs and offers superior value to competing alternatives.

Figure 21.1 : INTEGRATING THREE FUNCTIONAL IMPERATIVES

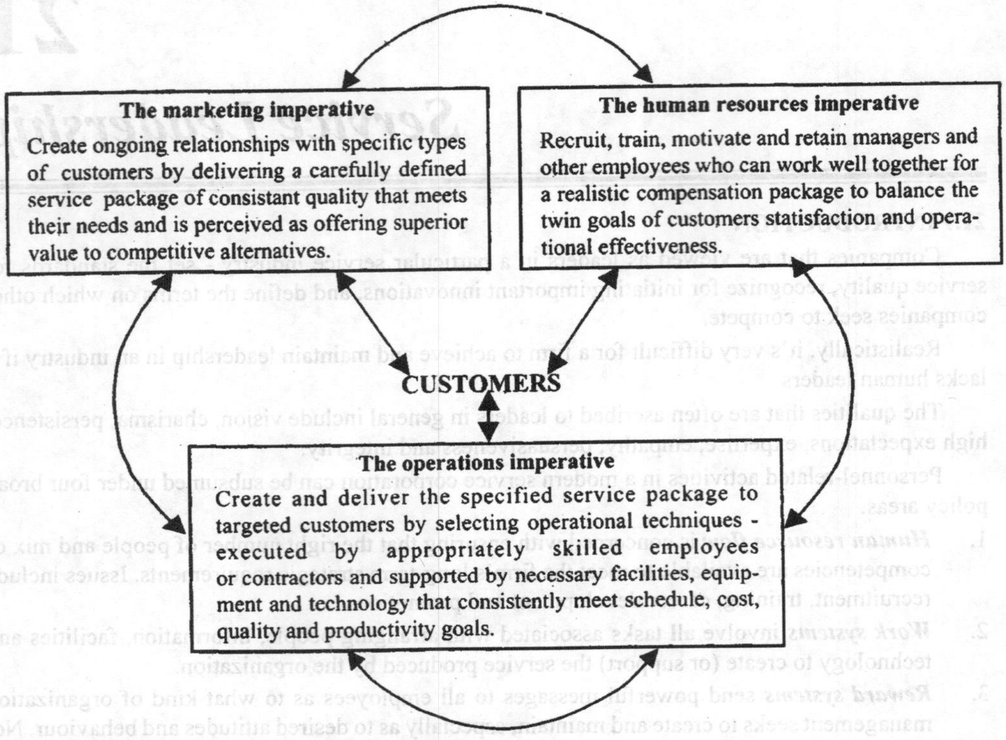

The operations imperative

To create and deliver the specified service package to targeted customers, the firm will select those operational techniques that allow it to consistently meet customer-driven cost, schedule and quality goals, and also enable the business to reduce its costs through continuing improvements in productivity. The chosen operational methods will match skills that employees or contractors currently possess or can be trained to develop. The firm will have the resources not only to support these operations with the necessary facilities, equipment and technology, but also to avoid negative impacts on employees and the broader community.

The human resources imperative

The firm will recruit, train and motivate managers, supervisors and employees who can work well together for a realistic compensation package to balance the twin goals of customer satisfaction and operational effectiveness. People will want to stay with the firm and to enhance their own skills because they value the working environment, appreciate the opportunities that it presents, and take pride in the services they help to create and deliver.

21.3 REDUCING INTRA-ORGANIZATIONAL TENSION

Top management's responsibility is to develop structures and procedures that harness the energy of managers in different departments, rather than allowing it to be dissipated in inter-functional disputes or permitting one department to dominate (and thereby frustrate) the others. There are a number of ways in which service firms seek to reduce inter-functional tension.

Transfers and cross-training

One approach is to transfer management from one functional department to another to ensure better understanding of differing perspectives. By working in another department, the transferred manager learns the language and concepts of the other function, understands its opportunities and constraints, and recognizes how its priorities are established. A related approach is to cross-train managers and employees to perform a broader variety of tasks, rather than remaining narrow specialists.

Creating cross-functional task forces

Another approach is to create a task force for a specific project, such as planning the introduction of a new service, improving quality or enhancing productivity. Some groups are normally formed on a temporary basis with a defined deadline for completing a specific task. Ideally, groups should be composed of individuals from each functional area who are well attuned to the others' viewpoints. In operations, this means looking for what one manager has termed 'field hands' - personnel who are practical and understand how to deal with people, rather than being totally systems and technology-oriented. For marketers, task force membership requires an orientation towards operating systems and what is involved in making them work from both a staffing and technical perspective; it doesn't necessarily require detailed technical training or an understanding of the inner workings of technology.

Task force participants should represent a microcosm of the organization yet be insulated from the pressures and distractions of day-to-day management activities. Properly planned and managed, the team environment provides a forum for discussion and resolution of many of the problems likely to occur during, say, the development and commercialization of an innovative service. There needs to be an external mechanism for settling any disputes which task force members cannot resolve among themselves. When a marketing manger is assigned the leadership role, top management's commitment to this individual must be explicit, because it flies in the face of the traditional seniority of operations.

New tasks and new people

Organizational change requires that new relationships be developed, jobs redefined, priorities restructured and existing patterns of thought and behaviour modified - often sharply. There are two schools of thought here. One involves taking the existing players and redirecting them. The other calls for replacing these people with new ones. The extent to which replacement is feasible depends not only on organizational policies and procedures, but also on the availability of suitable new people - either outside or inside the firm. Larger firms obviously have a bigger pool of people on whom to draw; they have mangers and specialists in other divisions or regions who have not been 'contaminated' by close exposure to the activity in question, yet are sufficiently knowledgeable about the organization that they can quickly be productive in a new project.

Process management teams

A more permanent form of team is that which is organized around a specific process. In a marketing context, this approach may include brand management organizations created to plan and coordinate the design and delivery of all frontstage elements for a particular product. One example is found in the brand management teams that are responsible for planning and managing each of the different classes of service offered by an international airline. Another example is found in the executive operating committees that manage individual hotel units in a chain.

Instituting gain-sharing programmes

These programmes allow employees to share in improved profits (or in the cost savings achieved at a nonprofit organization). The most significant form of sharing in the fortunes of a business comes through employee stock ownership programmes (ESOPs), especially when participation is broadly based and employees own a substantial share of the equity.

21.4 MARKETING ACTIVITIES AT DIFFERENT LEVELS IN THE ORGANIZATION

Large, dispersed service businesses are usually divided into operating regions, and sometimes subdivided into territories or divisions. In international markets, four different levels may exist:

headquarters, countries, regions and units. An important issue is what marketing tasks should be undertaken at what levels. Much depends on the degree of autonomy assigned to each level of operating management: is the product standardized or do unit (or territory or regional) managers have authority to customize? Even if the product is standardized, are country, regional or unit variations in pricing, delivery and communications appropriate? In an international context, a key strategic issue underlying such decisions is whether the firm wishes to operate on a truly transnational basis or whether it is content to preside over a loose confederation of largely independent national subsidiaries.

Staff marketing functions are most commonly associated with the head office. But in large service businesses where marketing strategies and markets must necessarily vary widely from unit to unit, certain staff functions may be performed at the country, regional or even unit level. The trade-off is one of responsiveness to local conditions versus the operating efficiencies and depth of expertise that can be obtained from centralization.

Where line marketing functions are concerned, another important issue is whether it makes sense to focus on geographic market segments served from the closest operating unit as opposed to segmenting customers in other ways and serving them across a broader geographic area. One of the great benefits of international expansion for a firm that targets a narrow niche in the market is that it can increase its market potential without departing from its niche focus. For information-based services, which can be delivered electronically, geographic segmentation may become irrelevant when there is little need for face-to-face contacts between customers and service personnel. Instead, segmentation may be based on other, more relevant criteria, such as language, national law, level of benefits desired and willingness to pay for them, usage frequency, and so forth.

21.5 ENSURING THAT SERVICE ENCOUNTERS ARE CUSTOMER-ORIENTED

One reason why a customer orientation has to extend well beyond the marketing function in a service business relates to service encounters between customers and service employees.

Frontstage procedures are those experienced by the consumer. In the case of low-contact services, such procedures represent a very small proportion of the service firm's total activities. For instance, the extent of personal contact between customers and credit card companies is limited to receiving and paying a monthly statement, and an occasional letter or telephone call if problems arise. Tasks such as review of credit card applications, credit checks and processing of credit card slips all take place behind the scenes.

By contrast, in a high-contact service such as a hotel the customer is exposed to the physical facilities and is likely to have service encounters with numerous hotel personnel, ranging from telephone reservation agent to doorman, from porter to receptionist, and from waiter/waitress to housekeeper. Whatever the nature of service encounters, they should be designed and executed with customer needs in mind.

21.6 IMPROVING CUSTOMER SERVICE IN RESPONSE TO COMPETITIVE PRESSURES

As business in general - and the service sector in particular - becomes more competitive, the need for meaningful competitive differentiation is sharpened. Increasingly this differentiation includes a search for superior performance not only on the core product but also on each of the supplementary service elements Achieving such differentiation requires a commitment to formalize standards for all service encounters that might reasonable by anticipated, in ways that reflect the nature of the industry, the culture of the organization and its desired position in the market. The necessary management tasks will require coordination between managers from different functional backgrounds. These task will require coordination between managers from different functional backgrounds. These tasks will include:

1. Conducting ongoing research to determine customer needs, wants and satisfaction levels concerning each of their service encounters.
2. Identifying the key sources of customer satisfaction (or dissatisfaction) and relating them to current service elements.
3. Setting service-level standards for different tasks.

4. Designing jobs and technological systems to meet these standards.
5. Periodically revising standards and delivery systems in the light of changing customer preferences, technological innovation and competitive activities.

Poor performance may include bad manners as well as substandard operational execution. In this instance, the responsibility of an expanded human resources function includes training in human relations skills as part of developing a stronger customer perspective on the part of all contact personnel.

21.7 CUSTOMER SERVICE UMBRELLA

In terms of job assignments, customer service may involve people who:

- provide information and technical advice in their capacity as members of the sales support staff;
- take orders and reservations over the phone and pass them along to those individuals responsible for order fulfillment;

Figure 21.2 : ESSENCE OF LEADERSHIP MODEL

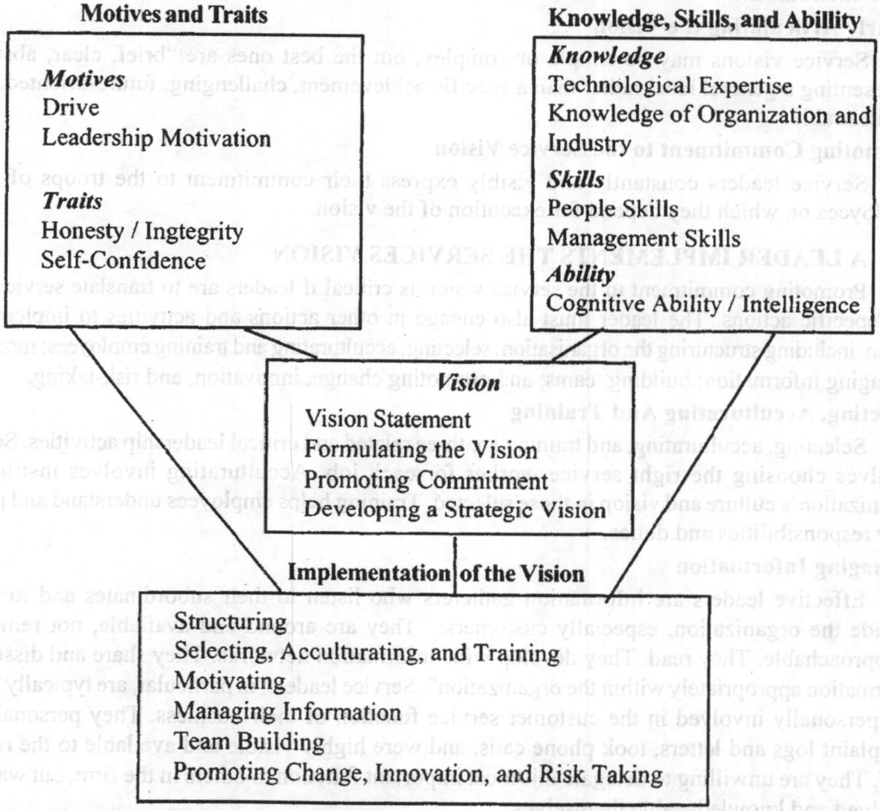

- communicate with customers following receipt of orders or reservations to provide information on availability, advise on shipping dates or reservation details, confirm shipment or trace missing orders;
- greet customers on arrival at a service facility, offer refreshments and attend to other needs;
- take responsibility for customers' cars, bags, coats or other possessions while they are at a service facility;
- maintain contact with customers while supervising assembly or completion of special or customized orders;
- schedule transportation and expedite deliveries to customers;
- handle installation and repairs.

21.8 A LEADER CREATES A SERVICE VISION

A leader must first have developed a mental image of a possible and desirable future state of the organization. This image, which we call vision, may be as vague as a dream or as precise as a goal or a mission statement. The critical point is that a vision articulates a view of a realistic, credible, attractive future for the organization, a condition that is better in some important ways than what now exists. A vision is a target that beckons (Figure 21.2).

Synthesizing the Vision

The ability to integrate information of various types is essential in creating a service vision. Synthesizing a vision requires foresight, to ensure that the vision will be appropriate for the future environment; hindsight, so that organizational tradition and culture are not overly violated; a world-view, to capitalize on the impact of new developments and trends; depth perception, to see the whole picture in detail and perspective; and peripheral vision, to foresee possible responses from competitors. The process must also include a mechanism for revision, so that the vision will reflect future changes in the environment.

Clearly Articulating the Vision

Service visions may be simple or complex, but the best ones are "brief, clear, abstract in representing a general ideal rather than a specific achievement, challenging, future-oriented, stable, and desirable.

Promoting Commitment to the Service Vision

Service leaders constantly and visibly express their commitment to the troops of service employees on which they depend for execution of the vision.

21.9 A LEADER IMPLEMENTS THE SERVICES VISION

Promoting commitment to the service vision is critical if leaders are to translate service vision into specific actions. The leader must also engage in other actions and activities to implement the vision, including structuring the organisation; selecting, acculturating and training employees; motivating; managing information; building teams; and promoting change, innovation, and risk-taking.

Selecting, Acculturating And Training

Selecting, acculturating, and training are three related and critical leadership activities. Selecting involves choosing the right service worker for each job. Acculturating involves instilling the organization's culture and vision in those selected. Training helps employees understand and perform their responsibilities and duties.

Managing Information

Effective leaders are information gatherers who listen to their subordinates and to sources outside the organization, especially customers: "They are around and available, not remote and unapproachable. They read. They develop wide information networks. They share and disseminate information appropriately within the organization". Service leaders, in particular, are typically "deeply and personally involved in the customer service function of their business. They personally read complaint logs and letters, took phone calls, and were highly visible and available to the rank and file". They are unwilling to delegate this most important function to others in the firm, but want to be involved and knowledgeable themselves.

Leaders who keep their ears tuned to employees are using upward communication to understand the activities and performance in the company. Specific types of communication that may be relevant are formal (e.g., reports of problems and exceptions in service delivery) and informal (e.g., discussions between contact people and upper-level managers). Leaders who stay close to their contact people benefit not only by keeping their employees happy but also by learning more about the customer.

Building Teams

Service leaders need to build cooperation among their followers, to teach subordinates to work effectively together to achieve goals. Amount the strategies used to ensure that employees work together are creating cooperative goals that can only be reached together, using project teams and task forces, and implementing group-based reward systems. Building an effective top-management team - to demonstrate to all the organization that teamwork is essential - is symbolic as well as practical.

21.10 KEY ELEMENTS

The key elements of the horizontal corporation are:

1. Organize around process, not task. Build three to five "core processes", with specific performance goals. Assign an "owner" to each process.
2. Flatten the hierarchy by eliminating work that fails to add value.
3. Use teams to manage everything; giving teams a common purpose and limiting supervision.
4. Let customers drive performance, making customer satisfaction (rather than profits or stock appreciation) the measure of performance.
5. Reward team performance rather than just individual performance.
6. Maximize supplier and customer contact.
7. Inform and train all employees and entrust employees with data.

21.11 THE SIX DIMENSIONS AND STYLES OF SERVICE LEADERSHIP

Figure 21.3 shows the six dimensions of service leadership namely vision and values; direction; persuasion; support; development and appreciation.

Figure 21.3 : THE SIX DIMENSIONS OF SERVICE LEADERSHIP

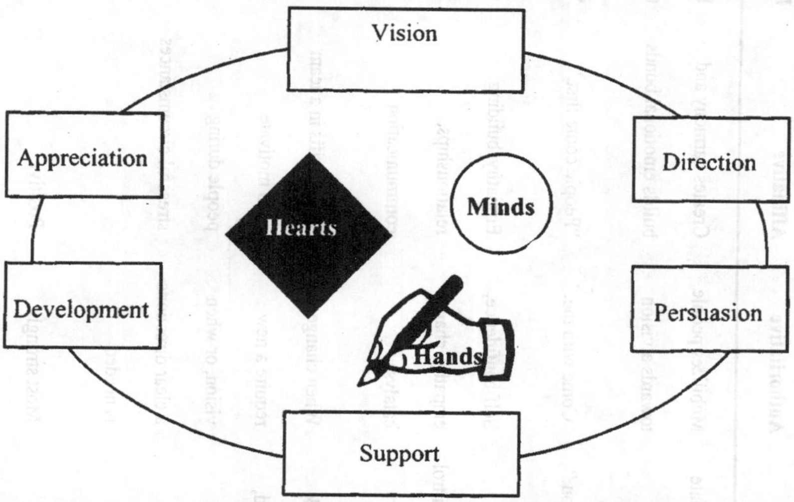

The six styles of leadership comprises Coercive, Authoritative, Affiliative, Democratic, Pacesetting and Coaching. These styles have been summarised in Table 21.1. In the coercive style, immediate compliance is demanded and its overall impact on the climate is negative. The authoritative style mobilises people towards a vision and its overall impact on the climate is mostly strongly positive. The affiliative style creates harmony and builds and emotional bonds. Its impact on climate is positive. Forging consensus through participation is the essence of democratic style and it has a positive impact on the climate. The pacesetting style sets high standards for performance and has a negative impact on the climate. The coaching style develops people for the future and has a positive impact on climate.

While the coercive style works best in a crisis, the authoritative style can be employed for facilitating changes. The affiliative style is used to relieve stress and close gaps. The democratic style is used to assimilate inputs and the pacesetting style for quick results. The coaching style is employed for long-term development.

Table 21.1 : THE SIX LEADERSHIP STYLES

	Coercive	Authoritative	Affiliative	Democratic	Pacesetting	Coaching
The leader's modus operandi	Demands immediate compliance	Mobilizes people towards a vision	Creates harmony and builds emotional bonds	Forges consensus through participation	Sets high standards for performance	Develops people for the future
The style in a phrase	"Do what I tell you."	"Come with me."	"People come first."	"What do you think?"	"Do as I do, now."	"Try this."
Underlying emotional intelligence competencies	Drive to achieve, initiative, self-control	Self-confidence, empathy, change catalyst	Empathy, building relationships, communication	Collaboration, team leadership, communication	Conscientiousness, drive to achieve, initiative	Developing others, empathy, self-awareness
When the style works best	In a crisis, to kick start a turnaround, or with problem employees	When changes require a new vision, or when a clear directions is needed	To heal rifts in a team or to motivate people during stressful circumstances	To build buy-in or consensus, or to get input from valuable employees	To get quick results from a highly motivated and competent team	To help an employee improve performance or develop long-term strengths
Overall impact on climate	Negative	Most strongly positive	Positive	Positive	Negative	Positive

21.12 LEADERSHIP SKILLS

The various skills required by a leader are depicted in Figure 21.4. The leadership should be focused on customer service as well as building employee competencies. The leader must encourage the employees to take initiative and to settle complaints quickly. He or she must encourage the assimilation of business knowledge and problem-solving skills. Team building and associative values must be fostered. Two-way communication must be facilitated and the employees must be empowered to take key decisions which are appropriate for the situation on hand. The concept of internal marketing must be dilligently promoted to create leadership qualities. Changes, based on feedback, must be implemented and resistance to change must be deftly handled. Adequate training and development and personal counselling would go a long way in making the employees understand the management's vision.

Figure 21.4 : LEADERSHIP SKILLS

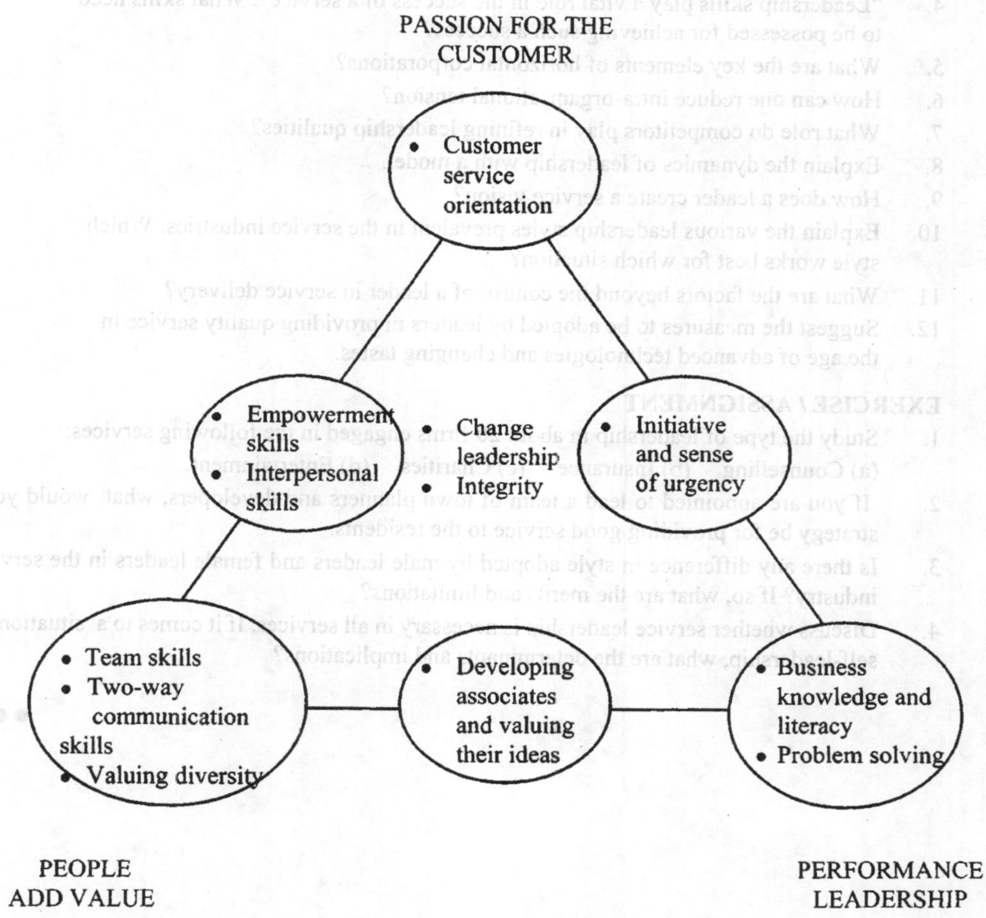

SHORT ANSWER QUESTIONS

1. What are the policy areas that deal with service leadership?
2. What do you understand by 'vision'? What sort of vision should leaders have?
3. List the different types of leadership styles.
4. Briefly explain the six dimensions of service leadership.
5. What is a customer service 'umbrella'? What is its link to leadership?
6. What do you understand by 'leadership style'?
7. Who is a leader? What type of service should he propagate?
8. Should leaders follow their heart of their mind? Give examples.
9. How do leaders manage information?
10. Describe the personality of an ideal leader.

ESSAY QUESTIONS

1. Do leaders in service industries have a vision? Justify your answer.
2. What are the imperatives for service leadership? What are the related issues?
3. How does a leader implement the service vision?
4. "Leadership skills play a vital role in the success of a service". What skills need to be possessed for achieving such a success?
5. What are the key elements of horizontal corporations?
6. How can one reduce intra-organisational tension?
7. What role do competitors play in refining leadership qualities?
8. Explain the dynamics of leadership with a model.
9. How does a leader create a service vision?
10. Explain the various leadership styles prevalent in the service industries. Which style works best for which situation?
11. What are the factors beyond the control of a leader in service delivery?
12. Suggest the measures to be adopted by leaders in providing quality service in the age of advanced technologies and changing tastes.

EXERCISE / ASSIGNMENT

1. Study the type of leadership in about 20 firms engaged in the following services:
   (a) Counselling (b) Insurance (c) Charities (d) Entertainment.
2. If you are appointed to lead a team of town planners and developers, what would your strategy be for providing good service to the residents.
3. Is there any difference in style adopted by male leaders and female leaders in the service industry? If so, what are the merits and limitations?
4. Discuss whether service leadership is necessary in all services. If it comes to a situation of self-leadership, what are the determinants and implications?

●●●

22

Service Profitability and Productivity

22.1 THE MEANING OF PRODUCTIVITY

The problem of productivity measurement is fundamental to any discussion of productivity in the service sector. Productivity is usually defined as the ratio of output of a production process to an aggregate value of inputs. As traditionally conceived the productivity concept contains two important assumptions:

a. that output and the factors of production are perfectly defined, homogeneous and can be measured. If these criteria can be met then it is possible to calculate the contribution of each factor of production, and changes in the input-output ratio resulting from changes in the use of factors. In addition information on the attainment of objectives and feedback on the consequences of action taken may be made and productivity trends compared.

b. the utility of the output is not questioned. It is assumed that there are no side effects beyond the satisfaction engendered by consumption of the goods produced. In other words, the traditional conception of productivity isolates the production process from the social setting: it assumes closed system characteristics.

The problems of measuring productivity in the service sector, therefore, stem from the continued use of traditional measures designed for goods contexts rather than services contexts. New kinds of measures have to be devised to take account of certain important characteristics of services and their marketing which influence productivity assessments. In particular the fact that services are ' performed' and not 'produced'; that services facilities must exist before they can be used; that services cannot be stockpiled; all have an influence upon the scope for productivity improvement. Another factor that influences productivity measurement is that many service settings are open systems, subject to external influences, rather than closed systems. Also with traditional productivity measures, quality is assumed to be constant; in the service sector of course quality varies greatly. One can increase the number of patients seen by a doctor but what of the quality of subsequent health care? One can increase the number of students taught by a lecturer but what effect might this have on the quality of their education?

The consumer's role in service productivity derives from the fact that:

a. Goods are produced whereas services are performed and the customer may be involved and. present while the service is being performed;

b. the place of marketing in the exchange process is different.

Productivity measures in services then require both quantitative and qualitative dimensions. In fact, in many services settings the qualitative dimensions of the service product (e.g. restaurants, business consultants) are fundamental in any consideration of productivity. A hypothetical positioning of major services classes according to their qualitative - quantitative mix has been proposed. It suggests that conventional productivity measures are less appropriate for the services shown on the right of Figure 22.1.

Figure 22.1 : PRODUCTIVITY OF SERVICES : OUTPUT MEASURES

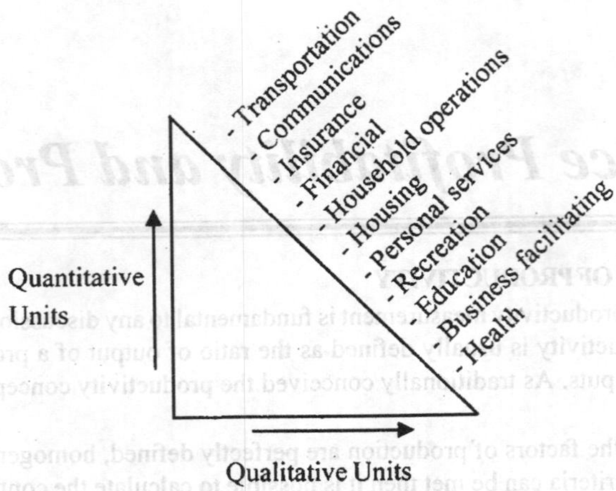

A final difficulty in measuring productivity in services is due to the linkage of demand for certain services with the demand for the output of other firms or agencies. The productivity of a consulting engineer or of an educational institution or of a fire service rests upon the value of the service provided to other individuals and institutions in the system affected by the services provided. There are great problems involved in evaluating the contribution of a service at such a general level and social costs and benefits enter any consideration of productivity in these settings.

22.2 THE PRODUCTIVITY FRAMEWORK

Two words in Figure 22.2 are frequently mentioned in everyday discussion often without clear understanding of their meaning. They are used loosely and often interchangeably. The words are, of course, efficiency and effectiveness. The meanings will become clearer as we look at some examples. However, in general they can be defined as follows:

- ***Efficiency*** - rate at which inputs are converted into outputs, e.g. calls per sales representative; customers served per catering assistant. The emphasis is often on quantitative measurement and the objective is one of securing the maximum output from the minimum input.
- ***Effectiveness*** - extent to which purposes/goals are achieved, e.g. the number of productive and profitable calls per sales representative and the nature of customer relationships established and fostered; the number of satisfied customers served per catering assistant. The emphasis is on qualitative measurement and the objective one of meeting customer needs and delivering service quality.

The distinction between efficiency and effectiveness has been defined as 'doing things right' (efficiency) and 'doing right things' (effectiveness). What this amounts to is that efficiency is 'the rate of which inputs are converted into outputs' and effectiveness ' the extent to which purposes are being achieved'.

Figure 22.2 : THE PRODUCTIVITY FRAMEWORK

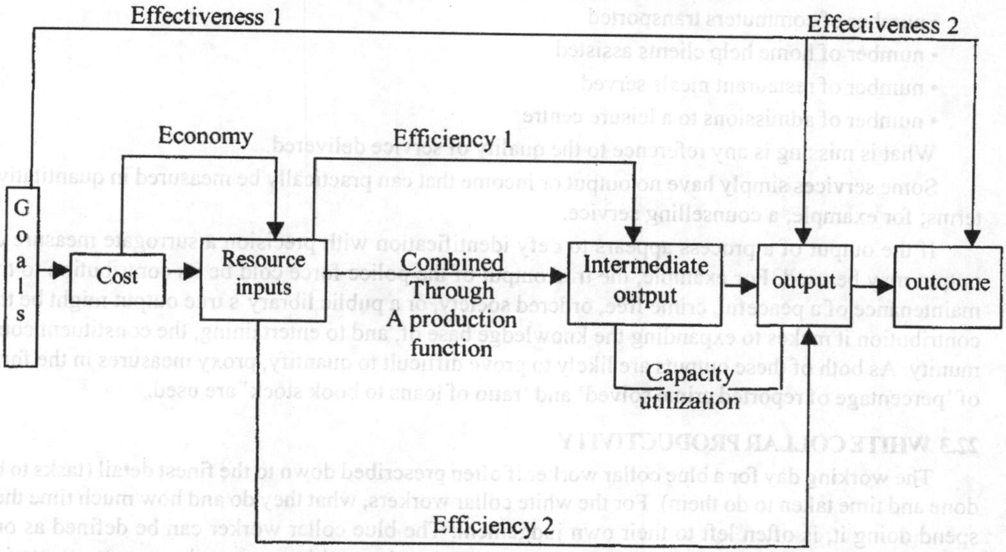

Figure 22.2 offers a guide to developing an understanding of the various elements and their relationships:

- ***Economy***: the cost of selecting and hiring people, materials and equipment and conversion through training and installation into resource inputs capable of providing service. It is not a measure of performance, but can have an impact on the level of performance.
- ***Efficiency1*** : the ratio of inputs of intermediate outputs, e.g. the cost per unit of capacity (cost per place in a private nursing home) or cost per anticipated level of demand (cost per meal prepared in a hotel).
- ***Production function*** : all the resources (staff, buildings, equipment, consumables) are combined to produce intermediate outputs, i.e. the capacity to produce the relevant service (school places, hospital beds, train seats, restaurant seats).
- ***Efficiency 2*** : the ratio of inputs to outputs, e.g. the cost per college graduate or cost per number of meals sold in a hotel.
- ***Capacity utilization*** : the ratio of intermediate output to final output, i.e. how good is management at converting the intermediate output into customer take-up. For example, what percentage of seats will be taken up by customers in a restaurant or what percentage of places will be taken up in a residential home. For services in general, and in particular where advance preparation is involved (meals in restaurant), accurate demand forecasting will become part of effective marketing management.
- ***Effectiveness 1 and 2*** : there is no overall agreement as to how effectiveness should be defined. Is it to be in terms of 'output' or 'outcome'?

Output means the service actually delivered to customers. Outcome, on the other hand, is the impact which the service may have on the recipients. It is the quality of the service delivered and its effectiveness in meeting users' needs or achieving its underlying purpose (Audit Commission). For example, a college educates students (output) but has a certain responsibility for graduate employability and destination (outcome). A management consultancy produces a report and advises a client (output) but has a certain responsibility for the impact of the report on the performance of the client company (outcome). In both cases, however, the outcome measure is not completely under the control of the service provider.

For many services, output is defined in a straightforward manner, as in:

- number of commuters transported
- number of home help clients assisted
- number of restaurant meals served
- number of admissions to a leisure centre

What is missing is any reference to the quality of service delivered.

Some services simply have no output or income that can practically be measured in quantitative terms; for example, a counselling service.

If the output of a process appears to defy identification with precision a surrogate measure of output may be used. For example, the true output of the police force cold be its contribution to the maintenance of a peaceful, crime free, ordered society, or a public library's true output might be the contribution it makes to expanding the knowledge base of, and to entertaining, the constituent community. As both of these outputs are likely to prove difficult to quantify, proxy measures in the form of 'percentage of reported crime solved' and 'ratio of loans to book stock' are used.

22.3 WHITE COLLAR PRODUCTIVITY

The working day for a blue collar worker if often prescribed down to the finest detail (tasks to be done and time taken to do them). For the white collar workers, what they do and how much time they spend doing it, is often left to their own judgement. The blue collar worker can be defined as one category in which the tasks are largely standardized and repetitive, e.g. railway porter, catering assistant, bus driver, street sweeper. The white collar category, on the other hand, includes a diversity of jobs, with differing sets of authority, responsibility and duties.

There are problems in measuring white collar productivity:

- Difficulties in determining the output or contribution
- Tendency to measure activities rather than the results, e.g. number of reports created says nothing about the quality of these reports.
- The input may not slow up in output until some time later. There is a lagged effect.
- Quality of output is even more difficult to determine than quantitv.
- Distinction of often not made between efficiency and effectiveness. The white collar worker may be efficient at developing reports but ineffective by not having enough to do, attending unproductive meetings, or assigned work outside the area of expertise.
- White collar workers are not accustomed to being measured.

Although there are difficulties, effort should be made to measure white collar productivity. The inputs may be relatively straightforward, e.g. number of hours worked, number of hours paid, resources used. It is the process and the output that pose the difficulties. The following issues are worthy of consideration:

- How creative are the white collar employees in the sense of developing and implementing new ideas.
- How efficient and effective is the utilization of the working day - this is an overriding factor upon which everything else depends.
- How satisfied are the customers - care needs to be exercised since no matter what the white collar worker does, the customer may remain dissatisfied, e.g. lecturer and student, doctor and patient.
- Ability to handle non-standard situations, i.e. crisis management.
- Communication skills and success in keeping people properly informed.

The above list is by no means exhaustive but simply indicates the kind of analysis that needs to be undertaken.

The single greatest challenge facing managers, according to Drucker is to raise the productivity of knowledge and service workers. He stresses that for all their diversity in knowledge, skill, responsibility, social status and pay, knowledge and service workers are remarkably alike in terms of:

What does and does not work in raising their productivity.

The first lesson that came as a rude shock, according to Drucker, is that the replacement of labour with technology does not, by itself, raise productivity. The key to raising productivity is working smarter rather than harder or longer. Drucker believes that fundamental questions need to be asked if the productivity of knowledge and service workers is to be raised. For example:

- What is task?
- What are we trying to accomplish?
- Why do it at all?

Drucker bemoans the fact that in many professional service jobs, e.g. nursing, teaching, a great deal of effort and time is taken up with paperwork and meetings, much of which contributes little if any value and has little if anything to do with what these professionals are qualified and paid for. The result is job impoverishment rather than enrichment and a reduction in motivation and morale.

Drucker recognizes that for a good many service jobs, e.g. making hospital beds, handling insurance claims, performance is defined on a quantity basis, very much like production jobs. The application of industrial engineering techniques will determine how long it should take, for example, to make up a hospital bed properly. For other service jobs, e.g. knowledge based, raising productivity, in Drucker's view, requires asking, 'What works?' plus analyzing the process step by step and operation by operation.

Process is the subject of a new approach that could achieve for office productivity what just-in-time techniques did for manufacturing practice. Business process redesign (BPR) looks at procedures and the way things are organized. BPR is attracting the interest of large service organizations looking for new ways of raising productivity and cutting costs. By simplifying the workflow and reducing the number of stages involved in a procedure, BPR can speed up customer service and involve fewer staff.

Of course, the most radical question of all in any discussion of white collar productivity would be, 'Why not give the workers a say?'

Giving subordinates a 'voice' in formal evaluation of their bosses can prove invaluable as a source of feedback for everyone concerned.

Employees can be asked their view of how effective the bosses are in, for example:

- Providing feedback on performance
- Looking for ways to improve existing systems
- Taking action on urgent requests
- Keeping people well informed
- Handling a disruptive employee

Care must be exercised over what to appraise and how to do it. Some might question the accuracy of subordinate appraisals. To some extent this misses the point. Their true value is in offering a view of management performance from those directly affected by it. That view can then be compared with management's view of itself.

A concluding comment about white collar productivity - it is not so readily observable and measurable as blue collar productivity, e.g. the bricklayer is both easily observed and measured - number of bricks laid per hour; whereas a nurse comforting a patient after a major operation may not be viewed as productive activity in the conventional wisdom.

Nowadays the term 'performance indictor' is often used to describe productivity measures. Given the distinctive characteristics of services, the pursuit of productivity measurement is a challenging one.

22.4 PRODUCTIVITY INDICATORS

Productivity is a measure of relationships between an input and an output, namely:

Productivity = [output / input]

It is a standard measure that has been used by manufacturing industries for a very long time, where for example:

Total productivity = [Total output / Sum of all inputs]

As total productivity can be difficult to determine and fail to detect explanations for poor performance, more specific measures are used:

P = [Production / Machine hours]

P = [Production / Number of employees]

P = [Sales / Number of square feet]

P = [Passenger miles (railway) / Number of guards]

Some examples are:

1. Inter-city railways passenger business

- Profit / (Loss) as a percentage of receipts %
- Receipts per train mile Rs.
- Receipts per passenger mile Rs.
- Passengers miles per loaded train mile (average train load) Passengers
- Total operating expenses per train mile Rs.
- Percentage of trains arriving within ten minutes of booked time %
- Percentage of trains cancelled %

2. Museums

(a) Education

- Number of courses/workshops arranged and their take-up
- Number of school visits
- Percentage of schools in the target areas reached

(b) Enquiries

- Number of enquiries dealt with each year
- Percentage of total enquiries successfully dealt with
- Average time/cost per specific enquiry

(c) Access

- Length of stay
- Number and type of visitors
- Return visitors
- Percentage from a given geographical area
- Relative performance with competition
- Measurement of visitor satisfaction

3. Further education

(a) Student success ratio =

[Number of students obtaining a qualification / Number of enrolled students]

(b) Post-course success ratio =

[Number of successful students who gain employment or progress to more advanced education or training / Number of successful students]

(c) Client satisfaction =

[Number of clients expressing satisfaction / Number of clients responding to requests for opinions]

(d) Utilization of teaching accommodation

Room utilization factor = [Room-hours used / Room hours available] × 100

That is, the percentage use of available rooms

Seat utilization factor = [Seat-hours used / Seat-hours available] × 100

That is, the percentage use of available seats.

4. Hospitals

(a) Activity indicators

- Average length of stay
- Average number of patients per bed per year
- Admission waiting lists in relation to the population served
- Turnover interval: average length of time a bed lies empty between admissions
- Urgent, immediate or emergency in-patient admissions in relation to the population served.

(b) Financial indicators

- Cost per day and cost per case by hospital
- In-patient catering costs per in-patient day
- Domestic and cleaning cost per cubic metre

(c) Manpower indicators

- Ratio or nursing staff to:
  (i) number of day cases and in-patient cases
  (ii) number of day cases and in-patient days

5. Hotel

Hotel ratios including labour, energy, capital and raw materials measures has been shown in Table 22.1.

Table 22.1 : EXAMPLE RATIOS OF HOTEL PRODUCTIVITY

	Physical measures	*Physical/financial measures combined*	*Financial Measures*
Labour measures	Kitchen meals produced / Kitchen staff	Restaurant revenue / Hours worked in restaurant	Banqueting revenue / Banqueting payroll
	Housecount / Total employee hours	Total room sales / Total reception employees	Hotel revenue / Total management salaries
	Restaurant covers / Hours worked in restaurant	Total room sales / Chambermaid day	Total added value / Hotel payroll
Energy measures	Total guest rooms / Total kilowatt hours	No. cooked meals / Total cooking costs	Hotel revenue / Total energy cost
Capital measures	Total hotel customers / Square foot of hotel	No. Rooms sold / Total capital expenditure	Net profit after tax / Equity capital
Raw materials measures	Chips prepared / Potatoes used	No. Bar customers / Cost of liquor used	Food revenue / Cost of food consumed
Total factor measures	No. Satisfied customers/ Total Hotel customers	Housecount / Cost of contributing resources	Net profit after tax / Cost of contributing resources

22.5 IMPROVING PRODUCTIVITY

Given the standard ratio there are, in theory, five ways to increase productivity:

1. Output increases faster than input
2. Output remains unchanged with fewer inputs
3. Output increases from the same inputs
4. Input decreases more than output
5. Maximum increase in the ratio through an ideal combination of outputs and inputs.

Whatever method is selected the true test will be the effect on the quality of service delivered. Improved productivity must, therefore, take into account effectiveness as well as efficiency.

Productivity improvements in the service sector are possible and a number of ways of improving service productivity are suggested.

Improving Staff

One way is through improving the knowledge, skills, attitudes and behaviour of existing and new staff involved in service delivery and performance through better systems of recruitment, training, development and motivation. Thus staff in contact with customers handling the visible elements of the service can be trained in handling queries and complaints, in product knowledge, in the operations of internal systems. Productivity bargaining schemes with considered measures of output and formulae for sharing gains can be operated to provide incentives for improved productivity. In other words staff can be encouraged to work harder and more skilfully.

Introducing Systems and Technology

Service organisations can reap productivity improvements if they become more systems and technology oriented. The systems approach looks at the task as a whole. It attempts to identify key operations to be undertaken, examines alternative ways of performing them, devises alternative methods, removes wasteful practices and improves co-ordination within the system as a whole. Alternative layouts, better job design and consideration of overall costs of the system are important features of the systems approach. For example productivity improvements in grocery retailing have been made possible by a systems approach to physical handling of goods, layout, job design and merchandising.

The systems approach to service can be applied in three ways: through hard technology, soft technology and hybrid technology.

(a) Hard technology means substituting machinery and tools for people (e.g. automatic car washes, airport x-ray surveillance equipment, automatic car parking, automatic vending equipment, audio visual equipment, computers.)

(b) Soft technology means substituting pre-planned systems for individual service operations. The systems may involve some technology, but their basic characteristic is the system itself which is designed for optimal results (e.g. fast food outlets, pre-packaged tours).

(c) Hybrid technology is where equipment is combined with planned systems to give greater order, speed and efficiency to the service process (e.g. limited service, fast repair facilities for car exhausts, tyres and brakes).

The approach to service activities can have important effects upon productivity. The systems approach, like the marketing approach, is as much about attitude and outlook as it is about tools, techniques and hardware or engineering. But the combination of division of labour with industrialization of service can produce new solutions to old problems.

The effects of this kind of thinking when applied to services are reflected in features like:

(a) greater standardization of performance and the mass production and greater impersonalization of services (e.g. telecommunications, group travel schemes);

(b) the appraisal of jobs. Attention is focused on how improvements can be made in the ways of doing the present job, what new methods can be employed to do jobs differently, and how the jobs and tasks themselves can be changed.

(c) reconsideration of the scale of operations. Economies of operation through chain operation or franchising may be sought;

(d) specialization of effort of markets to make labour more productive.

Reducing Service Levels

Productivity can also be improved by reducing the quantity of service and/or the quality of service (e.g. doctors could give less time to each patient). There are dangers in these approaches particularly where a service organization has promised to deliver a higher level of service in the past. Also competitors can differentiate their services by broadening and upgrading their service quantity and quality.

Substituting Products for Services

Productivity can be improved by providing a product substitute for the service (e.g. new data transfer technology has removed the need for the telegram service).

Introducing New Services

It is possible to design a more effective service that eliminates or reduces the need for the less effective service. For example, trans-atlantic travel by air has largely replaced trans-atlantic travel by sea; the credit card has replaced the former system for obtaining overdrafts.

Customer Interaction

It is possible to change the way in which customers interact with service providers. This is particularly possible with 'high contact' services. Using the consumer more in the production process demands greater understanding of consumer behaviour and its underlying causes. Ways have to be found to hardness consumers or to change the behaviour through education and persuasion for the benefit of service delivery. Consumers are involved in service delivery anyway, whether actively or passively. To improve the useful, active role of the customer in service delivery may mean new managerial approaches, changed organizations or organizational structures, the employment of para professionals and perhaps a changed role for the professional service manager. He may become more of a catalyst, stimulator, orchestrator or manager directing energies toward the maximum involvement of the consumer, student, client, parent or whatever. In other words more consumer-intensive designs have to be developed to maximize the contribution of the customer to service performance and delivery.

Reduce the Mismatch between Supply and Demand

A significant feature of many service organizations is the mismatch that often exists between supply of the service and demand for it. A major goal in marketing services is to get greater control over supply and demand and to obtain a better balance between the two. If more people want to use an airplane than there are seats available then business may be lost to competitors; unsold seats for a theatrical performance mean revenue lost forever. Service marketer may therefore face problems of:

Increasing demand (e.g. using up spare capacity);

Decreasing demand (e.g. where demand is excessive);

Obtaining a better balanced service supply (e.g. to meet fluctuating demand patterns).

Kotler has used the term 'demarketing' to describe the strategy which an organization may actively adopt to discourage additional customers on a temporary or a permanent basis. He uses the terms 'syncromarketing' to describe the strategy which an organization may actively adopt to bring supply and demand into better balance.

22.6 CUSTOMER RELATIONSHIP PROFITABILITY

The basic assumption is that customer satisfaction drives profitability. The assumption is based on the idea that by improving the quality of the provider's service, customers' satisfaction is improved. A satisfied customer creates a strong relationship with the provider and this leads to relationship longevity (or customer retention - customer loyalty). Retention again generates steady revenues and by adding the revenues over time customer relationship profitability is improved. Thus the firm can utilize potential customer relationship opportunities in a favourable way. A conceptual framework is depicted in Figure 22.3 and Table 22.2. The framework incorporates the basic sequence; service quality leads to customer satisfaction, which leads to relationship strength, which leads to relationship longevity, which leads to customer relationship profitability - but it also adds new perspectives to the sequence.

In order to structure the discussion we shall examine more closely the most important of the links between the different constructs. The first link deals with the relation between service quality and customer satisfaction. The second link deals with the relation between relationship strength and relationship longevity and the final link deals with how relationship longevity is connected to customer relationship profitability. In this sequence, the static perception of service quality inherent in most conceptual and measurement models is developed towards a dynamic concept of relationship quality.

Table 22.2 : DESCRIPTION OF CONCEPTS IN THE RELATIONSHIP PROFITABILITY MODEL

CONCEPT	DEFINITION
Perceived service quality	Customers' congnitive evaluation of the service across episodes compared with some explicit or implicit comparison standard
Perceived sacrifice	Perceived sacrifices (price, other sacrifices) across all service episodes in the relationship compared with some explicit or implicit comparison standard
Perceived value	Service quality compared with perceived sacrifice
Customer satisfaction	Customer's cognitive and affective evaluation based on the personal experience across all service episodes within the relationship
Commitment	Commitment is defined as the parties intentions to act and their attitude towards interacting with each other. High relationship value will affect commitment positively
Relationship strength	Measured both as purchase behaviour and as communication behaviour (word of mouth, complaints). Loyalty (repetitive purchase behaviour) which is based also on positive commitment by the customer indicates a stronger relationship. The behaviour is also affected by the bonds between the customer and the service provider.
Bonds	Exit barriers that tie the customer to the service provider and maintain the relationship. These are legal, economic, technological, geographical, time, knowledge, social, cultural, ideological and psychological bonds.
Critical episodes	Episodes that are of critical importance for the continuation of the relationship. Episodes can be critical based on the size of the values exchanges during the episode, compared with the parties' resources and based on the experiences during the episode
Patronage concentration	The share of the customer's cash flow in a certain industry in which the customer chooses to concentrate on one provider
Relationship longevity	The length of a relationship

Episode configuration	The episode types and number of each type that occur over time in a relationship between a provider and a customer
Relationship revenue	The total revenue generated from a customer relationship during a fiscal year
Relationship cost	The total cost incurred from serving a customer relationship - including direct and indirect costs - during a fiscal year
Relationship profitability	Relationship revenue - relationship costs

Figure 22.3 : A RELATIONSHIP PROFITABILITY MODEL

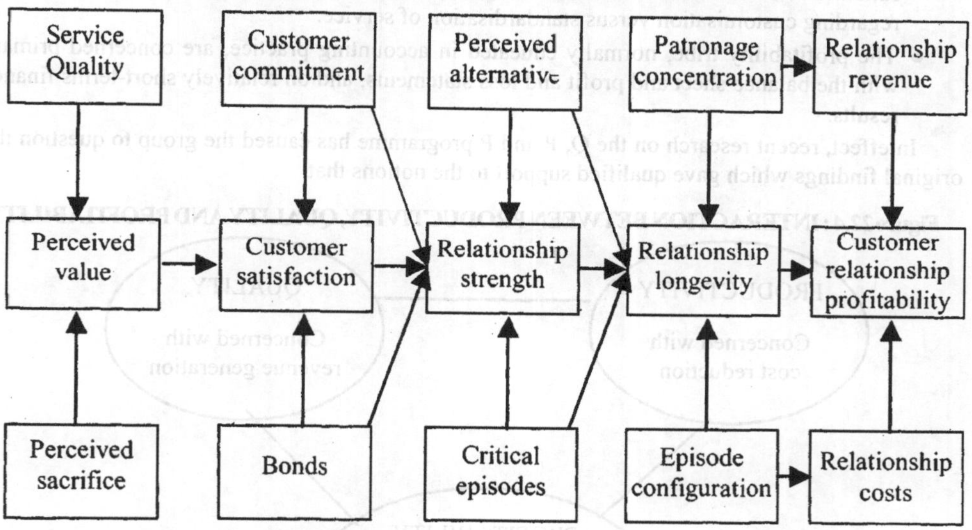

22.7 QUALITY, PRODUCTIVITY AND PROFITABILITY PROGRAMME

The Q, P and P programme, which examines the interactions between quality, productivity and profitability in service operations, is being undertaken by Gummesson and colleagues in Sweden. The programme, which was set up in 1993, regards quality, productivity and profitability as 'triplets' with the implication that 'separating one from the others creates an unhappy family. Unimpressed by current measures of productivity in particular, the group are seeking, through actual company case studies, to better understand the interactions between quality, productivity and profitability before attempting to quantify what is not yet fully understood.

A simple framework (Figure 22.4) shows the basic relationship, in financial terms, between the triplets:

1. A concentration, by a service company, on productivity means that the company will look towards an effective use of resources and towards producing more for less.
2. A concentration, by the company, on service quality means that it will look towards satisfying customers and, through customer retention and loyalty, increasing revenue.
3. A concentration on profitability means that the company will address the combined effect of cost reduction and revenue generation. This should involve an active interest in both productivity and quality.

According to the framework, all three elements of the triplets are pulling in the same direction. In practice, even within a single service organisation, the interactions between the elements may be affected by a tribal culture, where the different tribes - the productivity tribe, the quality tribe, and the profitability tribe - have different mindsets and do not necessarily understand one another or work together to a common aim.

Expanding on Gummesson's arguments it is suggested that

- The productivity tribe are concerned primarily with issues of definition of productivity and the various mathematical formulae to 'measure' productivity. Their concern is with, for example, the number of patients seen per hour in the surgery, or the average service time per supermarket customer.
- The quality tribe are concerned primarily with customer expectations, perceptions and levels of satisfaction. Their concern is with the quality of the service encounter and with arguments regarding customisation versus standardisation of service.
- The profitability tribe, normally educated in accounting practice, are concerned primarily with the balance sheet and profit and loss statements, and on relatively short-terms financial results.

In effect, recent research on the Q, P and P programme has caused the group to question their original findings which gave qualified support to the notions that

Figure 22.4 : INTERACTION BETWEEN PRODUCTIVITY, QUALITY AND PROFITABILITY

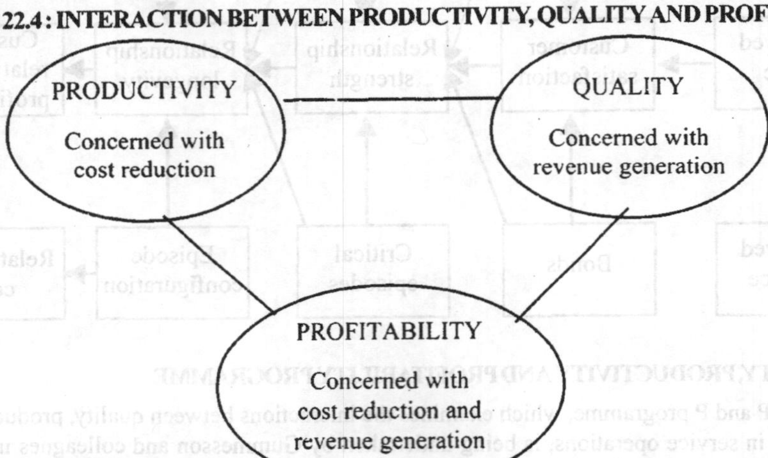

1. Productivity improvements lead to increased profits;
2. Quality improvements lead to increased productivity;
3. Quality improvements lead to increased profits.

The early conclusions were based on what the group now acknowledge as 'deceptively clear' definitions of the three triplets. They argue strongly that a premature move to quantifying relationships between the triplets will fail to address the many tribal and interpersonal contributions to an organisation's operation. This may result in measuring the wrong things, or only looking at variables which are of relevance or importance to members of a particular tribe.

22.8 THE SERVICE - PROFIT CHAIN

The current position on the relationships between loyalty (both customer and employee) and profitability is probably most easily visualised with reference to the 'service - profit chain', constructed by Heskett and his colleagues in 1994. The service - profit chain shows the *proposed* relationships between profitability, customer loyalty, and employee satisfaction, loyalty and productivity. It is reproduced here as Figure 22.5.

Figure 22.5: THE LINKS IN THE SERVICE-PROFIT CHAIN

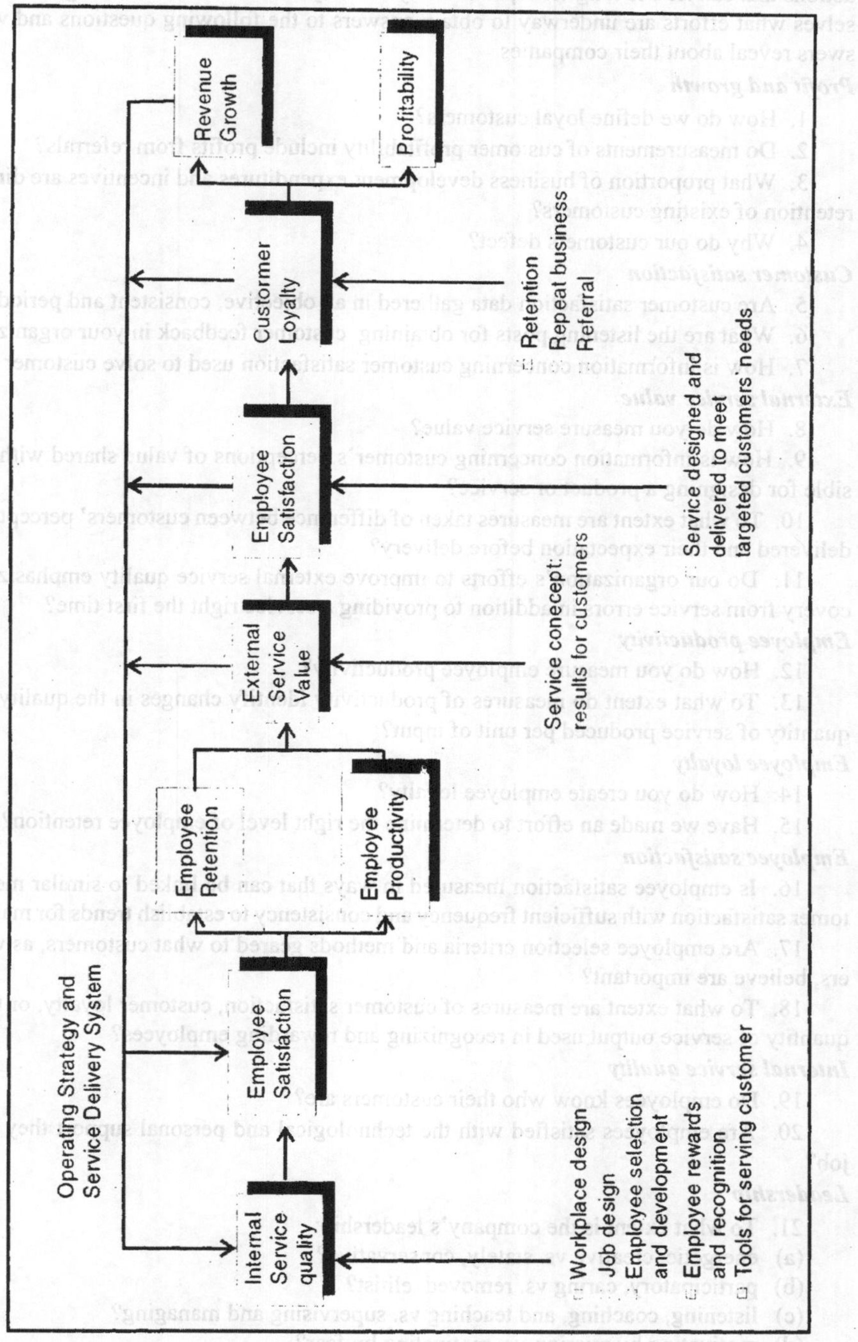

22.9 SERVICE - PROFIT CHAIN AUDIT

A service - profit chain audit helps companies determine what drives their profit and suggests actions that can lead to long-term profitability. As they review the audit, managers should ask themselves what efforts are underway to obtain answers to the following questions and what those answers reveal about their companies.

Profit and growth

1. How do we define loyal customers?
2. Do measurements of customer profitability include profits from referrals?
3. What proportion of business development expenditures and incentives are directed to the retention of existing customers?
4. Why do our customers defect?

Customer satisfaction

5. Are customer satisfaction data gathered in an objective, consistent and periodic fashion?
6. What are the listening posts for obtaining customer feedback in your organization?
7. How is information concerning customer satisfaction used to solve customer problems?

External service value

8. How do you measure service value?
9. How is information concerning customer's perceptions of value shared with those responsible for designing a product or service?
10. To what extent are measures taken of difference between customers' perceptions of quality delivered and their expectation before delivery?
11. Do our organization's efforts to improve external service quality emphasize effective recovery from service errors in addition to providing a service right the first time?

Employee productivity

12. How do you measure employee productivity?
13. To what extent do measures of productivity identify changes in the quality as well as the quantity of service produced per unit of input?

Employee loyalty

14. How do you create employee loyalty?
15. Have we made an effort to determine the right level of employee retention?

Employee satisfaction

16. Is employee satisfaction measured in ways that can be linked to similar measures of customer satisfaction with sufficient frequency and consistency to establish trends for management use?
17. Are employee selection criteria and methods geared to what customers, as well as managers, believe are important?
18. To what extent are measures of customer satisfaction, customer loyalty, or the quality and quantity of service output used in recognizing and rewarding employees?

Internal service quality

19. Do employees know who their customers are?
20. Are employees satisfied with the technological and personal support they receive on the job?

Leadership

21. To what extent is the company's leadership:
(a) energetic, creative vs. stately, conservative?
(b) participatory, caring vs. removed, elitist?
(c) listening, coaching, and teaching vs. supervising and managing?
(d) motivating by mission vs. motivating by fear?
(e) Leading by means of personally demonstrated values vs. institutionalized policies?

22. How much time is spent by the organization's leadership personally developing and maintaining a corporate culture centered around service to customers and fellow employees?

Relating the measures

23. What are the most important relationships in your company's service-profit chain?
24. To what extent does each measure correlate with profit and growth at the frontline level?
25. Is the importance of these relationships reflected in rewards and incentives offered to employees?

22.10 DETERMINANTS OF REVENUE GROWTH

The determinants of revenue growth (Figure 22.6) comprises attitude towards job, attitude towards company, behaviour of employees, helping tendency, value of goods and services, retention level of customers as well as recommendations put forth by customers. Impressions indeed are a major determinant of revenue growth which is in turn an indicator of better productivity and increased profitability.

Figure 22.6 : DETERMINANTS OF REVENUE GROWTH

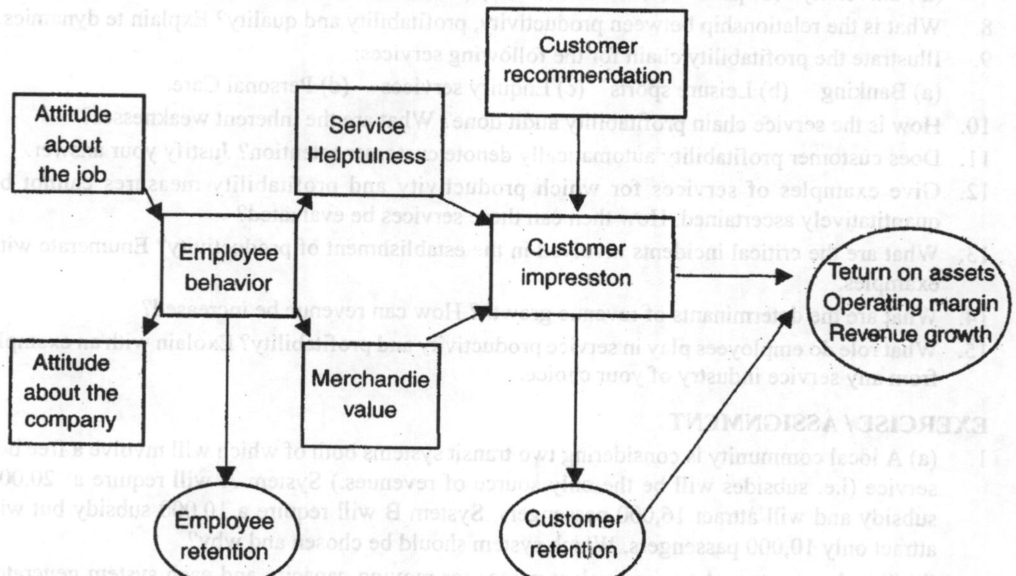

SHORT ANSWER QUESTIONS

1. How do definitions of service quality differ from those relating to the quality of manufactured products?
2. Why should manufacturers be concerned about service quality?
3. Why is productivity a more difficult issue for service firms than for manufactures?
4. Why is productivity improvement an important concern for service organizations?
5. What role does the consumer play in productivity in service organization?
6. Suggest six ways in which a service organization can improve the productivity of its operations?
7. What problems are involved in productivity measurement in services?
8. Why do technological methods of productivity improvement have their limitations in services?
9. Explain the relationship between service productivity and service quality.
10. List the productivity indicators for: (a) Tourism (b) Counselling (c) Public utility services

ESSAY QUESTIONS

1. How would you assess the productivity of : (a) college lecture (b) general practitioner (c) member of parliament (d) trading standards officer.
2. Under what circumstances will improvements in service quality and productivity lead to both increased value for customers and higher profits for the firm?
3. Review the dimension of service productivity. What do 'tangibles' mean in the context of (a) an airline, (b) a retail bank, (c) a hotel, (d) a telephone company?
4. In what ways can consumers help to improve service productivity? What distinctive characteristics of services make some of these actions possible?
5. Suggest methods you would use to measure the productivity of (a) fire man (b) marketing lecturer (c) business consultant (d) final year under graduate marketing student.
6. Is there a danger that increases in productivity may lead to reductions in quality? If there is, are there any particular services that are most at risk?
7. Describe the input-process-output relationships found in the following types of services: (a) university (b) prison (c) bank branch (d) restaurant.
8. What is the relationship between productivity, profitability and quality? Explain te dynamics.
9. Illustrate the profitability chain for the following services:
   (a) Banking (b) Leisure sports (c) Enquiry services (d) Personal Care.
10. How is the service chain profitability audit done? What are the inherent weaknesses?
11. Does customer profitability automatically denote customer retention? Justify your answer.
12. Give examples of services for which productivity and profitability measures cannot be quantitatively ascertained. How then can these services be evaluated?
13. What are the critical incidents involved in the establishment of productivity? Enumerate with examples.
14. What are the determinants of revenue growth? How can revenue be increased?
15. What role do employees play in service productivity and profitability? Exolain with an example from any service industry of your choice.

EXERCISE / ASSIGNMENT

1. (a) A local community is considering two transit systems both of which will involve a free bus service (i.e. subsides will be the only source of revenues.) System A will require a 20,000 subsidy and will attract 16,000 passengers, System B will require a 10,000 subsidy but will attract only 10,000 passengers. Which system should be chosen and why?

   (b) Two bus systems have equivalent passenger-moving capacity and each system generates 1,00,000 vehicle hours. The cost for systems A and B are \$2m and \$1.5m respectively. System A carries 3 million passengers and system B carries 1.5million passengers.

   (c) In a particular hospital 10 nurses and one doctor using 10 beds are able to do 20 minor operations. Another hospital performed 40 operations with the same number of staff. Which hospital is more efficient / effective?
2. Identify and describe six methods you have observed in which service industries have tried to improve productivity.
3. Develop measures of productivity indicators for as many services as possible. Consult wit others on the practicality of such measures prepared by you.

●●●

23

International Marketing of Services

23.1 WHAT IS A TRANSNATIONAL STRATEGY?

From a strategic perspective, planning and execution of the different management functions need to be integrated across national frontiers, rather than just taking place independently on domestic basis within each of a variety of different nations. Transnational strategy involves the integration of strategy formulation and implementation across all the countries in which the company elects to do business, in contrast to a multi-domestic (or 'multi-local') approach which provides for the independent development and implementation of strategy by management units within each country. In this broadest form, transnational strategy becomes global in form and we speak of globalization.

Although we can see a growing number of well-known service brand names popping up all over the world, this does not mean that the companies behind the brands have a truly global strategy. Many strategies today are basically multi-domestic in nature. For instance, even though a number of retail banks now have offices and even networks outside their countries of origin, in most instances, there is little transnational integration. One reason for this is that few retail customers need to conduct business in several different countries; when people travel within a country, their main financial need is usually to have a debit or credit card that can be used to make retail purchases and ATM withdrawals across the country. To achieve this, all that is needed is that the bank that issues the card should be affiliated with a global network such as Visa or Master Card. One key research theme is that globalization potential depends of industry characteristics - and particularly on specific industry drivers - such as market forces, cost factors, technology, government policies and competitive factors. A second key theme is that the use of global strategy should differ by dimension of strategy and for different elements of the value -adding chain.

How should different types of service firms move from multi-local strategies - that is, purely domestic marketing strategies within a variety of countries - to creation of truly transnational strategies? In the balance of this chapter, we discuss the elements.

23.2 WHY SERVICE FIRMS CHOOSE TO OPERATE INTERNATIONALLY

Some services were international in scope long before the term "scientific management" was ever invented or the first marketing course was taught. International services such as Shipping, banking, and insurance, for example, followed and facilitated early trade routes. With the advent of international air travel and telecommunications, both the opportunity and the need for global delivery of a wide array of services have grown dramatically, either displacing or complementing parallel delivery of similar services by purely domestic operations. Some firms follow their customers into new markets, others see new opportunities for building sales and expertise. We will examine few drivers that stimulate the globalization of an industry : market factors, costs, technology, favourable government policies, and competition.

As more and more firms offer services in foreign markets - often around the world - and as international trade in services increases, important questions are being raised concerning the design and implementation of global service marketing strategies. What do we mean by global strategy? How do the distinctive characteristics of service businesses affect globalization and development of a global strategy? How should different types of service firms move from multi-local strategies - that is, purely domestic marketing strategies within a variety of countries - to creation of truly transnational or global strategies? What should be the basis of competition against other global players in the service sector? These are questions for government policy makers as well as corporate managers. So it is essential to national competitiveness that governments, too, achieve a better understanding of how to develop effective global strategies for different types of service operations.

23.3 ELEMENTS OF GLOBAL TRANSNATIONAL STRATEGY

How do we determine whether a firm's international strategy can realistically be described as transnational rather than multi-local? And how might the distinctive characteristics of service businesses affect the ability or necessity to adopt and implement specific aspects of a transnational approach?

Five 'transnational strategy levers' serve to determine whether international strategy is primarily multi-local (recreated independently in each location) or primarily transnational. Within each dimension, strategic options cover a spectrum that ranges from a strictly multi-local orientation to a completely global one.

Judicious use of these global strategy levers can enable a firm to obtain one or more important benefits: cost reductions, improved quality of products and processes, greater customer preference and increased competitive leverage.

Global market participation

Management selects countries in which to market its services not just on the basis of stand-alone attractiveness; it also considers the potential of each market to contribute to broader globalization benefits.

Delivering global products

The firm offers a standardized core product (either a good or a service) that requires a minimum of local adaptation.

Global location of value-adding supplementary services

The value chain is broken up across different countries; with management adopting a strategy of creating supplementary services in one country (or a limited number of countries) for worldwide delivery, rather than duplicating each activity in many different countries. Looking at this another way, we would say that in a given location, the flower of service is pieced together with individual petals imported electronically from around the world. Technology allows information-based petals to be delivered in real time to the service site from anywhere with good telecommunication links.

Global marketing

Management employs a consistent marketing approach around the world, although not all elements of the marketing mix need be identical. Typically, corporate design is identical (except for language variations) and advertising themes and execution are recognizably similar. Market positioning, however, may vary somewhat in the light of local competitive offerings.

Global competitive moves

These are integrated across countries. The same type of move is made in different countries at the same time or in some systematic sequence. In highly competitive industries, a competitor may be targeted in one country in order to drain the resources that it was planning to apply in another country, or an assault by a competitor on the company's position in one country may be countered by a vigorous marketing campaign against that same competitor in a different country.

Services and transnational market participation

Certain types of services seem very easy to spread around the world and others, very difficult. In the 'easy' category fall simple service concepts that are easily replicable and therefore frachisable. Some 'essential' services, such as banking, telecommunications, hospitals and airlines, operate in heavily regulated environments, making it difficult to gain rapid penetration of foreign markets. But progress is being made in establishing global reputations for service businesses that are closely associated with a specific country (consider, for instance, American Express, BT, Credit Suisse, Lufthansa, mandarin-Oriental Hotels, Qantas, Royal Bank of Canada, Singapore Telecom and Zurich Insurance).

Historically, businesses that rely on trust and the reputation of their personnel - such as law firms and other professional service providers - have found it difficult to demonstrate quality to potential foreign customers and to adopt a professional style that fits the local culture. Ways to overcome such hurdles include not only extensive advertising and public relations, but also hiring host country nationals who have obtained education and work experience in other countries. Another approach is through mergers and alliances. Except for network organizations (notably airlines, logistics firms, travel services and financial services), it's hard to see how a service firm's presence or absence in India (or any other individual country) significantly affects its global strategic position, other than contributing revenues and profits. A few Western service companies have built successful businesses in India, either because their Western orientation (such as American-style fast food) appealed to Indian consumers or because they were creating an international network that could not afford to be absent from such a major market.

In the case of travel-related services, wider global market participation makes a brand more valuable to consumers. Thus, American Express traveller's cheques and credit cards are useful precisely because they are widely accepted in most countries. Similarly, international airlines enhance their appeal as they fly to more destinations and provide more connections at their hubs. There is a growing trend for airlines to form global partnerships with carriers that have complementary routes and then to coordinate their schedules so as to feed passengers to each other's services. In 1998, BA announced formation of the One world network in partnership with American Airlines, Canadian Airlines, Cathay Pacific and Qantas.

23.4 INTERNATIONAL BRANDING AND ADVERTISING

In general, services seem to make more use of international branding than do manufacturing firms, especially in consumer markets. The uncertainty created by intangibility can be offset by strong branding, so the primary task of the brand name or trademark for a service is to offer recognition and reassurance, rather than performing other functions such as positioning or local adaptation. McDonald's operates under the same name and 'golden arches' trademark around the world, so that both locals and travellers know that they will get the genuine McDonald's experience. Travel-related services virtually require the same brand name globally.

International branding is supported by transnational advertising and consistent corporate design, featuring recognizable colour schemes and an easily identified logo and trademark. Transnational or global advertising campaigns - sometimes termed 'strategic advertising' as distinct from local or 'tactical' promotions - often employ the same video sequences with voice-over in the local language. One of the challenges when creating global campaigns is to create visual themes that will travel well across different cultures. In recent years, for instance, British Airways' TV advertising has featured dramatic opening scenes followed by people of many races coming together in visually stunning locations. The need to be able to create and implement such campaigns for global clients has been an important factor in globalization of the advertising industry.

23.5 HOW THE NATURE OF THE PROCESS AFFECTS THE OPPORTUNITIES FOR GLOBALIZATION

Not all services are the same. So we will explore the effects of globalization drivers on three categories of services. (1) People-processing services that involve each customer directly in delivery of services targeted at the physical person; (2) possession-processing services targeted at physical objects belonging to the customer; and (3) information-based services targeted either at customers's mind or at their intangible assets.

People-processing services involve physical interactions with customers and necessarily require either that these people travel to the service "factory" of that service providers and equipment come to the customer. In both instances, the service provider needs to maintain a local geographic presence, stationing the necessary personnel, buildings, equipment, vehicles, and supplies within reasonable easy access of target customers. If the customers are themselves mobile-as in the case of business travellers and tourists, then the same customers are likely to be patronizing a company's offerings in many different locations, and making comparisons between them.

Possession-processing services may also be geographically constrained in many instances. A local presence is still required when the supplier must come to service objects in a fixed location; in the case of smaller, transportable items, certain services can be provided at more remote service centers - although transportation costs, customs duties, and government regulations may constrain shipment across large distances or national frontiers. On the other hand, modern technology now allows certain types of service processes to be administered from a distance through electronic diagnostics and transmission of so-called "remote fixes".

Information-based services are, perhaps, the most interesting category of services from the standpoint of global strategy development, because they depend upon the transmission or manipulation of data in order to create value. The advent of modern global telecommunications, linking intelligent machines to powerful databases, makes it increasingly easy to deliver information-based services around the world. Local presence requirements may be limited to a terminal-ranging from a simple telephone or fax machine to a computer or more specialized equipment like a bank ATM-connected to a reliable telecommunications infrastructure. If the local infrastructures is not of sufficiently high quality, then use of mobile or satellite communications may solve the problem in some instances.

23.6 INDUSTRY GLOBALIZATION DRIVERS

Five categories of industry drivers favour globalization and globally integrated strategy:

1. ***Market drivers*** comprise the following elements: common customer needs, global customers, global channels, transferable marketing and lead countries.
2. ***Competition drivers*** and composed of high levels of exports and imports in a specific industry, the presence of competitors from different continents, interdependence of countries, and the globalization policies of competitors themselves.
3. ***Technology drivers*** are composed of advances in the performance and capabilities of telecommunications, computerization, and software, miniaturization of equipment, and the digitization of voice, video, and text so that all can be stored and transmitted in the digital language of computers.
4. ***Cost drivers*** comprise global scale economies, steep experience curve effects, sourcing efficiencies, favourable logistics, differences in country costs (including exchange rates), high product development, and a rapid decline in the costs of key communication and transportation technologies relative to their performance.
5. ***Government drivers*** comprise favourable trade policies, compatible technical standards, common marketing regulations, government-owned competitors and customers, and host government policies.

How Drivers Affect Service Businesses

The relative significance of each driver varies by service category. In some instances, there may even be variations by industry.

Market globalization drivers. One factor of particular significance to many service industries is the presence of global customers who demand consistent service from suppliers around the world, and the availability of global channels in the form of fast-developing physical supply chains or electronic networks. As large corporate customers themselves become global, they often seek to standardize and simplify the suppliers they use in different countries for a wide array of business-to-business services.

A related trend can be found among some of the people-processing services used by international business travellers and tourists, who often feel more comfortable with predictable standards of performance worldwide for such travel-related services as airlines and lodging. In possession-processing services, the development of global logistics capabilities by firms such as Federal Express has encouraged a number of manufacturers to outsource responsibility for their logistics function to a single firm, which then coordinates transportation and warehousing operations around the world.

Competition drivers. These exercise a powerful force in many service industries. To the extent that customers who operate around the world are known to value global provision of services, a firm may be obliged to follow its competitors into new markets in order to protect its position in existing markets. Similarly, once a major player moves into a new foreign market, a scramble for territory among competing firms may ensue, particularly if the preferred mode of expansion involves purchasing or licensing the most successful local firms in each market.

Technology drivers. For information-based services, the growing availability of broadband telecommunication channels, capable of moving vast amounts of data at great speed, is playing a major role in opening up new markets. Access to the Internet or World Wide Web is accelerating around the world. But there may be no need to duplicate all informational elements in each new location. Significant economies may be gained by centralizing "information hubs" on a global basis. It may also be advantageous to take advantage of favorable labour costs and exchange rates by consolidating operations of supplementary services (such as reservations) or back office functions (such as accounting) in just one or a few selected countries.

Cost drivers. The effect of these drivers varies according to the level of fixed costs required to enter an industry and the potential for cost efficiencies. Lower operating costs for telecommunications and transportation, accompanied by improved performance, serve to facilitate entry into global markets. Barriers to entry caused by the upfront cost of equipment and facilities may be reduced by such strategies as equipment leasing (as in airlines), seeking investor-owned facilities such as hotels and then selling them on management contracts, or awarding franchises to local entrepreneurs. However, cost drivers may be less applicable for services that are primarily people based and so require recreating most element of the "service factory" in multiple locations. Under such circumstances, scale economies tend to be lower and experience curves relatively flatter. In service business on which new product development costs are low, cost drivers are also likely to be less significant.

Government drivers. We can expect government drivers to be more favourable for people-processing and possession-processing services that require a significant local presence, because these services can create local employment opportunities. In contrast, governments often impose regulations to protect home-based services, such as passenger and freight transportation, from attacks by foreign carriers operating on the same routes. A typical action involves restricting foreign airline's landing rights or their ability to pick up passengers at an intermediate stop on a scheduled flight between two other countries.

If transportation services are easily exported, information-based services are even more so. Data, after all, can move around the world almost instantaneously through electronic channels. Governments can play an important role in requiring adoption of internationally compatible technical standards. However, unrestricted imports of services in categories ranging from entertainments to finance are often seen as both an economic and cultural threat. Hence such government actions as regulating international banking (widely practiced), banning private ownership of satellite dishes (already implemented in China, Iran, Singapore and Saudi Arabia), or seeking to limit access to services on the Internet.

Overall Assessment of Drivers

Are some types of services more easily driven to globalize than others? Looking at the summary in Table 23.1, we can see important variations in the impact of each of the five groups of drivers. However, government drivers, expressed in terms of economic policy, regulation, and protections, are often specific to individual industries. Hence it's important to evaluate globalization drivers at the level of individual industries, as well as in terms of broader service categories.

Table 23.1 : IMPACT OF GLOBALIZATION DRIVERS ON DIFFERENT SERVICE CATEGORIES

Globalization Drivers	Services category: People processing	Possession processing	Information-Based
Competition	Simultaneity of production and consumption limits leverage of foreign-based competitive advantage in front-stage of service factory, but advantage in management systems can be basis for globalization.	Lead role of technology creates driver for globali zation of competitors with technical edge (e.g., Singapore Airlines technical servicing for other carrier's aircraft).	Highly vulnerable to global dominance by competitors with monopoly or com petitive advantage in infor mation (e.g. BBC, Holy-wood, CNN), unless restricted by governments.
Market	People differ economically, and culturally, so needs for service and ability to pay may vary. Culture and education may affect will ingnesss to do self-service.	Less variation for service to corporate possessions, but level of economic development impacts demand fro services to individually owned goods.	Demand for many services is derived to a significant degree from economic and educational levels. Cultural issues may affect demand for entertainment.
Technology	Use of IT for delivery of supplementary services may be a function of own ership and familiarity with technology, including tele-communications, and intelligent terminals.	Need for technology-based service delivery systems is a function of the types of possessions requiring service and the cost trade-offs in labour Substitution.	Delivering core services through remote terminals may be a function of invest ments in computerization, quality of telecom infrastructure and education levels.
Cost	Variable labour rates may impact on pricing in labour-intensive services (consider self-service in high-cost locations.)	Variable labour rates may favour low-cost locations if not offset by shipment costs. Consider substitu-ting equipment for labour.	Major cost elements can be centralized and minor cost elements localized.
Government	Social policies, (e.g., health) vary widely and may affect labour costs, role of women in front-stage jobs, and hours/days on which work can be performed.	Tax law, environmental reg-ulations, and technical standards may decrease/ increase costs and encourage/discourage certain types of activity.	Policies on education, censorship, public ownership of communications, and infra-structure standards may impact demand and supply and distort pricing.

23.7 MODES OF INTERNATIONALIZATION

Few firms are in a position to move swiftly from a purely domestic posture to a broad international presence. Typically, the move takes place over many years, beginning with expansion into selected markets. As with domestic expansion, several options are available.. Three broad modes of internationalization are highlighted in Figure 23.1.

The first, which is restricted to information-based service, involves capturing a service performance in some storage medium-a video cassette, diskette or CD-ROM, and then exporting what is now a physical good by mail order or local distributors. Customers obtain the value they are asking by self service through playback devices or computers. Entertainment, software and databases are all examples of such an approach. Alternatively, the service can be delivered through such channels as satellites, the internet, cinemas or broadcast stations.

The second approach involves reliance on third parties, through such arrangements as licensing agents, brokers, franchising and minority joint ventures. The extent of their responsibilities may vary from handling just a few supplementary services, such as provision of information and reservations, to delivering the entire service package and being responsible for all domestic marketing activities. Some intermediaries operate under their own names and simply identify themselves as agents or

Figure 23.1 : CLUSTERING OF SERVICES AND INTERNATIONALISATION MODES

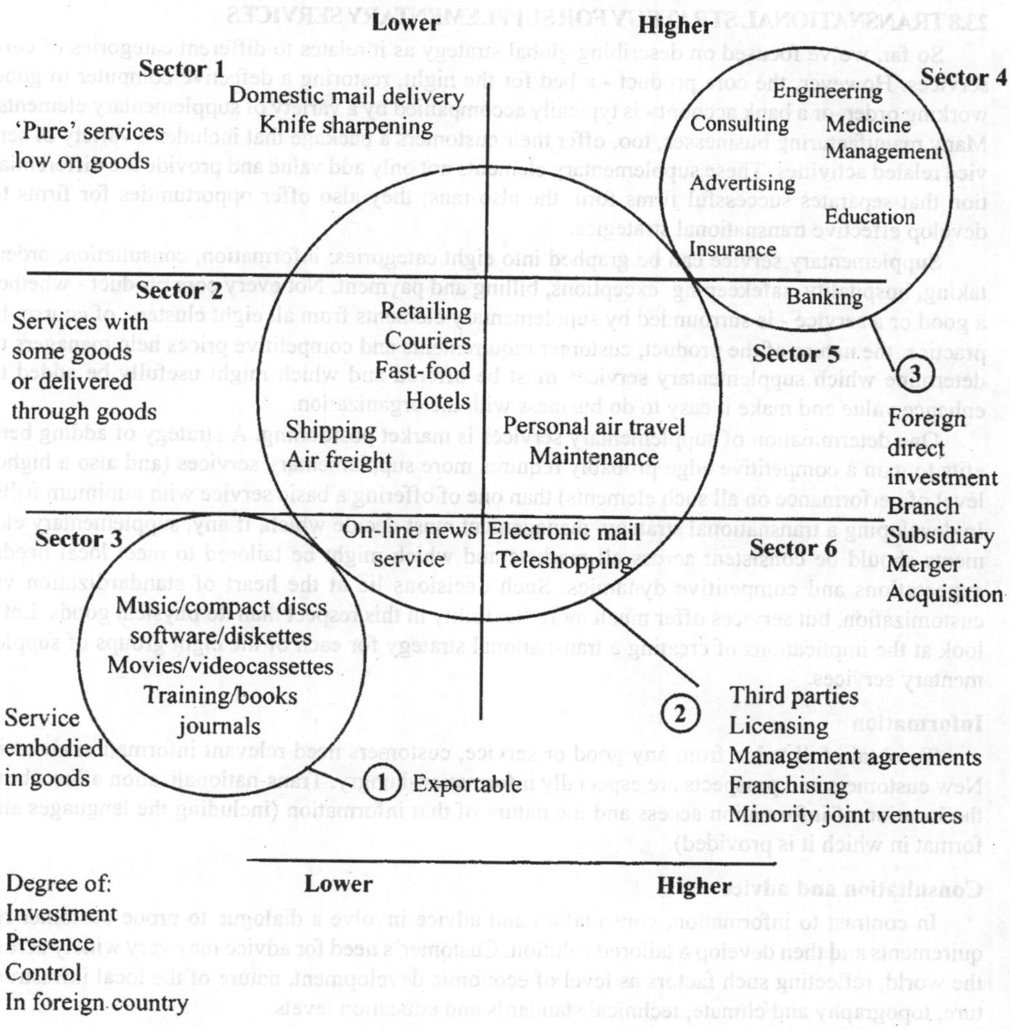

distributors, some link their name to that of the originating service organization (a common practice in international professional firms), while others (as in many franchises) completely assume the marketing identity of the original service organization and implement a global marketing strategy.

The third approach involves full control, achieved either through direct investment in a new operation or a buyout of an existing business which is then absorbed into the original company. International banks and express package firms have used both routes to gain presence in foreign markets, as have accounting firms. Buyouts are often favoured when the goal is to gain rapid access to a new client base and personnel who are already experienced in serving them, in contrast to following existing clients into new markets. The acquisition route is, of course, faster than internal expansion and allows immediate access to operating systems and personnel. The drawback is that substantial redirection and re-education may be needed to bring the new acquisition into alignment with the purchaser's existing operation. This task may result in a disruptive period during which quality declines, valued personnel leave and others are dismissed, leading to customer confusion and even defection to competitors. A big question is whether to adopt a consistent transnational marketing strategy or to create a strategy tailored to the local market.

23.8 TRANSNATIONAL STRATEGY FOR SUPPLEMENTARY SERVICES

So far, we've focused on describing global strategy as it relates to different categories of core services. However, the core product - a bed for the night, restoring a defective computer to good working order, or a bank account - is typically accompanied by a variety of supplementary elements. Many manufacturing businesses, too, offer their customers a package that includes a variety of service related activities. These supplementary elements not only add value and provide the differentiation that separates successful firms form the also-rans; they also offer opportunities for firms to develop effective transnational strategies.

Supplementary service can be graphed into eight categories: information, consultation, order-taking, hospitality, safekeeping, exceptions, billing and payment. Not every core product - whether a good or a service - is surrounded by supplementary elements from all eight clusters, of course. In practice, the nature of the product, customer requirements and competitive prices help managers to determine which supplementary services must be offered and which might usefully be added to enhance value and make it easy to do business with the organization.

One determination of supplementary services is market positioning. A strategy of adding benefits to gain a competitive edge probably requires more supplementary services (and also a higher level of performance on all such elements) than one of offering a basic service with minimum frills. In developing a transnational strategy, management must decide which, if any, supplementary elements should be consistent across all markets and which might be tailored to meet local needs, expectations and competitive dynamics. Such decisions lie at the heart of standardization vs. customization, but services offer much more flexibility in this respect than do physical goods. Let's look at the implications of creating a transnational strategy for each of the eight groups of supplementary services.

Information

To obtain full value from any good or service, customers need relevant information about it. New customers and prospects are especially information-hungry. Trans-nationalization affects both the location of information access and the nature of that information (including the languages and format in which it is provided).

Consultation and advice

In contrast to information, consultation and advice involve a dialogue to probe customer requirements and then develop a tailored solution. Customer's need for advice may vary widely across the world, reflecting such factors as level of economic development, nature of the local infrastructure, topography and climate, technical standards and education levels.

Order-taking (including reservations)

Once customers are ready to buy, a key supplementary element should come into play: accepting applications, orders and reservations. Trans-nationalization affects both the nature and location of order-taking access, such as the potential for instituting global reservation systems.

Hospitality: taking care of the customer

A well-managed business should try, at least in small ways, to treat customers as guests when they have to visit supplier's facilities (especially when, as is true for many-people processing operations, the period extends over several hours or more). Cultural definitions of appropriate hospitality may differ widely from one country to another, such as the tolerable length of waiting time (much longer in Russia than in Germany) and the degree of personal service expected (higher in France, for instance, than in the Scandinavian countries).

Safekeeping: looking after the customer's possessions

When visiting a service site, customers often want assistance with their personal possessions. Expectations often vary by country, reflecting culture and levels of affluence. For example, most restaurants in the United Stated bar dogs, but in France most will tolerate them, and in China some restaurants may even cook them for you!

Exceptions

Exceptions fall outside the routine of normal service delivery. They include special requests, problem-solving, handling of complaints/suggestions/compliments, and restitution (compensating customers for performance failures). Special requests are particularly common in people-processing services, as in the travel and hotel industries. International airlines, for example, find it necessary to respond to an array of medical and dietary needs, sometimes reflecting religious and cultural values. Problem solving is often more difficult for people who are travelling abroad than it would be in the familiar environment of their native country.

Billing

Customers need clear, timely bills that explain how charges are computed. With abolition of currency exchange restrictions in many countries, travellers from many nations now except to be able to make purchases on their credit cards almost anywhere and to have bills converted to their home currencies.

Payment

Ease and convenience of payment (including credit) are increasingly expected by customers when purchasing a broad array of goods and services. Acceptance of major credit cards and travellers' cheque solves the problem of paying in foreign funds for many retail purchases, but some shops go even further to accommodate customers.

23.9 PROBLEMS CONNECTED WITH MARKETING SERVICES INTERNATIONALLY

The principles of marketing services internationally are the same as those which apply to domestic markets. Clearly the notions of setting clear marketing objectives, defining and selecting target markets, developing appropriate marketing strategies and marketing mixes and controlling marketing efforts are the same. What is different are the environmental contexts - social, political, economic, legal and cultural - to which marketers need to adjust. The nature of such environmental forces are given detailed treatment in many texts on international marketing - albeit in product marketing settings - and will not be repeated here. Their absence is in no way a measure of their unimportance. There are however few illustrations of how such influences affect service organizations specifically.

a. the risk of international marketing for service organization

b. problems of adaptation to and operation in overseas markets;

c. barriers to trade in services.

The Risk of International Marketing for Service Organizations

While internationalization represents a growth strategy for service firms they also believe that:

a. out-of-country expansion is a more risky strategy for a service firm than, for example, concentric diversification of new service development in existing markets;

b. out-of-country expansion is more risky for a service business than it is for a manufacturer of physical items.

Problems of Adaptation to and Operation in Overseas Markets

Adjusting to foreign business practices, client expertise and the culture in general; gaining client confidence; and overcoming national hostilities were additional challenges faced by all firms initially. As a group, the adjustment to overseas practices and client expertise was the greatest barrier faced by advertising firms, while consulting firms experienced most difficulties in gaining client confidence and law firms had to meet the problems of overcoming national hostilities.

A major problem encountered today by both consulting and law firms is the maze of host government laws and industry rules.

Legal Barriers to Services Marketing

Because the production and marketing of services are closely inter-wined with the societies being served, often the barriers associated with trade in services are even more restrictive than those associated with trade in merchandise. Such barriers usually fall into four main categories: 1. quantitative or qualitative border prohibitions and restrictions, 2. law and regulations discriminating against foreign firms, 3. direct and indirect subsidies to local firms, and 4. infringement of international copyright and trademark law (and intellectual property rights).

a. **Borders Restrictions** Perhaps the simplest forms of restrictions are those that affect firms at the time their operations cross borders. For example, tariffs (taxes) are often assessed by one country when advertisements or computer services are produced in another country. Tariff rates seem to change almost on a monthly basis. Quotas are another common form or border restriction. Many countries have erected barriers to entry of foreign banks and insurance firms;

b. **Discriminatory Laws** A second common approach to protecting domestic firms from foreign competition is to let foreign firms in, but then discriminantly restrict their operations. Perhaps the best examples occur in the international banking and insurance industries. In Indonesia, foreign banks have been allowed to operate only in Jakarta, with limits on import financing. In Malaysia, foreign banks have had to meet racial employment quotas. In the EC, only the United Kingdom has no restrictions on foreign insurance companies. Even in the United States, some in congress have advocated higher taxes on subsidiaries of foreign firms.

c. **Subsidies** A more subtle form of protection from outside competition is government subsidies of domestic workers and industries. Subsidies to agriculture are the most well known, but local services industries are commonly supported financially by governments as well. For example, most countries around the world subsidize to some degree their local telecommunications companies. Likewise, most countries give their national airlines concessional loans, fare subsidies, and other financial assistance.

d. **Intellectual Property Rights** This last category is perhaps the most important from the perspective of American industry. The main thing the United States has to offer in trade to the rest of the world is technology. This often takes the form of ideas and innovations that are quite easily copied.

Cultural Barriers

Because trade in services frequently involves people-to-people contact, culture plays a much bigger role in such trade than in merchandise trade. Many a successful domestic marketer has come away from a foreign market "adventure" wondering what went wrong.

a. ***Language*** Language is an obvious difference between cultures. It reflects cultural values in its lexicon form, and structure. Communication is an essential part of the marketing task; therefore services marketers must communicate in the language of the market. Adaptation is needed in advertising and personal selling and in market research, which is often accomplished using national employees, distributors, and advertising agencies. When service provider and service customer are of different cultural backgrounds, sensitivity is especially needed to ensure a satisfactory service encounter.

Many business blunders result from simple errors in translation. The following examples illustrates some translation errors in service context.

- ***In a hotel lobby:***
  The lift is being fixed for the next day. During that time we regret that you will be unbearable.
- ***In a Hotel:***
  The flattening of underwear with pleasure is the job of the chambermaid.
- ***On the menu of restaurant:***
  Our wines leave you nothing to hope for.
- ***In an advertisement by dentist:***
  Teeth extracted by the latest Methodists.
- ***In a tourist agency:***
  Take one of our horse-driven city tours - we guarantee no miscarriages.
- ***In a airline ticket office:***
  We take your bags and send them in all directions
- ***From a brochure of a car rental firm:***
  When passenger of foot heave in sight, tootle the horn. Trumpet him melodiously at first, but if he still obstructs your passage then tootle him with vigour.

b. **Values and Attitudes** These help to determine what members of a culture think is right, important and/or desirable. Because behaviours, including consumer behaviours, flow from values and attitudes, services marketers who want their service adopted cross-culturally must understand these differences.

c. **Manners and Customs** These represent a culture's views of appropriate ways of behaving. It is important to monitor differences in manners and customs, as these can have a direct impact on the service encounter.

d. ***Material Culture*** Material culture consists of the tangible products of culture, "the stuff we own." What people own and how they use and display material possessions varies around the world. Cars, houses, clothes, and furniture are examples of material culture.

e. ***Aesthetics*** Aesthetics refers to cultural ideas about beauty and good taste. These are reflected in music, art, drama, and dance as well as the appreciation of colour and form.

f. ***Educational and Social Institutions*** Both kinds of institutions are affected by, and are transmission agents of, culture. Education includes the process of transmitting skills and knowledge, and thus may take place in schools and in less formal "training" circumstances. The structure and functioning of each are heavily influenced by culture. Culture manifests itself most dramatically in the people-to-people contact of our social institutions.

23.10 TRADE IN SERVICES

The advanced economies are primarily service economies in the sense that the services sector generates the major share of employment as well as income in these economies. In the industrial market economies, services produce, on an average, over 60 per cent of GDP and provide about 60 per cent of the total employment. It has been the experience that the share of the service in the GDP and total employment increases as the economy progresses. Thus, in the developing countries, the share of the services sector in the GDP increased from 40 per cent in 1965 to 47 per cent in 1990. In the low income countries, this ratio increased from 32 per cent to 35 per cent during this period. During the same period, the share of services in India's GDP increased from 34 per cent to 40 per cent.

Economic development is, thus, characterised by an increase of the share of the services in the GDP and total employment. This trend tends to increase the international trade in services.

The size of the international market for service is difficult to measure. However, it has been estimated that services, termed as invisibles, account for about one-quarter of the world trade. That the world trade in service is dominated by the developed countries is reflected by the fact that the developed nations run large surpluses and the developing countries show huge deficits on the invisible account.

International trade in services is subject, in general, to lot of restrictions. The General Agreement on Tariffs and Trade (GATT) which has been trying to liberalise the trade in goods does not cover the service. The industrialised nations, like the U.S.A. and the members of the EEC have been strongly arguing for the inclusion of trade in services in the GATT negotiations. The developing countries, like India on the other hand have strongly opposed such a move. The fear of the developing countries is that the liberalisation of trade in services will result in the destruction of their service industries by the multinationals. On the other hand, it is argued that the liberalisation and the resultant competition will improve the efficiency of the service sector in the developing countries and this will help improve the overall efficiency of the economy and the export competitiveness of the developing countries. It may also be pointed out that strategic considerations also discourage, both developed and developing countries, the opening up of certain services of foreigners and in certain cases even to domestic private firms.

Characteristics

An important characteristic of services that has far reaching implications for marketing of services is their inseparability, i.e. services cannot be separated from their providers, whether they are persons or machines. This does not, however mean that all service require the physical proximity of the provider and user.

There are two broad categories of services, viz., (1) those that necessarily require the physical proximity of the provider and the user; and (ii) those that do not, though such physical proximity may be useful.

The services where physical proximity is essential fall into three categories:

The first category is characterised by the **mobile provider** and **immobile user**. This involves cases where the mobility of the beneficiary to the place of the provider is not physically feasible. For example, an Indian firm which has a construction contract abroad will have to send the manpower required to the construction site for carrying out the work. Similarly, a technician may have to go to a plant abroad to rectify a problem with the plant.

The second category is characterised by **mobile user** and **immobile provider**. This category consists of services which involves some key elements which are not normally transferable to the user's location. For example, certain experiments can be done only in those laboratories equipped for them. A patient who wants an open-hearted surgery will have to go to a hospital where the required facilities are available.

The third category consists of **mobile user** and **mobile provider**; proximity may be achieved by either the provider going to the user or the user going to the provider.

Services for which physical proximity is not essential are known as **long distance services.** Examples of this category include transmission 'over the wire' of live music concerts or data. In advanced countries, traditional banking and insurance services fall into this category since loans or insurance policies can be secured by mail or phone. The scope for long distance transactions will increase with the advance of technology. This has important implications for broader issues such as the trend effect immigration restrictions on the relative wages of skilled and unskilled labour since skilled services may increasingly be transacted "long distance" whereas the latter cannot.

Even in respect of many long distance services, physical proximity between the provider and user will help increase the efficiency of the service. A large number of service firms will therefore like to have places of business in countries with sufficient market. The 'right to establish' is an essential aspect of free trade in services. The right to establish also involves the right to employ people without restrictions on the nationality.

International trade in many services involve international factor mobility. There are a number of international transactions involving **temporary-factor-relocation** services such as those requiring temporary residence by foreign labour to execute service transactions.

International trade in service, thus, involves intricate issues like right to establish factor mobility. These are special problems in liberalising trade in services compared to trade in goods.

Restrictions

Because of these characteristics and the socio-economic and political implications of certain services, they are, generally, subject to various types of national restrictions. Protective measures include visa requirements and investment regulations. Services in different countries include banking and insurance; transportation; television, radio, film and other forms of communication, and so on.

Several economists have tried to allay the fears of the developing countries in respect of liberalisation of trade in services. It has been pointed out that several developing countries have acquired enough strength in different services to successfully compete with developed countries. For example, countries like Korea, Brazil, India, Lebanon and Taiwan have done well in international construction and design contracts. Several developing countries have great potential in the field of professional services. Some already have considerable exports of tourism and shipping.

It has been argued that if developing countries protect more expensive or lower quality services produced by local firms, they run the risk of handicapping their exports of goods: many services are upstream or down stream services to producers. Access at reasonable cost to quality services can make the difference between success or failure in exporting. In many developing countries, the need for such services argues for at least selective liberalisation. If this encouraged the multinational corporations of the industrial countries to provide these services to developing countries, it would help developing countries' exports of manufacturers in three ways. First, it would lower their costs and help them to develop markets. Second, it would encourage the multinational corporations to move away from goods in favour of producing more services. Third, if industrial nations can sell more services, they may be more willing to lower protective barriers elsewhere.

These arguments, which sound theoretically very good many not be easily realised. It needs to be cautioned that unless the developing countries take measures to strengthen their services before liberalisation, it would adversely affect the domestic service industries.

India has great potential in a variety of services. The large number of scientists. Professional and skilled and semi-skilled personnel working abroad is indicative of India's potential in several fields. With such a resource potential, we should be able to develop a number of service industries capable of obtaining customers from abroad. For example, can't we provide health care instead of just exporting doctors and other medical personnel? Can't we provide education instead of just exporting teachers?.

23.11 THE 10-P MODEL OF GLOBAL STRATEGIC MANAGEMENT

The 10-P framework for globalization symbolizes the aspirations and needs of employees and organizations in the new competitive settings. It comes a long way from the initial impetus provided to the subject by Michael Porter in his book *Competitive Strategy* (1980), and goes beyond his purely industrial organization perspective. The framework operationalizes 4-Diamonds for a nation's competitive advantage of Porter. The 10-P framework integrates theory of strategic management and practice of business policy and provides a structure for the practising manager to evaluate competitiveness at regular intervals.

The 10-P framework (Figure 23.2) explores a fine 'fit' between the soft and hard strategic choices. It seeks a self-motivated network of stakeholders who are able to self-actualize a high sense of satisfaction, self-worth, liberty and freedom in business organizational settings.

True to the vision of a world-class organization, the central fulcrum in the framework is a people-orientation - both inside and outside the corporation. This approach presents a humane perspective to issues at hand and differentiates between a 'satisfying' approach and an 'excellent' approach. It realizes and reflects that modern economies and corporations thrive mainly on innovation in all respects of value-augmentation-creative thinking at the design stage, ensuring production at highest efficiency and minimum costs, and satisfying the customer in a most effective manner.

The rest of the 9-Ps are levered in a highly interactive mode with People and amongst themselves. A change in any of the Ps affects performance of the other levers and therefore the final outcome for the organization. The 9-Ps are : Purpose, Perspective, Positioning, Plans (and policies), Partnerships, Products, Productivity, Politics, and Performance (and profits). It may be mentioned explicitly that the suggestion is not to supplant frameworks such as McKinsey's 7-S, marketing's 4-Ps or overriding the importance of leadership in strategy formulation and implementation - these are important at their respective levels of analysis. Instead, the 10-P framework is higher-order framework appropriate for auditing strategic competitiveness, a monitoring of emerging opportunities and threats, devising a value-based action-plan and executing it in the context of globalizing organisations.

1. People

Organization is people : An organization is created by the people, it exists for the people, and continuously draws sanction from the people. From this humane perspective, the primary objective of an organization can only be to add value to the society by serving it with value-augmented products.

The people-focus implies that the primary purpose of an organization can never be to provide employment at the expense of customers or society in general - a drill routinely exercised in Third World countries, and especially in India by many public sector and government organizations during the height of regulated economic regimentation. Similarly, retrenchment of people (hire and fire) cannot be accepted as a non-holds-barred practice for maximizing organizational profits! Retrenchment is a myopic and non-creative response to the problem of cutting costs and improving productivity.

The corporate manager in the new paradigm has the unenviable role of maximizing 'people orientation' as well as 'task orientation'.

In these emerging work values, each employee is empowered to take decisions under certain norms. For instance, under Just-in-Time culture, an ordinary shop-floor worker is empowered to stop the whole machine assembly line if he finds that the product quality has gone out of control.

2. Purpose

Organizational purpose as used in strategy-making sense is interchangeable with mission, vision, core competence, strategic intent, and basic values. It is important not merely to produce and sell products, but to produce and sell quality products, without fail. Not only from the production side, but also from the distribution side, we must constantly review whether our customers are satisfied with our products and whether customers are satisfied with our service. We must be perfect in satisfying. Organizational purpose must be explicitly stated. An organization must enjoy social sanction by serving socially useful purpose.

Purposeless organizations are liable to drift and become marginal in the course of time. A sense of purpose is important for other organizational reasons, including facilitating inter- personal processes and formalization of relationships (the other characteristic of an organization) . Globalization connotes dynamic human will for achieving larger social and human purposes.

3. Perspective

Strategic management begins with a statement of clear perspective. Top-management perspective is not a bunch of hunches.

Organizational perspective must be well-researched. In facing global competitive challenges, it is important that the firm possesses a global perspective, even though it might be competing and managing locally.

Failure to develop an in-depth perspective results in missed opportunities. Polemical debates arise from lack of appreciation of multiple perspectives.

Some of the techniques for improving the perspective horizon and thereby quality of decisions are: scenario-building, process consultation, in-house training programmes, job rotation, and cross-functional teams.

4. Positioning

An important dimension in achieving world-class competitiveness relates to the positioning of the firm. This dimension has high interface with organizational purpose, planning and perspective, resulting in definitional confusion. Positioning of the firm is distinct from positioning of products in marketing. The term has remained mostly confined to abstract strategic management literature despite its obvious criticality to practice.

An important dimension in strategy is to understand 'where am I', 'why am I here', 'where do I want to be', and 'how do I reach there'. In other words, the strategic manager has to ascertain the existing position and future positioning of the firm.

Positioning means the place in the industry which the firm would like to occupy in relation to its competitors from the perspective of the consumers. Does the firm compete on lowest-cost mass-production, high-technology basis? Does it differentiate itself from others on the basis of superior and value-augmented products, or on high-ethic practices, employee policies, etc. which are unique in the industry?

An important technique for ascertaining positioning choices is by mapping the strategic groups in the industry. In this technique, clusters of competitors are identified based on their key strategic choices with regard to broad but critical dimensions of the industry structure.

Strategic positioning, like most other factors in business, is a dynamic concept. Firms must periodically review the strengths of their position viz-a-viz the existing as well as potential competitors and mobility barriers.

Once 'positioning' choice is made, many process- and product-related decisions flow. High-quality rice sellers in developed countries do agree generally that Indian basmati rice would have fetched a far higher premium if it was produced in a 'better imaged' country.

5. Partnerships

The partnership approach suggests a sense of belief and trust in other person's capabilities and skills. It opens the doors for people to look beyond the usual routine responses, and create an environment where people voluntarily come up with innovative solutions for seemingly intractable problems. Partnership is a 'perspective' as well as a 'position'. Partnership has softer (intangible) and harder (tangible) dimensions.

Going beyond the softer side of partnership-approach, development of long-term partners for weak competitors is essential for deriving sustainable advantages. Suppliers, bankers and other investors, employees, government, technology collaborators, transporters, and distributors do have a stake in the firm's well-being (and vice versa) and therefore have to be treated as key resources. In this approach, the perspective is that there can be no profits at the expense of any resource. For world-class performance, thus, an interactive, mutually reinforcing, and politically strong relationship between government, industry, and firms is necessary. To implement this strategy, a fresh perspective of treating each stakeholder as a partner has to be developed at all levels. The diverse groups are held together by shared values. The partnership approach precludes any superior-subordinate relationship. This is true at both the levels: employee-employee, and firm- firm. Government, industry, and firms are partners on one plane.

6. Productivity

Global competitiveness is largely an expression of firm's relative productive efficiency. A country's prosperity is indicated by the amount of value-added goods that are produced/made availabie for consumption. Labour productivity is generally the accepted measure of value- addition with the assumption that the same individual would have different capacities in different technological environments and organizational contexts.

A key managerial decision that vitally affects the firm's overall productivity pertains to capital intensity of the project in terms of investments in land, building and machinery. This decision also affects leverage position of firms.

Leverages are of two types: the first, called the degree of operating leverage (DOL), is the firm's commitment to fixed overhead expenses irrespective of business done. The second, degree of financial leverage (DFL), is the way the firm's funds are distributed, for example, the debt- ratio. The degree of combined leverage (DCL) of the firm is the product of its DOL & DFL.

7. Product

A product is a package of information which the customer interprets in his mind while going through the process of consumption. Therefore, the concept of any product must start with the customer in mind, and end with his total satisfaction. In this definition all products are ultimately service converted into information. Beyond quality, products must offer customers a satisfaction level where they become the best salesmen for the company forever.

8. Plans (and Policies)

The thrust of the 10-P framework is to integrate people's personal growth and development with organizational objectives through excellent all-round quality. The premise is that the tasks are executed with finesse by satisfied and motivated people. To ensure that people remain aligned with the common sense of purpose and do not drift, the organization must have a clear, documented statementans of objectives and broad plans.

A firm's plan' must contain a clear mission statement on the way it proposes to serve the customer.

The first task for the firms is to break open the rigidity of the work culture system which, over time has acquired characteristic air-tight compartmentalization of jobs. In pursuing globalization, functional distinctions evaporate. The firm has to acquire an integrated outlook in its business operations. Strategic manufacturing advantages such as high quality products, costs, productivity, and technology absorption become important and enduring competitive resources. Development of these resources calls for long-term investments in highly skilled and motivated multi-functional personnel backed up by committed professionals.

9. Politics

Organizational politics is a reality; it provides dynamism to individuals, groups and total organization. The orthodox organizational behaviour school holds that politics is an attempt to bypass the official channels or to influence outcomes for personal gains (impliedly, at the cost of organizational efficiency). Hence, this school holds that, politics being a negative power-bearing agent, should be discouraged. This cannot be true in a larger perspective. Political behaviour, in the positive sense of the word, is a highly democratic and peaceful form of conflict resolution process especially useful in high-uncertainty environments.

Political behaviour in the absence of strong organizational purpose becomes manipulative. There are various levels of politics - games are played by many.

10. Performance (and Profits)

Improving performance outcomes is the core of all strategic management theories. Achievement of goals and objectives is the basis of all strategic planning. It is important to realize that different stakeholders will possess different measures of performance. Organizational performance must have several parametres.

Performance parameters must include hard and soft measures such as Market Share, Time taken to develop and introduce new products, technological competitiveness, employee motivation and skills, throughput value-addition, etc.

In such, it may be noted that the ten Ps are not only dynamic, inter-related, but also overlapping. The task of the strategic manager is to strike a 'fit' between the various soft and hard components appropriate to the organizational values and need of the times. At this stage, He has to himself become a 'specialist-entrepreneurial-visionary-general manager'. The successful corporate manager is a combination of serval mutually contradictory attributes.

Figure 23.2 : 10-P FRAMEWORK

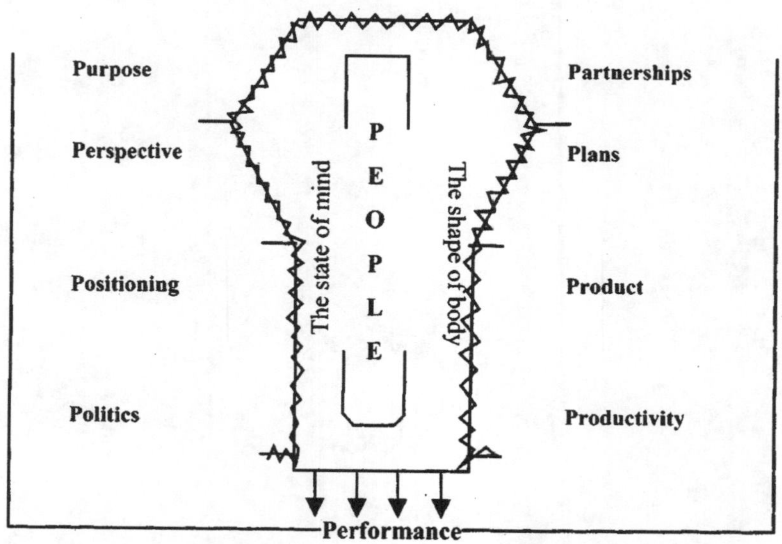

SHORT ANSWER QUESTIONS

1. What do you understand by 'transnational strategy'?
2. What are the drivers for globalisation?
3. Develop a global strategy for any pesonal care service.
4. What are the restrictions on trade in services?

ESSAY QUESTIONS

1 Discuss the impact of various globalisation drivers for the following services:
(a) Hotel (b) Airlines (c) Consultancy.
2. What are the elements of a global strategy?

3. How is international advertising achieved?
4. Discuss the various industry globalisation drivers with examples.
5. What are the modes of internationalisation? Elaborate.
6. How do transnational strategies differ for supplementary services?
7. What are the barriers for international marketing of services?
8. How do trade in services differ from trade in goods?
9. Explain the 10-P model of global strategic management for the following services:
   (a) Insurance (b) Telecommunications (c) Education.

EXERCISE/ASSIGNMENT

1. Make a list of services that have transcended borders. What obstacles have these services faced?
2. What are the policy guidelines issued by the Government of India with regard to entry of multinational firms in the services sector?
3. Discuss the prons and cons of global services taking any five service industries.

●●●

24

Case Studies

Note: This chapter contains case studies inspired by real incidents. Some of the case studies pertain to foreign markets while others deal with local issues. Also, some case studies do not have questions attached to them. It is left to the reader to address the issues in the case and to adopt different solutions and strategies to deal with the concepts and issues.

CASE STUDY 1: MYTHS OF PROFESSIONAL SERVICES MARKETING

For decades, professional service providers—including consultants, accountants, lawyers and others—were reluctant marketers. They thrived in a cozy world where networks of personal relationships and word-of-mouth brought them enough new clients to grow a profitable business. Those days aren't gone, but they're fading fast.

For many services buyers, personal relationships are still the driver of purchase decisions, but the cracks in that buying model are now apparent.

In a recent study of client buying behavior, analysts at Raintoday.com found that more than half of professional service purchasers are open to switching service providers. Golf, theatre tickets and other perks are still part of the business development game for many. But even those tactics are running out.

To compete for and win the most profitable work, professional service providers must rethink familiar marketing practices and focus their marketing strategies on the issues that really matter to clients.

Begin that shift in your marketing mindset by challenging four common myths.

Myth 1: Great work speaks for itself

Some believe that delivering outstanding results in the present is the foundation of a successful marketing strategy. That is, if you do great work, your client will hire you when new needs arise and will send you valuable referrals for new business. That logic seems reasonable, but don't bet your business on it.

It's true that flawless delivery is essential for long-term success. It's not likely that a professional service firm would survive a string of service failures. But you can't assume in today's business environment that word of your great performance will travel through your client's organization—and beyond that to others—without sustained effort on your part.

To get the word out, you need client-level communication plans for your current clients, and you need to integrate the details of the success you have helped clients achieve into your overall marketing plan.

Myth 2: A Web site is just a promotional tool

Even with a referral in hand, the majority of prospective clients head straight to your Web site before they call you. Often, that Web site visit is the prospective client's first step in a business relationship with you.

With a virtual handshake, your site has the power to create a positive first impression that can mean the difference between getting a follow-up call from the client and losing that opportunity.

Your Web site should be a critical part of your strategy to initiate and sustain relationships with clients, instead of just a promotional tool. Nothing substitutes for the power of personal interaction with clients, but your Web site can and should re-enforce your commitment to clients.

Professional service firms differ from one another in many ways, including size, scope of services, culture, client management philosophies and people. Yet, to clients, their Web sites make professional service firms look like clones of one another.

Look at the Web sites of a handful of firms, and you'll find similar, hollow marketing messages, such as these:

"Our passion is providing insights to small businesses which lead you and your organization to financial well-being."

"We have built our firm with the resources and support to help meet your long and short-term financial goals."

Clients buy services from people they believe in. Meaningless claims like those won't get the job done.

Your Web site should help you gain clients' trust. How? Build your site's content around specific client problems and issues, not your qualifications or generic mission statements. Give clients what they're looking for—a way to see that your firm understands exactly what they need.

Myth 3: You need to find the client's pain

Sales trainers often advise finding a client's "pain" as the first step to sales success. We're advised to ask prospective clients questions like What keeps you awake at night? What are your pain points? And, If you had a magic wand, what problem would you make disappear?

Not only do such questions make a client's eyes cross, they also expose two fatal flaws. First, they proclaim that you are fishing for answers rather than pursuing a substantive discussion; at the very least, they demonstrate a lack of preparation.

And, second, not all clients are looking for "pain" remedies. Sure, business advisors sort out tough problems for clients, but that doesn't mean they're painful. Maybe clients want to raise the bar on overall company performance, pursue a new business opportunity or improve some aspect of the business. The help you provide doesn't have to alleviate pain.

Myth 4: It's safe to follow the leader

Most professional service marketing follows a predictable strategy—a series of "safe" marketing decisions based on what's being done by others.

The result is me-too marketing that does little to differentiate you from competing firms. Marketing expert Seth Godin warns that "professional service marketing is certainly among the 'safest' I've ever seen. Because it appears to take no risks, it's actually quite risky."

Of course, there is value in learning from the success of others. Many firms face similar marketing challenges, so using the ideas of those who share your plight may seem like a good way to accelerate the development of your marketing strategy.

Unfortunately, relying on the marketing programs of others blurs the subtle differences between professional service firms, leading to a client perception that very different firms have the same characteristics.

Too often, professional service firms do just that—recycle the ideas of others. Review how 25 firms differentiate themselves, and you'll find marketing material that emphasizes attributes like quality service, best price, methodologies or service responsiveness. Because these differentiators are so overused, they've lost their strength.

Clients view such claims as table stakes—the minimum needed to get in the game, but not enough to win. You don't have to stop using those market differentiators completely. But lead your marketing communication with something more client-focused, such as your detailed understanding of the client's problem followed by how you helped others in a similar situation.

No More Myths

The marketing of professional services is evolving, with many new ways to attract and retain clients. Some marketing strategies have lost their magic, while others are emerging as winners.

One marketing truth won't change: Clients will continue to buy from trustworthy and competent people who can demonstrate, beyond a reasonable doubt, that they can produce the results they promise.

Demonstrate that to the market and you'll have clients lined up to work with you.

CASE STUDY 2: AIRLINES ACCOUNT MANAGEMENT AS A MARKETING INVESTMENT

From the time you book an airline flight until that plane lands, your pecking order in the airline's customer hierarchy determines your travel experience. To the airlines, all customers are not equal—they are segmented and managed according to profitability, loyalty, and frequency of travel.

Like the airlines, professional service and solution providers have embraced the concept of account relationship management, yet many struggle with execution. Account management is based on the premise that a subset of your clients will purchase most of your offerings, and so you should manage and market to them differently—and directly. All clients are important to your business, but some are more so than others.

More Eggs in Fewer Baskets

A relationship strategy that differentiates your clients can reduce your cost of sales, simplify your approach to complex relationships, help you deliver products and services to clients more efficiently, and increase the profitability of your business.

At the core of a productive relationship strategy is a shift in mindset. Solution providers are often too willing to chase every new opportunity, when instead they should focus on the clients they've got and the referrals that can flow from them.

Just as with an investment portfolio, though, you should spread your marketing resources among selected clients. Don't focus on a single client, and don't apply your marketing resources equally across all of your clients.

Is It Right for You?

The first step is to decide whether an account relationship program is right for you. For larger firms with long client lists, the decision is a no-brainer. Those firms should use a program to focus resources and people on targeted industries and clients.

In smaller firms, a commitment to client relationship building is desirable, but not every firm needs a formal strategy.

Build Your Portfolio

Choosing clients to include in an account management program is complex, no matter the size of your firm. Assign clients to action categories according to their relative importance to your business at a given point in time. This initial classification is a one-size-fits-none exercise. Let your culture and business objectives guide your decisions.

Consider these questions about your clients:

- **Relationship potential:** Is the client interested in a long-term relationship? Can you realistically expect to sustain a relationship based on mutual benefit?
- **Compatibility:** Is there a good match between the client's long-tern needs and your capabilities?
- **Profitability:** Do historic and forecasted account activity and profitability justify an investment in cultivating a long-term relationship?

Assess each client on two criteria: the strength of the existing relationship and the potential for mutual gain. Place each client in one of four action categories:

1. **Manage key accounts.** The clients you rate highest in both relationship strength and potential for mutual gain are your key accounts and the obvious choices for an account management program.
2. **Invest in relationship.** Clients with a high potential for mutual gain with whom you don't yet have strong relationships are the next generation of key clients—assuming you can build effective relationships with decision makers. Invest in building those relationships to convert those clients to key accounts.
3. **Transition to higher-value offerings.** You may have a solid relationship with clients who don't know about or understand the full extent of the business benefits you offer. Educate those clients on opportunities for mutual gain.
4. **Rethink.** In some cases, the potential for a mutually beneficial business relationship is just not in the cards. If so, consider reducing or eliminating your investment in those clients.

This point-in-time snapshot is just the beginning. Regularly revisit each client's potential and adjust your use of resources.

Take a First Cut at Your Strategy

To achieve the promise of account management, create a specific marketing strategy for each key client that includes eight elements:

1. The top five issues your client faces
2. How you can help with those problems
3. How you stand out from others in meeting the client's challenges
4. The status of your relationships with key decision makers
5. Which relationships you'll build and which you'll shore up
6. The marketing tactics you'll use to position yourself in the minds of key client decision makers and influencers
7. Your marketing budget for the client in terms of time and money
8. How you will measure the success of each client relationship.

Once you've created the outline for your plan, seek client input. The ideal relationship strategy is one that's developed with your partner, the client. Without consensus on what you hope to contribute, your plan is wishful thinking.

But Will It Fly?

It may seem risky to manage key clients this way. After all, you could invest the bulk of your marketing resources on a small group of clients who fail to generate the profit you need. So don't give up on other marketing activities that generate visibility for your business. As a guideline, commit roughly 60% of your marketing resources to your key accounts, and the remainder to other clients.

Patience is essential. If you've selected the right clients to include in a client relationship program, you work the plan consistently, and you have the right level of accountability, the program will pay dividends in the form of long-term profitable relationships, referrals for new business, and a simplified approach to marketing.

CASE STUDY 3: FACTORS THAT DISTINGUISH SERVICES MARKETING

It's been called "selling the invisible"—delivering intangible services as a core "product" offering.

Law firms, management consultants, IT services and telecom providers, architectural groups, healthcare and educational organizations, financial and insurance institutions, and a multitude of business-to-consumer operations profit from performing and delivering people-based services.

But invisibility, or intangibility, is just one factor that distinguishes services marketing from product marketing. Along with inseparability, variability, and perishability, these four characteristics affect the way clients behave during the buying process and the way organizations must interact with them.

Additionally, these characteristics influence the development of marketing strategies and the more tactical marketing mix—from the "packaging" and pricing of services bundles, to defining distribution plans and promotions options.

To ensure business success, services marketing professionals must clearly understand these characteristics, how they affect client behavior, and how their organization can respond to diminish engagement risk, improve customer perceptions, and enhance market opportunities.

Intangibility

Services are not physical and cannot be "possessed." Because they can't be seen, touched, or made tangible in some way, assessing their quality and value is difficult.

A services client will never know how good the service is until after he receives it. In some cases, it actually may be months or years before a trigger event occurs to activate the service, at which time the client hopes to experience the promised service quality (e.g., an IT crisis triggers service, or an accident initiates an insurance claim).

This can be unsettling for the client, whose response is to look for tangible signals about the service process and quality prior to purchase to reduce uncertainty and reservation.

The Marketing Response: Services marketing professionals must determine how to effectively communicate the services process, deliverables, and benefits in order to build client confidence. Tangible signals that indicate services quality and value come from personal interaction, trusted recommendations, clear communications, equipment used or processes followed, pricing, and the physical environment in which the business operates.

With promotions, a logo symbol can offer a sense of tangibility—the "good hands" of Allstate, the Merrill Lynch bull, the Prudential Insurance rock. Testimonials and case studies can be used to build client confidence and rapport. The communications material itself (paper, design, and content) can convey quality, too.

Pricing can also be an indicator of quality: Premium pricing often suggests higher quality, while prices that are too low may hint at the inexperience, limited depth, or vague processes of the services producer.

But tangibility must extend beyond promotions and price. Because positive personal interaction and "chemistry" is a gauge of quality to the client, marketing as a discipline must be influential in the training of sales and service associates. These individuals literally are the embodiment of marketing for the organization. Their ability to deliver on the brand promise affects business success.

Therefore, creating client relationships, setting appropriate expectations, and learning to represent the company in an acceptable way (e.g., through appearance, attitude, and communications) should augment standard knowledge and process training. Because it is critical to services delivery, the success of client interactions should be quantified, measured, and improved with regularity.

Inseparability

The *production* of the services can't be separated from its *consumption*. For example, the production and consumption of a medical exam happen together, as do many consulting services and IT maintenance contracts.

This leads to two important factors. First, the client is, essentially, "in the factory," watching production all along the way. It is very important for a service provider or consultant to carefully manage the "production process" as the client is able to observe it in action and make judgments about quality and value.

Second, the client often expects the service to be provided in a specific way or by a specific individual—and that can pose challenges in assigning staff, managing the process, and ensuring the frontline people display the appropriate knowledge, attitude, and appearance when delivering the service.

The Marketing Response: Services marketing professionals can encourage client participation during the delivery process. As the client is engaged through interviews, strategy sessions, regular communications, testing, and face-to-face updates at major milestones, he gains confidence and builds commitment to the engagement and relationship.

To manage distribution and pricing considerations in the face of inseparability, the marketing professional can identify the level of personalization that the client requires and the company can support. For example, interactions can be managed through conference calls versus on-site visits, or exchanges can be shifted from high-contact to low-contact operations (e.g., personalized banking to ATM or online banking). These changes should be carefully evaluated to ensure client acceptance and positive brand impact.

Variability

Sometimes called "heterogeneity," services quality and consistency are subject to great variability because they are delivered by people, and human behavior is difficult to control. Personal performance and quality can vary by time of day (people get tired), time of month or year (during tax time for CPAs), workload, experience, attitude, knowledge, and other factors. Maintaining client trust during lapses (which will happen) is critical.

Also, variability is why it can be risky to have one person make the sale and establish the relationship, and another deliver the service. The original contact person is the one who reduced risk for the client; when someone else delivers the service, the client may become agitated or wary.

The Marketing Response: Services marketing professionals particularly can overcome variability by developing special service packages.

For example, the level of quality to be received can be deliberately limited. IT maintenance contracts frequently offer a range of service packages (e.g., from "basic" with response in 4-6 hours, to "premium" with immediate, on-call support). Standardizing some service offerings enables the organization to be very specific in noting service and quality deliverables, thus decreasing variability and meeting client expectations simultaneously.

When this method is used, variability can become a point of differentiation as it enables flexibility and services customization.

When promoting services, marketers can overcome client concern about service consistency in two ways—through team introductions and through positive referrals. The sales leader should make it clear that a qualified team will work with the client, and schedule face-to-face introduction and discovery sessions to smooth the next-phase transition process.

In addition, positive word-of-mouth referrals, written testimonials and case studies, or referenceable accounts can dispel client concerns about variability.

Because things can and do go wrong, the services producer should know how to deliver a professional client response. How quickly the response is delivered is critical. The objective is to maintain client trust; so shifting blame, explaining it away, or ignoring it can further damage the relationship. The services producer should provide an apology, fix the problem or situation quickly, make up for the inconvenience with additional free services or a token of appreciation, and determine the reason for the error and fix it at the root—even if it means people or process changes.

Finally, research shows that employee satisfaction is the most important factor in providing high quality service. Potential client interaction problems can be minimized through adequate training, empowering employees to make more customer-focused decisions, and rewarding them for positive customer-oriented behavior.

Also, establishing employee feedback mechanisms so that management can hear and take action on issues of concern will strengthen employee perceptions of the company, increase satisfaction, and result in better client interactions.

Perishability

You can't store services for future use. When a client misses an appointment with his attorney, that time can never be recaptured. When hotel rooms are empty and theater tickets go unsold, the inherent value vanishes.

Perishability also affects performance, as balancing supply and demand can be difficult. Demand may be seasonal, time sensitive, or crisis driven. When demand fluctuates, it can be a challenge to maintain high performance levels.

For example, a CPA at tax time may have difficulty giving the same personalized attention as at other times of the year. In IT services, performance could be tested during peak times of disaster recovery, massive server outages, or when juggling new installation projects in four states. While product marketers handle supply/demand issues through production scheduling and inventory management, services marketers don't have that advantage.

The Marketing Response: Unlike the other three characteristics, perishability primarily is a concern of the service producer—the client is aware of this factor only when there is an insufficient supply and he has to wait for the service. For the services marketing professional, perishability affects pricing and distribution most distinctly.

If the services are particularly time sensitive, demand-based pricing can be instituted as with airline tickets, seasonal vacations, or even a partner's hourly fee structure. For many services, managing demand is handled by scheduling delivery through appointments, while increasing supply is addressed through multiple locations or additional site personnel.

Another way to balance supply-demand issues is through the use of retainer agreements. For those services that are long-term, maintenance, or consultative in nature, this pricing and delivery method ensures the client of ongoing services delivery with a greater consistency in quality and allows the services producer to establish a more predictable cash flow and forecasting scenario.

The Final Factor

What's right for your services organization? How can your company strengthen client relationships and improve its competitive position?

Understanding the characteristics of services can provide a unique opportunity for services producers to improve business success by rethinking their pricing models and packaging options, improving production processes and client participation, enhancing customer focus, and building employee relationship skills.

CASE STUDY 4: MARKETING CHALLENGE

How would you sell computer repair services? Fast, friendly, and reliable first come to mind as the main selling points. But that kind of language speaks to the company's opinion of itself, not necessarily much else.

Instead, focus on the customer—not the company. For example: "Your computer will not stall out after it leaves our shop." Or: "Bought a new gadget or computer? Let us set it up for you."

Previous Challenge: How to add a dash of creativity to service solutions

It's not uncommon for a person to move from a product-oriented business to a service-oriented one and vice versa. I come from a product environment, where we had a defined product and targeted customers, and I was consistently a top producer. I've moved into a service-oriented business and have taken a dive because I have trouble thinking creatively of solutions specifically tailored to my client. What works well for developing custom solutions, and is it possible to succeed in both product and service areas?

—AJ, business development

Put Yourself in Your Prospects' Shoes

Everyone who wrote in said to treat your service like a product and to try to understand how it addresses your customers' needs. It's about finding the value and communicating it. Sometimes you must get creative because selling services often has invisible value—so you won't always be able to put the value in numbers such as "increase your productivity by 10 percent!"

With computer support, for instance, having a computer or gadget ready for use is a valuable service. You can attempt to add numbers or statistics by claiming that all computers and gadgets are ready for use within 24 hours. This kind of claim may not always be possible, depending on the complexity of the problem. But it doesn't hurt to think creatively and see what kind of "solid" benefits you can offer.

Steve Beaman, president of Beaman Consulting Services, provides many questions that lead to treating a service like a product. He recommends you first step inside your clients' shoes:

What benefit do the customers receive from using the service? What is in it for them? Put yourself in their shoes. What benefit would you want to receive from the service? Is there a particular solution that the service addresses or a unique way that other services don't provide a particular aspect of the service (unique competitive advantage)?

Focus on the key points that are issues for other businesses like your prospect and that the service addresses. Do you have any testimonials, quotes, attention-getting headlines about the service? How has the service helped other businesses?

Bill Huffman, vice-president of interactive marketing with The Robin Shepherd Group, believes that everything is a product, whether tactile or not. He agrees with getting to know the prospect, including developing the "problem-solving skills" or "critical-thinking skills" that are necessary to solve your prospects' problems and design a creative sales pitch:

If you are in the service business, you should still have a targeted customer list. It sounds like you just have to learn how to think like your "new" customers. If you understand your customers, then you will become aware of the issues they face. This will allow you to more effectively use your service offering to solve the customers' problem.

Another way to get creative is to look at what the competition (or even your client) is currently doing and then take their pitch in a new direction. Tamara Halbritter, freelance writer, recently found a way to beat out the competition and woo a client:

A few weeks ago, I had an opportunity to pitch my writing services to a new client. I knew the client was looking at several other writers, so I wanted to find a way to stand out. I thought about the way many other writers sell their services and I tried to expand on some of the ideas I've seen in their campaigns for my pitch. And then it occurred to me: Look at what the business is doing now, and show them how my way (my writing service) would be even more effective.

So I perused the company's web site from another business's perspective and realized that they weren't addressing a big problem that many of their clients face. They had also left out some critical information that many clients would need before they could make a purchasing decision. So I wrote some web copy that addresses that particular problem and explains how their product does the trick (from the client point of view, providing all the necessary details) and the business thought it was so creative and liked it so much, they hired me soon after I submitted my pitch.

Learn to think like your customers and understand their specific problems. Then go beyond your competitors' current offerings to devise a creative, custom service solution to address your customers' exact needs. Your customers are sure to be impressed by your efforts.

CASE STUDY 5: SERVICE BRAND PREFERENCE

Imagine the strongman game at the carnival. You lift the sledgehammer over your head and swing it down onto the platform.

When it strikes its target, a metal cylinder rises up and up—20 feet up the pole, until it dings the bell. On its way down, the pole the cylinder passes the same words it passed on the way up: strongman, tough guy, athlete, junior, weakling.

In a way, establishing a services brand follows a similar process. You swing the hammer (your marketing tactics, the marketing mix you employ, the quality of your company's services), and the strength of your efforts determines whether your brand moves up the pole and makes it to the top to ring the bell.

The question is, "What stages must your brand pass through to ring the bell?"

Ringing the Branding Bell

Strip away the apparent complexity around what building a service brand is all about. You will find that the stages you have to reach with your own strongman efforts are straightforward:

- **Recognize:** Your target customers must recognize you.
- **Articulate:** They need to be able to articulate what you do.
- **Memorize:** When they need your service, your company should be the first option they think of.
- **Prefer:** Your target customers should prefer to use your service instead of all the other options available to them.

While there are several interim stages in the services branding process through which you must travel, the desired end result—the golden goose of branding—is to establish *preference* for your brand over your competitors. (Can you hear the bell ringing?)

To help you visualize your steps to a stronger brand, follow the what we call the Brand RAMP (Recognize, Articlulate, Memorize, Prefer). Within the RAMP framework and methodology, branding becomes approachable as a process and, at the same time, is focused on a worthwhile business outcome.

Let's take a brief look at each stage of the Brand RAMP and see how it leads to establishing a powerful services brand.

Recognize

Question: *What's the purpose of this marketing campaign?*

Answer: *Well, we really need to get our name out there. You know, establish our identity.*

We are about as impressed with this answer as we are with the salesperson who has a meeting with a prospective client and describes it "is a get-to-know-you meeting."

The purpose of a sales meeting is to find sales opportunities and advance a sale. Getting to know the client is part of what is done in that process. It's not a goal in and of itself.

In services branding, getting your name out there and establishing an identity is something that you do in the process of branding; it's not the goal. For most firms, focusing on standalone brand recognition leads to inefficent use of money, time and effort in the marketing process. You work hard to get your name out there, but you do not generate actual business development activity.

On the other hand, companies that don't have enough outbound activity leave their business fortunes to serindipity. Worse, they never know where the next lead will come from or how to plan for growth.

You need your prospective clients to recognize you. Without recognition, you're at the whim of your referral base. As you start to proactively generate recognition, though, you need to do it in a way that serves other, higher-return goals (namely the rest of the RAMP process).

Articulate

The core of brand messaging is getting your prospective clients to be able to state, in clear terms, what you do. This serves multiple ends:

- By their knowing what you do, you now have a chance that they will know how, where and when to apply your services.
- They may now be able to refer you to others who can use your services.
- They are able to explain your services internally so that they can create a coalition (if it's necessary) to purchase your services.

This is so important. Yet so many services firms struggle with how to articulate what they do. Regardless of your situation, whether your firm is large or small, singularly focused or with a range of complex services, you need to be able to get the message across.

The litmus test of whether it is getting across is asking a prospect, "Do you know what we do?" and hearing the answer you want. Let's assume you make it past the Recognition phase of the Brand RAMP. At this point, you want to avoid the following:

Question from the firm: *So you've heard of us. Do you know what we do?*

Answer from prospect: *Yes, I've heard of you. What you do...I'm not sure.*

Memorize

At some point we've all had the following thought, "This is a sticky problem…oh, I remember there's a firm out there that focuses 100% on fixing this problem and I've heard they're great…what was their name again… slipped my mind. Oh well, on to other things."

How often and what type of brand messaging you employ will effect how well people remember you at the time of need. If they know who you are and they know what you do, but your marketing mix and communications plan drop the ball in terms of creating a *lasting* impression, your business development efforts will never perform to their fullest potential.

Prefer

Prospective clients *recognize* you, can *articulate* what you do, and have a *memory* of you at the time of need. Still, all of this is for naught if they do not have a compelling reason to want to work with you and your firm.

Brand preference is created in many ways through both the marketing tactics and the actual service experiences with your company. How you create preference is the subject of many other articles (by us and others) on MarketingProfs. For this article, simply remember this: engage branding and marketing acticives with the idea of creating as much *preference* as you can for your services with your prospective and current clients.

Developing a brand identity without the RAMP methodology firmly embedded in the *beginning* of the process often leads to graphic design and marketing campaigns in a vacuum. Consequently, logos, Web sites, brochures, presentations and marketing tactics are developed without the end goal in mind: creating a client's preference for the brand.

At the Carnival

The carnival is your market. The sledge hammer is your branding program.

If you swing the hammer with the right force and aim it at the right spot, the prizes you win are more new clients and increased brand loyalty. And, unlike at the carnival, these prizes can be worth a great deal more than the cost of playing the games.

CASE STUDY 6: SUSTAINABLE DIFFERENTIATION

While the economy is beginning to show signs of recovery, companies continue to face a brutal business environment. Competitors are cutting prices, simultaneously introducing new products and adding features to their existing product portfolio. What can you do in this highly competitive environment?

Essentially, you are faced with one of two fundamental strategies: become the low-price provider in your category or industry, which requires a cost structure lower than your competitors, or substantively differentiate your products from your competitors'.

Many firms try to accomplish the latter by creating additional products or upgrading their existing products with incremental features. For example, Kellogg's Eggo waffles come in 16 flavors, and my local supermarket offers seven types of turkey breast. However, while the aforementioned companies are providing options, what meaningful value are these incremental product improvements really providing?

Additional products and upgrades are often competitively driven without any real understanding of how much additional value is being provided to the customer. Companies merely copycat their competitors without investigating what solutions their customers value.

This strategy of continually upgrading products, while seemingly a necessity to keep on a level playing field, provides little in the way of true differentiation.

The Consumer Electronics Association estimates that more devices have been launched from 1998 to 2003 than during the entire previous history of the industry. However, beyond a few core innovations, such as perhaps PDAs and digital cameras, what real value has been added? The path out of this reactive new product doodad strategy is to shift your perspective from being product driven to being customer-value driven.

A true differentiation needs to be somewhat sustainable and difficult to replicate. This is especially troublesome with physical products (versus service-related products), because the functions performed by your most-recent nifty product or feature is quickly copied. Research reflects that even the most sophisticated functionality provided by new products is replicated within three to six months.

Think of Proctor and Gamble spending all that money on developing the Swiffer only to have numerous competitors duplicate the functionality in a matter of months. While one might say that this is the inevitable nature of our competitive system, there are other approaches that will yield a more sustainable and difficult-to-replicate value proposition.

Specifically, delivering outstanding service to your customers will go a long way toward providing that advantage. Many of you are reading this and are thinking that you have heard this before. However, understanding a concept is a long way from implementing it.

The American Customer Satisfaction Index has consistently revealed that American business has not improved service delivery over the past decade. This finding clearly reflects that most companies, while understanding the value of service, are not delivering on this powerful means of differentiation.

One company that not only understands the value of service but also delivers is GE—by many accounts the best managed company in the world. It is known for a wide range of products, including light bulbs, jet engines, medical imaging equipment, locomotives, consumer appliances, and turbines.

But GE is changing its strategic direction and is emphasizing service to such an extent that a component of its overall corporate vision states that it will be "a service company which also manufactures products."

This direction is exemplified in the remote diagnostics service package that it sells with almost all of its engine-related products. A GE service center using satellite communication and sophisticated software will monitor a locomotive engine and, on the first sign of trouble, proactively take corrective action. That is real value!

Now, why is the supposedly best-managed company in the world making this transition to a service company? Service is a way to achieve sustainable differentiation and higher margins. Many organizations realize the importance of providing good service, but most don't grasp that great service delivery requires a tenacious focus on execution.

Excellent service delivery is hard work and operationally exhausting. It requires explicitly defining what customers want, measuring how well you deliver on customer requirements and hiring the type of people who are suited to providing good service. Once in the door, you must train those people well, provide them with outstanding systems and processes and reward them for excellent performance. Certainly not as romantic as developing that new doodad for your existing product.

Technology, especially Internet-related hardware and software, was supposed to automate many aspects of service. In other words, we were going to automate service—get rid of all those hard-to-hire, -train and -manage customer service representatives.

This technological promise was made once before with call centers—telecommunication tools were going to deliver better service and reduce costs. However, our frustration is legendary with this supposedly better approach to customer service. A recent comprehensive Pew Charitable Trust study discovered that 94% of a randomly selected sample of 2,013 adults were "very frustrated" with call centers.

Technology is an enabler. It is not the solution to delivering great service.

Amazon.com is an example of a company that uses technology to support great service delivery. Amazon is the highest-rated company in the American Customer Satisfaction Index. It has invested millions in technology that helps them meet and exceed customers' expectations. Its one-click ordering process is about as convenient as it gets. Its order confirmation and tracking services are easy to access and usable by even the most inexperienced computer user.

The key point is that Amazon uses technology as a tool to deliver great service—not as an end in itself. Without knowledge of the customers' needs and the specific measures required to ensure that those needs are met, the technology would mean nothing.

A vast amount of research has gone into what the American consumer values in service, and the results have consistently revealed that we highly value two attributes: reliability and responsiveness.

Reliability means being dependable, accurate and honest—and delivering on your commitments. Responsiveness means being eager to help, offering an appropriate number of choices, and demonstrating both flexibility and simplicity in those out-of-the-ordinary circumstances.

The Internet and related information technology can certainly help you become more reliable and responsive; however, technology also adds another layer of complexity. A great example of this is email. If your organization doesn't have standards for getting back to customers, emails will often languish and sometimes go unanswered.

In early 2003, Jupiter Research investigated customer expectations for email response times and discovered that over 50% expected email to be returned within a 24-hour period, but only 54% of companies surveyed met those expectations. In addition, Jupiter discovered that 29% of businesses did not respond to email at all!

Clearly, these companies do not have a clear picture of what customers expect when it comes to providing reliable service. You must make a commitment to respond to your customers' emails, faxes or phone calls within a timeframe they expect.

Responsiveness is the second core attribute of great service and should be a prime driver in all your service delivery processes, including your Web site. For example, shipping is a key consideration in online purchasing. How many sites do you know that provide a number of choices that meet your pricing requirements? Also, customers expect to use whatever communications medium is easiest for them. Is your company's 1-800-number clearly identified on all your Web pages, or are you instead using your Web site to coerce a customer into unwanted self-service?

Another key element of responsiveness is an easy-to-use Web site. Online consumers expect to complete a purchase in three clicks. Can your site do this? Some 60% of potential customers drop away with each additional click in the online ordering process. It is imperative that you design a Web site with the customers' service expectations in mind. You want customer loyalty, and providing great service is the prime determinant of Internet customer loyalty!

Creating sustainable differentiation is a daunting task, but providing great service does provide a business with a hard-to-replicate value proposition.

If you start with meeting customers' needs for reliability and responsiveness, you are well on your way to providing a competitively superior level of customer value.

CASE STUDY 7: REVENUE ROLLERCOASTER TRAP

Many consulting, professional, and technology service businesses find themselves trapped in the following vicious, no-growth cycle. The firm is either:

- Heavily marketing because they don't have enough leads and new business or
- Heavily billing and delivering—and thus have no time for marketing.

We call this the service revenue rollercoaster. It's a common trap for many professional service companies because when they get busy they can't sustain their marketing momentum...they're too busy with client work. Then, when the client work slows down, they must start marketing from square-one all over again, as all momentum from previous marketing efforts has stalled.

How to Avoid the Trap—Create a Revenue Engine

The ideal role of the marketing function for consulting and professional service companies is to generate a sustainable flow of leads and revenue—helping the company to avoid using only billable resources to intermittently generate leads for their practices when business is slow.

Consider the following six guidelines to help your firm establish and benefit from a sustainable lead and revenue generation engine:

- **Choose to Avoid the Services Revenue Rollercoaster:** The first step in avoiding the services revenue rollercoaster is to realize it exists, and to overtly declare, "We are going to maintain marketing energy by creating a lead and revenue generation engine—and avoid the pitfalls of the revenue rollercoaster."
- **Balance Billable and Non-Billable Resources:** When creating a revenue engine, assign a non-billable resource as the senior marketing leader. This person, whether full or part-time, should be able to set strategy for and lead the revenue engine, not merely implement tactics.

Senior billable resources may flow in and out of the marketing team as the busy-ness of their practices dictate, but it is imperative that the revenue engine continues to function and improve under the seamless leadership of a competent senior person.

- **Understand Services Marketing:** The person who heads your firm's marketing efforts doesn't necessarily need to be an industry insider (i.e. you don't need a CPA to run your CPA firm's marketing efforts), but you do need someone who understands how profitable services clients are attracted and retained.
- **Dedicate Management and Staff:** It may be trite to say so, but without senior management support, your revenue engine aspirations will turn into a "marketing department" that buys a few ads, sends some mail, maintains a website, and puts together your glossy brochures.

Senior managers must set the tone, fund the efforts, and involve themselves in the revenue engine. Revenue engines in services firms depend on the energy and efforts of all the professional staff—from the partners to the rising stars to the new associates.

Without senior management dedication the billable staff will not involve themselves with the revenue engine. Without the billable staff actively on board and working in concert with marketing you won't have a revenue engine.

- **Reward Business Development Success:** To get billable resources on board and involved with your ongoing marketing efforts, you must first consider what drives their behavior.

For example, if a professional is only compensated on billability, they will only focus on business development when it is absolutely necessary (producing revenue rollercoaster behavior). If they are compensated for some balance of the two, they will be more inclined to balance their energy on both—generating and delivering business simultaneously, thus helping to smooth out the revenue rollercoaster.

Consequences are also important. It's counterproductive if, for example, the most senior person in the firm frowns every time she sees someone not billable, even if the person is actively and energetically engaged in a business development activity that they're incented for and expected to do. Uncover and mitigate these "informal" disincentives to business development.

- **Maintain Client Satisfaction and Loyalty:** According to Fred Reicheld and Earl Sasser in the Harvard Business Review, "...for service companies...a 5% increase in customer loyalty can produce profit increases from 25% to 85%," and "customer satisfaction drives customer loyalty."

As your marketing efforts take hold and you grow, make sure you continue to focus your firm on maintaining loyalty and satisfaction. Though many don't, all firms should formally measure client loyalty and satisfaction. Marketing should have a major role in client satisfaction and loyalty measurement, and in driving firm behavior to increase satisfaction and loyalty.

By maintaining client satisfaction and loyalty, you smooth out the revenue rollercoaster because you increase your chances of the phone ringing with a new project waiting for you on the other end.

Consistent Lead and Client Generation

Avoiding the revenue rollercoaster by implementing a revenue engine takes time, focus, energy, funding, and, most important, organizational change. It can, however, be the key to breaking the vicious no-growth cycle of marketing/billing/marketing/and billing that traps many professional service firms.

By implementing a sustainable revenue engine you not only avoid the revenue rollercoaster trap, you wholly reverse it. Once business development and marketing energy are simultaneously sustained, success breeds success. Sustained marketing efforts tend to snowball over time; the longer they're sustained and continuously improved, the greater the payoff.

In this case, that success is measured in consistency of leads, revenue, and profit to your firm.

CASE STUDY 8: THEME PARK

A theme park based at Mumbai proposes to come out with a programme to attract the attention of School Children. The programme involves a package of games, drama and dance competitions. The winners would be given high value prizes.

Questions:

a) How would you go about marketing this programme?

b) Will this programme any way help to improve the image of theme park? How?

CASE STUDY 9: BZC BANK

In the last six months or so, the BZC bank in a small town found that a number of its important customers from the business sector have considerably reduced their business with the bank. It has come to the notice of BZC that these customers have opened accounts with the newly opened branch of the NST bank.

Questions:

(a) Formulate suitable hypotheses and research design to find out the reasons for this.

(b) What is the strategy to be adopted by BZC Bank?

CASE STUDY 10: PPP HOTEL

The PPP hotel, located in a narrow lane in a busy locality in Hyderabad, which serves 'Andhra Style' food has become very popular and has become very overcrowded. The owner of the hotel allowed his nephew to open a hotel in the same name in a nearby locality. The new hotel has a better building and seating arrangements. The food served in the new hotel is supplied from the old hotel on a cost plus basis. Within a short while, the new hotel began to attract more customers than the original one, although the prices in the new hotel are about 20 percent higher than in the older one.

Questions:

a) Why is the new hotel able to attract more customers?

b) Do you suggest any future strategy for the PPP?

CASE STUDY 11: HOTEL SNOW VIEW

Hotel Snow View located in Shimla was famous for its services. Till 1998, the tourists in seasons had to make advance bookings for accommodation. Now few more hotels established recently have started attracting tourists because of their proactive policies. The business of Snow View declined considerably. Even after few policy changes, the decline could not be arrested. Snow View has decided to go for a professional Director Marketing who would be solely responsible for formulating new strategies to bring the business back on stream.

Questions:

(a) If you are appointed as Director Marketing, will you accept the offer? Why?

(b) If you accept the offer what changes would you implement to bring back the hotel on rails?

(c) What value added services would you offer?

CASE STUDY 12: HIPPOCRATES HOSPITALS

Hippocrates Hospitals Ltd has become a well known corporate entity in the promotion of Health Care Services in this country. Recently the corporate planning division of the company has suggested to the Board of Directors that a Hospital should be established at New Delhi which would increase the coffers of the company. The corporate planning division had suggested that a unique range of

Health Care Services should be made available. At the same time the services offered should be affordable and available to all segments of the society at all times.

Question:

Evolve a marketing strategy for the marketing of health services at New Delhi.

CASE STUDY 13: SANJIVINI HOSPITAL

Sanjivini Hospital, established 22 years ago, had a fairly good reputation. The management has realised that of late the customers are not very happy and that many of them have started patronising other hospitals.

Question:

Suggest a framework for a study to identify the problems. The proposal should also pinpoint the services to be covered by the study.

CASE STUDY 14: SHAJAZ INTERNATIONAL

Shajaz International, a premier Five Star Hotel based at Kolkatta has started facing decline in its Corporate customer inventory. Corporate clients who had constant relationship for a long period with SHAJAZ have moved over to other competing star hotels. The CEO, expressed concern over this trend and worried that the same trend is likely to happen with their other client segments of both national and international individual customers. On this background if you are consulted:

Question:

What could be the strategy you would recommend to overcome the situation?

• • •

Appendix I

Table A.1 : CREATING BREAKTHROUGH SERVICES

Dimension	*"Merely Good" Service Providers*	*Breakthrough Service Providers*
Approach to the design of the service encounter	Regard the relationships in a service encounter as a series of trade-offs (higher quality vs. higher productivity, lower cost vs. lost customer loyalty)	Regard the relationships in a service encounter as a series of mutually reinforcing concepts forcing concepts (higher quality and higher productivity, lower costs and higher customer loyalty, etc.)
Emphasis on quality and value	Concentrate on producing services of the highest quality	Concentrate on producing services of the highest value to customers, taking into account quality in relation to price and other customer costs of service acquisition
Emphasis on sales delivery	Design marketing and building efforts for sales growth	Focus marketing and service service delivery efforts efforts on building the loyalty of existing customers while also attracting new ones
Approach to building customer satisfaction	Measure customer expectations and meet or exceed them	Measure both customer and server expectations and meet or exceed both, recognizing the self-reinforcing relationship between server and customer satisfaction.

Table A.2 : DEVELOPING A VISION OF THE SERVICE BUSINESS

Dimension	*"Merely Good" Service Providers*	*Breakthrough Service Providers*
Definition of service concept	Define their service concept and their businesses in terms of services, processes, or even equipment by which they are delivered	Define their service concept and their businesses in terms of results produced for customers
Customer targeting	Identify target customers primarily on demographic dimensions (age, income etc.)	Identify target customers primarily on psychographic dimensions (life-styles, perceived risks, etc.).
Operating strategy formulation	Formulate operating strategies to provide conventional 'low cost' or "differentiation" advantages over competitors	Develop operating strategies that leverage value for customers over cost, often achieving both low cost, and significant differentiation
Service delivery system design	Design service delivery systems that focus on reliable and timely service delivery	Design service delivery systems that offer customer assurance and tangible evidence of the service ("leave behinds," uniforms, etc.) as well as reliability and timeliness

Table A.3 : BUILDING CUSTOMER LOYALTY

Dimension	*"Merely Good" Service Providers*	*Breakthrough Service Providers*
Measurement of purchasing behavior	Track repeat purchasing behaviour of loyal customers	Track repeat purchasing behavior of loyal customers and follow up with those whose service usage has lapsed.
Cost-value measurement	Generally support the idea that loyal customers are valuable	Seek to measure the value of of customer loyalty and the cost of lost customers as the basis for budgeting efforts to preserve the existing customer base
Marketing budget patterns	Spend liberally to promote usage by old and new customers	Explicitly establish budgets for efforts to retain existing customers as well as engage in spending to promote usage by old and new customers
Strategy for serving existing customers	Develop methods for serving all customers more effectively, with	Activate specific initiatives to develop customer loyalty through measuring and managing expecta

	general purpose of increasing repeat service utilization	tions, carefully managing the initial service encounter, "membership" programs, customer "training," and efforts to make customers better at what they do

Table A.4 : FOCUSSING AND POSITIONING A SERVICE

Dimension	*"Merely Good" Service Providers*	*Breakthrough Service Providers*
Sources of focus	Focus on serving specific groups of customers, primarily through marketing emphasis	Focus on serving specific groups of customers with an operating strategy and service delivery system designed specifically to meet their needs, often requiring restrictions to discourage unwanted customers
Focus in operating strategies	Attempt to develop new markets or businesses that share a service delivery system with existing ones	Expand into new businesses with dedicated service delivery systems and management
Scope of positioning efforts	Center their positioning efforts around promotional themes that seek to help customers differentiate them from competitors on important dimensions	Regard positioning as something to be achieved first through operating strategy and service delivery system design and secondarily through marketing efforts that seek to help customers differentiate them from competitors on important dimensions
Primary bases for establishing a 'position' in relation to customers and competitors	Based on marketing research of customer needs and competitor capabilities develop operating strategies to deliver superior service on dimensions important to customers.	Based on marketing research of customer needs and competence capabilities, seek positions through operating strategies built on initia-tives that run counter to "industry myths" that change the way custom -ers feel or do business, altering the important dimensions of competition for the entire industry.

Table A.5 : DETERMINING THE TRUE COST OF POOR QUALITY

Dimension	*"Merely Good" Service Providers*	*Breakthrough Service Providers*
Management attitudes towards measurement	Realize the importance of measuring the cost of poor quality but do not have the means to do so in the firm's	Develop devices outside the accounting system for measuring service quality costs

	existing accounting system	
Scope of effort	Devise means of measuring and tracking explicit costs of appraisal (inspection, testing, and system auditing), error prevention, and correcting complaints (so-called external failure costs)	Track not only explicit cost of appraisal, error prevention, and external service failures but also the internal costs of poor service (lowered employee morale, increased turnover, and lowered productivity)
Use of information	Use measurements of the cost of poor quality to justify periodic programmes to improve quality at points that the tracking system indicates are important	Use this information as the basis for budgeting and launching companywide quality improvement efforts and tracking the value of quality improvement against the costs of such efforts
Emphasis on customer cost	Develop measure of customer costs that are limited to the cost of the defective service, which is reflected in the corrective action (often the replacement of the service)	Develop measures of customer costs that include the money, time and emotional costs spent in replacing defective services or complaining about them, which is reflected in a corrective action that goes beyond merely replacing the defective service

Table A.6: DEVELOPING DEVICES FOR ACHIEVING TOTAL CUSTOMER SATISFACTION

Dimension	*"Merely Good" Service Providers*	*Breakthrough Service Providers*
Uses of service guarantees	Use service guarantees primarily as marketing devices, providing a source of differentiation and assurances especially to new customers	Use service guarantees primarily as devices for achieving outstanding quality through improved error detection and eradication, and secondarily for marketing purposes
Type of service guarantee adopted	Introduce guarantees for specific, measurable aspects of a service to customers meeting carefully specified conditions, often developed by the firm's	Introduce unconditional guarantees of total customer satisfaction, with evaluation dependent on customers' judgments, and placement and collection of claims made easy

	legal department	
Role of recovery initiatives	Often regard service recovery initiatives, procedures, and training as secondary to efforts to encourage servers to "do it right the first time	Give high priority to service recovery initiatives, procedures, and training as a means of preserving total customer satisfaction even though performance on a particular dimension of service may be less than desired
Service recovery	Provide strict guidelines indicating what a server may and may not do in a recovery situation	Empower servers to do what is necessary to effect immediate service recovery, with review after the fact primarily for learning, not control, purposes

Table A.7 : MANAGING FOR QUALITY AND PRODUCTIVITY GAINS

Dimension	*"Merely Good" Service Providers*	*Breakthrough Service Providers*
Basic approach to quality and productivity improvement	Seek to improve quality through programs that reward the identification and correction of errors in service delivery	Seek to improve both quality and productivity through continuing efforts that motivate employees to "do it right the first time" and reward them for it as well as the identification and correction of errors in service delivery
Development and use of service standards	Measure customers expectations and seek to develop standards for quality that meet or exceed them, using them as the basis for performance measurements and reward	Measure customers expectations and competitors' performance and seek to develop standards for quality that exceed both, using them both as the basis for performance measurement and reward and as "bogies" to be continually improved upon
Selection of appropriate methods	Adopt a single, company wide approach to quality and productivity improve ment, often one utilized successfully elsewhere, thereby facilitating training, measurement, and the communication of results	Adopt the "what's right for us?" attitude, utilizing more than one approach to quality and productivity improvement, depending on (among other factors) the nature of the task being performed, its ease of description and measurement, and the ease with which causes of quality and productivity improve ment can be identified.

Marshaling of resources	Often focus quality and productivity efforts around facility design, information, technology, or the training and motivation of servers	Recognize the importance of calibrating and coordinating changes in facility design, information technology, and the training and motivation of servers in efforts to improve quality and productivity

Table A.8 : MANAGING DEMAND AND SUPPLY

Dimension	*"Merely Good" Service Providers*	*Breakthrough Service Providers*
Emphasis in managing demand and supply	Attack the problem primarily by managing either demand (through marketing, pricing, or demand inventorying practices) or supply of services	Attack the problem primarily by managing both demand (through marketing, pricing, or demand inventorying practices) and the capacity to supply a service
Forecasting of demand	Track demand by analyzing past sales and transaction data under various conditions using the result as an input for demand forecasting	Track demand patterns by capturing data for both actual customers and those who were not served because of capacity problems, using it as input to superior revenue control information systems
Capacity design	Determine the size of somewhat fixed capacity facilities, either by optimizing the cost of serving vs. not serving customers during peak periods or maintaining excess capacity to meet peak needs	In addition to using demand estimates to determine facilities of "optimum" size, look for ways to design flexible capacity by utilizing "floating" personnel, contracted services, high levels of organizational spirit, or other devices
Policies regarding customer queues	Seek to minimize customer waiting time during peak periods of demand	In addition to seeking ways to minimize customer waiting time during peak periods of demand, alter the customer's waiting experience through diversions that the customer finds relevant and useful, including the involvement of the customer in the service, with or without economic incentives

Table A.9 : MANAGEMENT OF NETWORKS

Dimension	*"Merely Good" Service Providers*	*Breakthrough Service Providers*
Emphasis in network management	Regard networks primarily as operating facilities connected by communications or transport routes	Regard networks both in a physical sense and as individuals linked by a common name or by relationships in channels of distribution for services
Major consideration in network design	Seek to optimize the length and complexity of networks as well as the "connectivity" (service to points on the network) they provide	Take into account both the cost of building and operating networks and the cost to customer (in time and convenience) in using networks of various configurations to maximize the overall value of networks to customers
Strategies for building and expanding networks	Build and expand networks works to accommodate reasonable levels of demand generated by marketing effort	Coordinate marketing, operations and network construction and expansion to ensure the most effective use of existing network facilities before making necessary additions
Management of network utilization	Price and market services to produce short-term balanced usage of shared network facilities	Price and market services to produce long-term balanced usage of shared network facilities

Table A.10 : MANAGING INFORMATION TECHNOLOGY

Dimension	*"Merely Good" Service Providers*	*Breakthrough Service Providers*
Attitude of leadership toward information	Regard information as an important resource for estimating and planning to accommodate demand as well as for internal control	Regard information as a primary device for delivering outstanding service as well as extending services to new dimensions and even into new businesses, often by making it available for direct use by customers
Strategy for developing information technology	Utilize the best "packaged" technology available from dependable sources, with the technology adapted to the task at hand where necessary	Set out to develop proprietary software in combination with available, proven hardware components, with the primary objectives or raising customer switching costs and tying

		customers to the server
Strategy for implementing information technology	Spend relatively heavily for technology in comparison with expenditures for training in its use	Spend relatively heavily for training in the use of technology in comparison with expenditures for the technology itself
Strategy for utilizing information technology	Utilize information technology as a means for empowering employees or customers, depending on the task being performed	Utilize information technology as a means of empowering employees and customers, often for the same task, as a means of providing a choice of methods to customers for accessing the serving organization and its information resource.

Table A.11 : MOBILISING PEOPLE

Dimension	*"Merely Good" Service Providers*	*Breakthrough Service Providers*
Recruiting and selection of people	Work hard at finding the best people available, depending on the techni cal and human skills needed for a particular job	Work hard at sorting out the best people available who find them, spending less effort than the "merely good" at recruiting and selection but hiring better people as the "employee of choice"
Personal development	Through job-related training and promotion to progressively more demanding jobs, develop people, particularly at middle to upper levels of the organization	Through training both for the job and in "life skills" and through the expansion of existing jobs, help people to develop at all levels in the organization, with particular emphasis on those directly serving customers
Empowerment of people	Empower employees according to the needs of the job, often by making authority commensurate with responsibility, with bottom -up processes for suggesting change subject to higher management approval	Empower employees beyond the needs of the job as a matter of principle, often through assigning responsibilities that exceed authority, with individuals encouraged to act first and documents actions later, all with the objective of creating an organization responsive to customer (and employee) needs.

Compensation and recognition practices	Pay at the upper end of the scale for comparable jobs in the industry, both in terms of salary and benefits, with a resulting modest amount of person nnel turnover at all or most levels of the organization and recognition provided both in the form of pay increases and promotions	Pay "off the scale" for the industry, both in terms of salary and benefits, by creating fewer, larger, noncomparable jobs with compensation on a pay-for-perform ance basis, resulting in turnover largely from "self-selection" in entry-level jobs and low turnover rates in other jobs, with recognition provided in ways other than hierarchical promotion

Table A.12 : ORGANISING WORK

Dimension	*"Merely Good" Service Providers*	*Breakthrough Service Providers*
Shape of the organization and the nature of internal communication	Organize on a traditional pyramid shape with levels of management and responsibilities added to provide maximum opportunities for promoting, requiring long lines of communication for concurrence and approval of operating decisions	Develop a flat organization with few levels comprising jobs somewhat scaled in size to the growing capabilities of the individual as a form of both personal development and promotion, allowing for short and often informal lines of communication
Structuring jobs	Structure jobs according to the demands of various tasks, with a clear, often somewhat rigid definition of responsibility, if not authority	More often structure jobs according to the needs and capabilities of individuals to foster growth in both individuals and their jobs, with an implicit but not rigid definition of responsibility
Emphasis on continuity in contact with customers	Emphasize the importance of continuity in contact with customers most of ten by developing information systems to facilitate the transfer of responsibility for customer contact from one employee to another, with an acceptance of the inev itability of promoting	Emphasize the importance of of continuity in contact with customers, primarily by devising ways, often through job expansion, of keeping good employees and managers in direct contact with customers as long as possible in their job progression

	good managers further and further away from customers	
Means of support for front-line servers	Continually emphasize the importance of support for front-line servers through means ranging from management exhor tations to headquarters staff to the creation of profit centers only at operating service facilities with authority there to purchase needed services	Emphasize the importance of support for front-line servers by "turning the organization upside down," making middle management largely a support as opposed to a control function, and organizing profit centers around front-line operating entitites

Table A.13 : ENVISIONING FUTURE BREAKTHROUGHS

Dimension	*"Merely Good" Service Providers*	*Breakthrough Service Providers*
Approach to new service design	Seek ways of improving services through existing methods	Continually monitor new methods of offering services that obsolete existing methods, both for defensive and potentially offensive reasons
Attitudes toward infor mation	Understand how information intensive services are different and seek to develop the most efficient information proce ssing methods available	See information as the learning curve of service, and a significant source of competitive advantage and devise ways of capturing and using it as the basis for previously unavailable services as well as a highly mobile means of service delivery
Approaches to service delivery	Seek to expand the avail ability of services in terms of form, location, and time	Embrace the concept of "future perfect" and explore the development of service delivery systems that can deliver anything, any time, any where, and now" and which themselves make use of such universal capabilities while incrementally improving existing services as well.
Environmental scanning	Are among the first to react to environmental changes such as the evolving nature of the available work force, international market oppor tunities, and technological developments	Conduct continuous environmental scanning, allowing them to anticipate and take advantage of social, economic, and technological change

Appendix II

Appendix A : LEADERSHIP QUALITIES CHECKLIST

Would they say that ...	*Often true of you*	*Sometimes true of you*	*Never true of you*
You provide a clear vision and direction that challenge and motivate your people	☐	☐	☐
You are an example of quality and service in the way towards your people	☐	☐	☐
You treat your people with the same respect as you would want them to treat customers	☐	☐	☐
You lead by example - It's 'do as I do' not 'do as I say'	☐	☐	☐
You always make the customer, quality and service your priorities	☐	☐	☐
You make clear what is required to achieve success and set standards to achieve this	☐	☐	☐
You are visible; when the going gets tough you are there, leading, encouraging and supporting	☐	☐	☐
You believe in the potential of other and push and support them to achieve success	☐	☐	☐
You set challenging targets and attract a team of people who want to be the best	☐	☐	☐
You give responsibility and expect people to take it	☐	☐	☐
You communicate, informing your team, listening and responding to them and their ideas	☐	☐	☐
You are visible and available; you show interest and enthusiasm	☐	☐	☐

You work on solutions rather than complaining about problems	☐	☐	☐
People enjoy working for you; you are a good 'people manager'	☐	☐	☐
You are trusted and listened to; your people know where they stand	☐	☐	☐
You involve people because you believe that everyone has something to contribute	☐	☐	☐
You take responsibility and show loyalty to those who work with and for you	☐	☐	☐
You are consistent	☐	☐	☐
You are honest and people trust you	☐	☐	☐
You admit mistakes and work to correct them	☐	☐	☐
You are interested in results; you set clear goals and talk to your people about success	☐	☐	☐
You develop people and don't feel threatened by their progress	☐	☐	☐
You are interested in your people as individuals, not just as workers	☐	☐	☐
You believe in teamwork and stress support and cooperation	☐	☐	☐
You keep promises and don't keep moving the goalposts	☐	☐	☐
You give people space to use their initiative	☐	☐	☐
You love success; you give recognition to people for their contribution and celebrate their achievements	☐	☐	☐
Total			

Appendix B : TEAM CHECK

So that we can make our working circumstances as positive as possible, I would value your views on the following:

On a scale of 0-10 (where 0 is low and 10 is high), how would you rate :

RATING SCORE

1. The way you are managed?

   What would make this better for you?

2. The quality of communication at work?

   What would make this better for you?

3 Working relationships?

   What would make these better for you?

4 The support you receive to help you do a quality job?

   What would make this better for you?

5 The recognition given to people for the job they do?

   What would make this better for you?

6 The opportunities to develop new skills and talents?

   What would make these better for you?

7. The clarity of goals and targets in your work?

   What would make this better for you?

8. The quality of teamwork?

   What would make this better for you?

9. The feedback on achievements?

   What would make this better for you?

Thank you for your views. These will provide a good guide to future action and requirements.

Appendix C : SERVICE MANAGEMENT QUESTIONNAIRE

	SCORE
Management, at every level, is conscious of the special challenge of managing in a service business, the need to model excellent service in all dealings with staff, and the requirement to manage ethically and positively	
Competence in people management is at least as important as technical competence when it comes to promotion in the organization	
Managers offer strong, visible leadership, setting challenging service performance goals and motivating people to achieve them	
The quality of communication between managers and staff is very high	
Managers play a key role in the delivery of excellent service by involving their teams in a programme of continuous improvement	
We have cross-functional teams who can address service improvements that involve different parts of the business	
Managers regularly make presentations on the organization's commitment to excellent service	
Senior managers give evidence of their commitment to excellent service by their involvement in quality planning, reviewing and training	
Quality service priorities are evident in management's communications with staff and in on-going management activities	
Management has a clearly written policy statement on excellent service and a clear strategy for involving all levels in quality performance, with procedures for regular reviews	

The total possible score for service management is 50

My score for service management is

Appendix D : VISION QUESTIONNAIRE **SCORE**

We have a clear vision for our business

The vision is challenging, inspiring and motivating for our people

In our business, we recognize that service excellence is a differentiator in the marketplace

Our vision drives performance in the business. People see their role and their jobs in terms of the vision

Our vision is marketed internally. Business leaders continually refer to it in their contact with staff

We have team / department visions that support the organization's vision

Our vision is used to evaluate decisions and policies at all levels in the business

The vision can be summed up as a 'one-liner', which everybody is conscious of as the ultimate purpose of the business

We have visible benchmarks by which we assess progress towards achieving the vision

The total possible score for vision is 50

My score for vision is

Appendix E : CUSTOMER SURVEY

Our service rating

We would like your help in rating the quality and service that we provide for you. We want to offer all our customers excellent standards and, to do this, we need feedback on our performance. Please give us your views.

Product and presentation	**Yes**	**No**
Were our premises clean and attractive?	☐	☐
Were our displays neat and tidy?	☐	☐
Were all floors and surfaces clean and free of dust and litter?	☐	☐
Were the aisles clear of boxes and packaging?	☐	☐
Were the displays appropriately full?	☐	☐
Were the areas you visited clean, tidy and pleasant smelling?	☐	☐
Was the till area neat, tidy and well presented?	☐	☐
Procedures		
Were opening hours clearly visible?	☐	☐
Were size and price tags easily identifiable?	☐	☐
Were graphics displaying new or sale items visible?	☐	☐
Were staff easily identifiable and wearing badges?	☐	☐
Was the refund policy explained?	☐	☐
Was the till point sufficiently staffed for the number of customers waiting?	☐	☐
Were there three or fewer customers waiting in the queue?	☐	☐
Did you feel that the queue was efficiently managed?	☐	☐
Was your transaction handled smoothly?	☐	☐
Was your change counted back to you?	☐	☐
Were purchases packed properly?	☐	☐
Was the receipt placed in the bag?	☐	☐
Was the bag handed to you?	☐	☐
Was there an obvious management presence?	☐	☐
Did you feel that the establishment was well/smoothly run?	☐	☐
People		
Were you acknowledged by a staff member on arrival?	☐	☐
If yes, was it within 30 seconds?	☐	☐
As you browsed, were you acknowledged by staff?	☐	☐
When you were in contact with staff, were they friendly and helpful?	☐	☐
Were you approached when you looked as if you needed help?	☐	☐
Were questions answered quickly and knowledgeably?	☐	☐
Did the assistant seem enthusiastic about the products?	☐	☐
Did the assistant ask questions to understand your requirements?	☐	☐
Were complementary/accessory products recommended?	☐	☐
If the product you wanted was unavailable, were efforts made to help you?	☐	☐
Were you encouraged to try the products?	☐	☐
Was there a member of staff on hand to help if required?	☐	☐
Were you acknowledged on arrival at the till?	☐	☐
Were you dealt with in a polite and friendly manner?	☐	☐
Were you thanked and bid a friendly farewell?	☐	☐

Appendix F : CREATING A POSITIVE CLIMATE

	Tick
Design events that give a positive start to each month, each year, to new projects and new phases of projects	☐
Make a positive start to days and weeks and to meeting - it may only be a matter of coffee, cakes, kind words and helpful ideas	☐
Have positive, encouraging notices or posters in your team's work area	☐
Make the work area beautiful - attractive settings lift people, whereas ugliness depresses. Have light rooms, pleasant colours, comfortable chairs and cheerful pictures	☐
Ask your team to draw up a list of '10 ways to improve our environment' and get them to implement the best ideas	☐
Have plenty of plants and trees around - these have a very positive psychological effect	☐
Give people the option of having occasional pleasant, inspiring music as a background to work	☐
Display photographs of your team and key customers, rather than just names, to help make people more real to each other	☐
If your workspace has a reception area, have an excellent receptionist to make that all-important first impression positive. Ensure that he/she is a model, not a substitute, for everybody else being welcoming	☐
Have special events for staff - theme days, trips out, special exhibitions, sports events, social outings, treasure hunts, music or cultural events, wine tasting etc.	☐
Display your best products, or features of them, in your work area Insist that all team energy is used positively - have a 'no gripes' contract	☐
Encourage attractive clothes and appearance - high standards promote self-esteem and convey respect for colleagues and customers	☐
Encourage and reward stylish ways of working and delivering products and services to your customers - 'it's not just what we do but the ways that we do it!'	☐
Go public with your vision when the time is ripe, so that your people and your customers know of your aspirations and ambitions	☐
Ban the phrase 'Yes, but ...,' which is the introduction to so many negative responses. Recognize and reinforce the response 'Yes, and ....' Challenge your people to adapt and build on ideas rather than rejecting them	☐
Make every job as interesting as it can be - ask the person who	

does the job regularly, 'How can what you do be made more interesting for you? Always ensure that people have challenge and achievement in their jobs ☐

Give people recognition for the job they do and reward them well ☐

Produce posters of what you want your customers and colleagues to say about the work of your team; challenge your team always to work to achieve that reputation ☐

Remember special details about people in your team - their birthdays, their children's names, their favourite colours, foods and music, their hobbies, special talents and skills - and find occasions to show that these are remembered ☐

Have a team contract that everyone has to perform one five-minute act of very special service to other team members every day ☐

Celebrate as a team - birthdays, anniversaries, spring, summer, autumn, Winter, the start of public holidays, new ideas, new projects, new contracts, Customer compliments, and anything else that recognizes people and their successes ☐

Support everybody as a way of life, but rally round those who carry heavy burdens and are under pressure at particular times ☐

Seek out any quality shortfalls or complaints, internal or external, seek fast, effective recoveries, and challenge your team with the question, 'What can we learn from that and how do we avoid a recurrence? ☐

Provide treats when they are least expected, or even least deserved! Chocolates, cakes, a glass of wine, a cup of special coffee, a long lunch break, a bunch of flowers and thank-you cards all register for people that they are the key to success ☐

Share out the more boring and mundane work, as well as the opportunities to do what is interesting and creative. Get others involved whenever anyone has an especially demanding task ☐

Develop a 10 ways to... pattern of thinking for your team - ask them to produce 10 suggestions for making customers welcome, celebrating achievements, having more fun, improving teamwork, offering even better customer service, or whatever else will make your team special. Produce copies of the ideas for team members and encourage them to use them. Every six months, have a 'creative party' with the challenge to introduce new ideas 'to make us even more successful in the future' ☐

Spend quality time with each other and organize happenings outside work ☐

Recruit positive, confident, energetic people, and support them at every opportunity. Use your best people to train new recruits ☐

Appendix G : CUSTOMERS QUESTIONNAIRE

	Score
We have a very clear profile of the customers that our business needs to attract	
We know exactly what those customers want and expect of us, and are committed to providing this	
We have a range of strategies for learning from customers and measuring their level of satisfaction with performance	
The data we collect from customers is used as a basis for management policies and decisions and in the design of products and services	
We use data from customers in our training of front-liners	
Our priorities are those given to us by our customers	
We guarantee customers standards of service excellence and measure performance against those standards	
Everybody in the business recognizes that the customer pays all wages and salaries, creates all profits and provides all jobs, and is the most significant person in the company	
Everybody knows the potential value of a typical customer who stays loyal to the company	
Everybody knows what our business performance is in terms of customer retention	
Total possible score for customer focus is 50	
My score for customer focus is	

Appendix H : INTERNAL SERVICE QUESTIONNAIRE

	Score
Everybody is clear who they provide service to (their customers) and who they receive service from	☐
Standards of performance are agreed for internal service between teams and departments and regularly reviewed	☐
People and departments have the resources to meet the reasonable expectations of their internal customers	☐
People and departments respond quickly and effectively to the unforeseen needs of their internal customers	☐
People and departments are flexible when circumstances require deviation from policy to meet the reasonable needs of internal customers	☐
We have high-quality communication between internal customers. There are no surprises when there are delays or problems	☐
People and departments are held accountable for their service commitments to internal customers	☐
There are high levels of understanding and trust between people and departments within the business	☐
The total possible score for internal service quality is 50	
My score for internal service quality is	☐

Appendix I : MOMENTS OF TRUTH CHECKLIST

	Good	Neutral	Poor
First impressions - entrance (visual impression)/ first contact (non- visual impression)	☐	☐	☐
Selection of services / products	☐	☐	☐
Quality of services/products	☐	☐	☐
Layout of premises/user-friendliness of processes	☐	☐	☐
Cleanliness of premises/simplicity of processes	☐	☐	☐
Staff greeting	☐	☐	☐
Availability of staff	☐	☐	☐

Physical appearance/professionalism of staff	☐	☐	☐
Availability of information	☐	☐	☐
Staff response to a request or query	☐	☐	☐
Friendliness of staff	☐	☐	☐
Way staff say goodbye	☐	☐	☐
Overall impression	☐	☐	☐

Appendix J : Ps CHECKLIST

	Can make a difference	***What I/ team can do***
People skills		
Approach to greeting customers	☐	
Approach to serving customers	☐	
Approach to saying goodbye to customers	☐	
Others		
Products		
The range of products we offer	☐	
The quality of products we offer	☐	
Others		
Presentation		
Display and layout of premises	☐	
Staff appearance	☐	
My personal appearance	☐	
Others		
Processes		
The approach to serving customers	☐	
Number of staff available	☐	
Is it easy to get staff attention?	☐	
Others		

Appendix K : MOMENTS OF TRUTH QUESTIONNAIRE

	Score
Everybody in the business is conscious of the importance of every moment of truth with customers	
We have a clear picture of what the moments of truth are with customers	
We are very clear about which staff create the customers' impression of the business	
These staff are clear that at every moment of truth there are three possible outcomes: the customer is impressed and pleased, the customer is left feeling neutral, or the customer is unimpressed and disappointed	
Front-line staff are respected; they are highly trained and well rewarded	
Front-liners feel that they are well supported by management, and colleagues in different departments and functions, in the task of providing excellent service to customers	
The business listens to front-liners, learns from them and responds to what they say	
Staff are conscious that moments of truth happen daily with internal customers and require the same skill and attention as with external customers	
Managers and team leaders are conscious of their moments of truth with their staff	
We have a clear picture of how well we perform at external and internal moments of truth	
The total possible score for moments of truth is 50	
My score for moments of truth is	

Appendix L : Ps QUESTIONNAIRE

	Score
People are very conscious that the customer's experience is made positive or negative by four factors: people skills, quality of products and services, features of our presentation and our processes to deliver what customers want	

The people skills of our front-liners, their ability to make customers feel special, are of a very high order	
The quality of products and services is excellent and invariable meets customers' requirements	
Features of the presentation of the business to customers - premises, paperwork, brochures, advertising and staff appearance - are very good	
Processes, practices and procedures are designed from the customer's point of view and are extremely customer friendly	
We are continuously improving the quality of products and services	
We are continuously improving how we present the business to customers	
We are continuously improving processes, practices and procedures so that they are customer friendly and cost effective	
Standards exist throughout the business defining required levels of performance in each of the 4 Ps	
The total possible score for the 4 Ps is 50	
My score for the 4 Ps is	

Appendix M : QUALITY SERVICE STANDARDS QUESTIONNAIRE

	Score
Quality service standards exist in every party of the business	
The standards address soft as well as hard service standards	
Service standards are worked out in dialogue with customers, and address what they regards as critical success factors	
Service standards are established in dialogue with staff and are not simply handed down from the top	
We regularly review performance against standards and communicate the findings to staff	
We know that the standards we offer customers compare with those offered by competitors	

We regularly review standards and seek to upgrade them	
Standards exist for internal service between people and departments in-house	
Service standards are part of the performance management system and individuals are appraised against them	
Performance against standards is linked to a reward system	
The total possible score for quality service standards is 50	
My score for quality service standards is	

Appendix N : MEASUREMENT QUESTIONNAIRE

	Score
We regard measurement of performance as a cornerstone of service excellence	
We are clear what the critical success factors are in the eyes of customers and measure performance against them	
We measure customer satisfaction regularly and in a range of ways	
We use findings from measurement activities to educate staff and inform management decisions	
We have clear goals and regularly measure achievements against them	
We measure internal service performance as a basis for continuous improvement	
We regularly monitor staff attitudes and opinions	
We measure the service performance of individual departments and functions, as distinct from our overall performance	
We use staff opinions and internal service measures to inform management performance and decision making	
We are continually seeking to upgrade the quality and scope of measurement factors affecting our customers	
To total possible score for measurements is 50	
My score for measurement is	

Appendix O : COMPLAINTS CHECKLIST

We are:	Tick if true
Always pleasant to customers, even if they are not pleasant to us	☐
Always ready to welcome suggestions from customers and colleagues about how we could improve	☐
Able to receive and handle complaints without feeling personally attacked	☐
Able to smile when we don't feel like it	☐
Always able to apologize to a customer, even if we are not at fault	☐
Willing to listen carefully and sympathetically to customers and find out what they want	☐
Able to give reasons and positive suggestions when we cannot do exactly what the customer wants	☐
Able to keep calm and behave professionally if a customer becomes upset	☐
Able to calm a customers if necessary and involve colleagues if any of us becomes upset	☐
Able to recover and profit from complaints and ensure that the customer goes away feeling that we were helpful, we solved the problem satisfactorily and wanting to return	☐

Appendix P : COMPLAINTS QUESTIONNAIRE

	Score
We are aware, as a business, that for every complaint received there could be 26 unhappy customers from whom we do not hear	
We know that an unhappy customer will on average tell 10 other people about the problem	
Complaints, although not pleasant, are welcomed. They are seen as second chances or moments of truth, providing another opportunity to impress the customers	
We make it easy for customers to complain	

Complaints are recorded, studied and learnt from

The level and nature of complaints are reported at the most senior level

We have effective recovery systems so that complaints are dealt with quickly and efficiently. The policy is to have a satisfied customer at the end of any problem or difficult situation

We train people in the skills of effective complaint handling

We empower front-liners to take fast, corrective action

We know why we lose any customer

The total possible score for profiting from complaints is 50

My score for profiting from complaints is

Appendix Q : CULTURE QUESTIONNAIRE

Score

We have a clearly identified organizational culture that supports our mission

Our people are clear on our values and priorities, and these are recognized as consistent with our business purpose and important to our success

Our top team members 'walk the talk" They promote the culture and senior and middle managers are seen as united in support of it. They live the values and there are no mixed messages about what the business needs, to be successful

We are clear about the competencies and qualities that individuals need to be successful in our culture and to make our business successful

We recruit the kind of people who will 'fit' our culture; you get on here by doing things 'our way'

Our training and development programmes enhance the competencies and values that we need to grow and maintain business success	
There is a strong sense of ownership of and pride in our culture, together with allegiance to it among line managers and front-liners	
There is a strong sense of ownership in and pride in our culture and allegiance to it across all areas of the business	
Our culture is one that will enable us to achieve our business ambitions for the next two to three years. There are no changes required	
The total possible score for a culture to support our mission is 50	
My score for a culture to support our mission is	

●●●